ORIGINAL INTENT

The Courts, the Constitution, & Religion

DAVID BARTON

Aledo, Texas

Original Intent: The Courts, The Constitution, and Religion
Copyright 2000 by David Barton
3rd Edition, 2nd Printing, September 2002

For additional copies of this book, or for information on other books and reprints, contact:
WallBuilders
P.O. Box 397
Aledo, TX 76008
(817) 441-6044
For orders and catalog, call (800) 873-2845
www.wallbuilders.com

Cover Design
Jeremiah Pent

ISBN 0-925279-75-7 (Hardback edition)
ISBN 0-925279-50-1 (Paperback edition)

342.73
Barton, David.
Original Intent: the courts, the constitution, and religion. - Aledo, TX: WallBuilder Press, 2000.
544 p; 21 cm.
Endnotes, list of cases cited, bibliography, index, and price list included.

1. United States - Constitutional history   2. Church and state - United States
3. United States - Constitutional law - Interpretation and construction I. Title

Printed in the United States of America

Table of Contents

Foreword

Our Constitution operates on long-standing principles which were recognized and incorporated into our government over two hundred years ago; each constitutional provision reflects a specific philosophy implemented to avoid a specific problem. Therefore, grasping the purpose for any clause of the Constitution is possible only through a proper historical understanding of the debates and the conclusions reached two hundred years ago.

For example, when adjudging the permissible in the realm of public religious expressions, courts revert to what they perceive to be the intent of those who, in 1789, drafted the religion clauses of the Constitution. Likewise, the perception of historical intent similarly affects the debates on gun control and the Second Amendment, States' Rights and the Tenth Amendment, abortion and the Ninth and Fourteenth Amendments, flag-burning and the First Amendment; etc. Therefore, if our understanding of historical facts and constitutional intent becomes confused or mistaken, the resulting policies may be not only ill-founded but may actually create the very abuses that the Founders originally intended to avoid.

Because the portrayal of history so affects current policy, some groups have found it advantageous to their political agenda to distort historical facts intentionally. Those particularly adept at this are termed "revisionists." (A thorough discussion of revisionism is presented in Chapter 16.) Not all dissemination of incorrect information, however, is deliberately intended to misinform; in many cases, it is the result of individuals innocently repeating what others have mistakenly reported.

In fact, there is an unhealthy tendency in many current books on the Founders—a tendency confirmed in their concluding bibliographies—to cite predominately contemporary "authorities" speaking *about* the Founders rather than citing the Founders' own words. Such evidence is termed "hearsay" and would never stand up in a court of law. *Original Intent,* however, has pursued the practice of "best evidence": it lets the Founders speak for themselves in accordance with the legal rules of evidence.

Furthermore, not only does *Original Intent* document the original intent on a number of constitutional issues debated today, it also documents how this essential information is often ignored under today's standard of "political correctness." Indicative of this deletion of information, the following questions are raised—and answered—in this book.

- Although there were fifty-five Founders who drafted the Constitution, and ninety more who drafted the Bill of Rights, why does the current Court invoke only Thomas Jefferson and James Madison as its spokesmen? Are there no constitutional authorities among the other one-hundred-forty-plus who framed those documents? Or, is it possible that their words would directly contradict the current Court's conclusions?

- Since Jefferson has over sixty volumes of written works and Madison has over twenty, why does the Court continually invoke only one or two select sentences from these exhaustive works? Is it perhaps that the rest of the statements made by Madison and Jefferson reveal the Court's intentional misportrayal of their intent?

- Since several signers of the Constitution were also Justices on the U. S. Supreme Court, why does the current Court avoid citing the declarations of those Justices on today's issues? Is it perhaps that the concise rulings of those who so clearly understood constitutional intent would contradict and thus embarrass the Court for its current positions?

Not only are these questions answered in this book, but the answers are established from the expansive writings of scores of Founders, not just inferred by narrow references from only a select few.

As more and more of the primary-source information documenting the views of the Founders has been publicized, it clearly has contradicted what the courts and some "scholars" have claimed. In fact, those individuals, to protect their own views and to diffuse growing criticism against them, have characterized the irrefutable historical facts which confront them as nothing more than "revisionism." Ironically, it is quite the contrary; for by reverting to primary-source historical documents, the true historical and legal revisionism which *has* occurred over recent generations is now being systematically exposed and rebutted.

Original Intent will provide hundreds of the Founders' direct declarations on many of the constitutional issues which America continues to face today. Their words, their conclusions, and especially their intent is clear; their wisdom is still applicable for today. Since these clear views may be new to many Americans, this work has been heavily footnoted, and the reader is strongly encouraged to investigate the sources cited in order to confirm the accuracy of the conclusions which have been reached.

Editor's Notes

The editors have utilized several helpful procedures and included seven beneficial appendices (discussed below) to augment the usefulness of this book.

1. Notes on Spelling

Prior to 1800, there was virtually no uniform standard for spelling in America. Consequently, the same word could be spelled several ways. (In fact, one colonial Governor allegedly spelled his own name six different ways!) Notice the spellings (words misspelled by today's standards are underlined) appearing in the Pilgrims' "Mayflower Compact" of 1620:

> We whose names are <u>underwriten</u>, the <u>loyall</u> subjects of our dread <u>soveraigne</u> Lord King James, by the grace of God, of Great <u>Britaine</u>, <u>Franc</u>, & Ireland king, defender of the faith, &c., <u>haveing</u> undertaken, for the <u>glorie</u> of God, and <u>advancemente</u> of the Christian faith, and <u>honour</u> of our king & <u>countrie</u>, a voyage to plant the first <u>colonie</u> in the <u>Northerne</u> parts of Virginia, <u>doe</u> by these presents solemnly & <u>mutualy</u> in the presence of God, and one of another, covenant & combine <u>our selves</u> <u>togeather</u> into a <u>civill</u> body <u>politick</u> . . .

In an effort to improve readability and flow, we have modernized all spellings in the historical quotes used throughout this work. This, however, will not change any meanings. By referring to the sources in the footnotes, the reader will be able to examine the original spelling should he/she so desire.

2. Notes on Capitalization and Punctuation

Similarly distracting is the early use of capitals and commas. For an example of the copious use of commas, refer to the previous example; to see the excessive use of capitals, notice this excerpt from a 1749 letter written by signer of the Declaration Robert Treat Paine (underlined words would not be capitalized today):

> I <u>Believe</u> the Bible to be the written word of God & to <u>Contain</u> in it the whole <u>Rule</u> of <u>Faith</u> & manners; I consent to the Assemblys Shorter Chatachism as being <u>Agreable</u> to the <u>Reveal'd</u> <u>Will</u> of God & to contain in it the <u>Doctrines</u> that are <u>According</u> to <u>Godliness</u>. I have for some time had a desire to attend upon the Lords Supper and to <u>Come</u> to that divine <u>Institution</u> of a <u>Dying</u> Redeemer, <u>And</u> I trust I'm now convinced that it is my <u>Duty</u> <u>Openly</u> to profess

him least he be ashamed to own me An Other day; I humbly therefore desire that you would receive me into your Communion & Fellowship, & I beg your Prayers for me that Grace may be carried on in my soul to Perfection, & that I may live answerable to the Profession I now make which (God Assisting) I purpose to be the main End of all my Actions.

In a further effort to improve readability, the modern rules of capitilization and punctuation have been followed in the quotes throughout this book.

3. The definition of a "Founding Father"
For the purpose of this work, a "Founding Father" is one who exerted significant influence in, provided prominent leadership for, or had a substantial impact upon the birth, development, and establishment of America as an independent, self-governing nation. While a more complete identification of a "Founding Father" appears at the beginning of Chapter 6, some two-hundred-fifty or so individuals fit within this category, including the fifty-six signers of the Declaration of Independence, the fourteen Presidents of Congress during the Revolution, the two-dozen or so prominent Generals who secured independence, the fifty-five delegates to the federal Constitutional Convention, the earliest State Governors largely responsible for the ratification and adoption of the Constitution, the ninety members of the first Congress who framed the Bill of Rights, the first members of the U. S. Supreme Court who helped set the judiciary on its feet, and the earliest members of the Executive department who helped establish that branch.

4. The usage of the word "court" and "constitution"
"Court" (capital "C") refers to the Supreme Court of the United States, whereas "court" (lower-case "c") indicates a State Supreme Court or any other court, whether federal or State. Similarly, "Courts" specifically refers to the decisions of collective U. S. Supreme Courts and "courts" refers to the judiciary in general, represented by jurisdictions from the lowest level local courts through the Supreme Court of the United States. Likewise, "Constitution" (capital "C") refers to the Constitution of the United States whereas "constitution" (lower-case "c") refers to a State constitution.

5. The various Appendixes

Appendixes "A" and "B" at the end of this book contain the Declaration of Independence and the Constitution of the United States. The reader is encouraged to read these two documents in their entirety and then refer to the appropriate sections as they are referred to or quoted in this book. Appendix "C" provides a brief biographical sketch of select individuals referenced in this book (nearly 300 biographies appear in this appendix). This section will be beneficial for most readers. Although most will recognize George Washington, Alexander Hamilton, James Madison, and Benjamin Franklin as signers of the Constitution, most have never heard of Abraham Baldwin, Rufus King, William Livingston, John Langdon, Roger Sherman, or the others who signed that document. Similarly, most will recognize John Hancock, Thomas Jefferson, John Adams, and Samuel Adams as signers of the Declaration of Independence, but few can identify the other fifty-two who signed America's birth certificate. In the overall scheme, while these other Founders are no less important, authors of history texts over the past two generations have inexplicably chosen to ignore these Founders. Therefore, if you come across a name in this book and don't recognize it, refer to this appendix to receive a quick historical "snapshot" of the life and accomplishments of that individual.

NOTE: The information for these nearly 300 biographical pieces is compiled from a number of sources, including the *Dictionary of American Biography* (22 volumes), *Appleton's Cyclopedia of American Biography* (6 volumes), *The Biographical Directory of the American Congress 1774-1927*, *The Biographical Directory of the United States Congress 1774-1989*, *The Signers of the Declaration of Independence* (1823, 9 volumes), *Encyclopedia Britannica* (1911 edition, 32 volumes), *World Book Encyclopedia* (1960 edition, 20 volumes), *Webster's American Biographies,* as well as numerous other individual biographies. Occasionally, there is discrepency between these works as to the date or year of a specific occurrence; therefore, the years given within each sketch are those on which most seem to agree. When necessary, the various historical societies and State archivists were also consulted for confirmation of facts and figures.

NOTE: There are a very few individuals mentioned in this book who were so historically obscure that no listing on that individual will appear in this appendix (for example, Benjamin Franklin wrote a letter to a "Dean Woodward" of whom little is known). However, very few will fall into this category.

<u>Appendix "D"</u> contains the endnotes—almost 1,400 citations! This quantity is provided in hope that the reader will avail him/herself of the opportunity to confirm both the context and the content of the quotes profusely provided throughout this work.

<u>Appendix "E"</u> contains a complete citation list of the legal cases referenced in this book so that not only attorneys and others in the legal profession but also every citizen can locate these cases for their own examination.

<u>Appendix "F"</u> contains the complete bibliographic listing of the works cited in this book—over 400 different sources. The bibliography section is subdivided into the categories of "books," "legal works," "documents," and "periodicals."

<u>Appendix "G"</u> is the index and will provide the page number where major names, cases, themes, issues, etc., are cited throughout this work. It provides an excellent quick locator for the reader.

Acknowledgments

In recent years, corporate jargon has undergone an amazing metamorphosis as books documenting the hallmarks of successful enterprises have popularized words like "teamwork" and "partnership." Despite their current vernacular popularity, such concepts are not new.

Three thousand years ago, Solomon, perhaps the wisest sage of that or any era, had already discovered these truths (see, for example, Proverbs 11:14; 15:22; 20:18b; 24:6; etc.). Then, a thousand years later, the learned scholar Paul specifically emphasized the teamwork principle with his illustration of the human body (see 1 Corinthians 12): although composed of many distinct members, each contributes an invaluable role and is part of the whole.

Original Intent affirms the wisdom both of this current age and of past millennia. While only my name appears on the cover as author, it would be inaccurate to conclude that this work was solely my product. It is the result of over two years of laborious work by numerous invaluable individuals.

The scope of their contributions encompasses extensive research in both rare and contemporary works, in both court cases and other legal writings, in biographical research, in data entry and typing (this work has gone through over thirty complete iterations in the past two years alone), in checking and comparing the accuracy of the entered data against the originals, in editing both for textual flow and grammar, in technical support for hardware and software, etc. This seemingly simple book is actually the result of a partnership of many able and dedicated individuals; while each has exhibited different strengths and functions, when coupled together they have formed—to use Paul's phraseology—a very adequate "body."

The individual "members" of that "body" have included—in random order—Bill Suggs, Leah Watson, Cheryl Barton, Brian Stone, Tom Smiley, Grady Barton, Mark Haynes, Sandy Grady, Knox Ross, Kit Marshall, Lynn Fowler, Rose Barton, Melissa Mullens, Fred McNabb, Barbara Smiley, Cindy Pettay, Liz McClendon, Bob Lewis, Kandi Hogan, Damaris Barton, Scarlett McClendon, Joni Gingles, Vicki Carter, and others. In addition to these staff workers, there has been the invaluable assistance of numerous historical societies—both federal and State, public and private, as well as those focusing on single individuals (e.g., the Noah Webster home in Hartford) as well as on collective groups (e.g., Independence Hall and the National Historical Park in Philadelphia).

Having acknowledged the help and assistance of these individuals and groups, there remains one final acknowledgment. With this, I have saved the best—and the most important—for last. Since the Scriptures direct that in all of our ways we should acknowledge God (Proverbs 3:5-6), I therefore wish to do so by repeating some of the similar acknowledgments frequently made by the Founding Fathers:

> Rendering thanks to my Creator for my existence and station among His works, for my birth in a country enlightened by the Gospel and enjoying freedom, and for all His other kindnesses, to Him I resign myself, humbly confiding in His goodness, and in His mercy through Jesus Christ for the events of eternity. **JOHN DICKINSON**, SIGNER OF THE CONSTITUTION

> Unto Him who is the author and giver of all good, I render sincere and humble thanks for His manifold and unmerited blessings, and especially for our redemption and salvation by His beloved Son. **JOHN JAY**, ORIGINAL CHIEF-JUSTICE OF THE U. S. SUPREME COURT

> My soul I resign into the hands of my Almighty Creator, whose tender mercies are all over His works, who hateth nothing that He hath made, and to the justice and wisdom of whose dispensations I willingly and cheerfully submit, humbly hoping from His unbounded mercy and benevolence, through the merits of my blessed Savior, a remission of my sins. **GEORGE MASON**, FATHER OF THE BILL OF RIGHTS

The Scriptures inform us that "in Him we live and move and have our being" (Acts 17:28); Jesus further declares that "apart from Me you can do nothing" (John 15:5). I firmly believe this.

In summary, while my name appears on the cover of this work, I would be foolish to take credit for what this work represents: the contributions of numerous workers—both seen and Unseen—without whose assistance this book would not exist either with its current content or in its current format. To all of these individuals, both human and Divine, I offer a sincere and heartfelt, "Thank you!"

David Barton
March 2000

~1~
Religion and the Courts

In recent years, controversies over public religious expressions have been among the most frequent to rise to the U. S. Supreme Court. Consequently, nine unelected individuals now exert more control over how, where, when, or if public religious activities will occur than any other body in America. In fact, for one Justice, the Court's current religious micromanagement is so inappropriate that he describes the Court as "a national theology board." [1]

The Court has arrived at this position through its usage of the phrase "separation of church and state." With these words as its standard for judging the propriety of a challenged religious expression, the Court has now declared many American customs and traditions unconstitutional. However, it doesn't stop here. Subsequent over-zealous applications by State and local officials not only of these court decisions, but also of this phrase in general, frequently lead to even greater religious restrictions than those handed down by the courts.

Through continuous usage over recent decades, the separation language has now become so commonplace that many Americans believe it to be a constitutional phrase found in the First Amendment. It is not. Concerning religion, that Amendment simply states:

> Congress shall make no law respecting an establishment of religion or prohibiting the free exercise thereof . . .

The current application of the "separation of church and state" metaphor actually represents a relatively recent concept rather than the enforcement of a long-standing constitutional principle. This is demonstrated by the fact that the separation idiom appeared in only two cases in the Supreme Court's first 150 years; [2] yet over the past 50 years, it has been cited in seemingly countless numbers of Court decisions.

The phrase became the contemporary standard for judicial policy in 1947 in *Everson* v. *Board of Education* when the Court announced:

> The First Amendment has erected a wall between church and state. That wall must be kept high and impregnable. We could not approve the slightest breach. [3]

Following this declaration, the Supreme Court—and numerous lower courts—began striking down religious activities and expressions which had been constitutional for the previous 150 years. Consider the following decisions delivered in the jurisdictions of contemporary courts:

☐ A verbal prayer offered in a school is unconstitutional, even if that prayer is both voluntary and denominationally neutral. ENGEL v. VITALE, 1962; [4] ABINGTON v. SCHEMPP, 1963; [5] COMMISSIONER OF EDUCATION v. SCHOOL COMMITTEE OF LEYDEN, 1971 [6]

☐ Freedoms of speech and press are guaranteed to students and teachers—unless the topic is religious, at which time such speech becomes unconstitutional. STEIN v. OSHINSKY, 1965; [7] COLLINS v. CHANDLER UNIFIED SCHOOL DIST., 1981; [8] BISHOP v. ARONOV, 1991; [9] DURAN v. NITSCHE, 1991 [10]

☐ It is unconstitutional for students to see the Ten Commandments since they might read, meditate upon, respect, or obey them. STONE v. GRAHAM, 1980; [11] RING v. GRAND FORKS PUBLIC SCHOOL DIST., 1980; [12] LANNER v. WIMMER, 1981 [13]

☐ If a student prays over his lunch, it is unconstitutional for him to pray aloud. REED v. VAN HOVEN, 1965 [14]

☐ A school song was struck down because it promoted values such as honesty, truth, courage, and faith in the form of a "prayer." Interestingly, the song occurred as a part of voluntary extracurricular student activities. DOE v. ALDINE INDEPENDENT SCHOOL DISTRICT, 1982 [15]

☐ It is unconstitutional for a war memorial to be erected in the shape of a cross. LOWE v. CITY OF EUGENE, 1969 [16]

☐ The Ten Commandments, despite the fact that they are the basis of civil law and are depicted in engraved stone in the U. S. Supreme Court, may not be displayed at a public courthouse. HARVEY v. COBB COUNTY, 1993 [17]

☐ When a student addresses an assembly of his peers, he effectively becomes a government representative; it is therefore unconstitutional for that student to engage in prayer. HARRIS v. JOINT SCHOOL DISTRICT, 1994 [18]

☐ It is unconstitutional for a public cemetery to have a planter in the shape of a cross, for if someone were to view that cross, it could cause "emotional distress" and thus constitute an "injury-in-fact." WARSAW v. TEHACHAPI, 1990 [19]

☐ Even though the wording may be constitutionally acceptable, a bill becomes unconstitutional if the legislator who introduced the bill had a religious activity in his mind when it was authored. WALLACE v. JAFFREE, 1985 [20]

☐ It is unconstitutional for a classroom library to contain books which deal with Christianity, or for a teacher to be seen with a personal copy of the Bible at school. ROBERTS v. MADIGAN, 1990 [21]

☐ It is unconstitutional for a Board of Education to use or refer to the word "God" in any of its official writings. OHIO v. WHISNER, 1976 [22]

☐ In a city seal composed of numerous symbols representing various aspects of the community (e.g., industry, its commerce, its history, its flora, its schools, etc.), it is unconstitutional for any of those symbols to depict the religious heritage or any religious element of the community. ROBINSON v. CITY OF EDMOND, 1995; [23] HARRIS v. CITY OF ZION, 1991; [24] KUHN v. CITY OF ROLLING MEADOWS, 1991; [25] FRIEDMAN v. BOARD OF COUNTY COMMISSIONERS, 1985; [26]

☐ It is unconstitutional for school officials to be publicly praised or recognized in an open community meeting if that meeting is sponsored by a religious group. JANE DOE v. SANTA FE INDEPENDENT SCHOOL DISTRICT, 1995 [27]

☐ Artwork may not be displayed in schools if it depicts something religious—even if that artwork is considered an historical classic. WASHEGESIC v. BLOOMINGDALE PUBLIC SCHOOLS, 1993 [28]

☐ It is unconstitutional for a kindergarten class to ask whose birthday is celebrated by Christmas. FLOREY v. SIOUX FALLS SCHOOL DISTRICT, 1979 [29]

☐ It is unconstitutional for a school graduation ceremony to contain an opening or closing prayer. HARRIS v. JOINT SCHOOL DISTRICT, 1994; [30] GEARON v. LOUDOUN COUNTY SCHOOL BOARD, 1993; [31] LEE v. WEISMAN, 1992; [32] KAY v. DOUGLAS SCHOOL DISTRICT, 1986; [33] GRAHAM v. CENTRAL COMMUNITY SCHOOL DISTRICT, 1985 [34]

☐ It is unconstitutional for a nativity scene to be displayed on public property unless surrounded by sufficient secular displays to prevent it from appearing religious. COUNTY OF ALLEGHENY v. ACLU, 1989 [35]

Numerous other absurdities have stemmed from the courts' "separation" doctrine:

☐ Because a prosecuting attorney mentioned seven words from the Bible in the courtroom—a statement which lasted less than five seconds—a jury sentence was overturned for a man convicted of brutally clubbing a 71-year-old woman to death. [36]

☐ A high ranking official from the national drug czar's office who regularly conducts public school anti-drug rallies was prohibited from doing so in Nacogdoches, Texas. The federal judge pointed out that even though the speaker was an anti-drug expert, he was also known as a Christian minister and thus was disqualified from delivering a secular anti-drug message. [37]

☐ In the Alaska public schools, students were prohibited from using the word "Christmas" at school, from exchanging Christmas cards or presents, or from displaying anything with the word "Christmas" on it because it contained the word "Christ." [38]

☐ In a high-school class in Dickson, Tennessee, students were required to write a research paper using at least four sources. Despite the fact that the students were allowed to write about reincarnation, witchcraft, and the occult, because student Brittney Settle chose to write her paper about the life of Jesus Christ, she was given a zero by her teacher. [39]

☐ Although States print hundreds of thousands of custom license plates purchased and ordered by individual citizens, Oregon refused to print "PRAY," Virginia refused to print "GOD 4 US," and Utah refused to print "THANK GOD," claiming that such customized license plates violated the "separation of church and state." [40]

☐ An elementary school principal in Denver removed the Bible from the school library, and an elementary school music teacher in Colorado Springs stopped teaching Christmas carols because of alleged violations of the "separation of church and state." [41]

☐ In DeFuniak Springs, Florida, a judge ordered the courthouse copy of the Ten Commandments to be covered during a murder trial for fear that jurors would be prejudiced against the defendant if they saw the command "Do not kill." [42]

☐ In Omaha, Nebraska, a student was prohibited from reading his Bible silently during free time, or even to open his Bible at school. [43]

Since the introduction of the 1947 *Everson* guideline, activities upheld as constitutional in prior years are now regularly prohibited. The *Everson* decision, however, was distinctive not only for its introduction of the modern "separation" doctrine but also because it dramatically expanded the role of the federal courts. How was this accomplished?

In *Everson*, the Court took the Fourteenth Amendment (which dealt with specific State powers) and attached to it the First Amendment's federal provision that "Congress shall make no law respecting an establishment of religion." The result of merging these two Amendments was twofold: first, the Court reversed the bedrock constitutional demand that the First Amendment pertain *only* to the federal government; second, the Court declared that federal courts were now empowered to restrict not only the religious activities of the federal government but also those of States and individuals as well.

This expansion of the Court's jurisdiction in the *Everson* decision was accomplished only by direct violations of the purposes for which both the First and the Fourteenth Amendments were enacted. This is demonstrated by the following brief historical review of those Amendments.

An Overview of the First Amendment

The prominent characteristic of the emerging national government both during and after the American Revolution (first under the Articles of Association, and then under the Articles of Confederation) was the strong zeal of each State not only to protect its own powers and rights but also to prevent the national government from usurping its powers.[†] As a reflection of this attitude, important policies under those national governments were enacted

---

[†] There are many indications of the degree of independent sovereignty zealously guarded by each State. For example, the Chief-Executive in some States was not called the "Governor" of the State, but rather the "President" of the State (e.g., Pennsylvania, Delaware, New Hampshire). Perhaps the best current parallel example would be Europe: although composed of many small and independent nations (sometimes called European States), yet they are joined together under a single European Parliament. Nevertheless, each still maintains its own individual sovereignty, and each individual nation/State—not the European Parliament—exercises powers over its own people.

not by a simple majority, but rather by a three-fourths supermajority. [44] Consequently, States could easily block the action of the entire government if they believed that their own rights or powers were being infringed.

Having this mindset, State delegates were selected and sent to a national gathering in Philadelphia in 1787. Although that meeting (now called the Constitutional Convention) did produce a new federal government, it also contained an element of strong opposition (only thirty-nine of the fifty-five delegates signed the Constitution). Several of those who refused to sign did so because of their ardent opposition to a potential centralization of federal power that might rival, invade, or usurp the State's sovereignty on a variety of specific issues. This group, termed "Anti-Federalists," warned that unless specific amendments were made to the Constitution to limit the federal powers, the federal government might first envelop and then annul the rights of States—and individuals. Perhaps Anti-Federalist Samuel Adams articulated those concerns most clearly when he declared:

> I mean . . . to let you know how deeply I am impressed with a sense of the importance of Amendments; that the good people may clearly see the distinction—for there is a distinction—between the federal powers vested in Congress and the sovereign authority belonging to the several States, which is the Palladium [the protection] of the private and personal rights of the citizens. [45]

The individual State conventions which convened to ratify the new federal Constitution resounded loudly with the Anti-Federal arguments. The Constitution thus received only marginal approval in several States, and North Carolina even refused to ratify unless clear restraints were placed on the power of the federal government (see Chapter 10 for greater details on how the States voted).

Subsequently, George Washington, in his "Inaugural Address," urged Congress to consider how the Constitution might be amended. [46] Congress did so, and the result was twelve proposed amendments specifying exactly what the *federal* government, and *only* the federal government, could not do. Of those twelve amendments, ten—the Bill of Rights—were ratified by the States to preserve State autonomy over the issues listed in those amendments. Thus the Court's 1947 decision to apply one of those amendments (the First Amendment) against the States completely reversed the protective jurisdiction of that Amendment.

An Overview of the Fourteenth Amendment

A similar improper expansion of jurisdiction occurred in the Court's reinterpretation of the scope of the Fourteenth Amendment. That Amendment was ratified in 1868 to guarantee State citizenship to recently emancipated slaves. (An in-depth examination of this Amendment is in Chapter 10.)

It is a peculiar interpretation by which the Court takes an amendment that provides citizenship to former slaves and applies it to prohibit religious activities in the schools and public affairs of States and local communities.

The Effect of the Coupling

When one understands the purposes of these two Amendments, it is not surprising that no previous Court had ever coupled them as did the 1947 Court. † In fact, in 1970, Justice William Douglas openly acknowledged that by coupling the Fourteenth Amendment and the Bill of Rights, the Court had not only removed State sovereignty over many areas, but it had also created an American revolution which . . .

. . . involved the imposition of new and far-reaching constitutional restraints on the States. *Nationalization* of many civil liberties has been the consequence of the Fourteenth Amendment, *reversing the historic position* that the foundations of those liberties rested largely in State law. . . . And so *the revolution occasioned by the Fourteenth Amendment* has progressed as Article after Article in the Bill of Rights has been incorporated in it and made applicable to the States. [47] (emphasis added)

The *Everson* decision—notable both for its introduction of the "separation" rhetoric and for its use of the Fourteenth Amendment to limit local religious expressions—represented a disturbing judicial paradigm shift.

Summary

Even though the Court today divides the religious clauses of the First Amendment into what it calls "The Establishment Clause" ("Congress shall make no law respecting an establishment of religion") and "The Free Exercise

---

† Justice William Douglas explained that although the Court had incorporated a portion of the First Amendment into the Fourteenth Amendment as early as 1940 in *Cantwell* v. *Connecticut* (310 U. S. 296), it was not until *Everson* in 1947 that the Establishment Clause was incorporated into the Fourteenth. See *Walz* v. *Tax Commission*, 397 U. S. 664 at 702 (1970).

Clause" ("nor prohibiting the free-exercise thereof"), it is still nonetheless very obvious that no portion of the separation phrase appears in any part of the First Amendment—nor in any other part of the Constitution.

In fact, the recent reliance by the Court on this non-constitutional phrase has prompted complaints by many jurists. For example, in *Baer* v. *Kolmorgen*, Judge Gallagher complained:

> Much has been written in recent years . . . to "a wall of separation between church and State." . . . [It] has received so much attention that one would almost think at times that it is to be found somewhere in our Constitution. [48]

Justice Potter Stewart observed:

> I think that the Court's task, in this as in all areas of constitutional adjudication, is not responsibly aided by the uncritical invocation of metaphors like the "wall of separation," a phrase nowhere to be found in the Constitution. [49]

Justice William Rehnquist described this phrase as a "misleading metaphor," [50] and then noted:

> But the greatest injury of the "wall" notion is its mischievous diversion of judges from the actual intentions of the drafters of the Bill of Rights. . . . The "wall of separation between church and State" is a metaphor based on bad history, a metaphor which has proved useless as a guide to judging. It should be frankly and explicitly abandoned. [51]

The public's current understanding (actually, misunderstanding) of the religious provisos of the First Amendment has been shaped by a phrase which does not even appear in the Constitution!

Yet, while all must truthfully concede that these words are not actually found in the Constitution, many nevertheless still argue that they accurately reflect the intent of the Framers—that is, while the words are not there, the concept of a complete separation was frequently demonstrated during the Founding Era. Is this assertion correct?

~2~
Religion and the Constitution

The question of what the Founders intended as the proper relationship between religious expressions and "public" life (whether in education, law, government, or throughout society in general) is clearly documented in their numerous writings on this subject. Those records establish their intent and thus clarify their two references to religion in the Constitution.

The first reference is in Article VI, Section 3:

> [N]o religious test shall ever be required as a qualification to any office or public trust under the United States.

The second is in the First Amendment:

> Congress shall make no law respecting an establishment of religion or prohibiting the free exercise thereof . . .

Through the years, these two constitutional requirements have formed the basis of many judicial decisions. Historically, legal scholars have examined both phrases when seeking the intent of either; the understanding of each was made more complete through the examination of both. [1] The goal was always to identify and establish the original context and purpose of those two religious provisos before attempting to apply them.

However, in *Everson* (1947) the modern Court discarded this objective. It first divorced the First Amendment from its original purpose and then reinterpreted it without regard to either historical context or previous judicial decisions. The result was that the Court abandoned the traditional constitutional meaning of "religion" as a single denomination or system of worship and instead substituted a new "modern" concept which even now remains vague and nebulous, having changed several times in recent years. By this substitution, the Court created a new and foreign purpose for the First Amendment and completely rewrote its scope of protections and prohibitions.

In attaching today's "enlightened" perceptions to yesterday's acts, the Court demonstrated an unscholarly, and even disquieting approach to both law and history. As explained by Founder Noah Webster,† not only misinterpretation

---

† Noah Webster (1758-1843) was among the first to call for the Constitutional Convention and was responsible for the copyright and patent protection clause found in Article 1, Section 8 of the Constitution. [2] Furthermore, Webster was a master of word usage, learning over twenty languages and compiling America's first dictionary that defined some 70,000 words.

but even serious error can result when original meanings are ignored:

> [I]n the lapse of two or three centuries, changes have taken place which in particular passages . . . obscure the sense of the original languages. . . . The effect of these changes is that some words are . . . being now used in a sense different from that which they had . . . [and thus] present wrong signification or false ideas. Whenever words are understood in a sense different from that which they had when introduced. . . . mistakes may be very injurious. [3]

To avoid the "injurious mistakes" which may arise from misinterpreting the First Amendment, one need simply establish the original intent of that Amendment. How can this be accomplished? As President Thomas Jefferson admonished Supreme Court Justice William Johnson:

> On every question of construction, carry ourselves back to the time when the Constitution was adopted, recollect the spirit manifested in the debates, and instead of trying what meaning may be squeezed out of the text, or invented against it, conform to the probable one in which it was passed. [4]

James Madison also declared:

> I entirely concur in the propriety of resorting to the sense in which the Constitution was accepted and ratified by the nation. In that sense *alone* it is the *legitimate* Constitution. And if that be not the guide in expounding it, there can be no security for a consistent and stable, more than for a faithful, exercise of its powers. . . . What a metamorphosis would be produced in the code of law if all its ancient phraseology were to be taken in its modern sense. [5] (emphasis added)

Justice James Wilson [†] similarly explained:

> The first and governing maxim in the interpretation of a statute is to discover the meaning of those who made it. [6]

---

† James Wilson (1742-1798) was a distinguished Founder; he was one of only six who signed both the Declaration of Independence and the Constitution; he was the second-most active member of the Constitutional Convention, speaking 168 times on the floor of the Convention; he was a law professor; he was nominated by President George Washington as an original Justice on the U. S. Supreme Court; and in 1792 he was co-author of America's first legal commentaries on the Constitution.

Justice Joseph Story † emphasized this same principle, declaring:

> The first and fundamental rule in the interpretation of all instruments [documents] is to construe them according to the sense of the terms and the intention of the parties. [8]

It was—and typically still is—a fundamental maxim of law to determine the intent of the authors of a statute before attempting to apply it. Therefore, to discover the legitimate scope of protections and prohibitions intended in either the First Amendment or Article VI, investigate the records from that era rather than relying on an interpretation concocted by the Court two hundred years *ex post facto*.

Begin, for instance, by investigating the various proposals for the First Amendment. Notice that of George Mason (a member of the Constitutional Convention and "The Father of the Bill of Rights"):

> [A]ll men have an equal, natural and unalienable right to the free exercise of religion, according to the dictates of conscience; and that no particular sect or society of Christians ought to be favored or established by law in preference to others. [9]

James Madison proposed:

> The civil rights of none shall be abridged on account of religious belief or worship, nor shall any national religion be established. [10]

The *Annals of Congress* from June 8, 1789, to September 25, 1789, contain the complete official records of those who drafted and approved the First Amendment. Notice some of their discussions on its intent:

> AUGUST 15, 1789. Mr. [Peter] Sylvester [of New York] had some doubts. . . . He feared it [the First Amendment] might be thought to have a tendency to abolish religion altogether. . . . Mr. [Elbridge] Gerry [of Massachusetts] said it would read better if it was that "no religious doctrine shall be established by law." . . . Mr. [James] Madison [of Virginia] said he apprehended the meaning of the words to be, that "Congress should not establish a religion, and enforce the legal observation of it by law." . . . [T]he State[s]. . . seemed to entertain an opinion that under the clause of the

---

† Joseph Story (1779-1845) was the son of one of the "Indians" at the "Boston Tea Party"; was the Founder of Harvard Law School; was called the "foremost of American legal writers" [7] and was nominated to the Supreme Court by President James Madison.

Constitution . . . it enabled them [Congress] to make laws of such a nature as might. . . establish a national religion; to prevent these effects he presumed the amendment was intended. . . . Mr. Madison thought if the word "national" was inserted before religion, it would satisfy the minds of honorable gentlemen. . . . He thought if the word "national" was introduced, it would point the amendment directly to the object it was intended to prevent. [11]

The State debates surrounding the ratification of the First Amendment reinforce this intended purpose. Notice, for example, Governor Samuel Johnston's comments during North Carolina's ratifying convention:

I know but two or three States where there is the least chance of establishing any particular religion. The people of Massachusetts and Connecticut are mostly Presbyterians. In every other State, the people are divided into a great number of sects. In Rhode Island, the tenets of the Baptists, I believe, prevail. In New York, they are divided very much: the most numerous are the Episcopalians and the Baptists. In New Jersey, they are as much divided as we are. In Pennsylvania, if any sect prevails more than others, it is that of the Quakers. In Maryland, the Episcopalians are most numerous, though there are other sects. In Virginia, there are many sects; you all know what their religious sentiments are. So in all the Southern States they differ; as also in New Hampshire. I hope, therefore, that gentlemen will see there is no cause of fear that any one religion shall be exclusively established. [12]

In that same convention, Henry Abbot further explained:

Many wish to know what religion shall be established. I believe a majority of the community are Presbyterians. I am, for my part, against any exclusive establishment; but if there were any, I would prefer the Episcopal. [13]

The records are succinct; they clearly document that the Founders' purpose for the First Amendment is *not* compatible with the interpretation given it by contemporary courts. The Founders intended only to prevent the establishment of a single national denomination, not to restrain public religious expressions.

Recall from the previous chapter that the First Amendment was designed to restrain *only* the federal government in the area of religion; it was well established that the States were free to do as they pleased. For example, in his *Commentaries on the Constitution*, Justice Joseph Story explained that because of the First Amendment . . .

> . . . the whole power over the subject of religion is left exclusively to the State governments to be acted upon according to their own sense of justice and the State constitutions. [14]

Thomas Jefferson had previously confirmed this same scope of power:

> I consider the government of the United States [the federal government] as interdicted by the Constitution from intermeddling with religious institutions, their doctrines, discipline, or exercises. This results not only from the provision that no law shall be made respecting the establishment or free exercise of religion [the First Amendment], but from that also which reserves to the States the powers not delegated to the United States [the Tenth Amendment]. Certainly, no power to prescribe any religious exercise or to assume authority in any religious discipline has been delegated to the General [federal] Government. *It must then rest with the States.* [15] (emphasis added)

Although it was completely permissible for the States to have their own State-established denominations, most simply made provision for the encouragement of religion, or for the public teaching of religion in general—as, for example, in the constitutions of New Hampshire and Massachusetts:

> As morality and piety rightly grounded on evangelical principles will give the best and greatest security to government and will lay in the hearts of men the strongest obligations to due subjection; and as the knowledge of these is most likely to be propagated through a society by the institution of the public worship of the Deity and of public instruction in morality and religion; therefore, to promote these important purposes, the people of this State have a right to empower, and do hereby fully empower, the legislature to authorize, from time to time, the several towns, parishes, bodies corporate, or religious societies within this State to make adequate provision at their own expense for the support and maintenance of public Protestant teachers of piety, religion, and morality. NEW HAMPSHIRE [16]

> As the happiness of a people and the good order and preservation of civil government essentially depend upon piety, religion and

morality; and as these cannot be generally diffused through a community but by the institution of the public worship of God and of public instructions in piety, religion and morality: Therefore to promote their happiness and to secure the good order and preservation of their government, the People of this Commonwealth have a right to invest their Legislature with power to authorize and require . . . the several towns, parishes, precincts, and other bodies politic or religious societies, to make suitable provision at their own expense for the institution of the public worship of God and for the support and maintenance of public Protestant teachers of piety, religion, and morality. MASSACHUSETTS [17]

Since the previous excerpts made express provision for Protestant teaching, a mention should be made here about Roman Catholics in America.

The Founders were *not* opposed to Catholics as individuals. This is clearly evidenced by the fact that signer of the Declaration Charles Carroll and signers of the Constitution Thomas FitzSimmons and Daniel Carroll were Roman Catholics. In fact, there were numerous Roman Catholic patriots and leaders in the struggle for American liberty, including Commodore John Barry, General Casimir Pulaski, and General Stephen Moylan. [†] The Founders were not fearful of Roman Catholics but rather of the aspect of Catholic doctrine which they viewed as repugnant to America's unique form of government. Specifically, they opposed the vesting of total, absolute, and irrevocable power in a single body (the Papal authority) without recourse by the people—and they were able to point to specific examples to bolster their argument.

For example, Dr. David Ramsay (a member of the Continental Congress, a surgeon during the Revolution, and an historian) noted that during America's struggle for independence:

[T]he Roman Catholic clergy [in Canada]. . . . used their influence in the next world as an engine to operate on the movements of the present. They refused absolution [forgiveness of sins] to such of their flocks as abetted [aided] the Americans. [18]

John Adams similarly criticized the Roman Catholic "power of deposing princes and absolving [releasing] subjects from allegiance." [19] Understandably, the Founders did not want individuals leading American government

---

† A brief biography of each of these individuals, as well as the other historical personalities referenced throughout this book, can be found in Appendix C: "Biographical Sketches of Select Individuals Referenced in Original Intent."

who maintained a sworn oath of allegiance to a "foreign power" (the Pope). The concern was that such individuals might be required to resist American government by their obedience to an authority who conceivably could issue a hostile decree. As Joseph Story explained:

> [If] men quarrel with the ecclesiastical establishment, the civil magistrate has nothing to do with it unless their tenets and practice are such as threaten ruin or disturbance to the state. He is bound, indeed, to protect. . . . papists [Roman Catholics]. . . . But while they acknowledge a foreign power superior to the sovereignty of the kingdom, they cannot complain if the laws of that kingdom will not treat them upon the footing of good subjects. [20]

It was the implications of this Roman Catholic doctrine which caused many States to exclude from office those who claimed a sole and absolute allegiance to a "foreign power." As the framers of the Massachusetts constitution explained:

> [W]e have . . . found ourselves obliged . . . to provide for the exclusion of these from offices who will not disclaim these principles of spiritual jurisdiction which Roman Catholics in some centuries have held and which are subversive of a free government established by the people. [21]

The North Carolina constitution similarly prohibited from office those who denied "the truth of the Protestant religion" or who held "religious principles incompatible with the freedom and safety of the State." [22] However, as already noted, this was not a rejection of Roman Catholics in general, just of those who embraced doctrines "subversive of a free government established by the people." In fact, when the people of North Carolina later amended their constitution, they maintained the clause excluding from office those who held "religious principles incompatible with the freedom and safety of the State," but they changed "Protestant" to "Christian," [23] thus acknowledging that many American Catholics did not embrace this doctrine.

However, returning to the issue of religion in the federal Constitution, the first ten amendments were enacted solely to limit the jurisdiction of the federal government. Furthermore, it was acknowledged that the States had the legitimate power to prescribe State religious establishments. Therefore, the sole purpose of the First Amendment was to prevent the federal government from usurping this specific State power.

Strikingly, however, although the States reserved this power, none of the State constitutions from the time of the American Revolution (or thereafter) established any single State denomination; most provided equal protection for all. [†] For example, in the framing of the Massachusetts constitution, John Adams explained that "the debates were managed by persons of various denominations" and that the "delegates did not conceive themselves to be vested with power to set up one denomination of Christians above another." [24] Numerous other States enacted similar provisions. Notice:

> And every denomination of Christians . . . shall be equally under the protection of the law: and no subordination of any one sect or denomination to another shall ever be established by law. NEW HAMPSHIRE [25]

> [T]here shall be no establishment of any one religious sect . . . in preference to another. NEW JERSEY [26]

> [T]here shall be no establishment of any one religious church or denomination in this State in preference to any other. NORTH CAROLINA [27]

> And each and every society or denomination of Christians in this State shall have and enjoy the same and equal powers, rights, and privileges. CONNECTICUT [28]

[†] It is a common charge that during the Founding Era at least nine of the thirteen States had State-established denominations. Yet, even a cursory reading of the various State Constitutions enacted following the Revolution disproves this assertion.

Because religious issues often fell within local controls, and because many localities were often of the same denomination (e.g., the overwhelming majority of those in Massachusetts and Connecticut were Congregationalists), what frequently appeared as State establishments were often nothing more than the almost universal preference of the people of that region. As a modern example, the State legislatures of both Arkansas and Hawaii are almost universally composed of Democrats; yet this is not the result of any State constitutional mandate on the establishment of the Democratic Party; it is simply the preference of the people in those States.

Additionally, the erroneous charge concerning the alleged State-establishments often results from critics applying the Supreme Court's current case-law whereby a State "establishment of religion" occurs if money is given to any religious group, or if any religious expression is permitted in government-sanctioned settings. However, this standard would have been almost universally rejected two centuries ago. Only under today's broad definition of "establishment" (i.e., condoning, sanctioning, or aiding any religious expression) rather than the previous narrow reading (i.e., the State-establishment of a single denomination, as in Great Britain's alternating establishment of Anglicanism and Catholicism), can the current charge be even partially defended.

Summarizing this tone, in 1793, Zephaniah Swift (author of America's first law textbook) explained:

> Christians of different denominations ought to consider that the law knows no distinction among them; that they are all established upon the broad basis of equal liberty, that they have a right to think, speak, and worship as they please, and that no sect has power to injure and oppress another. When they reflect that they are equally under the protection of the law, all will revere and love the constitution, and feel interested in the support of the government. No denomination can pride themselves in the enjoyment of superior and exclusive powers and immunities. † [29]

This was the prevalent sentiment across America. In fact, signer of the Declaration Charles Carroll (a Roman Catholic) even declared that the reason that he and many other Founders had entered the Revolution was to ensure that all Christian denominations were placed on an equal footing:

> To obtain religious as well as civil liberty I entered jealously into the Revolution, and observing the Christian religion divided into many sects, I founded the hope that no one would be so predominant as to become the religion of the State. That hope was thus early entertained, because all of them joined in the same cause, with few exceptions of individuals. [30]

Although this was the tone common among the States, it was **not** the result of any provision of the federal Constitution. The constitutional prohibition against "an establishment of religion" forbade only the *federal* establishment of a *national* denomination.

Earlier generations long understood this, and thus prevented any misapplied enforcements of those constitutional provisions. Notice, for example, Justice Story's clear articulation:

> We are not to attribute this [First Amendment] prohibition of a *national* religious establishment to an indifference to religion in general, and especially to Christianity (which none could hold in

---

† This 1793 declaration by Zephaniah Swift (1759-1823)—a leading Connecticut jurist, a U. S. Congressman, and the author of the first purely American law text—is one of many that clearly refutes today's errant claim that Connecticut had a State-established denomination until their 1818 constitution repealed that establishment.

more reverence, than the framers of the Constitution).... Probably, at the time of the adoption of the Constitution, and of the Amendment to it now under consideration, the general, if not the universal, sentiment in America was that Christianity ought to receive encouragement from the State.... An attempt to level all religions and to make it a matter of state policy to hold all in utter indifference would have created universal disapprobation [disapproval] if not universal indignation [anger]. [31] (emphasis added)

Notice, too, the same clear understanding expressed in the 1853-1854 House and Senate Judiciary Committee reports:

HOUSE JUDICIARY COMMITTEE: What is an establishment of religion? It must have a creed defining what a man must believe; it must have rites and ordinances which believers must observe; it must have ministers of defined qualifications to teach the doctrines and administer the rites; it must have tests for the submissive and penalties for the nonconformist. There never was an established religion without all these.... Had the people, during the Revolution, had a suspicion of any attempt to war against Christianity, that Revolution would have been strangled in its cradle. At the time of the adoption of the Constitution and the amendments, the universal sentiment was that Christianity should be encouraged, not any one sect [denomination]. Any attempt to level and discard all religion would have been viewed with universal indignation.... It [religion] must be considered as the foundation on which the whole structure rests. ... In this age there can be no substitute for Christianity; that, in its general principles, is the great conservative element on which we must rely for the purity and permanence of free institutions. That was the religion of the founders of the republic, and they expected it to remain the religion of their descendents. [32]

SENATE JUDICIARY COMMITTEE: The clause speaks of "an establishment of religion." What is meant by that expression? It referred, without doubt, to that establishment which existed in the mother-country.... [which was an] endowment, at the public expense, in exclusion of or in preference to any other, by giving to its members exclusive political rights, and by compelling the attendance of those who rejected its communion upon its worship or religious observances. These three particulars constituted that union of church and state of which our ancestors were so justly jealous, and against which they so wisely and carefully provided.... They [the Founders] intended, by this Amendment, to prohibit "an establishment of religion" such as the English Church presented, or any thing like it. But they had no fear or jealousy of religion itself, nor did they wish to see us an irreligious people ... they did not intend to spread over all the public authorities and the whole public action of the nation the dead and revolting spectacle of atheistical apathy. [33]

The First Amendment was enacted only for a very narrow purpose and to prohibit a very specific offense.

The Founders, however, not only chose **not** to establish federally any particular denomination of Christianity, they further never intended the First Amendment to become a vehicle to promote a pluralism of other religions. As Justice Story explained in his *Commentaries:*

The real object of the [First A]mendment was not to countenance, much less to advance, Mahometanism, or Judaism, or infidelity, by prostrating Christianity; but to exclude all rivalry among Christian sects. [34]

Some people raise two objections against the original intent of the First Amendment. First, they argue that its purpose is no longer valid today since at the time of the Founders the nation was completely homogeneous in its faith. This assertion is incorrect. The Founders openly acknowledged the presence of **numerous** religious groups in America, including Buddhists, Muslims, Jews, etc. In fact, in 1790, Dr. Benjamin Rush (a signer of the Declaration and one of America's top educators) authored the first work calling for free public schools. In that work, he declared:

Such is my veneration for *every* religion that reveals the attributes of the Deity, or a future state of rewards and punishments, that I had rather see the opinions of Confucius or Mohamed inculcated upon our youth than see them grow up wholly devoid of a system of religious principles. But the religion I mean to recommend in this place is that of the New Testament. .... [A]ll its doctrines and precepts are calculated to promote the happiness of society and the safety and well being of civil government. [35] (emphasis added)

Numerous religions *did* exist in America at the time of the Founders; and the Founders understood the potential value of *any* major religion to a society; but they specifically preferred Christianity—a fact John Adams made clear in a letter to Thomas Jefferson:

> Who composed that army of fine young fellows that was then before my eyes? There were among them Roman Catholics, English Episcopalians, Scotch and American Presbyterians, Methodists, Moravians, Anabaptists, German Lutherans, German Calvinists, Universalists, Arians, Priestleyans, Socinians, Independents, Congregationalists, Horse Protestants and House Protestants, Deists and Atheists, and Protestants "qui ne croyent rein." Very few, however, of several of these species; nevertheless, all educated in the general principles of Christianity. . . . Could my answer be understood by any candid reader or hearer, to recommend to all the others the general principles, institutions, or systems of education of the Roman Catholics? Or those of the Quakers? Or those of the Presbyterians? Or those of the Methodists? Or those of the Moravians? Or those of the Universalists? Or those of the Philosophers? No. The general principles on which the fathers achieved independence were. . . . the general principles of Christianity. . . . Now I will avow that I then believed, and now believe, that those general principles of Christianity are as eternal and immutable as the existence and attributes of God. . . . I could therefore safely say, consistently with all my then and present information, that I believed they would never make discoveries in contradiction to these general principles. [36]

Today, we might accurately describe the "general principles of Christianity" as the "Judeo-Christian Ethic" since the Founders showed great attachment to the "Hebrews" (see chapter 8 for detailed information of the Founders' views on this group). Yet, even though the Founders openly acknowledged their veneration for Judaism, they nonetheless believed that the teachings of Christ provided the greatest benefit for civil society. Thomas Jefferson explained:

> The precepts of philosophy, and of the Hebrew code, laid hold of actions only. He [Jesus] pushed his scrutinies into the heart of man; erected his tribunal in the region of his thoughts, and purified the waters at the fountain head. [37]

Zephaniah Swift similarly explained:

> Indeed moral virtue is substantially and essentially enforced by the precepts of Christianity, and may be considered to be the basis of it. But in addition to moral principles, the Christian doctrines inculcate a purity of heart and holiness of life which constitutes its chief glory. When we contemplate it in this light, we have a most striking evidence of its superiority over all the systems of pagan philosophy, which were promulgated by the wisest men of ancient times. [38]

Jefferson and Swift (and numerous others; see Chapter 17) present a compelling argument. Civil law (and most religions) focuses on stopping the act of murder, yet Christianity focuses on stopping the hate and anger which causes the murder. Similarly, the law and most religions try to prevent the act of adultery, but Christianity attacks the internal lust which results in that external behavior. The strongest civil code is impotent against malicious behavior unless the heart itself can be restrained, and even Benjamin Franklin joined Thomas Jefferson (two of the least religiously orthodox Founders) in believing that the teachings of Christianity best accomplished that goal. [39]

Does this mean that the Founders opposed pluralism? No—as long as the beliefs of other religions did not manifest in violent or deviant behavior which might threaten the stability of civil society. In fact, the Founders believed that pluralism survived only within the concept of religious liberty espoused by American Christianity.

Indeed, both modern and ancient history demonstrate that most, if not all other religious nations (whether Muslim, Jewish, Buddhist, monarchal Christian, etc.) rarely allow pluralism. However, independent America was different; it allowed the "free exercise" of other religions. In fact, early courts openly acknowledged that America was pluralistic and tolerant of other religions *only* because it was a Christian nation. †

The second argument raised against maintaining the original intent of the First Amendment is that times have changed; therefore, the meaning of that Amendment should be modernized. While the Founders would have agreed with this premise, they would have vehemently disagreed with the mechanism by which the change has occurred. The Founders made clear that *if* the meaning and application of *any* part of the Constitution

---

† Several of these court cases will be examined in detail in Chapter 4; note especially *Charleston v. Benjamin* and *Lindenmuller v. The People*.

was to be altered, it was to be at the hands of the people—*not* at the feet of the Court. (A discussion on the Founders' views of the proper way to alter or "evolve" the meaning of the Constitution is presented in Chapter 12.)

In summary, the First Amendment's prohibition on "an establishment of religion" was designed to restrict neither religious beliefs nor religious activities but only the federal establishment of a national denomination. Since the people had made no change in that, the Courts, therefore, long realized that just because religious expressions occurred in public, such actions did not "establish religion" under the First Amendment.

However, just as the Founders' massive documentation on the intent of the First Amendment has been ignored, their documentation on the Constitution's other reference to religion has also been disregarded. What was the intent of Article VI's prohibition of a religious test?

As with the First Amendment, Article VI was a provision which limited federal powers and jurisdiction. Since the issue of religion was left to the States, it was therefore not within the federal government's authority to examine the religious beliefs of any candidate. Consequently, as Justice Joseph Story explained, through Article VI it was possible that on the federal level . . .

> . . . the Catholic and the Protestant, the Calvinist and the Armenian, the Jew and the Infidel, may sit down at the common table of the national councils without any inquisition into their faith or mode of worship. [40]

Did this therefore mean—as many currently claim—that the Founders were attempting to prevent an investigation into the religious beliefs of a candidate, or that such beliefs were immaterial to his election? Definitely not (see the Founders' clear views on this issue in Chapter 18). The issue was not the investigation of the religious beliefs of candidates, but rather the jurisdiction for such investigations. The Founders believed that the investigation of the religious views of a candidate should not be conducted by the federal government, but rather by the voters in each State. What evidence supports this?

The discussion of this topic during the ratification debates provides extensive evidence. For example, in the North Carolina ratifying convention, Governor Samuel Johnston explained:

> It is apprehended that Jews, Mahometans, pagans, &c., may be elected to high offices under the government of the United States. Those who are Mahometans, or any others who are not professors of the Christian religion, can never be elected to the office of President or

other high office, but in one of two cases. First, if the *people* of America lay aside the Christian religion altogether, it may happen. Should this unfortunately take place, the people will choose such men as think as they do themselves. Another case is if any persons of such descriptions should, notwithstanding their religion, acquire the confidence and esteem of the people of America by their good conduct and practice of virtue, they may be chosen. [41] (emphasis added)

Signer of the Constitution Richard Dobbs Spaight also declared:

As to the subject of religion. . . . [n]o power is given to the general [federal] government to interfere with it at all. . . . No sect is preferred to another. Every man has a right to worship the Supreme Being in the manner he thinks proper. No test is required. All men of equal capacity and integrity are equally eligible to offices. . . . I do not suppose an infidel, or any such person, will ever be chosen to any office unless the *people* themselves be of the same opinion. [42] (emphasis added)

Supreme Court Justice James Iredell (nominated to the Court by President Washington) similarly explained:

But it is objected that the people of America may perhaps choose representatives who have no religion at all, and that pagans and Mahometans may be admitted into offices. . . . But it is never to be supposed that the *people* of America will trust their dearest rights to persons who have no religion at all, or a religion materially different from their own. [43] (emphasis added)

Article VI simply reaffirmed the Founders' belief that any provisos on religion should remain beyond federal jurisdiction.

The Court's initial abrogation of the original purpose of the Constitution's religious test clause occurred in *Torcaso* v. *Watkins* [44] (1961)—the Court's first-ever Article VI ruling. In that case, the Court used this federal constitutional provision to strike down Maryland's 200 year-old State constitutional requirement that a candidate must declare a belief in God to hold office. This utilization of Article VI obviously resulted in the breaking of new legal ground. As legal authorities observed:

Not until 1961 was this "declaration of belief [in God]". . . invalidated. [45]

The *Torcaso* ruling reflected two major mistakes by the Court: one in jurisdiction and one in interpretation. The jurisdiction error was that the Article VI prohibition against religious tests applied *only* to the federal and not to the State governments. The interpretation error was that the Founding Fathers did not consider a requirement to believe in God to be a religious test.

As an example, consider the provisions of the 1796 Tennessee Constitution (a document created with the help of Constitution signer William Blount [46]):

> Article VIII, Section II. No person who denies the being of God, or a future state of rewards and punishments, shall hold any office in the civil department of this State.
>
> Art XI, Section IV. That no religious test shall ever be required as a qualification to any office or public trust under this State. [47]

Article VIII first requires a belief in God to hold office; then Article XI prohibits a religious test. Clearly, then, requiring a belief in God was *not* a religious test in their view. In fact, the Founders believed that *any* oath or affirmation—including that of elected officials to uphold the Constitution—*presupposed* a belief in God.

For example, Supreme Court Justice James Iredell observed:

> According to the modern definition [1788] of an oath, it is considered a "solemn appeal to the Supreme Being for the truth of what is said by a person who believes in the existence of a Supreme Being and in a future state of rewards and punishments according to that form which would bind his conscience most." [48]

Signer of the Constitution Rufus King explained:

> [In o]ur laws . . . by the oath which they prescribe, we appeal to the Supreme Being so to deal with us hereafter as we observe the obligation of our oaths. The Pagan world were and are without the mighty influence of this principle which is proclaimed in the Christian system—their morals were destitute of its powerful sanction while their oaths neither awakened the hopes nor fears which a belief in Christianity inspires. [49]

George Washington, too, believed that an oath inherently contained a sense of religious obligation. In his "Farewell Address," he asked:

> [W]here is the security for property, for reputation, for life, if the sense of *religious* obligation desert the *oaths* . . . ? [50] (emphasis added)

Also indicative of this belief is the fact that when the convention of South Carolina ratified the Constitution in 1788, it proposed that in Article VI the word "other" should be inserted after the word "no," implying that an oath or affirmation to support the Constitution was itself a religious test. [51]

Numerous other sources further illustrate the fact that the taking of an oath presupposed a belief in God. For example, the 1799 Kentucky Constitution declared:

> The manner of administering an **oath** or affirmation . . . shall be esteemed by the General Assembly [the Legislature] the most **solemn appeal to God."** [52] (emphasis added)

Other constitutions contained the same declaration. [53]

Chancellor James Kent (a Father of American Jurisprudence) noted that an oath of office was a "religious solemnity" and that to administer an oath was "to call in the aid of religion." [54] In the case *People* v. *Ruggles* (1811), Kent ruled that "Christianity was parcel of the law and to cast contumelious [insulting] reproaches upon it tended to weaken . . . the efficacy [effectiveness] of oaths," [55] again affirming the intrinsic relationship between taking an oath and a belief in God.

In *Commonwealth* v. *Wolf* (1817), the Supreme Court of Pennsylvania explained that "laws cannot be administered in any civilized government unless the people are taught to revere the sanctity of an oath. . . . It is of the utmost moment, therefore, that they should be reminded of their religious duties," [56] thus again coupling an oath with a religious duty.

Early school books also taught that to take any oath inherently required a belief in God. One text explained, "An oath supposes that he who takes it believes that there is a God who will in a future life reward the worthy and punish the wicked." [57] An early House Judiciary Committee also declared:

> Laws will not have permanence or power without the sanction of **religious** sentiment—without a firm belief that there is a Power above us that will reward our virtues and punish our vices. [58] (emphasis added)

In his arguments before the U. S. Supreme Court, Daniel Webster, the great "Defender of the Constitution," queried:

> "What is an oath?" . . . [I]t is founded on a degree of consciousness that there is a Power above us that will reward our virtues or punish our vices. . . . [O]ur system of oaths in all our courts, by which we

hold liberty and property and all our rights, are founded on or rest on Christianity and a religious belief. [59]

He further noted:

We all know that the doctrine of the . . . law is that there must be in every person who enters court as a witness, be he Christian or Hindoo, there must be a firm conviction on his mind that falsehood or perjury will be punished either in this world or the next or he cannot be admitted as a witness. If he has not this belief, he is disfranchised [not admitted]. [60]

Justice Story confirms this, declaring that "infidels and pagans were banished from the halls of justice as unworthy of credit," [61] and the *New York Spectator* of August 23, 1831, reported:

The court of common pleas of Chester county (New York) a few days since rejected a witness who declared his disbelief in the existence of God. The presiding judge remarked that he had not before been aware that there was a man living who did not believe in the existence of God; that this belief constituted the sanction of all testimony in a court of justice: and that he knew of no cause in a Christian country where a witness had been permitted to testify without such belief. [62]

This had long been the practice of courts. For example, Zephaniah Swift declared:

All persons who believe in the existence of a God, let their religion be what it will, may be admitted to be witnesses. An oath is a solemn appeal to the Supreme Being that he who takes it will speak the truth, and an imprecation of His vengeance if he swears false. [63]

An oath, whether taken by a court witness or a public official, inherently signified a belief in God. There are abundant examples that this was not just an eighteenth century phenomenon. For instance, an 1834 legal guide for Tennessee judges declared:

Judges, justices of the peace, and all other persons who are or shall be empowered to administer oaths, shall . . . require the party to be sworn to lay his hand upon the holy evangelists of Almighty God in token of his engagement to speak the truth as he hopes to be saved in the way and method of salvation pointed out in that blessed volume; and in further token that if he should swerve from the truth, he may be justly deprived of all the blessings of the gospels and be made liable to that vengeance which he has imprecated on his own head; and after repeating the words, 'So help me God,' shall kiss the holy gospels as a scale of confirmation to said engagement. [64]

There were, however, some groups which held *religious* convictions for not conforming to this method of oath-taking (the Quakers, for example). Tolerant of such groups, the legal guide provided this recourse:

In all cases where . . . the person to be sworn shall be conscientiously scrupulous in taking a book oath . . . [then] the party . . . shall stand with his right hand lifted up towards Heaven in token of his solemn appeal to the Supreme God whose dwellings are in the highest Heavens, and also in token that if he should swerve from the truth he would draw down the vengeance of Heaven upon his head . . . with these words, viz: " 'You solemnly appeal to God, as a witness of truth and avenger of falsehood, as you shall answer for the same at the great day of judgment, when the secrets of all hearts shall be made known, that,' &c.. [65]

The evidence is clear: the Founders, and even legal authorities for generations afterwards, viewed a belief in God as an inherent part of taking an oath.

The Constitution required an oath of office, but prohibited a religious test; an oath, however, presupposed a belief in God; therefore, only under the most extreme and absurd application of Article VI could a belief in God have been considered a religious test. Consequently, when the *Torcaso* Court struck down the requirement of belief in God to hold office, it essentially struck down the requirement that public officials take an oath to uphold the Constitution. As signer of the Declaration John Witherspoon clearly explained, the two were inseparable:

An oath is an appeal to God, the Searcher of hearts, for the truth of what we say and always expresses or supposes an imprecation [a calling down] of His judgment upon us if we prevaricate [lie]. An oath, therefore, implies a belief in God and His Providence and indeed is an act of worship. . . . Persons entering on public offices are also often obliged to make oath that they will faithfully execute their trust. . . . In vows, there is no party but God and the person himself who makes the vow. [66]

Recall also that since Article VI pertained only to the federal government, it was within the legitimate jurisdiction of the States to establish whatever provisions the people wished. Significantly, many of the State requirements were often drafted by the same individuals who had signed the federal Constitution and who had approved Article VI.

For example, signers of the Constitution George Read [67] and Richard Bassett [68] also directed the drafting of the Delaware constitution. That constitution required:

> Every person who shall be chosen a member of either house, or appointed to any office or place of trust . . . shall . . . make and subscribe the following declaration, to wit: "I, _____, do profess faith in God the Father, and in Jesus Christ His only Son, and the Holy Ghost, one God, blessed for evermore; and I do acknowledge the holy scriptures of the Old and New Testament to be given by divine inspiration." [69]

Constitution signer Nathaniel Gorham helped author the Massachusetts constitution [70] which required:

> Any person chosen governor, or lieutenant-governor, counsellor, senator, or representative, and accepting the trust, shall before he proceed to execute the duties of his place or office, take, make and subscribe the following declaration, viz. "I, _____, do declare, that I believe the Christian religion, and have a firm persuasion of its truth." [71]

Other States had similar requirements—often authored by those who had signed the federal Constitution and had approved Article VI. Clearly, then, the Founders never intended that the prohibition in Article VI be applied to the States.

The imperative for understanding today the original purposes of the two religion clauses in the Constitution results from contemporary Courts often excusing their unpopular decisions with the specious claim that they are upholding the Constitution's original "intent" or "purpose." This claim is an historical absurdity. Furthermore, it has only been in recent generations that the original intent has been obscured—and that obscurity has been caused by the Courts.

Perhaps the most conclusive historical demonstration of the fact that the Founders never intended the federal Constitution to establish today's religion-free public arena is seen in their creation and passage of the "Northwest Ordinance." That Ordinance (a federal law which legal texts consider as one of the four foundational, or "organic" laws [72]) set forth the requirements of statehood for prospective territories. It received House approval on July 21, 1789; [73] Senate approval on August 4, 1789 [74] (this was the same Congress which was simultaneously framing the religion clauses of the First Amendment); and was signed into law by President George Washington on August 7, 1789. [75]

Article III of that Ordinance is the only section to address either religion or public education, and in it, the Founders couple them, declaring:

> Religion, morality, and knowledge, being necessary to good government and the happiness of mankind, schools and the means of education shall forever be encouraged. [76]

The Framers of the Ordinance—and thus the Framers of the First Amendment—believed that schools and educational systems were a proper means to encourage the "religion, morality, and knowledge" which they deemed so "necessary to good government and the happiness of mankind."

Subsequent to the passage of this Ordinance, when a territory applied for admission as a State, Congress issued an "enabling act" establishing the provisions of the Ordinance as criteria for drafting a State constitution. For example, when Ohio territory applied for statehood in 1802, its enabling act required that Ohio form its government in a manner "not repugnant to the Ordinance." [77] Consequently, the Ohio constitution declared:

> [R]eligion, morality, and knowledge being essentially necessary to the good government and the happiness of mankind, schools and the means of instruction shall forever be encouraged by legislative provision. [78]

While this requirement originally applied to all the territorial holdings of the United States in 1789 (the Northwest Territory—Ohio, Indiana, Illinois, Michigan, Wisconsin, and Minnesota), as more territory was gradually ceded to the United States (the Southern Territory—Mississippi and Alabama), Congress applied the requirements of the Ordinance to that new territory. [79]

Therefore, when Mississippi applied for statehood in 1817, Congress required that it form its government in a manner "not repugnant to the principles of the Ordinance." [80] Hence, the Mississippi constitution declared:

> Religion, morality, and knowledge, being necessary to good government, the preservation of liberty and the happiness of mankind, schools and the means of education shall be forever encouraged in this State. [81]

Congress later extended the same requirements to the Missouri Territory [82] (Missouri and Arkansas) and then on to subsequent territories. Consequently, the provision coupling religion and schools continued to appear in State constitutions for decades. For example, the 1858 Kansas constitution required:

> Religion, morality, and knowledge, however, being essential to good government, it shall be the duty of the legislature to make suitable provisions . . . for the encouragement of schools and the means of instruction. [83]

Similarly, the 1875 Nebraska constitution required:

> Religion, morality, and knowledge, however, being essential to good government, it shall be the duty of the legislature to pass suitable laws . . . to encourage schools and the means of instruction. [84]

Numerous other territorial papers and State constitutions—past and present [85]—make it clear that the Founding Fathers never intended to separate religious instruction or religious activities from the public or official life of America. Yet today the Courts have misinterpreted the First Amendment and Article VI to prohibit exactly what the Founders intended to protect.

The dilemma outlined in this chapter was succinctly described by Justice William Rehnquist in *Wallace* v. *Jaffree:*

> History must judge whether it was the Father of his Country in 1789, or a majority of the Court today, which has strayed from the meaning of the [First Amendment]. [86]

The historical "straying" from the Founders' original meaning for the First Amendment has been greatly facilitated by an overused, misused, and even regularly abused historical phrase: "the separation of church and state." Although these words are familiar to virtually the entire nation, few Americans know their history; where did this phrase originate?

~3~
The Misleading Metaphor

"Separation of church and state"—the expression Justice William Rehnquist described as "a misleading metaphor" [1]—appeared in an exchange of letters between President Thomas Jefferson and the Baptist Association of Danbury, Connecticut.

The election of President Jefferson—America's first Anti-Federalist President—elated many Baptists since that denomination was, by-and-large, strongly Anti-Federalist. [2] This political disposition by the Baptists was understandable; from the early settlement of Rhode Island in the 1630s to the time of the federal Constitution in the 1780s, the Baptists had often found themselves suffering from the centralization of power.

Consequently, now having a President who had not only championed the rights of Baptists in Virginia [3] but who also advocated clear limits on the centralization of government powers, the Danbury Baptists wrote Jefferson a letter of praise on October 7, 1801, telling him:

> Among the many millions in America and Europe who rejoice in your election to office, we embrace the first opportunity ... to express our great satisfaction in your appointment to the Chief Magistracy in the United States. ... [W]e have reason to believe that America's God has raised you up to fill the Chair of State out of that goodwill which he bears to the millions which you preside over. May God strengthen you for the arduous task which providence and the voice of the people have called you. ... And may the Lord preserve you safe from every evil and bring you at last to his Heavenly Kingdom through Jesus Christ our Glorious Mediator. [4]

However, in that same letter of congratulations, the Baptists also expressed to Jefferson their grave concern over the entire concept of the First Amendment:

> Our sentiments are uniformly on the side of religious liberty: that religion is at all times and places a matter between God and individuals, that no man ought to suffer in name, person, or effects on account of his religious opinions, [and] that the legitimate power of civil government extends no further than to punish the man

who works ill to his neighbor. But sir, our constitution of government is not specific. . . . [T]herefore what religious privileges we enjoy (as a minor part of the State) we enjoy as favors granted, and not as inalienable rights. [5]

The inclusion of Constitutional protection for the "free exercise of religion" suggested to the Danbury Baptists that the right was government-given (thus alienable) rather than God-given (hence inalienable), and that therefore the government might someday attempt to regulate religious expression. This was a possibility to which they strenuously objected—unless someone's religious practice caused him, as they explained, to "work ill to his neighbor."

Jefferson understood their concern; it was also his own. He made numerous statements declaring the inability of the government to regulate, restrict, or interfere with religious expression. For example:

[N]o power over the freedom of religion . . . [is] delegated to the United States by the Constitution. [6] KENTUCKY RESOLUTION, 1798

In matters of religion I have considered that its free exercise is placed by the Constitution independent of the powers of the general [federal] government. [7] SECOND INAUGURAL ADDRESS, 1805

[O]ur excellent Constitution . . . has not placed our religious rights under the power of any public functionary. [8] LETTER TO THE METHODIST EPISCOPAL CHURCH, 1808

I consider the government of the United States as interdicted [prohibited] by the Constitution from intermeddling with religious institutions . . . or exercises. [9] LETTER TO SAMUEL MILLER, 1808

Jefferson believed that the government was to be powerless to interfere with religious expressions for a very simple reason: he had long witnessed the unhealthy tendency of government to encroach upon the free exercise of religious expression. As he explained to Noah Webster:

It had become an universal and almost uncontroverted position in the several States that the purposes of society do not require a surrender of all our rights to our ordinary governors . . . and which experience has nevertheless proved they [the government] will be constantly encroaching on if submitted to them; that there are also certain fences which experience has proved peculiarly efficacious [effective] against wrong and rarely obstructive of right, which yet the governing powers have ever shown a disposition to weaken and remove. Of the first kind, for instance, is freedom of religion. [10]

Thomas Jefferson had no intention of allowing the government to limit, restrict, regulate, or interfere with public religious practices. He believed, along with the other Founders, that the First Amendment had been enacted only to prevent the federal establishment of a national denomination—a fact he made clear in a letter to fellow-signer of the Declaration of Independence Benjamin Rush:

> [T]he clause of the Constitution which, while it secured the freedom of the press, covered also the freedom of religion, had given to the clergy a very favorite hope of obtaining an establishment of a particular form of Christianity through the United States; and as every sect believes its own form the true one, every one perhaps hoped for his own, but especially the Episcopalians and Congregationalists. The returning good sense of our country threatens abortion to their hopes and they believe that any portion of power confided to me will be exerted in opposition to their schemes. And they believe rightly. [11]

Jefferson committed himself as President to pursuing what he believed to be the purpose of the First Amendment: not allowing the Episcopalians, Congregationalists, or any other denomination to achieve the "establishment of a particular form of Christianity."

Since this was Jefferson's view, in his short and polite reply to the Danbury Baptists on January 1, 1802, he assured them that they need not fear; the free exercise of religion would *never* be interfered with by the government. As he explained:

> Gentlemen,—The affectionate sentiments of esteem and approbation which you are so good as to express towards me on behalf of the Danbury Baptist Association give me the highest satisfaction. . . . Believing with you that religion is a matter which lies solely between man and his God; that he owes account to none other for his faith or his worship; that the legislative powers of government reach actions only and not opinions, I contemplate with sovereign reverence that act of the whole American people

which declared that their legislature should "make no law respecting an establishment of religion or prohibiting the free exercise thereof," thus building a wall of separation between Church and State. Adhering to this expression of the supreme will of the nation in behalf of the rights of conscience, I shall see with sincere satisfaction the progress of those sentiments which tend to restore to man all his natural rights, convinced he has no natural right in opposition to his social duties. I reciprocate your kind prayers for the protection and blessing of the common Father and Creator of man, and tender you for yourselves and your religious association assurances of my high respect and esteem. [12]

Jefferson's reference to "natural rights" invoked an important legal phrase which was part of the rhetoric of that day. The use of that phrase confirmed his belief that religious liberties were inalienable rights. While those words communicated much to people then, to most citizens today it means little.

By definition, "natural rights" included "that which the Books of the Law and the Gospel do contain." [13] Very simply, "natural rights" incorporated what God Himself had guaranteed to man in the Scriptures. Thus when Jefferson assured the Baptists that by following their "natural rights" they would violate *no* social duty, it was understood that he was affirming to them his belief that the free exercise of religion was their inalienable God-given right. They were therefore assured that the issue of religious expressions was above federal jurisdiction.

So clearly did Jefferson understand the Source of America's inalienable rights that he even doubted whether America could survive if we ever lost that knowledge. He queried:

And can the liberties of a nation be thought secure if we have lost the only firm basis, a conviction in the minds of the people that these liberties are the gift of God? That they are not to be violated but with His wrath? [14]

Jefferson believed that God, not government, was the Author and Source of our rights and that the government, therefore, was to be prevented from interference with those rights. Very simply, the "fence" of the Webster letter and the "wall" of the Danbury letter were *not* to limit religious activities in public; rather they were to limit the power of the government to prohibit or interfere with those expressions.

Earlier courts long understood Jefferson's intent. In fact, when Jefferson's letter was invoked by the Court (only once prior to the 1947 *Everson* case—the *Reynolds* v. *United States* case in 1878), unlike today's Courts which publish only his eight-word separation phrase, that Court published Jefferson's full letter, and then concluded:

> Coming as this does from an acknowledged leader of the advocates of the measure, it [Jefferson's letter] may be accepted almost as an authoritative declaration of the scope and effect of the Amendment thus secured. ***Congress*** was deprived of all ***legislative power*** over mere [religious] opinion, but was left free to ***reach actions which were in violation of social duties or subversive of good order.*** [15] (emphasis added)

That Court then succinctly summarized Jefferson's intent for "separation of church and state":

> [T]he rightful purposes of civil government are for its officers to interfere when principles break out into overt acts against peace and good order. In th[is] . . . is found the true distinction between what properly belongs to the church and what to the State. [16]

With this even the Baptists had agreed; for while wanting to see the government prohibited from interfering with or limiting religious activities, they also had declared it a legitimate function of government "to punish the man who works ill to his neighbor."

That Court, therefore, and others (for example, *Commonwealth* v. *Nesbit* [17] and *Lindenmuller* v. *The People* [18]), identified actions into which—if perpetrated in the name of religion—the government ***did*** have legitimate reason to intrude. Those activities included human sacrifice, polygamy, bigamy, concubinage, incest, infanticide, parricide, advocation and promotion of immorality, etc.

Such acts, even if perpetrated in the name of religion, would be stopped by the government since, as the Court had explained, they were "subversive of good order" and were "overt acts against peace and good order." However, the government was ***never*** to interfere with ***traditional*** religious practices outlined in "the Books of the Law and the Gospel"—whether public prayer, the use of the Scriptures, etc.

Therefore, if Jefferson's letter is to be used today, let its context be clearly given—as in previous years. Furthermore, that single letter should never be invoked as a stand-alone document. Earlier Courts had always viewed Jefferson's Danbury letter for what it was: a personal, private letter to a specific group. There is probably no other instance in America's history where words spoken by a single individual in a private letter—words clearly divorced from their context—have become the sole authorization for a national judicial policy. A proper analysis of Jefferson's views must include his numerous other statements on the First Amendment.

For example, Jefferson also declared that the "power to prescribe any religious exercise. . . . *must rest with the States*" [19] (emphasis added). Interestingly, the federal courts who misuse his separation phrase deliberately ignore this succinct declaration, regularly striking down scores of State laws which encourage or facilitate public religious expressions. Such rulings are a direct violation of the intent of the one on whom the courts claim so heavily to rely.

One further note should be made about the now infamous "separation" dogma. The *Congressional Records* from June 7 to September 25, 1789, record the months of discussions and debates of the ninety Founding Fathers who framed the First Amendment. Significantly, during those debates not one of those ninety Framers ever mentioned the phrase "separation of church and state." It seems logical that if this had been the intent of the Founding Fathers for the First Amendment—as is so frequently asserted—then at least one of those ninety would have mentioned that phrase; none did.

Since the "separation" phrase was used so infrequently by the Founders, and since early courts rarely invoked it, how did those courts rule on the religious issues and activities which confront today's courts? Were their conclusions different from those reached now? As demonstrated in the following chapter, the answer is an emphatic and a resounding, "Yes!"

~4~
The Judicial Evidence

Excerpts from twenty-one early cases will be presented in this chapter. These cases, representative of many others, will demonstrate that contrary to the actions of current courts, early courts protected, advanced, encouraged, and promoted the role and influence of religion throughout society. Significantly, several Judges who ruled in these early cases had personally participated in the drafting and ratification of the Constitution and thus were quite sure about its intent.

Church of the Holy Trinity v. *United States* (1892)
United States Supreme Court

This case provides a good starting point since it incorporates several previous decisions. At issue was an 1885 federal immigration law which declared:

> [I]t shall be unlawful for any person, company, partnership, or corporation, in any manner whatsoever to . . . in any way assist or encourage the importation . . . of any alien or . . . foreigners into the United States . . . under contract or agreement . . . to perform labor or service of any kind. [1]

Since this law, on its face, appeared to be a straightforward ban on hiring foreign labor, when the Church of the Holy Trinity in New York employed a clergyman from England as its pastor, the U. S. Attorney's office brought suit against the church. When the case reached the Supreme Court, the Court began by examining the legislative records surrounding the passage of that law and discovered that its sole purpose had been to halt the influx of almost slave-like foreign labor to construct the western railroads. Thus, while the church's hiring of the minister had violated the wording of the law, it clearly had fallen far outside the spirit and intent of that law. The Court therefore concluded that it would be an absurd application to prosecute the church under that law.

After vindicating the church, the Court spent the remainder of the case explaining that it would be completely repugnant to the spirit of the Constitution to in any way hinder, whether directly or indirectly, the spread or propagation of Christianity by legislative act. As the Court noted:

[N]o purpose of action against religion can be imputed to any legislation, State or national, because this is a religious people.... [T]his is a Christian nation. [2]

To support its conclusion that "this is a religious people. . . . this is a Christian nation," the Court paraded a veritable litany of precedents from American history:

From the discovery of this continent to the present hour, there is a single voice making this affirmation. The commission to Christopher Columbus ... [recited] that "it is hoped that by God's assistance some of the continents and islands in the ocean will be discovered," etc. The first colonial grant—that made to Sir Walter Raleigh in 1584— . . . and the grant authorizing him to enact statutes for the government of the proposed colony provided that "they be not against the true Christian faith. . . . " The first charter of Virginia, granted by King James I in 1606 . . . commenced the grant in these words: " . . . in propagating of Christian Religion to such People as yet live in Darkness . . . . "

Language of similar import may be found in ... the various charters granted to the other colonies. In language more or less emphatic is the establishment of the Christian religion declared to be one of the purposes of the grant. The celebrated compact made by the Pilgrims in the Mayflower, 1620, recites: "Having undertaken for the Glory of God, and advancement of the Christian faith . . . a voyage to plant the first colony in the northern parts . . . . "

The fundamental orders of Connecticut, under which a provisional government was instituted in 1638-1639, commence with this declaration: " . . . And well knowing where a people are gathered together the word of God requires that to maintain the peace and union . . . there should be an orderly and decent government established according to God ... to maintain and preserve the liberty and purity of the gospel of our Lord Jesus which we now profess ... of the said Gospel [which] is now practiced amongst us."

In the charter of privileges granted by William Penn to the province of Pennsylvania, in 1701, it is recited: " . . . no people can be truly happy, though under the greatest enjoyment of civil liberties, if abridged of . . . their religious profession and worship. . . . "

Coming nearer to the present time, the Declaration of Independence recognizes the presence of the Divine in human affairs in these words: "We hold these truths to be self-evident, that all men are created equal, that they are endowed by their Creator with certain unalienable Rights . . ."; " . . . appealing to the Supreme Judge of the world for the rectitude of our intentions . . ."; "And for the support of this Declaration, with a firm reliance on the Protection of Divine Providence, we mutually pledge to each other our Lives, our Fortunes, and our sacred Honor." [3]

After citing many additional historical examples, the Court then reviewed several legal precedents which further buttressed its declaration:

[W]e find that in *Updegraph* v. *The Commonwealth*, 11 S. & R. 394, 400, it was decided that, "Christianity, general Christianity, is, and always has been, a part of the common law . . . not Christianity with an established church . . . but Christianity with liberty of conscience to all men." And in *The People* v. *Ruggles*, 8 Johns. 290, 294, 295, Chancellor Kent, the great commentator on American law, speaking as Chief Justice of the Supreme Court of New York, said: "The people of this State, in common with the people of this country, profess the general doctrines of Christianity, as the rule of their faith and practice. . . . [W]e are a Christian people, and the morality of the country is deeply engrafted upon Christianity, and not upon the doctrines or worship of those impostors [other religions]." And in the famous case of *Vidal* v. *Girard's Executors*, 2 How. 127, 198, this Court . . . observed: "It is also said, and truly, that the Christian religion is a part of the common law." [4]

After several pages of similar discourse, the Court concluded:

There is no dissonance in these declarations. There is a universal language pervading them all, having one meaning; they affirm and reaffirm that this is a religious nation. These are not individual sayings, declarations of private persons: they are organic [legal, governmental] utterances; they speak the voice of the entire people. . . . These, and many other matters which might be noticed, add a volume of unofficial declarations to the mass of organic utterances that this is a Christian nation. [5]

As far as the Court was concerned, the issue was closed; it would never support any action which might have the effect of suppressing religion or of limiting religious expression.

Since the Court cited *Updegraph* v. *Commonwealth*, *People* v. *Ruggles*, and *Vidal* v. *Girard's Executors* in reaching its conclusion, it will be profitable to review these cases. However, before examining these three cases—and seventeen others—an observation should first be made about rulings issued by State Supreme Courts.

For 150 years following the ratification of the Constitution, States were considered the highest authority on any dispute involving the issues within the Bill of Rights. Only under unusual circumstances would a case involving those freedoms reach the federal courts. In fact, the *Holy Trinity* Court noted that federal courts rarely ruled on controversies involving religion. [6]

Therefore, since federal courts were less of an authority on these issues, they frequently cited State Supreme Court decisions as their authority—as did the Court in *Holy Trinity*. Only since the Court's federalization of the States in the mid-twentieth century have State Supreme Courts been viewed as subordinate to the federal courts. It will be helpful to recall this when reviewing the following cases.

Updegraph v. *The Commonwealth* (1824)
Supreme Court of Pennsylvania

This was the first case cited in *Holy Trinity*, and the facts of the case were described in the grand jury's indictment:

> Abner Updegraph . . . not having the fear of God before his eyes . . . contriving and intending to scandalize and bring into disrepute and vilify the Christian religion and the scriptures of truth in the presence and hearing of several persons . . . did unlawfully, wickedly and premeditatively, despitefully and blasphemously say . . . : "That the Holy Scriptures were a mere fable: that they were a contradiction, and that although they contained a number of good things, yet they contained a great many lies." To the great dishonor of Almighty God [and] to the great scandal of the profession of the Christian religion. [7]

Updegraph, indicted under the State law against blasphemy, was found guilty by the jury; that verdict was appealed.

Since the central question revolved around the issue of blasphemy, the court needed to establish a legal definition of that word. It therefore turned to the writings of the foremost legal authority of the day: William Blackstone.

Blackstone's *Commentaries on the Laws,* introduced in 1766, became ***the*** law book of the Founding Fathers. [8] (In fact, so strong was its influence in America that Thomas Jefferson once quipped that American lawyers used *Blackstone's* with the same dedication and reverence that Muslims used the Koran. [9]) It was therefore logical that the court should turn to this source to establish the legal definition of "blasphemy":

> Blasphemy against the Almighty is denying His being or Providence or uttering contumelious [insulting] reproaches on our Savior Christ. It is punished at common law by fine and imprisonment, for Christianity is part of the laws of the land. [10]

By the legal definition, Updegraph had clearly violated the law. His attorney, however, argued that his conviction should be overturned for two reasons: (1) Updegraph was a member of a debating association which convened weekly, and what he said had been uttered in the course of an argument on a religious question; (2) that both the State and federal Constitution protected freedom of speech, and that if any State law against blasphemy did exist, the federal Constitution had done away with it; Christianity was no longer part of the law. (Undoubtedly, defense arguments would differ little today.) The supreme court responded:

> The jury . . . finds a malicious intention in the speaker to vilify the Christian religion and the Scriptures and this court cannot look beyond the record nor take any notice of the allegation that the words were uttered by the defendant, a member of a debating association which convened weekly for discussion and mutual information. . . . That there is an association in which so serious a subject is treated with so much levity, indecency and scurrility [vulgar and obscene language] . . . I am sorry to hear, for it would prove a nursery of vice, a school of preparation to qualify young men for the gallows and young women for the brothel, and there is not a skeptic of decent manners and good morals who would not consider such debating clubs as a common nuisance and

disgrace to the city. . . . [I]t was the outpouring of an invective so vulgarly shocking and insulting that the lowest grade of civil authority ought not to be subject to it, but when spoken in a Christian land and to a Christian audience, the highest offence *contra bonos mores* [against proper standards]. [11]

Having rejected the defense argument concerning a debating society, the court concluded by refuting the defense contention that the constitution disregarded Christianity:

[T]he assertion is once more made that Christianity never was received as part of the common law of this Christian land; and it is added that if it was it was virtually repealed by the Constitution of the United States and of this State. . . .

We will first dispose of what is considered the grand objection— the constitutionality of Christianity—for, in effect, that is the question. Christianity, general Christianity, is and always has been a part of the common law . . . not Christianity founded on any particular religious tenets; not Christianity with an established church . . . but Christianity with liberty of conscience to all men.

Thus this wise legislature framed this great body of laws for a Christian country and Christian people. . . . This is the Christianity of the common law . . . and thus it is irrefragably [undeniably] proved that the laws and institutions of this State are built on the foundation of reverence for Christianity. . . . In this the Constitution of the United States has made no alteration nor in the great body of the laws which was an incorporation of the common-law doctrine of Christianity.

No free government now exists in the world unless where Christianity is acknowledged and is the religion of the country. . . . Its foundations are broad and strong and deep . . . it is the purest system of morality, the firmest auxiliary, and only stable support of all human laws. [12]

The People v. *Ruggles* (1811)
Supreme Court of New York

This was the second case cited in *Holy Trinity*, and the facts are described in the case:

The defendant was indicted . . . for that he did . . . wickedly, maliciously, and blasphemously utter and with a loud voice publish in the presence and hearing of divers good and Christian people, of and concerning the Christian religion, and of and concerning Jesus Christ, the false, scandalous, malicious, wicked and blasphemous words following: "Jesus Christ was a bastard and his mother must be a whore," in contempt of the Christian religion. . . . [T]he defendant was tried and found guilty and was sentenced by the court to be imprisoned for three months and to pay a fine of $500. [13]

The defendant's attorney had presented a simple defense:

There are no statutes concerning religion. . . . The constitution allows a free toleration to all religions and all kinds of worship. . . . Judaism and Mahometanism may be preached here without any legal animadversion [criticism]. . . . [T]he prisoner may have been a Jew, a Mahometan, or a Socinian: and if so, he had a right, by the constitution, to declare his opinions. [14]

The court's decision in this case was delivered by Chief Justice James Kent, who, along with Justice Joseph Story, is considered one of the two Fathers of American Jurisprudence. (In fact, Kent's four-volume *Commentaries on American Law* eventually replaced Blackstone's as the standard for American law.) Notice Judge Kent's decision in this case:

Nothing could be more offensive to the virtuous part of the community, or more injurious to the tender morals of the young, than to declare such profanity lawful. . . .

The free, equal, and undisturbed enjoyment of religious opinion, whatever it may be, and free and decent discussions on any religious subject, is granted and secured; but to revile . . . the religion professed by almost the whole community is an abuse of that right. . . . [W]e are a Christian people and the morality of the country is deeply engrafted upon Christianity and not upon the doctrines or worship of those impostors [other religions]. . . . [We are] people whose manners . . . and whose morals have been elevated and inspired . . . by means of the Christian religion.

Though the constitution has discarded religious establishments, it does not forbid judicial cognizance of those offenses against religion and morality which have no reference to any such establishment. . . . This [constitutional] declaration (noble and magnanimous as it is, when duly understood) never meant to withdraw religion in general, and with it the best sanctions of moral and social obligation from all consideration and notice of the law. . . . To construe it [the constitution] as breaking down the common law barriers against licentious, wanton, and impious attacks upon Christianity itself, would be an enormous perversion of its meaning. [15]

Vidal v. *Girard's Executors* (1844)
United States Supreme Court

This was the third case cited in *Holy Trinity,* and it involved the probation of the will of Frenchman Stephen Girard who had arrived in America before the Declaration of Independence was signed. Girard settled in Philadelphia and lived there until his death in 1831, whereupon his entire estate and personal property (valued at over $7 million) was bequeathed to the city on the condition that it construct an orphanage and a college according to his stipulations. Girard's heirs (the plaintiffs) filed suit contesting the will on two grounds: (1) that a private will could not be given to a public entity; and (2) that as a provision for the college, Girard had stipulated:

I enjoin and require that no ecclesiastic, missionary, or minister of any sect whatsoever, shall ever hold or exercise any station or duty whatever in the said college; nor shall any such person ever be admitted for any purpose, or as a visitor, within the premises. . . . My desire is that all the instructors and teachers in the college shall take pains to instill into the minds of the scholars the purest principles of morality. [16]

His requirement to exclude clergy and religious teachings from a school was unprecedented. The great Daniel Webster (the "Defender of the Constitution") and Walter Jones were the lawyers for the plaintiffs. Jones argued that:

[T]he plan of education proposed is anti-Christian and therefore repugnant to the law. [17]

Webster reminded the Court that:

> Both in the Old and New Testaments its importance [i.e., the religious instruction of youth] is recognized. In the Old it is said, "Thou shalt diligently teach them to thy children," and in the New, "Suffer little children to come unto me and forbid them not. . . ." No fault can be found with Girard for wishing a marble college to bear his name for ever, but it is not valuable unless it has a fragrance of Christianity about it. [18]

Webster believed that the single provision excluding clergy was sufficient to cause Girard's entire will to be set aside. The city's attorneys disagreed; although they, too, believed that it was wrong to exclude clergy, they claimed that instead of contesting the entire will, the plaintiffs should simply have:

> [J]oined with us in asking the State to cut off the obnoxious clause. [19]

As the city's attorneys explained to the Court, religion *must* be taught at the school:

> The purest principles of morality *are* to be taught. Where are they found? Whoever searches for them must go to the source from which a Christian man derives his faith—the Bible. . . . [T]here is an *obligation* to teach what the Bible alone can teach, viz. a pure system of morality. [20] (emphasis added)

After all the arguments were finished, the unanimous opinion of the Supreme Court was delivered by Justice Joseph Story. The Court first ruled that Girard's estate could be delivered to the city of Philadelphia, but that the teaching of Christianity could *not* be excluded from the school:

> Christianity . . . is not to be maliciously and openly reviled and blasphemed against to the annoyance of believers or the injury of the public. . . . It is unnecessary for us, however, to consider . . . the establishment of a school or college for the propagation of Judaism or Deism or any other form of infidelity. Such a case is not to be presumed to exist in a Christian country. [21]

The Court then pointed out to both sides that even though the will had prohibited clergy, it had not prohibited Christian instruction and was therefore constitutionally acceptable. As the Court explained:

> Why may not laymen instruct in the general principles of Christianity as well as ecclesiastics [the clergy]. . . . And we cannot overlook the blessings which such [lay]men by their conduct, as well as their instructions, may, nay *must* impart to their youthful pupils. Why may not the Bible, and *especially* the New Testament, without note or comment, be read and taught as a *divine revelation* in the college—its general precepts expounded, its evidences explained and its glorious principles of morality inculcated? . . . Where can the purest principles of morality be learned so clearly or so perfectly as from the New Testament? [22] (emphasis added)

While many legal controversies had marked this case, on the issue of Christian teachings in this government-run school, all parties had agreed: the plaintiff's lawyers said education without Christianity was "repugnant"; the city's lawyers declared it "obnoxious"; and the Supreme Court said that it couldn't be permitted—moral principles in schools *must* be taught from the Bible.

Commonwealth v. *Abner Kneeland* (1838)
Supreme Court of Massachusetts

This case, like both the *Updegraph* and the *Ruggles* cases, also involved an attack against God and Christianity. However, unlike those two cases, these attacks had been published rather than spoken. The indictment recorded Kneeland's published statements:

> "The Universalists believe in a god which I do not; but believe that their god, with all his moral attributes . . . is nothing more than a chimera of their own imagination"; "Universalists believe in Christ, which I do not; but believe that the whole story concerning him is . . . a fable and a fiction." [23]

The indictment against him invoked an interesting legal term—a term unknown to contemporary courts when associated with God:

> The defendant admitted the writing and publishing of the *libel*. [24] (emphasis added)

To libel means intentionally to write things about other persons that are false and would publicly injure their reputation or expose them to public ridicule. [25] While such attacks on individuals still remain illegal today, in

previous years, such attacks on God and Christ fell under the laws con-
structed to protect reputations—the laws against libel.

After Kneeland was convicted by the jury, he appealed, explaining that his
conviction should be overturned because: (1) he claimed he did not deny a
belief in god; he was a pantheist and only denied the belief in *a* God; he felt
that everything was god; (2) he argued that the law under which he was
convicted had been superseded and overturned by the constitution's guarantee of religious freedom; and (3) he believed that the laws against blasphemy
were a violation of the "freedom of the press," claiming that the constitution
"guarantees to me the strict right of propagating my sentiments, by way of
argument or discussion, on religion or any other subject." [26]

The court examined whether the law under which he was convicted had
been overturned by the constitution and concluded that it had *not* since the
law forbidding blasphemy . . .

> . . . was passed very soon *after* the adoption of the constitution and
> no doubt many members of the convention which framed the consti-
> tution were members of the legislature which passed this law. [27]
> (emphasis added)

The court next provided numerous precedents to demonstrate that prohibitions against blasphemy did not conflict with constitutional guarantees
for religious rights:

> In New Hampshire, the constitution of which State has a similar
> declaration of [religious] rights, the open denial of the being and
> existence of God or of the Supreme Being is prohibited by statute
> and declared to be blasphemy.
>
> In Vermont, with a similar declaration of rights, a statute was
> passed in 1797 by which it was enacted that if any person shall
> publicly deny the being and existence of God or the Supreme Being,
> or shall contumeliously reproach his providence and government,
> he shall be deemed a disturber of the peace and tranquility of the
> State and an offender against the good morals and manners of
> society and shall be punishable by fine. . . .
>
> The State of Maine also having adopted the same consti-
> tutional provision with that of Massachusetts in her declaration
> of rights in respect to religious freedom, immediately after the

adoption of the constitution reenacted the Massachusetts statute against blasphemy. . . .

In New York the universal toleration of all religious professions and sentiments is secured in the most ample manner. . . . Notwithstanding this constitutional declaration carrying the doctrine of unlimited toleration as far as the peace and safety of any community will allow, the courts have decided that blasphemy was a crime at common law and was not abrogated by the constitution. [28]

The court finally addressed the arguments of "freedom of the press" and emphasized the responsibility which limited that freedom:

According to the argument . . . every act, however injurious or criminal which can be committed by the use of language, may be committed . . . if such language is printed. Not only therefore would the article in question become a general license for scandal, calumny [slander] and falsehood, . . . all other crimes however atrocious, if conveyed in printed language, would be dispunishable. [29]

The Founders never intended the unlimited, unrestrained, and often unconscionable "freedom of the press" practiced today. In fact, Thomas Jefferson had declared:

While we deny that [the federal] Congress have a right to control the freedom of the press, we have ever asserted the right of the States, and their exclusive right, to do so. [30]

While many civil libertarians today cringe at the thought of "controlling" the press, the controls were actually those which common sense and reason dictated, and all were rooted within the concept of responsibility (in fact, responsibility and the duty of stewardship is intrinsic to the preservation of every liberty). Concerning the balance between the freedom of the press and the responsibility of the press, printer and publisher Benjamin Franklin explained:

If by the liberty of the press were understood merely the liberty of discussing the propriety of public measures and political opinions, let us have as much of it as you please; but if it means the liberty of affronting, calumniating [falsely accusing], and defaming one another, I, for my part . . . [am] willing to part with my share of it whenever our legislators shall please so to alter the law, and shall cheerfully consent to exchange my liberty of abusing others for the privilege of not being abused myself. [31]

Justice James Wilson agreed that responsibility was the central issue:

What is meant by the liberty of the press is that there should be no antecedent restraint upon it; but that every author is responsible when he attacks the security or welfare of the government, or the safety, character, and property of the individual. [32]

The exercise of any freedom without responsibility more often than not leads to licentiousness, and often to tyranny. As illustrated by the following statements, this was never intended:

"Congress shall make no law abridging the freedom of speech, or of the press." That this Amendment was intended to secure to every citizen an absolute right to speak, or write, or print, whatever he might please without any responsibility, public or private, therefore, is a supposition too wild to be indulged by any rational man. This would allow every citizen a right to destroy at his pleasure the reputation, the peace, the property, and even the personal safety of every other citizen. [33] **JOSEPH STORY,** U. S. SUPREME COURT JUSTICE; A FATHER OF AMERICAN JURISPRUDENCE

If a printer offends you, attack him in your paper, because he can defend himself with the same weapons with which you wound him; type against type is fair play; but to attack a man who has no types nor printing press, or who does not know anything about the manual of using them, is cowardly in the highest degree. [34] **BENJAMIN RUSH,** SIGNER OF THE DECLARATION

"[E]very citizen might freely speak, write, and print, on any subject, [but is] responsible for the abuse of that liberty." . . . Without such a check, the press, in the hands of evil and designing men, would become a most formidable engine [instrument] as mighty for mischief as for good. [35] **JAMES KENT,** A FATHER OF AMERICAN JURISPRUDENCE

While the issue of the press is really a sidenote to the central issue of the *Kneeland* case, it nonetheless underscores the fact that too often today the constitutional guarantees of freedom of the press and speech have been misinterpreted to protect irresponsible and even irrational exercises of personal vindictive prerogatives. Without the requirement of accountability, Justice Joseph Story warned that the press would "become the scourge of the republic, first denouncing the principles of liberty, and then, by rendering the most virtuous patriots odious through the terrors of the press, introducing despotism in its worst form." [36]

John M'Creery's Lessee v. Allender (1799)
Supreme Court of Maryland

Thomas M'Creery emigrated from Ireland to the United States where, upon his death, he left his American estate to a relative in Ireland. It was doubted whether M'Creery's estate could legally be left to an alien unless it could be proven that he had become a citizen of the United States before his death. The case was settled when a certificate was produced showing that he had indeed become a naturalized American citizen through an oath taken before Judge Samuel Chase. (Chase not only was a signer of the Declaration of Independence but was also nominated by President George Washington as a Justice for the United States Supreme Court.) Below is an excerpt from the document Chase executed in the naturalization of M'Creery; notice especially the requirement for naturalization:

> I, Samuel Chase, Chief Judge of the State of Maryland, do hereby certify all whom it may concern that . . . personally appeared before me Thomas M'Creery and did repeat and subscribe a declaration of his belief in the Christian Religion and take the oath required by the Act of Assembly of this State entitled "An Act for Naturalization." [37]

Runkel v. Winemiller (1799)
Supreme Court of Maryland

This case involved a conflict between a minister of a German Reformed Christian Church and the church from which he had been dismissed. The Judge who delivered the ruling noted that the court's decision had been unanimous. What was it upon which all the Judges concurred?

> Religion is of general and public concern and on its support depend, in great measure, the peace and good order of government, the

safety and happiness of the people. By our form of government, the Christian religion is the established religion; and all sects and denominations of Christians are placed upon the same equal footing and are equally entitled to protection in their religious liberty. [38]

The Commonwealth v. *Sharpless* (1815)
Supreme Court of Pennsylvania

This case, and two following it, deal with "morality;" and although many today assert that "you can't legislate morality," such charges are utter nonsense. Every law that exists *is* the legislation of morality. As signer of the Declaration John Witherspoon explained:

[C]onsider all morality in general as conformity to a law. [39]

Consequently, it is never a matter of *if* morality can be legislated, only *whose* morality will be legislated.

The Founders believed the Bible to be the perfect example of moral legislation and the source of what they called "the moral law." [40] For nearly 150 years, the Courts relied on that moral law as the basis for our civil laws—a fact clearly illustrated in the following three cases.

The indictment from the grand jury describes the offense in the first case:

Jesse Sharpless . . . designing, contriving, and intending the morals, as well of youth as of divers other citizens of this commonwealth, to debauch and corrupt, and to raise and create in their minds inordinate and lustful desires . . . in a certain house there . . . scandalously did exhibit and show for money . . . a certain lewd . . . obscene painting representing a man in an obscene . . . and indecent posture with a woman, to the manifest corruption and subversion of youth and other citizens of this commonwealth. [41]

A classic description of pornography—yet this occurred in 1815. The defense claimed that since this was only a "private viewing," it was not an indictable offense. The court disagreed, stating that many things occurring in private have a public effect and therefore are punishable:

This court is . . . invested with power to punish not only open violations of decency and morality, but also whatever secretly tends to undermine the principles of society. . . . [W]hatever tends to the destruction of morality in general may be punished criminally. Crimes are public offences not because they are perpetrated publicly, but because their effect is to injure the public. Burglary, though done in secret, is a public offense; and secretly destroying fences is indictable . . . hence, it follows, that an offence may be punishable if in its nature and by its example it tends to the corruption of morals; although it be not committed in public.

The defendants are charged with exhibiting and showing . . . for money, a lewd . . . and obscene painting. . . . [I]f the privacy of the room was a protection, all the youth of the city might be corrupted by taking them one by one into a chamber and there inflaming their passions by the exhibition of lascivious pictures. . . .

[A]lthough every immoral act, such as lying, etc., is not indictable, yet where the offence charged is destructive of morality in general . . . it is punishable at common law. The destruction of morality renders the power of the government invalid. . . . The corruption of the public mind, in general, and debauching the manners of youth, in particular, by lewd and obscene pictures exhibited to view, must necessarily be attended with the most injurious consequences. . . . No man is permitted to corrupt the morals of the people; secret poison cannot be thus disseminated. [42]

Davis v. *Beason* (1889)
United States Supreme Court

In this case, it was argued that what was immoral for one group might be moral for another. Under federal statutes, Samuel Davis had been convicted, fined, and sentenced to jail for bigamy and polygamy. He appealed, and before the Supreme Court his attorneys argued that laws against bigamy and polygamy: (1) were a violation of the First Amendment because they interfered with Davis and other Mormon's free exercise of religion; and (2) the Idaho law under which he was convicted was a violation of the Fourteenth Amendment which prohibited the States from making laws that interfered with the rights of their citizens. The Court rejected those arguments; its response was very straightforward and succinct:

Bigamy and polygamy are crimes by the laws of all civilized and Christian countries. They are crimes by the laws of the United States and they are crimes by the laws of Idaho. They tend to destroy the purity of the marriage relation, to disturb the peace of families, to degrade woman and to debase man. . . . To extend exemption from punishment for such crimes would be to shock the moral judgment of the community. To call their advocacy a tenet of religion is to offend the common sense of mankind. . . .

There have been sects which denied as a part of their religious tenets that there should be any marriage tie, and advocated promiscuous intercourse of the sexes as prompted by the passions of its members. . . . Should a sect of either of these kinds ever find its way into this country, swift punishment would follow the carrying into effect of its doctrines and no heed would be given to the pretence that . . . their supporters could be protected in their exercise by the Constitution of the United States. Probably never before in the history of this country has it been seriously contended that the whole punitive power of the government for acts recognized by the general consent of the Christian world . . . must be suspended in order that the tenets of a religious sect . . . may be carried out without hindrance.

The constitutions of several States, in providing for religious freedom, have declared expressly that such freedom shall not be construed to excuse acts of licentiousness [looseness and immorality]. . . . [T]he constitution of New York of 1777 provided as follows: "The free exercise and enjoyment of religious profession and worship, without discrimination or preference, shall forever hereafter be allowed within this State to all mankind: *Provided*, That the liberty of conscience hereby granted shall not be so construed as to excuse acts of licentiousness. . . ." The constitutions of California, Colorado, Connecticut, Florida, Georgia, Illinois, Maryland, Minnesota, Mississippi, Missouri, Nevada and South Carolina contain a similar declaration. [43]

Although the defendant claimed that his actions were not licentious—at least in his view—the Supreme Court rejected that argument on the basis that his behavior was a crime by "the laws of . . . Christian countries."

Murphy v. *Ramsey* (1885)
United States Supreme Court

This case also dealt with polygamy; and, as in the previous case, the Court upheld Biblical standards, declaring:

> [C]ertainly no legislation can be supposed more wholesome and necessary in the founding of a free, self-governing commonwealth ... than that which seeks to establish it on the basis of the idea of the family, as consisting in and springing from the union for life of one man and one woman in the holy estate of matrimony; [the family is] the sure foundation of all that is stable and noble in our civilization; the best guarantee of that reverent morality which is the source of all beneficent progress in social and political improvement. [44]

Despite the formerly long-standing legal protection for this traditional teaching, contemporary legal action now directly challenges teachings that a family "consists in and springs from the union for life of one man and one woman in the holy estate of matrimony." For example, California recently proposed legislation requiring that whenever sex education was taught:

> Course material and instruction shall stress that monogamous heterosexual [one man and one woman] intercourse within marriage is a traditional American value. [45]

The American Civil Liberties Union (ACLU) challenged this provision, explaining:

> It is our position that teaching that monogamous, heterosexual intercourse within marriage as a traditional American value is an unconstitutional establishment of a religious doctrine in public schools. There are various religions which hold contrary beliefs with respect to marriage and monogamy. We believe [this bill] violates the First Amendment. [46]

Ironically, those groups which so often advocate a complete toleration for any belief or behavior if done in the name of religion invoke Jefferson and Madison as their authorities. Such groups probably would be horrified to learn what the Court pointed out in *Reynolds* v. *United States* (1878):

It is a significant fact that on the 8th of December, 1788, *after* the passage of the act establishing religious freedom, and *after* the convention of Virginia had recommended as an amendment to the Constitution of the United States the declaration in a bill of rights that "all men have an equal, natural, and unalienable right to the free exercise of religion, according to the dictates of conscience," the legislature of that State substantially enacted the . . . death penalty [for polygamy]. [47] (emphasis added)

Even Jefferson and Madison, touted by today's liberal groups as champions of tolerance, strongly opposed anything *except* monogamous heterosexual relationships. This is established by the fact that they enacted the death penalty for bigamy and polygamy and that Jefferson himself proposed "castration" as the penalty for sodomy. [48]

Although the argument has been raised for generations that *any* moral behavior or belief should be protected by the Constitution—an argument which has always been consistently denied and refuted by responsible courts—the difference is that today's courts seem determined to sustain it.

City of Charleston v. *S. A. Benjamin* (1846)
Supreme Court of South Carolina

At issue in the following cases were violations of what today are called "Blue Laws," or Sunday closing laws. The question often surrounding such laws was whether they were a specific legislation of Christianity to the exclusion of all other beliefs. Many courts believed that this was not necessarily so; they pointed out, first, that no particular day had been established by God's decree as *the* Sabbath in the New Testament, and second, that the Apostles themselves allowed great latitude on this issue. [49] Consequently, these courts held that while Blue Laws were generally associated with religion, they were not necessarily religious mandates. Further, since days of rest had been proved to have clear secular benefits on both public health and morale, [†] these courts

---

† Following the French Revolution (1789), France made a calendar change so that workers were allowed one day rest in ten rather than the traditional religiously based one in seven. (See, for example, Noah Webster, *The Revolution in France Considered in Respect to Its Progress and Effects* (New York: George Bunce, 1794), p. 20). Apparently, the result on the workers' health and morale was so detrimental that the one day rest in seven was reinstituted.

ruled that such laws fell within the State's legislative prerogative—as the U. S. Constitution had phrased it—to "promote the general welfare" of its citizens. For example (emphasis added in each example):

> [T]he legislature of the State has the power, under the Constitution, to prohibit work on Sunday as a matter pertaining to the *civil* well-being of the community. [50] MELVIN v. EASLEY

> It [a day of rest] enables the industrious workman to pursue his occupation in the ensuing week with *health* and cheerfulness . . . [without it, he] would be worn out and defaced by an unremitted continuance of labor. [51] JOHNSTON v. COMMONWEALTH

> The legislative authority to provide for it [a day of rest] . . . is derived from its general authority to regulate the business of the community and to provide for its moral and *physical* welfare. [52] COMMONWEALTH v. HAS

> Sunday laws are based on the experience of mankind as to the wisdom and necessity for both the *physical* and moral welfare of man, of having at stated intervals a day of rest from customary labor. . . . [T]he purpose of Sunday statutes is to promote the *physical* and moral nature of man. [53] STATE v. MCGEE

Although many courts took this position on Blue Laws, others believed them to be legislative policies—although permissible legislative policies—which did reflect specific Christian beliefs. The next four cases reflect decisions from both sides. Yet, regardless of the stand taken by each court on whether Blue Laws were Christian mandates, they all agreed on the importance of and the interdependence between Christianity and the law in general.

In *City of Charleston v. Benjamin* (1846), the defendants argued that the Blue Laws were a violation of the constitution since they were based on specific Christian teachings. The prosecution responded to that argument, claiming that even if they were, they still would not be unconstitutional since:

> Christianity is a part of the common law of the land, with liberty of conscience to all. It has always been so recognized. . . . If Christianity is a part of the common law, its disturbance is punishable at common law. The U. S. Constitution allows it as a part of the common law. The President is allowed ten days [to sign a bill], with the exception

of Sunday. The Legislature does not sit, public offices are closed, and the Government recognizes the day in all things. . . . The observance of Sunday is one of the usages of the common law recognized by our U. S. and State Governments. . . . Christianity is part and parcel of the common law. . . . Christianity has reference to the principles of right and wrong . . . it is the foundation of those morals and manners upon which our society is formed; it is their basis. Remove this and they would fall. . . . it [morality] has grown upon the basis of Christianity. [54]

This court agreed with the prosecution, taking the position that Blue Laws were a legitimate recognition of Christianity:

The Lord's day, the day of the Resurrection, is to us who are called Christians, the day of rest after finishing a new creation. It is the day of the first visible triumph over death, hell and the grave! It was the birth day of the believer in Christ, to whom and through whom it opened up the way which, by repentance and faith, leads unto everlasting life and eternal happiness! On that day we rest, and to us it is the Sabbath of the Lord—its decent observance, in a Christian community, is that which ought to be expected. [55]

The defense argued that to legislate according to Christian standards violated religious toleration. However, the court vehemently disagreed with this argument, pointing out:

What gave to us this noble safeguard of religious toleration . . . ? It was Christianity. . . . But this toleration, thus granted, is a religious toleration; it is the free exercise and enjoyment of religious profession and worship, with two provisos, one of which, that which guards against acts of licentiousness [immorality], testifies to the Christian construction. . . .

What constitutes the standard of good morals? Is it not Christianity? There certainly is none other. . . . The day of moral virtue in which we live would, in an instant, if that standard were abolished, lapse into the dark and murky night of Pagan immorality. . . .

In the Courts over which we preside, we daily acknowledge Christianity as the most solemn part of our administration. A Christian witness, having no religious scruples about placing his hand upon the book, is sworn upon the holy Evangelists—the books of the New Testament which testify of our Savior's birth, life, death, and resurrection; this is so common a matter that it is little thought of as an evidence of the part which Christianity has in the common law. . . .

I agree fully to what is beautifully and appropriately said in *Updegraph* v. *The Commonwealth* . . . —Christianity, general Christianity, is, and always has been, a part of the common law: "not Christianity founded on any particular religious tenets; not Christianity with an established church . . . but Christianity with liberty of conscience to all men." [56]

In the view of the *Charleston* court, Christian principles had produced America's toleration for other religions; and while America did legislate according to Christian standards of conduct for *social* behavior, it did not tell other religions how, where, when, or even whether to worship. The only restraints placed on those religions were that their religious practices not be licentious or subversive of public morality or safety. Aside from these stipulations, America granted broad religious toleration to other religions *not in spite of,* but *because* of its Christian beliefs.

Lindenmuller v. *The People* (1860)
Supreme Court of New York

This court ruled that while Blue Laws could be considered a civil prerogative of the State to provide a day of rest for all people, it further explained that even if they were adjudged to be a specific legislation of Christianity, that this would be permissible since Christianity was part of the common law:

It would be strange that a people Christian in doctrine and worship, many of whom or whose forefathers had sought these shores for the privilege of worshipping God in simplicity and purity of faith, and who regarded religion as the basis of their civil liberty and the foundation of their rights, should, in their zeal to secure to all the freedom of conscience which they valued so highly, solemnly repudiate and put beyond the pale of the law the religion which was dear to them as life and dethrone the God who they openly and avowedly professed to believe had been their protector and guide as a people. [57]

The court further explained that maintaining an official respect for Christianity did not infringe upon the free exercise of religion for others; instead, it provided an umbrella of protection:

> Religious tolerance is entirely consistent with a recognized religion. Christianity may be conceded to be established religion to the qualified extent mentioned, while perfect civil and political equality with freedom of conscience and religious preference is secured to individuals of every other creed and profession.... [and] every man is left free to worship God according to the dictates of his conscience, or not to worship him at all, as he pleases.... Compulsory worship of God in any form is prohibited, and every man's opinion on matters of religion, as in other matters, is beyond the reach of the law. No man can be compelled to perform any act ... as a duty to God; but this liberty of conscience in matters of faith and practice is entirely consistent with the existence, in fact, of the Christian religion.... All agreed that the Christian religion was engrafted upon the law and entitled to protection as the basis of our morals and the strength of our government. [58]

Shover v. *State* (1850)
Supreme Court of Arkansas

This court accepted the fact that the establishment of Sunday laws was within the legitimate legislative power of the State, regardless of whether such laws were religious in nature. However, it did not hesitate to expound upon the important relationship between Christianity and the law:

> [T]he Christian religion .... is recognized as constituting a part and parcel of the common law and as such, all of the institutions growing out of it, or, in any way connected with it, in case they shall not be found to interfere with the rights of conscience, are entitled to the most profound respect and can rightfully claim the protection of the law-making power of the State. [59]

Commonwealth v. *Nesbit* (1859)
Supreme Court of Pennsylvania

In this final case on Blue Laws, the court ruled that such laws were both civil and religious in nature. It also took time to explain that such laws did not violate the constitutional guarantee for "liberty of conscience," because liberty of conscience *was* indeed to be protected:

> We are not forgetting that the public acts of our Pennsylvania ancestors abound with declarations in favor of liberty of conscience. [60]

However, the court pointed out that "liberty of conscience" had its limitations:

> They [the Founders] could not admit this [liberty of conscience] as a civil justification of human sacrifices, or parricide [killing one's parents or close kin], infanticide, or thuggism [religious murders], or of such modes of worship as the disgusting and corrupting rites of the Dionysia, and Aphrodisia, and Eleusinia, and other festivals of Greece and Rome.
>
> They did not mean that the pure moral customs which Christianity has introduced should be without legal protection because some pagan, or other religionist, or anti-religionist, should advocate as matter of conscience concubinage, polygamy, incest, free love, and free divorce, or any of them.
>
> They did not mean that phallic processions and satyric dances and obscene songs and indecent statues and paintings of ancient or of modern paganism might be introduced under the profession of religion, or pleasure, or conscience, to seduce the young and the ignorant into a Corinthian degradation; to offend the moral sentiment of a refined Christian people; and to compel Christian modesty to associate with the nudity and impurity of Polynesian or of Spartan women. No Christian people could possibly allow such things. . . .
>
> By our . . . laws against vice and immorality we do not mean to enforce religion; we admit that to be impossible. But we do mean to protect our customs, no matter that they may have originated in our religion; for they are essential parts of our social life. Instinctively we defend and protect them. It is mere social self-defence. . . .
>
> Law can never become entirely infidel; for it is essentially founded on the moral customs of men and the very generating principle of these is most frequently religion. [61]

United States v. *Macintosh* (1931)
United States Supreme Court

This case concerned a Canadian who applied for naturalization; although occurring 140 years after the ratification of the Constitution, the U. S. Supreme Court was still articulating the same message:

> We are a Christian people . . . according to one another the equal right of religious freedom and acknowledging with reverence the duty of obedience to the will of God. [62]

Zorach v. *Clauson* (1952)
United States Supreme Court

Although this case was after the 1947 *Everson* case announcing "the wall between church and state," the Court nevertheless continued to uphold the constitutionality of students receiving religious instruction during the school day. However, this case represented a major departure from historical precedent in that the Court ruled that the instruction must occur off campus. Even that decision, though radical at the time, was still light-years away from the Court's current position. That ruling declared:

> The First Amendment, however, does not say that in every and all respects there shall be a separation of Church and State. . . . Otherwise the State and religion would be aliens to each other— hostile, suspicious, and even unfriendly. . . .
>
> We are a religious people whose institutions presuppose a Supreme Being. . . . When the State encourages religious instruction or cooperates with religious authorities by adjusting the schedule of public events to sectarian needs, it follows the best of our traditions. For it then respects the religious nature of our people and accommodates the public service to their spiritual needs. To hold that it may not would be to find in the Constitution a requirement that the government show a callous indifference to religious groups. That would be preferring those who believe in no religion over those who do believe. . . . [W]e find no constitutional requirement which makes it necessary for government to

be hostile to religion and to throw its weight against efforts to widen the effective scope of religious influence. [63]

The Court concluded that the argument for separation of church and state did not apply to student religious instruction during school hours . . .

. . . unless separation of Church and State means that public institutions can make no adjustments of their schedules to accommodate the religious needs of the people. We cannot read into the Bill of Rights such a philosophy of hostility to religion. [64]

——————•••——————

As evident from the numerous cases excerpted above (and many others not presented in this chapter), contemporary courts have abundant legal precedents on which they may rely. The simple fact is that these precedents are ignored.

~ 5 ~
The Historical Evidence

When the *Holy Trinity* Court described America as a "Christian nation," it did so because, as it explained:

> This is historically true. From the discovery of this continent to the present hour, there is a single voice making this affirmation. . . . [T]hese are not individual sayings, declarations of private persons: they are organic utterances; they speak the voice of the entire people. . . . These and many other matters which might be noticed, add a volume of unofficial declarations to the mass of organic utterances that this is a Christian nation. [1]

According to the Court, it was the "organic utterances" which proved that America was a "Christian nation." "Organic utterances" are the bulk of historical documents and previous legal rulings which comprise what is called the "common law." The previous chapter examined several legal precedents which formed part of the "common law"; this chapter will survey some of its historical components.

These historical precedents will be presented in the same chronological order noted by the Court: "from the discovery of the continent to the present hour." The records from each period will sample the "volume" and "mass of organic utterances" which prompted the Court's declaration that "this is a Christian nation."

America's Discovery

The Court's allusion to the "discovery of this continent" immediately evokes an image of Christopher Columbus. Although Columbus clearly was not the first European to visit the "New World" (Vikings had traveled here centuries earlier), he first widely publicized, and thus "discovered," its existence to the Europeans.

Columbus undertook his first voyage facing the prospect of great danger. The professional opinion of that day not only assured him of the impossibility of his proposed endeavor, but it also warned him that dragons and death awaited him beyond the charted waters. With such advice coming from the intellectual leaders, his decision to embark on this unprecedented journey was certainly difficult. Why, then, did he set out? Columbus himself answered that question in his own writings:

> [O]ur Lord opened to my understanding (I could sense his hand
> upon me) so it became clear to me that it [the voyage] was feasible.
> . . . All those who heard about my enterprise rejected it with
> laughter, scoffing at me. . . . Who doubts that this illumination
> was from the Holy Spirit? I attest that He [the Spirit], with
> marvelous rays of light, consoled me through the holy and sacred
> Scriptures . . . they inflame me with a sense of great urgency. . . .
> No one should be afraid to take on any enterprise in the name of
> our Savior if it is right and if the purpose is purely for His holy
> service. . . . And I say that the sign which convinces me that our
> Lord is hastening the end of the world is the preaching of the
> Gospel recently in so many lands. [2]

America's First Colonies

Other explorers soon followed Columbus to the new continent, with
each making proprietary claims for his own king or monarch. Therefore,
when subsequent groups of colonists wished to settle in the New World,
they were required to beseech their particular sovereign for a land charter.
If granted, the resulting charter would present the reasons set forth by that
group for its proposed endeavor.

Hence, the motivations of the colonists who came to America can be documented from an examination of their approved intentions. For example, the
1606 charter for a colony in Virginia declared the settlers' desire:

> [T]o make habitation . . . and to deduce a colony of sundry of our
> people into that part of America commonly called Virginia . . . in
> propagating of Christian religion to such people as yet live in
> darkness. [3]

In 1609, another charter for Virginia stated:

> [T]he principal effect which we can desire or expect of this action
> is the conversion . . . of the people in those parts unto the true
> worship of God and Christian religion. [4]

In November of 1620, the Pilgrims arrived in America on the *Mayflower*. Having originally set out for an established settlement in Virginia,
they were blown far north by strong winds and severe storms, finally land-

ing in an uncolonized area. Before disembarking in that new area which had no established civil government, the Pilgrims drafted and signed the "Mayflower Compact"—the first government charter drafted solely in America. It declared:

> Having undertaken for the glory of God and advancement of the Christian faith . . . [we] combine ourselves together into a civil body politic for . . . furtherance of the ends aforesaid. [5]

William Bradford, one of their leaders, confirmed this purpose when he explained that the Pilgrims had come to the New World because . . .

> . . . a great hope and inward zeal they had of laying some good foundation, or at least to make some way thereunto, for the propagating and advancing the Gospel of the kingdom of Christ in those remote parts of the world. [6]

The Puritans, who began arriving in America nearly a decade after the Pilgrims, had come for a similar purpose. Their leader, John Winthrop, warned them of the consequences of forgetting their goal:

> [W]e are a company professing ourselves fellow-members of Christ . . . knit together by this bond of love. . . . [W]e are entered into covenant with Him for this work. . . . [F]or we must consider that we shall be as a city upon a hill, the eyes of all people are upon us; so that if we shall deal falsely with our God in this work we have undertaken and so cause Him to withdraw His present help from us, we shall be made a story and a byword through the world. [7]

Other charters documented the same goal for their respective groups. For example, the 1629 charter of Massachusetts declared:

> [O]ur said people . . . be so religiously, peaceably, and civilly governed [that] their good life and orderly conversation may win and incite the natives of . . . [that] country to the knowledge and obedience of the only true God and Savior of mankind, and the Christian faith, which . . . is the principal end of this plantation [colony]. [8]

The 1632 charter issued by King Charles II to Lord Baltimore set forth the goals for Maryland colony, noting that:

> [O]ur well beloved and right trusty subject Cæcilius Calvert, Baron of Baltimore . . . being animated with a laudable and pious zeal for

extending the Christian religion . . . hath humbly besought leave of us that he may transport . . . a numerous colony of the English nation to a certain region . . . having no knowledge of the Divine Being. [9]

When Lord Baltimore and his group finally arrived at the land designated by the charter, Father White, a member of the expedition, reported:

[W]e celebrated the mass. . . . This had never been done before in this part of the world. After we had completed the sacrifice [mass], we took on our shoulders a great cross which we had hewn out of a tree and advancing in order to the appointed place. . . . we erected a trophy to Christ the Savior. [10]

In 1653, Quakers and other Christian groups began to settle North Carolina; their 1662 charter explained that they were:

[E]xcited with a laudable and pious zeal for the propagation of the Christian faith . . . in the parts of America not yet cultivated or planted, and only inhabited by . . . people who have no knowledge of Almighty God. [11]

The 1663 charter for Rhode Island set forth the colonists' intent:

[P]ursuing with peace and loyal minds, their sober, serious and religious intentions of Godly edifying themselves and one another in the holy Christian faith, . . . a most flourishing civil state may stand and best be maintained . . . with a full liberty in religious concernments. [12]

The 1680-1681 charter for Pennsylvania declared:

William Penn . . . out of a commendable desire to . . . [convert] the savage natives by gentle and just manners to the love of civil society and Christian religion, hath humbly besought leave of us to transport an ample colony unto a certain country . . . in the parts of America not yet cultivated and planted. [13]

The charter of Connecticut, [14] and the early documents in New Hampshire, [15] New Jersey, [16] and other areas, were a virtual restatement of the Christian goals reflected above.

America's First Governments

Originally, a charter provided adequate civil government for most colonies. However, as population increased, so did the need for more elaborate governments. It was this need which resulted in the "Fundamental Orders of Connecticut"—not only the first constitution written in the United States but also the direct antecedent of our current federal Constitution. [17] The "Fundamental Orders" explained why that document had been created:

> [W]ell knowing when a people are gathered together, the word of God requires that to maintain the peace and union of such a people, there should be an orderly and decent government established according to God. [18]

That constitution next declared the colonists' desire to:

> [E]nter into combination and confederation together to maintain and preserve the liberty and purity of the Gospel of our Lord Jesus which we now profess . . . which, according to the truth of the said Gospel, is now practiced amongst us. [19]

Later that year (1639), when the colonists of Exeter, New Hampshire, established a government, that document similarly declared:

> [C]onsidering with ourselves the holy will of God, and our own necessity that we should not live without wholesome laws and civil government among us, of which we are altogether destitute; do in the name of Christ and in the sight of God combine ourselves together to erect and set up among us such government as shall be to our best discerning agreeable to the will of God. [20]

In 1643, the colonies of Massachusetts, Connecticut, New Plymouth, and New Haven joined together to form the New England Confederation—America's first "united" government. These colonies banded together because, as that document explained, each had similar goals:

> [W]e all came into these parts of America with one and the same end and aim, namely to advance the kingdom of our Lord Jesus Christ. [21]

In 1669, John Locke assisted in the drafting of the Carolina constitution under which no man could be a citizen unless he acknowledged God, was a member of a church, and used no "reproachful, reviling, or abusive language" against any religion. [22]

When Quaker minister William Penn established the 1682 "Frame of Government of Pennsylvania," he prefaced the document with a lengthy exegesis of the spiritual and Biblical nature of civil government, chronicling its general progress and referring to numerous Scripture references. [23] (Penn's introduction is recommended as excellent supplementary reading.)

These, and numerous similar documents, establish that Christianity was **the** prominent influence in the early growth and orderly development of civil government in the New World.

The Founding of Education in America

Many settlers to America had suffered persecution for their Christian beliefs at the hands of other "Christians" (many of the civil abuses of Europe inexcusably occurred under the banner of Christianity—the Inquisition, the Crusades, etc.). When Europe finally began to move away from such abuses, it did so because of the efforts of leaders like Martin Luther, John Wycliffe, John Huss, William Tyndale, and others. These individuals believed that it was the Biblical illiteracy of the people which had permitted so many civil abuses to occur; that is, since the common man was not permitted to read the Scriptures for himself, his knowledge of rights and wrongs was limited to what his civil leaders told him.

The American settlers, having been exposed to the Reformation teachings, believed that the proper protection from civil abuses in America could be achieved by eliminating Biblical illiteracy. In this way, the citizens themselves (rather than just their leaders) could measure the acts of their civil government compared to the teachings of the Bible. Consequently, one of the first laws providing public education for all children (the "Old Deluder Satan Law," passed in Massachusetts in 1642 and in Connecticut in 1647) was a calculated attempt to prevent the abuse of power which can be imposed on a Biblically-illiterate people. That public school law explained not only why students needed an education but also how it was to be accomplished:

> It being one chief project of that old deluder, Satan, to keep men from the knowledge of the Scriptures, as in former time. . . . It is therefore ordered . . . [that] after the Lord hath increased [the settlement] to the number of fifty householders, [they] shall then forthwith appoint one within their town, to teach all such children as shall resort to him, to write and read. . . . And it is further ordered, that where any town shall increase to the number of one hundred families or householders, they shall set up a grammar school . . . to instruct youths, so far as they may be fitted for the university. [24]

It was not uncommon for subsequent American literacy laws to stress the need to know the Scriptures. For example, the 1690 Connecticut law declared:

> This [legislature] observing that . . . there are many persons unable to read the English tongue and thereby incapable to read the holy Word of God or the good laws of this colony . . . it is ordered that all parents and masters shall cause their respective children and servants, as they are capable, to be taught to read distinctly the English tongue. [25]

The concern that caused this educational law to be passed was that many were illiterate and thereby "incapable to read the holy Word of God . . . "

The inseparability of Christianity from education, whether public or private, was evident at every level of American education. For example, the 1636 rules of Harvard declared:

> Let every student be plainly instructed and earnestly pressed to consider well the main end of his life and studies is to know God and Jesus Christ which is eternal life (John 17.3) and therefore to lay Christ in the bottom as the only foundation of all sound knowledge and learning. And seeing the Lord only giveth wisdom, let every one seriously set himself by prayer in secret to seek it of Him (Prov. 2, 3). Every one shall so exercise himself in reading the Scriptures twice a day that he shall be ready to give such an account of his proficiency therein. [26]

Those Harvard requirements changed little over subsequent years. For example, the 1790 rules required:

> All persons of what degree forever residing at the College, and all undergraduates . . . shall constantly and seasonably attend the worship of God in the chapel, morning and evening. . . . All the scholars shall, at sunset in the evening preceding the Lord's Day, lay aside all their diversions and. . . . it is enjoined upon every scholar carefully to apply himself to the duties of religion on said day. [27]

So firmly was Harvard dedicated to this goal that its two mottos were "For the Glory of Christ" and "For Christ and the Church." [28] This school and its philosophy produced signers John Adams, John Hancock, Elbridge Gerry, John Pickering, William Williams, Rufus King, William Hooper, William Ellery, Samuel Adams, Robert Treat Paine, and numerous other illustrious Founders.

In 1692, through the efforts of the Rev. James Blair, the College of William & Mary was founded in Williamsburg, Virginia, so that:

> [T]he youth may be piously enacted in good letters and manners and that the Christian faith may be propagated . . . to the glory of Almighty God. [29]

A century later, William & Mary was still pursuing this goal—as indicated by its 1792 requirements:

> The students shall attend prayers in chapel at the time appointed and there demean themselves with that decorum which the sacred duty of public worship requires. [30]

In 1699, Yale was founded by ten ministers [31] in order:

> [T]o plant, and under the Divine blessing, to propagate in this wilderness the blessed reformed Protestant religion. [32]

When classes began in 1701, Yale required:

> [T]he Scriptures . . . morning and evening [are] to be read by the students at the times of prayer in the school . . . studiously endeavor[ing] in the education of said students to promote the power and purity of religion. [33]

In 1720 Yale charged its students:

> Seeing God is the giver of all wisdom, every scholar, besides private or secret prayer, wherein all we are bound to ask wisdom, shall be present morning and evening at public prayer in the hall at the accustomed hour. [34]

Then in 1743, and again in 1755, Yale instructed its students:

> Above all have an eye to the great end of all your studies, which is to obtain the clearest conceptions of Divine things and to lead you to a saving knowledge of God in his Son Jesus Christ. [35]

Its 1787 rules declared:

> All the scholars are required to live a religious and blameless life according to the rules of God's Word, diligently reading the holy Scriptures, that fountain of Divine light and truth, and constantly attending all the duties of religion. . . . All the scholars are obliged

to attend Divine worship in the College Chapel on the Lord's Day and on Days of Fasting and Thanksgiving appointed by public Authority. [36]

It was this school and its philosophy which produced signers Oliver Wolcott, William Livingston, Lyman Hall, Lewis Morris, Jared Ingersoll, Philip Livingston, William Samuel Johnson, and numerous other distinguished Founders.

In 1746, Princeton was founded by the Presbyterians with the Rev. Jonathan Dickinson as its first president. He was followed by a long line of illustrious ministers who served as presidents, including Aaron Burr Sr., Jonathan Edwards, Samuel Davies, and Samuel Finley (all of whom were involved in America's greatest revival—the Great Awakening). [37] Its president immediately preceding the Revolution was the Rev. Dr. John Witherspoon, later a signer of the Declaration of Independence and a venerated leader among the patriots. Notice some of Princeton's requirements while John Witherspoon was president:

> Every student shall attend worship in the college hall morning and evening at the hours appointed and shall behave with gravity and reverence during the whole service. Every student shall attend public worship on the Sabbath. . . . Besides the public exercises of religious worship on the Sabbath, there shall be assigned to each class certain exercises for their religious instruction suited to the age and standing of the pupils. . . . and no student belonging to any class shall neglect them. [38]

Signers James Madison, Richard Stockton, Benjamin Rush, Gunning Bedford, Jonathan Dayton, and numerous other prominent Founders, graduated from Princeton (a seminary for the training of ministers).

In 1754, Dartmouth College of New Hampshire (made especially famous by alumnus Daniel Webster's defense of its charter before the U. S. Supreme Court in 1819 [39]) was founded by the Rev. Eleazar Wheelock. Its charter was very succinct as to its purpose:

> Whereas . . . the Reverend Eleazar Wheelock. . . . educated a number of the children of the Indian natives with a view to their carrying the Gospel in their own language and spreading the knowledge of the great Redeemer among their savage tribes. And . . . the design

became reputable among the Indians insomuch that a larger number desired the education of their children in said school. . . . [Therefore] Dartmouth-College [is established] for the education and instruction of youths . . . in reading, writing and all parts of learning which shall appear necessary and expedient for civilizing and Christianizing the children. [40]

That same year (1754), King's College was founded in New York. Following the American Revolution, its name was changed to Columbia College; and in 1787, Constitution signer William Samuel Johnson was appointed its first president. Columbia's admission requirements were straightforward:

No candidate shall be admitted into the College . . . unless he shall be able to render into English . . . the Gospels from the Greek. . . . It is also expected that all students attend public worship on Sundays. [41]

Johnson's commencement speech to the Columbia graduates further affirms the religious emphasis of American public education:

You this day, gentlemen, ... have . . . received a public education, the purpose whereof hath been to qualify you the better to serve your Creator and your country. . . . Your first great duties, you are sensible, are those you owe to Heaven, to your Creator and Redeemer. Let these be ever present to your minds and exemplified in your lives and conduct. Imprint deep upon your minds the principles of piety towards God and a reverence and fear of His holy name. The fear of God is the beginning of wisdom. . . . Remember, too, that you are the redeemed of the Lord, that you are bought with a price, even the inestimable price of the precious blood of the Son of God. . . . Love, fear, and serve Him as your Creator, Redeemer, and Sanctifier. Acquaint yourselves with Him in His Word and holy ordinances. Make Him your friend and protector and your felicity is secured both here and hereafter. [42]

In 1766, Rutgers University was founded through the efforts of the Rev. Theodore Frelinghuysen. Its official motto, "Sun of Righteousness, Shine upon the West Also," was an extension of the Netherlands' University of Utrecht motto: "Sun of Righteousness, Shine upon Us." [43]

Examination of other colleges and universities of the day reveals that the examples mentioned above were neither aberrations nor isolated selections—they represented the norm:

> [H]igher education in the United States before 1870 was provided very largely in the tuitional colleges of the different religious denominations, rather than by the State. Of the two hundred and forty-six colleges founded by the close of the year 1860 . . . seventeen were State institutions and but two or three others had any State connections. [44]

Perhaps George Washington, "The Father of the Country," provided the most succinct description of America's educational philosophy when Chiefs from the Delaware Indian tribe brought him three Indian youths to be trained in American schools. Washington first assured the chiefs that "Congress . . . will look upon them as their own children," [45] and then commended the Chiefs for their decision, telling them that:

> You do well to wish to learn our arts and ways of life, and above all, the religion of Jesus Christ. These will make you a greater and happier people than you are. Congress will do every thing they can to assist you in this wise intention. [46]

By George Washington's own words, what youths learned in America's schools "above all" was "the religion of Jesus Christ."

The American Revolution and the Acts of the Continental Congress

The seeds of separation between America and Great Britain had been sown as early as 1765 when Great Britain began to impose on the Colonies a number of tyrannical and, what the Colonists called, unlawful or "Intolerable Acts." Although the Americans faithfully sought redress from these arbitrary and often capricious policies, the response from the Crown was frequently hardfisted. The fact that British troops had even fired on their own citizens in the 1770 "Boston Massacre" further deepened the rift. As a result, some individuals understandably began to incite open insurrection; however, America's patriot leaders remained firmly committed both to lawful procedure and to a peaceful resolution of their differences with Great Britain.

Some today contend that the American Revolution represented a complete violation of basic Biblical principles. They argue from Romans 13 that since government is of God, then all government decrees are to be obeyed as proceeding from God. Interestingly, it was this same theological argument which had resulted in the "Divine Right of Kings" philosophy which reasoned that since the King was Divinely chosen by God, therefore God expected *all* citizens to obey the King in *all* cases; anything less, they reasoned, was rebellion against God.

The American Founding Fathers strenuously disagreed with this theological interpretation. For example, Founding Father James Otis (a leader of the Sons of Liberty and the mentor of Samuel Adams) openly struck against the "Divine Right of Kings" theology. In a 1766 work he argued that the only king who had any Divine right was God Himself; beyond that, God had ordained that the power was to rest with the people:

> Has it [government] any solid foundation? any chief cornerstone...?
> I think it has an everlasting foundation in the unchangeable will
> of God, the Author of Nature whose laws never vary. . . .
> Government. . . . is by no means an arbitrary thing depending
> merely on compact or human will for its existence. . . . The power
> of God Almighty is the only power that can properly and strictly
> be called supreme and absolute. In the order of nature immediately
> under Him comes the power of a simple democracy, or the power
> of the whole over the whole. . . . [God is] the only monarch in the
> universe who has a clear and indisputable right to absolute power
> because He is the only one who is omniscient as well as omnipotent.
> . . . The sum of my argument is that civil government is of God,
> that the administrators of it were originally the whole people. [47]

Even John Dickinson (not only a signer of the Constitution and the Governor of Pennsylvania, but also a devout Quaker and thus a member of a denomination favorably disposed toward the King) recognized the spiritual basis for the position taken by the Americans:

> Kings or parliaments could not give the rights essential to
> happiness. . . . We claim them from a higher source—from the
> King of kings, and Lord of all the earth. They are not annexed to
> us by parchments and seals. They are created in us by the decrees
> of Providence, which establish the laws of our nature. They are

born with us; exist with us; and cannot be taken from us by any human power without taking our lives. In short, they are founded on the immutable maxims of reason and justice. It would be an insult on the Divine Majesty to say that he has given or allowed any man or body of men a right to make me miserable. [48]

Despite their rejection of the theory that the King spoke for God, a generally submissive attitude prevailed among the Americans. Stephen Hopkins, a signer of the Declaration and the Governor of Rhode Island, confirmed this in his work, *The Rights of the Colonies Examined.* Hopkins explained:

We finally beg leave to assert that the first planters of these colonies were pious Christians; were faithful subjects; who, with a fortitude and perseverance little known and less considered, settled these wild countries by God's goodness and their own amazing labors [and] thereby added a most valuable dependence to the crown of Great-Britain; were ever dutifully subservient to her interests; so taught their children that not one has been disaffected to this day; but all have honestly obeyed every royal command and cheerfully submitted to every constitutional law; . . . have carefully avoided every offensive measure . . . have never been troublesome or expensive to the mother country; have kept due order and supported a regular government; have maintained peace and practiced Christianity; and in all conditions and in every relation have demeaned themselves as loyal, as dutiful, and as faithful subjects ought; and that no kingdom or state hath, or ever had, colonies more quiet, more obedient, or more profitable, than these have ever been. [49]

The evidence is clear that for years the Founders pursued peaceful reconciliation and entreaty and that it was Great Britain which terminated the discussions. In fact, separation from Great Britain was not selected as the American course of action until two years **after** King George III had drawn the sword and sent armed troops against his own citizens in America. As signer of the Declaration John Witherspoon made clear:

On the part of America, there was not the most distant thought of subverting the government or of hurting the interest of the people of Great Britain; but of defending their own privileges from unjust encroachment; there was not the least desire of withdrawing their allegiance from the common sovereign [King George III] till it became absolutely necessary—and indeed, it was his own choice. [50]

When the decision for a separation was made, the Founders still maintained their strong entreaty to God for the justness of their actions. For example, in a letter to British officials, Samuel Adams, the Father of the American Revolution, declared:

> There is One above us who will take exemplary vengeance for every insult upon His majesty. You know that the cause of America is just. You know that she contends for that freedom to which all men are entitled—that she contends against oppression, rapine, and more than savage barbarity. The blood of the innocent is upon your hands, and all the waters of the ocean will not wash it away. We again make our solemn appeal to the God of heaven to decide between you and us. And we pray that, in the doubtful scale of battle, we may be successful as we have justice on our side, and that the merciful Saviour of the world may forgive our oppressors. [51]

Adams also authored a manifesto for the Continental Congress which reflected a similar tone:

> We, therefore, the Congress of the United States of America, do solemnly declare and proclaim that. . . . [w]e appeal to the God who searcheth the hearts of men for the rectitude of our intentions; and in His holy presence declare that, as we are not moved by any light or hasty suggestions of anger or revenge, so through every possible change of fortune we will adhere to this our determination. [52]

After the separation occurred, despite the years of peaceful entreaties, some British leaders specifically accused the Americans of anarchy and rebellion. To this charge, John Quincy Adams forcefully responded:

> [T]here was no anarchy. . . . [T]he people of the North American union, and of its constituent States, were associated bodies of civilized men and Christians in a state of nature, but not of anarchy. They were bound by the laws of God, which they all, and by the laws of the Gospel, which they nearly all, acknowledged as the rules of their conduct. [53]

Francis Hopkinson, a signer of the Declaration of Independence (and a church choir leader, musician, noted poet and literary figure), similarly discounted any notion of anarchy or rebellion in his 1777 work "A Political Catechism":

> *Q. What is war?*
> A. The curse of mankind; the mother of famine and pestilence; the source of complicated miseries; and the undistinguishing destroyer of the human species.
> *Q. How is war divided?*
> A. Into offensive and defensive.
> *Q. What is the general object of an offensive war? . . .*
> A. [F]or the most part, it is undertaken to gratify the ambition of a prince, who wishes to subject to his arbitrary will a people whom God created free, and to gain an uncontrolled dominion over their rights and property. . . .
> *Q. What is defensive war?*
> A. It is to take up arms in opposition to the invasions of usurped power and bravely suffer present hardships and encounter present dangers, to secure the rights of humanity and the blessings of freedom, to generations yet unborn.
> *Q. Is even defensive war justifiable in a religious view?*
> A. The foundation of war is laid in the wickedness of mankind . . . . God has given man wit to contrive, power to execute, and freedom of will to direct his conduct. It cannot be but that some, from a depravity of will, will abuse these privileges and exert these powers to the injury of others: and the oppressed would have no safety nor redress but by exerting the same powers in their defence: and it is our duty to set a proper value upon and defend to the utmost our just rights and the blessings of life: otherwise a few miscreants [unprincipled individuals] would tyrannize over the rest of mankind, and make the passive multitude the slaves of their power. Thus it is that defensive is not only justifiable, but an indispensable duty.
> *Q. Is it upon these principles that the people of America are resisting the arms of Great Britain, and opposing force with force?*
> A. Strictly so. . . . And may Heaven prosper their virtuous undertaking! [54]

Quite simply, the American Revolution was **not** an act of anarchy. In fact, throughout the course of the struggle, the conflict was often described by the Americans as a civil war rather than a revolution; and a chronological survey of the acts before, during, and after America's separation from Great Britain provides numerous examples illustrating the Americans' consistent reliance on spiritual principles.

For example, in the early 1770s when English oppression had been steadily mounting and injustices increasing, there had been no reliable source from which the Colonists could receive either accurate news reports or patriotic inspiration. To meet this need, Samuel Adams of Massachusetts and Richard Henry Lee of Virginia formed the Committees of Correspondence—an early pony-express style news service. The original Committee in Boston had a threefold goal: (1) to delineate the rights the Colonists had as men, as Christians, and as subjects of the crown, (2) to detail how these rights had been violated, and (3) to publicize throughout the Colonies the first two items. [55]

Samuel Adams assumed personal responsibility for the first goal of the Committees, and his resulting work, "The Rights of the Colonists," was first circulated on November 20, 1772. In that work, Adams urged Americans to study the Scriptures to understand the basis of the struggle to preserve their God-given rights. He declared:

> The Rights of the Colonists as Christians. These may be best understood by reading and carefully studying the institutes of the great Law Giver and Head of the Christian Church, which are to be found clearly written and promulgated in the New Testament. [56]

In fact, the spiritual nature of the American resistance became so clear that even in the debates of the British Parliament:

> Sir Richard Sutton read a copy of a letter relative to the government of America from a [Crown-appointed] governor in America to the Board of Trade showing that. . . . If you ask an American, "Who is his master?" He will tell you he has none, nor any governor but Jesus Christ. [57]

On March 5, 1774, in an oration commemorating the Boston Massacre of 1770 in which British troops had opened fire on the Americans, John Hancock proclaimed:

I have the most animating confidence that the present noble struggle for liberty will terminate gloriously for America. And let us play the man for our God, and for the cities of our God; whilst we are using the means in our power, let us humbly commit our righteous cause to the great Lord of the Universe, who loveth righteousness and hateth iniquity. And having secured the approbation of our hearts by a faithful and unwearied discharge of our duty to our country, let us joyfully leave our concerns in the hands of Him who raiseth up and pulleth down the empires and kingdoms of the world as He pleases; and with cheerful submission to His sovereign will, devoutly say, "Although the fig tree shall not blossom neither shall fruit be in the vines, the labor of the olive shall fail and the field shall yield not meat, the flock shall be cut off from the fold and there shall be no herd in the stalls, yet we will rejoice in the Lord, we will joy in the God of our salvation" [Habakkuk 3:17-18]. [58]

As a consequence of the Colonists expressing their frustration at the "Boston Tea Party" following eight years of rejected appeals by the Crown, Parliament passed the Boston Port Bill to blockade Boston harbor. That bill, designed to eliminate all trade to or from that key port, was to take effect on June 1, 1774. How did the American Colonists respond? News accounts in Great Britain reported:

[T]he province of Virginia appointed the first of June, the day on which the Boston Port Bill took place, to be set apart for fasting, prayer, and humiliation, to implore the Divine interposition to avert the heavy calamity which threatened destruction to their civil rights with the evils of a civil war; and to give one heart and one mind to the people firmly to oppose every injury to the American rights. This example was either followed or a similar resolution adopted almost every where and the first of June became a general day of prayer and humiliation throughout the continent. [59]

Mercy Otis Warren, one of the first historians of the American Revolution and the wife of a patriot, reported that not only did the Colonists pray, but they also began to organize relief for the Bostonians. [60] For example, the citizens of Pepperell, Massachusetts, sent many loads of grain to Boston; and their leader, William Prescott, must have summed up the feelings of a great many Americans when he wrote the Bostonians:

> We heartily sympathize with you and are always ready to do all in our power for your support, comfort and relief; knowing that Providence has placed you where you must stand the first shock.... Our forefathers passed the vast Atlantic, spent their blood and treasure that they might enjoy their liberties both civil and religious, and transmit them to their posterity.... Now if we should give them up, can our children rise up and call us blessed?... Let us all be of one heart and stand fast in the liberty wherewith Christ has made us free; and may He of His infinite mercy grant us deliverance out of all our troubles. [61]

The other Colonies recognized that the British might continue their offensive tactics beyond Massachusetts and saw the need for a united strategy. Revolutionary surgeon and historian David Ramsay of South Carolina reported that:

> It was a natural idea that for harmonizing their measures a Congress of deputies from each province should be convened. [62]

This call for a joint "harmonizing of measures" resulted in America's first national Congress as leaders gathered in Philadelphia on September 5, 1774. The next day, they officially convened and:

> *Resolved*, That the Rev'd. Mr. Duché be desired to open the Congress tomorrow morning with prayers, at the Carpenter's Hall, at 9 o'clock. [63]

The records for the following day reported:

> *Wednesday, September 7, 1774, 9 o'clock a. m.* Agreeable to the resolve of yesterday, the meeting was opened with prayers by the Revd. Mr. Duché. *Voted*, That the thanks of Congress be given to Mr. Duché ... for performing Divine service and for the excellent prayer which he composed and delivered on the occasion. [64]

John Adams, in a letter to his wife Abigail, provided additional detail on that time of prayer:

> When the Congress first met, Mr. [Thomas] Cushing [of Massachusetts] made a motion that it should be opened with prayer.... [Mr. Samuel Adams] moved that Mr. Duché, an Episcopal clergyman, might be desired to read prayers to the

Congress tomorrow morning. The motion was seconded and passed in the affirmative. . . . Accordingly next morning he appeared with his clerk and in his pontificallibus [robes] and read several prayers. . . . After this Mr. Duché, unexpected to everybody struck out into an extemporary prayer which filled the bosom of every man present. I must confess I never heard a better prayer or one so well pronounced. . . . with such fervor, such ardor, such earnestness and pathos, and in language so elegant and sublime—for America, for the Congress, for the Province of Massachusetts Bay, and especially the town of Boston. It has had an excellent effect upon everybody here. [65]

Several of those who attended were greatly affected by Duché's prayer and commented upon it, including Samuel Adams, [66] Joseph Reed, [67] and Samuel Ward. [68] Silas Deane recorded:

The Congress met and opened with a prayer made by the Revd. Mr. Duché which it was worth riding one hundred mile to hear. He read the lessons of the day [Scriptures] which were accidentally extremely applicable, and then prayed without book about ten minutes so pertinently, with such fervency, purity, and sublimity of style and sentiment, and with such an apparent sensibility of the scenes and business before us, that even Quakers shed tears. [69]

In fact, so strong and compelling had been the prayer that:

Mr. Ward of Rhode Island moved that the thanks of the Congress be give to him [Rev. Duché] for his services which was unanimously agreed to; & Mr. Cushing & Mr. Ward were appointed a Committee for the purpose. It was then moved that he should be requested to print the prayer. [70]

However, for reasons noted by delegate James Duane, Congress decided against printing and distributing the prayer because:

It being objected that as this might possibly expose him [Rev. Duché] to some disadvantage, it was out of respect to him waived. [71]

Congress felt that the prayer had such a strong pro-American flavor that if a transcript of its words fell into British hands, Duché could be in danger.

Notice, however, that according to the delegates' records, not only the prayer, but also the "lessons" had strongly impacted the Congress. The "lessons" were the daily Scripture reading from the Psalter which, in the high-church tradition, had been selected years—actually, centuries—in advance. Yet the one for that day was unusually relevant. As John Adams had described it to Abigail:

> [Rev. Duché] then read the [lesson] for the seventh day of September, which was the thirty-fifth Psalm. You must remember this was the next morning after we heard the horrible rumor of the cannonade of Boston. I never saw a greater effect upon an audience. It seemed as if Heaven had ordained that Psalm to be read on the morning. . . . I must beg you to read that Psalm. . . . [R]ead this letter and the 35th Psalm to them [your friends]. Read it to your father. [72]

As Adams noted, the morning Congress read the 35th Psalm was the very morning that it had been informed that Great Britain had landed armed troops; that is, British citizens in Boston were now under attack by their own army and navy. Since Psalm 35 contained the prayers and pleadings of an innocent and defenseless person who had been attacked by one much stronger, it is easy to understand why that Psalm had such an impact on the delegates. Silas Deane had called it "accidentally extremely applicable"; [73] and John Adams said that it "was most admirably adapted, though this was accidental, or rather Providential." [74]

The Massachusetts legislature was concerned that the British use of force might spread beyond the Boston area. It therefore urged its inhabitants to band together as minutemen into local militias so that they might protect themselves from the British "so thirsty for the blood of this innocent people." [75] In its call, the Massachusetts legislature somberly reminded its citizens that:

> You are placed by Providence in the post of honor because it is the post of danger: and while struggling for the noblest objects, the liberties of your country, the happiness of posterity, and the rights of human nature, the eyes not only of North America and the whole British empire, but of all Europe, are upon you. Let us be therefore altogether solicitous that no disorderly behavior, nothing unbecoming our characters as Americans, as citizens, and Christians, be justly chargeable to us. [76]

Here was a governmental charge to the militias and minutemen to re-member their Christian witness during this struggle. This would thus pre-clude any opportunity to lodge accusations of misbehavior against Christianity in the United States. Such a charge was not incompatible with the nature of the minutemen, however, for they were often the men from a local church; and it was frequently a deacon, or sometimes a pastor, who was responsible for conducting their military drills. In fact, the editor of the *Boston Post* noted, "On the days of drill the citizen soldiers sometimes went from the parade-ground to the church, where they listened to exhor-tation and prayer." [77] And elsewhere:

> In Danvers, Massachusetts, the deacon of the parish was elected captain of the minutemen and the minister his lieutenant. The company, it is said, after its field exercise would sometimes repair to the "meetinghouse" to hear a patriotic sermon, or would partake of an entertainment at the town-house where the zealous "sons of liberty" would exhort them to fight bravely for God and their country. At Lunenburg, Massachusetts, the mute company, after drill, marched in procession to the "meeting house" where a sermon was delivered. Nor was the First Church, Boston, at all behind in patriotism. It voted to melt up the lead weights upon the church clock for bullets and use other metal in their stead. [78]

Although many loyalist voices urged calm and absolute submission, oth-ers—like Patrick Henry—cried for action. In his fiery speech before the Virginia House on March 23, 1775, Henry proclaimed:

> Shall we try argument? Sir, we have been trying that for the last ten years. . . . Our petitions have been slighted; our remonstrances [complaints] have produced additional violence and insult; our supplications have been disregarded; and we have been spurned with contempt from the foot of the throne. . . . An appeal to arms and to the God of hosts is all that is left us! They tell us, sir, that we are weak—unable to cope with so formidable an adversary. But when shall we be stronger? Will it be next week, or next year? Will it be when we are totally disarmed and when a British guard shall be stationed in every house? Shall we gather strength by irresolution and inaction? . . . Sir, we are not weak if we make a proper use of

those means which the God of nature hath placed in our power. Three millions of people armed in the holy cause of liberty and in such a country as that which we possess are invincible by any force which our enemy can send against us. Besides, sir, we shall not fight our battles alone. There is a just God who presides over the destinies of nations and who will raise up friends to fight our battles for us. The battle, sir, is not to the strong alone; it is to the vigilant, the active, the brave. . . . Gentlemen may cry peace, peace—but there is no peace! The war is actually begun! The next gale that sweeps from the north will bring to our ears the clash of resounding arms! Our brethren are already in the field! Why stand we here idle? What is it that gentlemen wish? What would they have? Is life so dear, or peace so sweet as to be purchased at the price of chains and slavery? Forbid it, Almighty God! I know not what course others may take; but as for me, give me liberty or give me death!!! [79]

On April 15, 1775, John Hancock, witnessing the growing and ominous storm clouds of full scale war, called Massachusetts to a day of prayer and fasting, explaining that:

In circumstances dark as these, it becomes us as men and Christians to reflect that whilst every prudent measure should be taken to ward off the impending judgments . . . all confidence must be withheld from the means we use and reposed only on that God who rules in the armies of heaven and without whose blessing the best human councils are but foolishness and all created power vanity.

It is the happiness of his church that when the powers of earth and hell combine against it . . . then the throne of grace is of the easiest access and its appeal thither is graciously invited by that Father of mercies who has assured it that when His children ask bread He will not give them a stone. . . .

That it be, and hereby is, recommended to the good people of this colony . . . as a day of public humiliation, fasting and prayer . . . to confess the sins . . . to implore the forgiveness of all our transgressions . . . and especially that the union of the American colonies in defence of their rights, for which, hitherto, we desire to thank Almighty God, may be preserved and confirmed. . . . and that America may soon behold a gracious interposition of Heaven. [80]

Only three days later, Paul Revere, William Dawes, and Samuel Prescott made their famous ride; and the next morning, April 19, the British began their march against Lexington and Concord which resulted in the "shot heard 'round the world.'"

The following day, British troops commenced military action in Virginia, seizing both public supplies and the Colonists' gunpowder stored in Williamsburg. Patrick Henry, unwilling to allow the British action to go unchecked, gathered the local militia, and on May 2 addressed them in an impassioned speech which . . .

> . . . inflamed their patriotism by calling up before them the fields of Lexington and Concord still warm with the blood of their brethren; he showed them that the object of the [British] ministry was to render the colonies powerless by seizing their military stores; that the late plunder of the magazine at Williamsburg was only part of the general system of warfare that the moment had come when they must decide whether they would assert their freedom or basely submit to be slaves. He reminded them of the pillar of cloud and the pillar of fire which guided the children of Israel; of the water gushing from the rock at Horeb; of the miraculous passage of the Red Sea, and then, with his eye uplifted, his arms aloft, and his whole soul burning with inspiration, declared that the same God still ruled in the heavens; that he was watching from his throne the oppressions of His people in America and that He was still strong to deliver and mighty to save. [81]

When word of the skirmishes in Massachusetts and Virginia reached Connecticut, the General Assembly secretly instructed Colonel Ethan Allen to enlist a group of men to disable Ticonderoga, a British stronghold in New York. Late in the evening on May 9, 1775, Allen and his Green Mountain Boys approached the unsuspecting garrison, quietly capturing the sentries and securing the barracks of sleeping British soldiers. Allen then pushed on to camp headquarters and roused the commandant, Captain De La Place. Allen himself described what next occurred:

> [T]he Captain came immediately to the door with his small clothes in his hand—when I ordered him to deliver to me the fort, instantly. He asked me by what authority I demanded it. I answered him—"In the name of the Great Jehovah and the Continental Congress." [82]

The fort was then handed over to Allen—without the loss of a single life. On June 12, Congress declared a day of prayer and fasting, [83] of which John Adams told his wife Abigail:

> We have appointed a continental fast. Millions will be upon their knees at once before their great Creator, imploring his forgiveness and blessing; his smiles on American councils and arms. [84]

On June 29, John Witherspoon (soon to become a signer of the Declaration of Independence) and a group of ministers in New York and Pennsylvania issued this admonition to American patriots:

> [T]here is no soldier so undaunted as the pious man, no army so formidable as those who are superior to the fear of death. There is nothing more awful to think of than that those whose trade is war should be despisers of the name of the Lord of hosts and that they should expose themselves to the imminent danger of being immediately sent from cursing and cruelty on earth to the blaspheming rage and despairing horror of the infernal pit. Let therefore every one who . . . offers himself as a champion in his country's cause be persuaded to reverence the name and walk in the fear of the Prince of the kings of the earth; and then he may with the most unshaken firmness expect the issue [God's protection] either in victory or death. [85]

On June 30, Congress passed the Articles of War to govern the Continental Army. In it, Congress directed that:

> It is earnestly recommended to all officers and soldiers diligently to attend Divine service; and all officers and soldiers who shall behave indecently or irreverently at any place of Divine worship, shall. . . . be brought before a court-martial. [86]

While calling both the nation and its army to pray, Congress did not neglect its own spiritual duties. On July 19, 1775, it voted:

Agreed, That the Congress meet here tomorrow morning at half after 9 o'clock in order to attend Divine service at Mr. Duché's Church; and that in the afternoon they meet here to go from this place and attend Divine service at Doctor Allison's church. [87]

Despite the continuing hostility and armed conflicts, no official separation had occurred between America and Great Britain; the Patriots yet remained British citizens. In July 1775, in another attempt to achieve a peaceful reconciliation, Congress approved "The Olive Branch Petition" which, in a completely conciliatory and submissive tone, pleaded for a full review of the unlawful policies being imposed upon them. By November, word returned that not only had the King and Parliament refused to give any hearing to their request, they had instead imposed a complete embargo against *all* the Colonies. As word of this rejected reconciliation attempt spread among the people—and as the British continued their military operations against the Colonists—public emotions and anger heightened, bringing action both at the State and national level.

For example, on the State level, the Massachusetts legislature acted to form its own navy. Even the naval emblems approved by the legislature on April 29, 1776, reflected the religious tone evident throughout the State:

Resolved, that the uniform of the officers be green, and that they furnish themselves accordingly, and the colors be a white flag with a green pine tree and the inscription, "Appeal to Heaven." [88]

At the national level, on March 13, 1776, William Livingston prepared a Congressional proclamation for a national day of prayer and fasting. [89] Congress designated May 17, 1776, as the day for its observance. That proclamation declared:

The Congress. . . . desirous . . . to have people of all ranks and degrees duly impressed with a solemn sense of God's superintending providence, and of their duty devoutly to rely . . . on His aid and direction . . . do earnestly recommend . . . a day of humiliation, fasting, and prayer; that we may with united hearts confess and bewail our manifold sins and transgressions and, by a sincere repentance and amendment of life, . . . and through the merits and mediation of Jesus Christ, obtain His pardon and forgiveness. [90]

With all channels of reconciliation exhausted, on July 2, 1776, Congress approved in principle a separation from Great Britain. Two days later, July 4, 1776, Congress approved the Declaration of Independence. (At this stage, it was signed only by John Hancock, President of Congress, and Charles Thomson, its Secretary.)

The fifty-six leaders who approved the separation from Great Britain realized that their struggle against the much superior British military could not be won solely through their own efforts. Thus, in their Declaration of Independence they openly acknowledged the Source of help on whom they would rely:

> " . . . the laws of nature and of *nature's God* . . ."; " . . . endowed by their *Creator* with certain unalienable rights . . ."; " . . . appealing to the *Supreme Judge of the World,* for the rectitude of our intentions . . . " (emphasis added)

Then, in the last line of that document, those Patriots announced:

> For the support of this Declaration, *with a firm reliance on the protection of Divine Providence,* we mutually pledge to each other our Lives, our Fortunes, and our sacred Honor. (emphasis added)

The Declaration of Independence was actually a dual declaration: a Declaration of *Independence* from Britain and a Declaration of *Dependence* on God.

This act preserved a lesson for future generations. As explained by signer of the Declaration Benjamin Rush:

> I sat next to John Adams in Congress, and upon my whispering to him and asking him if he thought we should succeed in our struggle with Great Britain, he answered me, "Yes—if we fear God and repent of our sins." This anecdote will, I hope, teach my boys that it is not necessary to disbelieve Christianity or to renounce morality in order to arrive at the highest political usefulness or fame. [91]

The day after the separation from Great Britain was approved, John Adams wrote Abigail two letters. The first was short and concise, jubilant that the separation had come; [92] the second was much longer and more pensive. In it, Adams cautiously noted:

> [This day] will be the most memorable epocha in the history of America. I am apt to believe that it will be celebrated by succeeding generations as the great anniversary festival. [93]

Amazingly, Adams foresaw that their move for independence on the previous day would be celebrated by future generations. Adams told Abigail that the day *should* be commemorated—but only in a particular manner and with a specific spirit. He explained:

> It ought to be commemorated as the day of deliverance by solemn acts of devotion to God Almighty. [94]

On the same day that Congress approved the Declaration, it appointed John Adams, Thomas Jefferson, and Ben Franklin to draft a seal to characterize the spirit of the new nation. Franklin proposed:

> Moses lifting up his wand, and dividing the Red Sea, and Pharaoh in his chariot overwhelmed with the waters. This motto: "Rebellion to tyrants is obedience to God." [95]

Jefferson proposed:

> The children of Israel in the wilderness, led by a cloud by day, and a pillar of fire by night. [96]

On July 8th, the Declaration had its first public reading (on the steps outside Independence Hall), and then the Liberty Bell was rung, fulfilling the Bible inscription emblazoned on its side:

> Proclaim liberty throughout the land unto all the inhabitants thereof. LEVITICUS 25:10

On July 9, the Rev. Mr. Duché was appointed chaplain of Congress [97] and shortly thereafter delivered this stirring prayer:

> O Lord our heavenly Father, high and mighty King of kings and Lord of lords . . . over all the kingdoms, empires, and governments; look down in mercy, we beseech thee, on these American States who have fled to thee from the rod of the oppressor, and thrown themselves on thy gracious protection, desiring to be henceforth dependent only on thee; to thee they have appealed for the righteousness of their cause; to thee do they now look up for that countenance and support which thou alone canst give; take them, therefore, heavenly Father, under thy nurturing care; give them wisdom in council, and valor in the field; defeat the malicious designs of our cruel adversaries; convince them of the unrighteousness of

their cause. . . . All this we ask in the name and through the merits of Jesus Christ, Thy Son, and our Savior, Amen! [98] †

On that same day (July 9), word reached General Washington in New York that four days earlier the Congress had authorized chaplains for the Continental Army. Washington promptly ordered chaplains appointed for each regiment and then, in his general orders, called on the men to attend to their spiritual duties:

> The Hon. Continental Congress having been pleased to allow a chaplain to each regiment . . . the Colonels or commanding officers of each regiment are directed to procure chaplains accordingly; persons of good characters and exemplary lives—To see that all inferior officers and solders pay them a suitable respect and attend carefully upon religious exercises. The blessing and protection of Heaven are at all times necessary but especially so in times of public distress and danger—The General hopes and trusts that every officer and man will endeavor so to live and act as becomes a Christian soldier defending the dearest rights and liberties of his country. [99]

On July 19, the Congress ordered that the Declaration of Independence be engrossed on parchment in beautiful script so that it could be signed by the entire Congress. On August 2, 1776, the members of the Congress placed their hands to that document, signing it in the form which is now so recognizable to the entire nation.

A year after signing the Declaration—and now nearly a full year into the British embargoes against the Colonies—America began experiencing a shortage of several important commodities—including Bibles. Therefore, on July 7, 1777, a request was placed before Congress to print or to import more. That request was referred to a committee of Daniel Roberdeau, John Adams, and Jonathan Smith [100] who examined the possibilities and then

---

† Nearly a year after his prayer, it did not appear as if it would be answered. Following a series of American defeats, British troops invaded and seized Philadelphia. In the midst of the gloomy outlook, Rev. Duché then wrote George Washington a letter predicting defeat for the Americans and urging Washington to retract the Declaration of Independence. Washington forwarded the report to Congress who declared Duché a traitor. Under that stigma, Duché promptly fled to Great Britain. Late in his life, after requesting permission from President Washington, Duché returned to America where he spent his remaining years.

on September 11, reported to Congress:

> [T]hat the use of the Bible is so universal, and its importance so
> great . . . your Committee recommend that Congress will order
> the Committee of Commerce to import 20,000 Bibles from
> Holland, Scotland, or elsewhere, into the different ports of the
> States of the Union. [101]

Congress agreed and ordered the Bibles imported. [102]

On October 31, in consequence of several unexpected American victo-
ries (Bennington, Stillwater, Saratoga, and others), Congress appointed
Samuel Adams, Richard Henry Lee, and Daniel Roberdeau to draft a proclamation for a national day of prayer and thanksgiving. [103] On November 1,
1777, Congress approved that proclamation, which declared:

> Forasmuch as it is the indispensable duty of all men to adore the
> superintending providence of Almighty God; to acknowledge with
> gratitude their obligation to Him for benefits received and to implore
> such farther blessings as they stand in need of . . . [to offer] humble
> and earnest supplication that it may please God, through the merits
> of Jesus Christ, mercifully to forgive and blot [our sins] out of
> remembrance . . . and to prosper the means of religion for the
> promotion and enlargement of that kingdom which consisteth "in
> righteousness, peace, and joy in the Holy Ghost." [104]

On December 15, 1777, John Adams reported to Abigail that the direct,
open, and frequent intervention of God was evident to most Americans:

> I have had many opportunities in the course of this journey to
> observe how deeply rooted our righteous cause is in the minds of
> the people. . . . One evening as I sat in one room, I overheard a
> company of the common sort of people in another [room] conversing
> upon serious subjects. . . . At length I heard these words: "It appears
> to me the eternal Son of God is operating powerfully against the
> British nation for their treating lightly serious things." [105]

That spiritual tone extended far beyond the passing conversation of just the
"common sort of people"; it was also evident among the people's leaders. For
example, when the General Assembly of Vermont asked the Rev. Peter Powers
to address them in an "election sermon" (a discourse on the application of Bib-

lical principles to civil government), Powers agreed. On March 12, 1778, he addressed the Assembly in a message entitled "Jesus Christ, the True King and Head of Government" based on Matthew 28:18. Powers declared:

> We have renounced the tyrant of Britain and declaimed loudly against monarchial power and have set up a free people. We own no other prince or sovereign but the Prince of Heaven, the great Sovereign of the Universe. To Him we swear allegiance and promise, through His abundant grace, to keep His laws. [106]

The General Assembly of Vermont ordered that address to be printed and distributed among the people. [107]

Throughout the struggle, the clergy played an important role from both sides of the pulpit. From the back side of the pulpit, they exhorted the people and provided Biblical guidance through numerous topical sermons, election sermons (like the one mentioned above), and artillery sermons (a discourse on the application of Biblical principles to the military). In fact, John Adams listed the Rev. Dr. Mayhew and the Rev. Dr. Cooper as two of the "characters . . . most conspicuous, the most ardent, and influential" in "an awakening and a revival of American principles and feelings . . . in 1775." [108]

From the front side of the pulpit, the clergy were often directing the troops as military leaders and officers—as, for example, the Rev. John Peter Muhlenberg. On January 21, 1776, Muhlenberg preached to his Virginia congregation concerning the crisis then facing America. He recounted to them how America had been founded in pursuit of religious and civil liberties and how they were now in danger of losing those liberties. He concluded with these words:

> [I]n the language of Holy Writ [Ecclesiastes 3], there [is] a time for all things, a time to preach and a time to pray, but those times have passed away. [109]

And then in a loud voice, he quoted from verse 8, saying:

> [T]here is a time to fight—and that time has now come! [110]

His sermon finished, he offered the benediction, and then deliberately disrobed in front of the congregation, revealing the uniform of a military officer beneath his clerical robes. He descended from the pulpit, marched to the back door of the church, and ordered the drums to beat for recruits. Three hundred men joined him, and they became the Eighth Virginia Regiment. [111] Pastor John Peter Muhlenberg went on to become one of the highest-ranking officers in the American Revolution, attaining the rank of Major-General. [112] Historian Daniel Dorchester reported numerous other similar incidents:

> Of Rev. John Craighead it is said that "he fought and preached alternately." Rev. Dr. Cooper was captain of a military company. Rev. John Blair Smith, president of Hampden-Sidney College, was captain of a company that rallied to support the retreating Americans after the battle of Cowpens. Rev. James Hall commanded a company that armed against Cornwallis. Rev. Wm. Graham rallied his own neighbors to dispute the passage of Rockfish Gap with Tarleton and his Britain dragoons. Rev. Dr. Ashbel Green was an orderly sergeant. Rev. Dr. Moses Hodge served in the army of the Revolution. [113]

In fact, so prominent were the clergy in the struggle that the British called them the "Black Regiment" [114] due to the black clerical robes they wore. †

On May 2, 1778, when the Continental Army was beginning to emerge from its infamous winter at Valley Forge, Commander-in-Chief George Washington commended his troops for their courage and patriotism and then reminded them that:

> While we are zealously performing the duties of good citizens and soldiers, we certainly ought not to be inattentive to the higher duties of religion. To the distinguished character of Patriot, it should be our highest glory to add the more distinguished character of Christian. [118]

Later that year, still in the midst of the Revolution, the help that America had already received from their "firm reliance on Divine Providence" was so obvious that George Washington told General Thomas Nelson:

> The hand of Providence has been so conspicuous in all this that he must be worse than an infidel that lacks faith, and more than wicked, that has not gratitude enough to acknowledge his obligations. [119]

---

† The exploits of many of these clergy-patriots are recorded in several older historical works, including *The Pulpit of the American Revolution*—1860; [115] *Chaplains and Clergy of the Revolution*—1861; [116] and *The Patriot Preachers of the American Revolution*—1860. [117]

On October 12, 1778, Congress again reaffirmed the importance of religion and made provision for its widespread encouragement when it issued the following act:

> Whereas true religion and good morals are the only solid foundations of public liberty and happiness: *Resolved,* That it be, and it is hereby earnestly recommended to the several States to take the most effectual measures for the encouragement thereof. [120]

As George Washington had noted, the fingerprints of God in America's behalf were often evident throughout the struggle; and in September of 1780, they were again manifested in the discovery of the plot by Benedict Arnold to betray American forces. In General Nathanael Greene's report to his troops and to the Congress on September 26, 1780, he reported:

> Treason of the blackest dye was yesterday discovered! General Arnold who commanded at Westpoint, lost to every sentiment of honor, of public and private obligation, was about to deliver up that important post into the hands of the enemy. Such an event must have given the American cause a deadly wound if not a fatal stab. Happily the treason has been timely discovered to prevent the fatal misfortune. The Providential train of circumstances which led to it affords the most convincing proof that the liberties of America are the object of Divine protection. [121]

When Congress learned of the Providential exposure of Arnold's intricately laid scheme, it promptly appointed Samuel Adams, William Houston, and Frederic Muhlenberg to draft a proclamation for a national day of prayer and thanksgiving. [122] On October 18, 1780, Congress approved the wording and distributed the proclamation throughout the Colonies:

> Whereas it hath pleased Almighty God, the Father of all mercies, amidst the vicissitudes [changes] and calamities of war, to bestow blessings on the people of these States which call for their devout and thankful acknowledgments, more especially in the late remarkable interposition of his watchful providence in rescuing the person of our Commander-in-Chief and the army from imminent dangers at the moment when treason was ripened for execution. . . .
> It is therefore recommended to the several States . . . a day of public thanksgiving and prayer; that all the people may assemble on that

day to celebrate the praises of our Divine Benefactor; to confess our unworthiness of the least of his favors, and to offer our fervent supplications to the God of all grace . . . to cause the knowledge of Christianity to spread over all the earth. [123]

That same year (1780), Samuel Adams reminded the troops:

May every citizen in the army and in the country have a proper sense of the Deity upon his mind and an impression of the declaration recorded in the Bible, "Him that honoreth me I will honor, but he that despiseth me shall be lightly esteemed" [I Samuel 2:30]. [124]

As the war prolonged, the shortage of Bibles remained a problem. Consequently, Robert Aitken, publisher of *The Pennsylvania Magazine*, petitioned Congress on January 21, 1781, for permission to print the Bibles on his presses here in America rather than import them. He pointed out to Congress that his Bible would be "a neat edition of the Holy Scriptures for the use of schools." [125] Congress approved his request and appointed a committee of James Duane, Thomas McKean, and John Witherspoon to oversee the project. [126]

In October 1781, amidst the work on the Bible, the Americans won the Battle of Yorktown and the British troops laid down their arms. The British press reported the activities surrounding the surrender:

It was on the 19th of October that lord Cornwallis surrendered himself and his whole army. . . . Two days after the capitulation took place, Divine service was performed in all the different brigades and divisions of the American army in order to return thanks to the Almighty for this great event; and it was recommended by General Washington to all the troops that were not upon duty, in his general orders, that they would assist at Divine service "with a serious deportment and with that sensibility of heart which the recollection of the surprising and particular interposition of Providence in their favor claimed." [127]

On October 24, 1781, Congress, too, set aside a time to honor God for this victory and:

Resolved, That Congress will at two o'clock this day go in procession to the Dutch Lutheran Church and return thanks to Almighty God for crowning the allied arms of the United States and France with success by the surrender of the whole British Army under the command of the Earl Cornwallis. [128]

Despite the victory, work on the new Bible continued. As it neared its final stage of readiness in late summer 1782, James Duane, chairman of the Congressional committee, reported to Congress:

> He [Mr. Aitken] undertook this expensive work at a time when from the circumstances of the war an English edition of the Bible could not be imported, nor any opinion formed how long the obstruction might continue. On this account particularly he deserves applause and encouragement. [129]

On September 12, 1782, the full Congress approved that Bible [130] which soon began rolling off the presses. Printed in the front of that Bible (the first English-language Bible ever printed in America) was the Congressional endorsement:

> Whereupon, *Resolved*, That the United States in Congress assembled . . . recommend this edition of the Bible to the inhabitants of the United States. [131]

Of this event, one early historian observed:

> Who, in view of this fact, will call in question the assertion that this is a Bible nation? Who will charge the government with indifference to religion when the first Congress of the States assumed all the rights and performed all the duties of a Bible Society long before such an institution had an existence in the world! [132]

A year after this Bible, and almost two years after the British had laid down their arms at Yorktown, there still was no treaty, and thus no official guarantee that the hostilities would not resume. Yet, since there had been no further fighting, and the prospect of a lasting peace appeared to be growing, George Washington began to anticipate his return to private life. In contemplation of this, on June 3, 1783, he explained:

> Before I retire from public life, I shall with the greatest freedom give my sentiments to the States on several political subjects. [133]

Consequently, five days later on June 8, Washington issued a circular letter to the Governors of all the States in which he told them:

I now make it my earnest prayer that God would have you and the State over which you preside in His holy protection . . . that He would most graciously be pleased to dispose us all to do justice, to love mercy, and to demean ourselves with that charity, humility, and pacific temper of mind which were the characteristics of the Divine Author of our blessed religion, without an humble imitation of whose example in these things, we can never hope to be a happy nation. [134]

Three months later, on September 8, 1783, the formal peace treaty with Great Britain was signed by John Adams, Benjamin Franklin, and John Jay. Like so many of the other official records of the Revolution, that document, too, openly acknowledged God. The opening line of the peace treaty declared:

In the name of the most holy and undivided Trinity. [135]

When word reached America that the peace was now official, there was first a time of great celebration; and then on October 17, 1783, Congress appointed James Duane, Samuel Huntington, and Samuel Holten to prepare a proclamation for a day of prayer and thanksgiving. [136] Congress approved that proclamation on October 18, 1783, and distributed it among the States, announcing:

Whereas it hath pleased the Supreme Ruler of all human events to dispose the hearts of the late belligerent powers to put a period to the effusion of human blood by proclaiming a cessation of all hostilities by sea and land, and these United States are not only happily rescued from the dangers and calamities to which they have been so long exposed, but their freedom, sovereignty and independence ultimately acknowledged. And whereas in the progress of a contest on which the most essential rights of human nature depended, the interposition of Divine Providence in our favor hath been most abundantly and most graciously manifested, and the citizens of these United States have every reason for praise and gratitude to the God of their salvation. Impressed, therefore, with an exalted sense of the blessings by which we are surrounded, and of our entire dependence on that Almighty Being from whose goodness and bounty they are derived, the United States in Congress assembled, do recommend it to the several States . . . a day of public thanksgiving that all the people may then assemble to celebrate with grateful hearts and united voices the praises of their Supreme and all bountiful Benefactor for his numberless favors and mercies. . . . and above all that he hath been pleased to continue to us the light of the blessed Gospel and secured to us in the fullest extent the rights of conscience in faith and worship. [137]

Many of the State Governors also issued their own individual proclamations for days of prayer, fasting, and thanksgiving, including John Hancock of Massachusetts, [138] William Livingston of New Jersey, [139] John Dickinson of Pennsylvania, [140] and others. This type of open acknowledgment of and reliance on God by our civic leaders was common practice. In addition to the fifteen national Congressional proclamations issued throughout the Revolution, [141] literally scores of similar proclamations—often strongly and openly Christian—were issued by individual Governors for their States.

Establishing a Stronger Government

With independence now a reality, the national legislators turned their full attention toward permanently securing America's newly gained liberty. To this end, delegates from each State were sent to Philadelphia in May 1787 to revise the Articles of Confederation (the document under which the national government had functioned during the Revolution). It soon became evident that revising the Articles was insufficient; a new government pact was needed. While the delegates had not originally convened to write a constitution, their work ultimately produced an entirely new document—the United States Constitution. Therefore, that Philadelphia gathering is now referred to as the "Constitutional Convention."

One of the longest speeches in the Convention was delivered by its elder statesman, Benjamin Franklin. James Madison, who kept fastidious personal records of the Convention's events and debates, recorded the stirring speech delivered by the 81 year-old statesman on June 28, 1787. Addressing George Washington, President of the Convention, Franklin declared:

Mr. President:

The small progress we have made after four or five weeks close attendance and continual reasonings with each other—our different sentiments on almost every question, several of the last producing as many noes as ayes is, methinks, a melancholy proof of the imperfection of the human understanding. We indeed seem to feel our own want of political wisdom since we have been running about in search of it. . . .

In this situation of this Assembly, groping as it were in the dark to find political truth, and scarce able to distinguish it when presented to us, how has it happened, sir, that we have not hitherto once thought of humbly applying to the Father of lights, to illuminate our understanding? In the beginning of the contest with Great Britain, when we were sensible of danger, we had daily prayer in this room for the Divine protection. Our prayers, sir, were heard, and they were graciously answered. All of us who were engaged in the struggle must have observed frequent instances of a superintending Providence in our favor. To that kind Providence we owe this happy opportunity of consulting in peace on the means of establishing our future national felicity. And have we now forgotten that powerful Friend? Or do we imagine we no longer need His assistance?

I have lived, sir, a long time, and the longer I live, the more convincing proofs I see of this truth—that God governs in the affairs of men. And if a sparrow cannot fall to the ground without His notice, is it probable that an empire can rise without His aid? We have been assured, sir, in the Sacred Writings, that "except the Lord build the House, they labor in vain that build it." I firmly believe this; and I also believe that without His concurring aid we shall succeed in this political building no better than the builders of Babel: we shall be divided by our little partial local interests; our projects will be confounded, and we ourselves shall become a reproach and byword down to future ages. And what is worse, mankind may hereafter from this unfortunate instance, despair of establishing governments by human wisdom and leave it to chance, war, and conquest.

I therefore beg leave to move—that henceforth prayers imploring the assistance of Heaven, and its blessings on our deliberations, be held in this Assembly every morning before we proceed to business, and that one or more of the clergy of this city be requested to officiate in that service. [142]

(This is a striking speech since it reflects the sentiments of one who is admittedly one of the least religious of the Founders.)

Roger Sherman of Connecticut seconded Franklin's motion for prayer, [143] but some opposed it, pointing out that since the Convention had no funds it could not pay for a chaplain. [144] Franklin's motion was therefore tabled. [145] (However, individual delegate accounts suggest that prayer did occur at some point during the Convention. [146]) Delegate Edmund Jennings Randolph of Virginia also proposed:

[T]hat a sermon be preached at the request of the Convention on the Fourth of July. [147]

To accommodate that proposal, on Monday, July 2, the Convention adjourned until Thursday, July 5, so that, as James Madison explained, "time might be given . . . to such as chose to attend to the celebrations on the anniversary of independence." [148] On July 4, many delegates attended that special service. For example, George Washington noted in his diary:

[W]ent to hear [at the Calvinist Church] an oration on the anniversary of independence. [149]

After the oration (delivered by a young law student), the Rev. William Rogers, minister of the Calvinist Church, concluded with this prayer:

[W]e fervently recommend to thy fatherly notice . . . our federal convention. . . . [F]avor them, from day to day, with thy inspiring presence; be their wisdom and strength; enable them to devise such measures as may prove happy instruments in healing all divisions and prove the good of the great whole; . . . that the United States of America may form one example of a free and virtuous government. . . . May we . . . continue, under the influence of republican virtue, to partake of all the blessings of cultivated and Christian society. [150]

When the Constitutional Convention finally concluded, some delegates opposed the final document. However, perhaps Benjamin Franklin summed up the sense of the thirty-nine who signed it when he declared:

I beg I may not be understood to infer that our general Convention was divinely inspired when it formed the new federal Constitution . . . yet I must own I have so much faith in the general government of the world by Providence that I can hardly conceive a transaction of such momentous importance to the welfare of millions now existing (and to exist in the posterity of a great nation) should be suffered to pass without being in some degree influenced, guided, and governed by that omnipotent, omnipresent, and beneficent Ruler, in whom all inferior spirits live, and move, and have their being. [151]

As the above examples indicate, the men who formed the Constitution neither precluded nor limited public or official religious acknowledgments. In fact, George Washington, President of the Convention, later told the Baptists of Virginia that:

> If I could have entertained the slightest apprehension that the Constitution framed in the Convention where I had the honor to preside might possibly endanger the religious rights of any ecclesiastical society, certainly I would never have placed my signature to it. [152]

However, not only did religious activities accompany the drafting of the federal Constitution, they also accompanied its ratification. This was evident throughout the various State conventions which gathered to approve that document. For example:

> On motion of the Hon. Mr. [John] Adams, *Voted*, That the Convention will attend morning prayers daily, and that the gentlemen of the clergy, of every denomination, be requested to officiate in turn. [153] MASSACHUSETTS

> After appointing the proper subordinate officers, and having ordered that the doors should be kept open . . . the business of the Convention opened every morning with prayer. [154] NEW YORK

> On the recommendation of Mr. Paul Carrington, the Rev. Abner Waugh was unanimously elected chaplain, to attend every morning to read prayers immediately after the bell shall be rung for calling the Convention. [155] VIRGINIA

Furthermore, in some States the ratification convention was held in a church. [156] Clearly, the proceedings of both the Constitutional Convention and the ratification conventions provide further organic utterances that the Framers not only supported, but even participated in both public religious activities and public endorsements of religion.

Under The Constitution
Practices of the Executive, Legislature, and Judiciary

On April 6, 1789, following the ratification of the Constitution, George Washington was selected President; he accepted the position on April 14, 1789; and his inauguration was scheduled in New York City (the nation's capital) for April 30, 1789. The April 23 *New York Daily Advertiser* reported on the planned inaugural activities:

> [O]n the morning of the day on which our illustrious President will be invested with his office, the bells will ring at nine o'clock, when the people may go up to the house of God and in a solemn manner commit the new government, with its important train of consequences, to the holy protection and blessing of the Most high. An early hour is prudently fixed for this peculiar act of devotion and . . . is designed wholly for prayer. [157]

On April 27, three days before the inauguration, the Senate:

> *Resolved*, That after the oath shall have been administered to the President, he, attended by the Vice-President and members of the Senate and House of Representatives, proceed to St. Paul's Chapel, to hear Divine service. [158]

The day before the inauguration, the House approved the same resolution; [159] and the next day (April 30th) after being sworn-in, George Washington delivered his "Inaugural Address" to a joint session of Congress. In it, Washington declared:

> [I]t would be peculiarly improper to omit, in this first official act, my fervent supplications to that Almighty Being who rules over the universe, who presides in the councils of nations, and whose providential aids can supply every human defect. . . . No people can be bound to acknowledge and adore the Invisible Hand which conducts the affairs of men more than those of the United States. Every step by which they have advanced to the character of an independent nation seems to have been distinguished by some token of providential agency. . . . [W]e ought to be no less persuaded that the propitious [favorable] smiles of Heaven can never be expected on a nation that disregards the eternal rules of order and right which Heaven itself has ordained. [160]

Following his address, the *Annals of Congress* reported that:

> The President, the Vice-President, the Senate, and House of Representatives, &c., then proceeded to St. Paul's Chapel, where Divine service was performed by the chaplain of Congress. [161]

Several months later, Congress contemplated whether it should request the President to declare a national day of thanksgiving. The *Annals of Congress* for September 25, 1789, record those discussions:

> Mr. [Elias] Boudinot said he could not think of letting the session pass over without offering an opportunity to all the citizens of the United States of joining with one voice in returning to Almighty God their sincere thanks for the many blessings He had poured down upon them. With this view, therefore, he would move the following resolution:
>
> *Resolved,* That a joint committee of both Houses be directed to wait upon the President of the United States to request that he would recommend to the people of the United States a day of public thanksgiving and prayer, to be observed by acknowledging with grateful hearts the many signal favors of Almighty God, especially by affording them an opportunity peaceably to establish a Constitution of government for their safety and happiness. . . .
>
> Mr. [Roger] Sherman justified the practice of thanksgiving, on any signal event, not only as a laudable one in itself but as warranted by a number of precedents in Holy Writ: for instance, the solemn thanksgivings and rejoicings which took place in the time of Solomon after the building of the temple was a case in point. This example he thought worthy of Christian imitation on the present occasion; and he would agree with the gentleman who moved the resolution. Mr. Boudinot quoted further precedents from the practice of the late Congress and hoped the motion would meet a ready acquiescence [approval]. The question was now put on the resolution and it was carried in the affirmative. [162]

(Strikingly, this request from Congress to the President was made the *same day* that Congress approved the final wording of the First Amendment. This clearly demonstrates that the same body which framed that Amendment did not believe that it was a violation for Congress to call for a national religious time of Thanksgiving.)

The Congressional resolution was delivered to President Washington who heartily concurred with its request. On October 3, 1789, he issued the following proclamation:

> Whereas it is the duty of all nations to acknowledge the providence of Almighty God, to obey His will, to be grateful for His benefits, and humbly to implore His protection and favor. . . . Now, therefore, I do recommend . . . that we may then all unite in rendering unto Him our sincere and humble thanks for His kind care and protection of the people of this country previous to their becoming a nation; for the signal and manifold mercies and the favorable interpositions of His providence in the course and conclusion of the late war; for the great degree of tranquility, union, and plenty which we have since enjoyed; for the peaceable and rational manner in which we have been enabled to establish constitutions of government for our safety and happiness, and particularly the national one now lately instituted; for the civil and religious liberty with which we are blessed. . . . And also that we may then unite in most humbly offering our prayers and supplications to the great Lord and Ruler of Nations, and beseech Him to pardon our national and other transgressions . . . to promote the knowledge and practice of true religion and virtue. [163]

During his Presidency, Washington remained just as outspoken about the importance of religion to government as he had been while he was Commander-in-Chief. For example, in October 1789, he declared:

> [W]hile just government protects all in their religious rights, true religion affords to government its surest support. [164]

And on March 11, 1792, he explained:

> I am sure there never was a people who had more reason to acknowledge a Divine interposition in their affairs than those of the United States; and I should be pained to believe that they have forgotten that Agency which was so often manifested during our revolution, or that they failed to consider the omnipotence of that God who is alone able to protect them. [165]

Washington, in addition to helping America traverse many stressful situations, had personally observed many others throughout the world. For example, the French Revolution, with its proponents of amorality and atheism, had produced a bloodbath and display of horrors in France during his Presidency. In the midst of this embarrassing French spectacle, his "Farewell Address" on September 17, 1796, delivered an articulate warning which summarized what had made the American experiment so successful:

> Of all the dispositions and habits which lead to political prosperity, religion and morality are indispensable supports. In vain would that man claim the tribute of patriotism, who should labor to subvert these great pillars of human happiness. . . . The mere politician . . . ought to respect and to cherish them. A volume could not trace all their connections with private and public felicity. Let it simply be asked, Where is the security for property, for reputation, for life, if the sense of religious obligation desert . . . ? And let us with caution indulge the supposition that morality can be maintained without religion. Whatever may be conceded to the influence of refined education on minds . . . reason and experience both forbid us to expect that national morality can prevail, in exclusion of religious principle. [166]

The visible and firm reliance on religious principles which Washington displayed in the Executive Branch was also just as visible in the practices of the Judicial Branch.

In the original Supreme Court, each Justice was assigned responsibilities over a specific geographic region. Although that practice still continues today, those early Justices, unlike today's Justices, traveled to the different geographic locations across the country to impanel grand juries to hear cases rather than requiring all parties to travel to the federal capital. Chancellor James Kent (considered one of the two Fathers of American Jurisprudence) observed that this was a practice with Biblical precedent:

> The Jewish judges rode the circuits, and Samuel judged Israel all the days of his life, and he went from year to year in circuit, to Bethel and Gilgal and Mizpeh, and judged Israel in all those places. I Sam. ch. 7, ver. 15 & 16. [167]

In preparation for these visits, local officials would correspond with the Supreme Court Justices to ensure that all necessary arrangements had been made prior to their arrival. For example, on February 24, 1790, Richard Law of New London, Connecticut, inquired of Chief-Justice John Jay . . .

> . . . which of the Judges are to ride the eastern circuit . . . and whether they would wish to give any directions relative to the

preparation for their reception in point of parade, accommodations or the like, whether any uniformity particularly formalities of dress [i.e., manner of judicial robe] is expectable, whether they would wish to have a clergyman attend. [168]

Chief-Justice Jay responded:

Judge Cushing is to ride with me the Northern Circuit; Judge Wilson, Judge Blair will take the Middle, and Judge Rutledge and Judge Iredell the Southern. . . . No particular dress has as yet been assigned for the Judges on the circuits. The custom in New England of a clergyman's attending, should in my opinion be observed and continued. [169]

Newspaper accounts of the Justices' visits from across the country confirm that prayer was a regular part of the Court's activities. Notice:

Pursuant to law, Court convened with Chief-Justice John Jay, Associate Justice William Cushing, and Judge John Sullivan in attendance. After the customary proclamations were made and the Grand Jury sworn— a short, though pertinent charge was given them by his Honor the Chief-Justice—when the Throne of Grace was addressed by the Rev. Dr. [Samuel] Haven [170] PORTSMOUTH, NEW HAMPSHIRE, 1791

Court opened on Saturday, May 12, with Chief-Justice John Jay, Associate Justice William Cushing, and Judge John Lowell in attendance. On Monday, May 14, Jay delivered a charge to the Grand Jury. . . . "replete with his usual perspicuity [wisdom] and elegance." The prayer was made by the Rev. Dr. [Samuel] Parker. His Excellency the Vice-President of the United States [John Adams], was in Court." [171] BOSTON, MASSACHUSETTS, 1792

Last Wednesday the Circuit Court of the United States opened in this town: When the Rev. Mr. Patten addressed the Throne of Grace in prayer—After which the Hon. Judge Wilson delivered to the Grand Jury a charge. [172] NEWPORT, RHODE ISLAND, 1793

On Monday last the Circuit Court of the United States was opened in this town. The Hon. Judge Paterson presided. After the Jury were impaneled, the Judge delivered a most elegant and appropriate charge. . . . Religion and morality were pleasingly inculcated and enforced as being necessary to good government, good order, and good laws, for "when the righteous are in authority, the people rejoice [Proverbs 29:2]." . . . After the charge was delivered, the Rev. Mr. [Timothy] Alden addressed the Throne of Grace in an excellent, well adapted prayer. [173] **PORTSMOUTH, NEW HAMPSHIRE, 1800**

These newspaper accounts are representative of scores of similar articles.

If many people today might be surprised by courtroom practices such as these, they probably would be shocked to discover that the practices of the Legislative Branch perhaps demonstrated an even greater direct support for religion than either those of the Executive or the Judicial.

In fact, in 1800 when the seat of federal government moved to Washington, D. C., the Congress authorized the Capitol building to serve also as a church building! [174] John Quincy Adams, a member of several Presidential administrations (first serving under George Washington), a U. S. Senator, a U. S. Representative, and himself a U. S. President, attended church in the Capitol building. For example, in his diary entries on October 23 and October 30, 1803, he wrote:

> Attended public service at the Capitol where Mr. Rattoon, an Episcopalian clergyman from Baltimore, preached a sermon. [175]

> [R]eligious service is usually performed on Sundays at the Treasury office and at the Capitol. I went both forenoon and afternoon to the Treasury. [176]

The practices of the original Executive, Legislative, and Judicial branches all repudiate today's doctrine of "separation of church and state" which purports that our Founding Fathers disapproved of religious activities in official public settings.

Foreign Observers

America's rapid rise as a successful nation was a wonder to many foreigners; how could a group of farmers and merchants have defeated what was arguably the world's greatest military power? Furthermore, how had America established a government which so quickly became envied across the world?

To answer questions such as these, many foreign writers traveled to America first to investigate and then to report their findings to their own countrymen. Consequently, their observations on America and American life are perhaps some of the more objective and informative.

One such visitor was Edward Kendall. He traversed America in 1807 and 1808 and then returned to Great Britain where in 1809 he published his three-volume work, *Travels in America*. Notice his description of election day in America (from his visit to Connecticut in 1807):

> At about eleven o'clock, his excellency [Governor Jonathan Trumbull] entered the statehouse and shortly after took his place at the head of a procession which was made to a meetinghouse or church at something less that half a mile distance. The procession was on foot and was composed of the person of the governor, together with the lieutenant-governor, assistants, high-sheriffs, members of the lower house of assembly, and, unless with accidental exceptions, all the clergy of the State. . . . The pulpit or, as it is here called, the desk, was filled by three if not four clergymen; a number which, by its form and dimensions, it was able to accommodate. Of these, one opened the service with a prayer; another delivered a sermon; a third made a concluding prayer, and a fourth pronounced a benediction. Several hymns were sung; and, among others, an occasional one [a special one for that occasion]. The total number of singers was between forty and fifty. The sermon, as will be supposed, touched upon matters of government. When all was finished, the procession returned to the statehouse. [177]

This observer, writing two decades *after* the Constitution, saw no evidence of the alleged "separation of church and state" which today would likely forbid this celebration from occurring. John Quincy Adams reports similar practices in Massachusetts. He related:

> This being the day of general election, at nine in the morning I repaired to the Senate Chamber, conformably to a summons which I received from the Governor [Caleb Strong] . . . . The Governor then came and administered to us the oaths required by the constitution. . . . The Governor and Council then came and with both Houses proceeded to the meeting house where a sermon was preached by Mr. Baldwin. [178]

Frenchman Alexis de Tocqueville traveled throughout the nation in the early 1830s and published his findings in 1835 in *The Republic of the States of America, and Its Political Institutions, Reviewed and Examined*—now called simply, *Democracy in America*. Notice some of his observations:

Upon my arrival in the United States, the religious aspect of the country was the first thing that struck my attention; and the longer I stayed there, the more did I perceive the great political consequences resulting from this state of things, to which I was unaccustomed. In France I had almost always seen the spirit of religion and the spirit of freedom pursuing courses diametrically opposed to each other; but in America I found that they were intimately united, and that they reigned in common over the same country. [179]

Achille Murat, another French observer of America, published his findings in 1833 in *A Moral and Political Sketch of the United States*. Murat personally disliked religion and found America's religious nature highly offensive. He exclaimed:

It must be admitted that looking at the physiognomy [discernible character] of the United States, its religion is the only feature which disgusts a foreigner. [180]

He continued:

[T]here is no country in which the people are so religious as in the United States; to the eyes of a foreigner they even appear to be too much so. . . . The great number of religious societies existing in the United States is truly surprising: there are some of them for every thing; for instance, societies to distribute the Bible; to distribute tracts; to encourage religious journals; to convert, civilize, educate the savages; to marry the preachers; to take care of their widows and orphans; to preach, extend, purify, preserve, reform the faith; to build chapels, endow congregations, support seminaries; catechize and convert sailors, Negroes, and loose women; to secure the observance of Sunday and prevent blasphemy by prosecuting the violators; to establish Sunday schools where young ladies teach reading and the catechism to little rogues, male and female; to prevent drunkenness, &c. [181]

Despite his dislike for religion, Murat nonetheless concluded that:

While a death-struggle is waging in Europe. . . it is curious to observe the tranquillity which prevails in the United States. [182]

Harriet Martineau of England traversed America from 1834 to 1836 before publishing her findings in 1837 in *Society in America*. Like Murat, she, too, was extremely harsh in her views toward Christianity, declaring:

> There is no evading the conviction that it [Christianity] is to a vast extent a monstrous superstition that is thus embraced by the tyrant, the profligate [immoral], the weakling, the bigot [obstinate, unreasonable], the coward, and the slave. [183]

Yet despite her own personal hostility toward Christianity, she concluded:

> The institutions of America are, as I have said, planted down deep into Christianity. Its spirit must make an effectual pilgrimage through a society of which it may be called a native; and no mistrust of its influences can forever intercept that spirit in its mission of denouncing anomalies, exposing hypocrisy, rebuking faithlessness, raising and communing with the outcast, and driving out sordidness [vileness] from the circuit of this, the most glorious temple of society that has ever yet been reared. [184]

Summary

The selections in this chapter, taken from both government documents and private writings, from both proponents and opponents of Christianity, all proclaim the same truth. Despite the immense quantity of citations presented here, they still represent only a minuscule portion of that which could be invoked. It was due to the massive amount of available documentation that the 1892 Supreme Court did not hesitate to declare:

> [T]his is a religious people. This is historically true. . . . These are not individual sayings, declarations of private persons: they are organic utterances; they speak the voice of the entire people. . . . These, and many other matters which might be noticed, add a ***volume*** of unofficial declarations to the ***mass*** of organic utterances that this is a Christian nation. [185] (emphasis added)

No other conclusion is possible after an honest examination of America's history. Nonetheless, revisionist historians and many contemporary courts have been effective in portraying a different view of American history. They overtly claim that both our heritage and the religious beliefs of our Founding Fathers mandate a religion-free public arena; that claim is clearly refuted by the facts.

~ 6 ~
The Religious Nature of the Founding Fathers

If the Founders were generally men of faith, then it is inconceivable that they would establish policies to limit expressions of that faith. However, if the contemporary portrayal is correct, and if, as many now claim, the Founders were by and large a collective group of atheists, agnostics, and deists, then it is logical that they would not want religious activities as a part of official public life. Therefore, a vital question to be answered in the current debate over the historical role of public religious expressions is, "What was the overall religious disposition of the Founding Fathers?"

Before delving into an investigation of their religious nature, it is important first to establish what constitutes a "Founding Father." As previously noted in the preface, for the purpose of this work, a "Founding Father" is one who exerted significant influence in, provided prominent leadership for, or had a substantial impact upon the birth, development, and establishment of America as an independent, self-governing nation.

This obviously includes the fifty-six signers of the Declaration of Independence, as well as the fourteen different Presidents who governed America from 1774 to 1789. (Under America's unicameral system prior to the Constitution, the President of the Continental Congress essentially served as the President of America.) Additionally, the handful of significant military leaders who provided leadership for, fought for, and secured our independence must be included. In other words, without the work of the fifty-six men who signed the Declaration, the fourteen Presidents of America who led the Continental Congress, or the three-dozen or so prominent military leaders, America as we know it undoubtedly would not exist today.

Included next are the fifty-five men at the Constitutional Convention as well as the major leaders responsible for the ratification of the Constitution (on many occasions, these were the State Governors—without whose efforts there would have been no United *States* of America). Therefore, without the work of the delegates at the Constitutional Convention and the leaders of the ratification movement, America would not have the form of government it has now enjoyed for over two centuries.

Following the ratification of the Constitution, the prognosis for a stable American government was uncertain until the end of Washington's administration, and probably that of Adams. Therefore, the final group of Founding Fathers includes those responsible for taking the vision written down in our Founding documents, working out the logistics of that vision, and then turning it into tangible reality. This group includes the ninety members of the First Congress (they created the Bill of Rights—an important part of the Constitution since it defines the scope of Constitutional powers), the earliest U. S. Supreme Court members who guided the development of the Judiciary, and the small group of men who served in Washington's cabinet during his administration. Without these groups, it is likely that the American experiment would have failed.

How many, then, may actually be counted as Founding Fathers? Even if one accounts for the fact that there is some overlap among the members of the groups outlined above (for example, six of the men who signed the Declaration also signed the Constitution), there still can be no exact number. The reason? There were many who, while they do not fit into any specific group, were nevertheless important leaders.

For example, Patrick Henry signed no document nor was he part of any of the outlined groups, but his leadership unquestionably contributed much to the success of the American Revolution. Similarly, Noah Webster, while fitting into no specific group, was among the first to call for the Constitutional Convention, [1] the man who contributed the copyright protection clause found in Article 1, Section 8 of the Constitution, and the man to whom many delegates in the Constitutional Convention repaired to lead the ratification efforts for the Constitution. [2] Therefore, allowing for overlap and the inclusion of leaders like Henry and Webster, approximately two-hundred-and-fifty individuals are considered here as "Founding Fathers."

To determine whether these "Founding Fathers" were generally atheists, agnostics, and deists, one must first define those terms. An "atheist" is one who professes to believe that there is no God; [3] an "agnostic" is one who professes that nothing can be known beyond what is visible and tangible; [4] and a "deist" is one who believes in an impersonal God who is no longer involved with mankind. (In other words, a "deist" embraces the "clockmaker theory" [5] that there was a God who made the universe and wound it up like a clock; however, it now runs of its own volition; the clockmaker is gone and therefore does not respond to man.)

Today the terms "atheist," "agnostic," and "deist" have been used together so often that their meanings have almost become synonymous. In fact, many dictionaries list these words as synonyms. [6]

Those who advance the notion that this was the belief system of the Founders often publish information attempting to prove that the Founders were irreligious. [7] Some of the quotes they set forth include:

> This would be the best of all possible worlds if there were no religion in it. **JOHN ADAMS**

> The government of the United States is in no sense founded on the Christian religion. **GEORGE WASHINGTON**

> I disbelieve all holy men and holy books. **THOMAS PAINE**

Are these statements accurate? Did these prominent Founders truly repudiate religion? An answer will be found by an examination of the sources of the above statements.

The John Adams' quote is taken from a letter he wrote to Thomas Jefferson on April 19, 1817, in which Adams illustrated the intolerance often manifested between Christians in their denominational disputes. Adams recounted a conversation between two ministers he had known:

> [S]eventy years ago. . . . Lemuel Bryant was my parish priest, and Joseph Cleverly my Latin schoolmaster. Lemuel was a jocular [humorous] and liberal scholar and divine. Joseph a scholar and a gentleman .... The parson and the pedagogue lived much together, but were eternally disputing about government and religion. One day when the schoolmaster [Joseph Cleverly] had been more than commonly fanatical and declared "if he were a monarch, he would have but one religion in his dominions;" the parson [Lemuel Bryant] coolly replied, "Cleverly! you would be the best man in the world if you had no religion." [8]

Lamenting these types of petty disputes, Adams declared to Jefferson:

> Twenty times in the course of my late reading have I been on the point of breaking out, "This would be the best of all possible worlds, if there were no religion in it!!!" But in this exclamation I would have been as fanatical as Bryant or Cleverly. Without religion this world would be something not fit to be mentioned in polite company, I mean hell. [9]

In reality, Adams' position on religion was exactly the opposite of what is put forth by many groups. Adams believed that it would be "fanatical" to desire a world without religion, for such a world would be "hell." Jefferson wrote back and declared that he agreed. [10]

Amazingly, while the assertion concerning Adams was completely inaccurate, the words attributed to Washington are totally false ("The government of the United States is in no sense founded on the Christian religion"). The 1797 Treaty of Tripoli is the source of Washington's supposed statement.

That treaty, one of several with Tripoli, was negotiated during the "Barbary Powers Conflict," which began shortly after the Revolutionary War and continued through the Presidencies of Washington, Adams, Jefferson, and Madison. [11] The Muslim Barbary Powers (Tunis, Morocco, Algiers, Tripoli, and Turkey) were warring against what they claimed to be the "Christian" nations (England, France, Spain, Denmark, and the United States). In 1801, Tripoli even declared war against the United States, [12] thus constituting America's first official war as an established independent nation.

Throughout this long conflict, the five Barbary Powers regularly attacked undefended American merchant ships. Not only were their cargoes easy prey but the Barbary Powers were also capturing and enslaving "Christian" seamen [13] in retaliation for what had been done to them by the "Christians" of previous centuries (e.g., the Crusades and Ferdinand and Isabella's expulsion of Muslims from Granada [14]).

In an attempt to secure a release of captured seamen and a guarantee of unmolested shipping in the Mediterranean, President Washington dispatched envoys to negotiate treaties with the Barbary nations. [15] (Concurrently, he encouraged the construction of American naval warships [16] to defend the shipping and confront the Barbary "pirates"—a plan not seriously pursued until President John Adams created a separate Department of the Navy in 1798.) The American envoys negotiated numerous treaties of "Peace and Amity" [17] with the Muslim Barbary nations to ensure "protection" of American commercial ships sailing in the Mediterranean. [18] However, the terms of the treaty frequently were unfavorable to America, either requiring her to pay hundreds of thousands of dollars of "tribute" (i.e., official extortion) to each country to receive a "guarantee" of safety or to offer other "considerations" (e.g., providing a warship as a "gift" to Tripoli, [19] a "gift" frigate to Algiers, [20] paying $525,000 to ransom captured American seamen from Algiers, [21] etc.).

The 1797 treaty with Tripoli was one of the many treaties in which each country officially recognized the religion of the other in an attempt to prevent further escalation of a "Holy War" between Christians and Muslims. [22] Consequently, Article XI of that treaty stated:

> As the government of the United States of America is not in any sense founded on the Christian religion as it has in itself no character of enmity [hatred] against the laws, religion or tranquility of Musselmen [Muslims] and as the said States [America] have never entered into any war or act of hostility against any Mahometan nation, it is declared by the parties that no pretext arising from religious opinions shall ever produce an interruption of the harmony existing between the two countries. [23]

This article may be read in two manners. It may, as its critics do, be concluded after the clause "Christian religion"; or it may be read in its entirety and concluded when the punctuation so indicates. But even if shortened and cut abruptly ("the government of the United States is not in any sense founded on the Christian religion"), this is not an untrue statement since it is referring to the *federal government.*

Recall that while the Founders themselves openly described America as a Christian nation (demonstrated in chapter 2), they did include a constitutional prohibition against a federal establishment; religion was a matter left solely to the individual States. Therefore, if the article is read as a declaration that the *federal government* of the United States was not in any sense founded on the Christian religion, such a statement is *not* a repudiation of the fact that America was considered a Christian nation.

Reading the clause of the treaty in its entirety also fails to weaken this fact. Article XI simply distinguished America from those historical strains of European Christianity which held an inherent hatred of Muslims; it simply assured the Muslims that the United States was not a Christian nation like those of previous centuries (with whose practices the Muslims were very familiar) and thus would not undertake a religious holy war against them.

This latter reading is, in fact, supported by the attitude prevalent among numerous American leaders. The Christianity practiced in America was described by John Jay as "wise and virtuous," [24] by John Quincy Adams as "civilized," [25] and by John Adams as "rational." [26] A clear distinction was drawn between American Christianity and that of Europe in earlier centuries. As Noah Webster explained:

The ecclesiastical establishments of Europe which serve to support tyrannical governments are not the Christian religion but abuses and corruptions of it. [27]

Daniel Webster [†] similarly explained that American Christianity was:

Christianity to which the sword and the fagot [burning stake or hot branding iron] are unknown—general tolerant Christianity is the law of the land! [28]

Those who attribute the Treaty of Tripoli quote to George Washington make two mistakes. The first is that no statement in it can be attributed to Washington (the treaty did not arrive in America until months *after* he left office); Washington never saw the treaty; it was not his work; no statement in it can be ascribed to him. The second mistake is to divorce a single clause of the treaty from the remainder which provides its context.

It would also be absurd to suggest that President Adams (under whom the treaty was ratified in 1797) would have endorsed or assented to any provision which repudiated Christianity. In fact, while discussing the Barbary conflict with Jefferson, Adams declared:

The policy of Christendom has made cowards of all their sailors before the standard of Mahomet. It would be heroical and glorious in us to restore courage to ours. [29]

Furthermore, it was Adams who declared:

The general principles on which the fathers achieved independence were. . . . the general principles of Christianity. . . . I will avow that I then believed, and now believe, that those general principles of Christianity are as eternal and immutable as the existence and attributes of God; and that those principles of liberty are as unalterable as human nature. [30]

Adams' own words confirm that he rejected any notion that America was less than a Christian nation.

---

† Daniel Webster (1782-1852) was a prominent leader in the second generation of American statesmen. As a young boy, he grew up listening to and reading the speeches of prominent Founders like Washington, Adams, Jefferson, Madison, et. al., and subsequently championed the Founders' ideas throughout the first half of the nineteenth century. He has been titled "The Defender of the Constitution" both for his understanding of that docu ment and his efforts to maintain its principles.

Additionally, the writings of General William Eaton, a major figure in the Barbary Powers conflict, provide even more irrefutable testimony of how the conflict was viewed at that time. Eaton was first appointed by President John Adams as "Consul to Tunis," and President Thomas Jefferson later advanced him to the position of "U. S. Naval Agent to the Barbary States," authorizing him to lead a military expedition against Tripoli. Eaton's official correspondence during his service confirms that the conflict was a Muslim war against a Christian America.

For example, when writing to Secretary of State Timothy Pickering, Eaton apprised him of why the Muslims would be such dedicated foes:

> Taught by revelation that war with the Christians will guarantee the salvation of their souls, and finding so great secular advantages in the observance of this religious duty [the secular advantage of keeping captured cargoes], their [the Muslims'] inducements to desperate fighting are very powerful. [31]

Eaton later complained that after Jefferson had approved his plan for military action, he sent him the obsolete warship "Hero." Eaton reported the impression of America made upon the Tunis Muslims when they saw the old warship and its few cannons:

> [T]he weak, the crazy situation of the vessel and equipage [armaments] tended to confirm an opinion long since conceived and never fairly controverted among the Tunisians, that the Americans are a feeble *sect of Christians.* [32] (emphasis added)

In a later letter to Pickering, Eaton reported how pleased one Barbary ruler had been when he received the extortion compensations from America which had been promised him in one of the treaties:

> He said, "To speak truly and candidly . . . . we must acknowledge to you that we have never received articles of the kind of so excellent a quality from any *Christian nation.*" [33] (emphasis added)

When John Marshall became the new Secretary of State, Eaton informed him:

> It is a maxim of the Barbary States, that "The Christians who would be on good terms with them must fight well or pay well." [34]

And when General Eaton finally commenced his military action against Tripoli, his personal journal noted:

> April 8th. We find it almost impossible to inspire these wild bigots with confidence in us or to persuade them that, being Christians, we can be otherwise than enemies to Musselmen. We have a difficult undertaking! [35]

> May 23rd. Hassien Bey, the commander in chief of the enemy's forces, has offered by private insinuation for my head six thousand dollars and double the sum for me a prisoner; and $30 per head for Christians. Why don't he come and take it? [36]

Shortly after the military excursion against Tripoli was successfully terminated, its account was written and published. Even the title of the book bears witness to the nature of the conflict:

> *The Life of the Late Gen. William Eaton . . . commander of the **Christian** and Other Forces . . . which Led to the Treaty of Peace Between The United States and The Regency of Tripoli* [37] (emphasis added)

The numerous documents surrounding the Barbary Powers Conflict confirm that historically it was *always* viewed as a conflict between Christian America and Muslim nations. Those documents completely disprove the notion that any founding President, especially Washington, ever declared that America was not a Christian nation or people. (Chapter 16 will provide numerous additional current examples of historical revisionism.)

Consider next the quote attributed to Thomas Paine: "I disbelieve all holy men and holy books." Is the accuracy of this quote any better than the previous ones imputed to Adams and Washington? In this case, the answer is probably yes—that is, while we were unable to locate this specific statement by Paine, it is certainly of a tone similar to several others he made in his *Age of Reason* and other writings which attacked religion generally and Christianity specifically. However, the real story is not the accuracy of Paine's quote, but rather how the other Founders reacted to Paine's declarations.

Consider first Benjamin Franklin's response. Paine sent a copy of his thoughts on religion to Franklin, seeking his response. Notice Franklin's strong and succinct reply, and keep in mind that those on all sides of the religion question would concede Franklin to be one of the least religious Founders:

> I have read your manuscript with some attention. By the argument it contains against a particular Providence, though you allow a

general Providence, you strike at the foundations of all religion. For without the belief of a Providence that takes cognizance of, guards, and guides, and may favor particular persons, there is no motive to worship a Deity, to fear his displeasure, or to pray for his protection. I will not enter into any discussion of your principles, though you seem to desire it. At present I shall only give you my opinion that . . . the consequence of printing this piece will be a great deal of odium [hate] drawn upon yourself, mischief to you, and no benefit to others. He that spits into the wind, spits in his own face. But were you to succeed, do you imagine any good would be done by it? . . . [T]hink how great a portion of mankind consists of weak and ignorant men and women and of inexperienced, inconsiderate youth of both sexes who have need of the motives of religion to restrain them from vice, to support their virtue. . . . I would advise you, therefore, not to attempt unchaining the tiger, but to burn this piece before it is seen by any other person. . . . If men are so wicked with religion, what would they be if without it. I intend this letter itself as a proof of my friendship. [38]

Of Paine's views, John Adams wrote:

The Christian religion is, above all the religions that ever prevailed or existed in ancient or modern times, the religion of wisdom, virtue, equity and humanity, let the Blackguard [scoundrel, rogue] Paine say what he will. [39]

In fact, when asked about several of Thomas Paine's disciples coming to America, Adams replied:

The German letter proposing to introduce into this country a company of schoolmasters, painters, poets, &c., all of them disciples of Mr. Thomas Paine, will require no answer. I had rather countenance [allow] the introduction of Ariel and Caliban [two evil spirits in Shakespearean plays] with a troop of spirits. [40]

Samuel Adams wrote Paine a stiff rebuke, telling him:

[W]hen I heard you had turned your mind to a defence of infidelity, I felt myself much astonished and more grieved that you had attempted a measure so injurious to the feelings and so repugnant to the true interest of so great a part of the citizens of the United States. The people of New England, if you will allow me to use a Scripture phrase, are fast returning to their first love. Will you excite among them the spirit of angry controversy at a time when they are hastening to amity and peace? I am told that some of our newspapers have announced your intention to publish an additional pamphlet upon the principles of your *Age of Reason.* Do you think that your pen, or the pen of any other man, can unchristianize the mass of our citizens, or have you hopes of converting a few of them to assist you in so bad a cause? [41]

Benjamin Rush, signer of the Declaration, wrote to his friend and signer of the Constitution John Dickinson that Paine's *Age of Reason* was "absurd and impious"; [42] Charles Carroll, a signer of the Declaration, described Paine's work as "blasphemous writings against the Christian religion"; [43] John Witherspoon said that Paine was "ignorant of human nature as well as an enemy to the Christian faith"; [44] John Quincy Adams declared that "Mr. Paine has departed altogether from the principles of the Revolution"; [45] and Elias Boudinot, President of Congress, even published the *Age of Revelation*—a full-length rebuttal to Paine's work. In a letter to his daughter, Susan, Boudinot described his motivations for writing that rebuttal:

> I confess that I was much mortified to find the whole force of this vain man's genius and art pointed at the youth of America. . . . This awful consequence created some alarm in my mind lest at any future day, you, my beloved child, might take up this plausible address of infidelity; and for want of an answer at hand to his subtle insinuations might suffer even a doubt of the truth, as it is in Jesus, to penetrate into your mind. . . . I therefore determined . . . to put my thoughts on the subject of this pamphlet on paper for your edification and information, when I shall be no more. I chose to confine myself to the leading and essential facts of the Gospel which are contradicted or attempted to be turned into ridicule by this writer. I have endeavored to detect his falsehoods and misrepresentations and to show his extreme ignorance of the Divine Scriptures which he makes the subject of his animadversions [criticisms]—not knowing that "they are the power of God unto salvation, to every one that believeth [Romans 1:16]." [46]

Patrick Henry, too, wrote a refutation of Paine's work which he described as "the puny efforts of Paine." [47] However, after reading Bishop Richard

Watson's *Apology for the Bible* written against Paine, Henry deemed that work sufficient and decided not to publish his reply. [48] When William Paterson, signer of the Constitution and a Justice on the U. S. Supreme Court, learned that some Americans seemed to agree with Paine's work, he thundered:

> Infatuated Americans, why renounce your country, your religion, and your God? Oh shame, where is thy blush? Is this the way to continue independent, and to render the 4th of July immortal in memory and song? [49]

Zephaniah Swift, author of America's first law book, noted :

> [W]e cannot sufficiently reprobate the beliefs of Thomas Paine in his attack on Christianity by publishing his *Age of Reason*. . . . He has the impudence and effrontery [shameless boldness] to address to the citizens of the United States of America a paltry performance which is intended to shake their faith in the religion of their fathers. . . . No language can describe the wickedness of the man who will attempt to subvert a religion which is a source of comfort and consolation to its votaries [devout worshipers] merely for the purpose of eradicating all sentiments of religion. [50]

John Jay, an author of the *Federalist Papers* and the original Chief-Justice of the U. S. Supreme Court, was comforted by the fact that Christianity would prevail despite Paine's attack:

> I have long been of the opinion that the evidence of the truth of Christianity requires only to be carefully examined to produce conviction in candid minds, and I think they who undertake that task will derive advantages. . . . As to *The Age of Reason*, it never appeared to me to have been written from a disinterested love of truth or of mankind. [51]

Many other similar writings could be cited, but these are sufficient to show that Paine's views were strongly rejected even by the least religious Founders. In fact, Paine's views caused such vehement public opposition that he spent his last years in New York as "an outcast" in "social ostracism" and was buried in a farm field because no American cemetery would accept his remains. [52]

Yet, even Thomas Paine cannot be called an atheist, for in the same work wherein he so strongly attacked Christianity, Paine also declared:

> I believe in one God . . . and I hope for happiness beyond this life. [53]

The Founding Fathers simply were *not* atheists—not even one of them. As Franklin had previously explained to the French:

> [B]ad examples to youth are more rare in America, which must be comfortable consideration to parents. To this may be truly added, that serious religion, under its various denominations, is not only tolerated, but respected and practised. Atheism is unknown there; infidelity [a disbelief in the Scriptures and in Christianity [54]] rare and secret; so that persons may live to a great age in that country, without having their piety shocked by meeting with either an atheist or an infidel. [55]

While there was some anti-organized-religion sentiment among the Founders (e.g., Thomas Paine, [56] Ethan Allen, [57] Charles Lee, [58] Henry Dearborn [59]), those with such views numbered very few among the total number of Founding Fathers.

In fact, even a cursory examination of the Founders' own declarations in their last wills and testaments [60] provides convincing evidence of the strong religious beliefs evident among so many of them. Observe:

> Principally and first of all, I recommend my soul to that Almighty Being who gave it and my body I commit to the dust, relying upon the merits of Jesus Christ for a pardon of all my sins. **SAMUEL ADAMS**, SIGNER OF THE DECLARATION

> Firstly I commit my Soul into the hands of God, its great and benevolent author. **JOSIAH BARTLETT**, SIGNER OF THE DECLARATION

> First and principally, I commit my Soul unto Almighty God. **DAVID BREARLEY**, SIGNER OF THE CONSTITUTION

> Rendering thanks to my Creator for my existence and station among His works, for my birth in a country enlightened by the Gospel and enjoying freedom, and for all His other kindnesses, to Him I resign myself, humbly confiding in His goodness and in His mercy through Jesus Christ for the events of eternity. **JOHN DICKINSON**, SIGNER OF THE CONSTITUTION

> I resign my soul into the hands of the Almighty who gave it in humble hopes of his mercy through our Savior Jesus Christ. **GABRIEL DUVALL**, SELECTED AS DELEGATE TO CONSTITUTIONAL CONVENTION; U. S. SUPREME COURT JUSTICE

[T]hanks be given unto Almighty God therefore, and knowing that it is appointed for all men once to die and after that the judgment [Hebrews 9:27] . . . principally, I give and recommend my soul into the hands of Almighty God who gave it and my body to the earth to be buried in a decent and Christian like manner . . . to receive the same again at the general resurrection by the mighty power of God. **JOHN HART,** SIGNER OF THE DECLARATION

This is all the inheritance I can give to my dear family. The religion of Christ can give them one which will make them rich indeed. **PATRICK HENRY**

Unto Him who is the author and giver of all good, I render sincere and humble thanks for His manifold and unmerited blessings, and especially for our redemption and salvation by his beloved Son. . . . Blessed be his holy name. **JOHN JAY,** ORIGINAL CHIEF JUSTICE U. S. SUPREME COURT

My soul I resign into the hands of my Almighty Creator, whose tender mercies are all over His works, who hateth nothing that He hath made, and to the justice and wisdom of whose dispensations I willingly and cheerfully submit, humbly hoping from His unbounded mercy and benevolence, through the merits of my blessed Savior, a remission of my sins. **GEORGE MASON,** FATHER OF THE BILL OF RIGHTS

With an awful reverence to the Great Almighty God, Creator of all mankind, being sick and weak in body but of sound mind and memory, thanks be given to Almighty God for the same. **JOHN MORTON,** SIGNER OF THE DECLARATION

I am constrained to express my adoration of the Supreme Being, the Author of my existence, in full belief of His Providential goodness and His forgiving mercy revealed to the world through Jesus Christ, through whom I hope for never ending happiness in a future state. **ROBERT TREAT PAINE,** SIGNER OF THE DECLARATION

To the eternal and only true God be all honor and glory now and forever. Amen! **CHARLES COTESWORTH PINCKNEY,** SIGNER OF THE CONSTITUTION

And as my children will have frequent occasion of perusing this instrument and may probably be particularly impressed with the last words of their father, I think it proper here not only to subscribe to the entire belief of the great and leading doctrines of the Christian religion, such as the being of God, the universal defection and depravity of human nature, the divinity of the person and the completeness of the redemption purchased by the blessed Saviour, the necessity of the operations of the Divine Spirit; of Divine faith accompanied with an habitual virtuous life, and the universality of the Divine Providence: but also, in the bowels of a father's affection, to exhort and charge them that the fear of God is the beginning of wisdom, that the way of life held up in the Christian system is calculated for the most complete happiness that can be enjoyed in this mortal state. **RICHARD STOCKTON**, SIGNER OF THE DECLARATION

These wills, and others like them, represent the tone of what was common among the Founders. Additionally, the personal writings of many other Founders reflect equally succinct declarations about their faith in Christ. Consider a few examples:

My hopes of a future life are all founded upon the Gospel of Christ and I cannot cavil or quibble away [evade or object to]. . . . the whole tenor of His conduct by which He sometimes positively asserted and at others countenances [permits] His disciples in asserting that He was God. [61] **JOHN QUINCY ADAMS**

Now to the triune God, The Father, the Son, and the Holy Ghost, be ascribed all honor and dominion, forevermore—Amen. [62] **GUNNING BEDFORD**, SIGNER OF THE CONSTITUTION

[T]he religion I have [is] to love and fear God, believe in Jesus Christ, do all the good to my neighbor, and myself that I can, do as little harm as I can help, and trust on God's mercy for the rest. [63] **DANIEL BOONE**, REVOLUTIONARY OFFICER; LEGISLATOR

You have been instructed from your childhood in the knowledge of your lost state by nature—the absolute necessity of a change of heart, and an entire renovation of soul to the image of Jesus Christ—of salvation thro' His meritorious righteousness only— and the indispensable necessity of personal holiness without which no man shall see the Lord. [64] **ELIAS BOUDINOT**, PRESIDENT OF CONGRESS (TO HIS DAUGHTER SUSAN BOUDINOT)

[D]on't forget to be a Christian. I have said much to you on this head and I hope an indelible impression is made. [65] **JACOB BROOM,** SIGNER OF THE CONSTITUTION

On the mercy of my Redeemer I rely for salvation and on his merits; not on the works I have done in obedience to his precepts. [66] **CHARLES CARROLL,** SIGNER OF THE DECLARATION

For my part, I am free and ready enough to declare that I think the Christian religion is a Divine institution; and I pray to God that I may never forget the precepts of His religion or suffer the appearance of an inconsistency in my principles and practice. [67] **JAMES IREDELL,** U. S. SUPREME COURT JUSTICE

I . . . am endeavoring . . . to attend to my own duty only as a Christian. . . . let us take care that our Christianity, though put to the test . . . be not shaken, and that our love for things really good wax not cold. [68] **WILLIAM SAMUEL JOHNSON,** SIGNER OF THE CONSTITUTION

My object in telling you this is that if anything happens to me you might know, and perhaps it would console you to remember, that on this point my mind is clear; I rest my hopes of salvation on the Lord Jesus Christ. [69] **JAMES KENT,** FATHER OF AMERICAN JURISPRUDENCE

[M]ay I always hear that you are following the guidance of that blessed Spirit that will lead you into all truth, leaning on that Almighty arm that has been extended to deliver you, trusting only in the only Saviour, and going on in your way to Him rejoicing. [70] **FRANCIS SCOTT KEY,** ATTORNEY; AUTHOR OF THE "STAR SPANGLED BANNER"

I desire to bless and praise the name of God most high for appointing me my birth in a land of Gospel Light where the glorious tidings of a Saviour and of pardon and salvation through Him have been continually sounding in mine ears. [71] **ROBERT TREAT PAINE,** SIGNER OF THE DECLARATION

Pardon, we beseech Thee, all our offences of omission and commission; and grant that in all our thoughts, words, and actions, we may conform to Thy known will manifested in our consciences, and in the revelations of Jesus Christ our Saviour. [72] **TIMOTHY PICKERING,** REVOLUTIONARY GENERAL; SECRETARY OF STATE

I am at last reconciled to my God and have assurance of His pardon through faith in Christ, against which the very gates of hell cannot prevail. Fear hath been driven out by perfect love. [73] **JOHN RANDOLPH OF ROANOKE,** U. S. CONGRESSMAN; U. S. DIPLOMAT

My only hope of salvation is in the infinite transcendent love of God manifested to the world by the death of his Son upon the Cross. Nothing but his blood will wash away my sins. I rely exclusively upon it. Come, Lord Jesus! Come quickly! [74] **BENJAMIN RUSH,** SIGNER OF THE DECLARATION

I believe that there is one only living and true God, existing in three persons, the Father, the Son, and the Holy Ghost, the same in substance equal in power and glory. That the scriptures of the old and new testaments are a revelation from God and a complete rule to direct us how we may glorify and enjoy Him. . . . I believe that the souls of believers are at their death made perfectly holy and immediately taken to glory: that at the end of this world there will be a resurrection of the dead and a final judgment of all mankind when the righteous shall be publicly acquitted by Christ the Judge and admitted to everlasting life and glory, and the wicked be sentenced to everlasting punishment. [75] **ROGER SHERMAN,** SIGNER OF THE DECLARATION; SIGNER OF THE CONSTITUTION

Jesus Christ has in the clearest manner inculcated those duties which are productive of the highest moral felicity and consistent with all the innocent enjoyments, to which we are impelled by the dictates of nature. Religion, when fairly considered in its genuine simplicity and uncorrupted state, is the source of endless rapture and delight. [76] **ZEPHANIAH SWIFT,** AUTHOR OF AMERICA'S FIRST LEGAL TEXT

[Pray t]hat God would graciously pour out His Spirit upon us and make the blessed Gospel in His hand effectual to a thorough reformation and general revival of the holy and peaceful religion of Jesus Christ. [77] **JONATHAN TRUMBULL,** GOVERNOR OF CONNECTICUT

I shall now conclude my discourse by preaching this Savior to all who hear me, and entreating you in the most earnest manner to believe in Jesus Christ, for "there is no salvation in any other" [Acts 4:12]. . . . [I]f you are not reconciled to God through Jesus Christ, if you are not clothed with the spotless robe of His righteousness, you must forever perish. [78] **JOHN WITHERSPOON,** SIGNER OF THE DECLARATION

There are numerous additional examples, and to apply the term "deist" to this group is a completely erroneous characterization.

Further testimony of the strong religious convictions of so many Founding Fathers is evidenced through their leadership roles in establishing and guiding numerous religious societies or through serving in active ministry. Notice these representative examples:

JOHN QUINCY ADAMS: Vice-President of the American Bible Society; [79] member of the Massachusetts Bible Society. [80]

ABRAHAM BALDWIN (SIGNER OF THE CONSTITUTION): Chaplain in the American Revolution for two years. [81]

JOEL BARLOW (DIPLOMAT UNDER WASHINGTON AND ADAMS): Chaplain in the American Revolution for three years. [82]

JOSEPH BLOOMFIELD (GOVERNOR OF NEW JERSEY): Member of the New Jersey Bible Society. [83]

ELIAS BOUDINOT (PRESIDENT OF THE CONTINENTAL CONGRESS): Founder and first President of the American Bible Society; [84] President of the New Jersey Bible Society; [85] member of the American Board of Commissioners for Foreign Missions; [86] member of the Massachusetts Society for Promoting Christian Knowledge. [87]

JAMES BOWDOIN (GOVERNOR OF MASSACHUSETTS): Member of the Society for Propagating the Gospel Among the Indians and Others. [88]

JOHN BROOKS (GOVERNOR OF MASSACHUSETTS; REVOLUTIONARY GENERAL): President of Middlesex County Bible Society. [89]

JAMES BROWN (U. S. SENATOR; DIPLOMAT): Original Officer of the American Bible Society. [90]

JAMES BURRILL, JR. (CHIEF-JUSTICE OF RHODE ISLAND SUPREME COURT; U. S. SENATOR): President of the Providence Auxiliary Bible Society. [91]

DEWITT CLINTON (GOVERNOR OF NEW YORK; U. S. SENATOR; INTRODUCED THE TWELFTH AMENDMENT): Manager and Vice-President of the American Bible Society. [92]

FRANCIS DANA (MEMBER OF CONTINENTAL CONGRESS; CHIEF-JUSTICE OF MASSACHUSETTS SUPREME COURT; U. S. MINISTER TO RUSSIA): Member of the Society for Propagating the Gospel Among the Indians and Others. [93]

JOHN DAVENPORT (REVOLUTIONARY OFFICER; U. S. CONGRESS): Member of the Missionary Society of Connecticut. [94]

SAMUEL DEXTER (SECRETARY OF WAR UNDER ADAMS; U. S. CONGRESSMAN; U. S. SENATOR): Society for Propagating the Gospel Among the Indians and Others. [95]

JONAS GALUSHA (GOVERNOR OF VERMONT): Original Officer of the American Bible Society. [96]

WILLIAM GASTON (CHIEF-JUSTICE OF NORTH CAROLINA SUPREME COURT; U. S. REPRESENTATIVE): Original Officer of the American Bible Society. [97]

CHARLES GOLDSBOROUGH (GOVERNOR OF MARYLAND; U. S. REPRESENTATIVE): Vice-President of the American Bible Society. [98]

WILLIAM GRAY (LT. GOVERNOR OF MASSACHUSETTS; U. S. SENATOR): Original Officer of the American Bible Society. [99]

FELIX GRUNDY (U. S. ATTORNEY GENERAL; U. S. SENATOR; U. S. CONGRESSMAN): Original Officer of the American Bible Society. [100]

ALEXANDER HAMILTON (SIGNER OF THE CONSTITUTION): Proposed formation of the Christian Constitutional Society to spread Christian government to other nations. [101]

JOHN HAMILTON (MAJOR-GENERAL IN THE REVOLUTION; U. S. CONGRESS): Member of the New Jersey Bible Society. [102]

JOHN JAY (ORIGINAL CHIEF-JUSTICE OF THE U. S. SUPREME COURT): President of the American Bible Society; [103] member of American Board of Commissioners for Foreign Missions. [104]

WILLIAM JONES (GOVERNOR OF RHODE ISLAND): Original Officer of the American Bible Society. [105]

FRANCIS SCOTT KEY (ATTORNEY; AUTHOR OF "THE STAR-SPANGLED BANNER"): Manager and Vice-President of the American Sunday School Union. [106]

RUFUS KING (SIGNER OF THE CONSTITUTION): Selected as manager †
of the American Bible Society. [107]

ANDREW KIRKPATRICK (CHIEF-JUSTICE OF NEW JERSEY SUPREME
COURT): Vice-President of the New Jersey Bible Society; [108] Vice-
President of the American Bible Society. [109]

MARQUIS DE LAFAYETTE (REVOLUTIONARY GENERAL): Member of
the American Sunday School Union. [110]

JOHN LANGDON (SIGNER OF THE CONSTITUTION): Vice-President
of the American Bible Society. [111]

BENJAMIN LINCOLN (REVOLUTIONARY GENERAL; LT. GOVERNOR OF
MASSACHUSETTS): Member of the Society for the Propagating of
the Gospel among the Indians and Others. [112]

JOHN LOWELL (REVOLUTIONARY OFFICER; MEMBER OF THE
CONTINENTAL CONGRESS): Member of the Society for the
Propagating of the Gospel among the Indians and Others. [113]

GEORGE MADISON (GOVERNOR OF KENTUCKY): Original Officer of
the American Bible Society. [114]

JOHN MARSHALL (CHIEF-JUSTICE OF THE U. S. SUPREME COURT;
SECRETARY OF STATE; REVOLUTIONARY GENERAL): Vice-President
of the American Bible Society; [115] officer in the American Sunday
School Union. [116]

JAMES MCHENRY (SIGNER OF THE CONSTITUTION): President of the
Baltimore Bible Society. [117]

DAVID LAWRENCE MORRIL (GOVERNOR OF NEW HAMPSHIRE; U. S.
SENATOR): Vice-President of the American Bible Society; [118]
Manager in the American Sunday School Union. [119]

JOSEPH NOURSE (REVOLUTIONARY OFFICER; U. S. TREASURY):
Original Officer of the American Bible Society. [120]

---

† Rufus King was selected as a member of the American Bible Society by his peers, but
declined the position on the recommendation of his Episcopal Bishop who desired that he
instead focus his efforts on his own denomination's Bible Society: the New York Bible and
Common Prayer Book Society. King therefore respectfully deferred to his Bishop's wishes.
For more information on Rufus King's feelings on the worthiness of the American Bible
Society, and on the establishment of, and of his financial support for, the New York Bible
and Common Prayer Book Society, read the complete letter cited in his endnote above.

ROBERT TREAT PAINE (SIGNER OF THE DECLARATION): Military Chaplain. [121]

ALBION PARRIS (GOVERNOR OF MAINE): Manager of the American Sunday School Union. [122]

WILLIAM PHILLIPS (LT. GOVERNOR OF MASSACHUSETTS FOR 11 TERMS): President of the Society for Propagating the Gospel Among the Indians; [123] President of the Massachusetts Bible Society; [124] a member of the American Board of Foreign Missions; [125] Vice-President of the American Bible Society; [126] President of the American Society for Educating Pious Youth for the Gospel Ministry. [127]

CHARLES COTESWORTH PINCKNEY (SIGNER OF THE CONSTITUTION): President of the Charleston Bible Society; [128] Vice-President of the American Bible Society. [129]

THOMAS POSEY (REVOLUTIONARY OFFICER; GOVERNOR OF INDIANA; U. S. SENATOR): Original Officer of the American Bible Society. [130]

RUFUS PUTNAM (REVOLUTIONARY GENERAL; FEDERAL JUDGE): President of the Ohio Bible Society. [131]

BENJAMIN RUSH (SIGNER OF THE DECLARATION): Founder and manager of the Philadelphia Bible Society. [132]

ISAAC SHELBY (REVOLUTIONARY OFFICER; GOVERNOR OF KENTUCKY): Original Officer of the American Bible Society. [133]

JOHN COTTON SMITH (GOVERNOR OF CONNECTICUT; U. S. CONGRESSMAN): President of the Litchfield County Foreign Missionary Society; [134] first President of the Connecticut Bible Society; [135] President of the American Bible Society; [136] President of the American Board of Foreign Missions. [137]

CALEB STRONG (CONSTITUTIONAL CONVENTION; U. S. SENATOR; GOVERNOR OF MASSACHUSETTS): Vice-President of the American Bible Society. [138]

JAMES SULLIVAN (GOVERNOR OF MASSACHUSETTS; U. S. CONGRESSMAN): Member of the Society for Propagating the Gospel Among the Indians and Others. [139]

INCREASE SUMNER (GOVERNOR OF MASSACHUSETTS): Member of the Society for Propagating the Gospel Among the Indians and Others. [140]

WILLIAM TILGHMAN (FEDERAL JUDGE; CHIEF-JUSTICE OF PENNSYLVANIA SUPREME COURT): Original Officer of the American Bible Society. [141]

SMITH THOMPSON (U. S. SUPREME COURT; SECRETARY OF NAVY): Vice-President of the American Bible Society. [142]

DANIEL TOMPKINS (GOVERNOR OF NEW YORK; VICE-PRESIDENT OF THE U. S.): Vice-President of the American Bible Society. [143]

JOHN TREADWELL (GOVERNOR OF CONNECTICUT; MEMBER OF CONTINENTAL CONGRESS): Member of the Missionary Society of Connecticut. [144]

ROBERT TROUP (FEDERAL JUDGE; SECRETARY OF WAR): Vice-President of the American Bible Society. [145]

PETER VROOM (GOVERNOR OF NEW JERSEY; U. S. CONGRESSMAN): Vice-President of the American Bible Society; [146] member of the American Board of Commissioners for Foreign Missions. [147]

BUSHROD WASHINGTON (U. S. SUPREME COURT JUSTICE): Vice-President of the American Bible Society; [148] Vice-President of the American Sunday School Union. [149]

WILLIAM WIRT (U. S. ATTORNEY-GENERAL UNDER TWO PRESIDENTS): Manager of the American Sunday School Union; [150] Vice-President of the American Bible Society. [151]

THOMAS WORTHINGTON (GOVERNOR OF OHIO; U. S. SENATOR): Original Officer of the American Bible Society. [152]

Other Founders were involved in numerous similar organizations. The evidence is clear that not only can *none* of them be called an atheist, only the smallest handful would fit today's definition of a deist. Nevertheless, despite this irrefutable evidence, the charge persists to the contrary—as, for example, evidenced in an article in *American Heritage* by Gordon Wood. Wood amazingly asserted:

> The Founding Fathers were at *most* deists . . . [and] were a very thin veneer on their society. [153] (emphasis added)

In a national article, Steven Morris similarly claimed:

> The early presidents and patriots were generally deists or Unitarians, believing in some form of impersonal Providence but rejecting the divinity of Jesus and the relevance of the Bible. [154]

Wood, Morris, and all who make such broad charges are totally incorrect, deliberately ignoring all historical facts to the contrary. They also randomly, recklessly, and even unethically impute the term "deist" to Founders who would vehemently deny it if they were alive today.

For example, some contemporary works incorrectly assert that Jefferson called himself a deist. Yet historical records are clear that not only did Jefferson *not* call himself a deist, *he* called *himself* a Christian:

> I am a real Christian, that is to say, a disciple of the doctrines of Jesus. [155]

Although Jefferson did call himself a Christian, he would probably fail the standard by any orthodox definition, for he viewed Jesus only as a great teacher and not as Divine. [156] Nonetheless, the fact remains that Jefferson did *not* call himself a deist; he called himself a Christian.

Even though a very few of the Founders did consider themselves deists (for example, Franklin did call himself a "deist" [157]), the definition of a deist in that day [158] is totally different from today's definition, evidenced by the fact that Franklin totally *rejected* the "clockmaker" concept and believed that prayer *was* worthwhile and that God *did* intervene in our daily affairs. [159]

The evidence is clear that atheism was rejected by the Founding Fathers and even the deism of that day was strongly frowned upon by most of them. For example:

> The idea of infidelity [a disbelief in the inspiration of the Scriptures or the divine origin of Christianity [160]] cannot be treated with too much resentment or too much horror. The man who can think of it with patience is a traitor in his heart and ought to be execrated [denounced] as one who adds the deepest hypocrisy to the blackest treason. [161] **JOHN ADAMS**

> I anticipate nothing but suffering to the human race while the present systems of paganism, deism, and atheism prevail in the world. [162] **BENJAMIN RUSH**, SIGNER OF THE DECLARATION

> The attempt by the rulers of a nation [France] to destroy all religious opinion and to pervert a whole people to atheism is a

phenomenon of profligacy [act of moral depravity]. . . . [T]o establish atheism on the ruins of Christianity [is] to deprive mankind of its best consolations and most animating hopes and to make a gloomy desert of the universe. [163] **ALEXANDER HAMILTON**

During my residence there [in France], I do not recollect to have had more than two conversations with atheists about their tenets. The first was this: I was at a large party, of which were several of that description. They spoke freely and contemptuously of religion. I took no part in the conversation. In the course of it, one of them asked me if I believed in Christ? I answered that I did, and that I thanked God that I did. . . . Some time afterward, one of my family being dangerously ill, I was advised to send for an English physician who had resided many years at Paris. . . . But, it was added, he is an atheist. . . . [D]uring one of his visits, [he] very abruptly remarked that there was no God and he hoped the time would come when there would be no religion in the world. I very concisely remarked that if there was no God there could be no moral obligations, and I did not see how society could subsist without them. . . . And he, probably perceiving that his sentiments met with a cold reception, did not afterwards resume the subject. [164] **JOHN JAY**, ORIGINAL CHIEF-JUSTICE OF THE U. S. SUPREME COURT

[T]he rising greatness of our country . . . is greatly tarnished by the general prevalence of deism which, with me, is but another name for vice and depravity. . . . I hear it is said by the deists that I am one of their number; and indeed that some good people think I am no Christian. This thought gives me much more pain than the appellation of Tory [being called a traitor], because I think religion of infinitely higher importance than politics. . . . [B]eing a Christian. . . is a character which I prize far above all this world has or can boast. [165] **PATRICK HENRY**

[I] have a thorough contempt for all men . . . who appear to be the irreclaimable enemies of religion. [166] **SAMUEL ADAMS**

[T]he most important of all lessons [from the Scriptures] is the denunciation of ruin to every State that rejects the precepts of religion. [167] **GOUVERNEUR MORRIS**, PENMAN AND SIGNER OF THE CONSTITUTION

> [S]hun, as a contagious pestilence, . . . those especially whom you perceive to be infected with the principles of infidelity or [who are] enemies to the power of religion. [168] Whoever is an avowed enemy of God, I scruple not to call him an enemy to his country. [169]
> **JOHN WITHERSPOON**, SIGNER OF THE DECLARATION

There is abundant evidence to refute any notion that the Founding Fathers were atheists, agnostics, or deists, or that they wanted to divorce religious principles from public affairs. The more one learns about their activities and writings, the easier it is not only to understand but also to agree with the characterization given by many of them concerning the Christian nature of the American nation and its government.

In fact, following the death of Richard Henry Lee (President of the Continental Congress and the man who officially introduced in Congress the call for America's independence [170]), his papers and correspondence, including numerous original handwritten letters from other patriots (e.g. George Washington, Benjamin Rush, John Dickinson, etc.), were passed on to his grandson who compiled those documents into a two-volume work published in 1825. After having studied those personal letters, the grandson described the great body of men who founded the nation in these words:

> The wise and great men of those days were not ashamed publicly to confess the name of our blessed Lord and Savior Jesus Christ! In behalf of the people, as their representatives and rulers, they acknowledged the sublime doctrine of his mediation! [171]

Despite the abundance of evidence on the highly religious nature of the Founding Fathers, many groups have ignored the clear historical records. Instead, they have promoted their own view of the alleged anti- or non-religious beliefs of our Founders in attempts to bolster their arguments for the current separation doctrine. The result is that the nation's policies concerning religion and government have been turned upside-down. In fact, not only does much of the nation not realize that the current "separation of church and state" is *not* constitutionally mandated, many are not even aware that "the free exercise" of religion *is*. (A recent study showed that "only a third [of the nation's citizens] knew freedom of religion was guaranteed by the Constitution's First Amendment." [172]) How did this reversal happen?

~7~
Safeguarding Original Intent

The Founders understood the multiple benefits of religion. They therefore aggressively promoted religion throughout American society. The departure from that practice was facilitated by the laxness of the citizenry in understanding, and of the Court in upholding the Constitution's original intent. When the intent undergirding a law is abandoned, then that law can be applied in a manner that is totally contrary to its intended purpose; the result can be devastating.

The controversy which resulted in the *Holy Trinity* case (1892) provided an excellent illustration of the abuse which can occur if a law's intent is ignored. Recall that a zealous U. S. Attorney had prosecuted a New York church for employing an English clergyman as its pastor under a law that Congress had enacted solely to halt the importation of slave-type foreign labor to construct western railroads.

When the Court concluded that to prosecute the church under that law would constitute an abuse and a misuse of the law, it explained:

> It is a familiar rule that a thing may be within the letter of the statute and yet not within the statute, because not within its spirit, nor within the intention of its makers. . . . [F]requently words of general meaning are used in a statute, words broad enough to include an act in question, and yet a consideration of the whole legislation, or of the circumstances surrounding its enactment, or of the absurd results which follow from giving such broad meaning to the words, makes it unreasonable to believe that the legislator intended to include the particular act. [1]

This is only common sense, for legislators are unable to foresee every circumstance that might arise under the enforcement of a law they enact. Furthermore, they vividly recall the extensive discussions in which their legislation was framed and often believe that the law communicates more clearly than it actually does. Yet those called upon to enforce that law years later do not always see the intent which the legislators felt was so obvious.

For this reason, it was an elementary principle of law, and thus a fundamental responsibility of the courts, to establish the spirit of a law before ruling on any issue. Signer of the Constitution John Dickinson had explained the importance of this principle:

> [N]othing is more certain than that the forms of liberty may be retained when the substance is gone. In government, as well as in religion, "the letter killeth, but the spirit giveth life." 2 Cor. 3:6 [2]

Courts, understanding this principle, long strove to establish the spirit (intent) of a law before issuing a ruling on any controversy touching that particular law. To illustrate the absurdities, and even atrocities, which could result if a law's intent were disregarded, the *Holy Trinity* Court cited numerous cases, including the following two.

The State v. *Smith Clark,* 1860
Supreme Court of New Jersey

The "offense" was described in the case:

> [T]he defendant [Smith Clark] did maliciously and willfully . . . break down . . . twenty panels of rail fence belonging to and in the possession of George Arnwine. The. . . . [law] provides that if any person or persons shall willfully . . . break down . . . or destroy any fences . . . belonging to . . . any other person . . . [they] shall be deemed guilty of a misdemeanor. [3]

Smith Clark had confessed to intentionally destroying George Arnwine's fence; therefore, under this law, he should be found guilty and sentenced. However, there was more:

> The defendant offered to show, by way of defence, that at the several times when he broke down the fence, he had title to the land upon which it was built, and . . . that the fence which was destroyed was erected . . . upon [his] land. [4]

The fence that Clark broke down was wrongly built by Arnwine on Clark's property. Despite its wording, the law clearly had **not** been designed to prosecute Clark for tearing down someone else's fence built on his property; Arnwine was the real abuser of the law. The court thus correctly concluded:

> The language of the act, if construed literally, evidently leads to an absurd result. If a literal construction of the words of a statute be absurd, the act must be so construed as to avoid the absurdity. [5]

The legislature felt the intent of the law was obvious; it could never have foreseen such an attempt to misapply its law by a zealous prosecutor. Had the court applied the law solely by its wording and not according to its intent, it would have created an injustice while supposedly administering "justice."

United States v. *Kirby*, 1868
United States Supreme Court

This "offense" was also described in the case:

> [T]he act of Congress . . . provides "that if any person shall knowingly and wilfully obstruct or retard the passage of the mail, or of any driver or carrier . . . he shall, upon conviction, for every such offence, pay a fine not exceeding one hundred dollars. . . . " The indictment contained four counts, and charged the defendants with knowingly and wilfully obstructing . . . the passage of one Farris, a carrier of the mail, while engaged in the performance of his duty. [6]

Congress clearly intended that "the mail must go through!" Since Kirby and the three with him had confessed to interfering with the mail-carrier, they should be punished; however, there was more. It turned out that:

> [T]wo indictments were found by the grand jury of the county against the said Farris [the mail-carrier] for murder . . . and placed in the hands of Kirby [the sheriff] . . . commanding him to arrest the said Farris and bring him before the court to answer the indictments; that in obedience to these warrants [Kirby] arrested Farris, and was accompanied by other defendants as a posse, who were lawfully summoned to assist him in effecting the arrest. [7]

By arresting Farris, the mail-carrier, Sheriff Kirby and his posse had indeed interfered with the delivery of the mail. But was the law intended to keep a Sheriff from arresting a mail-carrier charged with murder? The Court recognized that although his actions violated the letter of the law, they did not violate its intent. The Court thus noted:

> All laws should receive a sensible construction. General terms should be so limited in their application as not to lead to injustice, oppression, or an absurd consequence. . . . The reason of the law in such cases should prevail over its letter. [8]

That same Court provided some additional examples to buttress its point:

> The common sense of man approves the judgment mentioned by Puffendorf [a Christian philosopher quoted by numerous Founders] that the . . . law which enacted "that whoever drew blood in the streets should be punished with the utmost severity" did not extend to the surgeon who opened the vein of a person that fell down in the street in a fit. The same common sense accepts the ruling . . . which enacts that a prisoner who breaks prison shall be guilty of felony, does not extend to a prisoner who breaks out when the prison is on fire—"for he is not to be hanged because he would not stay to be burnt." And we think that a like common sense will sanction the ruling we make, that the act of Congress which punishes the obstruction or retarding of the passage of the mail, or of its carrier, does not apply to a case of temporary detention of the mail caused by the arrest of the carrier upon an indictment for murder. [9]

The *Holy Trinity* Court cited thirteen similar cases and then concluded by declaring emphatically that the spirit of a law should **always** prevail over its letter:

> [T]he legislature used general terms . . . and thereafter, unexpectedly, it is developed that the general language thus employed is broad enough to reach cases and acts which the whole history and life of the country affirm could not have been intentionally legislated against. It is the duty of the courts, under those circumstances, to say that, however broad the language of the statute may be, the act, although within the letter, is not within the intention of the legislature, and therefore cannot be within the statute. [10]

Previous courts had long applied this principle to cases on the First Amendment, consistently finding that the Founders' sole intent was to prevent the federal establishment of a single denomination of Christianity. However, the nation now finds itself under the "absurd results" stemming from the Courts' ignoring the Founders' massive documentation concerning the purpose of the First Amendment. Our Founders never envisioned that the First Amendment would become a weapon to excise Christian or traditional religious expressions from the public arena.

~8~
Rewriting Original Intent

Eight of the Supreme Court's contemporary landmark religious liberty cases will be reviewed in this chapter; each will demonstrate that the absurd results feared by previous Courts have now become commonplace.

As the Court's rulings in these eight cases are reviewed, rebuttals to the Court's rulings will also be presented. These rebuttals will be taken from two sources: (1) the statements and declarations of the Founding Fathers, and (2) the dissents of other Justices, thus presenting the other side of the Court's decision. According to the following proverb, such an examination is vital to determining truth:

> He who states his case first seems right until his rival comes and cross-examines him. **PROVERBS 18:17** (AMPLIFIED BIBLE)

> Any story sounds true until someone tells the other side and sets the record straight. **PROVERBS 18:17** (LIVING BIBLE)

Through the "cross-examination" provided both by the dissents and by the Founders' declarations, it will quickly become evident how extensively contemporary Courts not only have abandoned but also have contradicted the original intent of the First Amendment.

McCollum v. *Board of Education,* 1948

This case, decided the year following the *Everson* decision which introduced the separation phrase, was typical of an issue frequently raised in subsequent cases: can *voluntary* religious activities be unconstitutional?

The controversy in this case was over *elective* classes offered in Illinois schools. The Court delineated the facts:

> [I]nterested members of the Jewish, Roman Catholic, and a few of the Protestant faiths formed a voluntary association called the Champaign Council on Religious Education. They obtained permission from the Board of Education to offer classes in religious instruction to public school pupils in grades four to nine inclusive. Classes were made up of pupils whose parents signed printed cards requesting that their children be permitted to attend; they were held weekly, thirty minutes for the lower grades, forty-five minutes

for the higher. The council employed the religious teachers at no expense to the school authorities, but the instructors were subject to the approval and supervision of the superintendent of schools. The classes were taught in three separate religious groups by Protestant teachers, Catholic priests, and a Jewish rabbi. [1]

Not only were the classes voluntary, students could attend *only* with parents' written permission; yet the Court found these classes unacceptable. It reiterated its position taken the previous year:

[A]s we said in the *Everson* case, the First Amendment has erected a wall between Church and State which must be kept high and impregnable. [2]

Justice Felix Frankfurter further expounded on this position:

Separation means separation, not something less. . . . It is the Court's duty to enforce this principle in its full integrity. . . . Illinois has here authorized the commingling of sectarian with secular instruction in the public schools. The Constitution of the United States forbids this. [3]

The Court's assertion that it was wrong for Illinois to "commingle sectarian with secular instruction" seems ironic when one recalls that on August 7, 1789, George Washington signed the Northwest Ordinance [4] which encouraged schools in the territory that would become Illinois to teach "religion, morality, and knowledge." [5]

Furthermore, when Thomas Jefferson authored his plan of education in Virginia, he considered religious study an inseparable component in the study of law and political science. As he explained:

[I]n my catalogue, considering ethics, as well as religion, as supplements to law in the government of man, I had placed them in that sequence. [6]

Notice statements from additional Founders and early statesmen which further contradict the assertion made by the *McCollum* Court against commingling religious and secular instruction in public schools:

You have . . . received a public education, the purpose whereof hath been to qualify you the better to serve your Creator and your country. . . . Your first great duties, you are sensible, are those you owe to Heaven, to your Creator and Redeemer. Let these be ever present to your minds, and exemplified in your lives and conduct. [7] **WILLIAM SAMUEL JOHNSON**, SIGNER OF THE CONSTITUTION

As piety, religion and morality have a happy influence on the minds of men, in their public as well as private transactions, you will not think it unseasonable, although I have frequently done it, to bring to your remembrance the great importance of encouraging our University, town schools, and other seminaries of education, that our children and youth while they are engaged in the pursuit of useful science, may have their minds impressed with a strong sense of the duties they owe to their God. [8] If we continue to be a happy people, that happiness must be assured by the enacting and executing of the reasonable and wise laws expressed in the plainest language and by establishing such modes of education as tend to inculcate in the minds of youth the feelings and habits of "piety, religion and morality." [9] [E]ducation. . . . leads the youth beyond mere outside show [and] will impress their minds with a profound reverence of the Deity. . . . It will excite in them a just regard to Divine revelation. [10] **SAMUEL ADAMS**

[R]eason and experience both forbid us to expect that national morality can prevail in exclusion of religious principle. . . . Promote, then, as an object of primary importance, institutions for the general diffusion of knowledge. [11] **GEORGE WASHINGTON**

Religion is the only solid basis of good morals; therefore education should teach the precepts of religion and the duties of man towards God. [12] **GOUVERNEUR MORRIS**, PENMAN AND SIGNER OF THE CONSTITUTION

[T]he only foundation for a useful education in a republic is to be laid in religion. Without this there can be no virtue, and without virtue there can be no liberty, and liberty is the object and life of all republican governments. [13] Without religion, I believe that learning does real mischief to the morals and principles of mankind. [14] **BENJAMIN RUSH**, SIGNER OF THE DECLARATION

In my view, the Christian religion is the most important and one of the first things in which all children, under a free government, ought to be instructed. . . . No truth is more evident to my mind than that the Christian religion must be the basis of any government intended to secure the rights and privileges of a free people. [15] **NOAH WEBSTER**

The attainment of knowledge does not comprise all which is contained in the larger term of education. . . . [A] profound religious feeling is to be instilled and pure morality inculcated under all circumstances. All this is comprised in education. [16] **DANIEL WEBSTER**

Why may not the Bible, and especially the New Testament, without note or comment, be read and taught as Divine revelation in the college [school]—its general precepts expounded, its evidences explained and its glorious principles of morality inculcated? . . . Where can the purest principles of morality be learned so clearly or so perfectly as from the New Testament? [17] **JOSEPH STORY,** U. S. SUPREME COURT, FATHER OF AMERICAN JURISPRUDENCE

I cannot omit this occasion of inviting your attention to the means of instruction for the rising generation. To enable them to perceive and duly to estimate their rights; to inculcate correct principles and habits of morality and religion, and thus to render them useful citizens, a competent provision for their education is all essential. [18] **DANIEL TOMPKINS,** GOVERNOR OF NEW YORK; VICE-PRESIDENT OF THE U. S.

Just these few examples illustrate that our Founders *intended* to "commingle sectarian and secular instruction in the public schools."

When the Court struck down the elective classes and ruled in favor of Mrs. Vashti McCollum who had initiated action against the classes, Justice Jackson argued in his concurring opinion that the Court had awarded her too much and gone too far. He explained:

The plaintiff, as she has every right to be, is an avowed atheist. What she has asked of the courts is that they not only end the "released time" plan but also ban every form of teaching which suggests or recognizes that there is a God. She would ban all teaching of the Scriptures. She especially mentions as an example of invasion of her rights "having pupils [in the *voluntarily* attended, *elective* classes] learn and recite such statements as, 'The Lord is my Shepherd, I shall not want.'" And she objects to teaching that the King James version of the Bible "is called the Christian's Guide Book, the Holy Writ and the Word of God," and many other similar matters. This Court is directing the Illinois courts generally to sustain plaintiff's complaint without exception of any of these grounds of complaint. [19]

Despite the fact that students attended the elective classes only with signed parental permission, and that the instructors were non-school personnel paid through private funds, the Court ruled in favor of a single atheist *not* involved in the classes but who was *personally* offended by religion and therefore did not want *any* students taught religious principles.

This decision foreshadowed what was soon to become routine: a single individual, unable to advance his or her goals through legitimate political and legislative means, convincing a willing Court to violate the rights of the overwhelming majority of its citizens in order to accommodate the wishes of that individual.

One further note from this decision: a concurring Justice observed that, through this ruling, the Court was now assuming "the role of a super board of education for every school district in the nation" [20]—an ominous prediction of what has now become the norm.

Engel v. *Vitale*, 1962

For fourteen years following the *McCollum* case, the Court not only ceased to strike down voluntary religious activities for students, it actually upheld them, retreating significantly from its inflexible concept of "separation" introduced in 1947 in *Everson* (see *Zorach* v. *Clauson*, 1952 [21]). However, in the *Engel* case, the Court reverted to its *Everson* position; it attacked the long-standing tradition of school prayer and struck down this simple 22-word prayer from New York schools:

> Almighty God, we acknowledge our dependence upon Thee, and we beg Thy blessings upon us, our parents, our teachers and our Country. [22]

Contemporary reviewers often claim that the "real" issue in this prayer case was coercion since it involved a state-approved prayer. Yet this is a misportrayal; there was *no* coercion; even the Court conceded that . . .

> . . . the schools did not compel *any* pupil to join in the prayer over his or her parents' objection. [23] (emphasis added)

New York had taken great pains to provide that participation in these prayers be completely voluntary. Furthermore, in an attempt to be as inoffensive as possible, the prayer's wording was simply a nonsectarian acknowledgment of God. In fact, that acknowledgment was so bland that a later court described it "as a 'to-whom-it-may-concern' prayer." [24]

Since the prayer was both voluntary and nondenominational, it should have been upheld; yet the Court explained why it must be struck down:

> Neither the fact that the prayer may be denominationally neutral nor the fact that its observance on the part of the students is voluntary can serve to free it from the limitations of the Establishment Clause, as it might from the Free Exercise Clause, of the First Amendment. . . . [It] ignores the essential nature of the program's constitutional defects. . . . [P]rayer in its public school system breaches the constitutional wall of separation between Church and State. [25]

The real issue in this case was not the state-mandated coercion argument so often recited by today's reviewers; rather, as the Court acknowledged, it was simply the *presence* of "prayer in the public school system."

Additional proof that this ruling was a direct attack on all types of prayers is found in the manner in which the *Engel* case has been invoked by subsequent courts. If the impact of this ruling had been only to stop state-approved, allegedly state-mandated, coercive prayers, then this case would have been cited in no subsequent ruling since there have been no further cases involving such circumstances. Yet a perusal of court rulings over recent decades reveals that *Engel* has been cited in virtually *every* prayer case, [26] regardless of its dissimilarity to the New York case. Very simply, the *Engel* decision was an attack on *any* type of prayers in school.

In striking down this prayer, the Court explained that:

> [A] union of government and religion tends to destroy government and to degrade religion. [27]

While this might have been the Court's belief, it certainly was not representative of the beliefs of those who established this nation. Notice:

> [T]rue religion affords to government its surest support. [28] **GEORGE WASHINGTON**

> [R]eligion and virtue are the only foundations . . . of republicanism and of all free governments. [29] **JOHN ADAMS**

[G]overnment . . . is a firm compact sanctified from violation by all the ties of personal honor, morality, and religion. [30] **FISHER AMES,** AUTHOR OF THE HOUSE LANGUAGE OF THE FIRST AMENDMENT

[T]he happiness of a people and the good order and preservation of civil government essentially depend upon piety, religion, and morality. [31] **JAMES BOWDOIN,** GOVERNOR OF MASSACHUSETTS

Religion and morality . . . [are] necessary to good government, good order, and good laws. [32] **WILLIAM PATERSON,** SIGNER OF THE CONSTITUTION; U. S. SUPREME COURT JUSTICE

[The] liberty to worship our Creator in the way we think most agreeable to His will [is] a liberty deemed in other countries incompatible with good government and yet proved by our experience to be its best support. [33] **THOMAS JEFFERSON**

[T]he moral principles and precepts contained in the Scriptures ought to form the basis of all our civil constitutions and laws. [34] **NOAH WEBSTER**

The sanctions of religion compose the foundations of good government. [35] **DEWITT CLINTON,** INTRODUCED THE TWELFTH AMENDMENT; GOVERNOR OF NEW YORK; U. S. SENATOR

I do not believe that the Constitution was the offspring of inspiration, but I am as perfectly satisfied that the Union of the States in its form and adoption is as much the work of a Divine Providence as any of the miracles recorded in the Old and New Testament. [36] **BENJAMIN RUSH,** SIGNER OF THE DECLARATION

God grant that in America true religion and civil liberty may be inseparable and that the unjust attempts to destroy the one may in the issue, tend to the support and establishment of both. [37] **JOHN WITHERSPOON,** SIGNER OF THE DECLARATION

However, the Court was not particularly interested in the Founders' views on this subject; in fact, it openly acknowledged its contempt for America's heritage when it remarked:

[T]hat [New York] prayer seems relatively insignificant when compared to the governmental encroachments upon religion which were commonplace 200 years ago. [38]

The Court also claimed that to approve any specific wording made the prayer constitutionally infirm—an argument effectively dismantled by Justice Potter Stewart in his dissent:

> The Court today says that the State and federal governments are without constitutional power to prescribe any particular form of words to be recited by any group of the American people on any subject touching religion. One of the stanzas of "The Star-Spangled Banner," made our National Anthem by Act of Congress in 1931, contains these verses:
>
> > "Blest with victory and peace, may the heav'n rescued land
> > Praise the power that hath made and preserved us a nation!
> > Then conquer we must, when our cause it is just,
> > And this be our motto 'In God is our Trust.'"
>
> In 1954, Congress added a phrase to the Pledge of Allegiance to the Flag so that it now contains the words "one Nation under God, indivisible, with liberty and justice for all". . . . Since 1865 the words "In God We Trust" have been impressed on our coins. Countless similar examples could be listed, but there is no need to belabor the obvious. . . . I do not believe that this Court, or the Congress, or the President has by the actions and practices I have mentioned established an "official religion" in violation of the Constitution. And I do not believe the State of New York has done so in this case. What each has done has been to recognize and to follow the deeply entrenched and highly cherished spiritual traditions of our Nation—traditions which come down to us from those who almost two hundred years ago avowed their "firm reliance on the Protection of divine Providence." [39]

Aside from the fact that the Court had affronted the traditional interpretation of the First Amendment by striking down a voluntary prayer, in a comment the following year, the Court itself noted another irregularity of its decision:

> Finally, in *Engel* v. *Vitale*, only last year, these principles were so universally recognized that the Court, ***without the citation of a single case*** . . . reaffirmed them. [40] (emphasis added)

The Court had failed to cite even a single precedent to justify its prohibition of New York's voluntary prayers—a significant departure from a bedrock rule of jurisprudence. Why did it fail to cite precedent cases? There were none which would support its decision. For 170 years following the ratification of the Constitution and Bill of Rights, no Court had ever struck down any prayer, in any form, in any location.

While the Court invoked no judicial precedent to sustain its decision, it did employ some strategic psychological rhetoric. Recall the Court's comment that:

> ... these principles were so ***universally recognized*** ... [41] (emphasis added)

Lacking precedent, the Court simply alleged a widespread public support; that is, since "everybody" knew school prayer was wrong, the Court needed cite no precedent. However, the so-called "universally recognized" principles were actually foreign to most, and many observers commented on the Court's new direction. For example, the *World Book Encyclopedia 1963 Yearbook* observed:

> The significance of the [1962] decision regarding this [school] prayer was enormous, for the whole thorny problem of religion in public education ***was thus inevitably raised.*** [42] (emphasis added)

According to this source, prior to the *Engel* case, the issue of separating prayer from education had not been "raised." Legal authorities also noted:

> The Court has broken ***new ground*** in a number of fields. . . . Few Supreme Court decisions of recent years have created greater furor than *Engel* v. *Vitale.* [43] (emphasis added)

Actually, so few agreed with the Court's claims of "universally recognized" principles that the U. S. Congress even convened extensive hearings to deal with the widespread public outrage. [44] Nonetheless, in an attempt to purvey credibility, the Court invoked James Madison's statement that:

> [A]ttempts to enforce . . . acts obnoxious to so great a proportion of citizens tend to enervate [weaken] the laws in general and to slacken the bands of society. [45]

The Court equated school prayer to "acts obnoxious to so great a proportion of citizens." This, too, was a patent misrepresentation, evidenced by the fact that so many States *permitted* school prayers. [46] In fact, the next year the Court weakened its own assertion when it acknowledged that:

> [O]nly last year [1962] an official survey of the country indicated that . . . less than 3% profess no religion whatever. [47]

With such a strong religious adherence in this country, there simply was no factual basis for the Court's assertion that the generic acknowledgment of God embodied in the *Engel* prayer was something obnoxious to the mass of citizens.

In concluding its decision, the *Engel* Court claimed that to allow this voluntary prayer was to establish an "official state religion"—a conclusion strongly objected to by Justice Stewart:

> With all respect, I think the Court has misapplied a great constitutional principle. I cannot see how an "official religion" is established by letting those who want to say a prayer say it. On the contrary, I think that to deny the wish of these school children to join in reciting this prayer is to deny them the opportunity of sharing in the spiritual heritage of our Nation. . . . For we deal here not with the establishment of a state church, which would, of course, be constitutionally impermissible, but with whether school children who want to begin their day by joining in prayer must be prohibited from doing so. [48]

The *Engel* decision—the second occasion in which the Supreme Court had struck down a voluntary student religious activity—was based on a series of poorly grounded arguments punctuated by many erroneous and ill-advised statements. However, perhaps the most serious and longlasting effect of that case was the Court's transformation of the First Amendment prohibition against the establishment of a national church into the prohibition of a voluntary religious activity by students.

School District of Abington Township v. Schempp, 1963

This case involved yet another voluntary activity by students: the use of the Scriptures. At issue was a Pennsylvania policy which stated:

> Each school . . . shall be opened by the reading, without comment, of a chapter in the Holy Bible. . . . Participation in the opening exercises . . . is voluntary. The student reading the verses from the Bible may select the passages and read from any version he chooses. [49]

The Court explained:

> There are no prefatory statements, no questions asked or solicited, no comments or explanations made and no interpretations given at or during the exercises. The students and parents are advised that the student may absent himself from the classroom or, should he elect to remain, not participate in the exercises. [50]

Like the New York prayer, this seemed to be a relatively innocuous activity. It was voluntary; it was student-led; no additional instruction or comments were permitted. Yet today's civil libertarians portray this as a coercion case—so much so, they claim, that Edward Schempp thought himself forced to file suit to relieve his children from the coercion. However, the facts of the case disprove this assertion:

> Roger and Donna [two of the Schempp children] testified that they had *never* protested to their teachers or other persons of authority in the school system concerning the practices of which they now complain [in this lawsuit]. In fact, on occasion, Donna herself had volunteered to read the Bible. [51] (emphasis added)

Furthermore, so non-coercive was the policy that while other children were reading the Bible, one of the Schempp children had been permitted to read the Koran. [52] The facts in the case clearly establish that there was no coercion. (However, when this case finally reached the Supreme Court, these facts, presented in the District Court, were ignored.)

Another argument raised then (and still raised today) is that the school setting is no place for religious activities; if such activities are to occur, it should be at home—or in a private school. Justice Stewart, in his dissent, pointed out the constitutional fallacy of such arguments:

> It might be argued here that parents who wanted their children to be exposed to religious influences in school could . . . send their children to private or parochial schools. But the consideration which renders this contention too facile [simplistic] to be determinative [a factor] has already been recognized by the Court: "Freedom of speech, freedom of the press, freedom of religion are available to all, not merely to those who can pay their own way." *Murdock* v. *Pennsylvania*, 319 U. S. 105, 111. It might also be argued that parents who want their children exposed to religious influences

can adequately fulfill that wish off school property and outside school time. With all its surface persuasiveness, however, this argument seriously misconceives the basic constitutional justification for permitting the exercises at issue in these cases. For a compulsory state educational system so structures a child's life that if religious exercises are held to an impermissible activity in schools, religion is placed at an artificial and state-created disadvantage. Viewed in this light, permission of such exercises for those who want them is necessary if the schools are truly to be neutral in the matter of religion. And a refusal to permit religious exercises thus is seen, not as the realization of state neutrality, but rather as the establishment of a religion of secularism. [53]

Furthermore, the Founders' opinion of the Bible, and of its use in schools, was clear:

The great enemy of the salvation of man, in my opinion, never invented a more effectual means of extirpating [extinguishing] Christianity from the world than by persuading mankind that it was improper to read the Bible at schools. [54] [T]he Bible, when not read in schools, is seldom read in any subsequent period of life. . . . [It] should be read in our schools in preference to all other books from its containing the greatest portion of that kind of knowledge which is calculated to produce private and public temporal happiness. [55] **BENJAMIN RUSH,** SIGNER OF THE DECLARATION

[Why] should not the Bible regain the place it once held as a school book? Its morals are pure, its examples captivating and noble. The reverence for the Sacred Book that is thus early impressed lasts long; and probably if not impressed in infancy, never takes firm hold of the mind. [56] **FISHER AMES,** AUTHOR OF THE HOUSE LANGUAGE FOR THE FIRST AMENDMENT

Suppose a nation in some distant region should take the Bible for their only law book and every member should regulate his conduct by the precepts there exhibited. . . . What a Eutopia, what a Paradise would this region be. [57] I have examined all [religions] . . . and the result is that the Bible is the best Book in the world. It contains more of my little philosophy than all the libraries I have seen. [58] **JOHN ADAMS**

[T]he Bible. . . . [is] a book containing the history of all men and of all nations and . . . [is] a necessary part of a polite education. [59] **HENRY LAURENS**, PRESIDENT OF CONTINENTAL CONGRESS; U. S. DIPLOMAT; SELECTED AS DELEGATE TO THE CONSTITUTIONAL CONVENTION

The Bible itself [is] the common inheritance, not merely of Christendom, but of the world. [60] **JOSEPH STORY**, U. S. SUPREME COURT JUSTICE; FATHER OF AMERICAN JURISPRUDENCE

To a man of liberal education, the study of history is not only useful, and important, but altogether indispensable, and with regard to the history contained in the Bible . . . "it is not so much praiseworthy to be acquainted with as it is shameful to be ignorant of it." [61] **JOHN QUINCY ADAMS**

The reflection and experience of many years have led me to consider the holy writings not only as the most authentic and instructive in themselves, but as the clue to all other history. They tell us what man is, and they alone tell us why he is what he is: a contradictory creature that seeing and approving of what is good, pursues and performs what is evil. All of private and of public life is there displayed. . . . From the same pure fountain of wisdom we learn that vice destroys freedom; that arbitrary power is founded on public immorality. [62] **GOUVERNEUR MORRIS,** PENMAN AND SIGNER OF THE CONSTITUTION

[The Bible] is a book worth more than all the other books that were ever printed. [63] **PATRICK HENRY**

[T]o the free and universal reading of the Bible in that age, men were much indebted for right views of civil liberty. The Bible is . . . a book which teaches man his own individual responsibility, his own dignity, and his equality with his fellow man. [64] **DANIEL WEBSTER**

The Bible is the best of all books, for it is the word of God and teaches us the way to be happy in this world and in the next. Continue therefore to read it and to regulate your life by its precepts. [65] **JOHN JAY**, ORIGINAL CHIEF-JUSTICE OF THE U. S. SUPREME COURT

The Bible is the chief moral cause of all that is good and the best corrector of all that is evil in human society; the best book for regulating the temporal [secular] concerns of men. [66] **NOAH WEBSTER**

Bibles are strong entrenchments. Where they abound, men cannot pursue wicked courses. [67] **JAMES MCHENRY,** SIGNER OF THE CONSTITUTION

Not only did the Court disregard these stated beliefs of the Founders, it falsely asserted:

The [First] Amendment's *purpose* was not to strike merely at the official establishment of a single sect. . . . It was to create a complete and permanent separation of the spheres of religious activity and civil authority. [68] (emphasis added)

This absurd claim completely reverses the Founders' intent; their purpose for the First Amendment *was* to "strike at the official establishment of a single sect" and definitely was *not* to completely and permanently separate the religious and civil spheres. Notice (emphasis added in each quote):

Of all the dispositions and habits which lead to *political* prosperity, religion and morality are indispensable supports. [69] **GEORGE WASHINGTON**

The great pillars of all *government* and of social life . . . [are] virtue, morality, and religion. This is the armor, my friend, and this alone, that renders us invincible. [70] **PATRICK HENRY**

One of the beautiful boasts of our *municipal jurisprudence* is that Christianity is a part of the Common Law. . . . There never has been a period in which the Common Law did not recognize Christianity as lying at its foundations. . . . I verily believe Christianity necessary to the support of *civil* society. [71] **JOSEPH STORY,** U. S. SUPREME COURT JUSTICE; FATHER OF AMERICAN JURISPRUDENCE

We have been assured, Sir, in the Sacred Writings that except the Lord build the house, they labor in vain that build it. I firmly believe this; and I also believe that without His concurring aid, we shall succeed in this *political* building no better than the builders of Babel. [72] **BENJAMIN FRANKLIN**

[T]he Declaration of Independence first organized the social compact on the foundation of the Redeemer's mission upon earth.

. . . [and] laid the cornerstone of human *government* upon the first precepts of Christianity. [73] **JOHN QUINCY ADAMS**

[T]he Christian religion—its general principles—must ever be regarded among us as the foundation of *civil* society. [74] **DANIEL WEBSTER**

True religion always enlarges the heart and strengthens the *social* tie. [75] **JOHN WITHERSPOON**

Before any man can be considered as a member of *civil society*, he must be considered as a subject of the Governor of the Universe. [76] **JAMES MADISON**

The study and *practice of law* . . . does not dissolve the obligations of morality or of religion. [77] **JOHN ADAMS**

I have always considered Christianity as the strong ground of republicanism. . . . It is only necessary for republicanism to ally itself to the Christian religion to overturn all the corrupted *political* and religious institutions in the world. [78] **BENJAMIN RUSH**, SIGNER OF THE DECLARATION

[T]he religion which has introduced *civil* liberty is the religion of Christ and his apostles. . . . and to this we owe our free constitutions of government. [79] **NOAH WEBSTER**

[N]ational prosperity can neither be attained nor preserved without the favor of Providence. [80] **JOHN JAY**, ORIGINAL CHIEF JUSTICE OF THE U. S. SUPREME COURT

As guardians of the prosperity, liberty, and morals of the *State*, we are therefore bound by every injunction of patriotism and wisdom . . . to patronize public improvements and to cherish all institutions for the diffusion of religious knowledge and for the promotion of virtue and piety. [81] **DANIEL TOMPKINS**, GOVERNOR OF NEW YORK; VICE-PRESIDENT OF THE UNITED STATES

Nowhere can it be demonstrated that the Founders desired to secularize official society and "create a complete separation of the spheres of religious activity and civil authority." The *Abington* decision represented a further step in the devolution of the First Amendment by rewriting the intent of those who created the Constitution and Bill of Rights.

Walz v. *Tax Commission of the City of New York*, **1970**

Rather than any direct issue of religious expression, this case addressed the constitutionality of tax exemptions for churches. Ironically, the Court began by congratulating itself:

> [W]e have been able to chart a course that preserved the autonomy and freedom of religious bodies while avoiding any semblance of established religion. This is a "tight rope" and one we have successfully traversed. [82]

Justice Brennan continued that praise:

> [T]he line we must draw between the permissible and the impermissible is one which accords with history and faithfully reflects the understanding of the Founding Fathers. [83]

However, not only were these self-commendations self-serving, as already demonstrated, they also were false.

Yet, this case introduced a further step in the continuing rewriting of the First Amendment when Justice William Douglas claimed that its *purpose* was to enhance nonreligion and to promote pluralism:

> [O]ne of the mandates of the First Amendment is to promote a viable, pluralistic society [one which acknowledges no religion or system of belief above any other] and to keep government neutral, not only between sects, but also between believers and nonbelievers. [84]

It is unquestionably true that our Founders did respect many major religions. For example, while describing a federal parade in Philadelphia, Benjamin Rush commented:

> The rabbi of the Jews locked in the arms of two ministers of the Gospel was a most delightful sight. There could not have been a more happy emblem. [85]

George Washington's letter to the Hebrew congregation of Savannah showed a similar warmth:

> May the same wonderworking Deity, who long since delivered the Hebrews from their Egyptian oppressors and planted them in the promised land, whose Providential agency has lately been conspicuous

in establishing these United States as an independent nation, still continue to water them with the dews of Heaven and to make the inhabitants of every denomination participate in the temporal and spiritual blessings of that people whose God is Jehovah. [86]

Of the Hebrews, John Adams had declared:

I will insist that the Hebrews have done more to civilize men than any other nation. . . . [They] preserve and propagate to all mankind the doctrine of a supreme, intelligent, wise, almighty Sovereign of the Universe, which I believe to be the great essential principle of all morality, and consequently of all civilization. [87]

John Witherspoon, too, complemented the Jews:

To the Jews were first committed the care of the sacred Writings. . . . [Y]et was the providence of God particular manifest in their preservation and purity. The Jews were so faithful in their important trust. [88]

Elias Boudinot, President of Congress, was so fond of the "Hebrews" that he served as president of the "Society for Ameliorating the State of the Jews" and made personal provision to bring persecuted Jews to America where they could have an "asylum of safety" and have the opportunity, if they so chose, to inquire into Christianity "without fear or terror." [89]

However, the Founders' respect for other religions should not be confused or misinterpreted as a promotion of pluralism—evidenced by this statement from Benjamin Rush:

Such is my veneration for every religion that reveals the attributes of the Deity, or a future state of rewards and punishments, that I had rather see the opinions of Confucius or Mohamed inculcated upon our youth, than see them grow up wholly devoid of a system of religious principles. But the religion I mean to recommend in this place is that of the New Testament. [90]

Similarly, consider Justice Story's statement in his *Commentaries on the Constitution:*

The real object of the [First A]mendment was not to countenance, much less to advance Mahometanism, or Judaism, or infidelity by prostrating Christianity; but to exclude all rivalry among Christian sects and to prevent any national ecclesiastical establishment which should give to a hierarchy [a denominational council] the exclusive patronage of the national government. [91]

Representative quotes of many Founders demonstrate their preference for Christianity and provide no evidence of any alleged "mandate to promote a visible, pluralistic society." Notice:

You do well to wish to learn our arts and ways of life, and above all, the religion of Jesus Christ. . . . Congress will do everything they can to assist you in this wise intention. [92] **GEORGE WASHINGTON**

Let . . . statesmen and patriots unite their endeavors to renovate the age by . . . educating their little boys and girls . . . [and] leading them in the study and practice of the exalted virtues of the Christian system. [93] **SAMUEL ADAMS**

[W]ithout morals a republic cannot subsist any length of time; they therefore who are decrying the Christian religion, whose morality is so sublime and pure. . . are undermining the solid foundation of morals, the best security for the duration of free governments. [94] **CHARLES CARROLL**, SIGNER OF THE DECLARATION

However gradual may be the growth of Christian knowledge and moral reformation, yet unless it be begun, unless the seeds are planted, there can be no tree of knowledge and, of course, no fruit. The attempt to Christianize the heathen world and to produce peace on earth and goodwill towards men is humane, Christian, and sublime. [95] **WILLIAM ELLERY**, SIGNER OF THE DECLARATION

History will also afford frequent opportunities of showing the necessity of a public religion . . . and the excellency of the Christian religion above all others, ancient or modern. [96] **BENJAMIN FRANKLIN**

[O]nly one adequate plan has ever appeared in the world, and that is the Christian dispensation. [97] **JOHN JAY**, ORIGINAL CHIEF-JUSTICE U. S. SUPREME COURT

[T]he Christian religion is superior to every other. . . . But there is not only an excellence in the Christian morals, but a manifest superiority in them to those which are derived from any other source. [98] **JOHN WITHERSPOON,** SIGNER OF THE DECLARATION

[T]he Christian religion, in its purity, is the basis, or rather the source of all genuine freedom in government. . . . and I am persuaded that no civil government of a republican form can exist and be durable in which the principles of that religion have not a controlling influence. [99] **NOAH WEBSTER**

From the day of the Declaration, the people of the North American Union and of its constituent states were associated bodies of civilized men and Christians. . . . They were bound by the laws of God, which they all, and by the laws of the Gospel, which they nearly all, acknowledged as the rules of their conduct. [100] The Declaration of Independence cast off all the shackles of this dependency. The United States of America were no longer Colonies. They were an independent nation of Christians. [101] **JOHN QUINCY ADAMS**

Let us enter on this important business under the idea that we are Christians on whom the eyes of the world are now turned. . . . [L]et us earnestly call and beseech him for Christ's sake to preside in our councils. [102] **ELIAS BOUDINOT,** PRESIDENT OF THE CONTINENTAL CONGRESS

[T]he ethics, doctrines, and examples furnished by Christianity exhibit the best models for the laws. [103] **DEWITT CLINTON,** INTRODUCED THE TWELFTH AMENDMENT; GOVERNOR OF NEW YORK; U. S. SENATOR

An early House Judiciary Committee affirmed the Founders' lack of pluralistic intent when it declared:

Christianity. . . . was the religion of the founders of the republic, and they expected it to remain the religion of their descendants. [104]

The Founders *did* respect other religions; however, they neither promoted pluralism nor intended that the First Amendment do so.

Although the Court's decision in this case was favorable in the sense that tax exemptions for churches were preserved, the ruling demonstrated a major inconsistency by the Court: it upheld tax exemptions because of their historical precedent. As the Court explained:

[I]n resolving such questions of interpretation "a page of history is worth a volume of logic." ... The more long-standing and widely accepted a practice, the greater its impact upon constitutional interpretation. [105]

However, Justice William Douglas, who had voted to remove tax exemptions from churches, pointed out in his dissent that the Court's reliance on history and precedent to arrive at its conclusion in this case was the very practice it had *avoided* in previous First Amendment cases. He noted, for example, that although school prayer had been as equally a long-standing historical tradition as tax exemptions, this had not prevented it from being declared unconstitutional. [106] The *Walz* case, despite its favorable ruling, had introduced yet another new and different purpose to the First Amendment by claiming its *intent* was to promote pluralism.

Stone v. *Graham*, 1980

The issue in this case was the passive use of a portion of the Bible: specifically, the display of the Ten Commandments on the walls of schools in Kentucky. The posters of the Commandments were like the other numerous pictures and posters which adorned the school walls: they were passive displays. Students would look at them only if they wanted to and read them only if they were individually willing to take the time.

The Ten Commandments had been posted in the schools because the Kentucky legislature believed it beneficial to expose students to the historical code which had formed the basis of civil laws in the western world for over two thousand years. Reflective of this, at the bottom of each poster was printed: "The secular application of the Ten Commandments is clearly seen in its adoption as the fundamental legal code of Western Civilization and the Common Law of the United States." [107]

Despite both the passive and non-coercive nature of the poster, a legal challenge was lodged. When the Supreme Court heard the Kentucky legislature's assertion that the Ten Commandments had secular importance, the Court erupted in a surprising outburst of religious prejudice:

> The preeminent purpose for posting the Ten Commandments on schoolroom walls is plainly religious in nature. The Ten Commandments are undeniably a sacred text in the Jewish and Christian faiths, and no legislative recitation of a supposed secular purpose can blind us to that fact. [108]

When considering the Court's claim that the purpose for posting the Ten Commandments was "plainly religious in nature," one wonders if the Court had forgotten that depictions of the Ten Commandments appear in two different locations within the Supreme Court. As Chief-Justice Warren Burger noted in *Lynch* v. *Donnelly:*

> The very chamber in which oral arguments on this case were heard is decorated with a notable and permanent—not seasonal—symbol of religion: Moses with the Ten Commandments. [109]

Perhaps the Court had also forgotten that it is often easier to find the Ten Commandments displayed in government rather than in religious structures, and that our *civil* prohibitions against theft, murder, perjury, etc. are drawn from the Ten Commandments. There was much evidence—and much professional opinion—which disputed the Court's assertion that the display of the Commandments was "plainly religious in nature." In fact, Justices Marshall, Brennan, and Stevens—three liberal Justices—noted in *Allegheny* v. *ACLU:*

> [A] carving of Moses holding the Ten Commandments, if that is the only adornment on a courtroom wall, conveys an equivocal [*un*clear and *un*certain] message, perhaps a respect for Judaism, for religion in general, or for law. [110]

It was striking that in *Stone* the Supreme Court completely ignored the *facts* which led both the Kentucky legislature and the federal district court to acknowledge the *secular* importance of the Ten Commandments. This unprecedented rejection of fact by the Court drew sharp criticism from Justice Rehnquist in his dissent:

> [T]he Court concludes that the Kentucky statute involved in this case "has no secular legislative purpose," . . . and that "[t]he preeminent purpose for posting the Ten Commandments on schoolroom walls is plainly religious in nature. . . ." This even though, as the trial court found, "[t]he General Assembly thought the statute had a secular legislative purpose and specifically said so. . . . " The Court's summary rejection of a secular purpose articulated by the legislature and confirmed by the State court is without precedent in Establishment Clause jurisprudence. This Court regularly looks to legislative articulations of a statute's purpose in Establishment Clause

cases. . . . The Court rejects the secular purpose articulated by the State because the Decalogue is "undeniably a sacred text. . . . " It is equally undeniable, however, as the elected representatives of Kentucky determined, that the Ten Commandments have had a significant impact on the development of secular legal codes of the Western World. The trial court [also] concluded that evidence submitted substantiated this determination. . . . Certainly the State was permitted to conclude that a document with such secular significance should be placed before its students, with an appropriate statement of the document's secular import. [111]

Almost as amazing as the Court's claim that the Ten Commandments lacked secular purpose was the Court's complaint of what would occur if students were to view the Commandments:

If the posted copies of the Ten Commandments are to have any effect at all, it will be to induce the schoolchildren to read, meditate upon, perhaps to venerate and obey, the Commandments. [112]

The Court therefore concluded:

[This] . . . is not a permissible state objective under the Establishment Clause. . . . [T]he mere posting of the copies . . . the Establishment Clause prohibits. [113]

The Founding Fathers would have disagreed vehemently. For example:

The moment the idea is admitted into society that property is not as sacred as the laws of God, and that there is not a force of law and public justice to protect it, anarchy and tyranny commence. If "Thou shalt not covet," and "Thou shalt not steal," were not commandments of Heaven, they must be made inviolable precepts in every society, before it can be civilized or made free. [114] **JOHN ADAMS**

The law given from Sinai was a civil and municipal as well as a moral and religious code . . . laws essential to the existence of men in society and most of which have been enacted by every nation which ever professed any code of laws. [115] Vain indeed would be the search among the writings of profane antiquity [secular history] . . . to find so broad, so complete and so solid a basis for morality as this decalogue [Ten Commandments] lays down. [116] **JOHN QUINCY ADAMS**

[I]t pleased God to deliver, on Mount Sinai, a compendium of this holy law and to write it with His own hand on durable tables of stone. This law, which is commonly called the Ten Commandments or Decalogue. . . . was incorporated in the judicial law. [117] **WILLIAM FINDLEY**, REVOLUTIONARY SOLDIER; U. S. CONGRESSMAN

The opinion that human reason left without the constant control of Divine laws and commands will . . . give duration to a popular government is as chimerical [unlikely] as the most extravagant ideas that enter the head of a maniac. . . . Where will you find any code of laws among civilized men in which the commands and prohibitions are not founded on Christian principles? I need not specify the prohibition of murder, robbery, theft, [and] trespass. [118] **NOAH WEBSTER**

The sanctions of the Divine law . . . cover the whole area of human action. . . . The laws which regulate our conduct are the laws of man and the laws of God. [119] **DEWITT CLINTON**, INTRODUCED THE TWELFTH AMENDMENT; GOVERNOR OF NEW YORK; U. S. SENATOR

[T]he Ten Commandments . . . are the sum of the moral law. [120] **JOHN WITHERSPOON**, SIGNER OF THE DECLARATION

Clearly, prominent Founders saw the Ten Commandments—and religious codes in general—as the foundation of American civil law. In fact, the belief was clear that public adherence to religious principles was the greatest source of security for civil government:

[T]he Holy Scriptures. . . . can alone secure to society, order and peace, and to our courts of justice and constitutions of government, purity, stability, and usefulness. In vain, without the Bible, we increase penal laws and draw entrenchments [protections] around our institutions. [121] **JAMES MCHENRY**, SIGNER OF THE CONSTITUTION

Men, in a word, must necessarily be controlled either by a power within them or by a power without them; either by the Word of God or by the strong arm of man; either by the Bible or by the bayonet. [122] **ROBERT WINTHROP**, SPEAKER OF THE U. S. HOUSE

Human legislators can undertake only to prescribe the actions of men; they acknowledge their inability to govern and direct the sentiments of the heart. . . . It is one of the greatest marks of Divine favor bestowed upon the children of Israel that the legislator [God] gave them rules not only of action, but for the government of the heart. [123] **JOHN QUINCY ADAMS**

We seek to prevent in some measure the extension of the penal code by inspiring a salutary and conservative principle of virtue and of knowledge in an early age. . . . By general instruction we seek, as far as possible, to purify the whole moral atmosphere. . . and to turn the strong current of feeling and opinion, as well as the censures of the law and the denunciations of religion, against immorality and crime. [124] **DANIEL WEBSTER**

Had I a voice that could be heard from New Hampshire to Georgia, it should be exerted in urging the necessity of disseminating virtue and knowledge among our citizens. On this subject, the policy of the eastern States is well worthy of imitation. The wise people of that extremity of the union never form a new township without making arrangements that secure to its inhabitants the instruction of youth and the public preaching of the gospel. Hence their children are early taught to know their rights and to respect themselves. They grow up good members of society and staunch defenders of their country's cause. [125] **DAVID RAMSAY**, REVOLUTIONARY SURGEON; MEMBER OF THE CONTINENTAL CONGRESS

Let it simply be asked, "Where is the security for property, for reputation, for life, if the sense of religious obligation desert. . . ?" [126] **GEORGE WASHINGTON**

When the minds of the people in general are viciously disposed and unprincipled, and their conduct disorderly, a free government will be attended with greater confusions and evils more horrid than the wild, uncultivated state of nature. It can only be happy when the public principle and opinions are properly directed and their manners regulated. This is an influence beyond the reach of laws and punishments and can be claimed only by religion and education. [127] **ABRAHAM BALDWIN**, SIGNER OF THE CONSTITUTION

The first point of justice . . . consists in piety; nothing certainly being so great a debt upon us as to render to the Creator and

Preserver those acknowledgments which are due to Him for our being and the hourly protection He affords us. [128] SAMUEL ADAMS

All the miseries and evils which men suffer from vice, crime, ambition, injustice, oppression, slavery and war, proceed from their despising or neglecting the precepts contained in the Bible. [129] NOAH WEBSTER

The Court had declared unconstitutional the very embodiment of a system which the Founders had embraced as the basis of civilized society. Justice Rehnquist summarized the illogical position taken by the Court:

> The Establishment Clause does not require that the public sector be insulated from all things which may have a religious significance or origin. . . . The words of Justice Jackson, concurring in *McCollum* v. *Board of Education* . . . merit quotation at length: "I think it remains to be demonstrated whether it is possible, even if desirable, to comply with such demands as plaintiff's completely to isolate and cast out of secular education all that some people may reasonably regard as religious instruction. . . . The fact is that, for good or for ill, nearly everything in our culture worth transmitting, everything which gives meaning to life, is saturated with religious influences. . . . One can hardly respect the system of education that would leave the student wholly ignorant of the currents of religious thought that move the world society for a part in which he is being prepared." [130]

The Court's decision in this case not only struck down a passive, non-coercive display, it also reflected the hostility which has become characteristic of the Court's decisions on these issues.

Wallace v. Jaffree, 1985

This case was the challenge of an Alabama law which authorized a one-minute period of silence for students. When the case reached the federal court of appeals, although the court found that a one-minute period of silence for meditation *was* constitutional, it nevertheless struck down the law. The Supreme Court upheld that decision. Why? As the court of appeals had explained—and as the Supreme Court had repeated:

> It is not the activity itself that concerns us; it is the purpose of the activity that we shall scrutinize. [131]

In seeking "the purpose of the activity," the court had "discovered":

> The "prime sponsor" of the bill . . . explained that the bill was an "effort to return voluntary prayer to our public schools . . . ". He intended to provide children the opportunity of sharing in their spiritual heritage of Alabama and of this country. [132]

Consequently, based on this "discovery," the court struck down the voluntary silent activity and declared the statute . . .

> . . . invalid because the sole purpose . . . was "an effort on the part of the State of Alabama to encourage a religious activity". . . . [It] is a law respecting the establishment of religion within the meaning of the First Amendment. [133]

Chief-Justice Warren Burger was much disturbed by the Supreme Court's affirmation of this decision. For example, he was troubled by the judicial "discovery" which had resulted in the ruling:

> Curiously, the opinions do not mention that all of the sponsor's statements relied upon—including the statement "inserted" into the Senate Journal—were made *after* the legislature had passed the statute; indeed, the testimony that the Court finds critical was given well over a year *after* the statute was enacted. As even the appellees concede . . . there is not a shred of evidence that the legislature as a whole shared the sponsor's motive or that a majority in either house was even aware of the sponsor's view of the bill when it was passed. The sole relevance of the sponsor's statements, therefore, is that they reflect the personal, subjective motives of a single legislator. No case in the 195-year history of this Court supports the disconcerting idea that postenactment statements by individual legislators are relevant in determining the constitutionality of legislation. [134] (emphasis added)

The Alabama State legislature had simply *permitted* a voluntary, silent activity; the Court concluded that this was the equivalent of encouraging a religious activity and was thus an impermissible establishment of religion. Ironically, Alabama came under the provisions of the U. S. territorial ordinance which had declared that:

Religion, morality, and knowledge, being necessary to good government and the happiness of mankind, schools and the means of education *shall forever be encouraged.* [135] (emphasis added)

The Founders thought it *proper* for the government to promote religious activities. In fact, they frequently *encouraged* such activities. For example (emphasis added in each quote):

Sensible of the importance of Christian piety and virtue to the order and happiness of a state, I cannot but earnestly commend to you every measure for their support and *encouragement*. . . . [T]he very existence of the republics . . . depend much upon the public institutions of religion. [136] JOHN HANCOCK

[A] free government. . . . can only be happy when the public principle and opinions are properly directed. . . . by religion and education. It should therefore be among the first objects of those who wish well to the national prosperity to *encourage* and support the principles of religion and morality. [137] ABRAHAM BALDWIN, SIGNER OF THE CONSTITUTION

The *promulgation* of the great doctrines of religion, the being, and attributes, and providence of one Almighty God; the responsibility to Him for all our actions, founded upon moral accountability; a future state of rewards and punishments; the cultivation of all the personal, social, and benevolent virtues;— these never can be a matter of indifference in any well-ordered community. It is indeed difficult to conceive how any civilized society can well exist without them. [138] JOSEPH STORY, U. S. SUPREME COURT JUSTICE; FATHER OF AMERICAN JURISPRUDENCE

[T]o *promote* true religion is the best and most effectual way of making a virtuous and regular people. Love to God and love to man is the substance of religion; when these prevail, civil laws will have little to do. . . . The magistrate (or ruling part of any society) ought to *encourage* piety . . . [and] make it an object of public esteem. [139] Those who are vested with civil authority ought . . . to promote religion and good morals among all under their government. [140] JOHN WITHERSPOON, SIGNER OF THE DECLARATION

I had the honor of being one among many who framed that Constitution. . . . In order effectually to accomplish these great ends, it is incumbent upon us to begin wisely and to proceed in the fear of God; and it is especially the duty of those who bear rule to promote and *encourage* piety [respect for God] and virtue and to discountenance every degree of vice and immorality. [141] **HENRY LAURENS**, PRESIDENT OF CONTINENTAL CONGRESS; U. S. DIPLOMAT; SELECTED AS DELEGATE TO THE CONSTITUTIONAL CONVENTION

[T]he primary objects of government, are peace, order, and prosperity of society. . . . To the *promotion* of these objects, particularly in a republican government, good morals are essential. Institutions for the promotion of good morals are therefore objects of legislative provision and support and among these . . . religious institutions are eminently useful and important. [142] **OLIVER ELLSWORTH**, CONSTITUTIONAL CONVENTION; CHIEF-JUSTICE U. S. SUPREME COURT

[It is] the duty of all wise, free, and virtuous governments to countenance and encourage virtue and religion. [143] **JOHN JAY**, ORIGINAL CHIEF-JUSTICE U. S. SUPREME COURT

Since the Founders who prohibited an establishment of religion also encouraged religion, it is clear—contrary to the Court's assertion in this case—that the Founders did *not* equate encouraging or endorsing religion as an establishment of it.

Chief-Justice Burger struck out at the Court's new anti-endorsement criterion:

It makes no sense to say that Alabama has "endorsed prayer" by merely enacting a new statute "to specify expressly that voluntary prayer is one of the authorized activities during a moment of silence." . . . To suggest that a moment of silence statute that includes the word "prayer" unconstitutionally endorses religion, while one that simply provides for a moment of silence does not, manifests not neutrality but hostility toward religion. . . . The notion that the Alabama statute is a step toward creating an established church borders on, if it does not trespass into, the ridiculous. The statute does not remotely threaten religious liberty. . . . It accommodates the purely private, voluntary religious choices of the individual pupils who wish to pray while at the same time creating a time for nonreligious reflection for those who do not choose to pray. . . . The statute "endorses" only the view that the religious observances of others should be tolerated. [144]

Since this decision represented yet another in the Court's recent series of historically untenable rulings, Justice William Rehnquist undertook a review of the basic history of the First Amendment. (His dissent in this case is recommended reading as one of the best historical overviews of the First Amendment available from any source.) After his lengthy history lesson, he concluded:

There is simply no historical foundation for the proposition that the Framers intended to build the "wall of separation" that was constitutionalized in *Everson*. . . . But the greatest injury of the "wall" notion is its mischievous diversion of judges from the actual intentions of the drafters of the Bill of Rights . . . [N]o amount of repetition of historical errors in judicial opinions can make the errors true. The "wall of separation between church and State" is a metaphor based on bad history. . . . It should be frankly and explicitly abandoned. . . . Our perception has been clouded not by the Constitution but by the mists of an unnecessary metaphor. [145]

Rehnquist then noted with acerbity:

It would come as much of a shock to those who drafted the Bill of Rights, as it will to a large number of thoughtful Americans today, to learn that the Constitution, as construed by the majority, prohibits the Alabama Legislature from "endorsing" prayer. George Washington himself, at the request of the very Congress which passed the Bill of Rights, proclaimed a day of "public thanksgiving and prayer, to be observed by acknowledging with grateful hearts the many and signal favors of Almighty God." History must judge whether it was the Father of his Country in 1789, or a majority of the Court today, which has strayed from the meaning of the Establishment Clause. [146]

The *Jaffree* case was a ruling against a voluntary, and even a silent religious activity; further, it codified the "endorsement test" as the new replacement for the First Amendment prohibition against "establishment."

Allegheny County v. *Pittsburgh ACLU,* 1989

At the seat of government in Pittsburgh, Pennsylvania, many holiday symbols were displayed during the Christmas season—including a Christmas tree, a menorah (a multibranched candlestick used during Jewish celebrations), a Santa, a crèche (nativity scene), a patriotic sign, floral arrangements, etc. A legal challenge was lodged against the display of the menorah and the crèche.

Although this was the first case in which the Supreme Court had considered a menorah, only five years earlier in *Lynch* v. *Donnelly* it had upheld the use of a crèche because:

> [T]he [crèche] display is . . . to celebrate the Holiday recognized by Congress and national tradition and to depict the origins of that Holiday. . . . [T]he crèche . . . is no more an advancement or endorsement of religion than the congressional and executive recognition of the origins of Christmas. . . . It would be ironic if . . . the crèche in the display, as part of a celebration of an event acknowledged in the Western World for 20 centuries, and in this country by the people, the Executive Branch, Congress, and the courts for 2 centuries, would so "taint" the exhibition as to render it violative of the Establishment Clause. To forbid the use of this one passive symbol . . . would be an overreaction contrary to this Nation's history. [147]

Yet in this case, the Court reversed that ruling, declaring:

> The display of a crèche—a representation of the nativity of Jesus . . . conveys an endorsement of religion, in violation of the establishment of religion clause of the Federal Constitution's First Amendment and therefore must be permanently enjoined [prohibited]. [148]

Ironically, when the Court upheld the use of a crèche in *Lynch,* it had been government-owned; yet the crèche forbidden in this case had been privately-owned. This irony did not escape the notice of Justice Anthony Kennedy in his dissent:

> Nor can I comprehend why it should be that placement of a government-owned crèche on private land is lawful while placement of a privately-owned crèche on public land is not. If anything, I should have thought government ownership of a religious symbol

presented the more difficult question under the Establishment Clause, but as *Lynch* resolved that question to sustain the government action, the sponsorship here ought to be all the easier to sustain. [149]

Kennedy was dumbfounded that the Court was striking down a completely passive religious expression:

> There is no suggestion here that the government's power to coerce has been used to further the interests of Christianity or Judaism in any way. No one was compelled to observe or participate in any religious ceremony or activity. . . . The crèche and the menorah are purely passive symbols of religious holidays. Passersby who disagree with the message conveyed by these displays are free to ignore them, or even to turn their backs, just as they are free to do when they disagree with any other form of government speech. [150]

A major factor in the Court's order to remove the crèche was that it had been located in a portion of the courthouse from which Santa and the reindeer were not visible. Very simply, there had been nothing close enough to the crèche to secularize it. This prompted Justice Kennedy to observe:

> [T]he majority embraces a jurisprudence of minutiae [the trivial]. . . . This test could provide workable guidance to the lower courts, if ever, only . . . [by] using little more than intuition and a tape measure. . . . "It would be appalling to conduct litigation under the Establishment Clause as if it were a trademark case, with. . . . witnesses testifying they were offended—but would have been less so were the crèche five feet closer to the jumbo candy cane. . . . " This Court is ill-equipped to sit as a national theology board, and I question both the wisdom and the constitutionality of its doing so. [151]

The Court's decision repudiated both historical precedent and even its own recent case law. It also provided the Court another opportunity to continue its rewriting of the purpose of the First Amendment. Hence, the Court declared:

> [T]he Constitution mandates that the government remain secular. [152]

Obviously, the Founding Fathers disagreed. Notice:

> Has it [government] any solid foundation? Any chief corner stone?
> . . . I think it has an everlasting foundation in the unchangeable

will of God. . . . The sum of my argument is that civil government is of God. [153] **JAMES OTIS**

[T]he only true basis of all government [is] the laws of God and nature. For government is an ordinance of Heaven, designed by the all benevolent Creator. [154] **SAMUEL ADAMS**

[W]e will look for the permanency and stability of our new government to Him who bringeth princes to nothing and teacheth senators wisdom. [155] **JOHN HART**, SIGNER OF THE DECLARATION

[T]he rights essential to happiness. . . . We claim them from a higher source—from the King of kings and Lord of all the earth. [156] **JOHN DICKINSON**, SIGNER OF THE CONSTITUTION; GOVERNOR OF PENNSYLVANIA

[W]hatsoever State among us shall continue to make piety [respect for God] and virtue the standard of public honor will enjoy the greatest inward peace, the greatest national happiness, and in every outward conflict will discover the greatest constitutional strength. [157] **JOHN WITHERSPOON**, SIGNER OF THE DECLARATION

I . . . recommend a general and public return of praise and thanksgiving to Him from whose goodness these blessings descend. The most effectual means of securing the continuance of our civil and religious liberties, is always to remember with reverence and gratitude the source from which they flow. [158] **JOHN JAY**, ORIGINAL CHIEF JUSTICE U. S. SUPREME COURT

No people ought to feel greater obligations to celebrate the goodness of the Great Disposer of Events and of the Destiny of Nations than the people of the United States. . . . And to the same Divine Author of every good and perfect gift we are indebted for all those privileges and advantages, religious as well as civil, which are so richly enjoyed in this favored land. [159] **JAMES MADISON**

Religion and morality are the essential pillars of civil society. [160] **GEORGE WASHINGTON**

Our Constitution was made only for a moral and religious people. It is wholly inadequate to the government of any other. [161] **JOHN ADAMS**

These quotes, coupled with the numerous others already presented in this chapter, overwhelmingly confirm the blatant inaccuracy of the Court's assertion that the government remain secular.

The crowning irony of this case was that the Court upheld the menorah while striking down the crèche, thus evoking this strong criticism in the dissent:

> [T]he Supreme Court of the United States has concluded that the First Amendment creates classes of religions based on the relative numbers of their adherents. Those religions enjoying the largest following must be consigned to the status of least-favored faiths so as to avoid any possible risk of offending members of minority religions. [162]

The decision in this case clearly illustrates that when the standard of original intent is abandoned, Court decisions lack what Justice William Rehnquist termed "unified and principled results" [163]—demonstrated by the fact that within only a five-year period, the Court had completely reversed itself on the issue of crèches. As Justice Antonin Scalia accurately observed:

> [O]ur Nation's protection, that fortress which is our Constitution, cannot possibly rest upon the changeable philosophical predilections of the Justices of this Court, but must have deep foundations in the historic practices of our people. [164]

Lee v. Weisman, 1992

The issue in this case was prayer, specifically, invocations and benedictions delivered at school graduations. The facts were summarized by the Court:

> The city of Providence, Rhode Island had a policy of permitting its public high school and middle school principals to invite members of the clergy to offer invocation and benediction prayers as part of the school's formal graduation ceremonies. Pursuant to this policy, the principal of a middle school invited a rabbi to offer such prayers. The principal gave the rabbi a pamphlet entitled "Guidelines for Civic Occasions," which recommended that public prayers at nonsectarian civic ceremonies be composed with inclusiveness and sensitivity. Also, the principal advised the rabbi that the invocation and benediction should be nonsectarian. [165]

Although the rabbi prayed according to the "politically correct" guidelines given him, a suit was nevertheless filed by a student and her father, Daniel Weisman. When that case finally reached the Supreme Court, by a 5-4 vote the Court struck down the traditional practice of graduation invocations and benedictions offered by clergy. The Court provided the essence of its argument in this simple sentence:

> But it is not enough that the government restrain from compelling religious practices: it must not engage in them either. [166]

Notice the Court's conclusion that to *allow* a rabbi to offer a prayer was the equivalent of the government *engaging* in a religious practice—an incomprehensible stretch both of logic and of interpretation.

Nevertheless, even if it were true that the government allowing prayer is the same as engaging in it, then our history is replete with numerous examples of the government doing so—at the insistence of prominent Founding Fathers. Notice:

> Whereas it is the duty of all nations to acknowledge the providence of Almighty God, to obey His will, to be grateful for His benefits, and humbly to implore His protection and favor. . . . therefore, I do recommend [that] the people of these [United] States . . . may then all unite in rendering unto Him our sincere and humble thanks for His kind care and protection of the people of this country. [167]
> **GEORGE WASHINGTON**

> As the safety and prosperity of nations ultimately and essentially depend on the protection and the blessing of Almighty God, and the national acknowledgment of this truth is not only an indispensable duty which the people owe to Him. . . . I have therefore thought fit to recommend . . . a day of solemn humiliation, fasting, and prayer that the citizens of these [United] States . . . offer their devout addresses to the Father of Mercies. [168] **JOHN ADAMS**

> I do therefore issue this my proclamation, recommending to all who shall be piously disposed to unite their hearts and voices in addressing at one and the same time their vows and adorations to the Great Parent and Sovereign of the Universe . . . to render Him thanks for the many blessings He has bestowed on the people of the United States. [169] **JAMES MADISON**

The Supreme Ruler of the Universe, having been pleased in the course of His providence to establish the independence of the United States of America . . . we ought to be led by religious feelings of gratitude and to walk before Him in all humility according to His most holy law. . . . That with true repentance and contrition of heart we may unitedly implore the forgiveness of our sins through the merits of Jesus Christ and humbly supplicate our heavenly Father. [170] **SAMUEL ADAMS**

In the beginning of the contest with Great Britain, when we were sensible of danger, we had daily prayer in this room for the Divine protection. Our prayers, sir, were heard, and they were graciously answered. . . . I therefore beg leave to move—that henceforth prayers imploring the assistance of Heaven, and its blessings on our deliberations, be held in this Assembly every morning before we proceed to business. [171] **BENJAMIN FRANKLIN**

[W]e live in a republic thus highly favored of heaven, and under a social compact from which so many benefits result: and whilst these considerations should animate us with exalted sentiments of patriotism . . . they ought above all to inspire us with becoming gratitude to the great ruler of nations, on whose favor all our happiness depends. [172] **GEORGE CLINTON**, REVOLUTIONARY GENERAL; GOVERNOR OF NEW YORK

And I do hereby call upon the people. . . . [to] offer to our Almighty and all-gracious God, through our Great Mediator, our sincere and solemn prayers for his Divine assistance and the influences of His Holy Spirit. [173] **JONATHAN TRUMBULL**, GOVERNOR OF CONNECTICUT

[W]e can only depend on the all powerful influence of the Spirit of God, whose Divine aid and assistance it becomes us as a Christian people most devoutly to implore. Therefore I move that some minister of the Gospel be requested to attend this Congress every morning at o'clock [sic] during the sessions in order to open the meeting with prayer. [174] **ELIAS BOUDINOT**, PRESIDENT OF CONGRESS

Let us therefore implore Him to continue his benedictions upon our beloved country, and to grant us unanimity, patriotism, and wisdom, to pursue, at this important session, the most essential interest of this State and of the union. [175] **DANIEL TOMPKINS,** GOVERNOR OF NEW YORK; VICE-PRESIDENT OF THE U. S.

Numerous similar calls for public prayer were regularly issued by our Founding Fathers and by the Congress. This fact was so clear that it evidently caused the Court to refrain from even raising the issue of historical precedent. As the dissent noted, the Court's decision was "conspicuously bereft of *any* reference to history." [176] (emphasis added).

This statement, however, was not completely accurate. Justice Souter, in his concurring opinion, *had* acknowledged that the Founders allowed, encouraged, and participated in such prayers; but he then accused the Founders of not understanding the meaning of the Constitution they themselves had authored. Souter complained:

> [These] practices prove, at best, that the Framers simply did not share a common understanding of the Establishment Clause, and, at worst, that they, like other politicians, could raise constitutional ideals one day and turn their backs on them the next. [177]

Amazingly, Justice Souter asserts that his understanding of the constitutionality of prayer is more accurate than that of those who created the document! The dissent, however, quickly attacked Souter's implication that history contained confused precedents on this issue. Justice Antonin Scalia, speaking for Justices William Rehnquist, Byron White, and Clarence Thomas, explained:

> From our Nation's origin, prayer has been a prominent part of governmental ceremonies and proclamations. The Declaration of Independence, the document marking our birth as a separate people, "appeal[ed] to the Supreme Judge of the world for the rectitude of our intentions" and avowed "a firm reliance on the protection of divine Providence." In his first inaugural address, after swearing his oath of office on a Bible, George Washington deliberately made a prayer a part of his first official act as President. . . . Such supplications have been a characteristic feature of inaugural addresses ever since. Thomas Jefferson, for example, prayed in his first inaugural address. . . . In his second inaugural address, Jefferson acknowledged his need for divine guidance and invited his audience

to join his prayer. . . . Similarly, James Madison, in his first inaugural address, placed his confidence "in the guardianship and guidance of that Almighty Being . . . [with] fervent supplications and best hopes for the future." . . . The other two branches of the Federal Government also have a long-established practice of prayer at public events. . . . [T]here is simply no support for the proposition that the officially sponsored nondenominational invocation and benediction read by Rabbi Gutterman—with no one legally coerced to recite them— violated the Constitution of the United States. To the contrary, they are so characteristically American they could have come from the pen of George Washington or Abraham Lincoln himself. [178]

As previously noted, the Court's standard for what constitutes an unconstitutional religious activity had grown increasingly more narrow and restrictive from case to case; the *Weisman* case proved no exception. In it, the Court introduced a new test for constitutionality: the "psychological coercion test." Under this test, if a single individual finds himself uncomfortable in the presence of a religious practice in public, then that activity is unconstitutional.

The Court alleged that the unconstitutional "psychological coercion" had occurred when the crowd stood for Rabbi Gutterman's prayer:

What to most believers may seem nothing more than a reasonable request that the nonbeliever respect their religious practices, in a school context may appear to the nonbeliever or dissenter to be an attempt to employ the machinery of the State to enforce a religious orthodoxy. . . . The undeniable fact is that the school district's supervision and control of a high school graduation ceremony place public pressure, as well as peer pressure, on attending students to stand as a group or, at least, maintain respectful silence during the Invocation and Benediction. [179]

The dissent vehemently objected to this new test:

As its instrument of destruction, the bulldozer of its social engineering, the Court invents a boundless, and boundlessly manipulable, test of psychological coercion. . . . The opinion manifests that the Court itself has not given careful consideration to its test of psychological coercion. For if it had, how could it observe, with no hint of concern of disapproval, that students stood for the pledge of Allegiance, which immediately preceded Rabbi Gutterman's invocation?. . . . [S]ince the Pledge of Allegiance . . . included the phrase "under God," recital of the Pledge would appear to raise the same Establishment Clause issue as the invocation and benediction. If students were psychologically coerced to remain standing during the invocation, they must also have been psychologically coerced, moments before, to stand for (and thereby, in the Court's view, take part in or appear to take part in) the Pledge. Must the Pledge therefore be barred from the public schools (both from graduation ceremonies and from the classroom)? Logically, that ought to be the next project for the Court's bulldozer. [180]

In its decision, the majority had also implied that public prayers were disruptive and divisive, to which the dissent responded:

[N]othing, absolutely nothing, is so inclined to foster among religious believers of various faiths a toleration—no, an affection—for one another than voluntarily joining in prayer together, to God whom they all worship and seek. . . . The Baptist or Catholic who heard and joined in the simple and inspiring prayers of Rabbi Gutterman on this official and patriotic occasion was inoculated from religious bigotry and prejudice in a manner that can not be replicated. To deprive our society of that important unifying mechanism . . . is as senseless in policy as it is unsupported in law. [181]

Justices Scalia, Rehnquist, Thomas, and White concluded their argument with these strong words:

The reader has been told much in this case about the personal interest of Mr. Weisman and his daughter, and very little about the personal interests of the other side. They are not inconsequential. Church and state would not be such a difficult subject if religion were, as the Court apparently thinks it to be, some purely personal avocation that can be indulged entirely in secret, like pornography, in the privacy of one's room. For most believers it is not that, and has never been. Religious men and women of almost all denominations have felt it necessary to acknowledge and beseech the blessing of God as a people, and not just as individuals, because they believe in the "protection of divine Providence," as the Declaration of Independence put it, not just for individuals but for societies; because they believe God to be, as Washington's first Thanksgiving Proclamation put it, the "Great Lord and Ruler of Nations." One can believe in the effectiveness of such public worship, or one can deprecate and deride it. But the long-standing American tradition of prayer at official ceremonies displays with unmistakable clarity that the Establishment Clause does not forbid the government to accommodate it. The narrow context of the present case involves a community's celebration of one of the milestones in its young citizen's lives, and it is a bold step for this Court to seek to banish from that occasion, and from thousands of similar celebrations throughout this land, the expression of gratitude to God that a majority of the community wishes to make. [182]

The *Weisman* case fully illustrates the anti-religious bias which now dominates much of the Court's current jurisprudence. In fact, public expressions of prayer have been such a consistent loser over the past three decades that the district judge who issued the original ruling in the *Weisman* case had concluded:

> [T]he Constitution *as the Supreme Court views it* does not permit it [prayer]. . . . Unfortunately, in this instance there is no satisfactory middle ground. . . . Those who are anti-prayer have thus been deemed the victors. [183] (emphasis added)

———•••———

These eight representative cases, selected from scores of similar cases, confirm that the current First Amendment is unlike the one originally delivered by the Founders. In its remaking of the First Amendment over the past three decades, the Court has created four different standards: the "Establishment Test" (1947), the "Lemon Test" (1971—discussed in the following chapter), the "Endorsement Test" (1985), and the "Psychological Coercion Test" (1992). Observing these changes, one is reminded of Thomas Jefferson's warning:

> The Constitution . . . is a mere thing of wax in the hands of the judiciary which they may twist and shape into any form they please. [184]

Under the influence of the judiciary, the Constitution has indeed taken on a new "form," and even if an individual had absolutely no knowledge of our heritage or constitutional history, one must wonder at the logic behind the current interpretation.

The First Amendment's wording is explicit: "Congress shall make no law respecting an establishment of religion." Yet, amazingly, most of the contemporary rulings currently proceeding from that Amendment involve neither "Congress" nor the "making of a law." It is truly remarkable that the Court now considers a rabbi to be the equivalent of "Congress," and that offering an invocation or benediction is now the equivalent of "making a law."

The free exercise of religion is no longer the inalienable right recognized by our Founding Fathers. In fact, the First Amendment's guarantee for the free exercise of religion is now often ruled by the Court as the unconstitutional establishment of religion prohibited by that same Amendment. Therefore, because of the current Court's absurd interpretation, public free exercise of religion is now an unconstitutional establishment of religion, thus causing the First Amendment to violate itself.

~9~
Ignoring Original Intent

Recall that when school prayer was struck down in *Engel*, the Court acknowledged that it had failed to cite a single precedent. [1] From that point, the use of precedents by the Court has been haphazard and unpredictable. Quite simply, the Court makes its decisions almost solely on the basis of its own current prejudices rather than with any regard to original intent.

In fact, when invoking authority for its decisions, it almost exclusively cites only its own recent case law. To illustrate this, simply count the post-1947 citations the Court uses in its cases. Why use that year? Recall that it was the 1947 *Everson* case in which the Court began its radical reconstruction of the intent of the First Amendment, introducing not only its religion-hostile separation rhetoric but also extending its jurisdiction over religious issues into States and local communities rather than just the federal government.

Interestingly, despite the Court's haphazard use of historical precedents, it can invoke them with purpose if so inclined. For example, when the Court upheld the constitutionality of Congressional Chaplains in *Marsh* v. *Chambers*, 1983, it relied heavily upon history and original intent. However, such cases are infrequent. Today, the ability to enjoy "the free exercise of religion" and to participate in traditional religious activities is completely subject to the discretion and "good will" of the Court rather than to any constitutional provision.

The following cases will illustrate not only the Court's reliance upon its own recent case-law, but also its avoidance of historical citations that would tend to establish original intent.

Abington v. *Schempp*, 1963

In *Abington*, [2] the Court struck down the official use of the Bible in public education. Although the Court cited several pre-1947 cases in examining procedural questions, the count is still heavily skewed toward recent precedents. **Pre-1947: 112; Post-1947: 356.**

Epperson v. *Arkansas*, 1968

This case [3] challenged an Arkansas statute which made it unlawful for schools to teach "that mankind ascended or descended from a lower order of animals." [4] The U. S. Supreme Court ruled the statute violated the First Amendment. On what sources? **Pre-1947: 6; Post-1947: 12.**

However, the Arkansas law which the Court struck down in this case was identical to the one that the Tennessee Supreme Court had upheld in the 1927 *Scopes* decision. [5] Since the U. S. Supreme Court was in effect overturning the Tennessee Supreme Court decision of forty-three years earlier, it had been forced to reexamine that 1925 case, thus injecting several pre-1947 allusions into its decision. When these references are added, the final tally becomes: **Pre-1947: 23; Post-1947: 16.**

Board of Education of Central School District v. Allen, 1968

In this ruling, [6] the Supreme Court found that a New York law requiring public school authorities to lend textbooks to private schools—and thus possibly to religious schools—was not a violation of the Constitution. What was the basis of this decision? **Pre-1947: 8; Post-1947: 27.**

Lemon v. Kurtzman, 1971

In this case, [7] the Court struck down two State statutes: a Rhode Island law providing a salary supplement to nonpublic teachers if the "eligible teachers agree not to teach courses in religion," [8] and a Pennsylvania law which allowed the State to purchase "secular educational services" (including textbooks and instructional materials) from nonpublic schools if the materials contained no "religious teaching, or the morals or forms of worship of any sect." [9]

Despite the attempt to limit the State aid to purely secular aspects of education, the Court struck down both laws under what is now called the "Lemon Test." Under this test, a public religious activity is constitutional only if: (1) it has a predominately secular purpose; (2) it neither inhibits nor advances religion; and (3) it creates no "excessive entanglement" between government and religion. On which precedents did the Court construct this new test for constitutionality and strike down the State laws? **Pre-1947: 37; Post-1947: 105.**

Levitt v. Committee for Public Education, 1973

New York law mandated that all schools within the State—both public and nonpublic—keep certain secular administrative records (i.e., testing, attendance, etc.). The required record-keeping was costly; therefore, the legislature appropriated money for public schools to cover these expenses and felt it should do the same for the nonpublic schools upon whom it was forcing the requirements. The legislature therefore:

> Appropriated $28,000,000 for the purpose of reimbursing nonpublic schools throughout the State "for . . . the preparation and submission to the State of various other reports as provided for or required by law or regulation." [10]

Although the aid was for nonreligious, State-mandated activities, the Court ruled it unconstitutional. On what basis? **Pre-1947: 0; Post-1947: 21.**

Committee for Public Education v. Nyquist, 1973

To ensure that students had safe facilities in which to attend school, the New York legislature provided money for the " 'maintenance and repair' of facilities and equipment to ensure the students' 'health, welfare and safety.' " [11] The funding was made available in large amounts for public schools; and since the State also collected school taxes from private-school families, it provided funding in token amounts for qualifying nonpublic schools. The Court declared the legislature's action unconstitutional. On which precedents? **Pre-1947: 22; Post-1947: 177.**

Stone v. Graham, 1980

When the Court ruled it unconstitutional for students to view the Ten Commandments while at school, [12] what was the basis for its decision? **Pre-1947: 0; Post-1947: 15.**

Marsh v. Chambers, 1983

The *Marsh* case [13] involved a challenge against legislative chaplains. The Court ruled the chaplaincy to be constitutional, which is not surprising since it relied primarily on earlier sources. Which sources? **Pre-1947: 46; Post-1947: 13.**

Lynch v. Donnelly, 1984

This was the case [14] in which the Supreme Court upheld the display of a government owned crèche, ruling that the city of Pawtucket, Rhode Island, had a secular purpose with its nativity display, that it had not advanced religion, and that the display had not created an excessive entanglement between religion and government—thus satisfying all three prongs of the Court's "Lemon Test." What was the basis for this decision? **Pre-1947: 16; Post-1947: 118.**

Wallace v. Jaffree, 1985

This was the case [15] in which the Court struck down Alabama's statute authorizing a one-minute period of silence in schools. What precedents caused the Court to rule that a period for silent prayer by students was unconstitutional? **Pre-1947: 25; Post-1947: 197.**

Edwards v. Aguillard, 1987

The issue in this case [16] was a Louisiana statue mandating a so-called "balanced-treatment" in science instruction. The State law forbid "the teaching of the theory of evolution . . . unless accompanied by instruction in the theory of 'creation science.'" [17] The Court ruled the law violated the "Lemon Test" and therefore declared it unconstitutional. On which precedents? **Pre-1947: 13; Post-1947: 114.**

Allegheny v. ACLU, 1989

Here the Court struck down "stand-alone" créches displayed in public buildings. [18] On what basis? **Pre-1947: 0; Post-1947: 126.**

Westside v. Mergens, 1990

In this case, [19] the Court upheld the 1984 federal law which provided "Equal Access" to public school buildings for both religious and nonreligious groups. [20] Since Westside High School had allowed nonreligious clubs (e.g., Chess, Journalism, Scuba, etc.), the Court ruled that the school must also allow Christian clubs "equal access." On what precedents was this decision based? **Pre-1947: 0; Post-1947: 69.**

Lee v. Weisman, 1992

This was the case [21] in which the Court forbade clerical invocations and benedictions at student graduation ceremonies. From what sources did the Court derive its justification? **Pre-1947: 16; Post-1947: 112.**

However, recall that in Justice Souter's concurring opinion, he offered his "history" lesson before declaring that the Founding Fathers had "turned their backs" on the ideals in the First Amendment—at least according to his standards. [22] When his "precedents" are added, the final tally for the Court's decision becomes: **Pre-1947: 84; Post-1947: 182.**

Lamb's Chapel v. *Center Moriches Union Free School Dist.*, 1993

A New York law allowed equal-access rental of school property for after-hours use. When a school board prohibited a church which had rented the facility from showing a film series, the Court overturned the school board's policy. [23] On what basis? **Pre-1947: 0; Post-1947: 18.**

Zobrest v. *Catalina Foothills School District*, 1993

In this case, [24] the Court upheld a law which authorized the hiring of a sign-language interpreter for a deaf student, even though the student attended a religious high school. On what basis did the Court permit this service for the handicapped student? **Pre-1947: 0; Post-1947: 63.**

Rosenberger v. *Rector and Visitors of University of Virginia*, 1995

Student publications at the University of Virginia were reimbursed for printing costs from student activity funds. However, *Wide Awake*, a Christian publication, was denied reimbursement. The U. S. Supreme Court sided with the paper and ordered the reimbursement. [25] On what basis? **Pre-1947: 5; Post-1947: 159.**

———•••———

Clearly, in its numerous rulings on religious issues since 1947, whether ruling for or against religious expressions, the Court now relies almost exclusively upon its own recent case-law precedents—the very precedents under which it has essentially rewritten the First Amendment.

~10~
The Court's Selective Use of History

In recent decades, the Court has often avoided any reliance on historical records. However, when it has referred to history, it has been usually to its own series of carefully crafted misportrayals manipulated to add an appearance of the Founders' approval to its decisions. This chapter will expose five of the Court's frequent historical distortions; and although the Court has become adept in their use, each has fatal flaws.

1. The Fourteenth Amendment

Nearly every First Amendment case appearing before contemporary courts contains a phrase declaring "the First Amendment made applicable to the States by the Fourteenth Amendment . . . "

By using this phrase, the Court is invoking its decisions from the 1940s which reinterpreted the Fourteenth Amendment. That reinterpretation created a mechanism for the Court whereby, for the first time, it could intervene in virtually all practices of States and local communities, including religion.

The Fourteenth Amendment was the second of a succession of three Constitutional Amendments passed immediately following the Civil War. When the Thirteenth Amendment abolishing slavery was passed (1865), some voices in the South protested bitterly. While conceding that former slaves might now be legally free, those dissidents vowed to withhold from former slaves the rights belonging to a citizen in their State.

Congress' response was two more Amendments: the Fourteenth (1868), which guaranteed that freed slaves would enjoy all the privileges and rights conveyed by being a citizen either of the State or of the nation; [1] and the Fifteenth (1870), which secured for freed slaves the right to vote and thus to participate in the political affairs of their State.

The Fourteenth Amendment was a racial civil rights guarantee; and for seventy years following its ratification, the Courts applied it as it was intended. This is not surprising, however, for those Courts were simply following the elementary judicial principle described by Chief Justice John Marshall in *McCullough* v. *Maryland* (1819):

> An exposition of the Constitution deliberately established by legislative acts . . . ought not to be lightly disregarded. [2]

That is, determine the legislative intent for an act before applying it. The adherence to this principle was long practiced by the Courts. For example, the *Holy Trinity* Court reminded all courts of their primary responsibility of always first examining and establishing:

> [T]he evil which was intended to be remedied, the circumstances surrounding the appeal to Congress, the reports of the committee of each house . . . [and] the intent of Congress. [3]

In the Fourteenth Amendment, the "evil intended to be remedied" and "the intent of Congress" was clear: to make recently freed slaves citizens of the State in which they resided. Very simply—and very specifically—the Fourteenth Amendment was a badly needed racial civil rights amendment.

How, then, could the Courts of the 1940s manage so completely to rewrite the intent? Because the wording of the Fourteenth Amendment, if divorced from its purpose, seems to condone such an interpretation. The wording of the Fourteenth states:

> All persons born or naturalized in the United States, and subject to the jurisdiction thereof, are citizens of the United States and of the State wherein they reside. No State shall make or enforce any law which shall abridge the privileges or immunities of citizens of the United States.

As a result of separating the wording from its intent, in *Cantwell* v. *Connecticut* (1940), [4] *Murdock* v. *Pennsylvania* (1943), [5] *Everson* v. *Board of Education* (1947), [6] and other decisions, the Court substituted a totally revised and foreign interpretation for the Fourteenth Amendment. In those decisions, the Court declared that the ***purpose*** of the Fourteenth Amendment was to limit the States not just on racial civil rights issues, but on the numerous items contained within the Bill of Rights.

Under this reshaped purpose for the Fourteenth—and thereby under its new extended scope of power—the First Amendment would now limit every State and community, and no longer just the federal government as originally intended. (This process of individually subjugating issues from within the Bill of Rights to the jurisdiction of federal courts through the redefined scope of the Fourteenth Amendment is now described by the Court as "selective incorporation." [7])

Even though the selective incorporation of the First into the Fourteenth Amendment is a recent innovation, in *Abington*, the Court announced that the joining was now permanent and irrevocable:

> [T]his **Court** has **decisively settled** that the First Amendment's mandate that "Congress shall make no law respecting an establishment of religion, or prohibiting the free exercise thereof" has been made wholly applicable to the States by the Fourteenth Amendment. . . . The Fourteenth Amendment has rendered the legislatures of the States as incompetent as Congress to enact such laws. [8] (emphasis added)

What has been the effect? According to Justice William Douglas in *Walz v. Tax Commission* (1970), the result has been a national revolution . . .

> . . . reversing the historic position that the foundations of those liberties [in the Bill of Rights] rested largely in State law. . . . [T]he **revolution** occasioned by the Fourteenth Amendment has progressed as Article after Article in the Bill of Rights has been [selectively] incorporated in it [the Fourteenth] and made applicable to the States. [9] (emphasis added)

This description was entirely accurate; the Court unilaterally "*reversed the historic* position.*" What was that historic position? According to Samuel Adams, the Bill of Rights was created because the people wished . . .

> . . . to see a line drawn as clearly as may be between the federal powers vested in Congress and distinct sovereignty of the several States upon which the private and personal rights of the citizens depend. Without such distinction there will be danger of the Constitution issuing imperceptibly and gradually into a consolidated government over all the States. . . . [T]he population of the U. S. live in different climates, of different education and manners, and possessed of different habits and feelings [and] under one consolidated government cannot long remain free. [10]

Very simply, the purpose of the Bill of Rights was to keep the "education, manners, habits, and feelings" from being consolidated and micro-managed by the federal government. As Thomas Jefferson reminded Supreme Court Justice William Johnson:

> [T]aking from the States the moral rule of their citizens, and subordinating it to the general authority [federal government]. . . . would . . . break up the foundations of the Union. . . . I believe the *States* can best govern our home concerns, and the general [federal] government our foreign ones. [11] (emphasis added)

Jefferson made it clear that this was especially true with the First Amendment:

> Certainly, no power to prescribe any religious exercise or to assume authority in religious discipline has been delegated to the general [federal] government. It must, then, rest with the *States.* [12] (emphasis added)

The Bill of Rights was designed specifically to keep issues like that of the First Amendment's religious expression out of the hands of the federal government and in the realm of the States where the people would have effective recourse against any encroachments upon their liberties. For this reason, earlier Supreme Courts consistently rejected attempts to federalize the States or to usurp their powers. As Founding Father and Chief Justice John Marshall explained in *Barron v. Baltimore* (1833):

> In almost every convention by which the Constitution was adopted, amendments to guard against the abuse of power were recommended. These amendments demanded security against the apprehended encroachments of the general [federal] government—*not* against those of the local [State] governments. . . . These amendments contain *no* expression indicating an intention to apply them to the State governments. *This Court cannot so apply them.* [13] (emphasis added)

The documentation on the intent of the Bill of Rights as well as the intent of the Fourteenth Amendment was clear. Yet, the documentation on both of these Amendments has been not only ignored, but even rejected by the Court. Further, what makes the Court's coupling of the Fourteenth and the First even more reprehensible is the fact that those who framed and ratified the Fourteenth made clear that it was *not* to be applied to the First. What evidence indicates this intent?

Notice, for example, what occurred when the Blaine Amendment had been proposed in 1875. That proposed Amendment stated:

No *State* shall make any law respecting an establishment of religion or prohibiting the free exercise thereof.... No public property and no public revenue ... shall be appropriated to ... the support of any school ... under the control of any religious or anti-religious sect, organization, or denomination.... And no such particular creed or tenets shall be read or taught in any school or institution supported ... by such revenue. [14] (emphasis added)

This Amendment would have done to the States exactly what the Court did in the 1940s; yet it was *rejected* by the Congress which passed the Fourteenth. In fact, the *McCollum* Court (1948) noted that not only the Blaine Amendment but also five similar ones which would have applied the First Amendment against the States were *rejected* by that Congress. [15] The intent of the legislators who framed the Fourteenth was clear: it was *not* to be coupled to the First.

Therefore, even though the Court invokes the Fourteenth Amendment as its supposed constitutional authority to intrude into the issue of State and local religious expressions, history proves that the Fourteenth actually provides the Court *no* legitimate basis for that interference. History factually demonstrates the extent to which the Court has taken into its own hand the complete subverting of the Constitution by rewriting the intent of a number of its clauses.

2. The Efforts of James Madison and Thomas Jefferson in Virginia

A second ploy routinely utilized by contemporary Courts is to invoke the efforts of James Madison and Thomas Jefferson in Virginia as *the* national standard. For example:

This Court has previously recognized that the provisions of the First Amendment, in the drafting and adoption of which *Madison* and *Jefferson* played such leading roles, had the same objective and were intended to provide the same protection against governmental intrusion on religious liberty as the *Virginia* statute. [16] EVERSON v. BOARD OF EDUCATION (emphasis added)

In 1785-1786, those opposed to the established Church, led by *James Madison* and *Thomas Jefferson* ... opposed all religious establishments by law on grounds of principle [and] obtained the

enactment of the famous "*Virginia* Bill for Religious Liberty." [17]
ENGEL v. VITALE (emphasis added)

By the Court's use of such statements, one is led to believe that what Madison and Jefferson did with their celebrated "Virginia Bill for Religious Liberty" (often called the "Virginia Statute") was the prototype for the entire nation. It was not.

In Virginia, the Church of England (the Anglican church) was the *only* legally recognized and established denomination even though the members of other denominations (Baptists, Lutherans, Presbyterians, Quakers, etc.) were more numerous than the Anglicans. To rectify this inequity, Jefferson authored the Virginia Statute to disestablish the Anglican church and place all groups on an equal footing. However, before the passage of the Statute, Jefferson traveled overseas to represent American interests. James Madison assumed the mantle and led the successful fight for its passage.

Much of what Madison and Jefferson fought for in Virginia in 1786 had already occurred in many other States *prior* to the Virginia Statute. For example, New Jersey, [18] North Carolina, [19] and Delaware [20] had already given equal denominational protection well before Virginia; and New York, [21] Pennsylvania, [22] Georgia, [23] and Vermont [24] had established religious liberty *prior* to the Virginia Statute.

Furthermore, as early as 1773 (over a decade *before* the passage of the Virginia Statute) Samuel Chase and William Paca (signers of the Declaration) had led Maryland's fight to end the system of State-ordered tithes, [25] something Jefferson and Madison did not attempt in Virginia until years later. Clearly, many other States made progress in the area of religious liberty independent of the efforts of Jefferson and Madison in Virginia.

Despite what the Court claims, the efforts in Virginia were *not* the primary influence in America's movement to secure religious liberties. However, not only does the Court inaccurately claim that the Virginia Statute was the catalyst for the entire nation, it even claims that it served as the model for the First Amendment. This erroneous charge was ably rebutted by Justice William Rehnquist in *Wallace* v. *Jaffree* (1985):

> [T]he Court's opinion in *Everson*—while correct in bracketing Madison and Jefferson together in their exertions in their home State leading to the enactment of the Virginia Statue of Religious

Liberty—is totally incorrect in suggesting that Madison carried these views onto the floor of the United States House of Representatives when he proposed the language which would ultimately become the Bill of Rights. The repetition of this error in the Court's opinion in *Illinois ex rel. McCollum v. Board of Education*, 333 U. S. 203 (1948), and, *inter alia, Engel v. Vitale*, 370 U. S. 421 (1962), does not make it any sounder historically. Finally, in *Abington School District v. Schempp*, 374 U. S. 203, 214 (1963), the Court made the truly remarkable statement that "the views of Madison and Jefferson, preceded by Roger Williams, came to be incorporated not only in the Federal Constitution but likewise in those of most of our States." On the basis of what evidence we have, this statement is demonstrably incorrect as a matter of history. And its repetition in varying forms in succeeding opinions of the Court can give it no more authority than it possesses as a matter of fact; *stare decisis* [the reliance on previous precedent] may bind courts as to matters of law, but it cannot bind them as to matters of history. [26]

In summary, the Virginia Statute, while an important piece of legislation in the history of Virginia, was not the sole source of religious liberty for America. The concepts it embodied had already been advanced and pursued by many other Founders and many other States. Furthermore, contrary to the current misportrayal, Madison and Jefferson in their efforts with the Virginia Statute were *not* attempting to limit either Christianity or public religious expressions but rather were attempting to secure its uninhibited expression for all groups.

3. The Role of Thomas Jefferson and James Madison in the Formation of the First Amendment and the Bill of Rights

Although the contemporary courts apparently consider Jefferson and Madison as the only significant authorities on the First Amendment, the historical records are clear that the current portrayal of their influence is dramatically overstated. This heavy reliance on both Jefferson and Madison is a new and recent phenomenon.

In fact, the reason that Jefferson was rarely cited by earlier Courts was given by Jefferson himself when Dr. Joseph Priestly sent Jefferson a copy of an article he planned to publish. In that work, Priestly credited Jefferson with being a major influence in framing the Constitution. Jefferson knew this claim to be erroneous, and on June 19, 1802, he wrote Dr. Priestly, instructing him to correct that error:

> One passage in the paper you enclosed me must be corrected. It is the following, "And all say it was yourself more than any other individual, that planned and established it," i. e., the Constitution. I was in Europe when the Constitution was planned, and never saw it till after it was established. [27]

Jefferson knew that he could not be considered a leading figure in the creation of the Constitution; he was not even in America when it was framed. Jefferson properly disqualified himself.

Interestingly, Madison, too, disqualified himself from being the significant spokesman on the Constitution and its intent. As he explained to William Cogswell:

> You give me a credit to which I have no claim in calling me "the writer of the Constitution of the United States." This was not, like the fabled Goddess of Wisdom, the offspring of a single brain. It ought to be regarded as the work of many heads and many hands. [28]

Furthermore, one must also recognize that Madison—while undeniably an important influence during the Constitutional Convention—was often out of step with the majority of the delegates. This is evidenced by the fact that 40 of his 71 proposals during the Convention failed; [29] additionally, the Constitution that Madison initially sought was far removed from the final document. [30]

Earlier generations properly recognized the significant influence of many Founders which today are ignored by the courts and many quasi-political advocacy groups. Others from the Convention previously given lofty recognition included James Wilson; [31] Charles Pinckney (one early work called him "The Father of the Constitution"); [32] and George Washington (James Monroe believed that without his leadership, the entire Convention would have adjourned unsuccessfully). [33] In fact, in 1886, an eminent nineteenth century historian declared that Roger Sherman, George Washington, Charles Cotesworth Pinckney, James Madison, and Alexander Hamilton were the "master-builders of the Constitution." [34]

There indeed can be no legitimate single spokesman for the Constitution. However, this is not to say that Jefferson or Madison had no role; they definitely did. Yet, a serious consideration of the historical evidence makes it clear that they had much less impact than that which is attributed to them today.

For example, while Jefferson *was* a leading Anti-Federalist and *did* want a Bill of Rights, he was only one of the *many* loud Anti-Federalist voices calling for express protections (e.g., George Mason, Samuel Adams, Patrick Henry, Elbridge Gerry, etc.). In fact, as Jefferson explained, his influence was minimal:

> On receiving it [the Constitution while in France] I wrote strongly to Mr. Madison urging the want of provision for the freedom of religion, freedom of the press, trial by jury, *habeas corpus,* the substitution of militia for a standing army, and an express reservation to the States of all rights not specifically granted to the Union. . . . This is all the hand I had in what related to the Constitution. [35]

Jefferson wrote only a single letter broadly calling for a Bill of Rights.

Who, then, was responsible for the Bill of Rights? And what was Madison's role? A proper perspective on who was—and who was not—a major force in the formation of the Bill of Rights (and therefore in the formation of the First Amendment), can be provided by a brief review of the circumstances surrounding its creation.

While the Constitutional Convention had ended with a proposal for a new federal government, it had also ended on a divisive tone. During the Convention, Virginian George Mason had moved that a Bill of Rights be added to the Constitution to provide specific protection for States and individuals, [36] but the other Virginians at the Convention—including James Madison—opposed any Bill of Rights; their position prevailed. [37] For this reason, George Mason, Elbridge Gerry, Edmund Randolph, and others at the Convention refused to sign the new Constitution.

Mason and the others returned to their home States to lobby against the ratification of the Constitution until a Bill of Rights was added. As a result of their voices (and numerous others who agreed with them), the ratification of the Constitution almost failed in Virginia, [38] Massachusetts, [39] New Hampshire, [40] and New York. [41] Rhode Island flatly refused to ratify it, [42] and North Carolina refused to do so until limitations were placed upon the federal government. [43] Although the Constitution was eventually ratified, a clear message had been delivered: there was strong sentiment demanding the inclusion of a Bill of Rights.

The best source for examining the call for a Bill of Rights in the various State conventions is Elliot's *Debates in the Several State Conventions on the Adoption of the Federal Constitution* (1836). This is the original compilation of the records from each State's ratifying convention, and even today that work remains a primary reference, unrivaled in both scholarship and accuracy.

The Virginia reports from June 2 through June 25, 1788, make clear that during their convention, Patrick Henry, George Mason, and Edmund Randolph led the fight for the Bill of Rights over James Madison's *opposition*. [44]

Henry's passionate speeches of June 5th and June 7th resulted in Virginia's motion that a Bill of Rights be added to the federal Constitution; and on June 25, the Virginia Convention selected George Mason to chair a committee to prepare a proposed Bill of Rights, [45] with Patrick Henry and John Randolph as members. [46] Mason incorporated Henry's arguments as the basis of Virginia's proposal on religious liberty. [47]

Although Madison had opposed a Bill of Rights, he understood the grim political reality that without one, it was unlikely the new Constitution would receive widespread public acceptance. [48] Consequently, he withdrew his opposition, and in the federal House of Representatives he introduced his own versions of the amendments offered by his State.

Very little of Madison's proposed religious wording made it into the final version of the First Amendment; and even a cursory examination of the *Annals of Congress* surrounding the formation of that Amendment quickly reveals the influence of Fisher Ames and Elbridge Gerry of Massachusetts, John Vining of Delaware, Daniel Carroll and Charles Carroll of Maryland, Benjamin Huntington, Roger Sherman, and Oliver Ellsworth of Connecticut, William Paterson of New Jersey, and others on that Amendment. [49]

By utilizing Jefferson and Madison as the principal spokesmen for the First Amendment, the contemporary courts have chosen one who was out of the country at the time of the formation of the First Amendment and another who felt it unnecessary.

4. Jefferson, Madison, and Religion

Because of the manner in which Courts invoke Jefferson and Madison when striking down passive and voluntary religious activities, one is led to believe that these two were opposed *en toto* to religious activities in official public arenas; this is patently untrue—especially in the case of Jefferson.

Although Jefferson and Madison may certainly be considered two of the less overtly religious among the Founders, they certainly were *not* religion-hostile. Furthermore, the current portrayals of Madison and Jefferson fail to mention that these two did not even agree with each other on what was a permissible religious expression; each drew the line differently.

For example, Madison offered Presidential proclamations for national days of prayer, fasting, and thanksgiving; [50] but Jefferson refused to do so [51] because he believed it to be the responsibility of the State governments rather than the federal one. [52] Therefore, only as Governor of Virginia did Jefferson issue such calls. [53]

Similarly noteworthy is the fact that the Virginia Statute was only one from a group of bills simultaneously authored by Jefferson and subsequently introduced and promoted by Madison. These other bills (seldom mentioned by the social promoters of Madison and Jefferson) further clarify the views of Jefferson and Madison on religion. Those bills included: "A Bill for Saving the Property of the Church Heretofore by Law Established," "A Bill for Punishing Disturbers of Religious Worship and Sabbath Breakers," "A Bill for Appointing Days of Public Fasting and Thanksgiving," and "A Bill Annulling Marriages Prohibited by the Levitical Law and Appointing the Mode of Solemnizing Lawful Marriage." [54]

Additionally, today's so-called Jeffersonians ignore the fact that Jefferson designated space in the Rotunda of the University of Virginia for chapel services; [55] that he expected students to participate in the various religious schools which he personally had invited to locate adjacent to and upon the University property; [56] that he praised the use of the Charlottesville courthouse for religious services; [57] and that he stated that religion is "deemed in other countries incompatible with good government and yet proved by our experience to be its best support." [58]

In fact, Jefferson thought Christianity so important that he personally authored a work for the Indians entitled *The Life and Morals of Jesus of Nazareth* which set forth the teachings of Jesus as delivered in the Gospels. [59] While President of the United States, Jefferson even approved several measures appropriating federal funds to pay for Christian missionaries to the Indians. [60] Of one of these, Justice Rehnquist explained:

> Jefferson's treaty with the Kaskaskia Indians . . . provided annual cash support for the Tribe's Roman Catholic priest and church. . . . The treaty stated in part: "And whereas, the greater part of the Tribe have been baptized and received into the Catholic church, to which they are much attached, the United States will give annually for seven years one hundred dollars towards the support of a priest of that religion . . . [a]nd . . . three hundred dollars to assist the said Tribe in the erection of a church." [61]

Furthermore, Jefferson signed into law three separate acts setting aside government lands for the sole use of Christian missionaries to evangelize the Indians and others. [62]

While Jefferson's policies toward religious expressions are clear and consistent, an investigation of Madison on this subject is much more difficult. An understanding of Madison's views is complicated by the fact that his early actions were at direct variance with his later opinions. Consider six examples of his early actions.

First, Madison was publicly outspoken about his personal Christian beliefs and convictions. For example, he encouraged his friend, William Bradford, to make sure of his own spiritual salvation:

> [A] watchful eye must be kept on ourselves lest, while we are building ideal monuments of renown and bliss here, we neglect to have our names enrolled in the Annals of Heaven. [63]

Madison even desired that all public officials—including Bradford—would declare openly and publicly their Christian beliefs and testimony:

> I have sometimes thought there could not be a stronger testimony in favor of religion or against temporal enjoyments, even the most rational and manly, than for men who occupy the most honorable and gainful departments and [who] are rising in reputation and wealth, publicly to declare their unsatisfactoriness by becoming fervent advocates in the cause of Christ; and I wish you may give in your evidence in this way. [64]

Second, Madison was a member of the committee which authored the 1776 Virginia Bill of Rights and approved of its clause declaring that:

> It is the mutual *duty* of *all* to practice Christian forbearance, love, and charity toward each other. [65] (emphasis added)

Third, Madison's proposed wording for the First Amendment demonstrates that he opposed only the establishment of a federal denomination, not public religious activities. His proposal declared:

> The civil rights of none shall be abridged on account of religious belief or worship, nor shall any *national religion* be established. [66] (emphasis added)

(Madison reemphasized that position throughout the debates. [67])

Fourth, in 1789, Madison served on the Congressional committee which authorized, approved, and selected paid Congressional chaplains. [68]

Fifth, in 1812, President Madison signed a federal bill which economically aided a Bible Society in its goal of the mass distribution of the Bible. [69]

Sixth, throughout his Presidency (1809-1816), Madison endorsed public and official religious expressions by issuing several proclamations for national days of prayer, fasting, and thanksgiving. [70]

These were the early actions of Madison; yet, in later life in what is known as the *Detached Memoranda*, Madison retreated from many of these positions, even declaring his belief that having paid chaplains was unconstitutional. [71] He also reversed another previous position by avoiding discussions of his religious views in his latter years. [72]

Those who embrace Madison's later beliefs in preference to his earlier actions attempt widely to publicize his *Detached Memoranda*. Then, in an effort to make Madison's early actions conform to his latter beliefs, they even blatantly misportray his role in defeating Patrick Henry's 1784 "Bill for Establishing Teachers of the Christian Religion" into a supposed "proof" that Madison not only opposed, but that the entire nation also rejected, public endorsements of religion. Yet, consider the facts.

Henry's bill—today often titled the "Assessment Bill"—was an effort by Virginians to rebuild the spiritual foundation of their State. Understandably, those underpinnings had been ravaged during the Revolution because Virginia's official State denomination had been The Church of England. In an effort to restore an emphasis on some of the necessary spiritual values, Patrick Henry proposed a tax to support statewide religious instruction for *all* denominations. William Wirt Henry, Patrick Henry's biographer and grandson, described the tax:

> This was in effect a tax for the support of secular education, with the privilege to each taxpayer of devoting his tax to the support of the religious teachers of his own denomination. [73]

Henry's plan to introduce this bill sparked tremendous debate from both sides of the issue, and memorials both for and against the tax were ably written and broadly circulated in the State. However, the only one widely discussed today is that of Madison: his *Memorial and Remonstrance*.

In that work, Madison made clear his position that given time, everyone would eventually choose to become a Christian as a result of their own personal initiative and investigation. Madison was not disparaging Christianity in the *Memorial;* he just wanted religion practiced *only* in the private forum. [74]

It appeared, however, that Madison's position would fail; for numerous distinguished Virginians, including George Washington, John Marshall, Richard Henry Lee, and others, supported Henry's bill. [75] Yet, in the midst of the debates, Henry left the legislature to take his seat as Virginia's new Governor. With Henry's persuasive leadership absent from the Assembly, Madison believed he could now turn the tide in his favor. As he explained to James Monroe:

> The bill for a religious assessment has not been yet brought in. Mr. Henry, the father of the scheme, is gone up to his seat for his family and will no more sit in the House of Delegates, a circumstance very inauspicious [unfavorable] to his offspring [the bill]. [76]

With Henry gone, Madison's efforts prevailed. However, opposition to the new tax was not simply a matter of a religious debate; it was bolstered by the fact that the general state of postwar poverty which existed not only in Virginia but in all the States did not welcome new taxes of *any* kind. (For example, Shay's Rebellion and the Whiskey Rebellion were clear illustrations of the people's fervent opposition to new taxes.)

Today, one is led to believe that what Madison "accomplished" in defeating Henry's bill represented the national thinking; it did not. For example, in Massachusetts, [77] New Hampshire, [78] and Maryland, [79] bills similar to that defeated in Virginia were passed, showing only that the majority of those in Virginia—and not the nation—embraced Madison's position on this issue. And it is even debatable whether the majority of those in Virginia embraced Madison's view since the evidence suggests that had Henry remained in the legislature, the bill probably would have passed.

Another important factor ignored by those today who overly elevate Madison is that he was often in disagreement with many prominent Founding Fathers. For example, George Washington did publicly—and as the national leader—promote, encourage, and advance public religious expressions. With today's only measure of constitutionality being Madison's views, the absurd question becomes, "Did George Washington not understand the Constitution? Or did he intentionally violate it?" Such must be the case if Washington's actions—and those of many other Founders—are judged only by the Madisonian standards which many promote today.

In summary, in order to utilize Thomas Jefferson and James Madison to oppose public religious expression, Jefferson must be totally misportrayed, and Madison's opinions from decades *ex post facto* must be elevated over his actions—a theory which clearly would be rejected even under the elementary rules of evidence.

5. Omission of Facts

The final strategy used by the Court to bolster its arguments is one previously introduced: historical omission. Not only does the Court regularly omit cases prior to 1947 from its discussions, it also disregards quotes from prominent Founders other than Jefferson or Madison. As explained by one government researcher, such omission is an effective strategy:

> [L]iberal and secular bias is primarily accomplished by exclusion, by leaving out the opposing position. Such a bias is much harder to observe than a positive vilification or direct criticism, but it is the essence of censorship. It is effective not only because it is hard to observe—it isn't there—and therefore hard to counteract, but also because it makes only the liberal, secular positions familiar and plausible. [80]

The Court's failure to cite other Founders seems to imply either that no other Founders were qualified to address First Amendment issues, or that there exists no recorded statements from other Founders pertinent to the separation question. Both implications are wrong; numerous writings *do* exist; and since there were fifty-five at the Convention which framed the Constitution and ninety in the Congress which framed the First Amendment, numerous Founders *do* qualify as legitimate spokesmen.

For example, Gouverneur Morris of Pennsylvania was the most active member of the Constitutional Convention (speaking 173 times) and was the head of the committee which created the final wording for that document. As its penman, Gouverneur Morris certainly knew its intent, yet he never mentioned a "separation of church and state." On the contrary, he advocated that "education should teach the precepts of religion and the duties of man towards God." [81] Consequently, the Court omits Morris from its historical discussions.

Additionally, James Wilson was the second most active member of the Convention (speaking 168 times) and was appointed by President George Washington as an original Justice on the United States Supreme Court where he coauthored America's first legal text on the Constitution. James Wilson never mentions a "separation of church and state." On the contrary, in his legal writings he declared, "Far from being rivals or enemies, religion and law are twin sisters, friends, and mutual assistants." [82] Therefore, Wilson is not cited by the Court.

Similarly, it was Fisher Ames of Massachusetts who, on August 20, 1789, provided the final wording for the First Amendment as passed by the House of Representatives. [83] Fisher Ames therefore certainly knew the intent of the First Amendment, yet he never spoke of a "separation of church and state." On the contrary, he called for the Bible always to remain *the* principle textbook in America's classrooms. [84] Again, the Court chooses not to invoke Ames as an authority.

Furthermore, George Washington was the President of the Convention which framed the Constitution, and the President of the United States who called for and oversaw the formation of the Bill of Rights. Thus he fully understood the intent of those documents. Yet, not only did Washington never talk of a "separation of church and state," on the contrary, he advocated the inclusion of religious principles throughout national policies. [85] Clearly, the Court ignores his statements. Numerous other well-qualified Founders have similarly fallen into the Court's abyss of the forgotten or the forsaken.

— — — ··· — — —

Any objective, thorough examination of the five common historical "defenses" on which the contemporary Court so frequently relies to justify its separation doctrine proves that each is fatally flawed. Furthermore, they not only provide the Court no legitimate defense, they also reveal the Court's bias against the Founders' original intent for public religious expressions.

~11~

Establishing the American Philosophy of Government

Every human government ever established was the product of definable political theory; that is, each embraced a philosophy which, at least in its own eyes, justified its existence and manner of conducting affairs. The American government was no different.

The Declaration of Independence and the Constitution were well-devised plans for government based on specific political philosophies selected only after extensive research, study, and debate. This fact was acknowledged by Benjamin Franklin at the Constitutional Convention when he reminded the other delegates that:

> We have gone back to ancient history for models of government, and examined the different forms of those Republics. . . . And we have viewed modern states all round Europe. [1]

The result of our Founders' inquiries has been the longest ongoing constitutional-republic in the history of the world. Yet, from what sources did our Founding Fathers select the ideas for their successful political philosophy?

In an attempt to answer this question, a group of contemporary political scientists embarked on an ambitious ten-year project (beginning in the early nineteen seventies) to analyze more than 15,000 political writings from the Founding Era (1760-1805). [2] Those writings were examined with the goal of isolating and identifying the specific political sources cited amidst the debates in the establishment of American government. The identification of the sources which the Founders invoked would permit the origin of their political ideas to be determined.

From the 15,000 representative writings selected, the researchers first isolated some 3,154 quotations and then documented the original sources of those quotations. The following table presents the results of that study and identifies the specific political authorities used most frequently during the Founding Era:

Most Cited Thinkers [3]

Category	1760s	1770s	1780s	1790s	1800-05	% of total
Montesquieu	8%	7%	14%	4%	1%	8.3%
Blackstone	1%	3%	7%	11%	15%	7.9%
Locke	11%	7%	1%	1%	1%	2.9%
Hume	1%	1%	1%	6%	5%	2.7%
Plutarch	1%	3%	1%	2%	0%	1.5%
Beccaria	0%	1%	3%	0%	0%	1.5%
Cato	1%	1%	3%	0%	0%	1.4%
De Lolme	0%	0%	3%	1%	0%	1.4%
Puffendorf	4%	0%	1%	0%	5%	1.3%

Note: The total list contains more than 180 names. The use of 0% indicates less then .5% of the citations for a given decade rather than no citations whatsoever.

Baron Charles Secondat de Montesquieu

Montesquieu (1689-1755), a French attorney and author, was the most frequently invoked political source during the Founding Era; his *Spirit of Laws* (1748) provided a powerful influence on the thinking of our Founders. A fundamental premise of his political theory was that national stability and longevity could not be achieved unless a society was founded upon unchanging, transcendent laws:

> [S]ociety, notwithstanding all its revolutions, must repose on principles that do not change. [4]

What did Montesquieu believe to be the source of these immutable principles?

> The Christian religion, which ordains that men should love each other, would without doubt have every nation blest with the best civil, the best political laws; because these, next to this religion, are the greatest good that men can give and receive. [5]

Among many of Montesquieu's specific political theories that the Founders embraced was his belief that the powers of government should be kept separate and distinct, with one power able to check the power of another—what we now term "separation of powers" and "checks and balances." As John Quincy Adams noted:

At the time of the Declaration of Independence, Montesquieu was one of the most recent and esteemed writers upon government, and he had shown the division of powers to be essentially necessary to the preservation of liberty. [6]

Montesquieu had been very clear about "the division of powers":

> When the legislative and executive powers are united in the same person . . . there can be no liberty; because apprehensions may arise lest the same monarch or senate should enact tyrannical laws to execute them in a tyrannical manner. Again, there is no liberty if the power of judging be not separated from the legislative and executive powers. Were it joined with the legislative, the life and liberty of the subject would be exposed to arbitrary control; for the judge would then be the legislator. [7]

This separation of powers theory is rooted in the Biblical concept espoused in Jeremiah 17:9 that man naturally tends toward corruption. Following the religious teachings of the day, it was generally accepted that the unrestrained heart of man moved toward moral and civil degradation (what the Puritans, Calvinists, and others called the "depravity of man"). Thus it was logical that society would be much safer if all power did not repose in the same authority. With the power divided, if one branch became wicked, the others might still remain righteous and thus be able to check the wayward influence.

This reasoning was evident in the Founders' plan for government. For example, George Washington, in his "Farewell Address," confirmed that the Biblical teaching on the condition of the heart was sufficient reason for maintaining the separation of powers:

> A just estimate of that love of power, and proneness to abuse it, which predominates in the human heart, is sufficient to satisfy us for the truth of this position. The necessity of reciprocal checks in the exercise of political power by dividing and distributing it into different depositories . . . has been evinced [established]. [8]

Alexander Hamilton cited the same truth concerning the human heart:

> Why has government been instituted at all? Because the passions of men will not conform to the dictates of reason and justice without constraint. . . . [T]he infamy of a bad action is to be divided among a number, than . . . to fall singly upon one. [9]

The transcendency of laws and the separation of powers were two of the many identifiable aspects of Montesquieu's teachings to be found in the American system.

Sir William Blackstone

Blackstone (1723-1780), the second most invoked political authority during the Founding Era, was an English judge and law professor who authored the four-volume *Commentaries on the Laws of England (1765-69)*. His influence in America was so great that Edmund Burke told the British parliament:

> I hear that they have sold nearly as many of *Blackstone's Commentaries* in America as in England. [10]

Blackstone's *Commentaries* were purchased as the law book for the U. S. Senate, [11] and James Madison heartily endorsed Blackstone:

> I very cheerfully express my approbation of the proposed edition of Blackstone's *Commentaries*. [12]

Numerous other Founders also relied heavily on Blackstone, † and contributions from Blackstone's political theories may be found in the phraseology of the opening sentence of the Declaration of Independence:

> When in the course of human events it becomes necessary for one people to dissolve the political bands which have connected them with another and to assume among the powers of the earth the separate and equal station to which *the Laws of Nature and of Nature's God* entitles them ... (emphasis added)

The two phrases, "the Laws of Nature" and the laws "of Nature's God," had received significant attention in Blackstone's works. Notice his definition of "the law of nature," and the laws "of Nature's God"—or what was termed "the law of revelation":

> Man, considered as a creature, must necessarily be subject to the laws of his Creator, for he is entirely a dependent being. . . . And consequently, as man depends absolutely upon his Maker for every

---

† Blackstone is invoked as a key legal authority in the writings of Founders James Wilson, John Adams, Henry Laurens, Thomas Jefferson, John Marshall, James Madison, James Otis, James Kent, Joseph Story, Fisher Ames, *et. al.*

thing, it is necessary that he should in all points conform to his Maker's will. This will of his Maker is called the law of nature. . . . This law of nature, being coeval [coexistent] with mankind and dictated by God himself, is of course superior in obligation to any other. It is binding over all the globe, in all countries, and at all times: no human laws are of any validity, if contrary to this; and such of them as are valid derive all their force, and all their authority, mediately or immediately, from this original. . . . The doctrines thus delivered we call the revealed or divine law and they are to be found only in the holy Scriptures. These precepts, when revealed, are found upon comparison to be really a part of the original law of nature. . . . Upon these two foundations, the law of nature and the law of revelation, depend all human laws; that is to say, no human laws should be suffered to contradict these. [13]

These two aspects of natural law which Blackstone had identified (i.e., the law of nature and the Divine or revealed law of the Scriptures) are embodied in the Declaration's phrase "the Laws of Nature and of Nature's God"—the phrase the Founders invoked as the *legal* basis for their separation from Great Britain. Furthermore, Justice James Iredell (appointed to the Supreme Court by President George Washington) declares that Blackstone's views were relied upon by those who formed the Bill of Rights. [14]

Not only was Blackstone's influence apparent in our American government documents, it continued for decades afterwards as his *Commentaries* became the major foundation for the American system of jurisprudence. For example, in 1799, Justice Iredell noted:

[F]or near thirty years it [Blackstone's *Commentaries*] has been the manual of almost every student of law in the United States, and its uncommon excellence has also introduced it into the libraries, and often to the favorite reading of private gentlemen. [15]

And in 1810, Thomas Jefferson commented that American lawyers used Blackstone's with the same dedication and reverence that Muslims used the Koran. [16]

It was a fundamental precept under the natural law philosophy explained by Blackstone and embraced by the majority of the Founders that civil laws could not contradict the laws of God revealed either through nature or the Bible.

John Locke

Locke (1632-1704), a British philosopher and author, was the third most cited man in early American political thought. The Founders used many of his writings and especially drew from his *Two Treatises of Government* (1690). Locke concisely articulated the theory of social compact which helped the Founders formulate their belief on this issue. Social compact, as explained by Locke, is when:

> Men. . . . join and unite into a community for their comfortable, safe, and peaceable living one amongst another in a secure enjoyment of their properties and a greater security against any that are not of it. [17]

Of Locke's theory of social compact, William Findley, a Revolutionary soldier and a U. S. Congressmen, further explained:

> Men must first associate together, before they can form rules for their civil government. When those rules are formed and put in operation, they have become a civil society, or organized government. For this purpose, some rights of individuals must have been given up to the society but repaid many fold by the protection of life, liberty, and property afforded by the strong arm of civil government. This progress to human happiness being agreeable to the will of God, who loves and commands order, is the ordinance of God mentioned by the apostle Paul and . . . the apostle Peter. [18]

Locke's theory of social compact was manifested in the Declaration of Independence phrase that governments "derive their just powers from the consent of the governed."

Locke also believed that successful governments could be built only upon the transcendent, unchanging principles of natural law that were a subset of God's law:

> [T]he Law of Nature stands as an eternal rule to all men, legislators as well as others. The rules that they make for other men's actions must . . . be conformable to the Law of Nature, *i.e.* to the will of God. [19] "[L]aws human must be made according to the general laws of Nature, and without contradiction to any positive law of Scripture, otherwise they are ill made." [20]

So heavily did Locke draw from the Bible in developing his political theories that in his first treatise on government, he invoked the Bible in one thousand three hundred and forty nine references; in his second treatise, he cited it one hundred and fifty seven times. This is not surprising, however, since Locke was considered a theologian; [21] and among his many works were two major religious writings, *The Reasonableness of Christianity* (1696) and *A Vindication of the Reasonableness of Christianity* (1697).

Yet, despite his contributions as a theologian, many current political scientists and law professors claim that Locke was irreligious and even a deist. Interestingly, this same charge was raised during the Founding Era, and it drew a sharp response from law professor James Wilson—a signer of the Constitution and an original Justice on the U. S. Supreme Court. Wilson declared:

> I am equally far from believing that Mr. Locke was a friend to infidelity [a disbelief in the Bible and in Christianity [22]]. . . . The high reputation which he deservedly acquired for his enlightened attachment to the mild and tolerating doctrines of Christianity secured to him the esteem and confidence of those who were its friends. The same high and deserved reputation inspired others of very different views and characters . . . to diffuse a fascinating kind of lustre over their own tenets of a dark and sable hue. The consequence has been that the writings of Mr. Locke, one of the most able, most sincere, and most amiable assertors of Christianity and true philosophy, have been perverted to purposes which he would have deprecated and prevented [disapproved and opposed] had he discovered or foreseen them. [23]

From the works of John Locke, American political theorists drew the concept of social compact as well as a reinforcement of the concept that Natural Law was derived from God and the Scriptures.

Of the three theorists thus far examined, John Locke's writings chronologically preceded those of the other two; that is, he was the earliest of the preferred political theorists. Yet, from what source did he derive many of his political theories?

Richard Hooker

Many of Locke's ideas were specifically drawn from British theologian and legal philosopher Richard Hooker (1554-1600). [24] Hooker was a favorite not only of Locke but also of Founders like James Wilson who highly endorsed "the sublime language of the excellent Hooker," [25] "the judicious and excellent Hooker," [26] and "the sagacious Hooker." [27] Richard Hooker—as did Locke, Montesquieu, and Blackstone after him—began his legal discourses by first establishing the origin of all law. Hooker explained:

> And because the point about which we strive is the quality of our laws, our first entrance hereinto cannot better be made than with consideration of the nature of law in general . . . namely the law whereby the Eternal Himself doth work. Proceeding from hence to the law, first of Nature, then of Scripture, we shall have the easier access unto those things which come after to be debated. [28]

Hooker asserted that if God had specifically addressed an issue, that was the final word on that subject. He explained:

> For whereas God hath left sundry kinds of laws unto men, and by all those laws the actions of men are in some sort directed; they hold that one only law, the Scripture, must be the rule to direct in all things. [29]

Hooker believed that only God's principles provided a stable basis for government. He declared:

> [L]et polity [civil government] acknowledge itself indebted to religion. . . . So natural is the union of religion with justice that we may boldly deem there is neither where both are not. [30]

Hooker believed that man's natural rights proceeded from the Bible. He explained:

> The Scripture is fraught even with laws of Nature; insomuch that Gratian [a twelfth century philosopher] defining Natural Right . . . termeth "Natural Right, that which the 'Books of the Law and the Gospel do contain.' " [31]

These "natural rights" flowed from the "natural laws" given by God Himself and were never to be violated nor abridged by any government; hence, these rights were termed unalienable (several of them are listed in the Declaration of Independence).

Understanding "natural rights" as the unalienable rights listed in the Scriptures aids in understanding both the Danbury Baptists' complaint to President Jefferson and his response back to them in which he had invoked

Hooker's "natural rights" phraseology. Recall Jefferson's words:

> Believing with you that religion is a matter which lies solely between man and his God, that he owes account to none other for his faith or his worship, that the legislative powers of government reach actions only, and not opinions. . . . I shall see with sincere satisfaction the progress of those sentiments which tend to restore to man all his natural rights, convinced he has no **natural right** in opposition to his social duties. [32] (emphasis added)

The Baptists had been concerned that the government might try to regulate or limit public religious expression, but Jefferson had assured them that the exercise of any "natural right" ("that which the Books of the Law and the Gospel do contain") would never violate any civic standard.

Although Hooker was not among those most frequently cited by the Founders, he was nevertheless a clear influence upon the works of the major theorists utilized by the Founders.

David Hume

David Hume (1711-1776), a British philosopher and author of the three-volume work *Treatise of Human Nature* (1739-1740), was the fourth most cited political authority during the Founding Era. However, unlike the other preferred theorists of the Founders, Hume did not approach government theory from a Biblical viewpoint. As he himself explained:

> I expected, in entering on my literary course, that all the Christians . . . should be my enemies. [33]

Consequently, Hume was quoted by the Founders not so much to rely upon his political theories as to refute or to criticize them. For example, John Adams called Hume an "atheist, deist, and libertine [one not under the restraint of law or religion [34]]." [35] James Madison considered him a "bungling lawgiver" [36] with many of his theories being "manifestly erroneous"; [37] John Quincy Adams called him "the Atheist Jacobite"; [38] and Thomas Jefferson found him "endeavoring to mislead by either the suppression of a truth or by giving it a false coloring." [39] Jefferson actually lamented the influence that Hume had once had upon him:

> I remember well the enthusiasm with which I devoured it [Hume's work] when young, and the length of time, the research and

reflection which were necessary to eradicate the poison it had instilled into my mind. [40]

Signer of the Declaration John Witherspoon, in identifying many specific fallacies of Hume's theories, had urged:

> See David Hume's writings on morals throughout; where, besides leaving out entirely our duty to God (which he hath in common with many other late writers), he expressly founds justice upon power and conveniency, derides chastity, and turns many of the most important virtues into vices. [41]

In 1766, Dr. James Beattie, Professor of Moral Philosophy at Marisebal College in Scotland, authored his *Essay on the Nature and Immutability of Truth* to repudiate Hume's theories. Signer Benjamin Rush was thrilled with that work and wrote one of Beattie's friends, asking him to:

> Reverberate over and over my love to Dr. Beattie. I cannot think of him without fancying that I see Mr. Hume prostrate at his feet. He was the David who slew that giant of infidelity. [42]

Hume's fellow Englishman Richard Watson (who had written the rebuttal of Paine's work which had so pleased Patrick Henry [43]), described Hume as "revengeful, disgustingly vain, and an advocate of adultery and self-murder [suicide]." [44]

Of the Founders' most frequently invoked political authorities, Hume was the only non-Biblical theorist; and for those views he was attacked and discredited by many of the Founders.

Hugo Grotius and Baron Samuel de Puffendorf

In addition to Montesquieu, Blackstone, and Locke, several other political philosophers were highly esteemed by prominent Founders. For example, Alexander Hamilton recommended:

> Apply yourself, without delay, to the study of the law of nature. I would recommend to your perusal Grotius, Puffendorf, Locke, Montesquieu. [45]

Signer of the Declaration John Witherspoon similarly declared that "the chief writers upon government and politics are Grotius [and] Puffendorf." [46] These two were respected not only by Hamilton and Witherspoon, but also by

Benjamin Franklin, James Wilson, Samuel Adams, and numerous other Founders—a fact made clear in their political writings.

Hugo Grotius (1583-1645), a Dutch lawyer, theologian, and statesman, authored *Concerning the Law of War and Peace* (1625)—the first definitive text on international law—and *The Truth of the Christian Religion* (1627). Grotius' overall philosophy on law and civil government was clear; he argued that, "What God has shown to be His will that is law." [47] In fact, so important did Grotius consider God's principles to law and government that he declared:

> It may seem impossible for any state so long to subsist unless it were upheld by a constant particular care and by the power of a Divine hand. [48]

Baron Samuel de Puffendorf (1632-1694), a high political figure and Professor of the Law and Nature at universities both in Sweden and Germany, authored *Of the Law of Nature and Nations* (1672). Puffendorf also believed that civil societies and governments could not successfully exist apart from God and His principles. As he explained:

> 'Tis easier to build a city without ground to hold and support it than to make a Commonwealth either unite or subsist [survive] without the acknowledgment of a God and a Providence. [49]

In fact, Puffendorf explained that if a civil law violated the Divine law of God, men were required by God to disobey that civil law:

> [N]ot to obey God, and not to obey the Civil Magistrate if taken asunder, are both notoriously sins; and yet . . . when the Magistrate commands any thing contrary to the Divine Law, in this case disobedience to our earthly governors ceases to be evil because that law which binds us to conform to the will of human sovereigns is always understood with this provision and condition that they enjoin nothing repugnant to [in violation of] the laws of God. [50]

Grotius and Puffendorf were not only favorites among the Founders but were also considered the two men most responsible for establishing the "law of nature" as the basis of International Law.

The Law of Nature

As has been evident, the ideas of each political theorist embraced by the Founders were all built upon a common foundation: the "natural law," or "the laws of nature." Today, many claim that "natural law" was a purely secular standard. While it is true that in France "natural law" excluded all Divine revelation and was man-centered not God-centered, such was *not* the case in America. For example, according to James Wilson:

> In compassion to the imperfection of our internal powers, our all-gracious Creator, Preserver, and Ruler has been pleased to discover and enforce his laws by a revelation given to us immediately and directly from Himself. This revelation is contained in the Holy Scriptures. The moral precepts delivered in the sacred oracles form a part of the law of nature, are of the same origin and of the same obligation, operating universally and perpetually. . . . The law of nature and the law of revelation are both Divine: they flow, though in different channels, from the same adorable source. It is indeed preposterous to separate them from each other. The object of both is to discover the will of God and both are necessary for the accomplishment of that end. [51]

Zephaniah Swift, author of America's first law text, similarly explained:

> [T]he transcendent excellence and boundless power of the Supreme Deity . . . [has] impressed upon them those general and immutable laws that will regulate their operation through the endless ages of eternity. . . . These general laws . . . . are denominated the laws of nature. [52]

Other Founders were equally succinct that America's "natural law" was derived from God and His standards:

> In the supposed state of nature, all men are equally bound by the laws of nature, or to speak more properly, the laws of the Creator. [53]
> **SAMUEL ADAMS**

> [T]he laws of nature and of nature's God . . . of course presupposes the existence of a God, the moral ruler of the universe, and a rule of right and wrong, of just and unjust, binding upon man, preceding all institutions of human society and of government. [54] **JOHN QUINCY ADAMS**

> [T]he law of nature, "which, being coeval with mankind and dictated by God himself, is, of course, superior in obligation to

any other. It is binding over all the globe, in all countries, and at all times. No human laws are of any validity, if contrary to this." [55] **ALEXANDER HAMILTON** (quoting Blackstone)

[The] "Law of nature" is a rule of conduct arising out of the natural relations of human beings established by the Creator and existing prior to any positive precept [human law].... These ... have been established by the Creator and are, with a peculiar felicity of expression, denominated in Scripture, "ordinances of heaven." [56] **NOAH WEBSTER**

[T]he ... natural law was given by the Sovereign of the Universe to all mankind. [57] **JOHN JAY**, FIRST CHIEF-JUSTICE U. S. SUPREME COURT

The law of nature being coeval with mankind and dictated by God Himself is of course superior to [and] the foundation of all other laws. [58] **WILLIAM FINDLEY**, REVOLUTIONARY SOLDIER; U. S. CONGRESS

[T]he ... law established by the Creator, which has existed from the beginning, extends over the whole globe, is everywhere and at all times binding upon mankind. ... [This] is the law of God by which he makes his way known to man and is paramount to all human control. [59] **RUFUS KING**, SIGNER OF THE CONSTITUTION

God ... is the promulgator as well as the author of natural law. [60] **JAMES WILSON**, SIGNER OF THE CONSTITUTION; U. S. SUPREME COURT JUSTICE

These, and many other sources, clearly document that the Founders' view of the "law of nature" was *not* secular, but rather a Biblical view.

The Primary Influence

Despite the Founders' heavy reliance upon specific political theorists, the researchers referenced at the beginning of this chapter discovered that one direct source of inspiration for their ideas was cited far and away more than any other. In fact, the Founders cited this source four times more often than either Montesquieu or Blackstone and twelve times more often than Locke. What was that source? It was the Bible—accounting for 34 percent of the direct quotes in the political writings of the Founding Era. The following chart indicates the broad sources of the political quotes of the Founding Era:

Distribution of Citations [61]

Category	1760s	1770s	1780s	1790s	1800-05	% of total
Bible	24%	44%	34%	29%	38%	34%
Enlightenment [†]	32%	18%	24%	21%	18%	22%
Whig [††]	10%	20%	19%	17%	15%	18%
Common-Law [†††]	12%	4%	9%	14%	20%	11%
Classical [††††]	8%	11%	10%	11%	2%	9%
Other	14%	3%	4%	8%	7%	6%
Total	100%	100%	100%	100%	100%	100%
Number of citations	216	544	1,306	674	414	3,154

The fact that the Founders quoted the Bible more frequently than any other source is indisputably a significant commentary on its importance in the foundation of our government. In fact, some have even conceded that "historians are discovering that the Bible, perhaps even more than the Constitution, is our Founding document." [63]

---

† This category includes the eighteenth century philosophical writers who based their approaches to the political and social issues of the day upon scientific and intellectual reasonings. Nearly three-quarters of these citations are from conservative enlightenment writers (e.g., Montesquieu, Locke, Puffendorf, etc.) with the remainder coming from the more radical writers (e.g., Voltaire, Diderot, Rousseau, etc.). [62]

†† "Whigs" were those who advocated popular rights and were for American independence; Tories were those who advocated royal rights and were for submission.

††† "Common-Law" writers dealt with the "rules, principles, and customs which have been received from our ancestors and by which courts have been governed in their judicial decisions" (Webster's 1828 Dictionary).

†††† "Classical" refers to the ancient Greek and Roman authors (i.e., Aristotle, Plato, Cicero, Virgil, Tacitus, Plutarch, etc.).

~12~
A Changing Standard—
Toward A New Constitution?

The Founders' Biblical natural law philosophy remained the unques-tioned standard for law and government until the turn of this century. At that time, a different philosophy was beginning to gain strength among judges and educators. By the mid-twentieth century, this competing phi-losophy, often termed "relativism" (or "pragmatism"), had become main-stream in a number of academic disciplines. The encyclopedia describes the basic tenets of relativism:

> [V]iews are to be evaluated relative to the societies or cultures in which they appear and are not to be judged true or false, or good or bad, based on some overall criterion but are to be assessed within the context in which they occur. Thus, what is right or good or true to one person or group may not be considered so by others. . . . there [are] no absolute standards. . . . "Man is the measure of all things," and . . . each man [can] be his own measure. . . . [C]annibalism, incest, and other practices considered taboo are just variant kinds of behavior, to be appreciated as acceptable in some cultures and not in others. . . . [Relativism] urge[s] suspension of judgment about right or wrong. [1]

When applied in law, "relativism" is called "legal positivism." According to constitutional scholar and law professor John Eidsmoe, this philosophy is characterized by the following five major theses:

1. There are no objective, God-given standards of law, or if there are, they are irrelevant to the modern legal system.

2. Since God is not the author of law, the author of law must be man; in other words, the law is law simply because the highest human authority, the state, has said it is law and is able to back it up.

3. Since man and society evolve, therefore law must evolve as well.

4. Judges, through their decisions, guide the evolution of law.

5. To study law, get at the original sources of law—the decisions of judges. [2]

This philosophy ("positivism") was introduced in the 1870s when Harvard Law School Dean Christopher Columbus Langdell (1826-1906) applied Darwin's premise of evolution to jurisprudence. Langdell reasoned that since man evolved, then his laws must also evolve; and judges should guide both the evolution of law and the Constitution. Consequently, Langdell introduced the case-law study method under which students would study judges' decisions rather than the Constitution.

Under the case-law approach, history, precedent, and the views and beliefs of the Founders not only became irrelevant, they were even considered hindrances to the successful evolution of a society. As explained by a leading relativist (John Dewey) in 1927:

> The belief in political fixity, of the sanctity of some form of state consecrated by the efforts of our fathers and hallowed by tradition, is one of the stumbling-blocks in the way of orderly and directed change. [3]

Langdell's case-law approach was gradually embraced by other law schools, and the result was a diminishing belief in absolutes. In fact, within a few short years (by the 1930s), *Blackstone's Commentaries on the Law* had been widely discarded. *Blackstone's* was deemed to present an outdated approach to law since it taught that certain rights and wrongs—particularly those related to human behavior—did not change.

Roscoe Pound (1870-1964) strongly endorsed the positivistic philosophy introduced by Langdell. As a prominent twentieth-century legal educator, Pound helped institutionalize positivism. Having served as a professor at four different law schools and as Dean of the law schools at Harvard and at the University of Nebraska, his influence was considerable—and his vision for law was clear:

> We have . . . the same task in jurisprudence that has been achieved in philosophy, in the natural sciences, and in politics. We have to **rid ourselves of this sort of legality** and to attain a pragmatic [evolutionary], a **sociological** legal science. [4] (emphasis added)

According to Pound, no longer should it be the mission of jurisprudence to focus on the narrow field of legal interpretation; the goal should be to become a sociological force to influence the development of society.

The effects of these teachings by Langdell and Pound—and others like them—had a direct effect on the Supreme Court as individuals who embraced this philosophy were gradually appointed to the Court. For example, Oliver Wendell Holmes, Jr. (1841-1932), appointed to the Supreme Court in 1902, explained that original intent and precedent held little value:

> [T]he justification of a law for us cannot be found in the fact that our fathers always have followed it. It must be found in some help which the law brings toward reaching a social end. [5]

Consequently, during his three decades on the Court, Holmes argued that decisions should not be based upon natural law and its fixed standards, but rather upon:

> The felt necessities of the time, the prevalent moral and political theories . . . [for] the prejudices which judges share with their fellowmen have had a good deal more to do than the syllogism [legal reasoning process] in determining the rules by which men should be governed. [6]

Louis Brandeis (1856-1941), who served on the Court for 23 years following his 1916 appointment, also urged the Court to break new ground and to lead society in new directions. In *New State Ice Co.* v. *Liebmann* (1932), he declared:

> If we would guide by the light of reason, we must let our minds be bold. [7]

Benjamin Cardozo (1870-1938), appointed to the Supreme Court in 1932, openly refused to be bound by any concept of transcendent laws or fixed rights and wrongs:

> If there is any law which is back of the sovereignty of the state, and superior thereto, it is not law in such a sense as to concern the judge or lawyer, however much it concerns the statesman or the moralist. [8]

Like many of his predecessors, Cardozo also encouraged the Court to eliminate the use of its foundational precedents. He even condoned the prospect of the Court departing from its traditional role and instead assuming the function of lawmaker. As he explained:

> I take judge-made law as one of the existing realities of life. [9]

Reflective of this same philosophy, Charles Evans Hughes (1862-1948), the Court's Chief Justice from 1930 to 1941, declared that:

> We are under a Constitution, but the Constitution is what the judges say it is. [10]

Although prominent educators and individual Justices faithfully endeavored to advance this philosophy in the first half of the century, it was not until the late 1940s that their movement had gained the sufficiently widespread number of adherents to produce radical societal change. The overall change in direction was especially visible after 1953, when Earl Warren (1891-1974) became Chief Justice of the Court. Warren's words in *Trop* v. *Dulles* (1958) foreshadowed what was soon to become standard practice in American jurisprudence:

> The [Constitutional] Amendment must draw its meaning from the evolving standards of decency that mark the progress of a maturing society. [11]

During Warren's sixteen year tenure, the Court indeed became a powerful societal force, striking down numerous long-standing historical practices, while proudly acknowledging that it was doing so without precedent. [12] In other words, the Court publicly announced that it had finally arrived at its fully evolutionary state, no longer being bound by history or precedent.

Despite the fact that legal positivism is frequently accompanied by dramatic social upheavals, there is one of its tenets which the public finds appealing: the fact that governments *do* need to change from time to time (to "evolve") and to make some social adjustments (i.e., the ending of slavery, the granting of suffrage to women, etc.). However, despite the public's fascination with occasional change, such change must not occur through the Court. Article V of the Constitution establishes the proper means whereby the people may adjust, or "evolve," their government:

> The Congress, whenever two thirds of both Houses shall deem it necessary, shall propose amendments to this Constitution, or, on the application of the legislatures of two thirds of the several States, shall call a convention for proposing amendments.

Very simply, the *people* may amend the Constitution to update or modernize it as they think necessary. As Samuel Adams forcefully declared:

[T]he people *alone* have an incontestable, unalienable, and indefeasible right to institute government and to reform, alter, or totally change the same when their protection, safety, prosperity, and happiness require it. And the federal Constitution, according to the mode prescribed therein, has already undergone such amendments in several parts of it as from experience has been judged necessary. [13] (emphasis added)

George Washington, in his "Farewell Address," warned America to adhere strictly to this manner of changing the meaning of the Constitution:

If, in the opinion of the people, the distribution or the modification of the constitutional powers be in any particular wrong, let it be corrected by an amendment in the way which the Constitution designates. But let there be no change by usurpation [wrongful seizure of power]; for though this, in one instance, may be the instrument of good, it is the customary weapon by which free governments are destroyed. [14]

The real danger of positivism rests not in the fact that societal corrections are needed, but rather in the fact that they are made by unelected Justices—individuals whose personal values not only often do not reflect those of "we the people" but who are virtually unaccountable to the people. If change, or societal "evolution," is not directed by the people themselves, then our form of government becomes what Jefferson termed "an oligarchy," [15] and as Washington pointed out, "is the customary weapon by which free governments are destroyed."

If the evolution of society still rested in the hands of the people as originally intended, then America today would still retain much of what Courts have struck down over recent decades. (For example, national polls regularly show that some three-fourths of the nation approve of voluntary school prayer; [16] four-fifths of the nation oppose homosexual behavior; [17] nine-tenths oppose the use of abortion as a means of convenience birth control; [18] and similar numbers are recorded on numerous other issues.) Very simply, the allegedly evolving values of the nation have not been reflected in the Court's evolution of the Constitution.

~13~
A Constitution In a State of Flux

With the new measure of constitutionality being only the opinion of the Justices, standards now change as rapidly as the Justices. This causes an uncertainty for society; and, in fact, often establishes a dubious standard which, in effect, is no standard at all. For example:

- It is constitutional for congressional chaplains to pray (MARSH v. CHAMBERS, 1983 [1]), but unconstitutional for students to read those prayers (STATE BOARD OF EDUC. v. BOARD OF EDUC. OF NETCONG, 1970 [2]).

- It is constitutional to display the Ten Commandments on public property (ANDERSON v. SALT LAKE CITY CORP., 1973 [3]), but unconstitutional either to allow students to see them (STONE v. GRAHAM, 1980 [4]) or to display them at a courthouse (HARVEY v. COBB COUNTY, 1993 [5]).

- It is constitutional to begin public meetings with invocations (BOGEN v. DOTY 1979, [6] and MARSH v. CHAMBERS, 1983 [7]), but unconstitutional to allow students to hear invocations in a public meeting (LEE v. WEISMAN, 1992 [8] and HARRIS v. JOINT SCHOOL DIST., 1994 [9]).

- It was constitutional to display a créche and depict the origins of Christmas in 1984 (LYNCH v. DONNELLY [10]), but only five years later it was unconstitutional to do so (ALLEGHENY v. ACLU [11]).

Without a transcendent basis for laws (that which both Montesquieu and Benjamin Rush termed "principles that do not change" [12]), it is obvious that courts are unable to maintain a lasting consensus on virtually any issue. Notice several additional examples:

On Personal Appearance

On the one hand, the freedom to govern one's own personal appearance *is* a fundamental constitutional right:

> The Founding Fathers wrote an amendment for speech and assembly; even they did not deem it necessary to write an

amendment for personal appearance. . . . [T]he Constitution guarantees . . . the right to govern one's personal appearance. [13] BISHOP v. COLAW, 1971; see also WALLACE v. FORD, 1972 [14]

On the other hand, the right to govern one's personal appearance is *not* a fundamental constitutional right:

A public schoolteacher, while teaching, may not wear distinctly religious garb. [15] FINOT v. PASADENA CITY BOARD OF EDUCATION, 1967

On Student-led Prayers

On the one hand, student led, student-initiated graduation prayers *are* constitutional:

[P]ermitting public high school seniors to choose student volunteers to deliver nonsectarian, nonproselytizing invocations at their graduation ceremonies does *not* violate the Constitution's Establishment Clause. [16] JONES v. CLEAR CREEK INDEPENDENT SCHOOL DISTRICT, 1992 (emphasis added)

On the other hand, those same prayers are *not* constitutional:

[T]he fact that students set the assembly agenda and make decisions as to whether a prayer shall occur, who shall say it, and how it shall be said *is* . . . an Establishment Clause violation. [17] HARRIS v. JOINT SCHOOL DISTRICT, 1994 (emphasis added)

On Children

On the one hand, children are *not* wards of the state:

[T]he fundamental theory of liberty upon which all governments in this Union repose excludes any general power of the state to standardize its children. . . . The child is not the mere creature of the state. PIERCE v. SOCIETY OF SISTERS, 1925; [18] REED v. VAN HOVEN, 1965 [19]

On the other hand, children *are* wards of the state:

The courts for many years have held: Children are the wards of the state. [20] STATE BOARD OF EDUCATION v. BOARD OF EDUCATION OF NETCONG, 1970; see also HARRIS v. JOINT SCHOOL DISTRICT, 1994 [21]

However, not only do contemporary courts frequently repudiate themselves, they also regularly repudiate the rulings of their predecessors on identical issues. For example:

On Profanity

The current position:

> Appellant was . . . wearing a jacket bearing the words "F___ the Draft" in a corridor of the Los Angeles Courthouse. . . . [T]he [California statute prohibiting public use of such words] infringed his rights to freedom of expression guaranteed by the First and Fourteenth Amendments of the Federal Constitution. . . . This is not . . . an obscenity case. . . . That the air may at times seem filled with verbal cacophony [a harsh, jarring, discordant sound] is, in this sense not a sign of weakness but of strength. [22] COHEN v. CALIFORNIA, 1971

The previous position:

> Nothing could be more offensive to the virtuous part of the community, or more injurious to the tender morals of the young, than to declare such profanity lawful . . . and shall we form an exception in these particulars to the rest of the civilized world? [23] PEOPLE v. RUGGLES, 1811

On Lewdness and Indecency

In *Erznoznik v. City of Jacksonville*, the city sought to restrict adult movies shown in a public drive-in theater because the screen was facing a church and two public streets frequented by children. However, the Supreme Court struck down the ordinance, explaining that it could not "be justified as an exercise of the [city] . . . for the protection of children." [24]

Notice the previous position:

> The destruction of morality renders the power of the government invalid. . . . The corruption of the public mind, in general, and debauching the manners of youth, in particular, by lewd and obscene pictures exhibited to view, must necessarily be attended with the most injurious consequences. . . . No man is permitted to corrupt the morals of the people. [25] COMMONWEALTH v. SHARPLESS, 1815

On Blasphemy

In *Grove* v. *Mead School District* (1985), Cassie Grove, a high school sophomore, had been required to read *A Learning Tree* for her English Literature class. She filed suit to have that book removed from the curriculum because she objected to being forced to read several portions, including those:

> Declaring Jesus Christ to be a "poor white trash God," or "a long-legged white son-of-a-b___h." [26]

The court refused to rule in her favor or to remove the book from the school's required curriculum; all students taking that class would continue to use that book.

Notice the previous position:

> "Jesus Christ was a bast___d, and his mother must be a whore".... Such words . . . were an offense at common law. . . . [I]t tends to corrupt the morals of the people, and to destroy good order. Such offenses. . . . are treated as affecting the essential interests of civil society. [27] PEOPLE v. RUGGLES, 1811

On Deterring No Religious Belief

In *Walz* v. *Tax Commission* (1970), the Court stated, as it frequently does, that *all* religious beliefs were to be tolerated:

> The fullest realization of true religious liberty requires that government . . . effect no favoritism among sects or between religion and nonreligion, and that it *work deterrence of no religious belief.* [28] (emphasis added)

Notice the previous position:

> There have been sects which denied as a part of their religious tenets that there should be any marriage tie, and advocated promiscuous intercourse of the sexes as prompted by the passions of its members. . . . Should a sect of [these] kinds ever find its way into this country, swift punishment would follow the carrying into effect of its doctrines, and no heed would be given to the pretence that . . . their supporters could be protected in their

exercise by the Constitution of the United States. Probably never before in the history of this country has it been seriously contended that the whole punitive power of the government for acts, recognized by the general consent of the Christian world . . . must be suspended in order that the tenets of a religious sect . . . may be carried out without hindrance. [29] DAVIS v. BEASON, 1890

They [the Founders] could not admit this [religious tolerance] as a civil justification of human sacrifices, or parricide [killing one's parents], or infanticide, or thuggism [religious murders], or of such modes of worship as the disgusting and corrupting rites of the Dionysia, and Aphrodisia, and Eleusinia, and other festivals of Greece and Rome. They did not mean that the pure moral customs which Christianity has introduced should be without legal protection because some pagan, or other religionist, or anti-religionist, should advocate as matter of conscience concubinage, polygamy, incest, free love, and free divorce, or any of them. [30] COMMONWEALTH v. NESBIT, 1859

On Atheism and Non-Religion

The current position:

- [T]hese words [from the First Amendment] . . . are recognized as guaranteeing religious liberty and equality to "the infidel, the atheist." [31] ALLEGHENY v ACLU, 1989

- Excluding agnosticism and atheism from First Amendment religion clauses is too narrow a view. [32] THERIAULT v. SILBER, 1977

- Atheism may be a religion under the establishment clause. [33] MALNAK v. YOGI, 1977

- Secular humanism may be a religion for purposes of First Amendment. [34] GROVE v. MEAD SCHOOL DIST., 1985

- Also included under the protection of the religion clauses of the First Amendment would be religions which do not teach a belief in the existence of God, including Buddhism, Taoism, Ethical Culture, Secular Humanism, and others. [35] TORCASO v. WATKINS, 1961

The previous position:

> [The First Amendment] embraces all who believe in the existence of God as well . . . as Christians of every denomination. . . . [T]his provision does not extend to atheists, because they do not believe in God or religion; and therefore . . . their sentiments and professions, whatever they may be, cannot be called *religious* sentiments and professions. [36] COMMONWEALTH v. KNEELAND, 1838

In earlier decisions on the First Amendment, neither atheism nor secular humanism qualified as "religions"—for obvious reasons. Notice the comprehensive definition of "religion" from Webster's original dictionary:

> Religion: [I]ncludes a belief in the being and perfections of God, in the revelation of His will to man, and in man's obligation to obey His commands, in a state of reward and punishment, and in man's accountableness to God; and also true godliness or piety of life with the practice of all moral duties. . . . [T]he practice of moral duties without a belief in a Divine Lawgiver, and without reference to His will or commands, is *not* religion. [37] (emphasis added)

At a minimum, the Founders identified a religion by its belief in some Supreme Being; without that belief, there could be no "religion." Yet, by changing this standard of measurement, and by considering nonreligion as a religion, contemporary courts have created an irreconcilable conflict.

Recall that the Court has been very emphatic that no preference can be given either to religion or to nonreligion:

> [G]overnment [must] . . . effect no favoritism . . . between religion and nonreligion. [38] WALZ v. TAX COMMISSION, 1970

> The First Amendment mandates governmental neutrality between religion and religion, and between religion and nonreligion. [39] EPPERSON v. ARKANSAS, 1968

Consider the difficulty of maintaining this government neutrality when atheism and secular humanism are considered religions. For example, courts prohibit the inclusion of religious activities in schools because the presence of a religious activity constitutes an endorsement of religion; however, if religious activities are excluded, then nonreligion has been given preference and thus is being endorsed. Therefore, since either religion or nonreligion will be endorsed by its presence, how can "neutrality" and "no favoritism" be maintained under such standards?

Court decisions now regularly erect standards which Justice William Rehnquist described as being "neither principled nor unified." [40] To support this charge, Rehnquist detailed a litany of paradoxes arising under the Court's current standards:

> [A] State *may* lend to parochial school children geography textbooks that contain maps of the United States, but the State *may not* lend maps of the United States for use in geography class. A State *may* lend textbooks on American colonial history, but it *may not* lend a film on George Washington, or a film projector to show it in history class. A State *may* lend classroom workbooks, but *may not* lend workbooks in which the parochial school children write, thus rendering them nonreusable. A State *may* pay for bus transportation to religious schools but *may not* pay for bus transportation from the parochial school to the public zoo or natural history museum for a field trip. A State *may* pay for diagnostic services conducted in the parochial school but therapeutic services must be given in a different building; speech and hearing "services" conducted by the State inside the sectarian school are forbidden, but the State *may* conduct speech and hearing diagnostic testing inside the sectarian school. Exceptional parochial school students may receive counseling, but it must take place outside of the parochial school, such as in a trailer parked down the street. A State *may* give cash to a parochial school to pay for the administration of state-written tests and state-ordered reporting services, but it *may not* provide funds for teacher-prepared tests on secular subjects. Religious instruction *may not* be given in public school, but the public school *may* release students during the day for religion classes elsewhere, and *may* enforce attendance at those classes with its truancy laws. [41] (emphasis added)

Clearly, with the judicial departure from transcendent guidelines and values, and with the advent of positivism, the "standards" the courts now use are both confusing and contradictory, and therefore are not genuine standards at all.

~14~
Identifying the Spirit of the Constitution

As a result of the two distinctly differing philosophies of constitutional interpretation, there have now been two distinct eras of judicial decisions. The fundamental difference between these two was summed up by a U. S. Attorney General:

> [U]nder the old system the question was *how* to read the Constitution; under the new approach, the question is *whether* to read the Constitution. [1] (emphasis added)

The second era, which began with the slow accumulation of positivistic Justices on the Court throughout the 1930s and 1940s, was not fully actuated until the Court's 1962-63 decisions. Those decisions openly repudiated the transcendent, Biblical, natural-law standards which had prevailed—or had at least not been set aside—since the time of the Founders, and instituted legal positivism as the replacement.

Today, there are avid proponents of both systems; yet does either really make a difference? Does either actually affect our lifestyle? The answer to that question rests in this ancient proverb:

> Every good tree bears good fruit, but a bad tree bears bad fruit. Thus, by their fruit you will recognize them. MATTHEW 7:17, 20 (NIV)

Very simply, to determine if either philosophy had any substantial impact, compare the societal results from early years against those of more recent years—simply examine the "fruits." In support of this approach, signer of the Declaration John Witherspoon affirmed:

> [T]his rule of trying every principle . . . by its fruits. . . . is certain and infallible. . . . There seems, indeed, to be an exact analogy between this rule in religious matters, and reason in our common and civil concerns. Reason is the best guide and director of human life. [2]

The following charts are representative of several areas in which the Court has implemented its new approach and each accentuates the year in which positivism became the enforced standard. The correlations are striking.

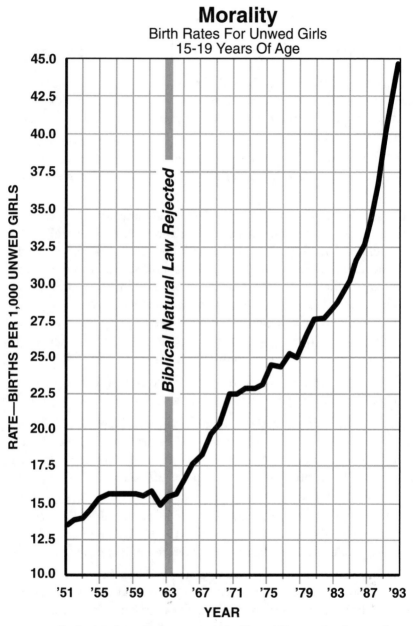

Morality
Birth Rates For Unwed Girls
15-19 Years Of Age

Biblical Natural Law Rejected

RATE—BIRTHS PER 1,000 UNWED GIRLS

YEAR

Basic data from Department of Health and Human Services and
Statistical Abstract of the United States.

Violent Behavior
Violent Crime: Number Of Offenses

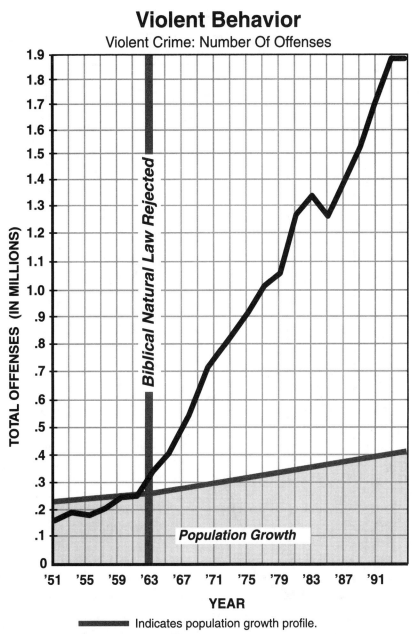

Biblical Natural Law Rejected

Population Growth

TOTAL OFFENSES (IN MILLIONS)

YEAR

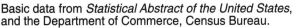 Indicates population growth profile.

Basic data from *Statistical Abstract of the United States*, and the Department of Commerce, Census Bureau.

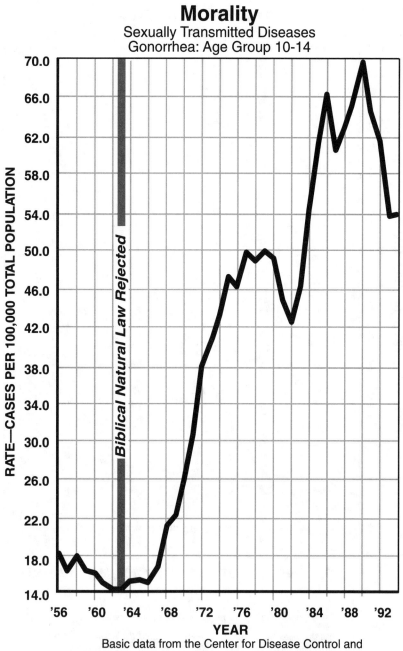

Morality
Sexually Transmitted Diseases
Gonorrhea: Age Group 10-14

Biblical Natural Law Rejected

RATE—CASES PER 100,000 TOTAL POPULATION

YEAR

Basic data from the Center for Disease Control and
Department of Health and Human Resources.

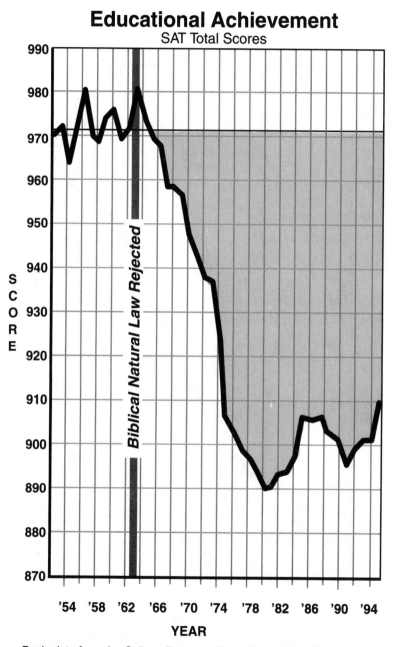

Educational Achievement
SAT Total Scores

Basic data from the College Entrance Exam Board, New York.

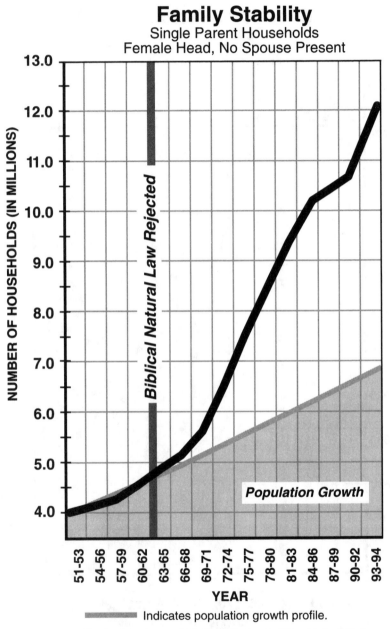

Family Stability
Single Parent Households
Female Head, No Spouse Present

NUMBER OF HOUSEHOLDS (IN MILLIONS)

Biblical Natural Law Rejected

Population Growth

YEAR

Indicates population growth profile.

Basic data from *Statistical Abstract of the United States,* and the Department of Commerce, Census Bureau.

The changes suggest that the new positivistic policies have resulted in drastic and unacceptable changes in morality, criminal behavior, education, and family stability—and these are but a few examples. [†] Nevertheless, these are sufficient to suggest strongly that the institutionalization of positivism and the abandonment of the transcendent Biblical natural law principles have not produced national improvement or prosperity but have worked in the opposite direction.

While the Court's change of standards has perhaps been a display of poor judgment, the Court's actions have actually been illegal under the standards of original intent. Furthermore, they have violated the value system of "the laws of nature and of nature's God" established in the Declaration of Independence.

Even though contemporary courts now regularly violate that legal standard, few today consider such violations significant for they believe the Constitution to be independent of the Declaration. This incorrect belief is of recent origin; in fact, it was rejected by earlier generations. As Samuel Adams pointed out:

> Before the formation of this Constitution. . . . [t]his Declaration of Independence was received and ratified by all the States in the Union and has *never* been disannulled. [3] (emphasis added)

For generations after the ratification of the Constitution, the Declaration was considered a primary guiding document in American constitutional government. In fact, well into the twentieth century, the Declaration and the Constitution were viewed as inseparable and *inter*dependent—not independent—documents.

Perhaps the proper relationship between the Declaration and the Constitution is best understood by a comparison with the relationship between a corporation's Articles of Incorporation and its By-Laws—the two documents vital to its legal existence. The Articles of Incorporation call the entity into legal existence, and the By-Laws then explain how it will be governed. However, the governing of the corporation under its By-Laws must always be within the framework and purposes set forth in its Articles; the By-Laws may neither nullify nor supersede the Articles.

---

† For an in-depth statistical examination, with numerous additional charts, see a separate work by David Barton: *America: To Pray or Not to Pray?*

Such is the relationship between the Declaration and the Constitution; the Declaration is America's articles of incorporation and the Constitution is its bylaws. The Constitution neither abolished nor replaced what the Declaration had established; it only provided the specific details of how American government would operate under the principles set forth in the Declaration.

Today, as the knowledge of this interdependent relationship has been widely lost or ignored, many individuals complain of the difficulties arising from the fact that the Founders placed no explicit moral values or rights and wrongs into the Constitution. However, the Founders needed to place no values in the Constitution (the bylaws) for they had already done so in the Declaration (the articles of incorporation).

Is there proof that the Founders believed that the Declaration was *the* foundational document in our Constitutional form of government? The answer is an emphatic, "Yes!" Notice, for example, that in Article VII, the Constitution attaches itself to the Declaration:

> Done in convention by the unanimous consent of the States present the seventeenth day of September in the Year of our Lord one thousand seven hundred and eighty seven, *and of the independence of the United States of America the twelfth.* (emphasis added)

Furthermore, under the Constitution, the Founders dated their government acts from the year of the Declaration rather than the Constitution. Notice a few examples (emphasis added in each quote):

> Given under my hand and the seal of the United States, in the city of New York, the 14th day of August, A.D. 1790, and *in the fifteenth year of the Sovereignty and Independence of the United States.* By the President: **GEORGE WASHINGTON** [4]

> In testimony whereof I have caused the seal of the United States to be affixed to these presents, and signed the same with my hand. Done at Philadelphia, the 22nd day of July, A.D. 1797, and *of the Independence of the United States* the twenty-second. By the President: **JOHN ADAMS** [5]

> In testimony whereof I have caused the seal of the United States to be hereunto affixed, and signed the same with my hand. Done at the city of Washington, the 16th day of July, A.D. 1803, and *in*

the twenty-eighth year of the Independence of the United States. By the President: THOMAS JEFFERSON [6]

Given under my hand and the seal of the United States at the city of Washington, the 9th day of August, A.D. 1809, and *of the Independence of the said United States* the thirty-fourth. By the President: JAMES MADISON [7]

Given under my hand, at the city of Washington, this 28th day of April, A.D. 1818, and *of the Independence of the United States the forty-second.* By the President: JAMES MONROE [8]

Given under my hand, at the city of Washington, this 17th day of March, A.D. 1827, and *the fifty-first year of the Independence of the United States.* By the President: JOHN QUINCY ADAMS [9]

Given under my hand, at the city of Washington, this 11th day of May, A.D. 1829, and *the fifty-third of the Independence of the United States.* By the President: ANDREW JACKSON [10] &c.

Additional evidence of the importance of the Declaration in our constitutional government is provided by the fact that the admission of territories as States into the United States was often predicated on an assurance by the State that its constitution would violate neither the Constitution nor the principles (i.e., the value system) of the Declaration. For example, notice these enabling acts granted by Congress for various States:

[T]he constitution, when formed, shall be republican, and not repugnant to the Constitution of the United States and *the principles of the Declaration of Independence.* COLORADO [11]

[T]he constitution, when formed, shall be republican, and not repugnant to the Constitution of the United States and *the principles of the Declaration of Independence.* NEVADA [12]

The constitution, when formed, shall be republican, and not repugnant to the Constitution of the United States and *the principles of the Declaration of Independence.* NEBRASKA [13]

The constitution shall be republican in form. . . and shall not be repugnant to the Constitution of the United States and *the principles of the Declaration of Independence.* OKLAHOMA [14]

In the Declaration, the Founders established the foundation and the core values on which the Constitution was to operate; it was never to be interpreted apart from those values. This was made clear by John Quincy Adams in his famous oration, "The Jubilee of the Constitution." Adams explained:

> [T]he virtue which had been infused into the Constitution of the United States . . . was no other than the concretion of those abstract principles which had been first proclaimed in the Declaration of Independence. . . . This was the platform upon which the Constitution of the United States had been erected. Its virtues, its republican character, consisted in its conformity to the principles proclaimed in the Declaration of Independence and as its administration . . . was to depend upon the . . . virtue, or in other words, of those principles proclaimed in the Declaration of Independence and embodied in the Constitution of the United States. [15]

Generations later, President Abraham Lincoln reminded the nation of that same truth:

> These communities, by their representatives in old Independence Hall, said to the whole world of men: "We hold these truths to be self-evident: that all men are created equal; that they are endowed by their Creator with certain inalienable rights; that among these are life, liberty, and the pursuit of happiness." . . . . They erected a beacon to guide their children, and their children's children, and the countless myriads who should inhabit the earth in other ages. . . . [T]hey established these great self-evident truths that . . . their posterity might look up again to the Declaration of Independence and take courage to renew that battle which their fathers began, so that truth and justice and mercy and all the humane and Christian virtues might not be extinguished from the land. . . . Now, my countrymen, if you have been taught doctrines conflicting with the great landmarks of the Declaration of Independence . . . let me entreat you to come back. . . . [C]ome back to the truths that are in the Declaration of Independence. [16]

The interdependent relationship between these two documents was clear, and even the U. S. Supreme Court openly affirmed it. At the turn of the century (1897), the Court declared:

The latter [Constitution] is but the body and the letter of which the former [Declaration of Independence] is the thought and the spirit, and it is always safe to read the letter of the Constitution in the spirit of the Declaration of Independence. [17]

The Constitution cannot be properly interpreted nor correctly applied apart from the principles set forth in the Declaration; the two documents must be used together. Furthermore, under America's government as originally established, a violation of the principles of the Declaration was just as serious as a violation of the provisions of the Constitution.

Nonetheless, Courts over the past half-century have steadily divorced the Constitution from the transcendent values of the Declaration, replacing them instead with their own contrivances. The results have been reprehensible— a series of vacillating and unpredictable standards incapable of providing national stability.

~15~
Maintaining Constitutional Integrity: A Government of the People

Just as the Founders defined the value system under which the government was to operate, they also defined the function of each of its three branches. And just as the Court has largely rejected the Founders' value system, it has also rejected the roles they assigned each branch. A major factor allowing the Court to ignore its constitutionally designed boundaries is the failure of most citizens to study the Constitution for themselves and thus to understand the function and role of each branch.

In a simple overview, Article I of the Constitution sets forth the responsibilities of the Legislative branch, dedicating 109 lines to describing its powers; Article II addresses the duties of the Executive branch in 47 lines; and Article III has a mere 17 lines in its description of the responsibilities of the Judiciary. The fact that the Legislative branch is listed first, coupled with the fact that nearly two-thirds of the lines describing the three branches of government are dedicated to the Congress, implies that our Founders believed it to be the most important and most powerful branch, with the Judiciary the least important and least powerful.

This is further confirmed by the fact that the Constitution makes many of the functions and operations of the Judiciary subject to the control of the other two branches. For example, the Executive selects and the Legislature confirms the members of the Judiciary; Congress sets the salaries for judges, determines the size of the Judiciary, and establishes the scope of their jurisdiction and the type of cases which might come before them; and Congress is given the power to remove judges with whom it is dissatisfied. Quite clearly, the Constitution places many functions of the Judiciary under the oversight of the other branches—a power not granted reciprocally to the Judiciary.

Additional indication of the overall lack of weight given the Judiciary is evident in the fact that the Founders, in their farsighted preparations and planning for the nation's capitol in Washington, D. C., provided distinct buildings for the Executive and the Legislature but no building for the Judiciary. In fact, the Supreme Court was housed in the basement below the Senate chambers for almost fifty years and did not have its own separate building until 1935. [1]

The clearest irrefutable proof concerning the ranking of the Judiciary is provided in the *Federalist Papers*. These papers were written by James Madison, Alexander Hamilton, and John Jay immediately following the Constitutional Convention to explain how the government would operate under the Constitution. How reliable is this work in establishing the Founders' intent? According to Madison, whose notes on the Convention are considered *the* authority:

> The "Federalist" may fairly enough be regarded as the most authentic exposition of the heart of the federal Constitution as understood by the body which prepared and the authority which accepted it. [2]

In establishing the relative weight assigned to each branch, Alexander Hamilton forcefully declared in *Federalist #51*:

> [T]he *Legislative* authority necessarily *predominates*. [3] (emphasis added)

Then, in *Federalist #78*, he declared:

> [T]he *Judiciary* is beyond comparison the *weakest* of the three departments of power. . . . [T]he general liberty of the people can never be endangered from that quarter. [4] (emphasis added)

That the Legislature was the superior force and the Judiciary the inferior is not surprising since the political theorists on whom the Founders relied taught the same. For example, John Locke declared:

> [T]he first and fundamental positive law of all commonwealths is the establishing of the Legislative power. . . . This Legislative is not only the supreme power of the commonwealth, but sacred and unalterable in the hands where the community have once placed it; nor can any edict [decision or decree] of anybody else . . . have the force and obligation of a law which has not its sanction [approval] from that Legislative which the public has chosen. [5]

Montesquieu, in discussing each of the three branches, declared:

> Of the three powers above mentioned [Executive, Legislative, Judicial], the Judiciary is in some measure, next to nothing. [6]

Logic demanded that those officials elected by the people to make laws held a more important position than those unelected officials who interpreted them. In fact, the approbation of the people was so important to policy-making that our founding documents declare that policies are to be established by "the consent of the governed." The Constitution defines what establishes that consent: usually a simple majority vote, although, on occasion, it can be two-thirds or three-fourths.

This principle of citizen approval was fundamental to government at all levels, both federal and State. For example (emphasis added in each example):

> [A]ll power is inherent in *the people* and all free governments are founded on their authority. [7] PENNSYLVANIA

> [A]ll power is originally vested in *the people* and all free governments are founded on their authority. [8] SOUTH CAROLINA

> [N]o authority shall, on any pretense whatever, be exercised over the people or members of this State, but such as shall be derived from and granted by them *[the people]*. [9] NEW YORK

> [A]ll political power is vested in and derived from the *people only.* [10] NORTH CAROLINA

> [P]ower is inherent in them *[the people]*, and therefore all just authority in the institutions of political society is derived from *the people.* [11] DELAWARE

> [A]ll power being originally inherent in, and consequently derived from *the people,* therefore all officers of government—whether Legislative or Executive—are their trustees and servants and, at all times in a legal way, accountable to them. [12] VERMONT

> [A]ll power is vested in and consequently derived from *the people.* [13] VIRGINIA

> [A]ll government of right originates from *the people,* is founded in consent, and instituted for the general good. [14] NEW HAMPSHIRE

> All power residing originally in *the people* and being derived from them, the several magistrates and officers of government vested with authority—whether Legislative, Executive, or Judicial—are their

substitutes and agents and are at all times accountable to them. [15]
MASSACHUSETTS

[A]ll government of right originates from *the people,* is founded in compact only, and instituted solely for the good of the whole. [16]
MARYLAND

Clearly, the will of the people is the fundamental principle of all sound government. [†] Therefore, it was the Legislature, not the Judiciary, which was the true guardian of the people's liberties—and logically so, for that branch was most responsive to the people. As Alexander Hamilton explained:

The members of the Legislative department . . . are numerous. They are distributed and dwell among the people at large. Their connections of blood, of friendship, and of acquaintance embrace a great proportion of the most influential part of the society. . . . they are more immediately the confidential guardians of their rights and liberties. [17]

This did not mean that the Judiciary was powerless. It did provide a level of checks and balances on the other branches by reviewing laws and judg-

---

[†] Critics will deprecatingly argue that at the time of the Founders, "the people," that is, the eligible voters, were only the now politically-incorrect "WEAMs" and "WASPs" (White European Anglo Males and White Anglo-Saxon Protestants) and excluded all others. This criticism, while largely accurate, still does not diminish the argument concerning the will of the majority, for in every case where a constitutional protection has been established for a minority, whether of race, gender, social status, or age, each protection was extended by the consent of the majority of eligible voters at that time. For example, it was predominantly Anglo males and a small portion of Free-Blacks who established the constitutional protections for former slaves given in the Thirteenth, Fourteenth, and Fifteenth Amendments. That is, former slaves received their rights by the majority consent of non-slaves in three-fourths of the States. Similarly, the constitutional rights accorded to women in the Nineteenth Amendment were awarded them by the majority approval of the males. In like manner, the constitutional rights accorded explicitly to the poor by the abolition of the poll tax in the Twenty-Fourth Amendment came at the approval of the majority. Additionally, the constitutional right granted in the Twenty-Sixth Amendment allowing eighteen-year-olds to vote was given by the approval of voters over the age of twenty-one.

Furthermore, all of the constitutional protections for individuals and minorities that were established in the original Bill of Rights were also established by the consent of the majority. That is, the majority, by its consent, agrees to tie its own hands on certain issues (e.g., speech, religion, petition, assembly, the bearing of arms, etc.). Once such explicit constitutional protections are accorded to individuals or minorities, they can at no time be abridged by a simple vote, or by any other group, short of the passage of a new constitutional amendment to explicitly alter or repeal those rights (as in the case of the Twenty-First Amendment repealing the Eighteenth Amendment). In other words, *all* minority rights in the Constitution, and *all* explicit protections for minorities, have been, in *all* cases, established by majority consent.

ing them against the Constitution—a process called "judicial review." † Under its current application, however, this term is misleading, for today the term too often is synonymous with judicial activism and judicial revision.

What, then, is the proper application of "judicial review"? The term was not used *per se* in early America; however, in its historic form, judicial review is protecting the Constitution through a judicial policing function whereby laws were judged against the clear meaning and original intentions of the Constitution.

Hamilton affirmed this in his *Federalist* essays, declaring that the courts were "faithful guardians of the Constitution." [18] Numerous other Founders agreed. For example:

A law violating a constitution established by the people themselves would be considered by the judges as null and void. [19] **JAMES MADISON**

[W]hen they [the judges] consider its [a law's] principles and find it to be incompatible with the superior power of the Constitution, it is their duty to pronounce it void. [20] **JAMES WILSON**, SIGNER OF THE CONSTITUTION, U. S. SUPREME COURT JUSTICE

If they [the federal government] were to make a law not warranted by any of the powers enumerated, it would be considered by the judges as an infringement of the Constitution which they are to guard. . . . They [the judges] would declare it void. [21] **JOHN MARSHALL**, REVOLUTIONARY OFFICER, SECRETARY OF STATE, CHIEF JUSTICE OF THE U. S. SUPREME COURT

The Judicial power . . . [is the] proper and competent authority to decide whether any law made by Congress . . . is contrary to or in violation of the federal Constitution. [22] **SAMUEL CHASE**, SIGNER OF THE DECLARATION, U. S. SUPREME COURT JUSTICE

They [judges] could declare an unconstitutional law void. [23] **LUTHER MARTIN**, DELEGATE TO THE CONSTITUTIONAL CONVENTION

[The Judiciary's] duty it must be to declare all acts contrary to the manifest tenor of the Constitution void. [24] **ALEXANDER HAMILTON**, SIGNER OF THE CONSTITUTION

---

† Current authorities suggest that this power is authorized by Article III, Section 2: "The judicial power shall extend to all cases in law and equity arising under this Constitution." However, in the extensive debates surrounding the scope of judicial powers and functions, *none* of the Founders cited this clause as authority for the judiciary to review laws.

> The Judicial department is the proper power in the government to determine whether a statute be or be not constitutional. [25] **JAMES KENT**, "FATHER OF AMERICAN JURISPRUDENCE"

> The power of interpreting the laws involves necessarily the function to ascertain whether they are conformable to the Constitution or not; and if not so conformable, to declare them void and inoperative. [26] **JOSEPH STORY**, U. S. SUPREME COURT JUSTICE

However, the consent for judicial review was not unanimous; some Founders did express opposition to this process. For example, during the Constitutional Convention, delegate John Mercer objected to "the doctrine that the judges, as expositors of the Constitution, should have authority to declare a law void." [27] Others, including John Dickinson, agreed. [28] Most, however, apparently supported it, for, as delegate Elbridge Gerry stated, this practice by the Judiciary had been accepted by the people "with general approbation." [29] In fact, one scholar documents that almost two-dozen of the fifty-five delegates to the Constitutional Convention expressly approved this function. [30]

On the basis of such historical evidence, Justice Story declared in his *Commentaries* that it was "indisputable that the Constitution was adopted under a full knowledge of this exposition of its grant of power to the Judicial department." [31] Very simply, the Constitutional framers supported judicial review; the *Federalist Papers* explained it; the ratification debates described it; and legal scholars confirmed it.

Yet, within judicial review, there were specific things which the Judiciary could **not** do. For example, laws were to be judged **only** against the specific, self-evident wording of the Constitution and nothing further. In other words, judicial review had a limited field of inquiry. Hamilton confirmed this in *Federalist #81:*

> [T]here is not a syllable in the plan [the Constitution] which directly empowers the national courts to construe the laws according to the *spirit* of the Constitution. [32] (emphasis added)

James Kent similarly explained that the Judiciary could compare a law **only** to "the true intent and meaning of the Constitution." [33]

According to Hamilton, the reason that the courts were **not** to construe the laws "according to the spirit of the Constitution" was that this would "enable the court to mold them [the laws] into whatever shape it may think proper" which was "as unprecedented as it was dangerous." [34] Very simply, if the Judiciary were allowed to place its own meaning on laws, or to strike down laws which did not necessarily violate the Constitution but with which it disagreed, then the Judiciary would become more powerful than the Legislature—a possibility repugnant to the Founders. As James Madison explained:

> [R]efusing or not refusing to execute a law, to stamp it with its final character. . . . makes the Judiciary department paramount in fact to the Legislature, which was *never* intended and can *never* be proper. [35] (emphasis added)

The Founders understood that under a broad judicial review, the Judiciary might become policy-makers—something they explicitly forbade. As signer of the Constitution Rufus King warned, "the judges must interpret the laws; they ought not to be legislators." [36] Hamilton similarly declared that the Judiciary was forbidden to "substitute [its] own pleasure to the constitutional intentions of the Legislature." [37]

Samuel Adams also offered strong opinions on this subject † and explained why Legislative intentions, rather than Judicial intentions, must always prevail:

> [I]f the public are bound to yield obedience to laws to which they cannot give their approbation [support], they are slaves to those who make such laws and enforce them. [40]

In fact, the Founders recognized that if national policies are enforced which lack popular support, the people will come to despise, and eventually resist, their government. As Luther Martin explained at the Constitutional Convention:

---

† Interestingly, almost a decade before the American Revolution, Samuel Adams had been one of the first to point out the abuses of the British judiciary in America. He long condemned the fact that British judges did not receive their salaries from the Legislature and, therefore, were not accountable to the people. [38] He also complained that the terms of British judges were not limited to the duration of good behavior, thus meaning they could continue to serve even if they usurped the rights of the citizens. [39] Very simply, Adams saw the British judiciary as a branch completely unaccountable to the people. Significantly, both of these complaints by Adams against the British judiciary were specifically incorporated in the U. S. Constitution to prevent a similar abuse of American judicial powers.

It is necessary that the supreme Judiciary should have the confidence of the people. This will soon be lost if they are employed in the task of remonstrating against [opposing and striking down] popular measures of the Legislature. [41]

Notwithstanding occasional attempts to expand its authority, the Judiciary, by-and-large, understood its role; and early courts expressed their keen understanding both of the elevated role of the Legislature and of the people's supreme power over that branch. For example, notice this excerpt from *Commonwealth* v. *Kneeland* (1838):

The Court, therefore, from its respect for the Legislature, the immediate representation of that sovereign power [the people] whose will created and can at pleasure change the Constitution itself, will ever strive to sustain and not annul its [the Legislature's] expressed determination. . . . [A]nd whenever the people become dissatisfied with its operation, they have only to will its abrogation or modification and let their voice be heard through the legitimate channel, and it will be done. But until they wish it, let no branch of the government, *and least of all the Judiciary,* undertake to interfere with it. [42] (emphasis added)

Constitutional scholar William Rawle affirmed this belief of the Judiciary, noting that early federal judges exercised "caution arising from a systematic anxiety not to exceed their jurisdiction." [43]

That scope of jurisdiction granted to the Judiciary by the Constitution precluded it from exerting either force or will. As Hamilton succinctly explained in *Federalist #78:*

The Judiciary . . . has *no* influence over either the sword or the purse; no direction either of the strength or of the wealth of the society, and can take no active resolution whatever. *It may truly be said to have neither force nor will.* [44] (emphasis added)

Obviously, the current Judiciary disdains this original plan and today exerts both force and will; it clearly has become the dominant policy-making branch in the federal government. Long ago, Thomas Jefferson predicted how this judicial increase of power might occur:

It has long, however, been my opinion, and I have never shrunk from its expression . . . that the germ of dissolution of our federal government is in the constitution of the federal Judiciary; . . . working like gravity by night and by day, gaining a little today and a little tomorrow, and advancing its noiseless step like a thief, over the field of jurisdiction, until all shall be usurped. [45]

Today's Judiciary, as Jefferson foresaw, accrued its additional powers by slowly advancing its field of jurisdiction. While earlier generations diligently guarded against the expansion of judicial powers, subsequent generations became careless. Consequently, if the Court "tested the waters," advanced a new self-assigned power and failed to meet serious resistance, it simply consolidated its new gain. The result has been that, over a period of decades, the Court has succeeded in completely redefining its own constitutional role and has usurped Executive, Legislative, and State powers, centralizing them in its own hands. Jefferson had forewarned that such a centralization of power would result in the loss of local controls:

[T]aking from the States the moral rule of their citizens, and subordinating it to the general authority [federal government] . . . . would . . . break up the foundations of the Union. . . . I believe the States can best govern our home concerns and the general [federal] government our foreign ones. I wish, therefore . . . never to see all offices transferred to Washington, where, further withdrawn from the eyes of the people, they may more secretly be bought and sold as at market. [46]

Indeed, today one would hardly recognize Jefferson's description whereby "the States would govern our domestic concerns and the federal government our foreign ones." Jefferson further warned that such a centralization of powers would effectively negate the checks and balances established in the Bill of Rights between the State and federal governments:

[W]hen all government, domestic and foreign, in little as in great things, shall be drawn to Washington as the center of all power, it will render powerless the checks provided of one government on another. [47]

Jefferson's fears have now become reality through the unchecked power of the Judiciary.

The means used by the Judiciary to increase its scope of power is to judge laws according to the "spirit," or what it calls the "penumbra," [48] or shadow, of the Constitution. This has enabled the Judiciary to impute any meaning it wishes to the Constitution, resulting in the creation of brand new constitutional "rights" which reflect not the will of the people but rather the personal values and prejudices of the judges.

Ironically, many of the new rights the Judiciary has discovered under this penumbra are neither explicitly mentioned nor even generally alluded to anywhere in the Constitution. In fact, these penumbral rights often repudiate the original intentions of the Constitution. For example:

- The Constitution protects free speech, but the courts created a new right—a "freedom of expression." They thus subverted a protection for *words* into a protection for *actions* and *behaviors,* judicially enshrining acts formerly forbidden, and still abhorred, by the citizenry (flag-burning, nude dancing, desecration of religious symbols, etc.).

- Under the "right of privacy" (a right found nowhere in the Constitution), overtly immoral acts against decency and good order that long were illegal are now judicially raised above the reach of the law (pornography, sodomy, etc.).

- The judicial grant of immunity for public officials prevents them from being sued by citizens for *deliberately* wrongful or malicious acts while in office. In fact, judges cannot be sued for *any* of their actions, even if they *intentionally* violate the Constitution.

- The judicial establishment of a "right to choose" enabled it to overturn State statutes which had existed from the time of the Constitution. That "right" has become a legal club used to inhibit citizen and State attempts to protect innocent, unborn human life.

- The judicial doctrine of "selective incorporation" completely reversed the purpose of the Bill of Rights, thus allowing the federal Judiciary to micromanage the smallest affairs of citizens and States.

When the Judiciary creates such new rights as these described above (and others), it promptly enshrines them in its case law. Courts then subsequently judge legislation not against the Constitution but rather against other court decisions, thus elevating judicial rulings to the level of the Constitution itself. In fact, the Courts have so thoroughly rewritten the intent of the Constitution that legal scholars now describe the contemporary Supreme Court as a "continuing Constitutional Convention." [49]

Even though judicial review is now misused and abused by the courts, nevertheless, it was, in its original form, established by the Founding Fathers. However, the Founders acknowledged that *any* of the three branches could exercise this review of the laws for constitutionality. For example, James Wilson (Supreme Court Justice and signer of the Constitution) declared that the President can "refuse to carry into effect an act that violates the Constitution." [50] An excellent example of this surrounds the passage of the four Alien and Sedition laws in 1798.

The catalyst for these four laws had been the XYZ scandal where French officials were demanding bribes from American diplomats before allowing them an audience with the French Foreign Minister. The largely Federalist Congress responded by crafting laws predominantly directed against foreigners; however, they also saw in those laws an opportunity to stifle their Jeffersonian critics.

The first law increased the residence requirements for would-be citizens from five to fourteen years. The second allowed the deportation of suspicious aliens. The third authorized the imprisonment of any alien suspected of aiding a nation hostile to the United States. The fourth, and most controversial, established a fine and/or imprisonment for *any* person, alien or otherwise, who criticized the government in writing or speech. It was this fourth law which provided the Federalists a mechanism to silence not only foreign critics but also the many domestic Anti-Federalist critics of President John Adams.

Under this law, twenty-five individuals were arrested, and ten convicted. The law was *not* declared unconstitutional by the courts, but when Jefferson became President, he believed the law was unconstitutional. Therefore, he promptly freed all of those imprisoned under it, without regard to the specifics of their particular offense. As he explained:

> I discharged every person under punishment or prosecution under the sedition law because I considered, and now consider, that law to be a nullity, as absolute and as palpable [obvious] as if Congress had ordered us to fall down and worship a golden image; and that it was as much my duty to arrest its execution in every stage as it would have been to have rescued from the fiery furnace those who should have been cast into it for refusing to worship the

image. It was accordingly done in every instance without asking what the offender had done or against whom they had offended, but rather the pains they were suffering were inflicted under the pretended sedition law. [51]

Jefferson was criticized by some for nullifying this law, yet notice his response to one critic:

> You seem to think it devolved on the judges to decide on the validity of the sedition law. But nothing in the Constitution has given them a right to decide for the Executive more than to the Executive to decide for them. Both magistracies are equally independent in the sphere of action assigned to them. The judges, believing the law constitutional, had a right to pass a sentence of fine and imprisonment because the power was placed in their hands by the Constitution. But the Executive, believing the law to be unconstitutional, were bound to remit the execution of it because that power has been confided to them by the Constitution. [52]

However, just as both the Judicial and the Executive had a right to expound the constitutionality of laws, so, too, did the Legislature. For example, at the Constitutional Convention, delegate Luther Martin had declared:

> A knowledge of mankind and of legislative affairs cannot be presumed to belong in a higher degree to the Judges than to the Legislature. [53]

Then, during congressional debates in 1789, James Madison forcefully rebutted a suggestion that the Legislature was not to expound the constitutionality of laws:

> But the great objection drawn from the source to which the last arguments would lead us is that the Legislature itself has no right to expound the Constitution; that wherever its meaning is doubtful, you must leave it to take its course until the Judiciary is called upon the declare its meaning. I acknowledge, in the ordinary course of government, that the exposition of the laws and Constitution devolves upon the Judiciary. But I beg to know upon what principle it can be contended that any one department draws from the Constitution greater powers than another in marking out the limits of the powers of the several departments. [54]

The following day, as the debate continued, Madison reasserted:

> Nothing has yet been offered to invalidate the doctrine that the meaning of the Constitution may as well be ascertained by the Legislative as by the Judicial authority. [55]

A decade later, Founder John Randolph reaffirmed the same belief during a congressional debate, explaining:

> The decision of a constitutional question must rest somewhere. Shall it be confided to men immediately responsible to the people [the Congress] or to those who are irresponsible [the judges]? . . . With all the deference to their talents, is not Congress as capable of forming a correct opinion as they are? Are not its members acting under a responsibility to public opinion which can and will check their aberrations from duty? [56]

Very simply, the original intent was that any of the three branches could interpret the Constitution. As Thomas Jefferson confirmed:

> [E]ach of the three departments has equally the right to decide for itself what is its duty under the Constitution without any regard to what the others may have decided for themselves under a similar question. [57]

Because any branch was capable of determining constitutionality, the Founders rejected the notion that the Judiciary was the final voice. In fact, in a letter to Judge Spencer Roane, Jefferson explicitly addressed the absurdity of such an assertion:

> [O]ur Constitution. . . . intending to establish three departments, co-ordinate and independent that they might check and balance one another, it has given—according to this opinion—to one of them alone the right to prescribe rules for the government of the others; and to that one, too, which is unelected by and independent of the nation. . . . The Constitution, on this hypothesis, is a mere thing of wax in the hands of the Judiciary which they may twist and shape into any form they please. [58]

To Abigail Adams he explained:

> [T]he opinion which gives to the judges the right to decide what laws are constitutional and what not, not only for themselves in their

own sphere of action, but for the Legislature and Executive also in their spheres, would make the Judiciary a despotic branch. [59]

And then, to William Jarvis, Jefferson declared:

> You seem . . . to consider the judges as the ultimate arbiters of all constitutional questions; a very dangerous doctrine indeed, and one which would place us under the despotism of an oligarchy. Our judges are as honest as other men and not more so. They have, with others, the same passions for party, for power, and the privilege of their corps. . . . [A]nd their power the more dangerous as they are in office for life and not responsible, as the other functionaries are, to the elective control. The Constitution has erected no such single tribunal. [60]

Jefferson did not oppose the courts expounding the Constitution, [61] but he stressed that the Judiciary was not the "final arbiter." It was merely one of three branches in a system where each was capable of reading the Constitution and determining constitutionality.

Generations later, President Lincoln, in his "Inaugural Address," affirmed that this was still the belief when he declared:

> I do not forget the position assumed by some that constitutional questions are to be decided by the Supreme Court. . . . At the same time, the candid citizen must confess that if the policy of the government upon vital questions affecting the whole people is to be irrevocably fixed by decisions of the Supreme Court, the instant they are made . . . the people will have ceased to be their own rulers, having . . . resigned their government into the hands of that eminent tribunal. [62]

Lincoln's statement had been prompted by the *Dred Scott* decision [63] in which the Supreme Court had declared that Congress could *not* prohibit slavery—that slaves were only property and not persons eligible to receive any rights of a citizen. Fortunately, the other two branches ignored the Court's ruling. On June 9, 1862, Congress *did* prohibit the extension of slavery into the free territories; [64] and the following year, President Lincoln *did* issue the "Emancipation Proclamation"—both were acts that were a direct affront to the Court's decision. Because Congress and President Lincoln were guided by their own understanding of the Constitution rather than by the Judiciary's opinion, both declared freedom for slaves.

As this example illustrates, if the other branches considered the Judiciary's opinion clearly wrong, they simply ignored it. Constitutional scholar William Rawle explained this prerogative of the branches to students in 1825:

> The Judicial power is general or limited according to the scope and objects of the government. In a word, it must be fully and exactly commensurate with that of the Legislature. It cannot by any terms of language be made to exceed the Legislative power, for such excess would be inconsistent with its nature. . . . But it is said that there is generally a propensity in public functionaries to extend their power beyond its proper limits, and this may at some future time be the case with the courts of the United States. . . . In such an extreme and therefore improbable case, as there would be no color of jurisdiction, the whole [judicial] proceedings would be void. [65]

Justice Story, too, acknowledged the right of the Executive and Legislative branches to make final and ultimate decisions within their spheres:

> [I]n many cases, the decisions of the Executive and Legislative departments, thus made, become final and conclusive, being from their very nature and character incapable of revision. Thus, in measures exclusively of a political, Legislative, or Executive character, it is plain that as the supreme authority as to these questions belongs to the Legislative and Executive departments, they cannot be re-examined elsewhere. [66]

Just as the Founders strongly believed that any of the three branches could interpret the Constitution, they also strongly opposed mixing the functions of each branch or blurring the distinct separations between them. Yet, today, the public's understanding of the function of each branch is distorted by the Judiciary's intrusion into the functions of the other branches; however, such obfuscation was never intended and was not always present. For example, in 1841, University of Virginia law professor Henry St. George Tucker [†] explained the clear function of each branch to his students:

[†] Henry St. George Tucker (1780-1848) was a soldier in the War of 1812, a judge, law professor, and a U. S. Congressman. Interestingly, he came from a family of distinguished legal scholars. His father was St. George Tucker (1752-1827) who served as a soldier in the American Revolution, a federal judge, and a law professor at William and Mary. His son was John Randolph Tucker (1823-1897) who was a U. S. Congressman, law professor at Washington and Lee University, and an early president of the American Bar Association.

[T]he power that makes them [the laws] exercises *de facto* the supreme power and constitutes the Legislature. But when laws have been made there must be somewhere vested the power of carrying them into execution. This power is clearly distinct from the Legislative, and is called the Executive. It consists in nothing more than in giving effect to what a superior power has commanded. As, if the law denounces death against the murderer, the duty of enforcing that law by the condign [deserved] punishment of the offender devolves upon the Executive or on some of those numerous officers who together constitute that branch of political power. But though the punishment of the guilty devolves upon the Executive, the ascertaining of his guilt belongs to an entirely different branch of the sovereign authority, and this branch is the Judiciary. For the power of judging constitutes no part either of Legislative or Executive authority. It is a separate and distinct attribute and in wise governments entrusted to different hands. Thus the Legislature makes the law, the Executive institutes its prosecutors against the infractors, the Judiciary decides on their guilt and pronounces judgment, and the Executive then again steps in and carries that judgment into execution. Such is a true and simple analysis of the powers of government. [67]

Historically, the separate role and function of each branch was clearly understood.

The Founders first made evident their opposition to blurring the lines of distinction between the branches during the Constitutional Convention when a "Council of Revision" was proposed. That Council would have combined representatives from the Judicial and Executives branches to review the constitutionality of legislation coming out of Congress. According to the records of the Convention:

Mr. [James] Wilson moved as an amendment . . . "that the Supreme National Judiciary should be associated with the Executive in the revisionary power." . . . The Judiciary ought to have an opportunity of remonstrating against [reviewing and protesting] projected encroachments on the people as well as on themselves. . . . Laws may be unjust, may be unwise, may be dangerous, may be destructive. . . . Let them [the judges] have a share in the revisionary power and they will have an opportunity of taking notice of those characters of a law and of counteracting by the weight of their opinions the improper views of the Legislature. [68]

The reaction of the other delegates to this proposal was unambiguous:

Mr. [Elbridge] Gerry. . . . [said] the motion was liable to strong objections. It was combining and mixing together the Legislative and other departments. . . . It was making statesmen of the judges and setting them up as the guardians of the rights of the people. He relied for his part on the Representatives of the people as the guardians of their rights and interests. It was making the expositors of the laws [the judges] the legislators which ought never to be done. . . . Mr. [Caleb] Strong thought with Mr. Gerry that the power of making ought to be kept distinct from that of expounding the laws. . . . Mr. [Luther] Martin considered the association of the judges with the Executive as a dangerous innovation as well as one which could not produce the particular advantage expected from it. [69]

The result was that even though three of the most influential of the Convention's participants (James Madison, James Wilson, and George Mason) championed this concept, it was voted down on four occasions. [70]

This rejection of mixing one branch into the affairs of another was also made evident in the *Marbury* v. *Madison* case (1803). [71] This case came as a result of actions taken during the final hours of the Presidency of John Adams. In those last hours before Jefferson took office, Adams, in an attempt to bolster the power of the Federalists in the Judiciary, issued several Federalist judicial appointments in the District of Columbia. When Jefferson entered office, those appointments, even though legally executed by President Adams, had not yet been delivered. President Jefferson refused to deliver the appointments.

William Marbury, one of the thwarted appointees—along with three others who did not receive their commissions—sued James Madison, Jefferson's Secretary of State, to receive the appointments. That suit reached the Supreme Court, where John Marshall was Chief Justice.

Interestingly, Marshall, a staunch Federalist, had simultaneously served as Secretary of State under John Adams and as Chief Justice of the Court. [72] The judicial appointments which were not delivered, and which had become the subject of the lawsuit, had actually been sitting on Marshall's own desk as Secretary of State; it was he who had failed to deliver them! Deeply grieved over this and foreseeing the problems he had created, Marshall told his brother, "I cannot help regretting it the more as I fear some blame may be imputed to me." [73] Now, as a Federalist Chief Justice of a Supreme Court still packed with Federalist members, the case had arrived before him and he was now to rule on whether those appointments should be delivered.

Marshall first determined that the Court had no judicial authority over the case. He then amazingly proceeded to strike down part of the 1789 Judiciary Act †—a law with which the Supreme Court on two previous occasions had found *no* fault. [76] Finally, he ruled that President Jefferson should deliver the appointments.

How did Jefferson and Madison respond to the Court's ruling? They ignored it—an act which outraged neither the public, the Congress, nor even the Court, for such a response was justified under the separation of powers. Jefferson later explained to Justice William Johnson (nominated to the Court by President Jefferson following the Marbury incident) the essence of the Court's wrongful decision in that case:

> The Court determined at once that, being an original process, they had no cognizance of it [no authority over the case] and therefore the question before them was ended. But the Chief-Justice went on to lay down what the law would be had they jurisdiction of the case, to wit: that they should command the delivery. . . . Besides the impropriety of this gratuitous interference, could anything exceed *the perversion of law?* [77] (emphasis added)

Jefferson considered it a "perversion of law" that the Judiciary should tell the Executive what to do. The precedent provided by Jefferson's and Madison's flat refusal to allow the Judiciary to interfere with Executive decisions was followed by other prominent Americans. For example, when the Court ruled that President Andrew Jackson was to take certain actions, [78] he also ignored the Court's order. [79] On what grounds? Jackson explained:

> Each public officer who takes an oath to support the Constitution swears that he will support it as he understands it, and not as it is

---

† Interestingly, the 1789 Judiciary Act had been framed in Congress under the supervision of at least a dozen members of the Constitutional Convention, including Gouverneur Morris, William Samuel Johnson, Robert Morris, William Few, George Read, Richard Bassett, Caleb Strong, James Madison, George Wythe, Abraham Baldwin, and Roger Sherman. [74] Furthermore, at least two of the Justices on the Courts that previously saw no fault with the law had also been members of the Convention—Justices William Paterson and Oliver Ellsworth. [75]

understood by others. . . . The opinion of the judges has no more authority over the Congress than the opinion of Congress has over the judges, and on that point the President is independent of both. The authority of the Supreme Court must not, therefore, be permitted to control the Congress or the Executive. [80]

President Abraham Lincoln once reminded his audience of another occasion when President Jackson had ignored the Court:

Do not gentlemen here remember the case of that same Supreme Court . . . deciding that a national bank was constitutional? [see *McCulloch* v. *Maryland* [81] and *Osborne* v. *United States Bank* [82]]. . . . [Jackson] denied the constitutionality of the bank that the Supreme Court had decided was constitutional . . . [saying] that the Supreme Court had no right to lay down a rule to govern a coordinate branch of the government, the members of which had sworn to support the Constitution—that each member had sworn to support that Constitution as he understood it. [83]

Very simply, the separation of powers wisely permitted each branch to determine within its own sphere what was and was not constitutional.

These separations had been established for specific reasons. It was the lesson of history that the tendency of human nature was to accrue and abuse power, and that tyranny occurred whenever government power was consolidated in one branch. Therefore, the Founders believed that America would remain secure only if power was divided; in this way, if one branch became corrupt, the others might still remain trustworthy and thus be able to check any wayward influence. As George Washington explained:

A just estimate of that love of power and proneness to abuse it which predominates in the human heart, is sufficient to satisfy us for the truth of this position. The necessity of reciprocal checks in the exercise of political power by dividing and distributing it into different depositories . . . has been evinced [established]. [84]

Alexander Hamilton similarly explained:

Why has government been instituted at all? Because the passions of men will not conform to the dictate of reason and justice without constraint. . . . [T]he infamy of a bad action is to be divided among a number [rather] than . . . to fall singly upon one. [85]

Quite simply, the security of the people in this form of government rested on maintaining the separation of powers. As Thomas Jefferson warned:

> [T]o preserve the republican form and principles of our Constitution and [to] cleave to the salutary distribution of powers which that [the Constitution] has established.... are the two sheet anchors of our Union. If driven from either, we shall be in danger of foundering. [86]

The Founders were therefore understandably emphatic: each branch must confine itself to its designated responsibilities, and each branch must ensure that the others not encroach. George Washington cautioned:

> [T]hose entrusted with its [the nation's] administration [must] confine themselves within their respective constitutional spheres, avoiding in the exercise of the powers of one department to encroach upon another. The spirit of encroachment tends to consolidate the powers of all the departments in one and thus to create, whatever the form of government, a real despotism.... [B]ut let there be no change by usurpation [wrongful seizure of power]; for though this in one instance may be the instrument of good, it is the customary weapon by which free governments are destroyed. [87]

James Madison admonished:

> The preservation of a free government requires not merely that the metes and bounds which separate each department of power be universally maintained but more especially that neither of them be suffered to overleap the great barrier which defends the rights of the people. The rulers who are guilty of such an encroachment exceed the commission from which they derive their authority and are tyrants. The people who submit to it are governed by laws made neither by themselves nor by an authority derived from them and are slaves. [88]

Samuel Adams similarly warned:

> In all good governments, the Legislative, Executive, and Judiciary powers are confined within the limits of their respective departments. If therefore it should be found that the constitutional rights of our federal and local governments should on either side be infringed, or

that either of the departments aforesaid should interfere with another, it will, if continued, essentially alter the Constitution, and may, in time, . . . be productive of such convulsions as may shake the political ground upon which we now happily stand. [89]

If it was essential that the separation of powers be maintained, was the integrity and honor of each branch the only safeguard against encroachment? Certainly not. Based on their healthy skepticism for consolidated power, the Founders provided checks and balances to impede unauthorized encroachments by one branch upon another. As Alexander Hamilton explained in *Federalist #73*, each branch was furnished "with constitutional arms" for its own "effectual powers of self-defense." [90]

For example, the Executive, in its check upon the Legislature, could veto legislative acts and convene the Congress into special sessions. Also, the Vice-President serves as the President of the Senate and thus is able to cast a deciding vote in case of a tie. Furthermore, even though Congress is given oversight and regulation of the military, the Executive is its Commander-in-Chief. The Constitution also offers the Executive further protection from the Legislature by at least two explicit provisions. First, it prohibits Congress from reducing the salary of the Executive during his term, thus preventing the Executive from being subject to economic extortion by Congress. Second, to remove the Executive from office required a majority vote of the House and a two-thirds vote of the Senate, thus making it virtually impossible for Congress to manipulate the Executive office in a purely partisan manner. Over the Judiciary, the Executive could exercise a check by its selection of judges as well as by granting pardons to those parties the Executive believed were wrongly convicted by the Judiciary.

The Judiciary could exercise a check over the Legislature by its proper use of judicial review. As Oliver Ellsworth explained:

> This Constitution defines the extent of the powers of the general government. If the general Legislature should at any time overleap their limits, the Judicial department is a constitutional check. If the United States go beyond their powers, if they make a law which the Constitution does not authorize, it is void: and the Judicial power . . . will declare it to be void. [91]

The Constitution also offered the Judiciary the same two protections from the Legislature that the Executive received: salaries could not be diminished during a judge's service, and the removal of a judge required a two-thirds vote by the Senate.

Finally, the Legislature exercised a check on the Executive by its role of "advise and consent," requiring Congressional approval of treaties negotiated by the Executive and approval of all Executive nominees, whether to the Judiciary or to head Executive departments. Furthermore, the Congress had the ability to override the Presidential veto of a legislative act. Over the Judiciary, the Legislature, as outlined earlier in this chapter, was given not only the ability to remove judges but was also given extensive regulatory power over the Judiciary.

It was because of these elaborate safeguards that Hamilton had declared "a phantom" [92] the fear that the Judiciary could mold the laws into "whatever shape it may think proper." [93] He especially considered this fear a phantom because of the congressional power to remove judges by impeachment. As he explained:

> This [impeachment] is alone a complete security. There never can be danger that the judges, by a series of deliberate usurpations on the authority of the Legislature, would hazard the united resentment of the body entrusted with it while this body [Congress] was possessed of the means of punishing their presumption by degrading them from their stations [impeachment]. [94]

Unfortunately, Hamilton's "phantom" has now become incarnate. Yet, in Hamilton's defense, he never imagined that the Judiciary would try to reinterpret the Constitution without the legislators impeaching any judge who tried; that is, he never imagined that the Legislature would refuse to exercise its own "constitutional arms for self-defense."

While today's defenders of judicial activism assert that a judge can be impeached only for criminal acts and not for political usurpations, the Founders emphatically disagreed. For example, Justice James Wilson declared:

> [I]mpeachments are confined to *political* characters, to *political* crimes and misdemeanors, and to *political* punishments. [95] (emphasis added)

Justice Story agreed:

> The offenses to which the power of impeachment has been and is ordinarily applied as a remedy. . . . are aptly termed *political* offences,

growing out of personal misconduct, or gross neglect, or usurpation, or habitual disregard of the public interests. [96] (emphasis added)

There is much additional evidence. For example, George Mason, the "Father of the Bill of Rights," explained that impeachment was for "attempts to subvert the Constitution," [97] and Alexander Hamilton declared that impeachment was to be used for "the abuse or violation of some public trust. . . . [or for] injuries done immediately to the society itself." [98] Constitutional Convention delegate Elbridge Gerry considered "mal-administration" as grounds for impeachment, [99] and William Rawle included "the inordinate extension of power, the influence of party and of prejudice" [100] as well as attempts to "infringe the rights of the people." [101] Justice Story also listed "unconstitutional opinions" and "attempts to subvert the fundamental laws and introduce arbitrary power." [102] Very simply, impeachment was the recourse when judges intruded on the domain of the other two branches, attempted to disregard public interests, affronted the will of the people, or introduced arbitrary power by seizing the role of policy-maker.

The Founders saw impeachment as a Legislative tool to maintain the separation of powers and to prevent Judicial encroachments. As Alexander Hamilton explained:

> [T]he practice of impeachments [is] a bridle in the hands of the Legislative body. [103]

Justice James Iredell, nominated to the Supreme Court by President Washington, also believed in using impeachment in this manner. He explained:

> Every government requires it [impeachment]. Every man ought to be amenable for his conduct. . . . It will be not only the means of punishing misconduct but it will prevent misconduct. A man in public office who knows that there is no tribunal to punish him may be ready to deviate from his duty; but if he knows there is a tribunal for that purpose although he may be a man of no principle, the very terror of punishment will perhaps deter him. [104]

Justice Story similarly declared:

> The provision in the Constitution of the United States [concerning impeachment] . . . holds out a deep and immediate responsibility as a check upon arbitrary power. They [Congress] must be

presumed to be watchful of the interests, alive to the sympathies, and ready to redress the grievances of the people. [105]

Yet, if such great power resided with Congress, and if, as Hamilton asserted, "the Legislative authority necessarily predominates," then what check would keep Congress from abusing its power and riding roughshod over the people? George Washington answered this question:

> The power under the Constitution will always be in the people. It is entrusted for certain defined purposes, and for a certain limited period to representatives of their own choosing; and whenever it is exercised contrary to their interest or not agreeably to their wishes, their servants can, and undoubtedly will be recalled. [106]

Very simply, the people and their use of the ballot box was the check upon Congress. Thomas Jefferson agreed:

> When the Legislative or Executive functionaries act unconstitutionally, they are responsible to the people in their elective capacity. The exemption of the judges from that is quite dangerous enough. I know no safe depository of the ultimate powers of the society but the people themselves; and if we think them [the people] not enlightened enough to exercise their control with a wholesome discretion, the remedy is not to take it from them, but to inform their discretion by education. This is the true corrective of abuses of constitutional power. [107]

Yet, isn't this what many legal activists decry as majoritarianism, that is, the so-called "tyranny of the majority"? Perhaps, but that does not mean that majoritarianism is unconstitutional. In fact, what is the acceptable alternative? That a small group should be able to annul the will of the people and enforce its own desires upon the masses? Certainly not, for as explained by President Washington:

> [T]he fundamental principle of our Constitution . . . enjoins [requires] that the *will of the majority shall prevail.* [108] (emphasis added)

Thomas Jefferson also emphatically declared:

> *[T]he will of the majority* [is] the natural law of every society [and] is the *only* sure guardian of the rights of man. Perhaps even this

may sometimes err. But its errors are honest, solitary and short-lived. [109] (emphasis added)

Does this therefore mean that minorities are to be disregarded or trodden upon? Of course not. As Jefferson further explained:

[T]hough the will of the majority is in all cases to prevail, that will to be rightful must be reasonable; that the minority possess their equal rights which equal law must protect. [110]

While the minority is not to prevail, with its constitutional guarantee of "free speech," it does have the equal right to attempt to persuade the majority to its point of view, or portions of its views, in the majority's policies. However, equal right is not the same as equal power; the minority is never the equivalent of the majority and is never to exercise control over it.

Every citizen, however, on occasion, will find himself in a minority on some issue. At that time, the appropriate response was expressed by Samuel Adams who, when he found himself on the losing side, declared:

[A]s it becomes a citizen, I will acquiesce in the choice of a majority of the people. [111]

Certainly, the majority will sometimes err, but as Jefferson observed, "its errors are honest, solitary, and short-lived." However, the errors created by Court decisions abrogating the will of the majority are more severe and longlasting. Today, the so-called "tyranny of the majority" has been replaced with "the tyranny of the minority." This is especially apparent in the recent reversals of numerous elections by citizen dissidents who, unable to prevail though normal governing processes, turn to activist judges to achieve their goals and to subvert the will of the people. For example:

- Washington and New York citizens voted down physician-assisted suicides; the Judiciary disagreed with the results and overturned the elections. [112]

- Colorado citizens voted that homosexual behavior should not qualify an individual for special rights; the courts again disagreed and set aside the election. [113]

- Arkansas and Washington citizens enacted term limits; the Judiciary overturned those results. [114]

- California citizens voted that equal treatment be the rule for everyone, and that those *illegally* in the country should *not* receive taxpayer-funded services; the courts overturned both elections. [115]

- Arizona citizens voted English as the official language of the State; some judges disagreed and set aside the election. [116]

- Missouri citizens voted down a tax-increase; the courts ordered one. [117]

There are numerous other examples.

Contrary to what is wrongly asserted by many today, the Bill of Rights was not enacted solely to protect the minority; rather it was enacted primarily to protect *everyone* from federal intrusion and micromanagement. And even though our founding documents never permit a national policy to be enacted by a minority group, today many policies in moral, social, educational, and religious arenas reflect not the will of the people but rather the judicially-established will of philosophical minorities whose genuine constitutional rights have not been violated. In too many cases, the true majority—despite extensive effort—has been absolutely powerless to overturn the will of the minority.

The Founders would be stunned by both the position and the power of today's Court. The separation of powers they so carefully crafted has now been obliterated. In fact, a foreign observer in modern America today would likely conclude that the President and Congress have taken oaths to uphold the Court's opinion of the Constitution. Yet, to allow themselves to be governed by the Court, both the President and Congress must relinquish their constitutional responsibilities and the purposes for which they were elected.

The people—not the courts—must control the destiny of the nation; national reforms and any "societal evolution" must be guided by the people rather than by the social engineering of an elite few. America must reclaim its right to be a republic, returning the Judiciary to its proper position—the least of three co-sovereign branches. The examples provided by our Founders of how to respond to overactive courts are worthy of emulation today.

~16~
Revisionism: A Willing Accomplice

The courts are not the only force reshaping American culture; a second major influence is revisionists. This group promulgates a message of radical moral and social change through its use of "historical revisionism"—a process by which historical fact is intentionally ignored, distorted, or misportrayed in order to maneuver public opinion toward a specific political agenda or philosophy. Historical revisionists accomplish their goals by:

1. Ignoring those aspects of American heritage which they deem to be politically incorrect and overemphasizing those portions which they find acceptable;

2. Vilifying the historical figures who embraced a position they reject; or

3. Concocting the appearance of widespread historical approval for a generally unpopular social policy.

Revisionists employ many methods to achieve these goals; nine will be examined in this chapter.

1. The Use of Patent Untruths

The use of untruths was one of the earliest tools effectively employed by revisionists. For example, Robert Ingersoll, a well known political lecturer of the 1880s and 1890s, falsely declared:

> [O]ur forefathers retired God from politics. . . . The Declaration of Independence announces the sublime truth that all power comes from the people. This was a denial, and the first denial of a nation, of the infamous dogma that God confers the right upon one man to govern others. . . . Our fathers founded the first secular government that was ever founded in this world. [1]

Charles and Mary Beard proclaimed a similarly false thesis in their 1930 *Rise of American Civilization*, stating that "national government was secular from top to bottom" [2] and that the Founders had "rear[ed] a national government on a secular basis." [3]

Even a young elementary student could quickly refute these charges by reading the Declaration of Independence. In fact, based on that document alone, the U.

S. Supreme Court noted that our government was *not* secular since in numerous references it invoked God and His principles into civil government. [4]

W. E. Woodward, a revisionist active in the 1920s, also employed the use of patent untruths, asserting:

> The name of Jesus Christ is not mentioned even once in the vast collection of Washington's published letters. [5]

And yet, on June 12, 1779, to the Delaware Indian Chiefs, Washington declared:

> You do well to wish to learn our arts and ways of life, and above all, the religion of Jesus Christ. These will make you a greater and happier people than you are. Congress will do every thing they can to assist you in this wise intention. [6]

Furthermore, in one single document (a well-worn, handwritten prayer book found among Washington's personal writings after his death), the name "Jesus Christ" was directly used sixteen times; [7] it also appeared numerous additional times in varied forms (e.g., "Jesus," "Lord Jesus," etc.).

In a similar patent untruth, the Beards proclaimed:

> In dealing with Tripoli, President Washington allowed it to be squarely stated that "the government of the United States is not in any sense founded upon the Christian religion." [8]

As already conclusively proved in Chapter 6, Washington did *not* make that—or any similar—statement.

What makes the revisionists' use of patent untruths effective is the failure of most readers to investigate revisionist claims.

2. The Use of Overly Broad Generalizations

Notice how this first technique is applied to George Washington's religious beliefs:

> A product of the Enlightenment, Washington's terms for God included "Divine Author of our blessed Religion," "Divine Providence," and "the Almighty Being who rules over the Universe." Like many Deists, Washington viewed the supreme being as an overseer and protector of all men, not simply the God of Presbyterians, Episcopalians or Baptists. [9] **JOHN P. RILEY**

George Washington. . . . seemed, according to the evidence, to have had no instinct or feeling for religion. . . . He refers to Providence in numerous letters, but he used the term in such a way as to indicate that he considered Providence as a synonym for Destiny or Fate. [10] **W. E. WOODWARD**

George Washington. . . . seems to have had the characteristic unconcern of the 18th century deist for the forms and creeds of institutional religions. . . . [H]e referred to Providence as an impersonal force, remote and abstract. [11] **STEVEN MORRIS**

Revisionists suggest that since Washington used general terms for God, he was therefore irreligious and a deist. The societal inference intended from this charge is that Washington, therefore, would disapprove of the public religious expressions sought by many today.

This generalization incorporates several historical fallacies. First, revisionists fail to mention that the broad, descriptive terms of God used by Washington were also frequently used by the *evangelical* Christian pastors of the day. [12] Those pastors described God in similar or identical terms not generally used in today's religious terminology; are those pastors, too, to be called "deists"? Second, revisionists deliberately withhold the fact that Washington *did* use *very* specific terms, such as "Jesus Christ" and "Christian." Finally, revisionists artfully omit the historical eyewitness testimonies which debunk their generalizations. For example, George Washington's adopted daughter declared:

I should have thought it the greatest heresy to doubt his [George Washington's] firm belief in Christianity. His life, his writings, prove that he was a Christian. [13]

His contemporaries offered similar impressive testimonies:

To the character of hero and patriot, this good man added that of Christian. . . . Although the greatest man upon earth, he disdained not to humble himself before his God and to trust in the mercies of Christ. [14] **GUNNING BEDFORD**, SIGNER OF THE CONSTITUTION

[H]e was a sincere believer in the Christian faith and a truly devout man. [15] **JOHN MARSHALL**, REVOLUTIONARY GENERAL; SECRETARY OF STATE; CHIEF JUSTICE U. S. SUPREME COURT

> [I]f we cannot aspire at his talents as a General, a President, or a Statesman, we may imitate his virtues as a man, a citizen, and a Christian. [16] **ABIEL HOLMES,** REVOLUTIONARY SURGEON; HISTORIAN

> He was a firm believer in the Christian religion . . . . For my own part, I trust I shall never lose the impression made on my own mind in beholding, in this house of prayer, the venerable hero, the victorious leader of our hosts, bending in humble adoration to the God of armies and great Captain of our salvation! [17] **JONATHAN SEWELL,** ATTORNEY

> Christianity is the highest ornament of human nature. Washington practiced upon this belief. . . . He was neither ostentatious nor ashamed of his Christian profession. [18] **JEREMIAH SMITH,** REVOLUTIONARY SOLDIER; U. S. CONGRESSMAN; GOVERNOR OF NEW HAMPSHIRE

To portray Washington as a deist, revisionists either must hide such testimonies or call these eye-witnesses liars.

The use of overly-broad generalization is often employed against the collective group of Founding Fathers. For example:

> Franklin, Washington, Jefferson, Paine and most of our other patriarchs were at best deists, believing in the unmoved mover of Aristotle, but not the God of the Old and New Testaments. [19] **MICHAEL MACDONALD**

Some 200 years ago, signer of the Declaration John Witherspoon clearly described the intent of this tactic:

> It is of no consequence to an infidel to make it appear that there are some . . . bad men. His great business is to transfer the faults of particulars to the whole order and to insinuate that "priests of all religions are the same." [20]

Notice how this strategy was employed by MacDonald: invoke Jefferson, Franklin, and Paine (the least overtly religious Founders) and then imply that *all* of the other Founders held similar convictions. Recall that there were some 200+ Founders; why not invoke Benjamin Rush, John Jay, Samuel Adams, Roger Sherman, Abraham Baldwin, Rufus King—and scores of other strongly religious Founders—and then claim accurately that they were much more representative of the collective group?

Note this use of overly-broad generalizations by Charles and Mary Beard in their *Rise of American Civilization:*

> And the First Amendment, added by the *radicals* in 1791, declared that "Congress shall make no law respecting an establishment of religion, or prohibiting the free exercise thereof." [21] (emphasis added)

The inference is that those who wanted to protect religious liberties (Patrick Henry, George Mason, Samuel Adams, etc.) were "radicals"; on this basis they were not representative of the more "mainstream" Founders. The societal implication intended from this charge is that those who today seek protections for public religious expression are also "radicals."

If revisionists can persuade the public that all of the Founders were deists, then they will have recast the Founders' religious beliefs, thus concocting a historical precedent for today's unpopular court decisions which limit public religious expressions. The use of overly broad generalizations induces erroneous impressions and wrong conclusions; therefore, any public policy built on these mistaken foundations will be inherently flawed.

3. The Use of Omission

Omission (the deletion of certain sections of text) is another effective tool of revisionists and can also completely transform the tone of a work. An excellent example of the use of omission is seen in the following quotes from a recent bestselling book on American history by Kenneth Davis:

> Is life so dear or peace so sweet as to be purchased at the price of chains and slavery? . . . I know not what course others may take, but as for me, give me liberty or give me death? [22] **PATRICK HENRY**, 1775

> We whose names are under-written . . . do by these presents solemnly and mutually in the presence of God, and one of another, covenant and combine our selves together into a civil body politick, for our better ordering and preservation and furtherance of the ends aforesaid. [23] **MAYFLOWER COMPACT**, 1620

The ellipses (" . . . ") indicate that a portion of the text was omitted. When used correctly, such deletions shorten the text but do not change its context; not so in this case. Notice (inserted in bold) what Davis deleted:

> Is life so dear or peace so sweet as to be purchased at the price of chains and slavery? ***Forbid it, Almighty God!*** I know not what course others may take, but as for me, give me liberty or give me death? [24]

We whose names are under-written *having undertaken, for the glory of God, and advancement of the Christian faith and honor of our king and country, a voyage to plant the first colonie in the Northern parts of Virginia* do by these presents solemnly and mutually in the presence of God, and one of another, covenant and combine ourselves together into a civil body politic, for our better ordering and preservation and furtherance of the ends aforesaid. [25]

By omitting these definitive portions, the revisionist changes the message from a God-centered to a secular tone.

Notice also the manner in which a popular library reference book presents the 1783 peace treaty which ended the American Revolution:

... ART. I.—His Britannic Majesty acknowledges the said United States, viz. New Hampshire, Massachusetts Bay, Rhode Island, and Providence Plantations, Connecticut, New York, New Jersey, Pennsylvania, Delaware, Maryland, Virginia, North Carolina, South Carolina, and Georgia, to be free, sovereign and independent States, &c. [26]

What was omitted by the editors at the beginning of the treaty? The section in which John Adams, John Jay, and Benjamin Franklin *officially* declared:

In the name of the Most Holy and Undivided Trinity. It having pleased the Divine Providence to dispose the hearts ... [27]

In another library reference book, the charter of Pennsylvania is presented in these words:

Charles the Second [&c.] ... Know ye ... that we, favoring the petition and good purpose of the said William Penn ... [28]

What is omitted from the charter? The section describing Penn's religious motivation for forming Pennsylvania:

Whereas our trusty and well beloved subject, William Penn, Esquire, son and heir of Sir William Penn, deceased, out of a commendable desire to enlarge our English Empire and promote such useful commodities as may be of benefit to us and our dominions, as also to reduce the savage natives by gentle and just manners to the love of civil society and Christian religion, hath humbly besought leave of us to transport an ample colony unto a certain country hereinafter describe in the parts of America not yet cultivated and planted ... [29]

Another example of the secularizing of history through omission is seen in the current reprint of Alexis de Tocqueville's classic 1835 work *Democracy in America*. The new edition (Richard D. Heffner, editor), touted as being "Specially Edited and Abridged for the Modern Reader," [30] contains *less than half* the content of the original. What has been omitted? Most of de Tocqueville's comments on the family, morality, and religion. Notice some of his observations deleted from the "modern" condensation:

> There is certainly no country in the world where the tie of marriage is more respected than in America or where conjugal happiness is more highly or worthily appreciated. [31]

> Upon my arrival in the United States, the religious aspect of the country was the first thing that struck my attention; and the longer I stayed there, the more did I perceive the great political consequences resulting from this state of things to which I was unaccustomed. In France I had almost always seen the spirit of religion and the spirit of freedom marching in pursuing courses diametrically opposed to each other; but in America, I found they were intimately united and they reigned in common over the same country. [32]

> The Americans combine the notions of Christianity and of liberty so intimately in their minds that it is impossible to make them conceive the one without the other. [33]

Apparently, the "modern" reader doesn't need to know about the influence of Christianity on American government and family.

Other similar examples of religious omissions from history texts were documented by researchers funded through the U. S. Department of Education. For example, at the elementary level they discovered:

> One social studies book has thirty pages on the Pilgrims, including the first Thanksgiving. But there is not one word (or image) that referred to religion as even a part of the Pilgrims' life. [34]

> Other examples of the washing out of religion are such explanations as, "Pilgrims are people who make long trips". . . . [T]he Pilgrims are described *entirely* without any reference to religion; thus at the end of their first year they "wanted to give thanks for all they had" so they had the first Thanksgiving. But no mention is made of the fact that it was God they were thanking. [35]

At the high-school level, one national textbook listed eighty-three important dates in American history, and only one (the first Thanksgiving in 1621) was religious; [36] revisionists would have us believe that there have been no religious events of historical importance since 1621.

Another national text listed 642 events. While only six referred to religion, the following "important" dates were among those listed: 1893, Yale introduces ice hockey; 1897, first subway completed in Boston; 1920, United States wins first place in Olympic Games; 1930, Irish Sweepstakes becomes popular; 1960, Pittsburgh Pirates win World Series; 1962, Twist—a popular dance craze. [37]

Again, the revisionists would have us believe that such trivia are vital components in our nation's development. The researchers document that the texts regularly omit positive references to religion, the family, marriage, free-enterprise economics, traditional values, entrepreneurialism, and other foundational American virtues. Certainly, the failure to acknowledge religion and its effect on America (or any of these other virtues) cannot be blamed on a lack of historical material. [38]

Educators in earlier generations believed that to omit such aspects—especially the religious elements and a Providential view of history—was to deprive students of a truthful portrayal of America. As Charles Coffin (a popular author of student history texts in the 1870s) explained:

> There is still one other point [to the teaching of history]: you will notice that while the oppressors have carried out their plans and had things their own way, there were other forces silently at work which in time undermined their plans, only no—as if a Divine hand were directing the counter-plan. Whoever peruses the "Story of Liberty" without recognizing this feature will fail of fully comprehending the meaning of history. There must be a meaning to history or else existence is an incomprehensible enigma [complete riddle]. [39]

Omission is an effective tool used to indoctrinate readers with a secular, religion-free view of American history. The goal of the revisionists' use of this tool is to continually expose readers to a truncated treatment of history. The intended effect is for students to grow up striving to "protect" the supposed religion-free atmosphere which they would have us believe made America great.

4. The Use of Insinuations and Innuendos

Because of the human tendency to couple a message with the messenger, one need only discredit the messenger if he wishes to attempt to discredit a message. This tactic has been employed for centuries.

For example, 2,000 years ago when large crowds were following Jesus, opponents of his teachings began to circulate the untruth that Jesus was "a winebibber and a glutton" (Matthew 11:19). The expected effect was that many would cease to follow Him, for who needs the teachings of a drunkard?

Such rumors may be termed "insinuations" (a hint or covert suggestion against someone) or "innuendos" (a derogatory allusion). The use of insinuations and innuendos have proven very effective, especially in the political arena. Notice, for example, this absurd application:

> George Smathers unseated incumbent Claude Pepper in Florida's 1950 Senate primary by the clever use of innuendo when speaking to unsophisticated audiences. In mock horror, Smathers would ask voters if they were aware that Pepper was a "shameless extrovert" who had "practiced celibacy" as a young man. To shock his listeners utterly, he would confide that Pepper's sister living in New York was a "known thespian" [in other words, Pepper was friendly, outgoing, and morally pure as a young man, and his sister was a dramatic actress]. [40]

The use of insinuation and innuendo has been so effective in politics that it continues today—evidenced by recent statewide elections in Virginia where:

> In the 1st House of Delegates District, residents were asked whether they would vote for Terry Kilgore if they knew he had taken $4,000 from a client; the caller didn't mention that the money was payment for a legal fee. Pollsters asked 8th District residents if they were aware that Republican Morgan Griffith once defended a child molester—but apparently failed to mention that Griffith had been appointed by the court to do so. [41]

This strategy is called a "whisper campaign"; its effects are illustrated by a children's game:

> Somebody whispers a story in someone's ear, and that someone whispers it in somebody else's ear, and so on and so forth—until the last person whispered to tells the story. Which, if the game's

going well, will be so different from the original that everybody laughs like crazy. [42]

Insinuations and innuendos distort a message and are very effective when applied to historical figures. Notice the utilization of this tactic by W. E. Woodward:

> The colonial forefathers were hard, cold, cruel and realistic. The idea that they were kindly and leisurely is a sentimental notion, and it is not true. . . . The conversation among prosperous folk at dinner was about land, money and religion; generally it was about the making of money by getting the better of somebody else. There is where religion helped. A deeply religious person could, of course, make more money than others not so religious because his transactions were under the cloak of sanctity and were not subject to criticism. [43]

Woodward implied that the Founders were manipulative, self-centered, and greedy; they used religion only to acquire wealth. He also charged:

> Washington had the inestimable faculty of being able to say nothing. He said nothing about religion—nothing very definite— and was willing to let people think whatever they pleased. Jefferson, on the contrary, talked a great deal about religion. His intellect was expansive, prolific, full of ideas. He was a deist, like Washington, and he wanted to convince others. [44]

Again, Woodward leads the readers to believe that the Founders never spoke of religion positively and, in fact, only spoke of it when trying to turn others from it.

Fairfax Downey, in his work *Our Lusty Forefathers* (the title is itself an insinuation), charged:

> All the men [of the Founding era] went wooing widows. They were most assiduous [diligent] in their courtship of a "warm" widow, as they termed a rich one. . . . The wealthy Widow Custis brought George Washington a marriage portion which included a fortune of fifteen thousand pounds sterling and one hundred and fifty slaves. Franklin, Jefferson, and Madison married widows. [45]

The insinuation is twofold: first, the Founders were selfish, greedy men, seeking wealth at any cost; and second, Washington sought slaves in his pursuit of wealth. The truth is that George Washington was already wealthy before he married Martha (he owned 8,000 acres at the time of his marriage), and he sought neither to promote nor to prolong slavery.

Even though the issue of slavery is often raised as a discrediting charge against the Founding Fathers, the historical fact is that slavery was *not* the product of, nor was it an evil introduced by, the Founding Fathers; slavery had been introduced to America nearly two centuries *before* the Founders. As President of Congress Henry Laurens explained:

> I abhor slavery. I was born in a country where slavery had been established by British Kings and Parliaments as well as by the laws of the country ages before my existence. . . . In former days there was no combatting the prejudices of men supported by interest; the day, I hope, is approaching when, from principles of gratitude as well as justice, every man will strive to be foremost in showing his readiness to comply with the Golden Rule ["do unto others as you would have them do unto you" Matthew 7:12]. [46]

In fact, prior to the time of the Founding Fathers, there had been few serious efforts to dismantle the institution of slavery. John Jay identified the point at which the change in attitude toward slavery began:

> Prior to the great Revolution, the great majority . . . of our people had been so long accustomed to the practice and convenience of having slaves that very few among them even doubted the propriety and rectitude of it. [47]

The Revolution was the turning point in the national attitude—and it was the Founding Fathers who contributed greatly to that change. In fact, many of the Founders vigorously complained against the fact that Great Britain had forcefully imposed upon the Colonies the evil of slavery. For example, Thomas Jefferson heavily criticized that British policy:

> He [King George III] has waged cruel war against human nature itself, violating its most sacred rights of life and liberty in the persons of a distant people who never offended him, captivating and carrying them into slavery in another hemisphere or to incur miserable death in their transportation thither. . . . Determined to keep open a market where men should be bought and sold, he has prostituted his negative for suppressing every legislative attempt

to prohibit or to restrain this execrable commerce [that is, he has opposed efforts to prohibit the slave trade]. [48]

Benjamin Franklin, in a 1773 letter to Dean Woodward, confirmed that whenever the Americans had attempted to end slavery, the British government had indeed thwarted those attempts. Franklin explained that . . .

. . . a disposition to abolish slavery prevails in North America, that many of Pennsylvanians have set their slaves at liberty, and that even the Virginia Assembly have petitioned the King for permission to make a law for preventing the importation of more into that colony. This request, however, will probably not be granted as their former laws of that kind have always been repealed. [49]

Further confirmation that even the Virginia Founders were *not* responsible for slavery, but actually tried to dismantle the institution, was provided by John Quincy Adams (known as the "hell-hound of slavery" for his extensive efforts against that evil). Adams explained:

The inconsistency of the institution of domestic slavery with the principles of the Declaration of Independence was seen and lamented by all the southern patriots of the Revolution; by no one with deeper and more unalterable conviction than by the author of the Declaration himself [Jefferson]. No charge of insincerity or hypocrisy can be fairly laid to their charge. Never from their lips was heard one syllable of attempt to justify the institution of slavery. They universally considered it as a reproach fastened upon them by the unnatural step-mother country [Great Britain] and they saw that before the principles of the Declaration of Independence, slavery, in common with every other mode of oppression, was destined sooner or later to be banished from the earth. Such was the undoubting conviction of Jefferson to his dying day. In the *Memoir of His Life*, written at the age of seventy-seven, he gave to his countrymen the solemn and emphatic warning that the day was not distant when they must hear and adopt the general emancipation of their slaves. [50]

In fact, Jefferson himself had introduced a bill in the Virginia Assembly designed to end slavery. [51] However, not all of the southern Founders were opposed to slavery; according to the testimony of Virginians James Madison, Thomas Jefferson, and John Rutledge, it was the Founders from North Carolina, South Carolina, and Georgia who favored slavery. [52]

Yet, despite the support for slavery in those States, the clear majority of the Founders opposed this evil. For instance, when some of the southern pro-slavery advocates invoked the Bible in support of slavery, Elias Boudinot, President of the Continental Congress, quickly reminded them:

> [E]ven the sacred Scriptures had been quoted to justify this iniquitous traffic. It is true that the Egyptians held the Israelites in bondage for four hundred years, . . . but . . . gentlemen cannot forget the consequences that followed: they were delivered by a strong hand and stretched-out arm and it ought to be remembered that the Almighty Power that accomplished their deliverance is the same yesterday, today, and for ever. [53]

Many of the Founding Fathers who had owned slaves as British citizens released them in the years following America's separation from Great Britain (e.g., George Washington, John Dickinson, Caesar Rodney, William Livingston, George Wythe, John Randolph of Roanoke, and others). Furthermore, many of the Founders had *never* owned any slaves. For example, John Adams proclaimed, "[M]y opinion against it [slavery] has always been known . . . [N]ever in my life did I own a slave." [54]

Notice a few additional examples of the strong anti-slavery sentiments held by great numbers of the Founders:

> [W]hy keep alive the question of slavery? It is admitted by all to be a great evil. [55] **CHARLES CARROLL,** SIGNER OF THE DECLARATION

> As Congress is now to legislate for our extensive territory lately acquired, I pray to Heaven that they may build up the system of the government on the broad, strong, and sound principles of freedom. Curse not the inhabitants of those regions, and of the United States in general, with a permission to introduce bondage [slavery]. [56] **JOHN DICKINSON,** SIGNER OF THE CONSTITUTION; GOVERNOR OF PENNSYLVANIA

> That men should pray and fight for their own freedom and yet keep others in slavery is certainly acting a very inconsistent as well as unjust and perhaps impious part. [57] **JOHN JAY,** PRESIDENT OF CONTINENTAL CONGRESS; ORIGINAL CHIEF JUSTICE U. S. SUPREME COURT

The whole commerce between master and slave is a perpetual exercise of the most boisterous passions, the most unremitting despotism on the one part, and degrading submissions on the other. . . . And with what execration [curse] should the statesman be loaded, who permitting one half the citizens thus to trample on the rights of the other. . . . And can the liberties of a nation be thought secure when we have removed their only firm basis, a conviction in the minds of the people that these liberties are of the gift of God? That they are not to be violated but with His wrath? Indeed I tremble for my country when I reflect that God is just; that his justice cannot sleep forever. [58] **THOMAS JEFFERSON**

Christianity, by introducing into Europe the truest principles of humanity, universal benevolence, and brotherly love, had happily abolished civil slavery. Let us who profess the same religion practice its precepts . . . by agreeing to this duty. [59] **RICHARD HENRY LEE**, PRESIDENT OF CONTINENTAL CONGRESS; SIGNER OF THE DECLARATION

I hope we shall at last, and if it so please God I hope it may be during my life time, see this cursed thing [slavery] taken out. . . . For my part, whether in a public station or a private capacity, I shall always be prompt to contribute my assistance towards effecting so desirable an event. [60] **WILLIAM LIVINGSTON**, SIGNER OF THE CONSTITUTION; GOVERNOR OF NEW JERSEY

[I]t ought to be considered that national crimes can only be and frequently are punished in this world by national punishments; and that the continuance of the slave-trade, and thus giving it a national sanction and encouragement, ought to be considered as justly exposing us to the displeasure and vengeance of Him who is equally Lord of all and who views with equal eye the poor African slave and his American master. [61] **LUTHER MARTIN**, DELEGATE AT CONSTITUTIONAL CONVENTION

As much as I value a union of all the States, I would not admit the Southern States into the Union unless they agree to the discontinuance of this disgraceful trade [slavery]. [62] **GEORGE MASON**, FATHER OF THE BILL OF RIGHTS

Honored will that State be in the annals of history which shall first abolish this violation of the rights of mankind. [63] **JOSEPH REED**, REVOLUTIONARY OFFICER; GOVERNOR OF PENNSYLVANIA

Domestic slavery is repugnant to the principles of Christianity. . . . It is rebellion against the authority of a common Father. It is a practical denial of the extent and efficacy of the death of a common Savior. It is an usurpation of the prerogative of the great Sovereign of the universe who has solemnly claimed an exclusive property in the souls of men. [64] **BENJAMIN RUSH**, SIGNER OF THE DECLARATION

Justice and humanity require it [the end of slavery]—Christianity commands it. Let every benevolent . . . pray for the glorious period when the last slave who fights for freedom shall be restored to the possession of that inestimable right. [65] **NOAH WEBSTER**

Slavery, or an absolute and unlimited power in the master over the life and fortune of the slave, is unauthorized by the common law. . . . The reasons which we sometimes see assigned for the origin and the continuance of slavery appear, when examined to the bottom, to be built upon a false foundation. In the enjoyment of their persons and of their property, the common law protects all. [66] **JAMES WILSON**, SIGNER OF THE CONSTITUTION; U. S. SUPREME COURT JUSTICE

[I]t is certainly unlawful to make inroads upon others . . . and take away their liberty by no better means than superior power. [67] **JOHN WITHERSPOON**, SIGNER OF THE DECLARATION

For many of the Founders, their feelings against slavery went beyond words. For example, in 1774, Benjamin Franklin and Benjamin Rush founded America's first anti-slavery society; John Jay was president of a similar society in New York. In fact, when signer of the Constitution William Livingston heard of the New York society, he, as Governor of New Jersey, wrote them, offering:

I would most ardently wish to become a member of it [the society in New York] and . . . I can safely promise them that neither my tongue, nor my pen, nor purse shall be wanting to promote the abolition of what to me appears so inconsistent with humanity and Christianity. . . . May the great and the equal Father of the human race, who has expressly declared His abhorrence of oppression, and that He is no respecter of persons, succeed a design so laudably calculated to undo the heavy burdens, to let the oppressed go free, and to break every yoke. [68]

Other prominent Founding Fathers who were members of societies for ending slavery included Richard Bassett, James Madison, James Monroe, Bushrod Washington, Charles Carroll, William Few, John Marshall, Richard Stockton, Zephaniah Swift, and many more. In fact, based in part on the efforts of these Founders, Pennsylvania and Massachusetts took decisive steps to end slavery in 1780; [69] Connecticut and Rhode Island did so in 1784; [70] Vermont in 1786; [71] New Hampshire in 1792; [72] New York in 1799; [73] and New Jersey did so in 1804. [74]

Additionally, the reason that Ohio, Indiana, Illinois, Michigan, Wisconsin, and Iowa all prohibited slavery was a Congressional act, authored by Constitution signer Rufus King [75] and signed into law by President George Washington, [76] which prohibited slavery in those territories. [77] It is not surprising that Washington would sign such a law, for it was he who had declared:

I can only say that there is not a man living who wishes more sincerely than I do to see a plan adopted for the abolition of it [slavery]. [78]

The truth is that it was the Founders who were responsible for planting and nurturing the first seeds for the recognition of black equality and for the eventual end of slavery. This was a fact made clear by Richard Allen.

Allen had been a slave in Pennsylvania but was freed after he converted his master to Christianity. A close friend of Benjamin Rush and several other Founding Fathers, Allen went on to become the founder of the A.M.E. Church in America. In an early address "To the People of Color," he explained:

Many of the white people have been instruments in the hands of God for our good, even such as have held us in captivity, [and] are now pleading our cause with earnestness and zeal. [79]

While much progress was made by the Founders to end the institution of slavery, what they began was not achieved until years later.

Yet, despite the strenuous effort of many Founders to recognize in practice that "all men are created equal," charges persist to the opposite. In fact, revisionists even claim that the Constitution demonstrates that the Founders considered one who was black to be only three-fifths of a person. This charge is yet another falsehood.

The three-fifths clause was not a measurement of human worth; rather, it was an *anti-slavery* provision to limit the political power of slavery's proponents. By including only three-fifths of the total number of slaves in the congressional calculations, Southern States were actually being denied additional pro-slavery representatives in Congress.

Based on the clear records of the Constitutional Convention, two prominent professors explain the meaning of the three-fifths clause:

> [T]he Constitution allowed Southern States to count three-fifths of their slaves toward the population that would determine numbers of representatives in the federal legislature. This clause is often singled out today as a sign of black dehumanization: they are only three-fifths human. But the provision applied to slaves, not blacks. That meant that free blacks—and there were many, North as well as South—counted the same as whites. More important, the fact that slaves were counted at all was a concession to slave owners. Southerners would have been glad to count their slaves as whole persons. It was the Northerners who did not want them counted, for why should the South be rewarded with more representatives, the more slaves they held? [80] **THOMAS WEST**

> It was slavery's *opponents* who succeeded in *restricting* the political power of the South by allowing them to count *only* three-fifths of their slave population in determining the number of congressional representatives. The three-fifths of a vote provision applied only to slaves, not to free blacks in either the North or South. [81] **WALTER WILLIAMS** (emphasis added)

Why do revisionists so often abuse and misportray the three-fifths clause? Professor Walter Williams (himself an African-American) further explained:

> Politicians, news media, college professors and leftists of other stripes are selling us lies and propaganda. To lay the groundwork for their increasingly successful attack on our Constitution, they must demean and criticize its authors. As Senator Joe Biden demonstrated during the Clarence Thomas hearings, the framers' ideas about natural law must be trivialized or they must be seen as racists. [82]

While this has been only a cursory examination of the Founders and slavery, it is nonetheless sufficient to demonstrate the absurdity of the insinuation that the Founders were a collective group of racists.

In a totally different type of insinuation, it is frequently charged that religion has been dangerously negative and even has an often harmful influence on a society. For example, Frank Swancara, in his *Obstruction of Justice by Religion*, claims:

> [R]eligion poisons the judicial mind just as it has often affected the mental condition of the persecuting bigot. [83]

This irrational conclusion is endorsed by those who, in an attempt to "prove" the adverse effect of religion on a society, point to several genuine atrocities perpetrated in the name of Christianity (e.g., the Salem Witch Trials, the Moors, the Crusades, the Inquisition, and even the World War II Holocaust, which many Jews attribute to Christians). In fact, if one tabulates the loss of lives occasioned by "Christian" conduct, the total which may be laid at the doorstep of Christianity over the past thousand years is perhaps 20 million.

It is true that leaders who have claimed a Christian adherence have definitely committed numerous atrocities, yet it is also irrefutable that those without Christian connections have committed abundantly more. In fact, the number of lives lost at the hands of non- and anti-Christian leaders in the twentieth-century alone is staggering. Consider the 62 million killed by the Soviet Communists; the 35 million by the Communist Chinese; the 1.7 million by the Vietnamese Communists; the 1 million in the Polish Ethnic Cleansing; the 1 million in Yugoslavia; the 1.7 million in North Korea; [84] etc.

Furthermore, consider the deaths perpetrated by individual anti-Christian or anti-religious leaders. For example, Joseph Stalin murdered 42.7 million; Mao Tse-tung, 37.8 million; Vladimir Lenin, 4 million; Tojo Hideki, 4 million; Pol Pot of the Khmer Rouge, 1 million; Yahya Khan, 1.5 million; [85] and numerous other anti-Christian leaders could be listed.

While the lives lost at the hands of Christians in the past thousand years number in the tens of millions, those lost at the hands of anti-Christians in only the past seventy-five years number in the hundreds of millions.

Furthermore, the lives lost under the guise of Christianity should be categorized in greater detail. For example, historian Daniel Dorchester pointed out that although inhumanities have occurred in the name of Christianity, very few have occurred under the banner of American Christianity:

> These "dreadful and disgusting inhumanities" were perpetrated by whom? Refined and cultivated Europeans. . . . Such are the facts of modern history which should moderate our denunciations and charges of severity, brutality and narrow-mindedness against

the colonial forefathers, who, it clearly appears, were much in advance of their times. [86]

Ironically, the charge of the harmfulness of Christianity to a society is not new; when it was raised two-hundred years ago, signer of the Declaration John Witherspoon had a very forceful response:

> Let us try it by its fruits. Let us compare the temper and character of real Christians with those of infidels and see which of them best merits the approbation of an honest and impartial judge. Let us take in every circumstance that will contribute to make the comparison just and fair and see what will be the result. . . . In which of the two is to be found the greatest integrity and uprightness in their conduct between man and man? the most unfeigned good-will? and the most active beneficence to others? Is it the unbeliever or the Christian who clothes the naked and deals his bread to the hungry? Ask the many and noble ancient structures raised for the relief of the diseased and the poor to whom they owe their establishment and support? [87]

The results, or what Witherspoon called the "fruits," do speak for themselves. While Christianity certainly does not make men perfect, as it is demonstrable both historically and statistically, it does tend to restrain their naturally destructive behavior. As Ben Franklin reminded religious critic Thomas Paine:

> If men are so wicked with religion, what would they be if without it? [88]

Insinuations and innuendos are applied against historical personalities for a simple purpose: if someone can be induced to reject the messenger, he will probably reject the message.

5. Impugning Morality

Impugning or belittling morality is a refined use of innuendoes and insinuations. Often, the charges which belittle morality are based on apparently viable historical evidence.

For example, when many current works claim that George Washington had an ongoing and longlasting love for Sarah [nicknamed Sally] Fairfax during his marriage to Martha, they appear to invoke a credible basis—as James Thomas Flexner's claim:

> That Washington fell in love with this wife of his friend and neighbor is proved by uncontrovertible documents. As we shall see

... as an old man who had been separated from Sally by the Atlantic Ocean for more than a quarter of a century, he wrote her that all the events of the Revolution and his presidency had not "been able to eradicate from my mind those happy moments, the happiest of my life, which I have enjoyed in your company." [89]

This reference by Flexner is taken from a letter written by Washington to Sarah Fairfax in which he told her:

None of which events, however, nor all of them together, have been able to eradicate from my mind the recollection of those happy moments, the happiest in my life, which I have enjoyed in your company. [90]

Certainly, on its surface, this portion of Washington's letter seems to imply that there was a special love relationship between him and Sarah Fairfax. Yet what is conspicuously absent from this revisionist claim is the rest of the letter, as well as the historical background providing the context for that letter.

There was indeed a special relationship between Washington and the Fairfaxes—a relationship which began while he was a youth. The property of the Fairfaxes (a prominent Virginia family for whom Fairfax County is named) directly adjoined that of the Washingtons. As a boy of fifteen, Washington had begun frequent visits to that estate (named "Belvoir") at which time William Fairfax, Sr., had befriended the young Washington, often taking him hunting. A strong and close friendship then developed between Washington and the family; and for a number of years, Washington spent many happy hours at that estate. When his dear friend, William, Jr., married Sarah, the strong friendship which Washington already enjoyed with William was broadened to include his new wife.

When the conflict with Britain commenced, Washington left behind both his home at Mount Vernon and his friendship with the Fairfaxes. Over the next twenty-five years, he returned home only infrequently due to his extended public service, including that in the Revolution, at the Constitutional Convention, as President, etc.

One of his rare visits home occurred in the interval between the conclusion of the Revolution and the convening of the Constitutional Convention. On that trip, Washington returned to Belvoir and, sadly, found it burned to the ground. On viewing the ruins of the house where he had passed so many happy hours, Washington was deeply moved. He wrote William, Jr., telling him:

But alas! Belvoir is no more! I took a ride there the other day to visit the ruins and ruins indeed they are. The dwelling house and the two brick buildings in front underwent the ravages of the fire; the walls of which are very much injured: the other houses are sinking under the depredation of time and inattention and I believe are now scarcely worth repairing. In a word, the whole are, or very soon will be a heap of ruin. When I viewed them, when I considered that the happiest moments of my life had been spent there, when I could not trace a room in the house (now all rubbish) that did not bring to my mind the recollection of pleasing scenes, I was obliged to fly from them and came home with painful sensations. [91]

Shortly after that letter, William, Jr., died, and Washington returned to the service of his country. Almost a decade passed before he finally returned home to spend the remaining three years of his life at Mount Vernon. In that period, shortly before his death, Washington wrote Sarah a letter expressing to her the sentiments similar to those he had earlier expressed to her husband. He told her:

My dear Madam: Five and twenty years nearly have passed away since I have considered myself as the permanent resident at this place [Mount Vernon] or have been in a situation to indulge myself in a familiar intercourse [social exchange] with my friends by letter or otherwise. During this period, so many important events have occurred and such changes in men and things have taken place, as the compass of a letter would give you but an inadequate idea of. None of which events, however, nor all of them together, have been able to eradicate from my mind the recollection of those happy moments, the happiest in my life, which I have enjoyed in your company [at Belvoir]. [92]

When divorced from its historical context, this last phrase enables revisionists to "prove" an affair between George Washington and Sarah Fairfax.

In a continuing attempt to impugn Washington's morality, Flexner further claimed:

Washington was in his later years to contrast unfavorably "the giddy rounds of promiscuous pleasure" with "the sequestered walks of connubial life." Was he judging from experience? [93]

By using these two phrases from a letter, Flexner insinuates that Washington had personally engaged in "the giddy rounds of promiscuous pleasure." Again, both the historical background and the full letter discredit Flexner's charge.

The subject of Washington's letter was the French General Charles Armand-Tuffin, the Marquis de la Rouerie. The French and their propensity for immorality had long been complained of by American leaders, [94] while in contrast, America had been known worldwide as the nation in which both marriage and marital fidelity were esteemed the highest. [95] When Washington was informed that the French General had announced his plans to be married, Washington wrote:

> I must confess, I was a little pleased, if not surprised, to find him think like an American on the subject of matrimony and domestic felicity. For in my estimation more permanent and genuine happiness is to be found in the sequestered walks of connubial life [married] than in the giddy rounds of promiscuous pleasure. [96]

Clearly, the full letter discredits Flexner's charge. Yet, Flexner nevertheless concocts an imputation of immorality against Washington. Such charges of immorality, once raised, often increase in tone and intensity until they reach ridiculous proportions—as has been the case with Washington.

For example, numerous students on college campuses across the nation have informed me that they were taught in their American history classes that Washington died from one of two causes: (1) either of syphilis (or a similar venereal disease) or (2) from contracting pneumonia as a result of making a hasty escape from a lover's bedroom window into a bitter winter storm as her husband approached the front door. Both of these charges are demonstrably false.

For example, Washington's adopted son testifies how that Washington contracted the illness while working on the grounds of Mount Vernon:

> On the morning of the 13th [of December, 1799], the General was engaged in making some improvements in the front of Mount Vernon. As was usual with him, he carried his own compass, noted his observations, and marked out the ground. The day became rainy, with sleet, and the improver remained so long exposed to the inclemency of the weather as to be considerably wetted before his return to the house. About one o'clock he was seized with chilliness and nausea, but having changed his clothes, he sat down to his indoor work—there being no moment of his time for which he had not provided an appropriate employment. [97]

John Marshall, George Washington's close friend and famous biographer, records what next occurred after Washington was thoroughly chilled:

> Unapprehensive of danger from this circumstance, he passed the afternoon in his usual manner; but in the night, he was seized with an inflammatory affection of the windpipe. The disease commenced with a violent ague, accompanied with some pain in the upper and fore part of the throat, a sense of stricture in the same part, a cough, and a difficult rather than a painful deglutition, which were soon succeeded by fever and a quick and laborious respiration. Believing bloodletting to be necessary, he procured a bleeder who took from his arm twelve or fourteen ounces of blood, but he would not permit a messenger to be dispatched for his family physician until the appearance of day. About eleven in the morning, Dr. Craik arrived: and perceiving the extreme danger of the case, requested that two consulting physicians should be immediately sent for. [98]

Notice the medical report filed by those physicians after the unsuccessful termination of their treatments. The three doctors who attended Washington during his final illness reported:

> Some time in the night of Friday the 13th instant, having been exposed to rain on the preceding day, General Washington was attacked with an inflammatory affection of the upper part of the windpipe, called in technical language, cynanche trachealis [currently called "quinsy"—a severe form of strep throat]. The disease commenced with a violent ague [shivering], accompanied with some pain in the upper and fore part of the throat, a sense of stricture in the same part, a cough, and a difficult rather than a painful deglutition [act of swallowing], which were soon succeeded by fever and a quick and laborious respiration. The necessity of bloodletting suggesting itself to the General [it was believed that fever was an "excitement" of the blood and that removing part of the blood would reduce the fever], he procured a bleeder in the neighborhood who took from his arm in the night twelve or fourteen ounces of blood. . . . Discovering the case to be highly alarming, and foreseeing the fatal tendency of the disease, two consulting physicians were immediately sent for who arrived, one at half after three, the other at four o'clock in the afternoon. In the interim were employed two copious bleedings; a blister [medical plaster] was applied to the part affected,

two moderate doses of calomel [a mercury mixture used to induce vomiting] were given, and an injection was administered which operated on the lower intestines—but all without any perceptible advantage; the respiration becoming still more difficult and distressing.—Upon the arrival of the first of the consulting physicians, it was agreed . . . to try the result of another bleeding, when about thirty-two ounces of blood were drawn without the smallest apparent alleviation of the disease. . . . The powers of life seemed now manifestly yielding to the force of the disorder. Blisters were applied to the extremities together with a cataplasm [a poultice] of bran and vinegar to the throat. . . . [R]espiration grew more and more contracted and imperfect till half after eleven o'clock on Saturday night when, retaining the full possession of his intellect, he expired without a struggle. [99]

The evidence, both medical and anecdotal, clearly disproves any charges that Washington died from a disease contracted or caused by any moral laxness. Furthermore, numerous eyewitnesses establish Washington's strong and pure moral character. For example:

His private character, as well as his public one, will bear the strictest scrutiny. . . . He was the friend of morality. [100] DAVID RAMSAY, SURGEON IN THE CONTINENTAL ARMY; MEMBER OF THE CONTINENTAL CONGRESS

We have seen that his private life was marked in an eminent degree with the practice of the moral virtues. . . . He taught (and his own practice corresponded with his doctrine) that the foundation of national policy can be laid only in the pure and immutable principles of private morality. [101] JEREMIAH SMITH, REVOLUTIONARY SOLDIER; JUDGE; U. S. CONGRESSMAN; GOVERNOR OF NEW HAMPSHIRE

The private virtues of this great man exactly corresponded with those exhibited in public life. . . . To crown all these moral virtues, he had the deepest sense of religion impressed on his heart; the true foundation-stone of all the moral virtues. This he constantly manifested on all proper occasions. [102] JONATHAN SEWELL, ATTORNEY

The purity of his private character gave effulgence to [was revealed by] his public virtue. [103] HENRY LEE, MAJOR-GENERAL UNDER GEORGE WASHINGTON

[H]is character will remain to all ages a model of human virtue, untarnished with a single vice. [104] **JOHN QUINCY ADAMS**

[T]he moral deportment in the character of this great man may be held up to view as the boast of the present and as a model for the imitation of future ages. [105] **CHARLES CALDWELL,** PHYSICIAN; EDUCATOR

The attacks on Washington's morality are solely the product of revisionists. As explained by early twentieth-century historian Alfred McCann:

Between 1759 and 1774 two letters, "G. W.," were sufficient to open all doors in Virginia. From 1774 to 1799 they opened all doors in America. In 1889 a feeble effort was made to put them in lower case—"g. w." In 1926 a new brand of courage appeared in the world. Two little men [definitely W. E. Woodward and apparently Charles Beard] with fountain pens restored the upper case, but made it read "Godless!" "Wanton!". . . . Perhaps it is well for the 1926 biographers that Washington is dead. Roosevelt could carry his libelers into court. The son of Gladstone, who describes Washington as "the purest figure of history," could meet his father's assailant in the presence of wig and gown [in the courts]. But the 1926 detractors need not fear civil or criminal action. The dead are without redress. So too the truth. . . . The spicy stories are all of recent origin. [106]

Jefferson also suffers from a contemporary attack on his morality. For example:

One of the greatest love stories in American history is also one of the least known, and most controversial. Thomas Jefferson, third president of the United States and author of the Declaration of Independence, had a mistress for thirty-eight years, whom he loved and lived with until he died, the beautiful and elusive Sally Hemings. But it was not simply that Jefferson had a mistress that provoked the scandal of the times; it was that Sally Hemings was a quadroon slave, and that Jefferson fathered a slave family. [107]

These charges appear in several contemporary works; for example, Fawn Brodie's *Thomas Jefferson: An Intimate History* and Barbara Chase-Riboud's *Sally Hemings.* (Even the highly publicized DNA testing results released in 1998 that reputedly "proved" that Jefferson fathered Hemings' children was ***retracted*** in 1999 due to both scientific and historical inaccuracies in the original report; yet, who heard of the retraction of the story?) Like the charges against

Washington, those against Jefferson also have an apparent "historical" basis—a basis identified by the eminent Jeffersonian historian Virginius Dabney:

> The debunking of Jefferson began when a vicious, unscrupulous disappointed office-seeker named James T. Callender disseminated to the nation in 1802 the allegation that Jefferson had slave Sally Hemings as his concubine. [108]

Were those charges credible? Consider Callender's personal history.

James T. Callender (1758-1803) began his career as a political pamphleteer in Scotland. His writings there were so libelous and seditious that being "oftimes called in court, did not appear, [Callender was] pronounced a fugitive and an outlaw." [109] Callender fled to America for refuge where he also resumed his former writing style—this time against prominent Americans—thus confirming "his genius as a scandalmonger." [110] In fact, his writings were so baseless and unscrupulous that, even in America, he was taken to court, fined, sentenced, and imprisoned. Ironically, it was Jefferson who secured his pardon. After his release, Callender resumed his previous practices—this time launching his attack on Jefferson, accusing him of "dishonesty, cowardice, and gross personal immorality." [111]

It is no wonder that with such a proven record of scurrility, eminent historians both then and now dismissed Callender's charges as frivolous:

> James Truslow Adams, the eminent [1922 Pulitzer Prize winning] historian, wrote that "almost every scandalous story about Jefferson which is still whispered or believed" may be traced to the scurrilous writings of Callender [rather than to any historical fact]. Others, including Merrill Peterson, [Professor of History at the University of Virginia], hold the same opinion. . . . John C. Miller, the Stanford University historian, describes Callender as "the most unscrupulous scandalmonger of the day . . . a journalist who stopped at nothing and stooped to anything. . . . Callender was not an investigative journalist; he never bothered to investigate anything; . . . truth, if it stood in his way, was summarily mowed down." [112]

On the charges of a single historical figure who was a proven liar, modern revisionists have attempted to sacrifice Jefferson's morality. In fact, as Virginius Dabney explained:

> Had it not been for Callender, recently revived charges to the same effect probably would never have come to national attention. [113]

Yet today's revisionists accept Callender's charges *carte blanche* and revive them as though they were undisputed fact in order to proclaim to today's generation that Jefferson was immoral.

Another example impugning the morality of the Founders comes from revisionist Randy Shilts, author of *Conduct Unbecoming*. Shilts claims:

> History tells us that the man who first instilled discipline in the ragtag Continental Army at Valley Forge was the Prussian Baron Frederick William von Steuben. . . . Von Steuben at first had declined Benjamin Franklin's offer of the job, because the Continental Congress could not pay him. But when von Steuben learned that ecclesiastical authorities were planning to try him for homosexuality, he renegotiated with Franklin and was appointed a major general to the Continental Army. . . . Some military historians have judged von Steuben as one of only two men whose contributions were "indispensable" toward winning the Revolutionary War; the other was George Washington. It is a crowning irony that anti-gay policies are defended in the name of preserving the good order and discipline of the U. S. military, when that very order and discipline was the creation of a gay man. [114]

Shilts seems to make a compelling argument and cites for his historical evidence the book *General Von Steuben* by John Palmer (perhaps the leading scholar on von Steuben). Shilts accurately depicted the charge against von Steuben but deliberately omitted Palmer's conclusion about that charge. Notice Palmer's conclusion:

> That it [the charge that von Steuben was a homosexual] grew out of jealousy and religious bigotry is not improbable; for it will be recalled that the Baron was a Protestant minister at the head of a Catholic court, the heretic favorite of an orthodox prince. If the story was credited at one time by the Prince of Hohenzollern-Hechingen, he was evidently convinced later of its falsity and cruel injustice. For, as we shall see, the Baron was eventually restored to his affectionate regard. It is impossible to prove the falsity of such a story. But it is perhaps pertinent for me to say that the charge is inconsistent with the conception of Steuben's personality that has grown up in my mind after eight years' study of every memorial [written representation of facts] of him that I could find. [115]

Further disproving Shilts' claim is the fact that an openly homosexual individual—as Shilts claims von Steuben was—would *never* have been accepted in the Continental Army. This is confirmed by the fact that the first time ever that a homosexual was drummed out of the American military was during the American Revolution—by Commander-in-Chief George Washington:

> At a General Court Martial whereof Colo. Tupper was President (10th March 1778), Lieut. Enslin of Colo. Malcom's Regiment [was] tried for attempting to commit sodomy, with John Monhort a soldier . . . [he was] found guilty of the charges exhibited against him, being breaches of 5th. Article 18th. Section of the Articles of War and [we] do sentence him to be dismiss'd [from] the service with infamy [public disgrace]. His Excellency the Commander in Chief approves the sentence and *with abhorrence and detestation of such infamous crimes* orders Lieut. Enslin to be drummed out of camp tomorrow morning by all the drummers and fifers in the Army never to return. [116] (emphasis added)

The overall attitude of the Founders toward homosexuality was similar to that of Blackstone, who found the subject so reprehensible that it was difficult for him even to discuss. [117] For example, James Wilson was so disgusted with homosexuality that in his legal works he declared:

> The crime not to be named [sodomy], I pass in a total silence. [118]

Similarly, Zephaniah Swift explained that homosexuality was "punished with death. . . . [because of] the disgust and horror with which we treat of this abominable crime." [119]

In fact, at the insistence of the Founding Fathers, the penalties for homosexuality were very severe. In States like New York, Connecticut, South Carolina, and Vermont, the penalty for homosexuality was death; [120] the laws of other States showed similarly harsh penalties. [121] In Virginia, according to Thomas Jefferson, "dismemberment" of the offensive organ was the penalty, [122] and Jefferson himself authored a bill to penalize sodomy by castration. [123]

Based on all evidence of that day, it is clear that any idea of homosexuals serving in the military was considered with repugnance; this is incontrovertible, with no room for differing interpretations. Shilts' conclusion is not only inconsistent with the source he claims to cite, but it is also repudiated by American military policy before, during, and after von Steuben.

Shilts, in a manner consistent with other revisionists, was attempting to concoct historical approval for a generally unacceptable social policy. Impugning morality remains an effective tool of revisionists in attempting to redirect and redefine the political morés of a society.

6. The Use of "Faction"

Another tactic commonly employed by revisionists is "faction" (presenting fiction as if it were fact)—an approach especially evident in many historical novels, plays, and dramas. While works of "faction" usually claim historical accuracy, they are typically characterized by a notable lack of references to primary-sources.

An excellent example of faction is "1776," which first appeared as a Broadway play (1969), as a book (1970), and later as a movie. Notice the author's and publisher's claim:

> The first question we are asked by those who have seen—or read—
> *1776* is invariably: "Is it true? Did it really happen that way?" The
> answer is: Yes. [124]

Recalling this claim of historical truth, observe the following conversations between Martha Jefferson, Ben Franklin, and John Adams:

JOHN: Franklin, look! He's [Jefferson] written something—he's done it! [He dashes after them, snatches the paper off the bow, and comes back to Franklin, delighted, and reads it.] "Dear Mr. Adams: I am taking my wife back to bed. Kindly go away. Y'r ob'd't, T. Jefferson."
FRANKLIN: What, again?
JOHN: Incredible! [125]

MARTHA: I am not an idle flatterer, Dr. Franklin. My husband admires you both greatly.
FRANKLIN: Then we are doubly flattered, for we admire very much that which your husband admires. [A pause as they regard each other warmly. They have hit it off].
JOHN: Did you sleep well, Madame? [Franklin nudges him with his elbow.] I mean, did you lie comfortably? Oh, d____! Y'know what I mean! [126]

Notice also the exchanges concerning John Hancock and Stephen Hopkins (the Governor of Rhode Island and a devout Quaker):

HANCOCK: Thank you, Mr. Thomson. [He swats a fly.] Mr. McNair, the stores of rum and other drinking spirits are hereby closed to the colony of Rhode Island for a period of three days.
MCNAIR: Yes, sir.
HOPKINS: John, y'can't do that!
HANCOCK: Sit down, Mr. Hopkins. You've abused the privilege. [127]

HOPKINS [joining Franklin and Hall, a mug of rum in his hand]: Ben, I want y'to see some cards I've gone 'n' had printed up that ought t'save everybody here a whole lot of time 'n' effort, considering the epidemic of bad disposition that's been going around lately. [He reads:] "Dear sir: You are without any doubt a rogue, a rascal, a villain, a thief, a scoundrel, and a mean, dirty, stinking, sniveling, sneaking, pimping, pocket-picking, thrice double-d____, no good son-of-a-b____"—and y'sign y'r name. What do y'think? [words deleted]
FRANKLIN [delighted]: Stephen, I'll take a dozen right now! [128]

Despite the author's and publisher's claim of an historical basis, there is **absolutely no** evidence to support **any** of these exchanges. In fact, concerning Stephen Hopkins' alleged drunkenness and gross profanity, all historical evidence points to an exactly opposite conclusion. Notice:

He went to his grave honored as a skillful legislator, a righteous judge, and able representative, a dignified and upright Governor. [129]

An affectionate husband, and a tender parent, he was greatly attached to the regular habits of domestic life. Exemplary, quiet, and serene in his family, he governed his children and domestics in an easy and affectionate manner. . . . As in life he had despised the follies, so in death he rose superior to the fears of an ignorant and licentious world; and he expected with patience and met with pious and philosophic intrepidity the stroke of death. [130]

Through life he had been a constant attendant of the religious meetings of Friends, or Quakers, and was ever distinguished among men as a sincere Christian. [131]

Another example of faction is the previously mentioned novel, *Sally Hemings*, by Barbara Chase-Riboud, detailing the supposedly lurid relationship between Thomas Jefferson and the slave girl, Sally Hemings. Of that work, the publisher claims:

In this moving novel, which spans two continents, sixty years, and seven presidencies, Barbara Chase-Riboud re-creates a love story, based on the documents and evidence of the day. [132]

Notice some of the story-line allegedly "based on the documents and evidence of the day":

"My dear . . . you mustn't worry if I seem . . . strange sometimes." Thomas Jefferson's voice had the familiar hesitancy of his public speaking. "This is so unexpected and for me, so unbidden. And you are . . . so young and yet so sure". . . . Thomas Jefferson fondled the delicate skin at the back of his slave's neck under the coiled hair. . . . The pallor, the soft eyes, the ribbon undone, the mouth softened by their kisses . . . He was smiling lazily at her. Even now after their moment of passion, there was a violence and a constraint about him that made her tremble. [133]

This is quite obviously a work of faction since there is absolutely *no* evidence to support *any* of these alleged exchanges (except the general charge made by the convicted libeler, James T. Callender). The lack of substance being no hindrance to the pursuit of scandal, the publisher nevertheless claims that this exchange was grounded in "the documents and evidence of the day."

Mary Higgins Clark, in her work *Aspire to the Heavens: A Portrait of George Washington*, writes in a similarly reckless manner about George Washington and Sally Fairfax:

The telltale blush had made him reckless. "Do you really think it necessary to teach me how to love," he demanded, "or don't you think you've taught me too well? Sally, oh Sally . . ." [134]

Through the use of faction, revisionists go beyond the indirect method of impugning morality and instead directly portray immorality as indisputable fact. The intended result is for the public's perception of its leaders' integrity and morality to be altered, thus destroying their credibility.

7. The Use of "Psychohistory" and "Psychobabble"

"Psychohistory" results when a psychological analysis is applied to the actions of persons long dead in an attempt to establish their "true" motives; "psychobabble" is the result of such an analysis. An example of this is Richard Rollins' psychoanalysis of why Noah Webster became a Christian in his book, *The Long Journey of Noah Webster:*

[H]is emotional conversion in the spring of that year [1808] was motivated by factors that were very much products of his own time. He had experienced intense anxiety over past and contemporary national events; the failure of Federalism as a viable means of controlling social trends and providing public leadership was quite evident. The negative view of human nature and need for strong authority he had affirmed since the 1790s had readied him for acceptance of evangelical Protestantism. A crisis in his personal relationships with his own family added to his preparation and brought home to him in personal terms the erosion of patriarchal influence throughout America. Altogether those factors provided an emotional matrix that made his conversion possible. The result was a psychological and intellectual acceptance of and the submission to authority that stemmed from a deep need within him and led to profound alterations of his views on every subject. [135]

Rollins portrayed the conversion of Noah Webster as a political expedient; contrast that psychobabble with Noah Webster's own simple explanation of the motives and circumstances surrounding his conversion:

Being educated in a religious family under pious parents, I had in early life some religious impressions, but being too young to understand fully the doctrines of the Christian religion, and falling into vicious company at college, I lost those impressions. . . . [I] fell into the common mistake of attending to the duties which man owes to man before I had learned the duties which we all owe to our Creator and Redeemer. . . . I sheltered myself as well as I could from the attacks of conscience for neglect of duty under a species of scepticism, and endeavored to satisfy my mind that a profession of religion is not absolutely necessary to salvation. In this state of mind I placed great reliance on good works or the performance of moral duties as the means of salvation. . . . About a year ago, an unusual revival of religion took place in New Haven. . . . and [I] was led by a spontaneous impulse to repentance, prayer, and entire submission and surrender of myself to my Maker and Redeemer. . . . I now began to understand and relish many parts of the Scriptures which before appeared mysterious and unintelligible, or repugnant to my natural pride. . . . In short, my view of the Scriptures, of religion, of the whole Christian scheme of salvation, and of God's moral government are very much changed, and my heart yields with delight and confidence to whatever appears to be the Divine will. . . . In the month of April last I made a profession of faith. [136]

Not being a professional psychologist, Noah Webster evidently didn't understand what had happened to him. Yet now, thanks to Richard Rollins, we "know" that Webster's conversion was due to "a psychological and intellectual acceptance of and the submission to authority" related both to his "intense anxiety over past and contemporary national events" and "the failure of Federalism as a viable means of controlling social trends and providing public leadership."

In *Thomas Jefferson: An Intimate History,* Fawn Brodie's psychobabble "proved" that Thomas Jefferson was enamored with Sally Hemings:

> The first evidence that Sally Hemings had become for Jefferson a special preoccupation may be seen in one of the most subtly illuminating of all his writings, the daily journal he kept on a seven-week trip through eastern France, Germany, and Holland in March and April of 1788. . . . Anyone who reads with care these twenty-five pages must find it singular that in describing the countryside between these cities he used the word "mulatto" eight times. [137]

Since Sally Hemings was a mulatto, Brodie concludes that Jefferson's use of that word proves that he had a relationship with her. Yet "mulatto" is used by Jefferson to describe the color of the soil. Notice:

> "The road goes thro' the plains of the Maine, which are mulatto and very fine. . . ."; "It has a good Southern aspect, the soil a barren mulatto clay. . . . "; "It is of South Western aspect, very poor, sometimes gray, sometimes mulatto. . . . "; "These plains are sometimes black, sometimes mulatto, always rich. . . . "; " . . . the plains are generally mulatto. . . ."; " . . . the valley of the Rhine . . . varies in quality, sometimes a rich mulatto loam, sometimes a poor sand. . . . "; " . . . the hills are mulatto but also whitish. . . . "; "Meagre mulatto clay mixt with small broken stones. . . . " [138]

Through psychoanalysis, Brodie is able to project Jefferson's farming observation of soil in Europe as "proof" of an affair with Sally Hemings!

This same approach was used against John Witherspoon (a signer of the Declaration and a chief among the patriots) in Mark Noll's, Nathan Hatch's, and George Marsden's *In Search of Christian America*. Despite the Rev. Dr. Witherspoon's firmly established reputation as one of America's leading evangelical Christian theologians, those authors concluded that Witherspoon lacked a Christian approach to public policy. They explained:

> The most serious difficulty in Witherspoon's political thought, however, was. . . . its frankly naturalistic basis. Witherspoon . . . was required to lecture on politics, and so we possess written statements of his thought. They present a disturbing picture inasmuch as they lack essential elements of a genuinely Christian approach to public life. That is, Witherspoon's lectures on politics and his public statements at the Congress nowhere expressed the conviction that all humans, even those fighting against British tyranny, were crippled by sin and needed redemption. [139]

Very simply, since Witherspoon did not behave or preach in the political arena as the three authors would have had him do, he therefore lacked a "genuinely Christian approach to public life." Certainly, a reading of Witherspoon's extensive theological and political writings [140] emphatically confirms his Christian approach to public life, even though the authors may not agree with every point of his Presbyterian theology.

"Psychohistory" and "psychobabble" are effective revisionist tools to create motives that cannot be proven on the basis of evidence. These tools enable an author not only to project but also to "prove" their personal opinions—regardless of what the facts or documents of the day might establish to the contrary.

8. A Failure to Account For Etymology

"Etymology" (the study of word derivations) deals with the manner in which the meanings of words change over the years. Even though word definitions and usage may change dramatically in only a few years, revisionists regularly ignore these changes, thus making completely inaccurate portrayals and assertions.

Noah Webster, a master of the meanings of words (having learned over twenty languages and having defined some 70,000 words in compiling America's first dictionary) explained why etymology is important:

> [I]n the lapse of two or three centuries, changes have taken place which, in particular passages, . . . obscure the sense of the original languages. . . . The effect of these changes is that some words are not understood . . . [and] being now used in a sense different from

that which they had . . . present wrong signification or false ideas. Whenever words are understood in a sense different from that which they had when introduced. . . . mistakes may be very injurious. [141]

Very simply, using today's definitions to define yesterday's words may lead to ridiculous historical conclusions.

For example, contemporary judicial leaders often rely on today's definition of religion when seeking to interpret that word in the First Amendment. For example, current dictionaries offer this definition:

Religion: A set of beliefs concerning the cause, nature, and purpose of the universe. [142]

Because this definition can allow almost any identifiable group to be considered religious, the Court, in *U. S. v. Seeger*, [143] extended the First Amendment's *religious* protection to virtually every group in America which has a "set of beliefs" on the "purpose of the universe." Consequently, many nonreligious groups (e.g., atheists, secular humanists, ethical culturalists, and numerous others) now receive "religious" protection. Yet notice the definition of "religion" at the time of the Founders (given in Noah Webster's 1828 dictionary):

Religion: Includes a belief in the being and perfections of God, in the revelation of His will to man, in man's obligation to obey His commands, in a state of reward and punishment, and in man's accountableness to God; and also true godliness or piety of life, with the practice of all moral duties. [144]

At a minimum, their definition of religion included the belief in a Supreme Being—a vital component conspicuously absent from today's definition (as previously demonstrated in Chapter 2). Consequently, because the Court failed to account for this etymology, today many *nonreligious* groups—groups which also existed at the time of the Founders—are accorded a protection under the *religion* clauses of the Constitution which the Founders did not intend.

Another case where a failure to account for etymology significantly alters a conclusion is illustrated in the claim by Charles and Mary Beard that:

Out of England Deism was borne to France by Voltaire, where. . . . the doctrine came into America, spreading widely among the intellectual leaders of the American Revolution. . . . It was not Cotton Mather's [a Puritan clergyman's] God to whom the authors of the Declaration of Independence appealed; it was to "Nature's God." [145]

Since the French usage of "Nature's God" was deistic, then the Beards claim that the Founders' use of that phrase was also deistic. Yet recall from Chapter 11 that the Founders were explicit that "Nature's God" was the God of the Bible, therefore refuting any French deistic definition.

Just as the failure to account for the variable meaning of words has resulted in inaccurate conclusions, so, too, has the related failure to account for historical changes in organizations. For example, many of the social teachings of today's Methodists, Quakers, Congregationalists, and others bear little resemblance to the teachings of those denominations two hundred years ago; is it thus to be assumed that the Founders who were then members of those denominations countenanced the social views which may be widespread in those denominations today?

For instance, John Adams, Daniel Webster, John Marshall, John Quincy Adams, Joseph Story, James Kent and others were associated with the Unitarians. Yet, because Unitarianism today is often non- and sometimes anti-Christian, and because it now embraces transcendentalist views and practices, are those Founders to be deprecated as cultists? Certainly not—that is, if one understands the doctrinal changes which have occurred in that group since its inception.

Historically, Unitarianism appeared in America as early as 1785; its doctrines were stated by William Ellery Channing in 1819, with the American Unitarian Association being formed in 1825. [146] The *Theological Dictionary* of 1823 described Unitarians in these words:

> In common with other Christians, they confess that He [Jesus] is the Christ, the Son of the Living God; and in one word, they believe *all* that the writers of the New Testament, particularly the four Evangelists, have stated concerning him. [147] (emphasis added)

In fact, the early Unitarians published a pamphlet entitled *An Answer to the Question, "Why Do You Attend a Unitarian Church?"* Notice some of the eighteen reasons:

> Because the Unitarians reject all human creeds and articles of faith, and strictly adhere to the great Protestant principle, "the Bible—the Bible only;" admitting no standard of Christian truth, nor any rule of Christian practice, but the words of the Lord Jesus and his Apostles. . . .
> Because at the Unitarian Church I hear Jesus of Nazareth who was crucified, preached as the Christ, the son of the living God. . . .

Because Unitarians teach the doctrine of "the true grace of God."—His unmerited, unpurchased favor to mankind,—that salvation and eternal life are his free gifts through Jesus Christ; which is clearly the doctrine of Scripture. . . .

Because there the crucified Jesus is exalted, as having attained His high dignity and glory, and His appointment to be the Saviour and Judge of the world. . . .

Because there the necessity of personal righteousness is insisted on, and the spirit of Christ and conformity to His example, made essential to genuine Christianity. [148]

As a further indication of the early Unitarian's reliance on the Bible, observers from that era noted "that several of the ablest defenders of Christianity against the attacks of infidels have been Unitarians." [149]

However, in 1838, Unitarianism took a radical turn when Ralph Waldo Emerson began slowly reshaping Channing's Christian teachings . . .

. . . into a Transcendentalist version of the ethical theism of Plato, the Stoics and Kant, coordinated with the nascent evolutionist science of the day and the newly explored mysticism of the ancient East. This new religious philosophy, as construed and applied by the Boston preacher Theodore Parker and other disciples of Emerson, included the other great ethnic faiths with Christianity in a universal religion of Humanity and through its intellectual hospitality operated to open Unitarian fellowship to evolutionists, monists, pragmatists and humanists. [150]

Certainly, these current views of Unitarians are totally unacceptable to most Christians. Yet even though Emerson began introducing these views in 1838, it was still some time before they took hold—demonstrated by the 1844 *History of Religious Denominations* which set forth Unitarian beliefs at that time:

Professing little reverence for human creeds, having no common standard but the Bible. . . . They [Unitarians] believe that He [God] earnestly desires their repentance and holiness; that His infinite, overflowing love led Him miraculously to raise up and send Jesus to be their spiritual deliverer, to purify their souls from sin, to restore them to communion with Himself, and fit them for pardon and everlasting life in His presence; in a word, to reconcile man to God. [151]

These early views and beliefs of Unitarians—views which included salvation and redemption only through Jesus Christ the Son of God—clearly are not now associated with Unitarians. But because today's Unitarians are both non- and anti-Christian, a failure to account for the historical changes in this organization have caused many contemporary reviewers to conclude wrongly that the Founders associated with the early Unitarians could not have been Christians.

This same failure to account for historical changes is also revealed in the analysis of many contemporary writers concerning the Founders and their involvement in Freemasonry—an organization which has also undergone a similar radical transformation over the years since its early introduction into America.

Revisionists either reveal their own laziness by failing to define terms according to original usage or they deliberately omit those meanings in an attempt to reach a conclusion different from that which was originally intended.

9. A Lack of Primary Source References

A simple means by which revisionism in any of its forms may be identified is its nearly universal failure to cite primary-source documents. Consider, for example, the work mentioned earlier, *The Search for Christian America*, [152] wherein three scholars purported to investigate whether America really did have a Christian founding.

They ultimately concluded that it did not, based in part on their use of "psychohistory" to impugn the Founders' motives, as well as on their rejection of the Founders' definitions of Christianity in deference to their own. In fact, by the standard these authors erected—a standard they claimed to be the Biblical standard—there never has been, nor will there ever be, a "Christian" nation.

Yet the most glaring evidence of their revisionist approach to the American founding is revealed by an examination of the bibliography list at the conclusion of their book. While allegedly examining the Founding Era, strikingly, 88 percent of the "historical sources" on which they rely postdate 1900, and 80 percent postdate 1950!

Conversely, in *Original Intent* the numbers are dramatically different. This book, unlike *The Search for Christian America*, examines not only the Founding Era but also the situation today and thus inevitably cites current works. Even with these citations, only 34 percent (rather than 88 percent) of its sources postdate 1900, and only 21 percent (rather than 80 percent) postdate 1950.

The difference between the sources relied upon in reaching the almost opposite conclusions between these two books is depicted in the two charts below:

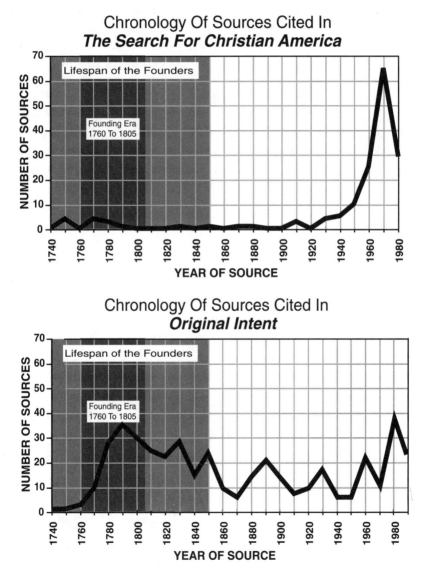

Chronology Of Sources Cited In
The Search For Christian America

Chronology Of Sources Cited In
Original Intent

When a book (e.g., *In Search of Christian America*) examining the founding of American government (1760-1805) does so by analyzing sources published primarily after 1950, the conclusions reached are not surprising. Consequently, whether intentionally or inadvertently, revisionism is further advanced.

———···———

There is no question that an activist judiciary has greatly altered American life in recent decades; however, not only have revisionists helped create an atmosphere conducive to those judicial decisions, but worse still, they have engendered an acceptance of those decisions by the American public.

While revisionists and an active judiciary do not necessarily conspire together to alter society, they are joined by the fact that leading individuals from each group often embrace common philosophical views and societal goals. Consequently, through the combined efforts of revisionist leaders in both the judicial and academic spheres of influence, legal protections for public religious expressions and public morality have been very nearly destroyed.

~17~
Religion and Morality:
The Indispensable Supports

The entire foundation for America's successful political existence was given by George Washington in his "Farewell Address" when he declared:

> Of all the dispositions and habits which lead to political prosperity, religion and morality are indispensable supports. In vain would that man claim the tribute of patriotism who should labor to subvert these great pillars of human happiness. [1]

Religion and morality—these were the Founders' indispensable supports for good government, political prosperity, and national well-being.

The Founders understood that self-governing nations are built upon self-governing individuals, and personal self-government is achieved only by adherence to moral and religious principles. In fact, they believed that our form of government, despite its worthy documents, was insufficient for governing immoral or irreligious citizens. As President John Adams proclaimed:

> [W]e have no government armed with power capable of contending with human passions unbridled by morality and religion. . . . Our Constitution was made only for a moral and religious people. It is wholly inadequate to the government of any other. [2]

The Founders believed that religion and morality were inseparable from good government and that they were essential for national success. Consequently, the promotion of the principles of religion and morality was accepted as sound public policy. Notice a few representative statements illustrating this fact:

> [I]t is religion and morality alone which can establish the principles upon which freedom can securely stand. [3] Religion and virtue are the only foundations . . . of republicanism and of all free governments. [4] **JOHN ADAMS**

> [T]hree points of doctrine, the belief of which, forms the foundation of all morality. The first is the existence of a God; the second is the immortality of the human soul; and the third is a

future state of rewards and punishments. Suppose it possible for a man to disbelieve either of these articles of faith and that man will have no conscience, he will have no other law than that of the tiger or the shark; the laws of man may bind him in chains or may put him to death, but they never can make him wise, virtuous, or happy. [5] **JOHN QUINCY ADAMS**

Religion and good morals are the only solid foundations of public liberty and happiness. [6] [N]either the wisest constitution nor the wisest laws will secure the liberty and happiness of a people whose manners are universally corrupt. [7] A general dissolution of the principles and manners will more surely overthrow the liberties of America than the whole force of the common enemy. While the people are virtuous, they cannot be subdued; but when once they lose their virtue, they will be ready to surrender their liberties to the first external or internal invader. [8] **SAMUEL ADAMS**

[G]overnment . . . is a firm compact sanctified from violation by all the ties of personal honor, morality, and religion. [9] **FISHER AMES**, AUTHOR OF THE HOUSE LANGUAGE OF THE FIRST AMENDMENT

[A] free government. . . . can only be happy when the public principles and opinions are properly directed. . . . by religion and education. It should therefore be among the first objects of those who wish well to the national prosperity to encourage and support the principles of religion and morality. [10] **ABRAHAM BALDWIN**, SIGNER OF THE CONSTITUTION

Without morals a republic cannot subsist any length of time; they therefore who are decrying the Christian religion whose morality is so sublime and pure . . . are undermining the solid foundation of morals, the best security for the duration of free governments. [11] **CHARLES CARROLL**, SIGNER OF THE DECLARATION

[T]he primary objects of government are the peace, order and prosperity of society. . . . To the promotion of these objects, particularly in a republican government good morals are essential. Institutions for the promotion of good morals are therefore objects of legislative provision and support: and among these . . . religious institutions are eminently useful and important. [12] **OLIVER ELLSWORTH**; DELEGATE TO THE CONSTITUTIONAL CONVENTION; U. S. SENATOR; CHIEF JUSTICE OF THE U. S. SUPREME COURT

[O]nly a virtuous people are capable of freedom. As nations become corrupt and vicious, they have more need of masters. [13] **BENJAMIN FRANKLIN**

Truth, honor, and religion are the only foundation to build human happiness upon. They never fail to yield a mind solid satisfaction, for conscious virtue gives pleasure to the soul. [14] **NATHANAEL GREENE**, REVOLUTIONARY GENERAL

Sensible of the importance of Christian piety and virtue to the order and happiness of a state, I cannot but earnestly commend to you every measure for their support and encouragement. . . . Manners, by which not only the freedom but the very existence of the republics are greatly affected, depend much upon the public institutions of religion. [15] **JOHN HANCOCK**

Righteousness alone can exalt them [America] as a nation. Reader! Whoever thou art, remember this; and in thy sphere practise virtue thyself, and encourage it in others. [16] [T]he great pillars of all government and of social life: I mean virtue, morality, and religion. This is the armor, my friend, and this alone, that renders us invincible. [17] **PATRICK HENRY**

We are now to rank among the nations of the world; but whether our Independence shall prove a blessing or a curse must depend upon our own wisdom or folly, virtue or wickedness. . . . Justice and virtue are the vital principles of republican government. [18] **GEORGE MASON**, FATHER OF THE BILL OF RIGHTS

The practice of morality being necessary for the well-being of society, He [God] has taken care to impress its precepts so indelibly on our hearts that they shall not be effaced by the subtleties of our brain. We all agree in the obligation of the moral precepts of Jesus and nowhere will they be found delivered in greater purity than in His discourses. [19] **THOMAS JEFFERSON**

It is certainly true that a popular government cannot flourish without virtue in the people. [20] **RICHARD HENRY LEE**, SIGNER OF THE DECLARATION; PRESIDENT OF THE CONTINENTAL CONGRESS

[T]he Holy Scriptures. . . . can alone secure to society, order and peace, and to our courts of justice and constitutions of government, purity, stability, and usefulness. In vain, without the Bible, we increase penal laws and draw entrenchments [defenses] around our institutions. Bibles are strong entrenchments [protections]. Where they abound, men cannot pursue wicked courses. [21] **JAMES McHENRY**, SIGNER OF THE CONSTITUTION; SECRETARY OF WAR

[F]or avoiding the extremes of despotism or anarchy . . . the only ground of hope must be on the morals of the people. [22] I believe that religion is the only solid base of morals and that morals are the only possible support of free governments. [23] [T]herefore education should teach the precepts of religion and the duties of man towards God. [24] **GOUVERNEUR MORRIS**, PENMAN AND SIGNER OF THE CONSTITUTION

Religion and morality . . . [are] necessary to good government, good order, and good laws, for "when the righteous are in authority, the people rejoice" [Proverbs 29:2]. [25] **WILLIAM PATERSON**, SIGNER OF THE CONSTITUTION; U. S. SUPREME COURT JUSTICE

Had I a voice that could be heard from New Hampshire to Georgia, it should be exerted in urging the necessity of disseminating virtue and knowledge among our citizens. On this subject, the policy of the eastern states is well worthy of imitation. The wise people of that extremity of the union never form a new township without making arrangements that secure to its inhabitants the instruction of youth and the public preaching of the gospel. Hence their children are early taught to know their rights and to respect themselves. They grow up good members of society and staunch defenders of their country's cause. [26] **DAVID RAMSAY**, REVOLUTIONARY SURGEON; MEMBER OF THE CONTINENTAL CONGRESS

Without this [religion] there can be no virtue, and without virtue there can be no liberty, and liberty is the object and life of all republican governments. [27] Without the restraints of religion and social worship, men become savages. [28] **BENJAMIN RUSH**, SIGNER OF THE DECLARATION

[C]herish and promote the interest of knowledge, virtue and religion. They are indispensable to the support of any free government. . . . Let it never be forgotten that there can be no genuine freedom where there is no morality, and no sound morality where there is no religion. . . . Hesitate not a moment to believe that the man who labors to destroy these two great pillars of human happiness . . . is neither a good patriot nor a good man. [29] **JEREMIAH SMITH,** REVOLUTIONARY SOLDIER; JUDGE; U. S. CONGRESSMAN; GOVERNOR OF NEW HAMPSHIRE

The promulgation of the great doctrines of religion; the being and attributes and providence of one Almighty God; the responsibility to Him for all our actions; founded upon moral freedom and accountability; a future state of rewards and punishments; the cultivation of all the personal, social, and benevolent virtues;—these never can be a matter of indifference in any well-ordered community. It is, indeed, difficult to conceive how any civilized society can well exist without them. And, at all events, it is impossible for those who believe in the truth of Christianity as a Divine revelation, to doubt that it is the especial duty of government to foster and encourage it among all the citizens and subjects. [30] It yet remains a problem to be solved in human affairs whether any free government can be permanent where the public worship of God and the support of religion constitute no part of the policy or duty of the state in any assignable shape. [31] **JOSEPH STORY,** U. S. SUPREME COURT JUSTICE; FATHER OF AMERICAN JURISPRUDENCE

Shun all giddy, loose and wicked company; they will corrupt and lead you into vice and bring you to ruin. Seek the company of sober, virtuous and good people, who will always show you examples of rectitude of conduct and propriety of behavior which will lead to solid happiness. [32] **THOMAS STONE,** SIGNER OF THE DECLARATION

[R]eason and experience both forbid us to expect that national morality can prevail in exclusion of religious principle. [33] Purity of morals [is] the only sure foundation of public happiness in any country. [34] [T]he [federal] government . . . can never be in danger of degenerating . . . so long as there shall remain any virtue in the body of the people. [35] [T]rue religion affords to government its surest support. [36] Religion and morality are the essential pillars of civil society. [37] **GEORGE WASHINGTON**

[T]he cultivation of the religious sentiment represses licentiousness ... inspires respect for law and order, and gives strength to the whole social fabric. [38] Moral habits ... cannot safely be trusted on any other foundation than religious principle nor any government be secure which is not supported by moral habits.... Whatever makes men good Christians, makes them good citizens. [39] **DANIEL WEBSTER**

Republican government loses half of its value where the moral and social duties are ... negligently practiced. To exterminate our popular vices is a work of far more importance to the character and happiness of our citizens, than any other improvements in our system of education. [40] [T]he moral principles and precepts contained in the Scriptures ought to form the basis of all our civil constitutions and laws.... All the miseries and evils which men suffer from vice, crime, ambition, injustice, oppression, slavery and war, proceed from their despising or neglecting the precepts contained in the Bible. [41] **NOAH WEBSTER**

Human law must rest its authority ultimately upon the authority of that law which is divine.... Far from being rivals or enemies, religion and law are twin sisters, friends, and mutual assistants. Indeed, these two sciences run into each other. [42] **JAMES WILSON,** SIGNER OF THE CONSTITUTION; U. S. SUPREME COURT JUSTICE

He who makes a people virtuous makes them invincible. [43] Nothing is more certain than that a general profligacy [depravity] and corruption of manners make a people ripe for destruction. A good form of government may hold the rotten materials together for some time but beyond a certain pitch even the best constitution will be ineffectual.... What follows from this? That he is the best friend to American liberty who is most sincere and active in promoting true and undefiled religion and who sets himself with the greatest firmness to bear down profanity and immorality of every kind. Whoever is an avowed enemy of God, I scruple not [would not hesitate] to call him an enemy to his country.... God grant that in America true religion and civil liberty may be inseparable and that the unjust attempts to destroy the one may in the issue tend to the support and establishment of both. [44] **JOHN WITHERSPOON,** SIGNER OF THE DECLARATION

The knowledge that the promotion of religion and morality was good public policy was a truth recognized not just by the Founders but even by early courts and Congresses. Notice:

Whereas true religion and good morals are the only solid foundations of public liberty and happiness . . . it is hereby earnestly recommended to the several States to take the most effectual measures for the encouragement thereof. [45] **CONTINENTAL CONGRESS, 1778**

Religion is of general and public concern and on its support depend, in great measure, the peace and good order of government, the safety and happiness of the people. [46] **RUNKEL v. WINEMILLER, 1799**

The morality of the country is deeply engrafted upon Christianity. . . . [We are] people whose manners are refined and whose morals have been elevated and inspired with a more enlarged benevolence by means of the Christian religion. [47] **PEOPLE v. RUGGLES,** 1811

No free government now exists in the world unless where Christianity is acknowledged and is the religion of the country. . . . Christianity is part of the common law. . . . Its foundations are broad and strong and deep. . . . It is the purest system of morality . . . and only stable support of all human laws. [48] **UPDEGRAPH v. COMMONWEALTH, 1824**

Why may not the Bible, and especially the New Testament . . . be read and taught as a divine revelation in the [school]? . . . Where can the purest principles of morality be learned so clearly or so perfectly as from the New Testament? [49] **VIDAL v. GIRARD'S EXECUTORS, 1844**

Christianity has reference to the principles of right and wrong; . . . it is the foundation of those morals and manners upon which our society is formed; it is their basis. Remove this and they would fall. . . . It [morality] has grown upon the basis of Christianity. [50] **CHARLESTON v. BENJAMIN, 1846**

Laws will not have permanence or power without the sanction of religious sentiment—without a firm belief that there is a Power above us that will reward our virtues and punish our vices. [51] **HOUSE JUDICIARY COMMITTEE, 1854**

[T]he happiness of a people and the good order and preservation of civil government essentially depend upon piety, religion and morality.... Religion, morality, and knowledge [are] necessary to good government, the preservation of liberty, and the happiness of mankind. [52] **CHURCH OF THE HOLY TRINITY v. U. S., 1892**

Consequently, the twin foundations of religion and public morality were long protected and zealously guarded in public policy. For example:

[W]hatever strikes at the root of Christianity tends manifestly to the dissolution of civil government . . . because it tends to corrupt the morals of the people, and to destroy good order.... [O]ffenses against religion and morality . . . strike at the root of moral obligation and weaken the security of the social ties. [53] **PEOPLE v. RUGGLES, 1811**

The destruction of morality renders the power of the government invalid. [54] **COMMONWEALTH v. SHARPLESS, 1815**

[A] malicious intention . . . to vilify the Christian religion and the Scriptures.... would prove a nursery of vice, a school of preparation to qualify young men for the gallows and young women for the brothel. . . . Religion and morality . . . are the foundations of all governments. Without these restraints no free government could long exist. [55] **UPDEGRAPH v. COMMONWEALTH, 1824**

What constitutes the standard of good morals? Is it not Christianity? There certainly is none other. Say that cannot be appealed to and . . . what would be good morals? The day of moral virtue in which we live would, in an instant, if that standard were abolished, lapse into the dark and murky night of pagan immorality. [56] **CHARLESTON v. BENJAMIN, 1846**

[Religion] must be considered as the foundation on which the whole structure rests.... In this age there can be no substitute for Christianity; that, in its general principles, is the great conservative element on which we must rely for the purity and permanence of free institutions. [57] **HOUSE JUDICIARY COMMITTEE, 1854**

> The great vital and conservative element in our system is the belief of our people in the pure doctrines and divine truths of the gospel of Jesus Christ. [58] **U. S. HOUSE OF REPRESENTATIVES, 1854**

Our Founders—as well as subsequent courts and Congresses—believed intensely that religion in general, and Christianity in particular, produced the public morality without which civil government would not long survive. On this basis, they neither created nor tolerated acts diminishing Christianity's effect; to have done so would have been to invite the demise of good government. No rational government would intentionally commit suicide by destroying its very foundation.

While the overall effects of religion on a society were well understood, there were also specific benefits of Christianity which were enumerated by the Founders. For example, Thomas Jefferson noted:

> The precepts of philosophy, and of the Hebrew code, laid hold of actions only. [Jesus] pushed his scrutinies into the heart of man, erected his tribunal in the region of his thoughts, and purified the waters at the fountain head. [59]

According to Jefferson, Christian principles, unlike those of other religions, went beyond merely addressing and attempting to regulate or restrain outward behavior. Consider murder as an example: civil law prohibits it; how can Christianity contribute anything more? Unlike civil statutes, Christianity addresses murder *before* it occurs—while it is still only a thought in the heart (see Matthew 5:22-28). Civil laws cannot address the heart, which is the actual seat of violence and of all crime. The true effectiveness of the teachings of Christianity were that, as Jefferson expressed it, they "purified the waters at the fountain head."

John Quincy Adams, who served not only as a President but also as a U. S. Representative and Senator, similarly explained why this aid from Christianity was so necessary to civil government. He declared:

> Human legislators can undertake only to prescribe the actions of men: they acknowledge their inability to govern and direct the sentiments of the heart; the very law styles it a rule of civil conduct, not of internal principles. . . . It is one of the greatest marks of Divine favor . . . that the Legislator gave them rules not only of action but for the government of the heart. [60]

To hate is not legally a crime, yet it often leads to a crime (assault, murder, slander, etc.). Similarly, to covet is not legally a crime; yet it too often leads to a crime (theft, burglary, embezzlement, etc.). Only religion effectively provides what John Quincy Adams termed "rules for the government of the heart" and thus prevents the crimes which originate internally.

This aspect of personal, internal self-government was long understood to be a direct societal benefit resulting from the widespread teachings of Christianity. As Zephaniah Swift explained:

> Indeed moral virtue is substantially and essentially enforced by the precepts of Christianity and may be considered to be the basis of it. But in addition to moral principles, the Christian doctrines inculcate a purity of heart and holiness of life which constitutes its chief glory. When we contemplate it in this light, we have a most striking evidence of its superiority over all the systems of pagan philosophy which were promulgated by the wisest men of ancient times. [61]

Signer of the Constitution Abraham Baldwin echoed this truth:

> When the minds of the people in general are viciously disposed and unprincipled and their conduct disorderly, a free government will be attended with greater confusions and evils more horrid than the wild, uncultivated state of nature. It can only be happy when the public principles and opinions are properly directed and their manners regulated. This is an influence beyond the reach of laws and punishments and can be claimed only by religion and education. [62]

John Witherspoon similarly explained:

> [V]irtue and piety are inseparably connected; then to promote true religion is the best and most effectual way of making a virtuous and regular people. Love to God and love to man is the substance of religion; when these prevail, civil laws will have little to do. [63]

Disregarding these direct societal benefits which result from the promotion of religious principles, government utilizes extensive manpower and expends massive financial sums attempting to restrain behavior which is the external manifestation of internal chaos and disorder.

If human behavior is not controlled by the internal restraints provided through religion, then the only other means to restrain misbehavior is the threat of sheer force. As Founder James Otis querried:

> When a man's will and pleasure is his only rule and guide, what
> safety can there be either for him or against him but in the point
> of a sword? [64]

Perhaps Robert Winthrop (a speaker of the U. S. House and a contemporary of John Quincy Adams and Daniel Webster) best summarized this principle when he declared:

> Men, in a word, must necessarily be controlled either by a power within
> them or by a power without them; either by the Word of God or by
> the strong arm of man; either by the Bible or by the bayonet. [65]

Because of the civil benefits, it is little wonder that basic religious teachings on behavior and morality have been long promoted throughout society in general and were specifically inculcated through public education. As Daniel Webster noted:

> We regard it [public instruction] as a wise and liberal system of police
> by which property, and life, and the peace of society are secured. We
> seek to prevent in some measure the extension of the penal code by
> inspiring a salutary and conservative principle of virtue and of
> knowledge in an early age. . . . [W]e seek . . . to turn the strong
> current of feeling and opinion, as well as the censures of the law and
> the denunciations of religion, against immorality and crime. [66]

In fact, so much were these religious teachings considered to be a fundamental part of a well-rounded education that the Founders feared what might transpire if education no longer included these teachings. As Benjamin Rush warned:

> In contemplating the political institutions of the United States, I lament
> that we waste so much time and money in punishing crimes, and take
> so little pains to prevent them. We profess to be Republicans and yet
> we neglect the only means of establishing and perpetuating our
> republican forms of government; that is, the universal education of
> our youth in the principles of Christianity by means of the Bible. [67]

Earlier generations understood that religion—which produced morality, internal restraints, and a basic knowledge of rights and wrongs—must be publicly encouraged and supported to ensure national longevity. In fact, history provides frequent proof of the national elevation of behavior resulting from the public promotion of religion and morality. It is only sensible, therefore, to insist on a continuation of this policy. As political philosopher Montaigne (1533-1592) observed:

> Were I not to follow the straight road for its straightness, I should follow it for having found by experience that, in the end, it is commonly the happiest and most useful track. [68]

Experience proves that in a nation such as ours, the promotion and encouragement of religion and morality allows government to concentrate on its primary function: serving, rather than restraining.

~18~
Returning To Original Intent

Our Founders established this government with both a strong dependence upon religious principles and a clear limitation on federal powers. The crumbling of their ideals, and the current departure from what the Founders intended, did not occur overnight. Abrogating the separation of powers, destroying the cooperative relationship between church and state, usurping State powers, restricting public religious expressions—each has been a slow process spanning years. Likewise, the correction of these problems may not occur quickly or through any single act.

A major factor contributing to the gradual devolution of each of the above areas has been a lack of accurate, factual information. For example, had the public been aware of our founding documents and understood the philosophy behind them, the Court could never have achieved its supremacy of recent decades. Similarly, had Americans better known our history and the Founders' abundant writings, we would never have accepted the assertion that our Founders were irreligious and disapproved of public religious expressions.

The solution for overcoming these travesties, therefore, depends on acquiring sound information. This process entails three steps: (1) identifying and eliminating wrong information; (2) obtaining correct information; (3) acting on the proper information. This book can satisfy only the first step and a part of the second (exposing wrong information and providing correct information); the remainder of the process (replacing the inaccuracy with truth and then acting on it) can be accomplished only by the reader.

Since proper knowledge is essential for the construction of sound public policy, this final chapter will suggest four standards against which proposed ideas or policies should be tested.

1 In evaluating a policy, a citizen should first ask, "What will be the result of this proposed policy in light of the principle of national accountability—or what the Founders called the principle of 'rewards and punishments'?"

The application of this principle was so vital to the establishment of public policy that an acknowledgment of it frequently appeared in early documents. For example (emphasis added in each quote):

> And each member, before he takes his seat, shall make and subscribe
> the following declaration, viz: "I do believe in one God, the Creator

and Governor of the universe, *the rewarder of the good and the punisher of the wicked.*" CONSTITUTION OF PENNSYLVANIA [1]

And each member, before he takes his seat, shall make and subscribe the following declaration, viz: "You do believe in one God, the Creator and Governor of the Universe, *the rewarder of the good and punisher of the wicked.*" CONSTITUTION OF VERMONT [2]

The qualifications of electors shall be that [he] . . . acknowledges the being of a God and believes in *a future state of rewards and punishments.* CONSTITUTION OF SOUTH CAROLINA [3]

No person who denies the being of God, or *a future state of rewards and punishments*, shall hold any office in the civil department of this State. CONSTITUTION OF TENNESSEE [4]

By such pronouncements, a public official was acknowledging his understanding that his actions in office would have consequences with God. As Constitution signer Rufus King explained:

Our laws constantly refer to this revelation and by the oath which they prescribe, we appeal to the Supreme Being so to deal with us hereafter as we observe the obligation of our oaths. The Pagan world were, and are, without the mighty influence of this principle. [5]

Speaking before the Connecticut legislature in 1803, Matthias Burnet described the consequences from ignoring the principle of Divine rewards and punishments:

[F]eeble . . . would be the best form of government, and ineffectual the most wise and salutary laws, . . . without a sense of religion and the terrors of the world to come. . . . In a word, banish a sense of religion and the terrors of the world to come from society and you dissolve the sacred obligation of conscience and leave every man to do that which is right in his own eyes. [6]

In the view of our Founders, understanding the inevitability of Divine consequences for political acts was vital to the preservation of sound government. In fact, according to John Adams, it was embracing this principle which distinguished a statesman (a leader who would *not* compromise principles) from a politician (a leader who would). Adams believed the main reason a statesman refused to compromise his principles was that he understood the principle of future rewards and punishments. Adams explained:

> [S]uch compliances [compromises] . . . of my honor, my conscience, my friends, my country, my God, as the Scriptures inform us must be punished with nothing less than hell-fire, eternal torment; and this is so unequal a price to pay for the honors and emoluments [profits from government] . . . that I cannot prevail upon myself to think of it [compromise]. The duration of future punishment terrifies me. If I could but deceive myself so far as to think eternity a moment only, I could comply and be promoted. [7]

A leader's understanding and acceptance of accountability to God for his political behavior helps restrain him from compromises of principle.

The Founders understood that the principle of Divine rewards and punishments applied not only to individual leaders but also to the nation and its policies. The primary difference was that rewards and punishments for nations occurred in *this* world rather than the next. As Samuel Adams explained:

> [Divine] Revelation assures us that "Righteousness exalteth a nation" [Proverbs 14:34]. Communities are dealt with in *this world* by the wise and just Ruler of the Universe. He rewards or punishes them according to their general character. [8] (emphasis added)

George Mason, the Father of the Bill of Rights, reminded the delegates at the Constitutional Convention:

> As nations cannot be rewarded or punished in the next world, so they must be in *this*. By an inevitable chain of causes and effects, Providence punishes national sins by national calamities. [9] (emphasis added)

At the same Convention, delegate Luther Martin echoed those sentiments:

> It was said, it ought to be considered, that national crimes can only be, and frequently are, punished in *this world* by national punishments. [10] (emphasis added)

Speaking before the Massachusetts legislature in 1791, Chandler Robbins similarly declared:

> The Supreme Governor of the World rewards or punishes nations and civil communities only in *this life*. . . . Political bodies are but

the creatures of time. They have no existence as such but in the present state; consequently, are incapable of punishments or rewards in a future. We can conceive no way in which the divine Being shall therefore manifest the purity of his nature . . . towards such societies but by rewarding or punishing them *here,* according to their public conduct. [11] (emphasis added)

President George Washington summarized this same principle in his "Inaugural Address" when he reminded the nation:

[T]he propitious [favorable] smiles of Heaven can never be expected on a nation that disregards the eternal rules of order and right which Heaven itself has ordained. [12]

It was understood that our political acts cause God to respond either as an ally or as an adversary. The widespread knowledge of this principle required that proposed laws and policies be judged with full cognizance of their spiritual implications. As Benjamin Franklin reminded the delegates at the Constitutional Convention:

And have we now forgotten that powerful Friend? Or do we imagine we no longer need His assistance? . . . [W]ithout His concurring aid . . . we ourselves shall become a reproach and a byword down to future ages. [13]

And Thomas Jefferson similarly cautioned:

I tremble for my country when I reflect that God is just: that His justice cannot sleep forever. [14]

Of course, considering the spiritual implications of a policy is important only *if* there is a God, only *if* He has established transcendent rights and wrongs, and only *if* He responds on that basis. However, if one accepts these "ifs," then public policy must be analyzed accordingly.

To help evaluate proposed policies, learn to ask, "Will this act violate God's clear standards, thus inviting Divine wrath (Thomas Jefferson) and 'national calamity' (George Mason), or will it rather produce 'the propitious smiles of Heaven' (George Washington) and God's 'concurring aid' (Benjamin Franklin)?"

2 A second question useful for judging a public policy is, "Is this act consistent with our form of government?"

This is a simple question; yet the answer may often be in error since many citizens today have been misled about our form of government. We have grown accustomed to hearing that we are a democracy; such was never the intent. The form of government entrusted to us by our Founders was a republic, *not* a democracy. [15]

Our Founders had an opportunity to establish a democracy in America and chose not to. In fact, the Founders made clear that we were not—and were never to become—a democracy:

> [D]emocracies have ever been spectacles of turbulence and contention; have ever been found incompatible with personal security, or the rights of property; and have, in general, been as short in their lives as they have been violent in their deaths. [16] **JAMES MADISON**

> Remember, democracy never lasts long. It soon wastes, exhausts, and murders itself. There never was a democracy yet that did not commit suicide. [17] **JOHN ADAMS**

> A democracy is a volcano which conceals the fiery materials of its own destruction. These will produce an eruption and carry desolation in their way. [18] The known propensity of a democracy is to licentiousness [excessive license] which the ambitious call, and ignorant believe to be liberty. [19] **FISHER AMES**, AUTHOR OF THE HOUSE LANGUAGE FOR THE FIRST AMENDMENT

> We have seen the tumult of democracy terminate . . . as [it has] everywhere terminated, in despotism. . . . Democracy! savage and wild. Thou who wouldst bring down the virtuous and wise to thy level of folly and guilt. [20] **GOUVERNEUR MORRIS**, SIGNER AND PENMAN OF THE CONSTITUTION

> [T]he experience of all former ages had shown that of all human governments, democracy was the most unstable, fluctuating and short-lived. [21] **JOHN QUINCY ADAMS**

> A simple democracy . . . is one of the greatest of evils. [22] **BENJAMIN RUSH**, SIGNER OF THE DECLARATION

> In democracy . . . there are commonly tumults and disorders. . . . Therefore a pure democracy is generally a very bad government. It is often the most tyrannical government on earth. [23] **NOAH WEBSTER**

> Pure democracy cannot subsist long nor be carried far into the departments of state—it is very subject to caprice and the madness of popular rage. [24] JOHN WITHERSPOON, SIGNER OF THE DECLARATION

> It may generally be remarked that the more a government resembles a pure democracy the more they abound with disorder and confusion. [25] ZEPHANIAH SWIFT, AUTHOR OF AMERICA'S FIRST LEGAL TEXT

Many Americans today seem to be unable to define the difference between the two, but there is a difference—a big difference. That difference rests in the source of authority.

A pure democracy operates by direct majority vote of the people. When an issue is to be decided, the entire population votes on it; the majority wins and rules. A republic differs in that the general population elects representatives who then pass laws to govern the nation. A democracy is rule by majority *feeling* (what the Founders described as a "mobocracy" [26]); a republic is rule by *law*.

If the source of law for a democracy is the popular feeling of the people, then what is the source of law for the American republic? According to Founder Noah Webster:

> [O]ur citizens should early understand that the genuine source of correct republican principles is the Bible, particularly the New Testament, or the Christian religion. [27]

The transcendent values of Biblical natural law were the foundation of the American republic. Consider the stability this provides: in our republic, murder will always be a crime, for it is always a crime according to the Word of God. However, in a democracy, if a majority of the people decide that murder is no longer a crime, murder will no longer be a crime.

America's immutable principles of right and wrong were not based on the rapidly fluctuating feelings and emotions of the people but rather on what Montesquieu identified as the "principles that do not change." [28] Benjamin Rush similarly observed:

> [W]here there is no law, there is no liberty; and nothing deserves the name of law but that which is certain and universal in its operation upon all the members of the community. [29]

In the American republic, the "principles which did not change" and which were "certain and universal in their operation upon all the members of the community" were the principles of Biblical natural law. In fact, so firmly were these principles ensconced in the American republic that early law books taught that government was free to set its own policy only if God had **not** ruled in an area. For example, *Blackstone's Commentaries* explained:

> To instance in the case of murder: this is expressly forbidden by the Divine. . . . If any human law should allow or enjoin us to commit it, we are bound to transgress that human law. . . . But, with regard to matters that are . . . not commanded or forbidden by those superior laws such, for instance, as exporting of wool into foreign countries; here the . . . legislature has scope and opportunity to interpose. [30]

The Founders echoed that theme:

> All [laws], however, may be arranged in two different classes. 1) Divine. 2) Human. . . . But it should always be remembered that this law, natural or revealed, made for men or for nations, flows from the same Divine source: it is the law of God. . . . Human law must rest its authority ultimately upon the authority of that law which is Divine. [31] **JAMES WILSON**, SIGNER OF THE CONSTITUTION; U. S. SUPREME COURT JUSTICE

> [T]he law . . . dictated by God Himself is, of course, superior in obligation to any other. It is binding over all the globe, in all countries, and at all times. No human laws are of any validity if contrary to this. [32] **ALEXANDER HAMILTON**, SIGNER OF THE CONSTITUTION

> [T]he . . . law established by the Creator . . . extends over the whole globe, is everywhere and at all times binding upon mankind. . . . [This] is the law of God by which he makes his way known to man and is paramount to all human control. [33] **RUFUS KING**, SIGNER OF THE CONSTITUTION

The Founders understood that Biblical values formed the basis of the republic and that the republic would be destroyed if the people's knowledge of those values should ever be lost.

A republic is the highest form of government devised by man, but it also requires the greatest amount of human care and maintenance. If neglected, it can deteriorate into a variety of lesser forms, including a democracy (a government conducted by popular feeling); anarchy (a system in which each person determines his own rules and standards); oligarchy (a government run by a small council or a group of elite individuals); or dictatorship (a government run by a single individual). As John Adams explained:

[D]emocracy will soon degenerate into an anarchy, such an anarchy that every man will do what is right in his own eyes and no man's life or property or reputation or liberty will be secure, and every one of these will soon mould itself into a system of subordination of all the moral virtues and intellectual abilities, all the powers of wealth, beauty, wit, and science, to the wanton pleasures, the capricious will, and the execrable [abominable] cruelty of one or a very few. [34]

Understanding the foundation of the American republic is a vital key toward protecting it. Therefore, in analyzing public policy, remember to ask, "Is this act consistent with our form of government?" and support or oppose the policy on that basis.

[3] Since history forms the basis for the creation of many public policies, a policy may be ill-founded unless we train ourselves to determine whether that policy is being built on a sound basis or on a flawed and erroneous historical assumption. Therefore, a third useful question for identifying sound policy is, "Is the information undergirding this policy verifiable in primary-sources or is it the product of revisionism?"

It is unfortunate that our citizens today rarely consult original sources. The extent of this national weakness is documented in a Department of Education report; it states that currently *less than five percent* of high-school juniors and seniors have the skills necessary to comprehend a primary-source historical document. [35]

The failure to delve into primary sources leads to widespread gullibility and is one of the reasons that the media has become a powerful political and societal force in America. The consequences resulting from such naiveté were accurately described in this 1830s educational maxim:

A demagogue would like a people half educated; enough to read what he says, but not enough to know whether it is true or not. [36]

As citizens, we should train ourselves to investigate the rhetorical basis of policies in order to affirm truth or to expose error. As Thomas Jefferson warned:

If a nation expects to be ignorant—and free—in a state of civilization, it expects what never was and never will be. [37]

John Adams expounded on this principle, declaring:

> We electors have an important constitutional power placed in our
> hands: we have a check upon two branches of the legislature. . . . It
> becomes necessary to every subject [citizen], then, to be in some degree
> a statesman and to examine and judge for himself . . . the . . . political
> principles and measures. Let us examine them with a sober . . . Christian
> spirit. [38]

Since citizens are entrusted with the responsibility to judge for themselves
"the political principles and measures," the first and primary standard for
measurement is the Constitution. As Chief Justice John Jay explained:

> Every member of the State ought diligently to read and to study
> the constitution of his country. . . . By knowing their rights, they
> will sooner perceive when they are violated and be the better
> prepared to defend and assert them. [39]

Each citizen must become familiar not only with the Constitution but
also with the standards expounded in America's other blueprint documents.
Samuel Huntington, signer of the Declaration and Governor of Connecticut, observed:

> While the great body of freeholders are acquainted with the duties
> which they owe to their God, to themselves, and to men, they will
> remain free. But if ignorance and depravity should prevail, they
> will inevitably lead to slavery and ruin. [40]

Previous generations maintained an unwavering belief that the preservation of our liberties was inseparable from a thorough familiarity with our
fundamental governing documents. Consequently, educational laws—even
as late as the turn of the twentieth century—required students to read the
Declaration of Independence, the U. S. Constitution, the State constitution (and other important documents), and to take a written exam on them
once a year for the first eight years of school. [41]

It is a tragedy that today the U. S. Constitution is rarely seriously examined in schools. As one prominent national figure has noted:

> I spent three years getting my law degree at Yale Law School. From
> the moment I enrolled, I was assigned huge, leather-bound editions
> of legal cases to study and discuss. I read what lawyers and judges,

professors and historians said *about* the Constitution. But never once was I assigned the task of reading the Constitution itself. . . . Over the last decade, however, I have become a student of the Constitution, searching each line for its meaning and intent. . . . It is amazing how much more you will learn when you quit studying about it and pick it up to read it for yourself. [42] (emphasis added)

Once you have read the Constitution and the Declaration (copies of which are provided in the Appendix), then read a copy of *The Federalist Papers* (authored by James Madison, John Jay, and Alexander Hamilton to explain the purpose of the Constitution); the *Anti-Federalist Papers* (the discussions of Founders like George Mason and Patrick Henry on the importance of limiting federal powers and the purpose of the Bill of Rights); George Washington's "Farewell Address" (setting forth national guiding principles); and continue your study in this manner by investigating other foundational works still widely available today. Learning to return to the original sources will help clear the 200 years of haze and speculation which now seem to cloud the Constitution.

Beyond individual self-education in primary-sources, it is vital that these same materials be studied in the collective education process. For far too long, large numbers of citizens have been complacent and uninvolved in the nation's schools. This has allowed many unproductive and unhealthy philosophies to flourish in students' texts and classrooms.

Citizens should heed Noah Webster's succinct warning that:

> The education of youth should be watched with the most scrupulous attention. [I]t is much easier to introduce and establish an effectual system . . . than to correct by penal statutes the ill effects of a bad system. . . . The education of youth . . . lays the foundations on which both law and gospel rest for success. [43]

The fundamental precept of any sound education—whether individual or collective—is that it be founded upon the pursuit of accuracy and truth. That pursuit can be greatly facilitated by asking, "Is the information and rhetoric undergirding this policy consistent with primary sources, or is this revisionist subterfuge?"

4 The fourth and most important practice vital to the creation of sound government policy is the election of leaders with moral and religious integ-

rity. [†] This entails much more than just voting; it presupposes a thorough investigation of the private life and personal beliefs of a candidate.

A justification for investigating the private life of a candidate was given by William Penn, who explained:

> Governments, like clocks, go from the motion men give them; and as governments are made and moved by men, so by them they are ruined too. Wherefore governments rather depend upon men than men upon governments. Let men be good and the government cannot be bad. . . . But if men be bad, let the government be never so good, they will endeavor to warp and spoil it to their turn. I know some say, "Let us have good laws and no matter for the men that execute them [that is, if you have good laws, it does not matter who is in office]." But let them consider that though good laws do well, good men do better; for good laws may want [lack] good men and be abolished or invaded by ill men; but good men will never want good laws nor suffer [allow] ill ones. [45]

Amplifying the truth of this principle, William Paterson, a signer of the Constitution and a Justice on the U. S. Supreme Court, would remind juries [46] of the following Scripture:

> When the righteous rule, the people rejoice; when the wicked rule, the people groan. PROVERBS 29:2

The quality of government in our republic depends more upon the quality and character of our leaders than upon our laws. Lax or incompetent individuals rarely enforce good laws, and a superb constitution is an inadequate guarantee for good government without competent and reliable leaders. For this reason, Noah Webster instructed students:

> When you become entitled to exercise the right of voting for public officers, let it be impressed on your mind that God commands you to choose for rulers just men who will rule in the fear of God. The preservation of a republican government depends on the faithful

---

[†] Signer of the Declaration Benjamin Rush provided what is perhaps the most concise method to recognize integrity when he offered the following definition: "By integrity I mean . . . a strict coincidence between thoughts, words, and actions." [44] Very simply, integrity is an alignment between words and actions regardless of whether in public or private matters.

discharge of this duty; if the citizens neglect their duty and place unprincipled men in office, the government will soon be corrupted; laws will be made not for the public good so much as for selfish or local purposes; corrupt or incompetent men will be appointed to execute the laws; the public revenues will be squandered on unworthy men; and the rights of the citizens will be violated or disregarded. If a republican government fails to secure public prosperity and happiness, it must be because the citizens neglect the Divine commands and elect bad men to make and administer the laws. [47]

In another text, Webster advised:

In selecting men for office, let principle be your guide. Regard not the particular sect or denomination of the candidate—look to his character. . . . It is alleged by men of loose principles or defective views of the subject that religion and morality are not necessary or important qualifications for political stations. But the Scriptures teach a different doctrine. They direct that rulers should be men "who rule in the fear of God, able men, such as fear God, men of truth, hating covetousness" [Exodus 18:21]. . . . [I]t is to the neglect of this rule of conduct in our citizens that we must ascribe the multiplied frauds, breaches of trust, peculations [white-collar larceny] and embezzlements of public property which astonish even ourselves; which tarnish the character of our country; which disgrace a republican government. [48]

The warnings were frequent that negligence in selecting Godly, moral leaders for office would certainly result in government corruption. For example, speaking before the Massachusetts legislature, Chandler Robbins declared:

How constantly do we find it inculcated in the sacred writings, that rulers be "just men—fearers of God—haters of covetousness." That they "shake their hands from holding bribes," because, "a gift blindeth the eyes of the wise, and perverteth the words of the righteous." [49]

And Matthias Burnet similarly reminded the Connecticut legislature:

[T]he man who . . . is not actuated by the fear and awe of Him [God], has in many cases no bond or restraint upon his conduct. . . . Think not that men who acknowledge not the providence of God nor regard his laws will be uncorrupt in office. [50]

Samuel Adams similarly explained:

> He who is void of virtuous attachments in private life is, or very soon will be, void of all regard of his country. There is seldom an instance of a man guilty of betraying his country who had not before lost the feeling of moral obligations in his private connections. . . . [P]rivate and public vices are in reality . . . connected. . . . Nothing is more essential to the establishment of manners in a State than that all persons employed in places of power and trust be men of unexceptionable characters. The public cannot be too curious concerning the characters of public men. [51]

Penman and signer of the Constitution Gouverneur Morris proclaimed:

> There must be religion. When that ligament is torn, society is disjointed and its members perish. The nation is exposed to foreign violence and domestic convulsion. Vicious rulers, chosen by vicious people, turn back the current of corruption to its source. Placed in a situation where they can exercise authority for their own emolument, they betray their trust. They take bribes. They sell statutes and decrees. They sell honor and office. They sell their conscience. They sell their country. By this vile traffic they become odious and contemptible. . . . But the most important of all lessons is the denunciation of ruin to every state that rejects the precepts of religion. [52]

John Witherspoon also warned:

> Those who wish well to the State ought to choose to places of trust men of inward principle, justified by exemplary conversation. Is it reasonable to expect wisdom from the ignorant? fidelity [faithfulness] from the profligate [unfaithful]? assiduity [diligence] and application to public business from men of a dissipated [careless] life? Is it reasonable to commit the management of public revenue to one who hath wasted his own patrimony [inheritance]? Those, therefore, who pay no regard to religion and sobriety in the persons whom they send to the legislature of any State are guilty of the greatest absurdity and will soon pay dear for their folly. [53]

The warnings were numerous and clear: if citizens became negligent in electing moral leaders to office—if they overlooked the private lives of candidates—their government *would* become corrupt.

Earlier generations understood that no institution—whether that of government, media, jurisprudence, education, or any other—has intrinsic, inherent value; that is, no institution is of itself either good or bad. Institutions simply reflect the values of those involved in them. For this reason, John Jay directed:

> Providence has given to our people the choice of their rulers, and it is the duty, as well as the privilege and interest of our Christian nation, to select and prefer Christians for their rulers. [54]

Matthias Burnet similarly urged:

> [L]ook well to the characters and qualifications of those you elect and raise to office and places of trust.... [L]et the wise counsel of Jethro ... be your guide: Choose ye out from among you able men, such as fear God, men of truth and hating covetousness and set them to rule over you. [Exodus 18:21]. [55]

John Witherspoon charged:

> [T]he people in general ought to have regard to the moral character of those whom they invest with authority either in the legislative, executive, or judicial branches. [56]

These warnings were rarely heard in other nations; why were they so abundant in America? It is because we have a unique form of government. As John Jay explained:

> The Americans are the first people whom Heaven has favored with an opportunity of deliberating upon and choosing the forms of government under which they should live. [57]

American government belonged to the people, and power over that government rested totally in the hands of the people. Therefore, whether it maintained that design or whether it degenerated would depend entirely on whether citizens took seriously the stewardship which God had given them. Consequently, voting, one of the simplest of citizen responsibilities, is also one of the most important. As Samuel Adams explained:

> Let each citizen remember at the moment he is offering his vote that he is not making a present or a compliment to please an individual—or at least that he ought not so to do; but that he is

executing one of the most solemn trusts in human society for which he is accountable to God and his country. [58] [He] may then reflect, each one on his own integrity, and appeal to the Monitor within his breast, that he has not trifled with the sacred trust reposed in him by God and his country—that he has not prostituted his honor and conscience to please a friend or a patron. [59]

Daniel Webster similarly warned that . . .

. . . the exercise of the elective franchise [the vote] is a social duty of as solemn a nature as man can be called to perform; that a man may not innocently trifle with his vote; that every free elector [voter] is a trustee as well for others as himself; and that every man and every measure he supports has an important bearing on the interests of others as well as on his own. [60]

In fact, so strongly did the Founders believe that the duration of our government rested upon the wise votes of its citizens that Noah Webster proclaimed:

When a citizen gives his suffrage [his vote] to a man of known immorality he abuses his trust [civic responsibility]; he sacrifices not only his own interest, but that of his neighbor; he betrays the interest of his country. [61]

In Webster's view, if an individual did not take seriously his responsibilities as a voter, and if he knowingly placed an immoral person into office, he was a traitor to his country, for he was intentionally installing leaders who practiced the principles that destroyed good government.

The Founders believed that we citizens understood our responsibilities so well that we would never neglect our charge. As George Washington explained:

No country upon earth ever had it more in its power to attain these blessings than United America. Wondrously strange, then, and much to be regretted indeed would it be, were we to neglect the means and to depart from the road which Providence has pointed us to so plainly; I cannot believe it will ever come to pass. [62]

In recent years, however, far too many God-fearing individuals have neglected their responsibilities as national stewards for a variety of excuses. For example, some have thought that the pursuit of civil government was unrelated to the practice of their spiritual activities. These individuals should reflect on the observation made by John Witherspoon that:

> There is not a single instance in history in which civil liberty was lost and religious liberty preserved entire. [63]

The maintenance of our civil liberties is inalterably united with the freedom to exercise our religious liberties.

Others have thought that time spent in the pursuit of our civil duties was time used unwisely since civil duties had no eternal consequence. When that same objection was raised two centuries ago, John Witherspoon promptly responded:

> Shall we establish nothing good because we know it cannot be eternal? Shall we live without government because every constitution has its old age and its period? Because we know that we shall die, shall we take no pains to preserve or lengthen our life? Far from it, Sir: it only requires the more watchful attention to settle government upon the best principles and in the wisest manner [so] that it may last as long as the nature of things will admit. [64]

The fact that something may not be eternal does not release Christian citizens from their duties of stewardship over the civil government which God has provided them.

Still others have mistakenly believed that involvement with civil activities detracted from the time necessary to build a strong family. Actually, the converse is true. While the overall well-being of a family depends upon a number of diverse factors, one of those factors clearly is the quality of our civil government. As Samuel Adams explained:

> [T]he importance of piety and religion; of industry and frugality; of prudence, economy, regularity and an even [stable] government; all . . . are essential to the well-being of a family. [65]

How does the preservation of sound government help build a strong family? If government is constituted of poor leaders, it will become an enemy to the values, beliefs, and practices necessary to the formation of stable families. In fact, even a cursory examination of America's family problems over recent decades reveals that all too frequently, government policies and programs lay at the root of those problems.

For the sake of our families, Christian citizens *must* be involved in their civil government. Samuel Adams exhorted:

> [E]very citizen will see—and I hope be deeply impressed with a sense of it—how exceedingly important it is to himself, and how intimately the welfare of his children is connected with it, that those who are to have a share in making as well as in judging and executing the laws should be men of singular wisdom and integrity. [66]

Daniel Webster also warned of the tragic consequence to our children which could result from citizen neglect of our political system:

> [I]f we and our posterity reject religious instruction and authority, violate the rules of eternal justice, trifle with the injunctions of morality, and recklessly destroy the political constitution which holds us together, no man can tell how sudden a catastrophe may overwhelm us that shall bury all our glory in profound obscurity. [67]

Despite these impassioned warnings, unwise arguments in recent years have contributed to the neglect of civic stewardship by God-fearing citizens. The current condition of our government and our country is simply a reflection of the action—or lack thereof—by the God-fearing community.

Perhaps this is best illustrated by the parable in which Jesus described a man who had a good field, growing good fruit. He awakened one morning to find that field filled with tares, weeds, and bad fruit. How did it change from good to bad? In Matthew 13:25, Jesus identified the problem: while the good men slept, the enemy came in and planted the tares. Jesus never faulted the enemy for doing what he did; the problem was that the good men went to sleep.

Strikingly, it was this danger of good men "going to sleep" which most concerned our early statesmen. John Dickinson declared:

> Let us take care of our rights and we therein take care of our prosperity. Slavery is ever preceded by sleep. [68]

Samuel Adams similarly warned:

> [A] state of indolence [laziness], inattention, and security . . . is forever the forerunner of slavery. [69]

Daniel Webster also cautioned:

> I apprehend no danger to our country from a foreign foe. The prospect of a war with any powerful nation is too remote to be a

matter of calculation. Besides, there is no nation on earth powerful enough to accomplish our overthrow. Our destruction, should it come at all, will be from another quarter. From the inattention of the people to the concerns of their government, from their carelessness and negligence. [70]

Early statesmen understood that if we "went to sleep," our government would become corrupt and tyrannical, resulting in political slavery of its citizens. Only if citizens remained alert and active stewards could this condition be avoided. Perhaps President James A. Garfield, himself a Christian minister, most succinctly articulated this truth when he reminded Americans:

Now, more than ever before, the people are responsible for the character of their Congress. If that body be ignorant, reckless, and corrupt, it is because the people tolerate ignorance, recklessness, and corruption. If it be intelligent, brave, and pure, it is because the people demand these high qualities to represent them in the national legislature. . . . [I]f the next centennial does not find us a great nation . . . it will be because those who represent the enterprise, the culture, and the morality of the nation do not aid in controlling the political forces. [71]

Christians must again become active in the civic arena and move beyond their self-imposed boundaries of church and home. It is time to remember the warning given by Charles Finney, a minister and leader in America's Second Great Awakening, who reminded Christians:

The Church must take right ground in regard to politics. . . . [T]he time has come that Christians must vote for honest men and take consistent ground in politics. . . . God cannot sustain this free and blessed country which we love and pray for unless the Church will take right ground. Politics are a part of a religion in such a country as this, and Christians must do their duty to the country as a part of their duty to God. . . . He [God] will bless or curse this nation according to the course they [Christians] take [in politics]. [72]

As the church reenters the political arena, however, it will be important to observe George Washington's warning against excessive allegiance to any political party:

Let me now . . . warn you in the most solemn manner against the baneful effects of the spirit of party. . . . The common and continual mischiefs of the spirit of party are sufficient to make it the interest and duty of a wise people to discourage and restrain it. It serves always to distract the public councils and enfeeble the public administration. It agitates the community with ill-founded jealousies and false alarms; kindles the animosity of one part against another. . . . In governments purely elective, it [the spirit of party] is a spirit not to be encouraged. [73]

Do not misread this passage; Washington was *not* saying to abolish political parties; political parties *are* necessary; for they are the mechanisms by which candidates are offered to the public. The tone of Washington's warning was not against political parties but only against excessive party allegiance—the "spirit of party."

God-fearing people of faith *should* be actively involved in a political party so that they may help select candidates, influence their party's platform, and vote in their party's primary to help Godly candidates advance. Yet, regardless of the party in which one is working, there will be times that someone in the other party will be more Godly than the candidate offered by his/her party and thus better for the community, the State, or the nation. At such times, faithfully support the best candidate without regard to party— a principle well illustrated by Benjamin Rush.

Benjamin Rush not only signed the Declaration of Independence, he also served in the Presidential administrations of John Adams, Thomas Jefferson, and James Madison—each of whom came from a different political party. How could Benjamin Rush serve for Presidents from three different parties, and what was his own party affiliation? He once proclaimed:

I have been alternately called an aristocrat and a democrat. I am now neither. I am a Christocrat. I believe all power . . . will always fail of producing order and happiness in the hands of man. He alone who created and redeemed man is qualified to govern him. [74]

Benjamin Rush made his choice of candidates based on which one better stood for Godly principles, no matter his party affiliation. As Proverbs 29:2 accurately states: "When the righteous"—not the Republicans, the Democrats, or any other party—but "When the righteous rule, the people rejoice; when the wicked rule, the people groan." The love of correct principles—not the love of a party—is the key to effective political involvement; the government of this nation will be blessed only to the extent that God-fearing and moral individuals are placed into office.

What legacy will we leave the next generation? Obviously, the choice is ours; but having this choice, we should heed the warning delivered to citizens in 1803 when the Reverend Matthias Burnet charged:

> Finally, ye . . . whose high prerogative it is to . . . invest with office and authority or to withhold them and in whose power it is to save or destroy your country, consider well the important trust . . . which God . . . [has] put into your hands. To God and posterity you are accountable for them. . . . Let not your children have reason to curse you for giving up those rights and prostrating those institutions which your fathers delivered to you. [75]

For the sake of this generation, as well as future ones, we must be active. As John Hancock urged:

> I conjure you, by all that is dear, by all that is honorable, by all that is sacred, not only that ye pray but that ye act. [76]

The responsibilities facing God-fearing citizens are somber, and the potential repercussions from our actions—or lack thereof—are both far-reaching and longlasting. Remember that where citizen complacency rules, wrong principles and policies will abound; and when it comes to sound government, the enemy is seldom "them"; it is generally citizen apathy.

Appendix A:
The Declaration of Independence

When in the course of human events, it becomes necessary for one people to dissolve the political bands which have connected them with another, and to assume among the powers of the earth the separate and equal station to which the laws of nature and of nature's God entitles them, a decent respect to the opinions of mankind requires that they should declare the causes which impel them to the separation.

We hold these truths to be self-evident, that all men are created equal, that they are endowed by their Creator with certain unalienable rights, that among these are life, liberty and the pursuit of happiness. That to secure these rights, governments are instituted among men, deriving their just powers from the consent of the governed. That whenever any form of government becomes destructive of these ends, it is the right of the people to alter or to abolish it and to institute new government, laying its foundation on such principles and organizing its powers in such form as to them shall seem most likely to effect their safety and happiness. Prudence, indeed, will dictate that governments long established should not be changed for light and transient causes; and accordingly, all experience hath shown that mankind are more disposed to suffer while evils are sufferable than to right themselves by abolishing the forms to which they are accustomed. But when a long train of abuses and usurpations, pursuing invariably the same object, evinces a design to reduce them under absolute despotism, it is their right, it is their duty, to throw off such government and to provide new guards for their future security. Such has been the patient sufferance of these Colonies; and such is now the necessity which constrains them to alter their former systems of governments. The history of the present King of Great Britain is a history of repeated injuries and usurpations, all having in direct object the establishment of an absolute tyranny over these States. To prove this, let facts be submitted to a candid world.

He has refused his assent to laws, the most wholesome and necessary for the public good.

He has forbidden his Governors to pass laws of immediate and pressing importance, unless suspended in their operation till his assent should be obtained; and when so suspended, he has utterly neglected to attend to them.

He has refused to pass other laws for the accommodation of large districts of people unless those people would relinquish the right of representation in the legislature, a right inestimable to them and formidable to tyrants only.

He has called together legislative bodies at places unusual, uncomfortable, and distant from the depository of their public records, for the sole purpose of fatiguing them into compliance with his measures.

He has dissolved representative Houses repeatedly for opposing with manly firmness his invasion on the rights of the people.

He has refused for a long time, after such dissolutions, to cause others to be elected; whereby the legislative powers, incapable of annihilation, have returned to the people at large for their exercise; the State remaining in the meantime exposed to all the dangers of invasion from without and convulsions within.

He has endeavored to prevent the population of these States; for that purpose obstructing the laws for naturalization of foreigners; refusing to pass others to encourage their migrations hither, and raising the conditions of new appropriations of lands.

He has obstructed the administration of justice by refusing his assent to laws for establishing judiciary powers.

He has made judges dependent on his will alone for the tenure of their offices and the amount and payment of their salaries.

He has erected a multitude of new offices and sent hither swarms of officers to harass our people and eat out their substance.

He has kept among us, in times of peace, standing armies without the consent of our legislature.

He has affected to render the military independent of and superior to the civil power.

He has combined with others to subject us to a jurisdiction foreign to our constitution and unacknowledged by our laws; giving his assent to their acts of pretended legislation:

For quartering large bodies of armed troops among us:

For protecting them, by a mock trial, from punishment for any murders which they should commit on the inhabitants of these States:

For cutting off our trade with all parts of the world:

For imposing taxes on us without our consent:

For depriving us in many cases of the benefits of trial by jury:

For transporting us beyond seas to be tried for pretended offenses:

For abolishing the free system of English laws in a neighboring province, establishing therein an arbitrary government, and enlarging its boundaries so as to render it at once an example and fit instrument for introducing the same absolute rule into these Colonies:

For taking away our charters, abolishing our most valuable laws, and altering fundamentally the forms of our government:

For suspending our own legislatures and declaring themselves invested with power to legislate for us in all cases whatsoever.

He has abdicated government here by declaring us out of his protection and waging war against us.

He has plundered our seas, ravaged our coasts, burnt our towns, and destroyed the lives of our people.

He is at this time transporting large armies of foreign mercenaries to complete the works of death, desolation, and tyranny, already begun with circumstances of cruelty and perfidy scarcely paralleled in the most barbarous ages, and totally unworthy the head of a civilized nation.

He has constrained our fellow citizens taken captive on the high seas to bear arms against their country, to become the executioners of their friends and brethren, or to fall themselves by their hands.

He has excited domestic insurrections amongst us and has endeavored to bring on the inhabitants of our frontiers the merciless Indian savages, whose known rule of warfare is an undistinguished destruction of all ages, sexes, and conditions.

In every stage of these suppressions we have petitioned for redress in the most humble terms. Our repeated petitions have been answered only by repeated injury. A Prince, whose character is thus marked by every act which may define a tyrant, is unfit to be the ruler of a free people.

Nor have we been wanting in attention to our British brethren. We have warned them from time to time of attempts by their legislature to extend an unwarrantable jurisdiction over us. We have reminded them of the circumstances of our emigration and settlement here. We have appealed to their native justice and magnanimity and we have conjured them by the ties of our common kindred to disavow these usurpations which would inevitably interrupt our connections and correspondence. They, too, have been deaf to the voice of justice and of consanguinity. We must, therefore, acquiesce in the necessity which denounces our separation and hold them, as we hold the rest of mankind, enemies in war, in peace friends.

We, therefore, the Representatives of the United States of America, in general Congress assembled, appealing to the Supreme Judge of the world for the rectitude of our intentions, do, in the name and by the authority of the good people of these Colonies, solemnly publish and declare that these United Colonies are, and of right ought to be, free and independent States; that they are absolved from all allegiance to the British Crown and that all political connection between them and the State of Great Britain is and ought to be totally dissolved; and that as free and independent States, they have full power to levy war, conclude peace, contract alliance, establish commerce, and do all other acts and things which independent States may of right do. And for the support of this Declaration, with a firm reliance on the protection of Divine Providence, we mutually pledge to each other our lives, our fortunes, and our sacred honor.

Appendix B:

The Constitution of the United States of America

Preamble to the Constitution of the United States

We the people of the United States, in order to form a more perfect Union, establish justice, insure domestic tranquility, provide for the common defence, promote the general welfare, and secure the blessings of liberty to ourselves and our posterity, do ordain and establish this Constitution for the United States of America.

ARTICLE I

Section 1. All legislative powers herein granted shall be vested in a Congress of the United States which shall consist of a Senate and House of Representatives.

Section 2. The House of Representatives shall be composed of members chosen every second year by the people of the several States, and the electors in each State shall have the qualifications requisite for electors of the most numerous branch of the State legislature.

No person shall be a Representative who shall not have attained to the age of twenty-five years and been seven years a citizen of the United States, and who shall not, when elected, be an inhabitant of that State in which he shall be chosen.

∞ [Representatives and direct taxes shall be apportioned among the several States which may be included within this Union, according to their respective numbers, which shall be determined by adding to the whole number of free persons, including those bound to service for a term of years, and excluding Indians not taxed, three fifths of all other persons.] The actual enumeration shall be made within three years after the first meeting of the Congress of the United States, and within every subsequent term of ten years, in such manner as they shall by law direct. The number of Representatives shall not exceed one for every thirty thousand but each State shall have at least one Representative; and until such enumeration shall be made, the State of New Hampshire shall be entitled to choose three, Massachusetts eight, Rhode Island and Providence Plantations one, Connecticut five, New York six; New Jersey four, Pennsylvania eight, Delaware one, Maryland six, Virginia ten, North Carolina five, South Carolina five, and Georgia three.

∞ (The preceding portion in brackets is amended by the Fourteenth Amendment, Section 2).

When vacancies happen in the representation from any State, the executive authority thereof shall issue writs of election to fill such vacancies.

The House of Representatives shall choose their Speaker and other officers; and shall have the sole power of impeachment.

Section 3. The Senate of the United States shall be composed of two Senators from each State, chosen by the legislature thereof, for six years; and each Senator shall have one vote.

Immediately after they shall be assembled in consequence of the first election, they shall be divided as equally as may be into three classes. The seats of the Senators of the first class shall be vacated at the expiration of the second year, of the second class at the expiration of the fourth year, and of the third class at the expiration of the sixth year, so that one-third may be chosen every second year; and if vacancies happen by resignation, or otherwise, during the recess of the legislature of any State, the Executive thereof may make temporary appointments until the next meeting of the legislature, which shall then fill such vacancies.

No person shall be a Senator who shall not have attained to the age of thirty years and been nine years a citizen of the United States, and who shall not, when elected, be an inhabitant of that State for which he shall be chosen.

The Vice-President of the United States shall be President of the Senate but shall have no vote unless they be equally divided.

The Senate shall choose their other officers, and also a President pro tempore, in the absence of the Vice-President, or when he shall exercise the office of President of the United States

The Senate shall have the sole power to try all impeachments. When sitting for that purpose, they shall be on oath or affirmation. When the President of the United States is tried, the Chief Justice shall preside: and no person shall be convicted without the concurrence of two thirds of the members present.

Judgment in cases of impeachment shall not extend further than to removal from office and disqualification to hold and enjoy any office of honor, trust, or profit under the United States: but the party convicted shall nevertheless be liable and subject to indictment, trial, judgment and punishment according to Law.

Section 4. The times, places, and manner of holding elections for Senators and Representatives shall be prescribed in each State by the legislature thereof; but the Congress may at any time by law make or alter such regulations except as to the places of choosing Senators.

The Congress shall assemble at least once in every year, and such meeting shall be on the first Monday in December, unless they shall by law appoint a different day.

Section 5. Each House shall be the judge of the elections, returns, and qualifications of its own members, and a majority of each shall constitute a quorum to do business; but a smaller number may adjourn from day to day and may be authorized to compel the attendance of absent members, in such manner, and under such penalties as each House may provide.

Each House may determine the rules of its proceedings, punish its members for disorderly behavior, and, with the concurrence of two thirds, expel a member.

Each House shall keep a journal of its proceedings and from time to time publish the same, excepting such parts as may in their judgment require secrecy; and the yeas and nays of the members of either House on any question shall, at the desire of one fifth of those present, be entered on the Journal.

Neither House, during the session of Congress, shall, without the consent of the other, adjourn for more than three days nor to any other place than that in which the two Houses shall be sitting.

Section 6. The Senators and Representatives shall receive a compensation for their services, to be ascertained by law, and paid out of the Treasury of the United States. They shall in all cases except treason, felony, and breach of the peace, be privileged from arrest during their attendance at the session of their respective Houses and in going to and returning from the same; and for any speech or debate in either House they shall not be questioned in any other place.

No Senator or Representative shall, during the time for which he was elected, be appointed to any civil office under the authority of the United States which shall have been created or the emoluments whereof shall have been increased during such time; and no person holding any office under the United States shall be a member of either House during his continuance in office.

Section 7. All bills for raising revenue shall originate in the House of Representatives; but the Senate may propose or concur with amendments as on other bills.

Every bill which shall have passed the House of Representatives and the Senate shall, before it becomes a law, be presented to the President of the United States; if he approve, he shall sign it, but if not he shall return it, with his objections, to that House in which it shall have originated, who shall enter the objections at large on their journal and proceed to reconsider it. If, after such reconsideration, two thirds of that House shall agree to pass the bill, it shall be sent, together with the objections, to the other House, by which it shall likewise be reconsidered, and if approved by two thirds of that

House, it shall become a law. But in all such cases, the votes of both Houses shall be determined by yeas and nays and the names of the persons voting for and against the bill shall be entered on the journal of each House respectively. If any bill shall not be returned by the President within ten days (Sundays excepted) after it shall have been presented to him, the same shall be a law in like manner as if he had signed it unless the Congress, by their adjournment, prevent its return, in which case it shall not be a law.

Every order, resolution, or vote to which the concurrence of the Senate and House of Representatives may be necessary (except on a question of adjournment) shall be presented to the President of the United States; and before the same shall take effect shall be approved by him, or, being disapproved by him, shall be repassed by two thirds of the Senate and House of Representatives according to the rules and limitations prescribed in the case of a bill.

Section 8. The Congress shall have power to lay and collect taxes, duties, imposts, and excises to pay the debts and provide for the common defense and general welfare of the United States; but all duties, imposts, and excises shall be uniform throughout the United States;

To borrow money on the credit of the United States;

To regulate commerce with foreign nations and among the several States and with the Indian tribes;

To establish an uniform rule of naturalization and uniform laws on the subject of bankruptcies throughout the United States;

To coin money, regulate the value thereof and of foreign coin, and fix the standard of weights and measures;

To provide for the punishment of counterfeiting the securities and current coin of the United States;

To establish post offices and post roads;

To promote the progress of science and useful arts by securing for limited times to authors and inventors the exclusive rights to their respective writings and discoveries;

To constitute tribunals inferior to the Supreme Court;

To define and punish piracies and felonies committed on the high seas and offences against the law of nations;

To declare war, grant letters of marque and reprisal, and make rules concerning captures on land and water;

To raise and support armies, but no appropriation of money to that use shall be for a longer term than two years;

To provide and maintain a Navy;

To make rules for the government and regulation of the land and naval forces;

To provide for calling forth the militia to execute the laws of the Union, suppress insurrections, and repel invasions;

To provide for organizing, arming, and disciplining the militia and for governing such part of them as may be employed in the service of the United States, reserving to the States respectively the appointment of the officers and the authority of training the militia according to the discipline prescribed by Congress;

To exercise exclusive legislation in all cases whatsoever over such district (not exceeding ten miles square) as may, by cession of particular States and the acceptance of Congress, become the seat of the government of the United States, and to exercise like authority over all places purchased by the consent of the legislature of the State in which the same shall be for the erection of forts, magazines, arsenals, dockyards, and other needful buildings;—and

To make all laws which shall be necessary and proper for carrying into execution the foregoing powers and all other powers vested by this Constitution in the government of the United States or in any department or officer thereof.

Section 9. The migration or importation of such persons as any of the States now existing shall think proper to admit shall not be prohibited by the Congress prior to the year one thousand eight hundred and eight, but a tax or duty may be imposed on such importation not exceeding ten dollars for each person.

The privilege of the writ of Habeas Corpus shall not be suspended unless when in cases of rebellion or invasion the public safety may require it.

No bill of attainder or ex post facto law shall be passed.

No capitation or other direct tax shall be laid unless in proportion to the census or enumeration herein before directed to be taken.

No tax or duty shall be laid on articles exported from any State.

No preference shall be given by any regulation of commerce or revenue to the ports of one State over those of another: nor shall vessels bound to or from one State be obliged to enter, clear, or pay duties in another.

No money shall be drawn from the Treasury but in consequence of appropriations made by law; and a regular statement and account of the receipts and expenditures of all public money shall be published from time to time.

No title of nobility shall be granted by the United States: and no person holding any office of profit or trust under them shall, without the consent of the Congress, accept of any present, emolument, office, or title of any kind whatever from any king, prince, or foreign State.

Section 10. No State shall enter into any treaty, alliance, or confederation; grant letters of marque and reprisal; coin money, emit bills of credit; make any thing but gold and silver coin a tender in payment of debts; pass any bill of attainder, ex post facto law, or law impairing the obligation of contracts, or grant any title of nobility.

No State shall, without the consent of the Congress, lay any imposts of duties on imports or exports except what may be absolutely necessary for executing its inspection laws: and the net produce of all duties and imposts laid by any State on imports or exports shall be for the use of the Treasury of the United States; and all such laws shall be subject to the revision and control of the Congress.

No State shall, without the consent of Congress, lay any duty of tonnage, keep troops, or ships of war in time of peace, enter into any agreement or compact with another State or with a foreign power, or engage in war, unless actually invaded, or in such imminent danger as will not admit of delay.

ARTICLE II

Section 1. The executive power shall be vested in a President of the United States of America. He shall hold his office during the term of four years and, together with the Vice-President chosen for the same term, be elected as follows:

Each State shall appoint, in such manner as the legislature thereof may direct, a number of electors equal to the whole number of Senators and Representatives to which the State may be entitled in the Congress: but no Senator or Representative or person holding an office of trust or profit under the United States shall be appointed an elector.

∞ ["The electors shall meet in their respective States and vote by ballot for two persons of whom one at least shall not be an inhabitant of the same State with themselves. And they shall make a list of all the persons voted for and of the number of votes for each; which list they shall sign and certify and transmit sealed to the seat of the government of the United States, directed to the President of the Senate. The President of the Senate shall, in the presence of the Senate and House of Representatives, open all the certificates and the votes shall then be counted. The person having the greatest number of votes shall be the President if such number be a majority of the whole number of electors appointed; and if there be more than one who have such majority and have an equal number of votes, then the House of Representatives shall immediately choose by ballot one of them for President; and if no person have a majority, then from the five highest on the list the said House shall in like manner choose the President. But in choosing the President, the votes shall be taken by States, the representation from each State having one vote; a quorum for this purpose shall consist of a member or members from two-thirds of the States, and a majority of all the States shall be necessary to a choice. In every case, after the choice of the President, the person having the greatest number of votes of the electors shall be the Vice-President. But if there should remain two or more who have equal votes, the Senate shall choose from them by ballot the Vice-President."]

∞ (The preceding section has been superseded by the Twelfth Amendment).

The Congress may determine the time of choosing the electors and the day on which they shall give their votes; which day shall be the same throughout the United States.

No person except a natural born citizen, or a citizen of the United States at the time of the adoption of this Constitution, shall be eligible to the office of President; neither shall any person be eligible to that office who shall not have attained to the age of thirty-five years and been fourteen years a resident within the United States.

In case of the removal of the President from office, or of his death, resignation, or inability to discharge the powers and duties of the said office, the same shall devolve on the Vice-President, and the Congress may by law provide for the case of removal, death, resignation, or inability, both of the President and Vice-President, declaring what officer shall then act as President, and such officer shall act accordingly until the disability be removed or a President shall be elected.

The President shall, at stated times, receive for his services a compensation which shall neither be increased nor diminished during the period for which he shall have been elected, and he shall not receive within that period any other emolument from the United States or any of them.

Before he enter on the execution of his office, he shall take the following oath or affirmation: — "I do solemnly swear (or affirm) that I will faithfully execute the office of President of the United States and will, to the best of my ability, preserve, protect, and defend the Constitution of the United States."

Section 2. The President shall be Commander in Chief of the Army and Navy of the United States, and of the militia of the several States when called into the actual service of the United States; he may require the opinion, in writing, of the principal officer in each of the executive departments upon any subject relating to the duties of their respective offices, and he shall have power to grant reprieves and pardons for offenses against the United States, except in cases of impeachment.

He shall have power, by and with the advice and consent of the Senate, to make treaties, provided two thirds of the Senators present concur; and he shall nominate, and by and with the advice and consent of the Senate, shall appoint Ambassadors, other public Ministers and Consuls, Judges of the Supreme Court, and all other Officers of the United States, whose appointments are not herein otherwise provided for and which shall be established by law: but the Congress may by law vest the appointment of such inferior officers as they think proper in the President alone, in the Courts of law, or in the heads of departments.

The President shall have power to fill up all vacancies that may happen during the recess of the Senate by granting commissions which shall expire at the end of their next session.

Section 3. He shall from time to time give to the Congress information of the state of the Union and recommend to their consideration such measures as he shall judge necessary and expedient; he may, on extraordinary occasions, convene both Houses, or either of them, and in case of disagreement between them with respect to the time of adjournment, he may adjourn them to such time as he shall think proper; he shall receive Ambassadors and other public Ministers; he shall take care that the laws be faithfully executed, and shall commission all the officers of the United States.

Section 4. The President, Vice-President, and all civil officers of the United States shall be removed from office on impeachment for and conviction of treason, bribery, or other high crimes and misdemeanors.

ARTICLE III

Section 1. The judicial power of the United States shall be vested in one Supreme Court and in such inferior Courts as the Congress may from time to time ordain and establish. The Judges, both of the Supreme and inferior Courts, shall hold their offices during good behavior and shall, at stated times, receive for their services a compensation which shall not be diminished during their continuance in office.

Section 2. The judicial power shall extend to all cases in law and equity arising under this Constitution, the laws of the United States, and treaties made, or which shall be made, under their authority:—to all cases affecting Ambassadors, other public Ministers and Consuls;—to all cases of admiralty and maritime jurisdiction;—to controversies to which the United States shall be a party;—to controversies between two or more States;—between a State and citizens of another State;—between citizens of different States,—between citizens of the same State claiming lands under grants of different States, and between a State, or the citizens thereof, and foreign States, citizens, or subjects.

In all cases affecting Ambassadors, other public Ministers and Consuls, and those in which a State shall be party, the Supreme Court shall have original jurisdiction. In all the other cases before mentioned, the Supreme Court shall have appellate jurisdiction both as to law and fact with such exceptions and under such regulations as the Congress shall make.

The trial of all crimes, except in cases of impeachment, shall be by jury; and such trial shall be held in the State where the said crimes shall have been committed; but when not committed within any State, the trial shall be at such place or places as the Congress may by law have directed.

Section 3. Treason against the United States shall consist only in levying war against them or in adhering to their enemies, giving them aid and comfort. No person shall be convicted of treason unless on the testimony of two witnesses to the same overt act or on confession in open court.

The Congress shall have power to declare the punishment of treason, but no attainder of treason shall work corruption of blood or forfeiture except during the life of the person attainted.

ARTICLE IV

Section 1. Full faith and credit shall be given in each State to the public acts, records, and judicial proceedings of every other State. And the Congress may by general laws prescribe the manner in which such acts, records, and proceedings shall be proved, and the effect thereof.

Section 2. The citizens of each State shall be entitled to all privileges and immunities of citizens in the several States.

A person charged in any State with treason, felony, or other crime, who shall flee from justice and be found in another State, shall on demand of the executive authority of the State from which he fled, be delivered up to be removed to the State having jurisdiction of the crime.

No person held to service or labor in one State under the laws thereof, escaping into another, shall, in consequence of any law or regulation therein, be discharged from such service or labor, but shall be delivered up on claim of the party to whom such service or labor may be due.

Section 3. New States may be admitted by the Congress into this Union; but no new State shall be formed or erected within the jurisdiction of any other State; nor any State be formed by the junction of two or more States or parts of States without the consent of the legislatures of the States concerned as well as of the Congress.

The Congress shall have power to dispose of and make all needful rules and regulations respecting the territory or other property belonging to the United States; and nothing in this Constitution shall be so construed as to prejudice any claims of the United States or of any particular State.

Section 4. The United States shall guarantee to every State in this Union a republican form of government and shall protect each of them against invasion; and on application of the legislature, or of the Executive (when the legislature cannot be convened), against domestic violence.

ARTICLE V

The Congress, whenever two thirds of both Houses shall deem it necessary, shall propose amendments to this Constitution or, on the application of the legislatures of two thirds of the several States, shall call a convention for proposing amendments which, in either case, shall be valid to all intents and purposes as part of this Constitution when ratified by the legislatures of three fourths of the several States or by conventions in three fourths thereof as the one or the other mode of ratification may be proposed by the Congress; provided that no amendment which may be made prior to the year one thousand eight hundred and eight shall in any manner affect the first and fourth clauses in the ninth section of the first article; and that no State, without its consent, shall be deprived of its equal suffrage in the Senate.

ARTICLE VI

All debts contracted and engagements entered into before the adoption of this Constitution shall be as valid against the United States under this Constitution as under the Confederation.

This Constitution and the laws of the United States which shall be made in pursuance thereof; and all treaties made or which shall be made, under the authority of the United States shall be the supreme law of the land; and the judges in every State shall be bound thereby, any thing in the Constitution or laws of any State to the contrary notwithstanding.

The Senators and Representatives before mentioned, and the members of the several State legislatures, and all executive and judicial officers both of the United States and of the several States, shall be bound by oath or affirmation to support this Constitution; but no religious test shall ever be required as a qualification to any office or public trust under the United States.

ARTICLE VII

The ratification of the conventions of nine States shall be sufficient for the establishment of this Constitution between the States so ratifying the same.

DONE in convention by the unanimous consent of the States present the seventeenth day of September in the Year of our Lord one thousand seven hundred and eighty seven, and of the independence of the United States of America the twelfth.

Amendments to the Constitution

AMENDMENT I
(First ten amendments adopted June 15, 1790)

Congress shall make no law respecting an establishment of religion or prohibiting the free exercise thereof; or abridging the freedom of speech, or of the press; or the right of the people peaceably to assemble and to petition the government for a redress of grievances.

AMENDMENT II

A well regulated militia being necessary to the security of a free State, the right of the people to keep and bear arms shall not be infringed.

AMENDMENT III

No soldier shall in time of peace be quartered in any house without the consent of the owner, nor in time of war but in a manner to be prescribed by law.

AMENDMENT IV

The right of the people to be secure in their persons, houses, papers, and effects, against unreasonable searches and seizures shall not be violated, and no warrants shall issue but upon probable cause supported by oath or affirmation, and particularly describing the place to be searched and the persons or things to be seized.

AMENDMENT V

No person shall be held to answer for a capital or otherwise infamous crime unless on a presentment or indictment of a grand jury, except in cases arising in the land or naval forces or in the militia when in actual service in time of war or public danger; nor shall any person be subject for the same offence to be twice put in jeopardy of life or limb; nor shall be compelled in any criminal case to be a witness against himself, nor be deprived of life, liberty, or property, without due process of law; nor shall private property be taken for public use without just compensation.

AMENDMENT VI

In all criminal prosecutions, the accused shall enjoy the right to a speedy and public trial by an impartial jury of the State and district wherein the crime shall have been committed, which district shall have been previously ascertained by law, and to be informed of the nature and cause of the accusation; to be confronted with the witnesses against him; to have compulsory process for obtaining witnesses in his favor, and to have the assistance of counsel for his defence.

AMENDMENT VII

In suits at common law, where the value in controversy shall exceed twenty dollars, the right of trial by jury shall be preserved, and no fact tried by a jury shall be otherwise reexamined in any Court of the United States than according to the rules of the common law.

AMENDMENT VIII

Excessive bail shall not be required nor excessive fines imposed, nor cruel and unusual punishments inflicted.

AMENDMENT IX

The enumeration in the Constitution of certain rights shall not be construed to deny or disparage others retained by the people.

AMENDMENT X

The powers not delegated to the United States by the Constitution nor prohibited by it to the States are reserved to the States respectively or to the people.

AMENDMENT XI
(Adopted January 8, 1798)

The judicial power of the United States shall not be construed to extend to any suit in law or equity commenced or prosecuted against one of the United States by citizens of another State or by citizens or subjects of any foreign State.

AMENDMENT XII
(Adopted September 25, 1804)

The electors shall meet in their respective States and vote by ballot for President and Vice-President, one of whom, at least, shall not be an inhabitant of the same State with themselves; they shall name in their ballots the person voted for as President and in distinct ballots the person voted for as Vice-President, and they shall make distinct lists of all persons voted for as President and of all persons voted for as Vice-President, and of the number of votes for each, which lists they shall sign and certify and transmit sealed to the seat of the government of the United States, directed to the President of the Senate;—the President of the Senate shall, in the presence of the Senate and House of Representatives, open all the certificates and the votes shall then be counted;—the person having the greatest number of votes for President shall be the President if such number be a majority of the whole number of electors appointed; and if no person have such majority, then from the persons having the highest numbers not exceeding three on the list of those voted for as President, the House of Representatives shall choose immediately by ballot the President. But in choosing the President, the votes shall be taken by States, the representation from each State having one vote; a quorum for this purpose shall consist of a member or members from two-thirds of the States and a majority of all the States shall be necessary to a choice. And if the House of Representatives shall not choose a President whenever the right of choice shall devolve upon them, before the fourth day of March next following, then the Vice-President shall act as President, as in the case of the death or other constitutional disability of the President. The person having the greatest number of votes as Vice-President shall be the Vice-President if such number be a majority of the whole number of electors appointed, and if no person have a majority, then from the two highest numbers on the list the Senate shall choose the Vice-President; a quorum for the purpose shall consist of two-thirds of the whole number of Senators and a majority of the whole number shall be necessary to a choice. But no person constitutionally ineligible to the office of President shall be eligible to that of Vice-President of the United States.

AMENDMENT XIII
(Adopted December 18, 1865)

Section 1. Neither slavery nor involuntary servitude, except as a punishment for crime whereof the party shall have been duly convicted, shall exist within the United States or any place subject to their jurisdiction.

Section 2. Congress shall have power to enforce this article by appropriate legislation.

AMENDMENT XIV
(Adopted July 21, 1868)

Section 1. All persons born or naturalized in the United States and subject to the jurisdiction thereof are citizens of the United States and of the State wherein they reside. No State shall make or enforce any law which shall abridge the privileges or immunities of citizens of the United States; nor shall any State deprive any person of life, liberty, or property, without due process of law; nor deny to any person within its jurisdiction the equal protection of the laws.

Section 2. Representatives shall be apportioned among the several States according to their respective numbers, counting the whole number of persons in each State, excluding Indians not taxed. But when the right to vote at any election for the choice of electors for President and Vice-President of the United States, Representatives in Congress, the Executive and Judicial officers of a State, or the members of the Legislature thereof, is denied to any of the male inhabitants of each State, being twenty-one years of age and citizens of the United States, or in any way abridged, except for participation in rebellion or other crime, the basis of representation therein shall be reduced in the proportion which the number of such male citizens shall bear to the whole number of male citizens twenty-one years of age in such State.

Section 3. No person shall be a Senator or Representative in Congress or elector of President and Vice-President, or hold any office, civil or military, under the United States or under any State who, having previously taken an oath as a member of Congress or as an officer of the United States or as a member of any State legislature or as an executive or judicial officer of any State, to support the Constitution of the United States, shall have engaged in insurrection or rebellion against the same or given aid or comfort to the enemies thereof. But Congress may by a vote of two-thirds of each House remove such disability.

Section 4. The validity of the public debt of the United States, authorized by law, including debts incurred for payment of pensions and bounties for services in suppressing insurrection or rebellion, shall not be questioned. But neither the United States nor any State shall assume or pay any debt or obligation incurred in aid of insurrection or rebellion against the United States or any claim for the loss or emancipation of any slave; but all such debts, obligations, and claims shall be held illegal and void.

Section 5. The Congress shall have power to enforce by appropriate legislation the provisions of this article.

AMENDMENT XV
(Adopted March 30, 1870)

Section 1. The right of citizens of the United States to vote shall not be denied or abridged by the United States or by any State on account of race, color, or previous condition of servitude.

Section 2. The Congress shall have power to enforce this article by appropriate legislation.

AMENDMENT XVI
(Adopted February 25, 1913)

The Congress shall have power to lay and collect taxes on incomes, from whatever source derived, without apportionment among the several States and without regard to any census or enumeration.

AMENDMENT XVII
(Adopted May 31, 1913)

The Senate of the United States shall be composed of two Senators from each State, elected by the people thereof for six years; and each Senator shall have one vote. The electors in each State shall have the qualifications requisite for electors of the most numerous branch of the State legislatures.

When vacancies happen in the representation of any State in the Senate, the executive authority of such State shall issue writs of election to fill such vacancies; Provided that the legislature of any State may empower the executive thereof to make temporary appointments until the people fill the vacancies by election as the legislature may direct.

This amendment shall not be so construed as to affect the election or term of any Senator chosen before it becomes valid as a part of the Constitution.

AMENDMENT XVIII
(Adopted January 29, 1919)

Section 1. After one year from the ratification of this article the manufacture, sale, or transportation of intoxicating liquors within, the importation thereof into, or the exportation thereof from the United States and all territory subject to the jurisdiction thereof for beverage purposes is hereby prohibited.

Section 2. The Congress and the several States shall have concurrent power to enforce this article by appropriate legislation.

Section 3. This article shall be inoperative unless it shall have been ratified as an amendment to the Constitution by the legislatures of the several States, as provided in the Constitution, within seven years from the date of the submission hereof to the States by the Congress.

AMENDMENT XIX
(Adopted August 26, 1920)

The right of citizens of the United States to vote shall not be denied or abridged by the United States or by any State on account of sex.

Congress shall have power to enforce this article by appropriate legislation.

AMENDMENT XX
(Adopted January 23, 1933)

Section 1. The terms of the President and Vice-President shall end at noon on the 20th day of January, and the terms of Senators and Representatives at noon on the 3rd day of January, of the years in which such terms would have ended if this article had not been ratified; and the terms of their successors shall then begin.

Section 2. The Congress shall assemble at least once in every year and such meeting shall begin at noon on the 3rd day of January unless they shall by law appoint a different day.

Section 3. If, at the time fixed for the beginning of the term of the President, the President elect shall have died, the Vice-President elect shall become President. If a President shall not have been chosen before the time fixed for the beginning of his term, or if the President elect shall have failed to qualify, then the Vice-President elect shall act as President until a President shall have qualified; and the Congress may by law provide for the case wherein neither a President elect nor a Vice-President elect shall have qualified, declaring who shall then act as President, or the manner in which one who is to act shall be selected, and such person shall act accordingly until a President or Vice-President shall have qualified.

Section 4. The Congress may by law provide for the case of the death of any of the persons from whom the House of Representatives may choose a President whenever the right of choice shall have devolved upon them, and for the case of the death of any of the persons from whom the Senate may choose a Vice-President whenever the right of choice shall have devolved upon them.

Section 5. Sections 1 and 2 shall take effect on the 15th day of October following the ratification of this article (Oct. 1933).

Section 6. This article shall be inoperative unless it shall have been ratified as an amendment to the Constitution by the Legislatures of three-fourths of the several States within seven years from the date of its submission.

AMENDMENT XXI
(Adopted December 5, 1933)

Section 1. The eighteenth article of amendment to the Constitution of the United States is hereby repealed.

Section 2. The transportation or importation into any State, territory, or possession of the United States for delivery or use therein of intoxicating liquors, in violation of the laws thereof, is hereby prohibited.

Section 3. This article shall be inoperative unless it shall have been ratified as an amendment to the Constitution by conventions in the several States, as provided in the Constitution, within seven years from the date of the submission hereof to the States by the Congress.

AMENDMENT XXII
(Adopted February 27, 1951)

Section 1. No person shall be elected to the office of the President more than twice, and no person who has held the office of President, or acted as President, for more than two years of a term to which some other person was elected President shall be elected to the office of the President more than once. But this Article shall not apply to any person holding the office of President when this Article was proposed by the Congress, and shall not prevent any person who may be holding the office of President, or acting as President, during the term within which this Article becomes operative from holding the office of President or acting as President during the remainder of such term.

Section 2. This article shall be inoperative unless it shall have been ratified as an amendment to the Constitution by the Legislatures of three-fourths of the several States within seven years from the date of its submission to the States by the Congress.

AMENDMENT XXIII
(Adopted March 29, 1961)

Section 1. The District constituting the seat of government of the United States shall appoint in such manner as the Congress may direct:

A number of electors of President and Vice-President equal to the whole number of Senators and Representatives in Congress to which the District would be entitled if it were a State, but in no event more than the least populous State; they shall be in addition to those appointed by the States, but they shall be considered, for the purposes of the election of President and Vice-President, to be electors appointed by a State; and they shall meet in the District and perform such duties as provided by the twelfth article of amendment.

Section 2. The Congress shall have power to enforce this article by appropriate legislation.

AMENDMENT XXIV
(Adopted January 23, 1964)

Section 1. The right of citizens of the United States to vote in any primary or other election for President or Vice-President, for electors for President or Vice-President, or for Senator or Representative in Congress, shall not be denied or abridged by the United States or any State by reason of failure to pay any poll tax or other tax.

Section 2. The Congress shall have power to enforce this article by appropriate legislation.

AMENDMENT XXV
(Adopted February 10, 1965)

Section 1. In case of the removal of the President from office or of his death or resignation, the Vice-President shall become President.

Section 2. Whenever there is a vacancy in the office of the Vice-President, the President shall nominate a Vice-President who shall take office upon confirmation by a majority vote of both houses of Congress.

Section 3. Whenever the President transmits to the President pro tempore of the Senate and the Speaker of the House of Representatives his written declaration that he is unable to discharge the powers and duties of his office, and until he transmits to them a written declaration to the contrary, such powers and duties shall be discharged by the Vice-President as acting President.

Section 4. Whenever the Vice-President and a majority of either the principal officers of the executive departments or of such other body as Congress may by law provide, transmit to the President pro tempore of the Senate and the Speaker of the House of Representatives their written declaration that the President is unable to discharge the powers and duties of his office, the Vice-President shall immediately assume the powers and duties of the office as acting President

Thereafter, when the President transmits to the President pro tempore of the Senate and the Speaker of the House of Representatives his written declaration that no inability exists, he shall resume the powers and duties of his office unless the Vice-President and a majority of either the principal officers of the executive department or of such other body as Congress may by law provide, transmit within four days to the President pro tempore of the Senate and the Speaker of the House of Representatives their written declaration that the President is unable to discharge the powers and duties of his office. Thereupon Congress shall decide the issue, assembling within forty-eight hours for that purpose if not in session. If the Congress, within twenty-one days after receipt of the latter written declaration, or, if Congress is not in session, within twenty-one days after Congress is required to assemble, determines by two-thirds vote of both houses that the President is unable to discharge the powers and duties of his office, the Vice-President shall continue to discharge the same as acting President; otherwise, the President shall resume the powers and duties of his office.

AMENDMENT XXVI
(Adopted July 1, 1971)

Section 1. The right of citizens of the United States, who are 18 years of age or older, to vote shall not be denied or abridged by the United States or any state on account of age.

Section 2. The Congress shall have the power to enforce this article by appropriate legislation.

AMENDMENT XXVII
(Adopted May 7, 1992)

No law varying the compensation for the services of the Senators and Representatives shall take effect until an election of Representatives shall have intervened.

Appendix C:
Biographical Sketches
of Select Individuals
Referenced in *Original Intent*

NOTE: The information for nearly 300 biographical pieces is compiled from a number of sources, including the *Dictionary of American Biography* (22 volumes), *Appleton's Cyclopedia of American Biography* (6 volumes), *The Biographical Directory of the American Congress 1774-1927*, *The Biographical Directory of the United States Congress 1774-1989*, *Encyclopedia Britannica* (1911 edition, 32 volumes), *World Book Encyclopedia* (1960 edition, 20 volumes), *Webster's American Biographies*, as well as numerous other individual biographies. Occasionally, there is discrepancy between these works as to the date or year of a specific occurrence; the years given within each sketch below are those on which most seem to agree.

Abigail Adams (1744-1818; Massachusetts) Wife of John Adams; mother of John Quincy Adams; married to John (1764) and had four children: John Quincy, Thomas, Charles, and Abby; a staunch supporter of the American Revolution, her voluminous letters during this period provide an insightful picture of the people and events surrounding the Revolution; served as First Lady (1797-1801); she and John were the first couple to occupy the White House (1800); she was the only woman to be the wife of a President and the mother of a President.

James Truslow Adams (1878-1949; New York) Historian and journalist; served in WW I and was on the staff of the U. S. delegation to the Versailles Peace Conference which officially ended that War (1919); a Pulitzer Prize winner (1922); contributed to *Encyclopedia Britannica* and the *Dictionary of American Biography;* he believed that work, morality, individualism, fiscal responsibility, and dedication to duty were the important American virtues.

John Adams (1735-1826; Massachusetts) Educator, attorney, jurist, diplomat, and public official; graduated from Harvard (1755); taught school at Worcester and considered entering the ministry but had theological problems with Calvinism; admitted to the bar (1758); leader in the opposition to the Stamp Act (1765); delegate to the Continental Congress (1774-77) where he signed the Declaration of Independence (1776); appointed Chief Justice of Superior Court of Massachusetts (1775); delegate to the Massachusetts constitutional convention (1779-80) and wrote most of the first draft of the Massachusetts Constitution; foreign ambassador to Holland (1782); signed the peace treaty which ended the American Revolution (1783); foreign ambassador to Great Britain (1785-88); served two terms as Vice-President under President George Washington (1789-97); second President of the United States (1797-1801); delegate to the Massachusetts constitutional convention (1820); he and his one time political-nemesis-turned-close-friend Thomas Jefferson both died on July 4, 1826, the fiftieth anniversary of the Declaration of Independence; Adams was titled by fellow signer of the Declaration Richard Stockton as the "Atlas of American Independence"; his son, John Quincy Adams, was also a President of the United States, making John Adams the first President who was also father of a President.

John Quincy Adams (1767-1848; Massachusetts) Public official, diplomat, and attorney; son of John and Abigail Adams; accompanied his father to France (1778) where he received training in French and Latin; attended Latin school in Amsterdam; attended Leyden University (1781) but was sent to St. Petersburg as Secretary to the Minister to Russia; studied classics at the Hague but was called to be the Secretary to John Adams during the peace negotiations ending the American Revolution (1783); graduated from Harvard (1787); admitted to the bar (1790); U. S. foreign ambassador under President George Washington to the Netherlands (1794) and Portugal (1796); under President John Adams to Prussia (1797-1801); under President James Madison to Russia (1809-14) and England (1815-17); a member of the Massachusetts legislature (1802); U. S. Senator (1803-08); Secretary of State under President James Monroe (1817-25); member of the Massachusetts Bible Society (1818); vice-president and long time member of the American Bible Society (1818-30); sixth President of the United States (1825-29); member of the U. S. House of Representatives (1831-48) where he was known both as "Old Man Eloquent" for his defense of the antislavery cause and as "the Hell-Hound of Slavery" for his intense opposition to slavery.

Samuel Adams (1722-1803; Massachusetts) Public official; second cousin to John Adams; leader in the opposition to the acts by British Parliament which precipitated the American Revolution (1765-76); member of the General Court of Massachusetts (1765-74); formed Boston's Committee of Correspondence (1772); was a member of the Continental Congress (1774-81) where he signed the Declaration of Independence (1776); helped draft the Articles of Confederation (1777); delegate to the Massachusetts constitutional convention (1779-80); president of the Massachusetts senate (1781); a member of the state convention to ratify the Federal Constitution (1788); Lieutenant-Governor of Massachusetts (1789-94); Governor of Massachusetts (1794-97); titled both the "Firebrand of the Revolution" and "The Father of the American Revolution" for his important leadership in the cause of American independence.

Robert Aitken (1734-1802; Pennsylvania) Publisher; opened a bookstore in Philadelphia (1771); published the *Pennsylvania Magazine* in which patriot leaders like Francis Hopkinson, the Rev. Dr. John Witherspoon, and Thomas Paine were contributors; printed "the Aitken Bible"—the first complete English Bible printed in America (1782).

Ethan Allen (1739-87; Connecticut, New Hampshire, New York, Vermont) Soldier and author; served in the French and Indian War at Fort William Henry (1757); captured Fort Ticonderoga (1775); without success he presented the Vermont claims to the Continental Congress (throughout the Revolution, Vermont was still considered to be part of New York; it was not recognized as an independent State until after the Revolution); awarded the rank of Colonel by George Washington (1778); received the rank of Major-General (1778) and given the command of the Vermont militia (1779-83); author of various books and pamphlets.

Richard Allen (1760-1831; Pennsylvania) Clergyman; born a slave; converted under the influence of the Methodists and became a religious worker; received his own freedom after he converted his master to Christianity; educated by private, independent studies; given appointments to preach at the St. George Methodist Church and began to conduct prayer meetings among other Blacks; established an independent organization known as the "Free African Society" (1787); ordained as a deacon in an independent Black Methodist church which he helped found (1799); ordained an elder in that same church (1816); is considered the founder and the first Bishop of the A. M. E. (African Methodist Episcopal) denomination.

Fisher Ames (1758-1808; Massachusetts) Public official; graduated from Harvard (1774); member of the Massachusetts House of Representatives (1788); member of the state convention to ratify the federal Constitution (1788); member of the U. S. House of Representatives (1789-97) where he helped frame the Bill of Rights and specifically the First Amendment; member of the Governor's Council (1798-1800); chosen by the Legislature of Massachusetts to deliver the oration at the death of George Washington (1800); declined the presidency of Harvard University because of poor health (1804); considered one of America's premier and most elegant orators.

Benedict Arnold (1741-1801; Connecticut) Soldier; became a druggist and bookseller (1762); a Captain in the Connecticut militia, helping in the capture of Fort Ticonderoga with Ethan Allen (1775); Brigadier-General (1776); war hero at the Battle of Saratoga (1777); turned traitor and made plans to deliver up the American post of West Point to the British (1780); fled to the British troops when the plot was exposed and was rewarded with a British commission as Brigadier-General (1780); led British attacks against Virginia and Connecticut (1780-81); after the surrender of the British at Yorktown (1781), Arnold fled to Great Britain where the people rejected and scorned him; traveled to Canada for the next ten years (1791-91); spent his remaining ten years in London where he died in deep depression (1791-1801).

Abraham Baldwin (1754-1807; Connecticut, Georgia) Minister, educator, attorney, and public official; attended local village school; graduated from Yale (1772); became minister (1775); served as tutor at Yale (1775-79); served as chaplain in the Revolutionary Army (1777-83); declined Professor of Divinity at Yale (1781); admitted to the bar (1783); moved to Georgia (1783); member of the Georgia State Legislature (1784-85); is titled "The Father of the University of Georgia" for the important role he played in founding that institution (1785); a delegate to the Constitutional Convention where he signed the federal Constitution (1787); member of the Continental Congress (1787-89); member of the U. S. House of Representatives (1789-99) where he helped frame the Bill of Rights; U. S. Senator (1799-1807).

Joel Barlow (1754-1812; Connecticut) Minister, educator, attorney, poet, and diplomat; tutored by Rev. Nathaniel Bartlett (1772-73); attended Moore's School, Dartmouth, and entered Yale in 1774 in the same class as Oliver Wolcott (signer of the Declaration), Zephaniah Swift (author of America's first law text), and Noah Webster (considered the "Schoolmaster of America"); graduated from Yale (1778); studied philosophy at Yale

(1779-87) but during those years he also taught school, managed a business, published a journal, wrote a version of the Psalms, served as chaplain in the Continental army (1780-83), and was admitted to the bar (1786); travelled to France and London (1788); made citizen of France (1792); Consul in Algiers (1795-97); foreign ambassador to France under President James Madison (1811); selected to meet with Napoleon (1812) but the disaster in Russia prevented that meeting; member of the United States Military Philosophical Society and the American Philosophical Society; director of the Bank of Washington; noted poet, author, and Statesman; died of pneumonia in Poland.

John Barry (1745-1803; Ireland, Pennsylvania) Sailor and soldier; born in Ireland and went to sea at an early age; no record of any formal education; settled in Philadelphia (1760); commissioned as Captain in the American Navy to command the *Lexington* (1776); captured the British sloop *Edward*—the first naval victory of the Revolution; given command of the *Effingham* but unable to use it because of the British blockade of Philadelphia; fought with the Continental Army at Philadelphia, Trenton, and Princeton (1776-77); was forced to burn the *Effingham* to prevent its capture (1778); later commanded the *Raleigh, Alliance,* and *United States* and was engaged in many sea battles— most of which he won; effected the capture of many British vessels and supplies destined for the British army; after the Revolution, he returned briefly to the merchant trade and then retired; recalled in 1794, but retired to Philadelphia in 1801; at his death, was a senior officer of the Navy and is generally rated second only to John Paul Jones.

Josiah Bartlett (1729-1795; New Hampshire) Physician, jurist, and public official; educated in common schools and tutored in Greek and Latin; began the study of medicine in Massachusetts (1745); entered practice in New Hampshire (1750); member of the State legislature (1765-75); justice-of-the-peace and Colonel of the militia, but was dismissed from both because of his support for the Colonies; member of the Continental Congress (1775-76, 78) where he signed the Declaration of Independence (1776); helped draft the Articles of Confederation (1777); Chief-Justice of the Court of Common Pleas (1778); justice of the Superior Court (1784-89) and its Chief-Justice (1788); elected to the U. S. Senate but declined to serve (1789); founded the New Hampshire Medical Society (1791); delegate to the New Hampshire constitutional convention (1792); President (Governor) of New Hampshire (1790-94).

Richard Bassett (1745-1815; Delaware) Attorney, jurist, and public official; read for law at Philadelphia and licensed to practice (1770); member of the Council of Safety (1776-86); delegate to the State constitutional convention (1776); member of both the State House (1782) and the State Senate (1786); member of the Continental Congress (1787); delegate to the Constitutional Convention where he signed the federal Constitution (1787); U. S. Senator (1789-93) where he helped frame the Bill of Rights and was the first member to vote in favor of locating the national capital on the Potomac; member of an abolition society (1795); presidential elector (1797); U. S. Circuit Judge (1798-1801); was one of the "midnight appointments" of President John Adams, but President Thomas Jefferson abolished his office, after which Bassett retired from public life.

Charles and Mary Beard (Charles: 1874-1948; Mary: 1876-1958; Indiana) Political scientists and "historians"; authors of numerous books and articles on United States history, government, foreign policy, and public issues, including *The History of the United States* (1921), *The Rise of American Civilization* (1927), *America in Midpassage* (1939), and *The American Spirit* (1942); Mary wrote about labor problems and the position of women; they are described as revisionist historians for their tendency to misportray or omit specific facts or incidents in order to alter the tone surrounding an event.

James Beattie (circa 1735-1803; Scotland) Educator and author; attended Marischal College in Aberdeen; appointed schoolmaster (1753); appointed Professor of Moral Philosophy at Marischal College (1760-96); authored *Nature and Immutability of Truth* which refuted David Hume's works—this work pleased numerous of the Founding Fathers, particularly Benjamin Rush (1770); authored numerous other philosophical and theological treatises and is remembered in literary history for the popular romantic poem, *The Minstrel* (1771).

Beccaria (Cesare Beccaria-Bonesana) (1735-94; Italy) Italian attorney, economist, and political philosopher; educated in the Jesuit college at Parma; studied Montesquieu; formed a literary society and published a small journal; appointed to the chair of law and economy (1768); his lectures were published in the collection of Italian writers on political economy; member of the Supreme Economic Council (1771); appointed one of the board for the reform of Italy's judicial code (1791).

Gunning Bedford, Jr. (1747-1812; Delaware) Attorney, soldier, jurist, and public official; graduated as valedictorian from Princeton and was in the same class with James Madison, who was his roommate (1771); admitted to the bar (c. 1773-74); apparently served as an aide to George Washington during the Revolution; member of the Continental Congress (1783-85); Attorney-General of Delaware (1784-89); delegate to the Constitutional Convention where he signed the federal Constitution (1787); member of the state convention to ratify the federal Constitution (1788); member of the State Senate (1788); appointed U. S. federal judge by President George Washington (1789-1812); presidential elector (1789, 1793).

Sir William Blackstone (1723-80; England) Attorney, jurist, and political philosopher; educated at Oxford where he became a professor of law there; admitted to the bar, but spent most of his time lecturing on law; appointed to the Vinerian Professorship of Law (1758); was elected to Parliament and achieved the rank of King's Counsel (1761); was so successful at the bar that he resigned his chair (1766); judge in the Court of Common Pleas (1770-80); his four-volume *Commentaries on the Laws of England* (1766-69) were probably more respected in America than in Great Britain and they became the premier legal work used by the Founders.

Rev. James Blair (1658-1743; Scotland) Episcopal clergyman and educator; educated in a Scottish university; moved to England, met Dr. Compton (Bishop of London), and was sent as a missionary to Virginia (1685); appointed Commissary of the Bishop of London for the Province of Virginia and thus received a seat in the council of the colonial government where he presided over any trials involving clergymen (1689-1743); King William and Queen Mary favored his plan of establishing a college and a charter was granted for William & Mary College (1692); was named its president, but did not assume duties until 1729; minister in

Bruton Parish Church in Williamsburg (1710-43); his one published work was *Our Saviour's Divine Sermon on the Mount* (1722) although he helped compile works with other authors.

Joseph Bloomfield (1753-1823; New Jersey) Attorney, soldier, and public official; educated at the Rev. Enoch Green's Classical Academy; studied law under the Colony's Attorney General; admitted to the bar (1774); commissioned Captain in a New Jersey regiment (1775); as General Phillip Schuyler's guard officer, he personally carried the Declaration of Independence to Fort Stanwix (1776); participated in the Quebec expedition (1775); became Major and Judge Advocate of the Northern Army; participated in the Battles of Brandywine (1777) and Monmouth (1778); resigned from the Army (1778); member of the Abolition Society (1794, 1796-97); Mayor of Burlington (1795-1800); Governor (1801, 1803-12); signed the "Gradual Emancipation Act" virtually ending slavery in that State (1804); member of the New Jersey Bible Society (1810); appointed Brigadier-General by President James Madison (1812); U. S. House of Representatives (1817-21).

William Blount (1749-1800; North Carolina, Tennessee) Public official; no record of any formal education; he, his two brothers, and his father participated in the Revolution; Blount served as paymaster of the Continental troops (1777); member of the North Carolina House of Commons (1780-84); member of the Continental Congress (1782-83, 1786-87); delegate to the Constitutional Convention where he signed the federal Constitution (1787); member of the North Carolina State Senate (1788-90); appointed Governor of the Territory South of the Ohio River by President George Washington (1790); Superintendent of Indian Affairs (1790-96); chairman of the convention which framed the first constitution of Tennessee (1796); U. S. Senator from Tennessee from August 2, 1796, until he was expelled from the Senate on July 8, 1797 for his sharp criticism of Congress and for his participation in "Blount's Conspiracy"— a plan to use the British, Indians, and frontiersmen to take Florida and Louisiana from Spain; elected to the State Senate of Tennessee (1798) and then chosen its president.

Daniel Boone (1734-1820; Virginia, Kentucky) Frontiersman, expert hunter, trapper, fighter, and public official; served with George Washington in the French and Indian War (1755); explored Florida (1765); explored Kentucky (1767); brought first division of settlers into Kentucky where they founded Boonesborough (1775); captured by the Shawnees and adopted by their chief (1778); was Major in the militia; served in the Virginia legislature (1781, 1787); purchased many tracts of land, but began losing them due to carelessness in preparing the titles (1785); by 1798-99, had lost all of his Kentucky land and moved west of St. Louis, Missouri; was given 845 acres from Spain, but when the United States made the "Louisiana Purchase" (1803) he was dispossessed from that land, again due to an improper title; regained the land by act of Congress (1814); spent his last years mostly at a son's home.

Elias Boudinot (1740-1821; New Jersey) Attorney, public official, author, and philanthropist; converted to Christianity during the Great Awakening and was baptized by the Rev. George Whitefield; received a classical education and studied law under Richard Stockton (who would become a signer of the Declaration) at Princeton; (interestingly, Richard Stockton married his sister in 1755 and he married Stockton's sister in 1762); admitted to the bar (1760); member of the Board of Trustees of Princeton (1772-1821);

member of the New Jersey Assembly (1775); Commissary General of Prisoners for the Continental Army, where he organized the care of American prisoners and even spent $30,000 from his own pocket in the process (1776-1779); member of the Continental Congress (1778-79, 1781-84) where he served as its president (1782-83); signed the Treaty of Peace with Great Britain (1783); member of the U. S. House of Representatives (1789-95) where he helped frame the Bill of Rights; published the *Age of Revelation* in rebuttal to Thomas Paine's *Age of Reason* (1790); first attorney admitted to the Supreme Court bar (1790); Director of the U. S. Mint under Presidents George Washington and John Adams (1795-97); member of the Massachusetts Society for Promoting Christian Knowledge (1811); member of the American Board of Commissioners for Foreign Missions (1812); helped found and served as the first president of the American Bible Society (1816-21); president of the New Jersey Bible Society (1818); published *A Star in the West* (1816) in which he attempted to prove that the American Indians were the ten lost tribes of Israel.

James Bowdoin (1726-90; Massachusetts) Public official; graduated from Harvard (1745); member of the General Court of Massachusetts (1753-56); member of the Executive Council of Massachusetts (1757-74); selected as delegate to the Continental Congress, but because of his poor health, John Hancock attended in his place (1774); member of the State Executive Council (1775-77); president of the State constitutional conventional (1779-80); founder and first President of the American Academy of Arts and Sciences (1780); Governor (1785-87); delegate to the State convention to ratify the federal Constitution and influential in securing its ratification (1788); Bowdoin College, founded in 1794, is named for him.

William Bradford (1755-95; Pennsylvania) Attorney, jurist, soldier, theologian, and public official; graduated from Princeton as a close friend of James Madison (1772); studied theology under the Rev. Dr. John Witherspoon (1776); Captain in the Continental Army (1776) and then Colonel (1777); survived the infamous winter at Valley Forge (1777-78); admitted to the bar (1779); Attorney General of Pennsylvania (1780-91); justice on the Supreme Bench of Pennsylvania (1791); appointed as U. S. Attorney General by President George Washington (1794).

Louis Brandeis (1856-1941; Kentucky) Attorney and jurist; attended Harvard Law School during the time that Law Dean Christopher Columbus Langdell was replacing the study of constitutional law with the case-law study method; appointed to the Supreme Court by President Woodrow Wilson (1916-39); many of the positivistic concepts in use by courts today were introduced or popularized by Justice Brandeis, including the application of the Bill of Rights to the States via the Fourteenth Amendment, a constitutional right to privacy, and the evolution of legal standards and principles.

David Brearly (1745-1790; New Jersey) Attorney, jurist, soldier, and public official; educated at Princeton but did not graduate; studied law and admitted to the bar (c. 1767); was so outspoken for the cause of America that he was arrested for high treason by Great Britain but was later freed by a mob of citizens; Lieutenant-Colonel of New Jersey militia (1776-79); member of the State constitutional convention (1776); Chief Justice of the Supreme Court of New Jersey (1779); one of the compilers of the Episcopal prayer book (1786); delegate to the Constitutional Convention where he signed the federal Constitution (1787); presided over the State ratification convention for the federal Constitution (1788); presidential elector (1789); U. S. District Judge (1789-90).

William Brennan (1906-   ; New Jersey) Attorney and jurist; was the second of eight children of an Irish-Catholic Democratic immigrant family; his father shoveled coal in a brewery and later became a labor leader and municipal reformer; Brennan graduated with honors from Wharton School of the University of Pennsylvania and ranked high in his law class at Harvard (1931); admitted to the bar (1931); entered and remained in private practice for a number of years; appointed to the U. S. Supreme Court by President Dwight Eisenhower (1956-90); Brennan believed that the Constitution's meaning should evolve to fit the changing standards of society; he struck down school prayer, upheld flag desecration, and upheld abortion.

John Brooks (1752-1825; Massachusetts) Physician, soldier, and public official; became a medical apprentice (1766); early involved in the cause of American Independence and was present with the Minutemen at the Battle of Lexington (1775); Lieutenant-Colonel in the Continental Army (1777); associated with General Baron von Steuben in the introduction of a system of tactics at the Battle of Monmouth (1778); delegate to the State convention that ratified the federal Constitution (1788); Governor (1816-22); president of the Middlesex County Bible Society.

Jacob Broom (1752-1810; Delaware) Farmer, surveyor, businessman, public official, and philanthropist; educated at home; prepared military maps for General George Washington prior to the Battle of Brandywine (1777); held numerous local political positions throughout his life; member of the State legislature (1784-86, 1788); delegate to the Constitutional Convention where he signed the federal Constitution (1787); Wilmington's first Postmaster (1790-92); chairman of the board of Delaware Bank.

James Brown (1766-1835; Virginia, Kentucky, Louisiana) Attorney, soldier, diplomat, and public official; attended Washington College (now Washington and Lee College) and William and Mary; admitted to the bar (c. 1788); began practice in Frankfort, Kentucky; commanded a company of sharpshooters in an expedition against the Indians (1789); secretary to the Governor (1792); Secretary of the New Orleans Territory (1804); U. S. District Attorney of New Orleans Territory (c. 1805); U. S. Senator from Louisiana (1812-17, 1819-23); appointed Minister to France by President James Monroe (1823-29); vice-president of the American Bible Society.

Warren Burger (1907-95; Minnesota) Attorney and jurist; worked as an insurance salesman and took extension courses from the University of Minnesota for two years; studied law at night at St. Paul and graduated with high honors (1931); member of a St. Paul law firm and also part of the College faculty until 1953; Assistant Attorney General under President Dwight D. Eisenhower (1953); appointed to the U. S. Federal Court of Appeals for Washington, D. C. by President Dwight D. Eisenhower (1955); appointed to the U. S. Supreme Court by President Richard Nixon to succeed Earl Warren; served as its fifteenth Chief-Justice (1969-86); would be considered a moderate, or at times a conservative, but was often in the minority; during his tenure the Court made controversial rulings on the issues of abortion, affirmative action, welfare rights, and separation of church and state.

Rev. Matthias Burnet (1749-1806; New York) Clergyman; graduated from Princeton (1769); received his license to preach and pastored the Presbyterian church in Jamaica, Long Island (1775-85); pastored the Congregational church in Norwalk, Connecticut (1785-1806); enjoyed a lengthy, successful, and influential career as a minister, and many of his sermons were published and distributed.

Rev. Aaron Burr (1715-57; New Jersey) Presbyterian clergyman and college president; father of Aaron Burr and son-in-law of Jonathan Edwards; graduated from Yale with highest honors and won a scholarship for advanced work in the classics (circa 1734) but underwent a marked religious experience which turned him to theological study; licensed to preach (1736); called to the First Church of Newark and became involved in extensive religious revivals during the Great Awakening; named one of seven trustees of Princeton (1746); elected the second president of the college (1748-57).

James Burrill, Jr. (1772-1820; Rhode Island) Attorney, jurist, and public official; graduated from Rhode Island College—now Brown University (1788); studied law and admitted to the bar (1791); State Attorney-General (1797-1813); member of the General Assembly (1813-16) and Speaker of the House (1814-16); Chief-Justice of the Supreme Judicial Court of Rhode Island (1816); U. S. Senator (1817-20); president of the Providence Auxiliary Bible Society.

Charles Caldwell (1772-1853; Kentucky) Physician, educator, and author; completed his medical education in the University of Pennsylvania under Benjamin Rush and began his medical practice (1793); served as a military surgeon during the squashing of the Whiskey Rebellion (1794); wrote much concerning the War of 1812; was a founder of the Medical Department of Transylvania University at Lexington, Kentucky (1819); first Professor at Louisville Medical Institute (1837-49); titled "the first introducer of true medical science into the Mississippi Valley"; medical career spanned sixty years during which he authored some two hundred works.

James T. Callender (1758-1803; England, Virginia) Political pamphleteer; British Messenger at Arms (1792) but because of his pamphlet, *The Political Progress of Britain,* he was indicted for sedition and called a fugitive and outlaw (1793); fled to America and wrote the *History of the United States* (1796) in which he "uncovered" the intimate affairs of Alexander Hamilton; for remarks about President John Adams he was tried under the Sedition Law, sentenced, and fined; President Thomas Jefferson secured his release, but after the U. S. government refused to meet his monetary demands he accused Jefferson of dishonesty, cowardice, and gross personal immorality. As a result of intoxication, Callender drowned in three feet of water.

Cecilius Calvert (1605-75; England) The second Lord Baltimore. The charter for Maryland was originally intended for his father but was subsequently issued to him, giving him authority as Lord Proprietor with the rights of a feudal sovereign; he never visited Maryland himself, but sent an expedition there under the direction of his brother.

Charles Calvert (1637-1715; England) The third Lord Baltimore, and second proprietor of the province of Maryland.

Benjamin Cardozo (1870-1938; New York) Attorney and jurist; attended Columbia College and Law School and began his law practice in New York City; member of the New York Court of Appeals (1914-32) and its Chief-Judge (1926-32); appointed to the United States Supreme Court by President Herbert Hoover (1932-38); he advocated judicial positivism and sociological jurisprudence.

Charles Carroll (1737-1832; Maryland) Farmer and public official; educated in France and Bohemia (1748-54); studied law in France and in London (1754-57); returned to Annapolis (1765); member of the Committee of Correspondence (1774); member of the State Council of Safety (1775); helped draft the Maryland Constitution (1776); member of the Continental Congress (1776-78) where he signed the Declaration of Independence (1776); selected as a delegate to the Constitutional Convention (1787) but did not attend; U. S. Senator (1789-92) where he helped frame the Bill of Rights; opposed the War of 1812; at his death, he was the longest lived and last surviving signer of the Declaration and was considered the wealthiest citizen in America; he was the only Roman Catholic signer of the Declaration.

Daniel Carroll (1730-1796; Maryland) Public official; cousin of Charles Carroll; his older brother John was the first Roman Catholic Bishop in America; Carroll was educated at Flanders (1742-48); little is known of his life between 1753-81; member of the Continental Congress (1781-83); signed the Articles of Confederation (1781); delegate to the Constitutional Convention where he signed the federal Constitution (1787); U. S. Senator and helped draft the Bill of Rights (1789-91).

Richard Caswell (1729-89; North Carolina) Attorney, soldier, and public official; born in Maryland to a merchant father; moved to Raleigh (1746); deputy surveyor of the colony (1750); clerk of the Court of Orange County (1752-54); studied law, admitted to the bar, and commenced practice in Hillsboro, North Carolina (1754); member of the colonial House of Delegates (1754-71) and served as its speaker the last two years; military commander at the Battle of Alamance (1771); member of the Continental Congress (1774-76); commanded the patriots at the Battle of Moore's Creek Bridge (1776); Colonel of the North Carolina Rangers (1776-77); Brigadier-General (1776); president of the State constitutional convention (1776); Governor (1776-80, 1785-88) and served without pay (1776-78); commanded the North Carolina troops at the Battle of Camden (1780); Major-General in the State militia (1780); Comptroller-General of the militia (1782); member and Speaker of the State senate (1782-84); selected as delegate to the Constitutional Convention but did not attend (1787); member of the State convention to ratify the federal Constitution (1789); member and speaker of the State House (1789).

Cato (Marcus Porcius Cato) (95-46 B.C.; Rome) Distinguished Roman philosopher; fought in the ranks against Spartacus; became a military tribune (67); obtained a provincial appointment in Asia.

Rev. William Ellery Channing (1780-1842; Rhode Island) Unitarian clergyman; graduated from Harvard (1798); opponent of slavery due to his firsthand observations of it; acquired a reputation as a preacher of remarkable power when he was installed as minister of the Federal Street Church in Boston (1803-42); his opposition to Calvinism led him to became an early advocate and spokesman for the Unitarian movement; published a sermon entitled *Unitarian Christianity* which outlined its fundamental beliefs at that time (1819).

Samuel Chase (1741-1811; Maryland) Attorney, jurist, and public official; son of an Anglican clergyman; mother died soon after his birth; educated at home by his father and then raised by his grandparents; studied law in Annapolis (1759); admitted to the bar (1761); member of the General Assembly of Maryland (1764-84); member of the Maryland Committee of Correspondence (1774); member of the Continental Congress (1774-78) where he signed the Declaration of Independence (1776); sent on a special mission to recruit Canadian resistance to the British (1776); judge of the Baltimore Criminal Court (1788); judge of the General Court of Maryland (1791); appointed to the U. S. Supreme Court by President George Washington (1796-1811); articles of impeachment filed against him for what would be considered judicial activism, or taking a political position in a judicial issue (1804); acquitted of all charges (1805) and remained on the Court until his death.

DeWitt Clinton (1769-1828; New York) Attorney and public official; graduated from Columbia College (1786); studied law three years and was admitted to the bar (1790); private secretary to the Governor (1790-95); member of the State Assembly (1798); member of the State Senate (1798-1802, 1806-11); delegate to the State constitutional convention (1801); U. S. Senator (1802-03) and introduced the Twelfth Amendment changing the manner in which the Vice-President of the United States was selected (1803); Mayor of New York City (1803-07, 1810-11, 1813-14); Governor of New York (1817-21, 1825-28); manager and vice-president of the American Bible Society (1816-27).

George Clinton (1739-1812; New York) Sailor, soldier, attorney, and public official; completed prep studies and went to sea (1758); officer in the French and Indian War (1758); Clerk of the Court of Common Pleas (1759); studied law and admitted to bar (c. 1762); District Attorney (1765); member of State Assembly (1768-75, 1800-01); served on the State Committee of Correspondence (1774); member of Continental Congress (1775-76); appointed Brigadier-General of militia (1775); voted for Declaration of Independence but unable to sign because of military duties (1776); Brigadier-General in the Continental Army (1777); Governor (1777-95, 1801-05); president of State ratification convention for the federal Constitution (1788); Attorney-General (1789); U. S. Senator (1791); Vice-President of the United States (1804-08); ran unsuccessfully for President, losing to James Madison (1808); known as the "Father of New York."

Charles Carleton Coffin (1823-96; Massachusetts) Journalist, author, and public official; gained fame under his pen-name, Carleton, and found a direction for his later writing by his success as a correspondent in the Civil War; made his first great success by his eyewitness account of Bull Run; installed the first electric fire-alarm system in Boston; a temperance advocate from both liquor and tobacco; his children's books had a tremendous popularity; elected to the State Assembly (1884-85) and the State Senate (1890).

Rev. William Cogswell (1787-1850; New Hampshire, Massachusetts) Clergyman and educator; graduated from Dartmouth (1811); ordained to the ministry and became pastor of the South Church in Dedham, Massachusetts (1815); chosen as general agent of the American Education Society (1829); trustee of Andover Theological Seminary (1837).

Christopher Columbus (1451-1506; Italy) Sailor and explorer; he went to sea early in life; shipwrecked off the coast of Portugal (1476); made a number of voyages to Iceland, the Madeiras, etc. and began slowly formulating his ideas on sailing west in order to reach Cathay (China); from 1486-92, his plan to sail west was under consideration; permission and money were finally granted from King Ferdinand and Queen Isabella of Spain; on August 3, 1492, the three-ship fleet—the *Nina,* the *Pinta,* and the *Santa Maria*—sailed; land was sighted in the Bahamas on October 12; Columbus disembarked on the island he named San Salvador and tarried only briefly; he discovered more islands, including Guadelupe, Puerto Rico, and Jamaica; his administration of the region was tyrannical, and some colonists returned to Spain to lodge complaints; in 1496, he returned to Spain; in 1498, he set out on his third voyage, landing this time on Trinidad; his governorship of Hispanola resulted in growing hostility among the natives and rebellion among his men, and in 1500 he was replaced as Governor; in 1502, he made his final voyage where, although he did not recognize it as such, he had discovered the mainland of Central America; beset by difficulties, his fleet disintegrated; became seriously ill, and returned to Spain (1504).

Rev. Samuel Cooper (1725-83; Massachusetts) Clergyman; graduated from Harvard (1743); became pastor of the puritan Brattle Square Church in Boston (1747); member of the Corporation of Harvard (1767) and declined its presidency (1774); a strong advocate in behalf of American independence, and British authorities even ordered his arrest (1775); his church was seized and used as a British barracks, suffering damage from cannonade; was a close friend of Adams, Franklin, and other patriots; first vice-president of the Academy of Arts and Sciences (1780); patron of the Society for the Promotion of the Gospel Among the Indians and Others.

William Cushing (1732-1810; Massachusetts) Attorney and jurist; graduated from Harvard (1751); admitted to the bar (1755); often associated in cases with John Adams; became judge of the Superior Court (1772); became Massachusetts' Chief-Justice after John Adams resigned (1777); member of the Convention which framed the first State constitution of Massachusetts (1779-80); vice-president of the State convention which ratified the federal Constitution (1788); appointed as an original Justice on the U. S. Supreme Court by President George Washington (1789-1810); administered the oath of office to President George Washington for his second term (1793); was the last American judge to wear the full-bottomed powdered judicial wig.

Francis Dana (1743-1811; Massachusetts) Attorney, jurist, public official, and diplomat; graduated from Harvard (1762); studied law, and admitted to bar (1767), delegate to the Provincial Congress (1774); a "Son of Liberty" and member of the Massachusetts Council (1776-80); member of the Continental Congress (1777-78); a signer of the Articles of Confederation for the national government (1778); as chairman of a congressional committee of the army, he went to Valley Forge to cooperate with General Washington in making plans for a general reorganization of the American forces (1778); spent two years in England endeavoring to adjust differences between Great Britain and the American Colonies (1779); commissioned by Congress as Minister to Russia (1780) but was never received there as such; appointed by Governor John Hancock as an associate justice of the Supreme Court of Massachusetts (1785-1800); member of the State ratifying convention for the federal Constitution (1788); original member of the Society for Propagating the Gospel Among the Indians and Others (1787-1810).

John Davenport (1752-1830; Connecticut) Attorney, soldier, and political leader; graduated from Yale (1770); tutored at Yale (1773-74); admitted to the bar (1773); member of the State House of Representatives (1776-96); Major in the Continental Army (1777); member of U. S. House of Representatives (1799-1817).

Rev. Samuel Davies (1723-61; Virginia) Clergyman and educator; educated at a Presbyterian "log college" in Pennsylvania; ordained as a minister (1747); influential in the Great Awakening revival; commissioned by the Presbyterian Synod of New York to go to the British Isles to raise funds for Princeton (1753); while in England and Scotland he delivered some sixty sermons, many of which were distributed and widely read; became President of Princeton (1759), succeeding his friend, the Rev. Jonathan Edwards.

William Dawes (1745-99; Massachusetts) Merchant; learned tanner's trade and had a tanning yard; one of those who rode with Paul Revere in his famous midnight ride to warn of the invasion of British troops (April 18, 1775); he and Paul Revere warned John Hancock and John Adams in time for them to avoid capture; joined the Continental Army and fought at Bunker Hill (1775); Congress appointed him a Commissary to the Continental Army.

Jonathan Dayton (1760-1824; New Jersey) Attorney, soldier and public official; graduated from Princeton in 1776; Captain in the Continental Army (1776-83); studied law after the war, and admitted to the bar; member of the State General Assembly (1786-88); youngest delegate to the Constitutional Convention (27 yrs. old) and a signer of the federal Constitution (1787); served in the State Council (1789); served in House of Representatives (1790-99); Speaker of the U. S. House of Representatives (1795-99); U. S. Senator (1799-1805); arrested on the charge of conspiring with Aaron Burr in treasonable projects (1807) but was never brought to trial; member of the New Jersey assembly (1814-15).

Silas Deane (1737-89; Connecticut) Attorney, diplomat, and public official; graduated from Yale (1758); taught school, studied law, and admitted to the bar (1761); opened his law office (1762); secretary of the legislative Committee of Correspondence (1773); member of the First Continental Congress (1774); sent as Minister to France (1776); along with Benjamin Franklin and Authur Lee, negotiated several treaties with the French government (1778); accusations by Authur Lee questioning his efforts in France, which Deane was unable to clarify, led to his recall by Congress (c. 1778); lost faith in the American cause and was accused of being a traitor after writing letters encouraging friends to seek reconciliation with England (1781).

Henry Dearborn (1751-1829; Massachusetts) Physician, soldier, and public official; attended local common schools and then studied medicine; entered practice (1772); Captain of a militia company and participated in the Battle of Bunker Hill (1775); served in the military expedition to Quebec (1776); survived the infamous winter at Valley Forge (1777-78); participated in the battles of Stillwater, Saratoga,

Monmouth, and Newton; joined Washington's staff and served at the siege of York-town (1781); promoted to Brigadier-General and later to Major-General of the militia (1787); U. S. Marshal for the District of Maine (1790); U. S. Representative (1793-97); Secretary of War under President Thomas Jefferson (1801-09).

Samuel Dexter (1761-1816; Massachusetts) Attorney and public leader; graduated from Harvard (1781); admitted to the bar (1784); member State House of Representatives (1788-90); member of the U. S. House of Representatives (1792-95); U. S. Senator (1799-1800); Secretary of War, under President John Adams (1800); also served under Adams as Secretary of the Treasury and Secretary of State; administered the oath of office to John Marshall on his appointment as Chief-Justice of the U. S. Supreme Court (1801); was offered but declined appointment by President James Madison as Minister to Spain (1815); member of the Society for Propagating the Gospel Among the Indians and Others.

John Dickinson (1732-1808; Pennsylvania, Delaware) Attorney, soldier, public official; home-schooled by a tutor; studied law in Philadelphia (1750); further studies in London (1753-57); returned to American and began his own practice (1757); member of the Pennsylvania Assembly from the "Lower Counties" (1760, 1762, 1764) [in 1776, the three "Lower Counties" separated from Pennsylvania to form the State of Delaware]; delegate to the Stamp Act Congress (1765); chairman of the Philadelphia Committee of Correspondence (1774); member of the Continental Congress (1774-76, 1779); Brigadier-General of Pennsylvania Militia (1775-77); President (Governor) of the State of Delaware (1781); President (Governor) of Pennsylvania (1782-85); delegate to the Constitutional Convention and a signer of the federal Constitution (1787); retired to private life and farming.

Rev. Jonathan Dickinson (1688-1747; New Jersey) Clergyman; after his graduation from Yale College (1706) he turned his attention to theology; ordained pastor of the Congregational church at Elizabethtown, New Jersey (1709); persuaded his congregation to join the Presbyter of Philadelphia (1717); for nearly forty years he labored in behalf of the Presbyterian church, and when the College of New Jersey (Princeton) was formally opened, he became its first president (1747).

William Orville Douglas (1898-1980; Maine, Minnesota) Attorney, author, and jurist; graduated from Whitman College (1920), and Columbia Law School (1925); professor at Columbia (1925-28); served on the Securities and Exchange Commission, to include Chairmanship (1936-39); appointed to the U. S. Supreme Court by President Franklin Roosevelt (1939-75); served on the Supreme Court longer than any other member in its history; traveled widely and authored numerous books, including *Of Men and Mountains* (1950), *Strange Lands and Friendly People* (1951), and *An Almanac of Liberty* (1954), and *The Bible in Schools* (1966); a supporter of increased government regulation of private enterprise.

James Duane (1733-97; New York) Attorney, jurist, and public official; admitted to the bar (1754); involved in some of the pre-revolutionary activities in New York in which he attempted to subdue the Stamp Act mob (1765); Attorney General of New York (1767); member of the Committee of Correspondence (1774); member of the Continental Congress (1774-84); sat in the New York Provincial Convention (1776-77); helped write final draft of the Articles of Confederation (1781); member of State Senate (1782-85); appointed mayor of New York (1784-89); delegate to the State convention to ratify the federal Constitution (1788); appointed U. S. District Judge of New York by President George Washington (1789-94).

Jacob Duché (1737/38?-1798; Pennsylvania) Anglican clergyman; graduated from the College of Philadelphia (1757); Assistant Rector of the united parishes of Christ Church and St. Peters (1759-77); strong and early supporter of American independence; authored political sermons, one of which was dedicated to George Washington (1775); chaplain of the Continental Congress (1776); after the British invaded Philadelphia, he was imprisoned by General Howe (1777); consequently, he advised General George Washington that Congress should recall the Declaration of Independence; was branded a traitor by Congress; fled to England (1777); later wrote President George Washington asking for permission to return to Philadelphia and it was granted by Congress (1792).

Gabriel Duvall (1752-1844; Maryland) Public official, soldier, attorney, and jurist; received a classical education; Clerk of State convention (1774); member of Council of Safety (1774); served as militiaman in the Battle of Brandywine (1777); member of the State House (1777); admitted to the bar (1778); member of the State Council (1782-85); selected as a delegate to the Constitutional Convention but declined (1787); Chief-Justice of the General Court of Maryland (1796); appointed by President Thomas Jefferson as first Comptroller of the United States Treasury, (1802); appointed to the U. S. Supreme Court by President James Madison (1811-35).

William Eaton (1764-1811; Connecticut, Massachusetts) Soldier and public official; graduated from Dartmouth College (1790); Captain in the United States Army (1792); appointed Consul to Tunis by President John Adams (1798); appointed Naval Agent to the Barbary States by President Thomas Jefferson (1804); led a military attack against Tripoli (1804); had been closely affiliated with Aaron Burr and was summoned to witness in the Aaron Burr trial (1807) where Eaton cleared himself; elected to the Massachusetts legislature (1807).

Rev. Jonathan Edwards (1703-58; Connecticut) Congregational clergyman, theologian, and philosopher; graduated from Yale (1720); began ministry in a Presbyterian church in New York (1722); elected tutor at Yale (1724-25); pastored at a congregational church in Northhampton (1726-1750); strong advocate of the Calvinist doctrine of absolute Divine sovereignty, and his preaching brought many to repentance, and started many revivals; a leading figure in the Great Awakening national revival (1740s); his famous sermon *Sinners in the Hands of An Angry God* had great effect during that revival; president of Princeton College (1757-58); he authored several writings and theological works.

William Ellery (1727-1820; Rhode Island) Sailor, attorney, jurist, and public official; graduated from Harvard (1747); naval officer in Rhode Island (1754); Clerk of the Court of Common Pleas (1768-69); began law practice (1770); member of the Continental Congress (1776-79; 1781; 1783-85) where he signed the Declaration of Independence (1776); Chief-Justice of Rhode Island (1785); Commissioner of the Continental Loan Office (1786); Collector of the Port of Newport (1790-1820).

Oliver Ellsworth (1745-1807; Connecticut) Public official, jurist; graduated from Princeton (1766); studied theology and law; admitted to bar (1771); State's attorney in 1775; member of the Continental Congress (1778-83); delegate to the Constitutional Convention but refused to sign the federal Constitution (1787); member of the Governor's Council (1780-85, 1801-07); judge of the Superior Court (1785-89); U. S. Senator (1789-96); appointed to the U. S. Supreme Court as its Chief Justice by President George Washington (1796-1800).

Ralph Waldo Emerson (1803-1882; New Hampshire) Unitarian clergyman; graduated from Harvard (1821); graduated from Harvard Divinity School (1826); assumed the pastorate of the Second Unitarian Church in Boston (1829); an abolitionist; formed the Transcendental Club (1836); was the leading figure in removing all vestiges of Christianity from Unitarianism by the introduction of mysticism and transcendentalism into that movement; the transcendentalist group published a periodical called *The Dial* of which Emerson was a regular contributor; was elected to their Hall of Fame in 1900.

The Fairfaxes — The Honorable William Fairfax (1689-1781; England, Virginia) Agent for Thomas Lord Fairfax to lay out his lordship's lands in the Shenandoah for leaseholders; President of the Council of Virginia and second in station only to the Governor; his own estate, Belvoir, was situated just below Mount Vernon. **George William Fairfax** (1725-87; Virginia) Oldest son of the Honorable William Fairfax; lived at Belvoir; grew up as a close friend of George Washington; Burgess for Frederick County (1748-49); Colonel of militia (1755-56); held various customs offices; pursued business interests in England (1773) and was there where the Revolution broke out (1776); member of His Majesty's Council (1776) but was sympathetic to the Americans; died in Bath, England. **Sarah Cary Fairfax** (1730-1811; Virginia) Oldest daughter of Col. William Cary; she married George William Fairfax (1748); she is erroneously alleged to be the woman in Washington's illicit love affair.

William Few (1748-1828; Georgia) Attorney, jurist, and public official; born in Maryland and educated in North Carolina; studied law, and admitted to the bar in Georgia (1776); member of State Assembly, and appointed one of the Council (1776) member of Continental Congress (1780-82); Lieutenant-Colonel of the Richmond County Militia (1779); original trustee for establishing the University of Georgia (1785); delegate to the Constitutional Convention and a signer of the federal Constitution (1787); U. S. Federal District Judge (1796-99); inspector of State prisons; director and later President of the Manhattan Bank (1804-14).

William Finley (1741-1821; Ireland, Pennsylvania) Public official, author; limited formal education; emigrated to America (1763); engaged in agricultural pursuits; served as a captain in the Continental Army; member of the elite Council of Censors responsible for monitoring violations of the State constitution (1783-90); delegate to the State constitutional convention (1789-90); member of the U. S. House of Representatives (1791-98; 1804-17); was in opposition to the government during the Whiskey Rebellion (1794) and wrote a book, *The History of the Insurrection in the Four Western Counties of Pennsylvania* (1796), defending his course; served in the State Senate (1799-1803).

Rev. Samuel Finley (1715-66; Ireland, New Jersey, Maryland, Pennsylvania) Clergyman, theologian, and educator; educated in Philadelphia; received advanced degrees from University of Glasgow; studied for the ministry and was ordained by the New Brunswick Presbytery (1742); settled in Maryland, and while pastoring a church he conducted an academy preparing young men for the ministry (1744); taught Signer of the Declaration Benjamin Rush and Jacob Rush in his academy; president of Princeton (1761-66); published numerous sermons and theological pieces.

Charles Finney (1792-1875; New York, Ohio) Attorney, clergyman, and educator; prepared to enter Yale, but his schoolmaster convinced him to study privately; entered the study of law and was admitted to the bar (1818); underwent a traumatic religious conversion (1821); ordained as a minister in the Presbyterian church (1824); gave up law to devote himself to evangelism, and as a result revivals spread throughout New York, New England, and the Middle Atlantic States (1824-34); his lectures on revivals were printed weekly in the *New York Evangelist* and were later published in book form (1835); pastor at First Congregational Church in Oberlin (1837-72); president of Oberlin College (1851-66); was an abolitionist and an anti-Mason.

Thomas FitzSimons (1741-1811; Ireland, Pennsylvania) Merchant, soldier, and public official; entered mercantile business in Philadelphia (1761); raised a company of militia and participated in several battles in the Revolution; helped build several military ships; influential in establishing the first bank of America (1781); member of the Continental Congress (1782-83); member of the elite Council of Censors responsible for monitoring violations of the State constitution (1783); member of the State House of Representatives (1786-87); delegate to the Constitutional Convention where he signed the federal Constitution (1787); member of the U. S. House of Representatives (1789-95) where he helped frame the Bill of Rights; served on a committee of Philadelphia businessmen organized to induce Congress to recharter the United States Bank (1810); founder and a director of the Insurance Company of North America; trustee of the University of Pennsylvania.

Felix Frankfurter (1882-1965; New York) Attorney and jurist; graduated from the College of New York City (1902); Professor of Administrative Law at Harvard (1914); participated in the founding of the American Civil Liberties Union (1920); close adviser to Governor Franklin D. Roosevelt; appointed to the U. S. Supreme Court by President Franklin D. Roosevelt (1939-62).

Benjamin Franklin (1706-90; Pennsylvania) State printer, author, inventor, scientist, philanthropist, statesman, diplomat, and public official; Clerk of the Pennsylvania General Assembly (1736-50); Postmaster of Philadelphia (1737); member of the Provincial Assembly (1744-54); first president of the Pennsylvania Society for Promoting the Abolition of Slavery (1774); member of the Continental Congress (1775-76) where he signed the Declaration of Independence (1776); President of the Pennsylvania constitutional convention (1776); sent by the Continental Congress as a Minister to France (1776-85); a negotiator and signer of the final treaty of peace with Great Britain (1783); President of the Executive Council of Pennsylvania (1785-88); delegate to the Constitutional Convention where he signed the federal Constitution (1787); President of the trustees of the University of Pennsylvania; also served as Consul, Judge of Admiralty, and Director of Naval Affairs; some of his numerous inventions include the Franklin Stove (1740), the lightning rod (1752), and bifocal glasses (1789); his many discoveries concerning electricity were compiled in a small volume titled *Experiments and Observations on Electricity* (1751); was one of only six men who signed both the Declaration and the Constitution; wrote his own epitaph, which declared: "The body of Benjamin Franklin, printer, like the cover of an old book, its contents torn out, stripped of its lettering, and guilding, lies here, food for worms. But the work shall not be lost; for it will, as he believed, appear once more in a new and more elegant edition, revised and corrected by the Author."

Jonas Galusha (1753-1834; Vermont) Soldier, jurist, and public official; led two companies of soldiers in the Battle of Bennington (1775); served in numerous local political offices; justice of the Vermont Supreme Court for two years; presidential elector (1808, 1820, 1824); Governor of Vermont (1809-13, 1815-20); president of the State constitutional conventions (1814 and 1822); member of the Baptist Church; vice-president of the American Bible Society.

James A. Garfield (1831-81; Ohio) Attorney, Minister, educator, soldier, and public official; experienced a dramatic conversion to Christianity in his youth while working on the Ohio canal and was later licensed as a minister in the Christian Church; studied at Geauga Seminary in Ohio (1849); graduated from Williams College (1856); Professor of Ancient Languages and Literature in Hiram College, Ohio (1856); President of Hiram College (1857-61); U. S. Senator (1859); admitted to the bar (1860); entered the Union side in the Civil War as Lieutenant-Colonel (1861); won a victory at Middle Creek and gained the rank of Brigadier-General (1862); promoted to Major-General (1863) and then resigned; member of the U. S. House of Representatives (1863-80); elected the twentieth President of the United States (1880); shot by an assassin at the Washington railroad station en route for a northern trip (1881) and died 81 days later.

William Gaston (1778-1844; North Carolina) Attorney, jurist, and public official; graduated from Princeton (1796); admitted to the bar (1800); member of the State Senate (1800-12, 1818-19); member of the State House (1807-1809, 1824, 1827-29, 1831); member of the U. S. House of Representatives (1813-17); vice-president of the American Bible Society; justice on the State Supreme Court (1833-44)—there was a question of his eligibility because he was a Roman Catholic and the State constitution forbade civil office to anyone who would "deny the truth of the Protestant religion," but he was later able to change the article to read "Christian" instead of "Protestant" (expanded explanation in Chapter 2).

King George III (1738-1820; England) Monarch; reigned as King of Great Britain during the American Revolution; oldest son of Frederick, Prince of Wales; and his grandfather was King George II; George III was said to be a poor student in his youth and mentally unstable; reigned not only during the American Revolution, but also during the defeat of Napoleon as well as during the overall decline of British monarchial power.

Elbridge Gerry (1744-1814; Massachusetts) Merchant, and public official; graduated from Harvard (1762); entered mercantile business; member of the Massachusetts Court (1772-74); member of the Committee of Correspondence (1772-74); member of the State Provincial Congress (1774-76); member of the Committee of Safety (1774-76); member of the Continental Congress (1776-80, 1783-85) where he signed the Declaration of Independence (1776) and the Articles of Confederation (1778); member of the Massachusetts House of Representatives (1786); delegate to the Constitutional Convention but refused to sign the federal Constitution because it provided no protection for States' rights (1787); Governor of Massachusetts (1810-11); Vice-President of the United States under President James Madison.

William Giles (1762-1830; Virginia) Attorney, and public official; graduated from Princeton (1781); admitted to the bar (1786); member of the U. S. House (1790-98, 1801); U. S. Senator (1803-15); strong Jefferson ally and strong opponent of Hamilton's centralizing policies; opposed the Jay Treaty (1794)—(a second treaty with the British to settle difficulties remaining from the treaty which ended the American Revolution); was much behind the exposure of the XYZ Papers (1797)—(Charles Pinckney, John Marshall, and Elbridge Gerry were seeking a treaty with France; three agents of France— X, Y, and Z—suggested that a U. S. "loan" to France and a bribe of $240,000 to the French Foreign Minister would help in securing the treaty); considered a "War Hawk" but an opponent of the Madison administration in the War of 1812; Governor of Virginia (1827-30); delegate to the State constitutional convention (1829-30).

Stephen Girard (1750-1831; France, Pennsylvania) Sailor, philanthropist; earned his masters rating on a merchant ship; voyaged to the West Indies as a captain (1774); sailed for a New York mercantile house (1776); settled in Philadelphia during the Revolution (1776); worked tirelessly to aid victims during the Philadelphia yellow fever epidemics of 1793 and 1797; when the charter of the Bank of the United States expired, he bought the institution's building and opened the Bank of Stephen Girard (1812), establishing credit with both American and European banks; expedited the sale of government bonds during the War of 1812; underwrote nearly the entire 3 million needed to capitalize the Second Bank of the United States; became known as the "sheet anchor" of government credit; upon his death, left 7 million dollars to the city of Philadelphia for the founding of Girard College.

Charles Goldsborough (1765-1834; Maryland) Attorney, and public official; graduated from the University of Pennsylvania (1784); admitted to the bar (1790); member of the State senate (1791-95, 1799-1801); member of the U. S. House of Representatives (1805-17) where he voted against the declaration of war in 1812; Governor of Maryland (1818-19); retired from public life in 1820; vice-president of the American Bible Society (1819-1834).

Nathaniel Gorham (1738-96; Massachusetts) Merchant, public official, and jurist; apprenticed under a merchant at fifteen; became a successful businessman; served in the State legislature (1771-75); delegate to the Provincial Congress (1774-75); member of the Board of War (1778-81); delegate to the Continental Congress (1782-83, 1787) where he served as President of Congress (1786); delegate to the State constitutional convention (1779-80); member of the State Senate (1780); member of the State House (1781-87); judge of Court of Common Pleas (1785-1796); delegate to the Constitutional Convention where he signed the federal Constitution (1787); delegate to the State convention which ratified the federal Constitution (1788).

Gratian (circa 1100-55) Theologian; monk of the order of St. Benedict; lecturer at the monastery of Saints Felix and Nabor in Bologna, Italy; his *The Harmony of Conflicting Canons* (most commonly known as *Gratian's Decrees*) was at the time thought by Popes and Bishops to be the most important book on church law; is considered the "Father of Canon Law."

William Gray (1750-1825; Massachusetts) Merchant, soldier, and public official; one of the first New England merchants to trade abroad; owned many privateer ships in the American Revolution; Second-Lieutenant in the militia (1775-76); delegate to the Massachusetts ratification convention for the federal Constitution (1788); State Senator (1807-08); Lieutenant-Governor (1810-12); president of the Boston branch of the Bank of the United States (1816-22); delegate to the State constitutional convention (1820); vice-president of the American Bible Society.

Rev. Ashbel Green (1762-1848; New Jersey) Soldier, clergyman, and educator; Sergeant in the Continental Army; studied theology under the Rev. Dr. John Witherspoon and graduated from Princeton (1783); licensed to preach (1786); minister at Second Presbyterian Church of Philadelphia (1787-1812); chaplain to Congress (1792-1800); member of the Presbyterian General Assembly for twenty years between 1790 and 1839 and wrote its historic declaration against slavery (1818); one of the founders of America's first Bible society—the Philadelphia Bible Society (1808); president of Princeton (1812-22); authored the plan for Princeton Theological Seminary and was president of its board of directors (1812- 48); wrote, edited, and published a monthly magazine, *The Christian Advocate,* as well as numerous other sermons, discourses, and theological treatises.

Nathanael Greene (1742-86; Rhode Island, South Carolina, Georgia) Soldier; tutored in Latin and geometry, and gradually studied the works of Locke, Watts, and Swift; Deputy to the Rhode Island General Assembly (1770-72, 1775); was a Quaker until he was expelled from the Society of Friends for his interest in military matters (circa 1774-1776); served in the Continental Army as a Brigadier-General (1776) and was an important leader in the Battle of Brandywine (1777); promoted to Major-General (1776); appointed Quarter-Master General (1778); when Washington was in Hartford to meet with the French allies, it was Greene who received the report of Benedict Arnold's treason attempt (1780); appointed Commander of the Southern Army to replace General Gates who was highly critical of Washington (1780); largely responsible for ending the war in South Carolina (1781-82); South Carolina, North Carolina, and Georgia voted him a large remuneration with which he bought expansive South Carolina estates (1784); moved to a plantation in Georgia given him by the grateful people of that State (1785).

Hugo Grotius (1583-1645; Holland) A Dutch lawyer, theologian, statesman, and poet; graduated from the University of Leiden; Chief-Magistrate of Rotterdam (1613); condemned to life in prison because he opposed strict Calvinism, however, he escaped with the aid of his wife (1619); authored *On the Law of War and Peace* (1625) and consequently is considered, along with Puffendorf, a founder of international law; Swedish Ambassador to France (1635-45).

Felix Grundy (1777-1840; Tennessee, Kentucky) Attorney, jurist, and public official; no formal education; admitted to the bar (1797); delegate to the Kentucky constitutional convention (1799); member of the Kentucky House of Representatives (1800-05); justice of the Supreme Court of Kentucky, (1806-07); member of the U. S. House of Representatives from Tennessee (1811-14); vice-president of the American Bible Society (1816-30); U. S. Senator from Tennessee (1829-40); member of the Tennessee House of Representatives (1819-25); U. S. Attorney-General under President Martin Van Buren (1838-39).

Rev. James Hall (1744-1826; North Carolina) Clergyman, and soldier; studied theology under the Rev. Dr. John Witherspoon at Princeton where he graduated (1774); licensed to preach (1775); accepted the pastorate of Fourth Creek church in Concord/Bethany, North Carolina (1776); accompanied an expedition against the Cherokee Indians during the Revolution; held double office as commander of troops and chaplain; established a mission at Natchez under the commission of the Presbyterian General Assembly (1800); moderator of the General Assembly of the Presbyterian Church (1803); a regular attendant at the Synod of the Carolinas and later became its last moderator (1812); active in the American Bible Society.

Rev. Lyman Hall (1724-90; Georgia) Clergyman, physician, public official, and jurist; graduated from Yale (1747); studied theology and began preaching (1749); studied medicine and commenced practice in Wallingford (1751); member of the State conventions held in Savannah (1774-75); member of the Continental Congress (1775-80) where he signed the Declaration of Independence (1776); Governor of Georgia (1783); judge of the Court of Chatham County until his death.

Alexander Hamilton (1757-1804; New York) Attorney, soldier, and public official; attended King's College but left to join the Revolution; Captain of artillery in the Continental Army (1776); Lieutenant-Colonel and aide-de-camp to General Washington (1777-81); admitted to the bar (1782); member of the Continental Congress (1782-83, 1787-88); delegate to the Annapolis Convention (1786); member of the New York State Assembly (1787); delegate to the Constitutional Convention where he signed the federal Constitution (1787); member of the State ratification convention for the federal Constitution (1788); one the three coauthors, along with James Madison and John Jay, of the *Federalist Papers* instrumental in securing the ratification of the Constitution (1788); appointed Secretary of U. S. Treasury by President George Washington (1789-95) and then Inspector General with the rank of Major-General (1798); Hamilton called Aaron Burr "dangerous" and held a poor private opinion of him, causing Burr to challenge him to a duel in which Hamilton was killed (1804).

John Hamilton (1754-1837; Pennsylvania) Soldier, public official, and jurist; Lieutenant-Colonel of militia (1786); sheriff of Washington County (1793-96); member of the State Senate (1796-1805, 1820-37); Brigadier-General (1800); associate judge of Washington County (1802-05); member of the Board of Trustees of Jefferson College in Washington, Pennsylvania (1802-31); member of the U. S. House of Representatives (1805-07); Major-General (1807); associate judge of Washington County (1820-37).

John Hancock (1737-93; Massachusetts) Soldier, public official; graduated from Harvard (1754); served several terms as a Selectman of Boston; member of the Provincial Legislature (1766-72); member of the Continental Congress (1774-78) where he was the first signer of the Declaration of Independence (1776) and President of Congress (1774-77); Senior Major-General of Massachusetts Militia (1778); delegate to the State constitutional convention (1779); Governor of Massachusetts (1780-85, 1787-93).

John Hart (1711-79; New Jersey) Jurist and public official; attended private school, with little formal education; Justice-of-the-Peace (1755, 1761); judge of the New Jersey Court of Common Claims (1761-76); member of the Provincial Assembly of New Jersey (1761-71); chairman of the township committees of Hunterdon County (1768-75); member of the New Jersey Provincial Congress (1775 -76); member of the Continental Congress (1776) where he signed the Declaration of Independence (1776); chairman of the New Jersey Council of Safety (1777-78); forced to flee his estate and the bedside of his dying wife when British troops invaded New Jersey (1778); spent a year living in the forest evading British capture (1779); when he returned home his entire estate had been devastated, his family of twelve children scattered, and his wife dead; he died shortly thereafter, supposedly of deep sorrow.

Patrick Henry (1736-99; Virginia) Attorney, and public official; educated by his father; at 15 years of age was a clerk at a small store (1751); opened his own store at 16 (1752); began law practice (1760) member of the House of Burgesses (1765); member of the Continental Congress (1774-75); member of the State Assembly where on March 23, 1775, he delivered his famous "Give me liberty, or give me death" speech; Governor of Virginia (1776-79, 1784-86); member of the State convention which ratified the Constitution (1788); offered but declined numerous appointments, including U. S. Senator (1794) and Secretary of State under President George Washington (1795); elected to the State Senate (1799) but died before he took office.

William Wirt Henry (1831-1900; Virginia) Attorney, and public official; grandson of Patrick Henry and named for William Wirt, the prominent statesman and first biographer of Patrick Henry; graduated from the University of Virginia (1850); entered legal practice (1853); member of the State House of Delegates (1877-79); member of the State Senate (1879-80); compiler of *The Addresses, Papers and Speeches of Patrick Henry* (1891).

Rev. Abiel Holmes (1763-1837; Massachusetts) Congregational clergyman and historian; graduated from Yale (1783); ordained at New Haven (1784); taught at Yale (1786-87); pastor of the First Church in Cambridge (1792-1829); member of the Massachusetts Historical Society (1798-1837); as a historian, wrote *Annals of America from* *the Discovery by Columbus in the Year 1492 to the Year 1826*—the first attempt at an extensive, orderly history of America as a whole; father of jurist Oliver Wendell Holmes.

Oliver Wendell Holmes, Jr. (1841-1932; Massachusetts) Attorney and jurist; educated in private schools; Lieutenant in the Union army in the Civil War (1861-63); graduated Harvard Law School (1866); admitted to the bar (1867); member of the Supreme Judicial Court of Massachusetts (1882-1901) and its Chief-Justice (1899-1901); appointed to the U. S. Supreme Court by President Theodore Roosevelt (1902-32); considered an early positivist and judicial evolutionist.

Samuel Holton (1738-1816; Massachusetts) Physician, jurist, and public official; began practice in Gloucester, Massachusetts (1765); member of the General Court (1768); member of the Committees of Correspondence (1774-75); member of the Continental Congress (1778); delegate to the State constitutional convention (1778-79); probate judge (1796-1815); member of the U. S. House of Representatives (1793-95); involved in the temperance movement in Massachusetts (1812-13).

Rev. Richard Hooker (1553-1600; England) Theologian and political philosopher; wrote the first four books of *The Laws of Ecclesiastical Polity* which defended the Church of England against the dissenters and the Puritans; known as "The Father of Anglicanism."

William Hooper (1742-90; North Carolina) Attorney and public official; graduated from Harvard (1760); admitted to the bar and began his practice in Wilmington, N. C. (1767); member of the Colonial Assembly of North Carolina (1773-76); member of the Continental Congress (1774-77) where he signed the Declaration of Independence (1776); member of the State Assembly (1777-78); member of a commission to settle a boundary dispute between Massachusetts and New York (1786).

Stephen Hopkins (1707-85; Rhode Island) Public official and jurist; an avid reader, but without a formal education; member of the General Assembly (1732-52, 1770-75) and its speaker (1738-44, 1749); Chief-Justice of the Court of Common Pleas (1739); founder of the town library of Providence (1750); Chief-Justice of the Superior Court (1751-54); delegate to the Colonial Congress (1754); Colonial Governor of Rhode Island (1755- 56, 1758-61, 1763-64, 1767); Chief-Justice of the Superior Court (1773); member of the Continental Congress (1774-76) where he signed the Declaration of Independence (1776); member of the committee to prepare the Articles of Confederation (1777); member of the General Assembly (1777-79).

Francis Hopkinson (1737-91; Pennsylvania, New Jersey) Attorney, public official, jurist and poet; graduated from University of Pennsylvania at Philadelphia (1757); admitted to the bar (1761); secretary of a commission of the Provincial Council of Pennsylvania which formed a treaty between with several Indian tribes (1761); member of the Provincial Council in New Jersey (1774-76); declined the office of Associate Justice of the Supreme Court of New Jersey (1776); member of the Continental Congress (1776) where he signed the Declaration of Independence (1776); judge of Pennsylvania admiralty court (1779-89); U. S. federal Judge (1789-91); first president of the American Philosophical Society (1769); noted literary figure, poet, and satirist; author of the first purely American hymn book, setting the Psalms to music.

William Churchill Houston (1746-88; New Jersey) Graduated from Princeton (1768); Professor of Mathematics and Natural Philosophy at Princeton (1771); deputy secretary of the Continental Congress (1775-76); Captain during the Revolution; member of the New Jersey Assembly (1777-79); member of the New Jersey Council of Safety (1778); admitted to the bar (1781); member of the Continental Congress (1784-85); delegate to the Annapolis Convention which preceded the Constitutional Convention (1786); delegate to the Constitutional Convention but he did not sign the Constitution because of illness (1787).

Charles Evans Hughes (1862-1948; New York) Public official and jurist; father was a methodist preacher, but Hughes converted to the Baptist church; Hughes entered Madison University at fourteen, then graduated from Brown University (1881); graduated from Columbia Law School and began practice (1884); taught law at Cornell University (1891-93); served as legislative council (1905); Governor of New York (1906-10); appointed as Associate Justice to the U. S. Supreme Court by President Howard Taft (1910-16); Secretary of State under Presidents Warren G. Harding and Calvin Coolidge (1921-25); appointed Chief-Justice of the U. S. Supreme Court by President Herbert Hoover (1930-41).

David Hume (1711-76; Scotland) Scottish political philosopher, educator, and soldier; unsuccessful in both law and business; spent a year in England as a tutor then became an officer and an aide-de-camp on an expedition to France, Vienna and Turin; authored *A Treatise of Human Nature* (1739) in three volumes later republished as *An Enquiry Concerning Human Understanding* (1748), *An Enquiry Concerning the Principles of Morals* (1751), and *Part Two of Four Dissertations* (1757); many of his theories were harshly criticized by America's Founding Fathers.

Benjamin Huntington (1736-1800; Connecticut) Attorney, public official, and jurist; graduated from Yale (1761); admitted to the bar (1765); member of the State House of Representatives (1771-80) and its Speaker (1778-79); member of the Continental Congress (1780, 1782-83, 1788); member of the State Senate (1781-90, 1791-93); mayor of Norwich (1784-96); member of the U. S. House of Representatives (1789-91) where he helped frame the Bill of Rights; judge of the Superior Court of the State (1793-98).

Samuel Huntington (1731-96; Connecticut) Attorney, jurist, and public official; studied Latin and law on his own and was admitted to the bar (1758); member of the State General Assembly (1764); justice-of-the-peace for New London County (1765-75); member of a Committee for the Defense of the Colony (1775); member of the Continental Congress (1775-84) where he signed the Declaration of Independence (1776) and served as President of Congress (1779); Chief-Justice of the Superior Court of Connecticut (1784); Lieutenant-Governor of Connecticut (1785); Governor of Connecticut (1786-96); received a doctorate from Dartmouth (1785) and from Yale (1787).

John Huss (circa 1373-1415; Bohemia) Catholic priest, Bohemian reformer, and martyr; rector or curate of the Bethlehem Chapel (1402); in his independent study of the Scriptures, found many teachings which he believed exposed wrong church practices and he became critical of those corruptions; his studies eventually led him to agree with the teachings of Wycliffe; participated in the meeting in Constance between Sigismund and Pope John XXIII for the restoration of the unity of the church and its reform (1413); was charged with heretical teaching and inflammatory preaching, seized and thrown into prison; he was given an opportunity to recant his beliefs but he declined; was burned at the stake (1415).

Jared Ingersoll (1749-1822; Pennsylvania) Public official, and jurist; graduated from Yale (1766); member of the Continental Congress (1780-81); delegate to the Constitutional Convention where he signed the federal Constitution (1787); Attorney-General of Pennsylvania (1790-99, 1811-17); U. S. District Attorney (1800-01); unsuccessful candidate for Vice-President of the United States (1812); judge of the District Court of Philadelphia County (1821-22).

Robert Ingersoll (1833-99; Illinois) Attorney, soldier, public official, and philosopher; son of a Congregational clergyman; no formal education; admitted to the bar (1854); unsuccessful Democratic candidate for the House of Representatives and then converted to Republicanism (1860); Colonel of a calvary regiment during the Civil War (1861-63); Attorney-General of Illinois (1867); during the spread of Darwinism, Ingersoll took to the lecture platform in its support and traveled widely, teaching on scientific and humanistic rationalism; was titled "The Great Agnostic."

James Iredell (1751-99; England, North Carolina) Attorney, public official, and jurist; no formal education; sailed from England to become Comptroller of His Majesty's Customs (1768); admitted to the bar (1770); judge of the State Superior Court (1777-78); State Attorney-General (1779-81); appointed by President George Washington to the U. S. Supreme Court (1790-99).

Andrew Jackson (1767-1845; Tennessee) Attorney, soldier, jurist, and public official; as a young boy was captured and injured by the British during the Battle of Hanging Rock (1780); studied law in Salisbury, North Carolina, and admitted to the bar (1787); delegate to the State constitutional conventions (1791 and 1796); member of the U. S. House of Representatives (1796-97); U. S. Senator (1797-98, 1823-25); judge of the State Supreme Court of Tennessee (1798-1804); commander of the Tennessee forces in the Creek Indian War (1813); Major-General in the U. S. Army (1814); claimed the victory in the Battle of New Orleans (1815); commanded an expedition which captured Florida (1817); Governor of Florida (1821); Seventh President of the United States, serving two terms (1828-37); known as "Old Hickory."

Robert Houghwout Jackson (1892-1954; New York) Attorney and jurist; entered Albany Law School; admitted to the bar (1913); appointed by President Franklin D. Roosevelt as General Counsel for the Bureau of Internal Revenue (1934); Department of Justice (1936); Assistant Attorney-General of the Antitrust Division, Solicitor General (1938-39); Attorney-General under Franklin D. Roosevelt (1940-41); appointed to the U. S. Supreme Court by Roosevelt (1941-45); appointed to the International Military Tribunal (Nürnberg Trials) by President Harry S. Truman (1945).

John Jay (1745-1829; New York) Attorney, public official, diplomat, jurist; graduated from Columbia (1766); admitted to bar (1766); member of the Continental Congress (1774-76, 1778-79) where he was President of Congress (1778-79); helped write the New York State constitution (1777); authored first manual on military discipline (1777); Chief-Justice of New York Supreme Court (1777-78); appointed minister to Spain (1779); signed the final peace treaty with Great Britain (1783); one of the three coauthors, along with James Madison and Alexander Hamilton, of the *Federalist Papers* instrumental in securing the ratification of the Constitution (1788); appointed first Chief-Justice of the U. S. Supreme Court by President George Washington (1789-95) and later declined a reappointment as Chief-Justice by President John Adams; Governor of New York (1795-1801); vice-president of the American Bible Society (1816-21) and its president (1821-27); member of American Board of Commissioners for Foreign Missions.

Martha Jefferson (1748-82; Virginia) Wife of Thomas Jefferson; first marriage was at eighteen to Bathurst Skelton (1766) who died two years later; next married Thomas Jefferson (1772); forced to flee to avoid British capture (1779); never recovered her health and eventually died (1782); they had six children, five daughters and one son, and only three daughters survived their mother.

Thomas Jefferson (1743-1826; Virginia) Attorney, diplomat, public official, educator; member of the Virginia House of Burgesses (1769-75); member of Virginia Committee of Correspondence; member of the Continental Congress (1775-76) where he was a signer and the principle author of the Declaration of Independence (1776); member of the Virginia House of Delegates (1776-79) where he introduced proposals for the complete abolition of the slave trade and total religious freedom; Governor of Virginia (1779-81); reelected to the Continental Congress (1783); sent with Benjamin Franklin and John Adams to negotiate treaties with European nations (1784); after returning (1789), Jefferson served as Secretary of State under President George Washington (1790-93) and as Vice-President under President John Adams (1797-1801); elected as third President of the United States he served two terms (1801-09); retired to Monticello where he helped found the University of Virginia (1819); died on the fiftieth anniversary of the Declaration of Independence (July 4, 1826) a few hours before fellow-signer John Adams; wrote his own epitaph, which declared, "Here was buried Thomas Jefferson, author of the Declaration of American Independence, of the Statute of Virginia for Religious Freedom, and Father of the University of Virginia."

William Samuel Johnson (1727-1819; Connecticut) Public official, jurist, and educator; graduated from Yale (1744) and Harvard (1747); member of the Colonial House of Representatives (1761, 1765); delegate to the Stamp Act Congress (1765); member of the Upper House (1766, 1771-75); judge of Connecticut Supreme Court (1772-74); member of Continental Congress (1785-87); delegate to the Constitutional Convention where he signed the federal Constitution (1787); first president of Columbia College (1787-1800); U. S. Senator (1789-91); late in life, helped to organize the Protestant Episcopal Church in America.

William Johnson (1771-1834; South Carolina) Attorney, public official, and jurist; graduated from Princeton (1790); admitted to the bar (1793); member of the State House of Representatives (1794-98) and became its Speaker (1798); elevated to the State Constitutional Court (1799); appointed to the U. S. Supreme Court by President Thomas Jefferson (1802-31); often at conflict with Justice Joseph Story and only Justices John Marshall and Joseph Story authored more opinions than Johnson.

Samuel Johnston (1733-1816; North Carolina) Attorney, public official, and jurist; studied law and admitted to the bar (1754); member of the State Assembly (1759-75); member of the Committee of Correspondence (1773); member of the Council of Safety (1775); member of the State Senate (1779, 1783, 1784); member of the Continental Congress (1780); Governor of North Carolina, (1787-89); delegate to the State convention which refused to ratify the federal Constitution (1788) and delegate to the State convention which eventually ratified (1789); U. S. Senator (1789-93) and helped frame the Bill of Rights; superior court judge (1800-03); first trustee of the University of North Carolina and remained such for twelve years.

Walter Jones (1776-1861; Virginia) Attorney, soldier, and public official; read law in Richmond under Bushrod Washington (the U. S. Supreme Court Justice and nephew of George Washington) and was admitted to the bar of Virginia (1796); appointed U. S. Attorney for the District of Potomac by President Thomas Jefferson (1802); fought in the battle of Bladensburg and commissioned by President James Monroe as a Brigadier-General of militia (1821); served as co-counsel with Daniel Webster in *Vidal* v. *Girard's Executors* (1844).

William Jones (1753-1822; Rhode Island) Merchant, soldier, public official; varied career including four years service in the military during the Revolution (commissioned as a Lieutenant in 1776); Justice-of-the-Peace; member of the General Assembly of Rhode Island (1807-11); Governor (1811-17); president of the Rhode Island Bible Society; vice-president of the American Bible Society.

Anthony Mcloed Kennedy (1936-   ; California) Attorney and jurist; graduated from Stanford University (1958); Harvard Law School (1961); pursued private practice (1961-75); appointed to the Ninth Federal Circuit Court of Appeals by President Gerald Ford (1975-1988); appointed to the U. S. Supreme Court by President Ronald Reagan (1988-   ); difficult to categorize him philosophically since he has shown a proclivity to reverse his own positions in Supreme Court decisions; heavily criticized by both conservative and liberal members of the Court for his inconsistency.

James Kent (1763-1847; New York) Attorney, jurist, public official, educator; graduated from Yale (1781); admitted to the bar (1785); member of the New York Assembly (1791-93, 1796-97); first Professor of Law at Columbia College (1793-98, 1824-25); judge on the State Supreme Court (1798-1814) and its Chief-Justice (1804-14); Chancellor (Chief-Judge) of the New York Court of Chancery (Equity) (1814-23); wrote the celebrated *Commentaries on American Law* (1826-30) which retained the major principles of Blackstone's *Commentaries* while supplying American precedents; credited with originating the practice of issuing written opinions in judicial decisions; his contributions to American law have caused him to be called, along with Justice Joseph Story, the "Father of American Jurisprudence."

Francis Scott Key (1779-1843; Maryland) Attorney; graduated from St. John's College (1796); began law practice (1801) known especially for his authorship of the National Anthem, "The Star Spangled Banner"; his words for that song came from events surrounding the British retreat from Washington, D. C., in the War of 1812 when prominent physician Dr. William Beanes was seized and confined aboard a ship in the British fleet; Key was asked to undertake his release but was detained on an American ship pending the projected British attack on Baltimore; Key watched the British bombardment of Ft. McHenry throughout the night and was overjoyed to see the flag still flying over that Fort the next morning; in intense emotional excitement, he then composed the now famous words which were officially adopted by Congress in 1931; Key was of a warmly religious nature and in 1814 seriously considered entering the ministry; he was a delegate to the general conventions of the Episcopal Church (1814-26); was U. S. Attorney for the District of Columbia (1833-41) was a manager and vice-president of the American Sunday School Union from its inception until his death (1791-1843); was a vice-president of the American Bible Society.

Rufus King (1755-1827; Massachusetts, New York) Soldier, attorney, public official, diplomat; graduated from Harvard (1777); served in the Revolution as an aide to General Glover on an ill-fated expedition to Rhode Island (1778); admitted to the bar (1780); delegate to the Massachusetts General Court (1783-85); member of the Continental Congress (1784-87); delegate to the Constitutional Convention where he signed the federal Constitution (1787); member of the State ratification convention for the federal Constitution (1788); member of the New York Assembly (1788-89); U. S. Senator from New York (1789-96; 1813-25) helping frame the Bill of Rights; appointed Minister to Great Britain by President George Washington (1796-1803); unsuccessful candidate for Vice-President of the United States (1804); unsuccessful candidate for Governor of New York (1815) and for President of the United States (1816); delegate to the State constitutional convention (1821); appointed Minister to Great Britain by President John Quincy Adams (1825-26); manager of the American Bible Society.

Andrew Kirkpatrick (1756-1831; New Jersey) Attorney, public official, jurist, educator; expelled from his father's home for deserting theology to study law; graduated from Princeton (1775); admitted to the bar (1785); member of the New Jersey House (1797); associate justice on the New Jersey Supreme Court (1798-1824) where he became its Chief-Justice (1804?-24); firm believer in capital punishment and the whipping post and had little faith in the efficacy of confining criminals in State prisons because he believed it was too easy for them to escape or to secure release; trustee of Princeton (1807-31); vice-president of the New Jersey Bible Society (1810); an original trustee of Princeton Theological Seminary and Chairman of the Board (1822-31); vice-president of the American Bible Society (1818-31).

Rev. Abner Kneeland (1774-1844; New Hampshire, Massachusetts) Public official, jurist, Universalist clergyman and anti-theist (literally, against one God); early joined the Baptist Church at Putney, Vermont; became a Universalist (1803); became minister at Langdon, New Hampshire (1805); member of the State legislature (1810-11); became minister of a Universalist Society at Charlestown, Massachusetts (1812); editor of five papers championing very theologically and politically liberal views (1819-24); translated the New Testament (1822); pastor of the newly organized Second Universalist Society (1827); began editing the *Olive Branch and Christian Inquirer,* a paper devoted to "free inquiry, pure morality and rational Christianity"; because of his radicalism, he asked permission to suspend himself from fellowship from the Universalists (1829); began to expound on his pantheistic views in the *Boston Investigator* (1831); tried and convicted for both libel and blasphemy (1835); after several appeals, served his sentence (1838).

Marquis de Lafayette (1757-1834; France) Achieved the rank of Captain in a regiment of French dragoons (1774); through Silas Deane, he arranged to join the Continental Army in America (1777) where he agreed to serve as a Major-General without pay; quickly grew to be a longtime, trusted friend of Washington; after serving under Washington for a period, he was given his own command (1777); fought and was wounded at the Battle of Brandywine (1777); shared the hardships at Valley Forge (1777-78) and earned the title "the soldier's friend"; liaison for the French fleet which arrived in Rhode Island (1778); Congress granted him a furlough to return to France to help gain support for the American cause (1778); returned to America and was given command of the Virginia Light Troops (1779); held a major position in the final campaign which ended the Revolution—the Battle of Yorktown (1781); returned to France (1782); played a significant role in the French Revolution and, next to the King, was the most powerful figure in France (1790); French Lieutenant-General (1791-97); U. S. Congress voted him $24,424 in payment for his services as a Brigadier-General which he refused to accept (1794); Congress also voted him a grant of 11,520 acres which he accepted, having lost most of his fortune in the French conflict (1803); member of the French Chamber of Deputies (1815, 1818-24, 1827-34); returned for a final tour of America at the request of President James Monroe (1824); was a lifetime member of the American Sunday School Union; was known as the "Hero of two worlds" and "America's Marquis."

Christopher Columbus Langdell (1826-1906; Connecticut) Attorney, jurist, educator; taught school (1844); entered Harvard Law School (1851); began his law practise in New York City (1854); became the Dane Professor of Law at Harvard Law School (1870-95); although he continued to instruct until 1900, he finally gave it up because of poor eyesight; married with no children; originator of the case-law method of study which resulted from his applying Darwin's thesis of evolution to law; under the case-law method of study, law students take the decisions of judges as the standard of law rather than the literal wording of the Constitution.

John Langdon (1741-1819; New Hampshire) Public official; attended a local grammar school, served an apprenticeship as a clerk, went to sea, and undertook his own commercial ventures; an active supporter of the Revolutionary movement in various patriot assemblies; member of the Continental Congress (1775-76, 1787); member of the New Hampshire House of Representatives (1801-05) and its speaker his last two terms; member of the New Hampshire Senate (1784); delegate to the Constitution Convention where he signed the federal Constitution (1787); U. S. Senator (1789-1801) and helped frame the Bill of Rights; Governor of New Hampshire (1805-08,

1810-11); declined the nomination as vice-president (1812); vice-president of the American Bible Society (1816-19).

Henry Laurens (1724-92; South Carolina) Merchant, soldier, public official, diplomat; received his business education in England (1744-47); returned to America and began mercantile pursuits (1747); Lieutenant-Colonel in a campaign against the Cherokees in the French-Indian War (1757-61); member of the House of Assembly (1757-74); lived in Europe (1771-74); member of the American Philosophical Society (1772-92); member of the Continental Congress (1775-76, 1777-80); vice-president of South Carolina (1776-77); was appointed Minister to Holland (1780) but was captured en route to his post and held prisoner in the Tower of London for fifteen months until finally released in exchange for Lord Cornwallis (1781); was one of the commissioners who arranged the peace with Great Britain and was a signer of the preliminary Treaty of Paris (1782); returned to America (1784); essentially retired, turning down positions in the Continental Congress, the State congress, and as a delegate to the federal Constitutional Convention.

Richard Law (1733-1806; Connecticut) Attorney, jurist, public official; graduated from Yale (1751); studied law under Jared Ingersoll and was admitted to the bar (1754); judge of the county court (1784); member of the General Assembly (1765); member of the State Council of Safety (1776-86); delegate to the Continental Congress (1777, 1781-82); along with Roger Sherman, he revised and codified the statute laws of Connecticut; member of the State Supreme Court (1784-86) and its Chief-Justice (1786); appointed U. S. district judge for Connecticut by President Washington (1789); mayor of New London (1784-1806).

Charles Lee (1731-1782; England, Virginia) Soldier; served during the French and Indian War and was part of Braddock's defeat in Pennsylvania (1755); adopted into the Mohawk tribe and married the daughter of a Seneca chief; wounded in Battle of Ticonderoga (1758); present at the capture of Ft. Niagara and Montreal (1760); appointed Major and fought in Portugal (1761); served in Poland and Constantinople (1763-65); granted 20,000 acres in Florida (1766); fought with Russia against Turkey (1769-1770); moved to Virginia (1775); when the conflict broke out between America and Great Britain, he renounced Britain and was given a Major-General position in the Continental Army (1775); supervised fighting in South Carolina and Georgia (1776); became extremely haughty and sharply criticized General Washington; the next day, he was captured in a humiliating manner by the British (1776); held prisoner by the British for a year; unknown to the Americans, he helped draw up a British plan for the defeat of the Americans; released in a prisoner exchange (1778); resumed command of a portion of the army but during the Battle of Monmouth demonstrated gross cowardice and was court-martialed (1778); because of his insulting remarks to Washington, several of Washington's friends challenged Lee to duels (e.g., John Laurens, Anthony Wayne) in which he was wounded (1778); retired to Virginia and then moved to Philadelphia, where he died.

Henry Lee (1756-1818; Virginia) Soldier, public official; graduated from Princeton (1773); served in the Revolutionary War as Captain of a company of the Virginia Dragoons (1776); became part of the First Continental Dragoons (1777); Lieutenant-Colonel

(1780-83) and was known as "Light Horse Harry"; member of the Continental Congress (1786-88); delegate to the State convention to ratify the federal Constitution (1788); Governor of Virginia (1792-95); commanded the U. S. forces in the Whiskey Rebellion (1794); Major-General (1798-1800); pronounced the eulogy on George Washington as the man "first in war, first in peace, and first in the hearts of his countrymen" (1800); injured in the Baltimore riots (1812) and his health never fully recovered.

Richard Henry Lee (1732-94; Virginia) Public official; educated in England and then returned to America (1751); member of the House of Burgesses (1758-75); member of the Continental Congress (1774-79, 1784-85) where he made the resolution which led to the Declaration of Independence, proposing that "these States are of a right and ought to be free and independent States," signed the Declaration of Independence (1776), and served as President of Congress (1784); member of the State House of Delegates (1777, 1780, 1785); authored the first national Thanksgiving Day Proclamation issued by Congress (1777); member of the State ratification convention for the federal Constitution (1788); U. S. Senator (1789-92), where he helped frame the Bill of Rights.

Abraham Lincoln (1809-65; Illinois) Attorney, soldier, public official; born in Kentucky; attended a log cabin school and was self-educated in early years; served in the Black Hawk Indian War (1832); unsuccessfully ran for Illinois House of Representatives (1832); Post-Master of New Salem (1833-36); Deputy County Surveyor (1834-36); admitted to the bar (1836); member of the State House of Representatives (1834-41); member of the U. S. House of Representatives (1847-49); declined the Governorship of the Oregon Territory; unsuccessfully ran for U. S. Senate (1855, 1858); elected as the sixteenth U. S. President, and then elected to a second term which was cut short by his assassination (1860-65).

Benjamin Lincoln (1733-1810; Massachusetts) Farmer, soldier, public official, jurist; member of the militia during the French and Indian War (1755); town clerk in Hingham, Massachusetts (1757); justice-of-the-peace (1762); member of the State legislature (1772-73); member of the Provincial State Congress (1774-75); Brigadier-General (1775); Major-General (1776); instrumental in the defeat of General John Burgoyne at the battle of Saratoga (1777); appointed Secretary of War by the Continental Congress (1781); was handed General Cornwallis' sword at the surrender at the Battle of Yorktown (1781); took part in suppressing Shay's Rebellion (1787); a federal commissioner appointed to form a treaty with the Creek Indians (1789); negotiated with the Indians north of the Ohio (1793); member of the Society for Propagating the Gospel Among the Indians and Others (1794-1810).

Phillip Livingston (1716-78; New York) Merchant, public official; graduated from Yale (1737); engaged in the mercantile business in New York City; member of the board of aldermen (1754-62); member of the Provincial House of Representatives (1763-69) and its Speaker (1768); delegate to the Stamp Act Congress (1765); member of the State Committee of Correspondence; member of the Continental Congress (1774-78) where he signed the Declaration of Independence (1776); president of the New York Provincial Convention (1775); member of the State Assembly (1776); member of the State Senate

(1777); prominent in commercial and educational societies; died while attending the sixth session of the Continental Congress.

William Livingston (1723-90; New Jersey) Attorney, public official, soldier; graduated from Yale (1741); admitted to the bar (1748); commissioner to settle boundary dispute with Massachusetts (1754); member of the New Jersey Provincial Assembly (1759-60); commissioner to settle boundary dispute with New York (1764); member of the Continental Congress (1774-76); Brigadier-General in the New Jersey militia (1775-76); Governor of New Jersey (1776-90); delegate to the Constitutional Convention where he signed the federal Constitution (1787); brother of signer of the Declaration Philip Livingston and cousin of Robert R. Livingston, who was on the committee which drafted the Declaration of Independence.

John Locke (1632-1704; England) Political philosopher, theologian, educator, diplomat; son of English gentry; entered Christ Church College of Oxford University (1652); received his bachelor's degree (1656) and his master's degree (1658); lectured at the College on Greek, rhetoric, and philosophy (1660); accepted a brief diplomatic mission to Madrid (1665); left London for France for health reasons (1675); went to Holland in 1683 and returned to England in 1688; his major works include *A Letter Concerning Toleration* (1689), *Two Treatises of Government* (1690), *An Essay Concerning Human Understanding* (1693), *Some Thoughts Concerning Education* (1693), and *The Reasonableness of Christianity* (1695).

John Lowell (1743-1802; Massachusetts) Attorney, soldier, public official, jurist; graduated from Harvard (1760); admitted to the bar (1762); officer in the militia (1776); member of the State House of Representatives (1778, 1780-82); delegate to the State constitutional convention (1780); founder of the American Academy of Arts and Sciences (1780); member of the Continental Congress (1782-83); member of the State Senate (1784-85); judge of the Court of Appeals (1784-89); U. S. federal judge (1789-1802).

Rev. Martin Luther (1483-1546; Germany) Clergyman, son of a minister; largely responsible the Protestant Reformation in Germany; received a master's degree from the University of Erfurt (1504); entered the monastery of the Augustinian order at Erfurt and was ordained a priest (1507); appointed Professor of Philosophy at the University of Wittenberg (1508); became one of the most popular professors and many of his students supported him during his struggles with the officials of the Roman Catholic Church; when Luther denied the supreme power of the Pope, the Pope excommunicated him, but Luther burned that papal bull; as a protest against the work of Johann Tetzel, a Dominican monk whose teachings Luther thought harmed the church, Luther nailed his protest of those teachings to the door of All Saints' Church in Wittenberg (1517); those points of contention are now known as Luther's Ninety-Five Theses; although Luther had not intended to revolt against the Roman Catholic Church, his actions began the Protestant Reformation; he was ordered by the Pope to retract his beliefs and teachings (1521); Luther responded, "Unless I am refuted and convicted by testimonies of the Scriptures or by clear arguments . . . my conscience is bound in the Word of God: I cannot and will not recant anything"; Luther was seized and carried to the Castle of Wartburg and was held as prisoner for 10 months (1521-22); contributed to German literature with his translation of the Bible (1521-22) in March 1522, Luther returned to Wittenberg to begin the work of organizing the new reformed church; from that point on, the story of his life is the story of the Reformation. (In the beginning, Luther had intended only to reform the Church of Rome but found instead that a new reorganized church was preferable. The Reformation was actually a spiritual revolution aimed at limiting and reducing ecclesiastical power over all phases of life, especially government. Its thrust was to replace centralized spiritual power with more popular control and self-government. Luther began by opposing corruptions in the church but moved toward pointing individuals to Christ and salvation through Him rather than through works; as he helped develop the image that God was not just a God of wrath but also a God of love and forgiveness.)

George Madison (1763-1816; Kentucky) Soldier and public official; became a soldier in the Revolution (1780); Major in the Kentucky volunteers; long history of military service, including several battles against the Indians (wounded in one such fight in 1792) and several battles in the War of 1812, including that of Frenchtown (1813) where he was taken prisoner and held until 1814; he was also auditor of public accounts in Kentucky for at least twenty years and was elected Governor of Kentucky, but died a few weeks before he entered office (1816); vice-president of the American Bible Society.

James Madison (1751-1836; Virginia) Public official; graduated from Princeton (1771); member of the Committee of Safety (1774); delegate to the State constitutional convention (1776); member of the State legislature (1776); member of the Governor's Council (1778-79); member of the Continental Congress (1779-83); member of the Virginia House of Delegates (1784-86); delegate to the Constitutional Convention where he signed the federal Constitution (1787); along with Alexander Hamilton and John Jay, he co-authored the *Federalist Papers* which were instrumental in securing the ratification of the Constitution (1788); member of the U. S. House of Representatives (1789-97) where he helped frame the Bill of Rights; member of the Virginia Assembly (1799); Secretary of State under President Thomas Jefferson (1801-09); served two terms as the President of the United States (1809-17); after his Presidency, retired to his estate, "Montpelier"; served as a delegate to the Virginia constitutional convention (1829).

William Marbury (specific dates unavailable, but the major historical event of his life occurred around 1800); was appointed as a Federalist justice-of-the-peace in the District of Columbia in the waning days of the Federalist administration of President John Adams; when incoming Anti-Federalist President Thomas Jefferson refused to honor the appointment, Marbury sued Jefferson's Secretary of State, James Madison, to receive his appointment; that suit led to the infamous 1803 *Marbury* v. *Madison* case which today's legal and judicial activists claim validated the principle of judicial review.

John Marshall (1755-1835; Virginia) Soldier, attorney, public official, diplomat, jurist; informally educated at home by his parents; became an officer in the Minutemen; fought in the Battles of Great Bridge (1775), Brandywine (1777), Germantown (1777), and Monmouth (1778); studied law at William & Mary College and admitted to the bar (1780); delegate to the Virginia House of Delegates (1780); member of the Executive Council (1782-95); member of the House of Burgesses (1782-88); delegate to the State ratification convention for the federal Constitution (1788); Commissioner to France (1797-98); declined appointment from President John Adams as Associate-Justice of the U. S. Supreme Court (1798); member of the U. S. Congress (1799-1800); declined the post of Secretary of War but accepted the appointment as Secretary of State under President John Adams (1800); appointed to the U. S. Supreme Court as Chief-Justice by President John Adams (1801-35); due to his unorthodox ruling in *Marbury* v. *Madison* in 1803, he is credited with being the principal founder of judicial review; delegate to the Virginia constitutional convention (1829); vice-president of the American Bible Society; officer in the American Sunday School Union.

Thurgood Marshall (1908-93; Maryland) Attorney, and jurist; graduated from Lincoln University (1930); studied Law at Howard University (1933); worked for the NAACP as director of its Legal Defense and Educational Fund; in charge of a number of cases argued before the Supreme Court challenging racism and racial oppression (*Smith* v. *Allwright*, 1944; *Shelly* v. *Kraemer*, 1948; *Brown* v. *Board of Education*, 1954); nominated to be circuit judge on the U. S. Court of Appeals for the Second Circuit by President John Kennedy (1961); appointed to the U. S. Supreme Court by President Lyndon Johnson, becoming the first African American to serve on the Court (1967-92); considered a liberal, and his opinions included affirming the rights of individuals to have obscene materials in their home, upholding affirmative action, and strongly opposing the constitutionality of the death penalty.

Luther Martin (1744-1826; Maryland) Attorney, educator, public official, jurist; graduated from Princeton (1766); taught school in Queenstown, Maryland (1766-71); admitted to the bar (1771); delegate to the Annapolis Convention (1774); Attorney-General of Maryland (1778-1805, 1818-20); declined appointment to the Continental Congress (1784); was a delegate to the Constitutional Convention but refused to sign the federal Constitution because it failed to end slavery and inadequately protected States' Rights (1787); counsel in the impeachment trial of Justice Samuel Chase (1805) and in the Aaron Burr treason trial (1807); Chief-Justice of the Court of Oyer and Terminer in Baltimore (1814-16); was an alcoholic, which led to a stroke (1820) after which he resigned from the bench (1822).

Harriet Martineau (1802-76; England) Educated under the supervision of her uncle; became deaf when very young and her interest turned to literary composition; travelled extensively in the United States (1834-36) and later recorded her impressions in a book entitled *Society in America*; her writings are numerous and diverse, including books on travel, history, politics, philosophy, as well as children's books.

George Mason (1725-92; Virginia) Public official; educated by private tutors and his own independent study; became member of the Virginia House of Burgesses (1759); drafted Virginia's first constitution which contained the famous Declaration of Rights from which Thomas Jefferson drew for the Declaration of Independence; member of the Virginia House of Delegates (1776-88); delegate to the Constitutional Convention but refused to sign the federal Constitution because it neither abolished slavery nor adequately protected States' rights (1787); returned to Virginia and led the opposition in the Virginia ratification convention largely responsible for the addition of the federal Bill of Rights (the first Ten Amendments to the Constitution); declined position as one of Virginia's first two U. S. Senators in order to retire to private life; titled "The Father of the Bill of Rights."

Rev. Cotton Mather (circa 1662-1727; Massachusetts) Puritan clergyman, theologian, educator; graduated from Harvard (1678); assisted his father at the Second Church in Boston (1680); was associated with the Salem Witch Trials, but advocated principles which—if they had been followed—would have prevented the executions (1688-93); wrote several works relating to witchcraft in which he promoted prayer and fasting rather than execution as the solution; appointed by the House of Representatives as president of Harvard, but as he was considered too conservative, that appointment was overruled by Harvard trustees (1703); invited to become the president of the Connecticut College (1721); he was the founder of many societies for good causes and was a prolific author, writing over 450 books.

Rev. Jonathan Mayhew (1720-66; Massachusetts) Clergyman; graduated with honors at Harvard (1774); called to pastor the West Church, Boston (1747); he preached what he considered a rational and practical Christianity based on the Scriptures rather than on Calvin's teachings; a true Puritan, he was a staunch defender of civil liberty and published many sermons related to the preservations of those liberties, including one immediately following the repeal of the Stamp Act entitled *The Snare Broken* (1766); highly thought of by many patriots, including John Adams.

James McHenry (1753-1816; Ireland, Maryland) Physician, soldier, public official; born and educated in Ireland; moved to Philadelphia (1771); studied medicine under Benjamin Rush in Philadelphia and was assigned to the military hospital there (1775); captured by the British (1776) and exchanged (1778); abandoned medicine and was assigned as military secretary to General George Washington (1778-80); transferred to Lafayette's staff (1780); commissioned as a Major (1781); member of the State Senate (1781-86); member of the Continental Congress (1783-86); member of the State Assembly (1789-91); delegate to the Constitutional Convention where he signed the federal Constitution (1787); member of the State convention to ratify the federal Constitution (1788); Secretary of War under Presidents George Washington and John Adams (1796-1800); a founder and president of the Baltimore Bible Society (1813).

Thomas McKean (1734-1817; Pennsylvania, Delaware) Attorney, public official, jurist; educated at Rev. Francis Allison's academy in New London, Connecticut (1744-51); deputy clerk and recorder for probate and wills in New Castle County (1752); studied law and admitted to the bar (1755); Deputy Attorney General for Sussex County (1756-58); member of the Delaware House of Assembly (1762-75); member of the Stamp-Act Congress (1765); member of the Continental Congress (1774-76, 1778-82) where he signed the Declaration of Independence (1776) and served as President of Congress (1781); member of the Delaware House of Representatives (1776-77); helped author the Delaware constitution (1776); President (Governor) of the State of Delaware (1777); Chief-Justice of the Supreme Court of Pennsylvania (1777-99); member of the Pennsylvania State convention to ratify the federal Constitution (1787); delegate to the Pennsylvania State constitutional convention (1790); Governor of Pennsylvania (1799-1808); he was the only signer of the Declaration to be the chief executive of two States and a concurrent office-holder in two States.

James Monroe (1758-1831; Virginia) Soldier, attorney, public official, diplomat; entered William & Mary (1774) but left school to join the Continental Army as a Lieutenant (1776); studied law under Governor Thomas Jefferson (1780); elected to Virginia House of Delegates (1782, 1787); one of nine judges to decide the boundary dispute between Massachusetts and New York (1784); delegate to the State ratification convention for the federal Constitution (1788) where he assented to the ratification on condition that certain amendments should be adopted (the Bill of Rights); U. S. Senator (1790-94); envoy to France (1794); Governor of Virginia (1799-1802); U. S. Secretary of State under President James Madison (1811-17); also served as Secretary of War under President Madison (1814-15); elected fifth President of the United States and served two terms (1816-25).

Michel de Montaigne (1533-92; France) Attorney, public official; political philosopher; sent to college at Guienne at Bordeaux (1539-46); entered the study of law (1546); became magistrate at the Parliament at Bordeaux (1554); inherited the family estate (1568) and retired there (1571); awarded the order of Saint-Michel (1571) and served Henry III; wrote and published his political *Essays* in two volumes (1580); traveled widely, had an audience with the Pope, and was made a Roman citizen (1581); elected mayor of Bordeaux (1584-85); republished his *Essays* with an additional third volume (1588); an illness paralyzed his tongue, although he retained his other senses for some time; in 1592, he called together his friends in a final farewell and requested mass to be celebrated in his room; he died during the mass.

Charles Louis Secondat Baron de la Brede et de Montesquieu (1689-1755; France) Political philosopher; Counsellor of the Parliament of Bordeaux (1714) and its President (1716-28); he toured Europe to observe the way of life and government in other areas (1728-30); authored numerous essays on law, government, the military, taxation, economics, religion, etc.; wrote *The Spirit of Laws* (1748) advocating that political reform could be achieved peacefully and political freedom maintained by separating political powers into three distinct branches ; his theory of "the separation of powers", and "checks and balances" became an integral part of American constitutional philosophy.

Rev. David Lawrence Morril (1772-1849; New Hampshire) Physician, clergyman, public official; studied medicine and began practice in Epsom, N. H. (1793-1800); studied theology and was ordained pastor of the Presbyterian Church of Goffstown (1802-11); member of the State House of Representatives (1808-17) and its speaker (1816); U. S. Senator (1817-23); member and president of the State Senate (1823-24); Governor (1824-27); vice-president of the American Bible Society (1821-30); manager in the American Sunday School Union.

Gouverneur Morris (1752-1816; New York, Pennsylvania) Attorney, public official, soldier, and diplomat; graduated from Kings College (1768); studied law and admitted to the bar (1771); member of the New York Provincial Congress (1775-77); on the committee to form a government for New York (1776); Lieutenant-Colonel in the New York militia (1776); member of the first New York State Assembly (1777-78); member of the Continental Congress (1778-79); signed the Articles of Confederation (1778); Pennsylvania delegate to the Constitutional Convention and a signer of the federal Constitution (1787); the most active member of the Constitutional Convention, speaking 173 times on the floor of the Convention; titled "the penman of the Constitution" because he was the head of the Committee on Style responsible for the final wording of the Constitution; Minister Plenipotentiary to France (1792-94); U. S. Senator (1800-03); authored numerous legal and political works.

Lewis Morris (1726-98; New York) Jurist and public official; half-brother to Gouverneur Morris; graduated from Yale (1746); engaged in agricultural pursuits; appointed by the Crown as a judge in the Court of Admiralty (1760-74); delegate to the Provincial Convention of New York (1775); member of the Continental Congress (1775-77) where he signed the Declaration of Independence (1776); deputy to the State Provincial Congress (1776-77); State Senator (1777-81, 1784-88); delegate to the State convention to ratify the federal Constitution (1788); member of the first board of regents of the University of New York (1784-98).

John Morton (1724-77; Pennsylvania) Jurist and public official; attended common school and received tutoring in surveying; became a land surveyor; justice-of-the-peace (1757-64); member of the colonial General Assembly (1756-66, 1769-75) where he served as its speaker (1771-75); member of the Stamp Act Congress (1765); High Sheriff (1766-70); appointed president judge of the Court of General Sessions and Common Pleas (1770-74); associate justice of the Supreme Court of Appeals of Pennsylvania (1774); member of the Continental Congress (1774-76) where he signed the Declaration of Independence (1776); he believed that his "signing the Declaration of Independence to have been the most glorious service that I ever rendered my country."

Stephen Moylan (1734-1811; England, Pennsylvania) Soldier and businessman; in his early years was educated and lived in England; when the Revolution erupted, he joined the Continental Army and was placed in the commissariat department (1775); General Washington appointed him one of his aides-de-camp (1776); appointed by Congress as Quartermaster-General (1776); raised the first Pennsylvania regiment of cavalry (1777-78); served in the infamous winter at Valley Forge (1777-78); participated in the campaigns in the Hudson River (1779) and Connecticut (1780) as well as in Wayne's expedition to Bull's Ferry (1780); commissioned Brigadier-General (1783); after the Revolution, he returned to mercantile pursuits and for several years prior to his death he was the U. S. Commissioner of Loans.

Rev. Frederick Augustus Conrad Muhlenberg (1750-1801; Pennsylvania, New York) Clergyman, public official; brother of John Peter Gabriel Muhlenberg; was educated at Halle, Germany; ordained to the ministry of the Lutheran Church (1770); preached in Lebanon, Pennsylvania (1770-74); pastor of Christ German Lutheran congregation in New York City (1773-76); forced to flee New York when British troops occupied it (1776); member of the Continental Congress (1779-80); member of the Pennsylvania Legislature (1780-83) and its speaker (1780); president of the State convention to ratify the federal Constitution (1787); member of the U. S. Congress and the original speaker of the U. S. House of Representatives (1789-97) where he helped frame the Bill of Rights.

Rev. John Peter Gabriel Muhlenberg (1746-1807; Virginia, Pennsylvania) Clergyman, soldier, public official; brother of Frederick Augustus Conrad Muhlenberg; was educated in Germany (1763-66); entered the Lutheran ministry (1768); on a visit to England, he was ordained in the Anglican Church (1772); member of the Virginia House of Burgesses (1774); while pastoring at Woodstock, Virginia he raised the 8th Virginia regiment, of which he became Colonel (1775); member of the Virginia convention (1776); Brigadier-General in the Continental Army (1777); fought in the Battles of Brandywine (1777), Germantown (1777), Monmouth (1778), and at Yorktown (1781) and passed the infamous winter at Valley Forge (1777-1778); Major-General (1783); vice-president of the Supreme Executive Council of Pennsylvania (1787-88); member of the U. S. House of Representatives (1789-91, 1793-95, 1799-1801) where he helped frame the Bill of Rights; U. S. Senator (1801); Collector of the Port of Philadelphia (1803-06).

Napoleon Achille Murat (1801-47; France, Florida) Public official; born in Paris, was the son of the King of Naples, who was Napoleon's most famous calvary General; moved to America and settled in Tallahassee (1821); accompanied Lafayette through most of his final American tour (1824); elected alderman of the Tallahassee (1824) and then mayor (1825); appointed postmaster (1826-38); nominated for Congress but declined (1832); published several essays on the United States of which his last was the most popular and was translated into numerous other languages.

Thomas Nelson, Jr. (1738-1789; Virginia) Public official, and soldier; graduated from Cambridge (1761); member of the House of Burgesses (1774); member of the first provincial convention held in Williamsburg (1774); Colonel of the Virginia militia (1775); delegate to the State constitutional convention (1776); member of the Continental Congress (1775-77, 1779) where he signed the Declaration of Independence (1776); appointed commander-in-chief of the State forces of Virginia (1777-81); elected Governor of Virginia (1781) but resigned shortly thereafter due to poor health; retired to his home.

Joseph Nourse (1754-1841; England; Virginia) Soldier and public official; emigrated with his family to Virginia (1769); entered the Revolutionary army as military secretary to General Charles Lee (1776); clerk and paymaster for the Board of War (1777-81); U. S. Assistant Auditor-General; Register of the U. S. Treasury (1781-1829); vice-president of the American Bible Society (1816-41).

James Otis (1725-83; Massachusetts) Attorney, public official, jurist, and soldier; graduated from Harvard (1743); studied law and admitted to the bar (1748); became Advocate-General of the Court System but resigned in order to argue against the Writs of Assistance (1761); (John Adams credited that argument with beginning the movement for American Independence); member of the Massachusetts General Court for years, authoring numerous State papers for the Colonies against British oppressions; became recognized in England as a chief of "the rebellious spirit"; member of the Stamp Act Congress (1765); authored a famous defence of the Colonies' position (1766); mentor of Samuel Adams and the Sons of Liberty (1761-69) and was considered *the* acknowledged political leader of Massachusetts Bay; a physical attack upon Otis by a British customs commissioner resulted in a severe head wound which left Otis greatly affected both physically and mentally (1769); despite his occasional attacks of temporary insanity brought on by the head injury, he was reelected to the General Court (1771); volunteered at the Battle of Bunker Hill (1775); argued his last case in 1778; ironically, according to his wish, he was mercifully struck by lightning thus ending his tormented physical condition.

William Paca (1740-99; Maryland) Attorney, public official, jurist; graduated from the College of Philadelphia (1759); admitted to the bar (1764); elected to the Provincial Legislature (1768); member of the Provincial Assembly (1771-74); member of the Continental Congress (1774-79) where he signed the Declaration of Independence (1776); member of the State Senate (1777-79); Chief-Judge of the Maryland General Court (1778-80); Chief-Justice of the Court of Appeals (1780-82); Governor (1782-85); helped establish Washington College (1786); delegate to the State ratification convention for the federal Constitution (1788); appointed U. S. federal Judge by President George Washington (1789-99).

Rev. Robert Treat Paine (1731-1814; Massachusetts) Clergyman, attorney, public official, and jurist; graduated from Harvard (1749); studied theology and acted as chaplain of troops on the northern frontier (1755); preached in the pulpits of the regular clergy in Boston and its vicinity; admitted to the bar (1757); delegate to the State Convention (1768); member of the Colonial House of Representatives (1773); delegate to the federal Provincial Congress (1774-75); member of the Continental Congress (1774-76) where he signed the Olive Branch Petition (1775) and the Declaration of Independence (1776); reelected to the Continental Congress but declined in order to serve as speaker of the State House of Representatives (1777); first Attorney General of Massachusetts (1777-90); member of the Governor's Council (1779-80); delegate to the State constitutional convention (1779); a founder of the American Academy of Arts and Sciences (1780); judge of the Massachusetts Supreme Court (1790-1804); helped suppress Shay's Rebellion (1786-87); retired from the Massachusetts court due to advanced deafness (1804).

Thomas Paine (1737-1809; England, Pennsylvania) Soldier and public official; Paine met Benjamin Franklin in London where Franklin encouraged him to seek his fortune in the United States (1774); after arriving in Philadelphia, Paine worked as an editor for the *Pennsylvania Magazine* (1774); at the suggestion of, and with the help of Benjamin Rush, Paine published the pamphlet *Common Sense* calling for independence from England (1776) (that pamphlet was credited by many with raising the fervor for independence to a fever pitch); served as an aide to General Nathanael Greene (1776); appointed secretary of the congressional committee on foreign affairs (1777-79); clerk of the Pennsylvania assembly (1779); went to England where he was indicted for treason by the British government for the publication of his *Rights of Man* (1787) ; escaped to France and was elected to the Revolutionary Convention (1792); as the terrors of the French Revolution grew, he was imprisoned by one of its factions (1793-94); released at the request of U. S. Minister to France James Madison; published his *Age of Reason*, a deistic work which brought him much criticism from his former American friends (1794); upon his return to the United States (1802), he found no welcome and lived and eventually died as an outcast.

Albion Parris (1788-1857; Maine) Attorney, public official, jurist; graduated from Dartmouth College (1806); admitted to the bar (1809); prosecuting attorney for Oxford County (1811); member of the State Assembly (1813); State Senator (1814); member of the U. S. Congress (1815-19); appointed U. S. District Judge by President James Monroe (1818); delegate to the State constitutional convention and a member of the committee for drawing up the constitution (1819); appointed judge of probate (1820); Governor (1821-26); U. S. Senator (1826-28); judge of the Supreme Court of Maine (1828-36); second comptroller of the U. S. Treasury (1836-50).

William Paterson (1745-1806; Ireland, New Jersey) Attorney, public official, and jurist; parents were from Ireland, but he was born at sea; parents brought him to America when he was two years old; graduated from Princeton (1763); studied law in the office of signer of the Declaration Richard Stockton (1764); admitted to the bar (1769); along with others he founded a literary society titled the "Well-Meaning Society" (1765-68); member of the New Jersey Provincial Congress (1775); member of the convention that formed the State constitution (1776); Attorney General of New Jersey (1776); delegate to the Constitutional Convention where he signed the federal Constitution (1787), being one of seven foreign born signers of that document; U. S. Senator and helped write the Judiciary Act, as well as the Bill or Rights (1789-90); Governor (1790-93); helped to codify the State laws (1792); appointed to the U. S. Supreme Court by President George Washington (1793-1806); published the *Laws of the State of New Jersey* (1800).

William Penn (1644-1718; England, Pennsylvania) Clergyman and public official; began attending meetings of the Quakers in England and was imprisoned by authorities for attending those meetings (1667); declared himself a Quaker instead of an Anglican; he began writing while in prison and vigorously advocated the doctrines of the Quakers (1668); subsequently authored many religious and political tracts; the land now known as Pennsylvania had been given to his father by Charles II in payment for a loan, and William Penn inherited that land on his father's death (1670); went on a missionary journey through Holland and Germany and then to America (1677); proposed to establish a civil government in Pennsylvania founded on tolerance, which he called his "holy experiment" (1681); negotiated several treaties with the Indians for that land; established a public grammar school in Philadelphia (1689); presented the Board of Trade in London the first plan for a union of all the American colonies (1697); labored to end slavery; returned to London on urgent business (1701) and never again returned to Pennsylvania.

Claude Pepper (1900-89; Alabama, Florida) Attorney and public official; graduate of the University of Alabama at Tuscaloosa (1921) and Harvard Law School (1924); practiced law in Florida; member of the Florida State legislature (1929-30); moved to Tallahassee and held various State offices; U. S. Senator (1938-50); member of the U. S. House of Representatives (1962-89) where he served as chairman of the House Select Committee on Aging (1977-83); sponsored the bill that halted mandatory retirement for most federal employees and raised the retirement age to seventy for workers in industry (1978); served as chairman of the House Rules Committee (1983).

William Phillips (1750-1827; Massachusetts) Public official and philanthropist; educated in Boston but due to his poor health, his education was repeatedly interrupted; entered business with his father who was a successful businessman; toured Britain, Holland, and France (1773); member of the Massachusetts General Court (1805-12); Lieutenant Governor for eleven consecutive terms beginning in 1812; delegate to the State constitutional convention (1820); State Senator (1823); in addition to his political service, he was involved in many philanthropic and religious organizations; for example, member of the Society for Propagating the Gospel Among the Indians and Others (1792-1821), serving as its president (1807-10); a deacon of the Old South Church (1794-1827); an original incorporator of the American Board of Foreign Missions; president of the American Society for Educating Pious Youth for the Gospel Ministry (1816); member of the Massachusetts Bible Society (1817); vice-president of the American Bible Society (1820-1827); also helped found the Massachusetts General Hospital, the American Education Society, as well as several other endeavors.

John Pickering (1737/38-1805; New Hampshire) Attorney, public official, and jurist; graduated from Harvard (1761); admitted to the bar; started his law practice in Greenland, then moved to Portsmouth; held various civil posts during the Revolution; delegate to the State constitutional convention (1781); member of the State House of Representatives (1783-87); selected as delegate to the Constitutional Convention for the federal Constitution but declined to serve (1787); delegate to the State ratification convention for the federal Constitution (1788); Presidential elector (1788, 1792); member of the New Hampshire Senate; delegate to the State constitutional convention (1791-92); Chief-Justice of the Superior Court (1790-95); appointed U. S. federal judge by President George Washington (1795-1804); suffered a mental breakdown in 1801 which led to his impeachment from the court in 1804.

Timothy Pickering (1745-1829; Massachusetts) Attorney, soldier, jurist, public official; graduated from Harvard (1763); commissioned as Lieutenant of militia (1766); admitted to the bar (1768); Colonel in the Continental Army (1775); justice-of-the-peace (1775); member of the General Court (1776); Adjutant-General in the Continental Army (1776); participated in the Battles of Brandywine (1777) and Germantown (1777); Quarter Master-General (1780); was present at the surrender of Cornwallis at Yorktown (1781); delegate to the State ratification convention for the federal Constitution (1788); delegate to the State constitutional convention (1789-90); Postmaster General under President George Washington (1791-95) and then Secretary of War, and Secretary of State (1795-97); Secretary of State under President John Adams (1797-1800); appointed Chief-Justice of the Court of Common Pleas (1802); U. S. Senator (1803-11); member of the Executive Council of Massachusetts (1812-13).

Pilgrims (circa 1620s) The term "pilgrim" means "a wanderer traveling to a holy place" and is generally applied to the group of spiritual refugees who arrived in America in pursuit of both practicing and advancing their religious beliefs in the New World. The Pilgrims were typically of the Congregational belief; that is, the spiritual form of church government they embraced was closer to that in a republic than that of a monarchy or oligarchy (i.e., a Pope, King, Bishop, high church council, etc.). The pilgrims had originated in England and opposed the high-handed tactics of the Church of England, but were persecuted and forced to flee to Amsterdam, Holland where they remained before embarking for America. They arrived in what is now called Plymouth, Massachusetts in the Fall of 1620, and they authored the first government document originated solely in America: the "Mayflower Compact." The Pilgrims became known in America for their hard-work ethic, their community form of government based on equality rather than aristocracy, and their firm reliance on the Bible and its principles as the basis for decisions in all aspects of life, whether spiritual or civil.

Charles Cotesworth Pinckney (1746-1825; South Carolina) Public official, attorney, and soldier; educated at Oxford; member of the State provincial assembly (1769); admitted to the bar (1770); Captain of South Carolina troops (1775); participated in the Battles of Brandywine and Germantown (1777); commanded a regiment in the campaign in the Floridas (1778); member of the State House (1778); member of the State Senate (1779); taken prisoner when Charleston fell (1780) and held until 1782; member of the State House (1782); Brigadier-General (1783); a delegate to the Constitutional Convention where he signed the federal Constitution (1787); Minister to France (1796); a founder of South Carolina College (1801); first president of the Charleston Bible Society (1810-25); vice-president of the American Bible Society (1816-25).

Plutarch (c. 350-430; Greece) Greek philosopher; studied under Aristotle and Plato; believed that reason is the basis and foundation of all consciousness and that reason is the transcendental or pure intelligence of God; authored numerous works, including *Parallel Lives of Illustrious Greeks and Romans* and *Morals*, which were his essays on historical, religious, and philosophical topics.

Thomas Posey (1750-1818; Virginia, Kentucky, Louisiana, Indiana) Soldier, and public official; early educated in common school; joined the 7th Virginia Continental Regiment (1774); active in many engagements, including the Battle of Saratoga (1777) and numerous excursions against the Indians on the Pennsylvania frontier; began as a Captain, was advanced to Major, to Lieutenant-Colonel (1782), and finally Brigadier-General (1793); member of the Kentucky State Senate (1805-06); Major-General in charge of organizing Kentucky troops (1809); chosen as Speaker of the State Senate and thereby ex-officio Lieutenant-Governor of Kentucky (1805-06); U. S. Senator from Louisiana (1812-13); Governor of the Indiana Territory (1813); vice-president of the American Bible Society.

Roscoe Pound (1870-1964; Nebraska) Educator and legal scholar; passed the bar exam without a law degree (1890); earned a Ph. D. from the University of Nebraska (1897); taught law at the University of Nebraska (1899-1903), and then became dean of its law school (1903-07); taught at Northwestern University (1907); taught at the University of Chicago (1909-10); dean of the Harvard Law School (1916-36); spent several years in Taiwan reorganizing the Nationalist Chinese government's judicial system; is considered a legal positivist, making many innovations in and departures from the traditional practices of legal interpretation; during his later years he shared with Learned Hand the reputation of being the nation's leading jurist outside the U. S. Supreme Court bench.

William Prescott (1726-95; Massachusetts) Farmer, soldier, and public official; served during the French and Indian War (1755-56); at the outset of the Revolution, he was instrumental in sending supplies of food to Boston during the British blockade (1774); Colonel of a regiment of Minute men (1775); during the Battle of Breed's Hill, he walked along the top of the hill in a broad-brimmed hat and conspicuous coat— both of which are depicted in the statue of him at Bunker Hill; he is alleged to have declared during that battle, "Don't fire until you see the whites of their eyes!" (1775); member of the council of war (1775); participated in the evacuation of New York (1776) and Burgoyne's surrender (1777); member of the General Court; helped in the suppression of Shay's Rebellion (1786-87).

Rev. Joseph Priestley (1733-1804; England, Pennsylvania) Clergyman, scientist, and author; attended Daventry, a dissenting academy (1751); took his first parish in the village of Needham Market, Surrey (1755); ordained to the ministry (1762); master several languages including Latin, Greek, Hebrew, French, German, Italian, Arabic, Syriac, etc. and studied both chemistry and electricity; made a fellow in the Royal Society (1766); made a foreign associate of the French Academy of Sciences (1772); spent time in France (1774); because of his sympathies for the French Revolution, his house, chapel, scientific and religious works, etc. were burned by a mob (1791); made a citizen of France by the French Assembly (1792); because of his longing for political and religious freedom, he sailed for America (1794); invited to become professor of chemistry at Philadelphia but declined (1794); made important discoveries in physics and chemistry (including isolating oxygen and eight other gases) but was never invited to preach; authored numerous religious and scientific works.

Samuel de Puffendorf (1632-94; Sweden) Educator, political philosopher, and public official; the son of a Lutheran minister; studied theology at the University of Leipzig but changed to legal studies at the University of Jena; traveled to Copenhagen, and as a result of the war between Denmark and Sweden, spent 8 months in prison (1658); after his release, traveled to Leiden and published a complete system of universal law (1660); accepted a new professorial position at the University of Lund in Sweden (1670); published his greatest work, "The Eight Books on the Law of Nature and Nations" (1672); a summary was published the following year, "On the Duty of Man and Citizen" (1673); turned to the study of history and became the official historian to the Swedish King (1677).

General Casimir Pulaski (1748-79; Poland) Soldier; joined the military at an early age; arrested and condemned to death because of an unsuccessful revolt against Russia; escaped and fled to Turkey and then France where he heard about the American cause from Benjamin Franklin (1775); sailed for America (1777); appointed by Congress as Brigadier-General in charge of cavalry (1777); fought in the Battles of Brandywine (1777) and Germantown (1777); helped supply troops at Valley Forge (1777-78); sent to Charleston where, although defeated by the British, he managed to save the city (1779); joined in the siege of Savannah (1779) where he was wounded, dying two days later; a statue to him was erected in Savannah with the cornerstone being laid by Lafayette (1824); the statue was completed in 1855.

Puritans Puritanism is the name given to the religious movement which generally sought greater strictness of life, simpler religious beliefs and manners of worship, and simpler church structure. The movement originated in the 16th century in the Church of England among those who thought there was too much attachment to the Church of Rome. The Puritans sought to "purify" the Church of England from vestments and elaborate ceremonies, and generally objected to icons (statues), stained glass windows, and church music. They further believe not only that all the clergy should be of equal rank rather than have a hierarchy of Archbishops, Bishops, etc., but that a local congregation should select its own pastor or even that a member of the congregation could preach. Some of the Puritans broke completely with the Church of England (also termed "separatists") largely made up the group of "Pilgrims" which settled Plymouth Colony. The Puritan movement was much influenced by John Calvin and John Knox, and modern descendants of many of the Puritans' teachings include the Baptists, Congregationalists, United Churches of Christ, and the Presbyterians.

Rufus Putnam (1738-1824; Massachusetts) Soldier, jurist, and public official; his father died when he was seven, and he was raised by relatives and apprenticed to a millwright; his academic studies were self-taught math, geography, history, etc.; served in the French and Indian War (1755-56); after the War, farmed, surveyed, and built mills; entered the Revolution as a Lieutenant-Colonel and organized the batteries on Dorchester Heights that forced the British to evacuate Boston (1775-76); served in the Battle of Saratoga (1777) as well as the Battles of Stonypoint and Verplanck Point (1779); Brigadier-General (1783); helped end Shays' Rebellion (1786-87); established the first settlement in the Northwest Territory at Marietta, Ohio (1788); appointed judge in the Northwest Territory by President George Washington (1796); Surveyor-General of the United States under Presidents George Washington, John Adams, and Thomas Jefferson (1796-1803); delegate to the first Ohio constitutional convention (1802); president of the Ohio Bible Society (1816); sometimes called "The Father of Ohio."

Sir Walter Raleigh (1552-1618; England) Sailor, soldier, explorer, and merchant; studied at Oxford (1568); served with the French Hugenots (1569-72); involved in two piratical ventures against Spain (1578-79); captain of infantry in suppressing the rebellion in Ireland (1580-81); became Court favorite and was knighted (1584); given 40,000 acres in Ireland; inherited from his half-brother a patent for land in America; sent two ships to Florida and up to North Carolina; his first 108 settlers landed on Roanoke Island (1585); those settlers ran short of food and were unable to get along with the Indians and so returned to England with Francis Drake (1586); a second group of settlers arrived but only fifteen stayed (1586); another expedition of 150, including 17 women, was sent to Roanoke where they found no trace of the previous fifteen (1587); while there, Virginia Dare was born—the first English child born on this continent; another expedition was sent to Roanoke but found no trace of the previous colonists except the word "Croatan" carved on a tree (1590); Raleigh lost so much money that in 1589 he gave his rights to a company of businessmen who eventually established Jamestown—the first permanent English settlement on the continent; Raleigh made numerous sea voyages, including one to South America (1595), Cadiz (1596), the Azores (1597), and again to South America (1617); he was executed in 1618 under an old sentence for piracy.

David Ramsay (1749-1815; South Carolina) Physician, public official, and author; graduated from Princeton (1765); graduated from the medical department of the University of Pennsylvania at Philadelphia (1772); moved to South Carolina (1773); member of the State House of Representatives (1776-83); served as surgeon in the Continental Army (1780-81); member of the Continental Congress (1782-86) and served as its President Pro Tempore during the last term; member of the State Senate (1792, 1794, 1796, 1801-15) and served as president of that body for seven years; prominent historian and author of several historical works, including *History of the Revolution of South Carolina* (1785), *History of the American Revolution* (1789), *Life of Washington* (1807), *History of South Carolina* (1809), *History of the United States* (published posthumously in 1816-17); Ramsay was gunned down by an insane assassin (1815).

Edmund Randolph (1753-1813; Virginia) Attorney, public official; graduated from William and Mary (1773); studied law under his father and admitted to the bar; appointed by Washington as aide-de-camp (1775); mayor of Williamsburg (1776); first Attorney-General of Virginia (1776-86); delegate to the State convention that adopted the first constitution for the State (1776); member of the Continental Congress (1779-82); Governor (1786); delegate to the Annapolis Convention which preceded the Constitutional Convention (1786); delegate to the Constitutional Convention (1787) but, along with George Mason, he declined to sign the completed Constitution because he thought it insufficiently protected States' rights; became a significant voice in leading the successful fight for a Bill of Rights; the first Attorney-General of the United States, appointed by President George Washington (1789-94); Secretary of State under President George Washington (1794-95); senior counsel for Aaron Burr in his treason trial (1807).

John Randolph of Roanoke (1773-1833; Virginia) Public official, and diplomat; a descendant of John Rolfe and Pocahontas; studied at Princeton, Columbia, and William & Mary; member of the U. S. House of Representatives (1799-1813, 1815, 1819-25, 1827-29); U. S. Senator (1825-27); delegate to the State constitutional convention at Richmond (1829); appointed minister to Russia by President Andrew Jackson (1830).

George Read (1733-98; Delaware) Attorney, and public official; studied independently; began the study of law at age of 15 and was admitted (1753); Crown Attorney-General for Delaware (1763-74); protested the Stamp Act (1765); member of the Continental Congress (1774-77) where he signed the Declaration of Independence (1776); president of the State constitutional convention (1776); State vice-president (1776-78); member of the State House of Representatives (1779-80); judge of the Court of Appeals (1782-88); delegate to the Constitutional Convention where he signed the federal Constitution (1787); U. S. Senator where he helped frame the Bill of Rights (1789-93); Chief-Justice of Delaware (1793-98); one of only six men who signed both the Declaration and the Constitution.

Joseph Reed (1741-85; Pennsylvania) Attorney, public official, and soldier; graduated from Princeton (1757); studied law and admitted to the bar (1763); two additional years of legal study at the Middle Temple in London before returning to the U. S. (1765); deputy secretary of New Jersey (1767); member of the Committee of Correspondence for Philadelphia (1775-75); Lieutenant-Colonel in the Pennsylvania militia and then General Washington's military secretary and aide-de-camp during the Revolution (1775); became Adjutant General (1776-77); was appointed first Chief-Justice of the Court of Pennsylvania but declined in order to remain on Washington's staff; served with distinction at the Battles of Brandywine (1777), Germantown (1777), and Monmouth (1777); member of the Continental Congress (1778); President of the Supreme Executive Council of Pennsylvania (1778-81); trustee of the University of Pennsylvania (1782-85); the British are said to have offered £10,000 and any office Reed wished if he would abandon the cause of independence; his reply was, "I am not worth purchasing, but, such as I am, the king of Great Britain is not rich enough to do it"; elected to Congress in 1784 but declined to serve because of poor health.

William Rehnquist (1924-   ; Wisconsin, Arizona) Attorney, public official, and jurist; graduated from Stanford Law School (1951); law clerk for Justice Jackson (1952); Assistant Attorney-General for the office of Legal Counsel in Washington (1969-71); appointed to the U. S. Supreme Court by President Richard Nixon (1972) and elevated to Chief-Justice by President Ronald Reagan (1986-   ); considered a conservative and is one of the Court's best historical scholars.

Paul Revere (1735-1818; Massachusetts) Merchant and soldier; educated at North Grammar School in Boston and entered apprenticeship as silversmith under his father; fought in the expedition against Crown Point in the French and Indian War (1756); one of fifty other "Indians" who were involved in the Boston Tea Party (1773); carried the news of the Tea Party of New York City (1773); made the famous midnight-ride to warn the patriots in Lexington and Concord of the impending British attack and to alert Hancock and Adams to flee (1775); member of the Committee of Correspondence (1776); made the first official seal for the Colonies; made the State seal for Massachusetts; joined in the ill-fated expeditions to Rhode Island (1778) and Penobscot Bay (1779); manufactured gunpowder, copper balls, and cannons; made metal protective plating for frigates, including the *Constitution*—"Old Ironsides"; worked with Robert Fulton to develop boilers for steamboats; wore uniforms of the Revolution every day until his death.

Rev. Chandler Robbins (1758-99; Massachusetts) Congregational clergyman and educator; son of a clergyman; graduated from Yale (1756); became a teacher in Dr. Wheeler's "Indian School" (Dartmouth College); studied theology and licensed to preach; became pastor of a church in Plymouth (1759-99); ordained (1760); received his Doctorate of Divinity from Dartmouth (1792); in 1795, that church numbered 2,500 members and was believed to be the largest in the State; he published numerous orations and sermons.

Daniel Roberdeau (1727-95; Pennsylvania) Merchant, soldier, and public official; member of the State Assembly (1756-60); manager of the Pennsylvania Hospital (1756-58, 1766-76); Warden of Philadelphia (1756-61); Brigadier General (1776); member of the Continental Congress (1777-79); volunteered in Congress to establish a lead mine (1778) and then built Fort Roberdeau to protect the mine; spent a year traveling in Europe (1783-84).

Caesar Rodney (1728-84; Delaware) Soldier, public official, and jurist; no formal education; High Sheriff of Kent County (1755-58); Captain of the Kent County Militia (1756); member of the State Assembly (1762-69); associate justice of the State Supreme Court (1769-77); member of the Continental Congress (1774-76) where he signed the Declaration of Independence (1776); interestingly, he had been called away from Congress on June 22, 1776, and later received emergency notification that his vote for Independence was drastically needed; he therefore rode eighty miles on horseback, arriving just in time to cast his vote for Independence; Brigadier-General (1777); Major-General (1777); President of Delaware (1778-82); he finally died from face cancer, which for ten years had consumed both his face and his health (1784).

Rev. William Rogers (1751-1824; Pennsylvania) Clergyman and educator; graduated from Rhode Island college (1769); also received degrees from the University of Pennsylvania (1773 and another in 1790), Yale (1780), and Princeton (1786); pastor of the 1st Baptist church in Philadelphia (1772-75); chaplain of the Pennsylvania rifle regiment (1776-78); brigade chaplain in the Continental army (1778-81); Professor of Oratory and English Literature at the College of Philadelphia (1789-92) and the University of Pennsylvania (1792-1811); vice-president of the Pennsylvania society for the gradual abolition of slavery (1794, 1796); chaplain to the Philadelphia militia (1805) chaplain to the Pennsylvania legislature (1816-17); vice-president of the Religious Historical Society of Philadelphia (1819); published numerous moral, religious, and political pieces.

Benjamin Rush (1745-1813; Pennsylvania) Physician, educator, philanthropist, and public official; graduated from Princeton (1760); studied medicine in Philadelphia, Edinburgh, London, and Paris; began practice in Philadelphia (1769); member of the Continental Congress (1776-77) where he signed the Declaration of Independence (1776); suggested to Thomas Paine that he write *Common Sense* (1776) and supplied the title for it as well as helped publish it; Surgeon-General of the Continental Army (1777-78); Treasurer of the U. S. Mint (1797-1813); joined the staff of the Pennsylvania Hospital in Philadelphia (1783); one of the founders of Dickinson College (1783); an influential delegate to the State ratification convention for the federal Constitution (1787); along with James Wilson, one of the principal coauthors of the Pennsylvania constitution (1789-90); Treasurer of the U. S. Mint under Presidents John Adams, Thomas Jefferson, and James Madison (1797-1813); mediated reconciliation between long time political rivals John Adams and Thomas Jefferson; among his philanthropic involvements, was a founder of the Pennsylvania Society for Promoting the Abolition of Slavery (1774) and its president; founder and Vice-president of the Philadelphia Bible Society (1808-13); member of the First Day Society of Philadelphia (1790); member of the Abolition Society (1794-97); called the "Father of American Medicine" for his numerous medical discoveries.

John Rutledge (1739-1800; South Carolina) Attorney, public official, and jurist; educated by his father, who was a physician and clergyman; studied law in London and admitted to the bar (1760); elected to the State Commons House (1761); delegate to the Stamp Act Congress (1765); member of the Continental Congress (1774-75); wrote South Carolina's new constitution (1776); president of the State House of Representatives (1776-78); Governor (1779-82); when Charleston fell to the British, his property was confiscated (1780); with General Nathanael Greene, reestablished the State government (1781); member of the State House of Representatives (1782, 1784-90); member of the Continental Congress (1782-83); judge on the State chancery court (1784); delegate to the Constitutional Convention where he signed the federal Constitution (1787); appointed to the U. S. Supreme Court by President George Washington (1789-91); Chief-Justice of South Carolina (1791-95); briefly served as Chief-Justice of the U. S. Supreme Court, succeeding John Jay, but his nomination was ultimately rejected by the Senate (1795); after his wife's death (1792), he suffered periodic fits of insanity which ended his career.

Antonin Scalia (1936-   ; New Jersey) Attorney, public official, and jurist; received his law degree from Harvard (1960); joined a Cleveland law firm but resigned to teach at the University of Virginia Law School (1967); served in the Nixon and Ford administrations in various positions including Assistant Attorney-General (1971-77); taught at University of Chicago Law School (1977-82); nominated for the U. S. Court of Appeals for the District of Columbia by President Ronald Reagan (1982); nominated to the U. S. Supreme Court by President Ronald Reagan (1986-   ); considered one of the more conservative and outspoken Justices and a strong supporter of original intent and judicial restraint.

Dred Scott (1795-1858; Virginia, Missouri) Slave; spent the early part of his life on the Virginia plantation of his master Captain Peter Blow, but the moved to Missouri (1827); after his master's death, Scott was assigned to his master's daughter (1831); he was purchased two years later by John Emerson, a surgeon in the United States Army; he married a slave woman named Harriet (1836); became the body servant of Colonel Henry Bainbridge at Jefferson Barracks (1838); after Emerson's death (c. 1840) was passed to his widow, Irene; with her, Scott spent three years in the States of Illinois and Wisconsin; Mrs. Emerson married Calvin Chaffee of Maine, a rabid anti-slavery Congressman; when she moved to Maine, she returned Scott to St. Louis (1845); Taylor and Henry T. Blow, the wealthy sons of Peter Blow, felt partially responsible for Scott and instituted and financed suits in the Missouri State courts to secure the freedom of Scott and his family (1846), arguing that after sojourning in free territory (Illinois and Wisconsin), that Scott was free upon his return to Missouri; after an unfavorable decision by Judge William Scott (1852) the case went before the federal courts (1854-57); the United States Supreme Court declared that Scott was not free by reason of his removal either to Illinois or to Wisconsin Territory (1857); he was transferred to Taylor Blow, who emancipated him that same year (1857); he spent the remainder of his life as the porter at Barnum's Hotel in St. Louis and died of tuberculosis (1858); Henry Blow paid for his funeral.

Jonathan Mitchell Sewell (1748-1808; Massachusetts, New Hampshire) Attorney, poet, orator; his parents died early and he was raised by an uncle; studied law and admitted to the bar (1773); became a poet and authored a ballad called "War and Washington" which became popular in the Continental Army (1776); authored three odes which were sung when

President George Washington visited Portsmouth, New Hampshire (1789); authored "A Verification of President Washington's Excellent Farewell Address" (1798); after Washington's death in December 1799, Sewell pronounced a eulogy which was published in 1800; authored "Miscellaneous Poems" (1801).

Isaac Shelby (1750-1826; Maryland, Virginia, Tennessee, Kentucky, North Carolina) Soldier and public official; born in Maryland and spent early years there; no record of any formal education; moved to Tennessee (c. 1771); Surveyor for Transylvania, Kentucky (1775); Captain of Virginia Minutemen (1775); appointed Commissary General of Virginia forces by Governor Patrick Henry (c. 1776); served in the Virginia legislature (1779) but because of border dispute, became resident of North Carolina; Colonel of the guerilla fighters in Sullivan County (1779-80); led part of the campaign of "Kings" Mountain (1780) and Cowpens (1781); member of the North Carolina legislature (1781-82); moved to Kentucky and became active in helping obtain Statehood; delegate to the Kentucky State constitutional convention (1792); first governor of Kentucky (1792-96) and was elected to another term (1812-16); offered but declined Secretary of War under President James Monroe (1817); helped General Andrew Jackson negotiate treaty with the Chickasaw Indians (1818); vice-president of the American Bible Society.

Roger Sherman (1721-93; Massachusetts, Connecticut) Born in Massachusetts and grew up as a farmer and cobbler; no formal education, although he independently studied math, law, and theology; moved to Connecticut (1743); county surveyor (1745); held a number of local offices; admitted to the bar (1754); Justice-of-the-Peace for Litchfield County (1755-61); Justice-of-the-Peace and member of the Court of Connecticut (1765-66); member of the State Senate (1766-85); Judge of the Superior Court (1766-67, 1773-88); member of the Council of Safety (1777-79); member of the Continental Congress (1774-81, 1784) where he signed the Declaration of Independence (1776); mayor of New Haven (1784-93); delegate to the Constitutional Convention where he signed the federal Constitution (1787); one of his major contributions in that Convention was the introduction of the plan for two houses in Congress; member of the U. S. House of Representatives (1789-91) where he helped frame the Bill of Rights; U. S. Senator (1791-93); one of only six Founders who signed both the Declaration and the Constitution and the only Founder who signed the Declaration, the Articles of Association, the Articles of Confederation, and the Constitution.

Peter Sylvester (1734-1808; New York) Attorney and public official; studied law and was admitted to the bar (1763); member of Council of Safety (1774); member of Provincial Congress (1775-76); County Judge (1786); regent of the University of New York (1787-1808); member of the State Assembly (1788, 1803-06); member of the U. S. House of Representatives (1789-93) where he helped frame the Bill of Rights; State senator (1796-1800).

George Smathers (1913-   ; Florida) Attorney, soldier, and public official; born in New York but educated in public schools in Florida; graduated from the University of Florida (1936); graduated from the University of Florida law school and admitted to the bar (1938); Major in the U. S. Marine Corp (1942-45); special assistant to the U. S. Attorney General (1945-46); U. S. Representative (1947-51); U. S. Senator (1951-69); retired to law practice in Washington, D. C. and Miami (1969).

Jeremiah Smith (1759-1842; New Hampshire) Soldier, attorney, public official, and jurist; attended Harvard College (1777) but graduated from Rutgers (1780); served in the Revolution under General Stark in the Battle of Bennington (1777); studied law and admitted to the bar (1786); member of the State House of Representatives (1788-91); delegate to the State constitutional convention (1791-92); member of the U. S. House of Representatives (1791-97); appointed U. S. federal judge by President John Adams (1801-02); Chief-Justice of the Superior Court of Judicature of New Hampshire (1802-1809); presidential elector (1808); Governor (1809-10); Chief-Justice of the Supreme Judicial Court of New Hampshire (1813-16); resumed law practice, but retired in 1820; served as president of a bank and treasurer of Phillips Exeter Academy.

John Cotton Smith (1765-1845; Connecticut) Attorney, public official, jurist, and philanthropist; graduated from Yale (1783); studied law and admitted to the bar (1787); member of the State House of Representatives (1793, 1796, 1800) and its speaker (1800); U. S. Representative (1800-06); judge of the Supreme Court of Connecticut (1809); Lieutenant-Governor (1810); Governor (1813-18); president of the Litchfield County Foreign Missionary Society; president of the County Temperance Society; first president of the Connecticut Bible Society; vice-president of the American Bible Society (1816-31) and its president (1831-45); member of the American Board of Foreign Missions (1826-45).

Jonathan Bayard Smith (1742-1812; Pennsylvania) Soldier, public official, educator, and jurist; graduated from Princeton (1760); active promoter of the Revolutionary cause; secretary of the Committee of Safety (1775); secretary of Philadelphia Committee of Safety (1775-77); member of the Continental Congress (1777-78); founder of the University of the State of Pennsylvania (1778); justice of the Court of Common Pleas, Quarter Sessions, and Orphans Court (1778); trustee of Princeton (1779-1808); Auditor of Accounts of Pennsylvania Troops in the Service of the United States (1781); trustee of University of Pennsylvania (1791-1812); Auditor-General of Pennsylvania (1794); member of the American Philosophical Society.

Richard Dobbs Spaight (1758-1802; Ireland, North Carolina) Soldier and public official; orphaned at 8, was early schooled in Ireland; graduated from the University of Glasgow, Scotland; returned to North Carolina as military aide to General Richard Caswell (1778); involved in the Battle of Camden (1780); member of the North Carolina House of Commons (1779-83) and was its Speaker (1785-87); member of the Continental Congress (1783-85); delegate to the Constitutional Convention where he signed the federal Constitution (1787), being one of the youngest signers; Governor (1792); presidential elector (1793-97); member of Congress, (1798-1801); member of the State Senate (1801-02); both his son and grandson were U. S. Representatives; died from wounds received in a duel with a political rival.

Baron Frederick William Augustus von Steuben (1730-94; Germany) Soldier; served in the Prussian Army under Frederick II (the Great); he was sent by Benjamin Franklin to serve in the American Continental Army under Washington (1777); drilled and trained the troops at Valley Forge after the hard winter (1777-78); turned the troops into an effective, disciplined, strategic fighting force; put in command of Virginia and participated in the Yorktown siege (1781); retired from the army (1784); became a citizen by acts of the Pennsylvania and New York legislatures.

John Paul Stevens (1920-   ; Illinois) Attorney, sailor, educator, and jurist; graduated from the University of Chicago (c. 1942); received his law degree from Northwestern University (c. 1943); spent three years in the Navy in WWII; law clerk to Justice Rutledge (1947-48); private practice specialized in anti-trust law; taught at Northwestern University law school; appointed to the United States Court of Appeals for the Seventh Circuit by President Gerald Ford and was President Ford's only nomination (1975-   ); an inconsistent Justice in that he is very liberal on social issues but conservative in many other areas.

Potter Stewart (1915-85; Ohio) Attorney, sailor, public official, and jurist; attended University School, Hotchiss, Yale, and Cambridge; graduated from Yale law school (1941); began law practice on Wall Street, but following the attack on Pearl Harbor, he joined the Navy as an officer and received three battle stars for service on tankers in the Atlantic and Mediterranean; returned to law practice on Wall Street but then moved to Cincinnati as a litigator; served two terms on the city council and one term as mayor; served as a judge on the sixth circuit federal court of appeals (1954-58); appointed to the U. S. Supreme Court by President Dwight D. Eisenhower (1958-81); on many significant issues he became the swing vote and is considered a moderate, being termed a liberal on a conservative Court and a conservative on a liberal Court.

Richard Stockton (1730-81; New Jersey) Attorney, jurist, and public official; graduated from Princeton (1748); admitted to the bar (1754); (interestingly, Stockton married the sister of Elias Boudinot and Elias Boudinot married Stockton's sister); those who studied under Stockton include Elias Boudinot (President of Congress), William Paterson (signer of the Constitution); and Joseph Reed (a general and the Governor of Pennsylvania); recruited the Rev. Dr. John Witherspoon for the presidency of Princeton (1768); member of the Executive Council of New Jersey (1768-74); member of the Provincial Supreme Court (1774-76); associate justice of the State Supreme Court (1774-76); member of the Continental Congress (1776) where he signed the Declaration of Independence (1776); elected but declined to sit as Chief-Justice of the State Supreme Court (1776); betrayed by Loyalists and captured by the British (1776); treated harshly but released (1777); health shattered, his estate and fortune pillaged, he died an invalid at age 50.

Thomas Stone (1743-87; Maryland) Attorney and public official; received a classical education under a Scottish schoolmaster; studied law and admitted to the bar (1764); State senator (1775-87); member of the Continental Congress (1775-76, 1778, 1784) and although he initially opposed independence because he hated the thought of war, he eventually signed the Declaration of Independence (1776); helped draft the Articles of Confederation (1778); selected as delegate to the Constitutional Convention but declined to serve because of poor health of wife who died in June 1787; heartbroken, he retired from all public life and decided to visit England but died at the age of 44.

Joseph Story (1779-1845; Massachusetts) Attorney, public official, educator, and jurist; grew up being strongly instructed in the principles of American liberty since his father was one of the "Indians" in the Boston Tea Party (1773); graduated from Harvard second in his class (1798); delivered a eulogy on the death of Washington (1800); admitted to the bar (1801); member of the Massachusetts Legislature (1805-07, 1811) and its Speaker (1811); U. S. Representative (1808-09); appointed to the U. S. Supreme Court by President James Madison (1811-45); considered the founder of Harvard Law School and its Professor of Law (1829-45); authored numerous legal works; is considered one of the most prolific judicial writers; in fact, of his 34 years on the Supreme Court (much of the time when John Marshall was Chief-Justice), Story authored opinions in 286 cases, of which 269 were reported as the majority opinion or the opinion of the Court; his contributions to American law have caused him to be called, along with Chancellor James Kent, the "Father of American Jurisprudence."

Caleb Strong (1745-1819; Massachusetts) Attorney and public official; graduated from Harvard (1764); on way home from Harvard, contracted smallpox which permanently injured his sight; studied law and admitted to the bar (c. 1768); member of State House of Representatives (1776-78); member of State senate (1780-88); elected to the Continental Congress but did not attend (1780); delegate to the Constitutional Convention but did not sign the federal Constitution (1787); member of the State ratification convention for the federal Constitution (1788); U. S. Senator (1789-96); Governor of Massachusetts (1800-07, 1812-15); opposed the War of 1812 and withheld the State militia until 1814; vice-president of the American Bible Society (1816-1819).

James Sullivan (1744-1808; Massachusetts) Attorney, jurist, public official, and philanthropist; completed prepatory studies and entered the study of law; admitted to the bar (1770); member of King's Council (1770); early advocate of the Revolutionary cause; member of the State Provincial Congress (1775); judge of the Supreme Court of Massachusetts (1776); elected to the Continental Congress but did not attend (1782); State Attorney-General (1790-1807); Governor (1807-08); influential in the adoption of the Eleventh Amendment regarding judicial powers; member of the Society for Propagating the Gospel Among the Indians and Others; member of the American Academy of Arts and Sciences; principle founder of the Massachusetts Historical Society, serving as president for many years.

Increase Sumner (1746-99; Massachusetts) Educator, attorney, jurist, and public official; graduated from Harvard with distinction (1767); taught school at Roxbury (1768-70); studied law and admitted to the bar (1770); representative in the General Court (1776-79); delegate to the State constitutional convention (1779-80); State Senator (1780-82); associate justice of the Supreme Judicial Court of Massachusetts (1782); delegate to the State ratification convention for the federal Constitution (1788); Governor (1797-99), and was sworn in for his third term while on his death bed.

Zephaniah Swift (1759-1823; Connecticut) Attorney, public official, author, and jurist; graduated from Yale in the same class with several other notables, including Joel Barlow, Uriah Tracy, and Oliver Wolcott (1778); studied law and admitted to the bar (1783); member of the State House of Representatives (1787-93) and its speaker (1792); Clerk of the State House (1788-91); authored the *System of Laws in Connecticut,* the first American legal text (1792); member of the U. S. Congress (1793-97); member of the Abolition Society (1795); secretary of the French mission (1800); judge of the State Superior Court (1801-19) and its Chief-Justice (1806-19); member of the Hartford Convention for framing a State constitution (1814); member of the State House of Representatives (1820-22); authored both legal and religious works.

Clarence Thomas (1948-   ; Georgia) Attorney, public official, and jurist; graduated from Yale Law School (1974); served as Assistant Secretary of Education and the Chairman of the Equal Employment Opportunity Commission under President Ronald Reagan; as a conservative, he often found himself at odds with much of the civil right movement; appointed by President George Bush to the District of Columbia Federal Circuit Court of Appeals (1990); nominated by President George Bush as the 106th Justice of the Supreme Court (1991); unsubstantiated charges of sexual harassment raised against him by a former disgruntled employee, Anita Hill, caused his confirmation to the Court to be approved by a margin of only 52-48—the smallest margin in over 100 years; has proven himself to be a conservative on all issues and a strict constructionist in upholding the original intent of the Constitution.

Smith Thompson (1768-1843; New York) Educator, attorney, public official, and jurist; graduated from Princeton (1788); while teaching school, studied law under Chancellor James Kent and was admitted to the bar (1792); member of the State legislature (1800); delegate to the State constitutional convention (1801); associate justice of the State Supreme Court (1802-18) and its Chief-Justice (1814-18); Secretary of the Navy under President James Monroe (1818-23); appointed to the U. S. Supreme Court by President James Monroe (1823-43); was opposed to many of the views of Chief Justice John Marshall; vice-president of the American Bible Society (1816-30).

William Tilghman (1756-1827; Maryland) Public official, jurist, and philanthropist; entered the College, Academy, and Charitable School of Philadelphia (now the University of Pennsylvania) and graduated (1772); studied law (1772-76); was considered a loyalist and consequently remained on his estate during the Revolution; admitted to legal practice (1783); member of the State Assembly (1788-90); delegate to the State ratification convention for the federal Constitution (1788); member of the State Senate (1791); admitted to the bar (1794); appointed by President John Adams as a "midnight judge" and Chief-Judge of the Third Circuit Court (1800); trustee of the University of Pennsylvania (1802-27); Judge of the Court of Common Pleas; judge of the Pennsylvania High Court of Errors and Appeals; Chief-Justice of the Pennsylvania Supreme Court (1806-27); president of the American Philosophical Society (1824-27); vice-president of the American Bible Society; was also an active member of the Society for Promoting Agriculture and for the last ten years of his life, he refused to wear any clothing not made in the United States.

Alexis Henri Charles Maurice Clerel Comte de Tocqueville (1805-59; France) French observer of America; assistant magistrate (1830); sent on a mission from the government to examine prisons and penitentiaries in America, and later published a report of his full tour, *De la Démocratie en Amérique [Democracy in America]* (1835); vice-president of the French assembly (1849); minister of foreign affairs; wrote the first book of reasoned politics on democratic government in America and concluded that equality of condition was the foundation of American democracy and was amazed that without violence America had been transformed from what was essentially aristocratic rule to a more extended suffrage.

Daniel Tompkins (1774-1825; New York) Public official and jurist; graduated from Columbia College (1795); studied law and admitted to the bar (1797); delegate to the State constitutional Convention (1801); member of the State Assembly (1803); elected to the U. S. Congress in 1804, but resigned before he took office to become Associate Justice of the State Supreme Court (1804-07); Governor (1807-17); during the War of 1812, he helped finance the defense of New York largely from personal and from borrowed funds; declined appointment as Secretary of State under President James Madison (1814); served as Vice-President under President James Monroe (1817-25); was reimbursed for his expenses in the War of 1812 (1823-24); president of the State constitutional convention (1821); died from broken health and overwork.

John Treadwell (1745-1823; Connecticut) Attorney, public official, and jurist; graduated from Yale (1767); studied law and admitted to the bar (c. 1770); member of the State legislature (1776-84); Clerk of the Court of Probate (1777-84); member of the Continental Congress (1784, 85, 87); member of the Governor's Council (1785); member of the State Council (1786-97); Judge of Probate and of the Supreme Court of Errors (1789-1809); Lieutenant-Governor (1798-1809); delegate to the State ratification convention for the federal Constitution (1788); Governor (1809-11); delegate to the State constitutional convention (1818).

Robert Troup (1757-1832; New York) Attorney, public official, and jurist; graduated from King's College (1774); studied law under John Jay; Lieutenant in the Continental Army; captured by the British and exchanged (1776); Lieutenant-Colonel (1777); present at Burgoyne's surrender (1777); Secretary of the Board of War (1778-79); Secretary of the Board of Treasury (1779-80); returned to private life and continued legal studies under William Paterson; campaigned for the adoption of the federal Constitution (1788); member of the State Assembly (c. 1790); judge of the U. S. District Court of New York (1796); helped develop and settle the western part of the State (1800-32); helped found Geneva (now Hobart) College (1822); vice-president of the American Bible Society (1830-32).

Rev. Jonathan Trumbull (1710-1785; Connecticut) Clergyman, businessman, jurist, and public official; his name was spelled "Trumble" until 1766; graduated from Harvard (1727); returned home to prepare for the ministry and was licensed to preach and called to a church at Colchester (1731); studied law, but no record of admission to the bar (1731); when his older brother—his father's business partner—died, Trumbull assumed his position from a sense of duty and became a successful merchant for thirty-five years; member of the General Assembly (1733-40) and its Speaker (1739-40); member of the Governor's Council (1740-50); member of the General Assembly (1751-54) and its Speaker (1753-54); member of the Governor's Council (1754-66); Deputy Governor and Chief-Justice of the State Supreme Court (1766-69); Governor (1769-84); was a staunch supporter of American rights and was the only Colonial Governor to take the American side; was the only Governor who served from the start to the finish of the American Revolution; he probably contributed more to the Revolution in the way of arms, munitions, supplies, men, etc. than any other Governor; was a close counsel of General Washington throughout the War; on his retirement following the close of the Revolution, he returned to theological pursuits.

William Tyndale (1490-1536; England) Theologian and reformer; graduated from Oxford (1515); ordained to the priesthood (c. 1521); translated the New Testament, the Pentateuch, Jonah, and sections from Joshua and Chronicles but could not get them published in England; traveled to Hamburg, visited Luther at Wittenberg, and settled in Cologne (1524); had some success printing there but was stopped by a church leader; went to Worms and completed his octavo edition of the Bible (1526); threatened with arrest and thus fled to Marbury (1526); abandoned formal Romanism and published *Parable of the Wicked Mammon* and *Obedience of a Christian Man* which delineated the two main principles of the English Reformation: (1) the supremacy of the Scriptures in the church and (2) the supremacy of the King in the state (1528); moved to Antwerp (1529); published *Practice of Prelates*—a strong indictment of Roman Catholicism and of Henry VIII's divorce of Catherine (1530); was betrayed by a supposed follower, imprisoned in Brussels (1535); despite efforts by Thomas Cromwell (Henry VIII's parliamentary representative), Tyndale was tried for heresy, condemned, and strangled at the stake; his body was later burned (1536).

John Vining (1758-1802; Delaware) Attorney and public official; studied law and admitted to the bar (1782); member of the Continental Congress (1784-85); U. S. Representative (1789-93) where he helped frame the Bill of Rights; member of the State Senate (1793); U. S. Senator (1793-98).

Peter Vroom (1791-1873; New Jersey) Attorney, public official, jurist, and diplomat; graduated from Columbia (1808); studied law and admitted to the bar (1813); member of the State Assembly (1826-27, 1829); Governor (1829, 1831, 1833-36); appointed a commissioner to adjust the claims of the Choctaw Indians (1837); U. S. Representative (1839-41); delegate to the State constitutional convention (1844); Chief-Justice of the State Supreme Court (1853); appointed Minister to Prussia by President Franklin Pierce (1854-57); member of peace conference which attempted to prevent the Civil War (1861); law reporter for New Jersey Supreme Court (1865-73); vice-president of the American Bible Society; vice-president of the American Colonization Society; member of the American Board of Commissioners for Foreign Missions.

Samuel Ward (1725-76; Rhode Island) Farmer and public official; attended only grammar school and then began agricultural pursuits; member of the General Assembly (1756-59); Chief-Justice of Rhode Island (1761-62); one of the founders and trustees of Rhode Island College—now called Brown (1764-76); member of the Continental Congress

(1774-76); helped secured the appointment of George Washington as Commander-in-Chief (1775); died of smallpox in Philadelphia.

Earl Warren (1891-1974; California) Attorney, soldier, public official, and jurist; graduated from the University of California (1912); graduated from University of California law school (1914); admitted to the bar (1914); served in the Army as Lieutenant; Clerk of State legislative committee (1919); Deputy City Attorney of Oakland (1919-20); Deputy District Attorney of Alameda County (1920-25) and then District Attorney (1925-39); State Attorney General (1939-43); Governor (1943-53); in 1946 when he ran for Governor, he was the first candidate for Governor ever to win both the Democratic and the Republican nominations; ran for Vice-President with Dewey (1948); ran for President against Dwight D. Eisenhower (1952); appointed as Chief-Justice of the U. S. Supreme Court by President Dwight D. Eisenhower (1953-69); Chairman of Presidential Commission to investigate the assassination of President John F. Kennedy (1963-64); a liberal who was devoted to extremes in the area of civil liberties and to the reshaping of the Constitution into a progressive, evolutionary document; under his leadership, the Court began its assault on public religious expressions.

Mercy Otis Warren (1728-1814; Massachusetts) Author and historian; sister of James Otis; married James Warren, a prominent Massachusetts political leader and a descendent of the Pilgrims who arrived on the Mayflower (1754); knew personally most of the leaders of the Revolution and was continually in the center of events; very astute in both literature and politics; strong leader and advocate of women's political abilities; wrote several plays, poetry, and political satire; authored the three-volume work *A History of the Rise, Progress, and Termination of the American Revolution* (1805).

Bushrod Washington (1762-1829; Virginia) Soldier, attorney, public official, and jurist; nephew of George Washington; early educated by a tutor in the home of Richard Henry Lee, the signer of the Declaration and the President of Congress; graduated from William & Mary (1778); enlisted in the Continental Army (1781); studied law in Philadelphia under James Wilson and admitted to the bar (c. 1784); member of the Virginia House (1787); delegate to the State ratification convention for the federal Constitution (1788); appointed to the U. S. Supreme Court by President John Adams to fill the vacancy caused by the death of Justice James Wilson (1798); was the executor of George Washington's will and inherited Mount Vernon after Martha Washington died as well as Washington's private library; supervised the preparation of John Marshall's *Life of George Washington;* vice-president of the American Bible Society (1816-29); one of the original vice-presidents of the American Sunday School Union.

George Washington (1732-99; Virginia) Soldier, jurist, and public official; commissioned Lieutenant-Colonel and then Colonel of a Virginia regiment during the French and Indian War (1754-55); served as aide-de-camp to British General Edward Braddock in the ill-fated expedition against Fort Duquesne in which Braddock was killed (1755); appointed Commander of all Virginia forces (1755-58); member of the State House (1758-74); justice-of-the-peace (1760-74); delegate to the Williamsburg Convention of August (1774); member of the Continental Congress (1774-75); unanimously chosen as the Commander-in-Chief of the American forces and served in that position until the successful conclusions of the American Revolution (1775-83); president of the Constitutional Convention and signer of the Constitution (1787); unanimously elected as the first President of the United States (1789) and then unanimously re-elected (1792); after declining renomination as President, he was appointed as Lieutenant-General and Commander of the United States Army (1798) which position he held until his death (1799); known as "The Father of His Country" and eulogized by Henry Lee as "First in War, First in Peace, and First in the Hearts of his Countrymen."

Martha Dandridge Custis Washington (1732-1802; Virginia) Daughter of Colonel John Dandridge; her mother died early and her father remarried; Martha married Colonel Daniel Parke Custis by whom she had two sons and two daughters (although one of those sons and one daughter died in early childhood); her husband died, leaving her one of the richest women in Virginia (1757); married George (1759); her remaining daughter died in 1773 and her son died in 1781, leaving four children, two of whom George adopted; she managed the estate at Mount Vernon during the Revolutionary War and spent the winters at camp with Washington; she was America's first "First Lady."

Rev. Bishop Richard Watson (1738-1816; England) Educator, scientist, and author; graduated from Trinity College (1760); Professor of Chemistry (1764); Professor of the Regius Chair of Divinity (1771); published several works on chemistry; answered Gibbon's attack on Christianity from his *Decline and Fall of the Roman Empire* (1776); was one of only two opponents which Gibbons respected; Arch-Deacon of Ely (1779); Bishop of Llandaff (1782); authored his *Apology for the Bible* in answer to Thomas Paine's work (1796); opposed the war with America; denounced the slave trade; advocated union with Ireland.

Daniel Webster (1782-1852; Massachusetts, New Hampshire) Attorney and public official; graduated from Dartmouth (1801); admitted to the bar (1805); U. S. Representative from New Hampshire (1813-17); moved to Boston (1816); delegate to the Massachusetts constitutional convention (1820); member of the Massachusetts House (1823); U. S. Representative from Massachusetts (1823-27); U. S. Senator from Massachusetts (1827-41, 1845-50); candidate for U. S. President (1836); U. S. Secretary of State (1841-43, 1850-52).

Noah Webster (1758-1843; Massachusetts, Connecticut) Soldier, attorney, educator, public official, and author; graduated from Yale (1778); left Yale on two occasions to march to participate in battles during the Revolution; admitted to bar (1781); taught classics in New York (1782-83); published his *Grammatical Institute of the English Language*—America's first speller (1783-85); advocate of a strong federal government, he printed *Sketches of American Policy*—one of the earliest calls for a Constitutional Convention (1785); began to campaign for copyright protections which finally were included in Article I, Section 8 of the U. S. Constitution (1787); printed pamphlet urging ratification of the federal Constitution (1787); visited with Franklin for ten months in Philadelphia on Americanization of spellings and consequently authored *Dissertations on the English Language* (1789); practiced law (1789-93); served in the Massachusetts Legislature, (1815-19); authored *The American Dictionary of the English Language* (1828); helped found Amherst College.

Eleazer Wheelock (1711-79; Connecticut, New Hampshire) Clergyman and educator; graduated from Yale (1733); licensed to preach (1734); accepted pastorate (1735); popular preacher throughout the Great Awakening; began plan for educating and converting Indians, specifically the Mohegans and the Delawares (1743); began More's Indian Charity School (1754); sent ten graduates as missionaries and schoolmasters to the Six Indian Nations (1765); obtained charter from Governor of New Hampshire for his college (1769) and established it as Dartmouth (1770); remained its president until his death.

Byron White (1917-   ; Colorado) Sailor, attorney, public official, and jurist; graduated valedictorian from University of Colorado (1938); received nine letters in sports and was nicknamed "Whizzer" for his abilities as a football running back; played for the Pittsburgh Steelers for a year after his graduation and led the league in rushing; accepted Rhodes scholarship to Oxford (1939); World War II broke out and he returned home (1939); studied law at Yale; played football with the Detroit Lions (1940-41); joined Navy shortly after Pearl Harbor and served in the Pacific as a naval officer with John Kennedy; after War, completed law school at Yale with high honors (1946); law clerk for Chief-Justice Vinson (1946-47); practiced law in Denver (1947-60); Deputy Attorney-General under President John F. Kennedy (1961); appointed to U. S. Supreme Court by President John F. Kennedy (1962-93).

Father Andrew White (1579-c. 1633; England) Attended St. Alban's College at Valladolid (1595); involved in the ministry in the English missionfield; exiled to France and entered the Society of Jesus (1605-09); went to Lisbon to the seminary founded by Father Persons (c. 1611); took final vows (1617); as a professor he taught Theology, Greek and Hebrew; while involved in the English mission he met Lord Baltimore and learned about the plans for the American colony, soon after he applied for the Maryland mission (1630); he wrote the famous *Declaration Coloniae* which provided the purposes of the colony as well as the terms and conditions offered to the settlers; known as "The Apostle of Maryland."

Roger Williams (1603-84; England, Rhode Island) Clergyman; born in London; graduated from Pembroke (1624); received holy orders (c. 1628); emigrated to the Puritan Colony at Massachusetts Bay (1630); non-conformist and an extreme separatist, he insisted on complete repudiation of the Church of England and refused the call to a pastorate in Boston (1631); pastored at Plymouth (1632-33); pastored at Salem in defiance of the General Court (1634); convicted of spreading "dangerous opinions" (1635); banished and attempted to organize separate Colony of Narragansett Bay; forced out of Massachusetts; founded Providence and Colony of Rhode Island on basis of complete religious toleration (1636); founded the very first Baptist church in America (1639); traveled to England to obtain patent for Rhode Island (1643); got along well with Indians but gave up trying to convert them and was skeptical of existing churches; first President of Rhode Island (1654-57).

William Williams (1731-1811; Connecticut) Soldier, public official, and jurist; son of a Congregational minister; graduated from Harvard (1751); studied theology for a year under his father; member of a military expedition to Lake George during the French and Indian War (1755); member of the State House (1757-76, 1780-84) and its Speaker

(1775, 1781-83); member of the Continental Congress (1776-78, 1783-84) where he signed the Declaration of Independence (1776); member of the Council of Safety; judge of the County Court of Windham (1776-1804); judge of probate (1776-1808); delegate to the State ratification convention for the federal Constitution (1788).

James Wilson (1742-98; Scotland, Pennsylvania) Attorney, educator, public official, and jurist; born in Scotland; attended University of St. Andrews and University of Glasgow; immigrated to New York (1765); moved to Philadelphia as tutor of Latin at College of Philadelphia (1766); studied law under John Dickinson and admitted to the bar (1767); member of the Continental Congress (1774-77, 1783, 1785-86) where he signed the Declaration of Independence (1776); member of the Board of War (1776-77); delegate to the Constitutional Convention where he signed the federal Constitution (1787); delegate to the State ratification convention for the federal Constitution (1788); appointed to the U. S. Supreme Court as one of its original Justices by President George Washington (1789-98); authored much of the State constitution (1789-90); first Professor of Law in the College of Philadelphia (1790) and in the University of Pennsylvania (1791); along with Thomas McKean, he co-authored America's first Commentaries on the Constitution (1792); laid the foundation for American jurisprudence; one of only six men who signed both the Declaration and the Constitution.

John Winthrop (1588-1649; Massachusetts) Attorney, jurist, and public official; attended Trinity College (1603-05); his father was an attorney and he studied law under his father; admitted to practice law (1613); justice-of-the-peace at Groton (1609-26?); appointed an attorney to the Court of Wards and Liveries (1626); admitted to the Inner Temple (1628); became the first Governor of Massachusetts Bay Colony because he wanted to establish a Bible Commonwealth free from the "corruption" of the Church of England (1629-34, 1637-40, 1642-44, 1646-49—he died in office); helped establish the first church in Boston; became the first president of the New England Confederation (1643); authored *History of New England*—a valuable source book of American history.

Robert Winthrop (1809-94; Massachusetts) Attorney and public official; graduated from Harvard (1828); studied law under Daniel Webster and admitted to the bar (1831); member of the State House (1834-40) and its Speaker (1838-40); U. S. Representative (1840-50) and Speaker of the House (1847-49); U. S. Senator appointed to replace Daniel Webster (1850-51); member of Massachusetts Historical Society (1839-94) and its president for thirty years; noted orator of his day.

William Wirt (1772-1834; Virginia) Attorney, author, and public official; parents died while a youth—raised by uncle; tutored privately; studied law and admitted to the bar (1792); clerk of the State House (1800); member of the State House (1808); appointed U. S. Attorney by President James Madison and was counsel for the prosecution in the Aaron Burr conspiracy trial (1816); authored numerous books but perhaps his best known was *Sketches of the Life and Character of Patrick Henry* (1818); appointed U. S. Attorney-General under President James Monroe (1817-29) and argued several landmark Supreme Court cases including *McCulloch* v. *Maryland* (1819), Dartmouth College case (1819), *Gibbons* v. *Ogden* (1824); practiced law in Baltimore (1829-34);

was presidential candidate for the Anti-Masonic party (1832); early manager of the American Sunday School Union; vice-president of the American Bible Society.

John Witherspoon (1723-1794; Scotland, New Jersey) Clergyman and public official; graduated from University of Edinburgh (1739); received Divinity degree (1743); licensed to preach in Presbyterian church and was ordained (1745); received his doctorate from University of St. Andrews (1764); conservative, orthodox, and Calvinist churchman; refused call to become President of Princeton (1766) but later accepted after being requested by Benjamin Rush (1768-76); member of the Committee of Correspondence (1775); member of the Provincial Congress of New Jersey (1776); member of the Continental Congress (1776-82) where he signed the Declaration of Independence (1776); labored strongly to rebuild Princeton after the Revolution (1782-94); member of the New Jersey State Assembly (1783-89); member of the State ratification convention for the federal Constitution (1787); authored numerous theological works.

Oliver Wolcott (1726-97; Connecticut) Soldier, jurist, and public official; graduated from Yale College (1747); commissioned a captain by the Governor of New York (1747); raised a company of volunteers and served on the northwestern frontier; studied medicine; practiced law; first Sheriff of Litchfield (1751-71); member of the State Council (1774-86); judge of the County Court of Common Pleas (1774-86); Major-General of militia; appointed by the Continental Congress as one of the commissioners of Indian affairs for the Northern Department and was intrusted with the task of inducing the Iroquois Indians to remain neutral (1775); member of the Continental Congress (1776-78, 1780-83) where he signed the Declaration of Independence (1776); commander of fourteen Connecticut regiments sent for the defense of New York (1776); divided his time between Army service and congressional service; commanded a brigade of militia which took part in the defeat of General Burgoyne (1777); Lieutenant-Governor of Connecticut (1786-96); Governor (1796-97); both his father and his son served as Governors of Connecticut.

William E. Woodward (1874-1950; South Carolina) Author; after graduating from the South Carolina Military Academy (the Citadel), he went into newspaper work and advertising; become an executive vice-president and a director of several banks (1918); bored with his job, he quit and went to Paris for a year where he began to write a novel (1920); authored several novels and biographies and *New American History;* is considered a blatant revisionist.

Thomas Worthington (1773-1827; Virginia, Ohio) Public official; finished preparatory studies and went to sea; moved to Ohio (1796); member of the first and second territorial legislatures (1799-1803); delegate to the State constitutional convention (1803); U. S. Senator (1803-07, 1810-14); member of the State House (1807, 1821-22); Governor (1814-18); Canal Commissioner (1818-27); vice-president of the American Bible Society (1816-27).

John Wycliffe (c.1320-84; England) Clergyman; studied at Oxford; became master of Balliol College (1361); he discovered that a relationship with God could be obtained without the help of a priest or sacraments; he criticized the church for what he felt was folly and corruption in the clergy and felt that the church hierarchy had too much authority; taught that the Holy Scriptures were the supreme authority; the church of Rome pronounced him a heretic and declared that his teachings were dangerous (1377); England refused to deliver him up to the church; was the first person to undertake a systematic translation of the Bible into English; the full translation of the Latin Vulgate Bible into English was published after his death (1388); Wycliffe's followers become known as the Lollards; John Huss was one of his followers who helped spread his doctrine to the degree of a national religion; called "The Morning Star of the Reformation"; Luther quoted extensively from his beliefs and his emphasis on the Bible; Pope Martin V ordered Wycliffe's bones to be dug up and burned (1428).

George Wythe (1726-1806; Virginia) privately instructed by his mother; studied law at William & Mary and admitted to the bar (1746); member of the State House (1754-55, 1758-68); Mayor of Williamsburg (1768); clerk of the State House (1769-75); member of the Continental Congress (1775-76) where he signed the Declaration of Independence (1776); member of the committee to prepare a seal for Virginia (1776); Speaker of the State House (1777); Judge of State Chancery Court (1777); Chancellor of Virginia (1778); professor of law at College of William & Mary—the first chair of law at a college in America (1779-90); he trained Thomas Jefferson, John Marshall, James Monroe, and Henry Clay; selected as delegate to the Constitutional Convention but did not remain long at the Convention (1787); member of the State ratification convention for the federal Constitution (1788); moved to Richmond and formed and conducted a private law school (1791-1806); was poisoned by a greedy grand-nephew seeking his estate, but Wythe lived long enough to write that nephew out of his will.

Appendix D:
Endnotes

Chapter 1
Religion and the Courts

1. *County of Allegheny* v. *American Civil Liberties Union,* 106 L. Ed. 2d 472, 550 (1989), Kennedy, J. (concurring in the judgment in part and dissenting in part).

2. *Reynolds* v. *United States,* 98 U. S. 145, 164 (1878), and *Pierce* v. *Society of Sisters,* 268 U. S. 510, 513 (1925).

3. *Everson* v. *Board of Education,* 330 U. S. 1, 18 (1947).

4. *Engel* v. *Vitale,* 370 U. S. 421 (1962).

5. *Abington* v. *Schempp,* 374 U. S. 203 (1963).

6. *Commissioner of Education* v. *School Committee of Leyden,* 267 N. E. 2d 226 (Sup. Ct. Mass. 1971), *cert. denied,* 404 U. S. 849.

7. *Stein* v. *Oshinsky,* 348 F. 2d 999 (2nd Cir. 1965), *cert. denied,* 382 U. S. 957.

8. *Collins* v. *Chandler Unified School District,* 644 F. 2d 759 (9th Cir. 1981), *cert. denied,* 454 U. S. 863.

9. *Bishop* v. *Aronov,* 926 F. 2d 1066 (11th Cir. 1991).

10. *Duran* v. *Nitsche,* 780 F. Supp. 1048 (E.D. Pa. 1991).

11. *Stone* v. *Graham,* 449 U. S. 39 (1980).

12. *Ring* v. *Grand Forks Public School District,* 483 F. Supp. 272 (D.C. ND 1980).

13. *Lanner* v. *Wimmer,* 662 F. 2d 1349 (10th Cir. 1981).

14. *Reed* v. *van Hoven,* 237 F. Supp. 48 (W.D. Mich. 1965).

15. *Doe* v. *Aldine Independent School District,* 563 F. Supp. 883 (U.S.D.C., S.D. Tx. 1982).

16. *Lowe* v. *City of Eugene,* 451 P. 2d 117 (Sup. Ct. Or. 1969), *cert. denied,* 434 U. S. 876.

17. *Harvey* v. *Cobb County,* 811 F. Supp. 669 (N.D. Ga. 1993); *affirmed,* 15 F. 3d 1097 (11th Cir. 1994); *cert. denied,* 114 S. Ct. 2138 (1994).

18. *Harris* v. *Joint School District,* 41 F. 3d 447 (9th Cir. 1994).

19. *Warsaw* v. *Tehachapi,* CV F-90-404 EDP (U.S.D.C., E.D. Ca. 1990).

20. *Wallace* v. *Jaffree,* 472 U. S. 38, 86 (1985).

21. *Roberts* v. *Madigan,* 702 F. Supp. 1505 (D.C. Colo. 1989), 921 F. 2d 1047 (10 Cir. 1990), *cert. denied,* 112 S. Ct. 3025; 120 L. Ed. 2d 896.

22. *State of Ohio* v. *Whisner,* 351 N. E. 2d 750 (Sup. Ct. Ohio 1976).

23. *Robinson* v. *City of Edmond,* 68 F. 3d 1226 (10th Cir. 1995).

24. *Harris* v. *City of Zion,* 927 F. 2d 1401 (7th Cir. 1991), *cert. denied,* 112 S. Ct. 3054 (1992).

25. *Kuhn* v. *City of Rolling Meadows,* 927 F. 2d 1401 (7th Cir. 1991), *cert. denied,* 112 S. Ct. 3025 (1992).

26. *Friedman* v. *Board of County Commissioners,* 781 F. 2d 777 (10th Cir. 1985), *cert. denied,* 476 U. S. 1169 (1986).

27. *Jane Doe* v. *Santa Fe Independent School District,* Civil Action No. G-95-176 (U.S.D.C., S.D. Tx. 1995).

28. *Washegesic* v. *Bloomingdale Public School,* 813 F. Supp. 559 (W.D. Mi., S.D. 1993); *affirmed,* 33 F. 3d 679 (6th Cir. 1994); *cert. denied,* 63 U.S.W.L. 3786 (May 1, 1995).

29. *Florey* v. *Sioux Falls School District,* 464 F. Supp. 911 (U.S.D.C., SD 1979), *cert. denied,* 449 U. S. 987 (1980).

30. *Harris* v. *Joint School District No. 241,* 41 F. 3d 447 (9th Cir. 1994).

31. *Gearon* v. *Loudoun County School Board,* 844 F. Supp. 1097 (U.S.D.C., E.D. Va. 1993).

32. *Robert E. Lee* v. *Daniel Weisman,* 112 S. Ct. 2649; 120 L. Ed. 2d 467 (1992).

33. *Kay* v. *Douglas School District,* 719 P. 2d 875 (Or. App. 1986).

34. *Graham* v. *Central Community School District of Decatur County,* 608 F. Supp. 531 (U.S.D.C., Ia. 1985).

35. *County of Allegheny* v. *American Civil Liberties Union;* 106 L. Ed. 2d 472 (1989).

36. *Commonwealth* v. *Chambers;* 599 A. 2d 630, 643-644 (Sup. Ct. Pa. 1991), *cert. denied,* case no. 91-1597, May 26, 1992, petition for rehearing denied August 18, 1992.

37. *Alexander* v. *Nacogdoches School District,* Civil Action 9:91CV144 (U.S.D.C., E.D. Tx. 1991).

38. *The New American,* June 20, 1988, p. 19, "America Without God."

39. *Brittney Kay Settle* v. *Dickson County School Board,* 53 F. 3d 152 (6th Cir. 1995), *cert. denied,* 64 L. W. 3478 (1995); see also *Dallas Morning News,* "Court rejects case of girl who wrote Jesus paper," November 28, 1995, 4-A; picked up on wire service from *Los Angeles Times.*

40. *Gloria Iverson* v. *Forbes,* 93-3-232 (Or. Cir. Ct. 1993); *Terry Reidenbach* v. *Pethtel,* 3:93CV632 (E.D. Va. 1993); *Bebout* v. *Leimbaugh,* 93-C-1079 J (C.D. Ut. 1993).

41. *The Washington Times,* December 12, 1988, "Parent silences teaching of carols" (p. A-7), and "School officials deny banning Bible" (p. B-6).

42. *Olean Times Herald,* Monday, April 6, 1992, p. A-1; see also *State of Florida* v. *George T. Broxson,* Case no. 90-02930 CF (1st Jud. Cir. Ct., Walton County, Fl., 1992).

43. *Gierke* v. *Blotzer,* CV-88-0-883 (U.S.D.C. Neb. 1989).

44. *The Constitutions of the Several Independent States of America* (Boston: Norman and Bowen, 1785), pp. 178-179, from the Articles of Confederation.

45. William V. Wells, *The Life and Public Services of Samuel Adams* (Boston: Little, Brown, and Company, 1865), Vol. III, p. 273, to Richard Henry Lee on August 24, 1789; see also Samuel Adams, *The Writings of Samuel Adams,* Harry Alonzo Cushing, editor (New York: G. P. Putnam's Sons, 1904), Vol. IV, p. 334.

46. George Washington, *The Writings of George Washington,* Jared Sparks, editor (Boston: Ferdinand Andrews, 1838), Vol. XII, p. 4, Inaugural Speech on April 30, 1789; see also *The Debates and Proceedings of the Congress of the United States* (Washington: Gales and Seaton, 1834), Vol. I, pp. 28-29, April 30, 1789.

47. *Walz* v. *Tax Commission,* 397 U. S. 664, 701, 703 (1970), Douglas, J. (dissenting).

48. *Baer* v. *Kolmorgen,* 181 NYS 2d. 230, 237 (Sup. Ct. NY 1958).

49. *Engel* v. *Vitale,* 370 U. S. 421, 445-446 (1962), Stewart, J. (dissenting).

50. *Wallace* v. *Jaffree,* 472 U. S. 38, 92 (1984), Rehnquist, J. (dissenting).

51. *Wallace* at 107, Rehnquist, J. (dissenting).

Chapter 2
Religion and the Constitution

1. For example, see John Randolph Tucker, *The Constitution of the United States* (Chicago: Callaghan & Co., 1899), Vol. II, p. 667, § 326; see also House Report 154, March 27, 1854, House Judiciary Committee, p. 1.

2. See Noah Webster's *Sketches of American Policy* (Hartford: Hudson and Goodwin, 1785). James Madison confirms Noah Webster's call as the second, following Pelatiah Webster's call (Pelatiah Webster, *A Dissertation on the Political Union and Constitution of the Thirteen United States* (Hartford: Hudson & Goodwin, 1783)); see also James Madison, *The Papers of James Madison,* Henry D. Gilpin, editor (Washington: Langtree & O. Sullivan, 1840), Vol. II, pp. 706-708, in Madison's preface to his Notes on the Debates in the Convention.

3. Noah Webster, *The Holy Bible . . . With Amendments of the Language* (New Haven: Durrie & Peck, 1833), p. iii.

4. Thomas Jefferson, *Memoir, Correspondence, and Miscellanies, From the Papers of Thomas Jefferson*, Thomas Jefferson Randolph, editor (Boston: Gray and Bowen, 1830), Vol. IV, p. 373, to Judge William Johnson on June 12, 1823.

5. James Madison, *The Writings of James Madison*, Gaillard Hunt, editor (New York and London: G. P. Putnam's Sons, 1910), Vol. IX, p. 191, to Henry Lee on June 25, 1824.

6. James Wilson, *The Works of the Honourable James Wilson*, Bird Wilson, editor (Philadelphia: Bronson and Chauncey, 1804), Vol. I, p. 14, from "Lectures on Law Delivered in the College of Philadelphia; Introductory Lecture: Of the Study of the Law in the United States."

7. *Dictionary of American Biography*, s.v. "Story, Joseph."

8. Joseph Story, *Commentaries on the Constitution of the United States* (Boston: Hilliard, Gray, and Company, 1833), Vol. III, p. 383, §400.

9. Kate Mason Rowland, *The Life of George Mason* (New York: G. P. Putnam's Sons, 1892), Vol. I, p. 244.

10. *The Debates and Proceedings in the Congress of the United States* (Washington, D. C.: Gales and Seaton, 1834), Vol. I, p. 451, James Madison, June 8, 1789.

11. *Debates and Proceedings* (1834), Vol. I, pp. 757-759, August 15, 1789.

12. *The Debates in the Several State Conventions on the Adoption of the Federal Constitution*, Jonathan Elliot, editor (Washington, D. C.: Jonathan Elliot, 1836), Vol. IV, p. 199, Governor Samuel Johnston, July 30, 1788.

13. Elliot's *Debates*, Vol. IV, pp. 191-192, Henry Abbot, July 30, 1788.

14. Story, *Commentaries*, Vol. III, p. 731, §1873.

15. Jefferson, *Memoir*, Vol. IV, pp. 103-104, to Samuel Miller on January 23, 1808.

16. *The Constitutions of the Several Independent States of America* (Boston: Norman and Bowen, 1785), p. 4, New Hampshire, 1783, Article 1, Section 6, "Bill of Rights."

17. *A Constitution or Frame of Government Agreed Upon By the Delegates of the People of the State of Massachusetts-Bay* (Boston: Benjamin Edes & Sons, 1780), pp. 7-8, Article III "Declaration of Rights."

18. David Ramsay, *The History of the American Revolution* (Dublin: William Jones, 1795), Vol. I, p. 212.

19. John Adams, *The Works of John Adams*, Charles Frances Adams, editor (Boston: Charles C. Little and James Brown, 1851), Vol. III, p. 449, "Dissertation on the Canon and the Feudal Law."

20. Story, *Commentaries*, Vol. III, pp. 706-707, §1841-1842, quoting Blackstone.

21. John Adams and John Bowdoin, *An Address of the Convention for Framing A New Constitution of Government For the State of Massachusetts-Bay to their Constituents* (Boston: White and Adams, 1780), p. 17.

22. *Constitutions* (1785), p. 138, North Carolina, 1776, Section 32.

23. *The Constitutions of the Several States Composing the Union* (Philadelphia: Hogan and Thompson, 1838), p. 202; 1835 amendments to the North Carolina Constitution of 1776, Article 4, Section 2.

24. John Adams, *Address of the Convention*, p. 17.

25. *Constitutions* (1785), p. 4, New Hampshire, 1783, Article 1, Section 6, "Bill of Rights."

26. *Constitutions* (1785), p. 73, New Jersey, 1776, Section 19.

27. *Constitutions* (1785), p. 138, North Carolina, 1776, Section 34.

28. *Constitutions* (1838), p. 110, Connecticut, 1818, Article 7, Section 1.

29. Zephaniah Swift, *The Correspondent* (Windham: John Byrne, 1793), p. 138.

30. Kate Mason Rowland, *The Life of Charles Carroll of Carrollton, 1737–1832, With His Correspondence and Public Papers* (New York: G. P. Putnam's Sons, 1898), Vol. II, p. 357-358, to the Rev. John Stanford on October 9, 1827.

31. Joseph Story, *A Familiar Exposition of the Constitution of the United States* (New York: Harper & Brothers, 1854), p. 259-261, §441, 444; see also Story, *Commentaries,* Vol. III, p. 726, §1868.

32. *Reports of Committees of the House of Representatives Made During the First Session of the Thirty-Third Congress* (Washington: A. O. P. Nicholson, 1854), pp. 1, 6, 8-9.

33. *The Reports of Committees of the Senate of the United States for the Second Session of the Thirty-Second Congress, 1852–53* (Washington: Robert Armstrong, 1853), pp. 1-4.

34. Story, *Commentaries,* Vol. III, p. 728, §1871.

35. Benjamin Rush, *Essays, Literary, Moral and Philosophical* (Philadelphia: Thomas & Samuel F. Bradford, 1798), p. 8, "Of the Mode of Education Proper in a Republic."

36. John Adams, *Works,* Vol. X, pp. 45-46, to Thomas Jefferson on June 28, 1813.

37. Jefferson, *Memoir,* Vol. III, p. 509, from his *"Syllabus of an Estimate of the Merits of the Doctrines of Jesus, Compared with Those of Others"* sent with a letter to Benjamin Rush on April 21, 1803.

38. Swift, *Correspondent,* p. 119.

39. Benjamin Franklin, *Proposals Relating to the Education of Youth in Pennsylvania* (Philadelphia: 1749), p. 22.

40. Story, *Commentaries,* Vol. III, p. 731, §1873.

41. Elliot's *Debates,* Vol. IV, pp. 198-199, Governor Samuel Johnston, July 30, 1788.

42. Elliot's *Debates,* Vol. IV, p. 208, Richard Dobbs Spaight, July 30, 1788.

43. Elliot's *Debates,* Vol. IV, p.194, James Iredell, July 30, 1788.

44. *Torcaso* v. *Watkins,* 367 U. S. 488 (1961).

45. Leonard F. Manning, *The Law of Church-State Relations in a Nutshell* (St. Paul: West Publishing Co., 1981), p. 3.

46. *The Constitutions of the Sixteen States* (Boston: Manning and Loring, 1797), p. 282, Tennessee, 1796.

47. *Constitutions* (1797), Tennessee, 1796, p. 274, Article VIII, Section II; p. 277, Article XI, Section IV.

48. Elliot's *Debates,* Vol. IV, p. 196, James Iredell, July 30, 1788.

49. *Reports of the Proceedings and Debates of the Convention of 1821, Assembled for the Purpose of Amending The Constitution of the State of New York* (Albany: E. and E. Hosford, 1821), p. 575, Rufus King, October 30, 1821.

50. George Washington, *Address of George Washington, President of the United States . . . Preparatory to His Declination* (Baltimore: George and Henry S. Keatinge, 1796), p. 23.

51. Israel Ward Andrews, *Manual of the Constitution of the United States* (New York: Wilson, Hinkle & Co., 1874), p. 259.

52. *The Constitutions of the United States of America With the Latest Amendments* (Trenton: Moore and Lake, 1813), p. 293, Kentucky, 1799, Article VI, Section 7.

53. *The Constitutions of All the United States* (Lexington, KY: Thomas T. Skillman, 1817), p. 418, Indiana, 1816, Article XI, Section 4; see also *Church of the Holy Trinity* v. *U. S.,* 143 U. S. 457, 468 (1892).

54. James Kent, *Memoirs and Letters of James Kent,* William Kent, editor (Boston: Little, Brown, and Company, 1898), p. 164.

55. *People* v. *Ruggles,* 8 Johns 545, 546 (1811).

56. *Commonwealth* v. *Wolf,* 3 Serg. & R. 48, 50 (1817).

57. William Sullivan, *The Political Class Book* (Boston: Richardson, Lord, and Holbrook, 1831), p. 139, §392.

58. *Reports of Committees of the House*, p. 8.

59. Daniel Webster, *Mr. Webster's Speech in Defence of the Christian Ministry and in Favor of the Religious Instruction of the Young, Delivered in the Supreme Court of the United States, February 10, 1844, in the Case of Stephen Girard's Will* (Washington: Gales and Seaton, 1844), pp. 43, 51.

60. Daniel Webster, *Speech in Defence*, p. 43.

61. Joseph Story, *Life and Letters of Joseph Story*, William W. Story, editor (Boston: Charles C. Little and James Brown, 1851), Vol. II, pp. 8-9.

62. Alexis de Tocqueville, *The Republic of the United States of America and Its Political Institutions, Reviewed and Examined*, Henry Reeves, translator (New York: A. S. Barnes & Co., 1851),Vol. I, p. 334, n.

63. Swift, Vol. II, pp. 238.

64. James Coffield Mitchell, *The Tennessee Justice's Manual and Civil Officer's Guide* (Nashville: Mitchell and C. C. Norvell, 1834), pp. 457-458.

65. *Id.*

66. John Witherspoon, *The Works of John Witherspoon* (Edinburgh: J. Ogle, 1815), Vol. VII, pp. 139-140, 142, from his "Lectures on Moral Philosopy," Lecture 16 on Oaths and Vows.

67. *Dictionary of American Biography*, s.v. "George Read."

68. *Dictionary of American Biography*, s.v. "Richard Bassett."

69. *Constitutions* (1785), pp. 99-100, Delaware, 1776, Article 22.

70. *Dictionary of American Biography*, s.v. "Nathaniel Gorham."

71. *Constitution . . . of Massachusetts-Bay*, p. 44, Chapter VI, Article I.

72. *United States Code Annotated* (St. Paul: West Publishing Co., 1987), *"The Organic Laws of the United States of America,"* p. 1. This work lists America's four fundamental laws as the Articles of Confederation, the Declaration of Independence, the Constitution, and the Northwest Ordinance.

73. *Debates and Proceedings* (1834), Vol. I, p. 685, July 21, 1789.

74. *Debates and Proceedings* (1834), Vol. I, p. 57, August 4, 1789.

75. *Acts Passed at a Congress of the United States of America Begun and Held at the City of New-York, on Wednesday the Fourth of March, in the Year 1789* (Hartford: Hudson & Goodwin, 1791), p. 104, August 7, 1789.

76. *Constitutions* (1813), p. 364, "An Ordinance of the Territory of the United States Northwest of the River Ohio," Article III.

77. *Debates and Proceedings in the Congress of the United States* (Washington D. C.: Gales and Seaton, 1851), Seventh Congress, First Session, p. 1350; see also *The Public Statutes at Large of the United States of America* (Boston: Little, Brown and Company, 1854), Vol. II, p. 174, April 30, 1802.

78. *Constitutions* (1813), p. 334, Ohio, 1802, Article 8, Section 3.

79. *Acts Passed at a Congress . . . in the Year 1789*, pp. 178-179, May 26, 1790.

80. *Debates and Proceedings* (1854), Fourteenth Congress, Second Session, p. 1283, March 1, 1817; see also, *The Public Statutes at Large of the United States of America* (Boston: Little, Brown and Co., 1854), Vol. III, p. 349, March 1, 1817.

81. *The Constitutions of All the United States According to the Latest Amendments* (Lexington, KY: Thomas T. Skillman, 1817), p. 389, Mississippi, 1817, Article 9, Section 16.

82. *Laws of Arkansas Territory, Compiled and Arranged . . . Under the Direction and Superintendance of John Pope, Esq., Governor of the Territory of Arkansas* (Little Rock, Ark. Ter.: J. Steele, Esq., 1835), p. 31, "Organic Law. Chapter I, Section 14."

83. House of Representatives, Mis. Doc. No. 44, 35th Congress, 2nd Session, February 2, 1859, pp. 3-4, Article 1, Section 7, of the Kansas Constitution.

84. M. B. C. True, *A Manual of the History and Civil Government of the State of Nebraska* (Omaha: Gibson, Miller, & Richardson, 1885), p. 34, Nebraska, 1875, Article 1, Section 4..

85. States which currently have this provision include *The Constitution of North Carolina* (Raleigh: Rufus L. Edmisten, Secretary of State, 1989), p. 42, Article 9, Section 1; *Constitution of the State of Nebraska* (Lincoln: Allen J. Beermann, Secretary of State, 1992), pp. 1-2, Article 1, Section 4; *Page's Ohio Revised Code Annotated* (Cincinnati: Anderson Publishing Co., 1994), p. 24, Article 1, Section 7.

86. *Wallace v. Jaffree*, 472 U. S. 38, 113, Rehnquist, J. (dissenting).

Chapter 3
The Misleading Metaphor

1. *Wallace v. Jaffree*, 472 U. S. 38, 92 (1984), Rehnquist, J. (dissenting).

2. See, for example, John Eidsmoe, *Christianity and the Constitution* (MI: Baker Book House, 1987), p. 353, where that of all the clergy who attended the various State ratifying conventions for the federal Constitution, the **only** denomination from which the majority of its representatives voted **against** the ratification of the Constitution was the Baptists. Eidsmoe compiled the figures from a dissertation by James Hutchinson Smylie, *American Clergyman and the Constitution of the United States of America* (Princeton, 1954).

3. Thomas Jefferson, *Writings of Thomas Jefferson*, Albert Ellery Bergh, editor (Washington D. C.: The Thomas Jefferson Memorial Association, 1904), from see, for example, from Vol. XVI his letters to the Baltimore Baptist Association on October 17, 1808 (pp. 317-318); the Ketocton Baptist Association on October 18, 1808 (pp. 319-320); the Baptist Church of Buck Mountain in Albemarle on April 13, 1809 (pp. 363-363); the General Meeting of Correspondence of the Six Baptist Associations Represented at Chesterfield, Virginia on November 21, 1808 (pp. 320-321); &c.

4. Letter of October 7, 1801, from Danbury (CT) Baptist Association to Thomas Jefferson, from the Thomas Jefferson Papers Manuscript Division, Library of Congress, Washington, D. C.

5. *Id.*

6. *The Jeffersonian Cyclopedia*, John P. Foley, editor (New York: Funk & Wagnalls, 1900), p. 977; see also *Documents of American History*, Henry S. Commager, editor (NY: Appleton-Century-Crofts, Inc., 1948), p. 179.

7. *Annals of the Congress of the United States* (Washington: Gales and Seaton, 1852), Eighth Congress, Second Session, p. 78, March 4, 1805; see also James D. Richardson, *A Compilation of the Messages and Papers of the Presidents, 1789-1897* (Published by Authority of Congress, 1899), Vol. I, p. 379, March 4, 1805.

8. Jefferson, *Writings*, Vol. XVI, p. 325, to the Society of the Methodist Episcopal Church on December 9, 1808.

9. Thomas Jefferson, *Memoir, Correspondence, and Miscellanies, From the Papers of Thomas Jefferson*, Thomas Jefferson Randolph, editor (Boston: Gray and Bowen, 1830), Vol. IV, pp. 103-104, to the Rev. Samuel Millar on January 23, 1808.

10. Jefferson, *Writings*, Vol. VIII, p. 112-113, to Noah Webster on December 4, 1790.

11. Jefferson, *Memoir*, Vol. III, p. 441, to Benjamin Rush on September 23, 1800.

12. Jefferson, *Writings*, Vol. XVI, pp. 281-282, to the Danbury Baptist Association on January 1, 1802.

13. Richard Hooker, *The Works of Richard Hooker* (Oxford: University Press, 1845), Vol. I, p. 207.

14. Thomas Jefferson, *Notes on the State of Virginia* (Philadelphia: Matthew Carey, 1794), Query XVIII, p. 237.

15. *Reynolds* v. *U. S.*, 98 U. S. 145, 164 (1878).

16. *Reynolds* at 163.

17. *Commonwealth* v. *Nesbit*, 84 Pa. 398 (Pa. Sup. Ct. 1859).

18. *Lindenmuller* v. *The People*, 33 Barb 548 (Sup. Ct. NY 1861).

19. Jefferson, *Memoir*, Vol. IV, p. 104, to the Rev. Samuel Millar on January 23, 1808.

Chapter 4
The Judicial Evidence

1. *Church of the Holy Trinity* v. *U. S.*, 143 U. S. 457, 458 (1892).

2. *Holy Trinity* at 465, 471.

3. *Holy Trinity* at 465-468.

4. *Holy Trinity* at 470-471.

5. *Holy Trinity* at 470-471.

6. *Holy Trinity* at 470.

7. *Updegraph* v. *The Commonwealth*, 11 Serg & R. 393, 394 (Sup. Ct. Penn. 1824).

8. Numerous early American lawyers, legal scholars, and politicians cited Blackstone's work as a key legal source. For example, Blackstone is invoked as an authority in the writings of James Kent, James Wilson, Fisher Ames, Joseph Story, John Adams, Henry Laurens, Thomas Jefferson, John Marshall, James Madison, James Otis, *et. al.*

9. Thomas Jefferson, *The Writings of Thomas Jefferson*, Albert Ellery Bergh, editor (Washington, D. C.: The Thomas Jefferson Memorial Association, 1904), Vol. XII, p. 392, to Governor John Tyler on May 26, 1810.

10. *Updegraph* at 396, citing William Blackstone, *Commentaries on the Laws of England* (Oxford: Clarendon Press, 1769), Vol. IV, p. 59.

11. *Updegraph* at 398-399.

12. *Updegraph* at 399, 402-403, 406-407.

13. *People* v. *Ruggles*, 8 Johns 545 (Sup. Ct. NY. 1811).

14. *Ruggles* at 545.

15. *Ruggles* at 545-547.

16. *Vidal* v. *Girard's Executors*, 43 U. S. 126, 132 (1844).

17. *Vidal* at 143.

18. *Vidal* at 175.

19. *Vidal* at 152.

20. *Vidal* at 153, 171.

21. *Vidal* at 198.

22. *Vidal* at 200.

23. *Commonwealth* v. *Abner Kneeland*, 37 Mass. (20 Pick) 206, 207 (Sup. Ct. Mass. 1838).

24. *Kneeland* at 208.

25. John Bouvier, *A Law Dictionary* (Philadelphia: George W. Childs, 1870), s.v. "libel."

26. *Kneeland* at 210.

27. *Kneeland* at 217.

28. *Kneeland* at 218.

29. *Kneeland* at 219.

30. Thomas Jefferson, *Memoir, Correspondence, and Miscellanies, From the Papers of Thomas Jefferson*, Thomas Jefferson Randolph, editor (Boston: Gray and Bowen, 1830), Vol. IV, p. 27, to Abigail Adams on September 11, 1804.

31. Benjamin Franklin, *The Works of Benjamin Franklin,* John Bigelow, editor (New York: G. P. Putnam's Sons, 1904), Vol. XII, p. 131, from "An Account of the Supremest Court of Judicature in Pennsylvania, viz., The Court of the Press."

32. *Debates in the Several State Conventions on the Adoption of the Federal Constitution,* Jonathan Elliot, editor (Washington: Printed for the Editor, 1836), Vol. II, p. 449, December 1, 1787, James Wilson.

33. Joseph Story, *Commentaries on the Constitution of the United States* (Boston: Hilliard, Gray, and Company, 1833), Vol. III, pp. 731-732, §1874.

34. Benjamin Rush, *Letters of Benjamin Rush,* L. H. Butterfield, editor (Princeton University Press, 1951), Vol. I, p. 488, to Andrew Brown on October 1, 1788.

35. James Kent, *Commentaries on American Law* (New York: O. Halsted, 1827), Vol. II, pp. 17-18, Lecture XXIV, "Of the Rights of Persons," quoting Louisiana constitution, Article VI, §21.

36. Story, *Commentaries,* Vol. III, pp. 731-732, §1874.

37. *M'Creery's Lessee* v. *Allender,* 4 Harris & McHenry 256, 259 (Sup. Ct. Md. 1799).

38. *Runkel* v. *Winemiller,* 4 Harris & McHenry 276, 288 (Sup. Ct. Md. 1799).

39. John Witherspoon, *The Works of John Witherspoon* (Edinburgh: J. Ogle, 1815), Vol. VII, p. 70, from his "Lectures on Moral Philosophy," Lecture 9.

40. See, for example, Witherspoon, *Works,* Vol. IV, p. 95, from "Seasonable Advice to Young Persons," Sermon XIX, February 21, 1762; Thomas Jefferson, *Writings,* Vol. III, p. 228, April 28, 1793; John Jay, *The Correspondence and Public Papers of John Jay,* Henry P. Johnston, editor (New York: G. P. Putnam's Sons, 1893), Vol. IV, pp. 391-393, October 12, 1816; William Findley, *Observations on "The Two Sons of Oil"* (Pittsburgh: Patterson & Hopkins, 1812), pp. 22-23; *et. al.*

41. *Commonwealth* v. *Jesse Sharpless and Others,* 2 Serg. & R. 91, 92 (Sup. Ct. Penn. 1815).

42. *Sharpless* at 97, 101, 104.

43. *Davis* v. *Beason,* 133 U. S. 333, 341-343, 348 n. (1890).

44. *Murphy* v. *Ramsey,* 144 U. S. 15, 45 (1885).

45. "Governor Signs Abstinence Bill," California Voter's Guide, Vol. 5, No. 10 (Sacramento: California Coalition for Traditional Values), Fall 1988.

46. From a letter by the ACLU California Legislative Office to Senator Newton Russell dated April 18, 1988.

47. *Reynolds* v. *United States,* 98 U. S. 145, 165 (1878).

48. Thomas Jefferson, *Notes on the State of Virginia* (Philadelphia: Matthew Carey, 1794), p. 211, Query XIV.

49. See, for example, the explanations in *Lindenmuller* v. *The People,* 33 Barb 548, (Sup. Ct. NY 1861); *Melvin* v. *Easley,* 52 N.C. 276, 280 (Sup. Ct. NC 1860), Manly, J. (concurring); *Commonwealth* v. *Has* (1877); *Johnston* v. *The Commonwealth,* 22 Pa 102 (Sup. Ct. Penn. 1853); *State* v. *Williams,* 26 N.C. 296, 297 (Sup. Ct. NC 1844); *State* v. *McGee,* 75 S.E. 2d 783 (Sup. Ct. NC 1953); *Commonwealth* v. *Wolf,* 3 Serg. & R. 48 (Sup. Ct. Penn. 1817); *et al.*

50. *Melvin* at 280, Manly, J. (concurring).

51. *Johnston* at 111.

52. *Has* at 42.

53. *McGee* at 788.

54. *City Council of Charleston* v. *S.A. Benjamin,* 2 Strob. 508, 518-520 (Sup. Ct. S.C. 1846).

55. *Charleston* at 521.

56. *Charleston* at 522-524.

57. *Lindenmuller* at 561-562.

58. *Lindenmuller* at 562, 564, 567.

59. *Shover* v. *State*, 10 English 259, 263 (Sup. Ct. Ark. 1850).
60. *Commonwealth* v. *Nesbit*, 84 Pa 398, 406 (1859).
61. *Nesbit* at 406-407, 411.
62. *United States* v. *Macintosh*, 283 U. S. 605, 625 (1931).
63. *Zorach* v. *Clauson*, 343 U. S. 306, 312-314 (1952).
64. *Zorach* at 315.

Chapter 5
The Historical Evidence

1. *Church of the Holy Trinity* v. *U. S.*, 143 U. S. 457, 465, 470-471 (1892).
2. Christopher Columbus, *Christopher Columbus's Book of Prophecies*, Kay Brigham, translator (Barcelona, Spain: CLIE, 1990; Ft. Lauderdale: TSELF, 1991), pp. 178-179, 182-183.
3. *Historical Collections: Consisting of State Papers and other Authentic Documents: Intended as Materials for an History of the United States of America*, Ebenezer Hazard, editor (Philadelphia: T. Dobson, 1792), Vol. I, pp. 50-51.
4. Hazard's *Historical Collections*, Vol. I, p. 72.
5. *Holy Trinity* at 466; see also Hazard's *Historical Collections*, Vol. I, p. 119.
6. William Bradford, *History of Plymouth Plantation* (Boston: Little, Brown, and Company, 1856), p. 24.
7. John Winthrop, *The Winthrop Papers*, Stewart Mitchell, editor (Massachusetts Historical Society, 1931), Vol II, pp. 292-295, "A Model of Christian Charity," 1630.
8. Hazard's *Historical Collections*, Vol. I, p. 252.
9. Hazard's *Historical Collections*, Vol. I, pp. 327-328; see also William MacDonald, *Select Charters and Other Documents* (New York: The MacMillan Company, 1899), pp. 53-54.
10. J. Moss Ives, *The Ark and the Dove* (NY: Cooper Square Publishers, Inc., 1936, 1969), p. 119; see also Joseph Banvard, *Tragic Scenes in the History of Maryland and the Old French War* (Boston: Gould and Lincoln, 1856), p. 32.
11. *North Carolina History*, Hugh Talmage Lefler, editor (Chapel Hill: University of North Carolina Press, 1934, 1956), p. 16.
12. Hazard's *Historical Collections*, Vol. II, p. 612.
13. *A Collection of Charters and Other Public Acts Relating to the Province of Pennsylvania* (Philadelphia: B. Franklin, 1740), p. 1.
14. Benjamin Trumbull, *A Complete History of Connecticut, Civil and Ecclesiastical, From the Emigration of its First Planters from England* (Hartford: Hudson & Goodwin, 1797), pp. 528-533.
15. Hazard's *Historical Collections*, Vol. I, p. 463.
16. *The Grants, Concessions, and Original Constitutions of the Province of New-Jersey*, Aaron Leaming and Jacob Spicer, editors (Philadelphia: W. Bradford, 1758), Preface.
17. John Fiske, *The Beginnings of New England* (Boston: Houghton, Mifflin & Co., 1898), pp. 127-128.
18. *The Code of 1650, Being a Compilation of the Earliest Laws and Orders of the General Court of Connecticut* (Hartford: Silus Andrus, 1822), p. 2; see also *Holy Trinity* at 467.
19. *Code of 1650*, p. 2; see also *Holy Trinity* at 467.
20. Hazard's *Historical Collections*, Vol. I, p. 463.
21. Hazard's *Historical Collections*, Vol. II, p. 1.
22. John Locke, *A Collection of Several Pieces of Mr. John Locke Never Before Printed or Not Extant in His Works* (London: J. Bettenham for R. Francklin, 1720), pp. 41, 45, 46.

23. *A Collection of Charters*, pp. 10-12; see also Thomas Clarkson, *Memoirs of the Private and Public Life of William Penn* (London: Longman, 1813), Vol. I, p. 299-305.

24. *Code of 1650*, pp. 90-92; see also *Holy Trinity* at 467.

25. Edward Kendall, *Kendall's Travels* (New York: I. Riley, 1809), Vol. I, pp. 270-271.

26. Benjamin Pierce, *A History of Harvard University* (Cambridge, MA: Brown, Shattuck, and Company, 1833), Appendix, p. 5.

27. *The Laws of Harvard College* (Boston: Samuel Hall, 1790), pp. 7-8

28. *The Harvard Graduates' Magazine* (Manesh, WI: George Barna Publishing Co.), September 1933, p. 8, from the article "Harvard Seals and Arms" by Samuel Eliot Morison. English translation also confirmed to the author in an October 18, 1995, letter from a curatorial associate at the Harvard University Archives.

29. *The Charter and Statutes of the College of William and Mary in Virginia* (Williamsburg, VA: William Parks, 1736), p. 3.

30. *William & Mary Rules* (Richmond: Augustine Davis, 1792), p. 6

31. Noah Webster, *Letters to a Young Gentleman Commencing His Education* (New Haven: Howe & Spalding, 1823), p. 237.

32. *Documentary History of Yale University*, Franklin B. Dexter, editor (New Haven: Yale University Press, 1916), p. 27, November 11, 1701, Proceedings of the Trustees.

33. *Documentary History of Yale University*, Franklin B. Dexter, editor (New Haven: Yale University Press, 1916), p. 32, November 11, 1701, Proceedings of the Trustees.

34. Daniel Dorchester, *Christianity in the United States* (New York: Hunt and Eaton, 1890), p. 245.

35. *The Catalogue of the Library of Yale College in New Haven* (New London: T. Green, 1743), prefatory remarks; see also *The Catalogue of the Library of Yale College in New Haven* (New Haven: James Parker, 1755), prefatory remarks.

36. *The Laws of Yale College in New Haven in Connecticut* (New Haven: Josiah Meigs, 1787), pp. 5-6, Chapter II, Article 1, 4.

37. *Appleton's Cyclopedia of American Biography*, James Grant Wilson and John Fiske, editors (New York: D. Appleton and Company, 1888), s. v. "Aaron Burr," "Timothy Edwards/Jonathan Edwards," Samuel Davies," and "Samuel Finley."

38. *The Laws of the College of New-Jersey* (Trenton: Isaac Collins, 1794), pp. 28-29.

39. See, for example, Rufus Choate, *A Discourse Delivered Before The Faculty, Students, and Alumni of Dartmouth College* (Boston: James Monroe and Company, 1853), p. 33, where he declares that Daniel Webster's arguments in *Dartmouth College* v. *Woodward*, 17 U. S. 518 (1819), "established the inviolability of the charter of Dartmouth College."

40. *The Charter of Dartmouth College* (Dresden: Isaiah Thomas, 1779), pp. 1, 4.

41. *Columbia Rules* (New York: Samuel Loudon, 1785), pp. 5-8.

42. Edwards Beardsley, *Life and Times of William Samuel Johnson* (Boston: Houghton, Mifflin and Company, 1886), pp. 141-142.

43. *Rutgers' Fact Book of 1965* (New Jersey: Rutgers University, 1965), p. 2. (The motto was based on the Bible verses of Malachi 4:2 and Matthew 13:43.)

44. E. P. Cubberley, *Public Education in the United States* (Boston: Houghton, Mifflin Co., 1919), p. 204; see also Luther A. Weigle, *The Pageant of America: American Idealism*, Ralph Henry Gabriel, editor (Yale University Press, 1928), Vol. X, p. 315.

45. George Washington, *The Writings of Washington*, John C. Fitzpatrick, editor (Washington, D. C.: U. S. Government Printing Office, 1932), Vol. XV, p. 55, from his speech to the Delaware Indian Chiefs on May 12, 1779.

46. *Id.*

47. James Otis, *The Rights of the British Colonies Asserted and Proved* (Boston: J. Williams 1766), pp. 11, 12, 13, 98.

48. John Dickinson, *The Political Writings of John Dickinson* (Wilmington: Bonsal and Niles, 1801), Vol. I, pp. 111-112.

49. Stephen Hopkins, *The Rights of Colonies Examined* (Providence: William Goddard, 1765), pp. 23-24.

50. John Witherspoon, *The Works of John Witherspoon* (Edinburgh: J. Ogle, 1815), Vol. IX, p. 250, "The Druid," Number III.

51. Samuel Adams, *The Writings of Samuel Adams,* Harry Alonzo Cushing, editor (New York: G. P. Putnam's Sons, 1904), Vol. IV, p. 38, to the Earl of Carlisle and Others on July 16, 1778.

52. Samuel Adams, *Writings,* Vol. IV, p. 86, "Manifesto of the Continental Congress" on October 30, 1778.

53. John Quincy Adams, *An Address Delivered at the Request of the Committee of Arrangements for the Celebrating the Anniversary of Independence at the City of Washington on the Fourth of July 1821 upon the Occasion of Reading The Declaration of Independence* (Cambridge: Hilliard and Metcalf, 1821), p. 28.

54. Francis Hopkinson, *The Miscellaneous Essays and Occasional Writings of Francis Hopkinson, Esq.* (Philadelphia: T. Dobson, 1792), Vol. I, pp. 111-116.

55. Samuel Adams, *The Life and Public Services of Samuel Adams,* William V. Wells, editor (Boston: Little, Brown, and Company, 1865), Vol. I, pp. 496-497.

56. Samuel Adams, *Life,* Vol. I, p. 504.

57. Hezekiah Niles, *Principles and Acts of the Revolution in America* (Baltimore: William Ogden Niles, 1822), p. 198.

58. John R. Musick, *John Hancock* (Chicago: H. G. Campbell Publishing Company, 1898), pp. 118, 156.

59. *The Annual Register, or a View of the History, Politics, and Literature, from the Year 1775* (London: J. Dodsley, 1776), p. 5.

60. Mercy Otis Warren, *History of the Rise, Progress and Termination of the American Revolution, Interspersed with Biographical, Political and Moral Observations* (Boston: E. Larkin, 1805), Vol. I, p. 133.

61. George Bancroft, *History of the United States* (Boston: Little, Brown and Company, 1858), Vol. VII, p. 99.

62. David Ramsay, *The History of the American Revolution* (Dublin: William Jones, 1795), Vol. I, p. 107.

63. *The Journals of the American Congress, from 1774 to 1788* (Washington, D. C.: Way and Gideon, 1823), Vol. I, p. 8, September 6, 1774.

64. *Journals of Congress* (1823), Vol. I, p. 8, September 7, 1774.

65. John Adams, *Letters of John Adams, Addressed to His Wife,* Charles Francis Adams, editor (Boston: Charles C. Little and James Brown, 1841), Vol. I, pp. 23-24, to Abigail Adams on September 16, 1774.

66. *Boston Gazette,* September 26, 1774, containing an extract of a letter from Samuel Adams to Joseph Warren on September 9, 1774; see also *Letters of the Delegates to the Continental Congress,* Paul H. Smith, editor (Washington D. C.: Library of Congress, 1976), Vol. I, p. 55.

67. John Adams, *The Works of John Adams, Second President of the United States,* Charles Francis Adams, editor (Boston: Little, Brown and Company, 1850), Vol. II, p. 378, from his diary entry of September 10, 1774; see also *Letters of Delegates,* Vol. I, p. 60.

68. *Letters of Delegates,* Vol. I, p. 45, from Samuel Ward's diary for September 7, 1774.

69. Silas Deane, *The Deane Papers: Collections of the New York Historical Society for the Year 1886* (New York: Printed for the Society, 1887), Vol. I, p. 20, Wednesday, September 7, 1774; see also *Letters of Delegates,* Vol. I, p. 35.

70. *Letters of Delegates,* Vol. I, p. 35, from James Duane's "Notes of the Debates in Congress," September 7, 1774.

71. *Id.*

72. John Adams, *Letters,* Vol. I, pp. 23-24, to Abigail Adams on September 16, 1774.

73. Deane, Vol. I, p. 20, September 7, 1774; see also *Letters of Delegates,* Vol. I, p. 35.

74. John Adams, *Works,* Vol. II, p. 368, diary entry for September 7, 1774.

75. *The Journals of Each Provincial Congress of Massachusetts in 1774 and 1775,* William Lincoln, editor (Boston: Dutton and Wentworth, 1838), p. 71, December 10, 1774.

76. *Journals of . . . Massachusetts,* p. 70, December 10, 1774.

77. Richard Frothingham, *Rise of the Republic of the United States* (Boston: Little, Brown & Co., 1872), p. 393.

78. Dorchester, pp. 264-265

79. William Wirt, *Sketches of the Life and Character of Patrick Henry* (Philadelphia: James Webster, 1818), pp. 121-123.

80. *Journals of . . . Massachusetts,* pp. 144-145, proclamation of John Hancock from Concord, April 15, 1775.

81. A. G. Arnold, *The Life of Patrick Henry of Virginia* (Auburn and Buffalo: Miller, Orton and Mulligan, 1854), pp. 118-119.

82. Hugh Moore, *Memoir of Col. Ethan Allen* (Plattsburgh, NY: O. R. Cook, 1834), pp. 94-95.

83. *Journals of Congress* (1823), Vol. I, pp. 81-82, June 12, 1775.

84. John Adams, *Letters,* Vol. I, p. 46, to Abigail Adams on June 17, 1775.

85. Witherspoon, *Works* (1815), Vol. IV, p. 170, from "A Pastoral Letter . . . to be read from the Pulpits on Thursday, June 29, 1775, being the day of the General Fast."

86. *Journals of Congress* (1823), Vol. I, p. 90, June 30, 1775. Furthermore, George Washington ordered that the Articles of War be read to the soldiers weekly—see George Washington, *Writings* (1931), Vol. IV, p. 527, from General Orders of April 28, 1776.

87. *Journals of the Continental Congress* (Washington: Government Printing Office, 1905), Vol. II, p. 192, July 19, 1775.

88. *House Journals, 1775. A Journal of the . . . House of Representatives* (Watertown, MA: 1776), pp. 196-197, April 29, 1776.

89. *Journals of Congress* (1906), Vol. IV, p. 201, March 13, 1776.

90. *Journals of Congress* (1905), Vol. IV, pp. 208-209, May 17, 1776.

91. Benjamin Rush, *Letters of Benjamin Rush,* L. H. Butterfield, editor (NJ: American Philosophical Society, 1951), Vol. I, pp. 532-536, to John Adams on February 24, 1790.

92. John Adams, *Letters,* Vol. I, pp. 123-125, to Abigail Adams on July 3, 1776.

93. John Adams, *Letters,* Vol. I, p. 128, to Abigail Adams on July 3, 1776.

94. John Adams, *Letters,* Vol. I, p. 128, to Abigail Adams on July 3, 1776.

95. John Adams, *Letters,* Vol. I, p. 152, to Abigail Adams on August 14, 1776.

96. John Adams, *Letters,* Vol. I, p. 152, to Abigail Adams on August 14, 1776.

97. *Journals of Congress* (1906), Vol. V, p. 530, July 9, 1776.

98. James Thacher, *A Military Journal* (Boston: Richardson and Lord, 1823), p. 145; see also B. F. Morris, *The Christian Life and Character of the Civil Institutions of the United States* (Philadelphia: George W. Childs, 1864), p. 213, and J. T. Headly, *The Chaplains of the Revolution* (Springfield: G. & F. Bill, 1861), pp. 58-86.

99. Washington, *Writings* (1932), Vol. V, pp. 244-245, July 9, 1776. This statement of George Washington was also used by Abraham Lincoln in his November 15, 1862, order to his troops to maintain regular Sabbath observances; see also Abraham Lincoln, *Letters and Addresses and Abraham Lincoln* (NY: Unit Book Publishing Co., 1907), p. 261.

100. *Journals of . . . Congress* (1907), Vol VIII, p. 536, July 7, 1777.

101. *Journals of . . . Congress* (1907), Vol. VIII, p. 734, September 11, 1777.

102. *Journals of . . . Congress* (1907), Vol. VIII, p. 735, September 11, 1777.

103. *Journals of . . . Congress* (1907), Vol. IX, p. 851, October 31, 1777.

104. *Journals of . . . Congress* (1907), Vol. IX, 1777, pp. 854-855, November 1, 1777.

105. John Adams, *Letters*, Vol. II, pp. 18-19, to Abigail Adams on December 15, 1777.

106. Peter Powers, *Jesus Christ the True King and Head of Government. A Sermon Preached Before the General Assembly of the State of Vermont, on the Day of their First Election, March 12, 1778 at Windsor* (Newburyport: John Mycall, 1778), p. 29.

107. See Powers, *Jesus Christ the True King*, which contains this copy of the Assembly's resolution: State of Vermont, In General Assembly, March 13, 1778: "This Assembly have this day appointed Col. John Barret, and Capt. John G. Bayley, a Committee to wait on the Rev. Mr. Peter Powers with the thanks of this House for his Sermon delivered them yesterday, at the opening of this session, and to request a copy thereof for the press."

108. John Adams, *Works*, Vol. X, p. 284, to Hezekiah Niles on February 13, 1818.

109. Paul Wallace, *The Muhlenbergs of Pennsylvania* (Pittsburg: University of Pennsylvania Press, 1950), p. 118; see also Henry A. Muhlenberg, *The Life of Major-General Peter Muhlenberg of the Revolutionary Army* (Philadelphia: Carey and Hart, 1849), p. 53.

110. Wallace, p. 118; see also Muhlenberg, p. 53.

111. Muhlenberg, pp. 53-54.

112. Muhlenberg, p. 456; *see also Appleton's Cyclopedia of American Biography* (New York: D. Appleton and Company, 1888), s.v. "John Peter Muhlenberg."

113. Dorchester, pp. 264-265

114. Peter Oliver, *Peter Oliver's Origin & Progress of the American Rebellion*, Douglass Adair and John A. Schutz, editors (San Marino, California: The Huntington Library, 1961), pp. 29, 41-45; see also Carl Bridenbaugh, *Mitre and Sceptre* (New York: Oxford University Press, 1962), p. 334.

115. John Wingate Thornton, *Pulpit of the American Revolution* (Boston: Gould and Lincoln, 1860).

116. J. T. Headly, *The Chaplains and Clergy of the Revolution* (MA: G. & F. Bill, 1861).

117. *The Patriot Preachers of the American Revolution, With Biographical Sketches, 1766-1783* (Printed for the Subscribers, 1860).

118. Washington, *Writings* (1932), Vol. XI, pp. 342-343, General Orders of May 2, 1778.

119. George Washington, *The Writings of George Washington*, Jared Sparks, editor (Boston: American Stationers' Company, 1838), Vol. VI, p. 36, to Brigadier General Nelson on August 20, 1778.

120. *Journals of Congress* (1823), Vol. III, p. 85, October 12, 1778.

121. Washington, *Writings* (1932), Vol. XX, pp. 94-95, General Orders of September 26, 1780.

122. *Journals of . . . Congress* (1910), Vol. XVIII, p. 919, October 13, 1780.

123. *Journals of . . . Congress* (1910), Vol. XVIII, pp. 950-951, October 18, 1780.

124. Samuel Adams, *Writings*, Vol. IV, p. 189, Samuel Adams article signed "Vindex" in *Boston Gazette* on June 12, 1780.

125. Memorial of Robert Aitken to Congress, 21 January 1781, obtained from the National Archives, Washington, D. C.; see also the introduction to the *Holy Bible As Printed by Robert Aitken and Approved & Recommended by the Congress of the United States of America in 1782* (Philadelphia: R. Aitken, 1782) or the New York Arno Press reprint of 1968.

126. *Journals of . . . Congress* (1914), Vol. XXIII, p. 572, September 12, 1782..

127. *The New Annual Register, or General Repository of History, Politics, and Literature, for the Year 1781* (London: G. Robinson, 1782), pp. 169-170.

128. *Journals of . . . Congress* (1823), Vol. III, p. 679, October 24, 1781.

129. *Journals of . . . Congress* (1914), Vol. XXIII, p. 573, September 1, 1782.

130. *Journals of . . . Congress* (1914), Vol. XXIII, p. 574, September 12, 1782; see also cover page of the "Bible of the Revolution," either the 1782 original or the 1968 reprint by Arno Press.

131. *Journals of . . . Congress* (1914), Vol. XXIII, p. 574, September 12, 1782.

132. W. P. Strickland, *History of the American Society from its Organization to the Present Time* (New York: Harper and Brothers, 1849), pp. 20–21.

133. Washington, *Writings* (1938), Vol. XXVI, p. 467, to Superintendent of Finance Robert Morris on June 3, 1783.

134. George Washington, *The Last Official Address of His Excellency George Washington to the Legislature of the United States* (Hartford: Hudson and Goodwin, 1783), p. 12; see also *The New Annual Register or General Repository of History, Politics, and Literature, for the Year 1783* (London: G. Robinson, 1784), p. 150.

135. *Annual Register for the Year 1783*, p. 113. Opening line of final Treaty of Peace.

136. *Journals of . . . Congress* (1914), Vol. XXV, p. 699, October 18, 1783.

137. *Journals of . . . Congress* (1914), Vol. XXV, p. 699, proclamation for October 18, 1793.

138. John Hancock, *A Proclamation for a Day of Thanksgiving* (Boston, 1783) for November 8, 1783.

139. *Thanksgiving Proclamation of November 11, 1783* (Trenton: Issac Collins, 1783).

140. See the Thanksgiving Proclamation of October 30, 1783 by the President and the Supreme Executive Council of the Commonwealth of Pennsylvania, *A Proclamation* (Philadelphia: Francis Bailey, 1783).

141. See the *Journals of Congress* (1833) for June 12, 1775; March 16, 1776; December 11, 1776; November 1, 1777; March 7, 1778; November 17, 1778; March 20, 1779; October 20, 1779; March 11, 1780; October 18, 1780; March 20, 1781; October 26, 1781; March 19, 1782; October 11, 1782; October 18, 1783.

142. James Madison, *The Papers of James Madison*, Henry D. Gilpin, editor (Washington: Langtree and O'Sullivan, 1840), Vol. II, pp. 984–986, June 28, 1787.

143. Madison, *Papers* (1840), Vol. II, p. 986, June 28, 1787.

144. Madison, *Papers* (1840), Vol. II, p. 986, June 28, 1787.

145. Madison, *Papers* (1840), Vol. II, p. 986, June 28, 1787.

146. Luther Martin, *The Genuine Information* (Philadelphia: Eleazer Oswald, 1788), pp. 56–57; see also *The Debates in the Several State Conventions*, Jonathan Elliot, editor (Washington, D. C.: Printed for the Editor, 1836), Vol. I, p. 373, from Luther Martin's "Letter on the Federal Convention of 1787," January 27, 1788, delivered to the Maryland State Legislature.

147. Madison, *Papers* (1840), Vol. II, p. 986, June 28, 1787.

148. Madison, *Papers* (1840), Vol. II, pp. 1023–1024, July 4, 1787.

149. George Washington, *The Diaries of George Washington*, John C. Fitzpatrick, editor (New York: Houghton Mifflin Co., 1925), Vol. III, p. 226, July 4, 1787.

150. Morris, pp. 253–254.

151. Benjamin Franklin, *The Works of Benjamin Franklin*, Jared Sparks, editor (Boston: Tappan, Whittemore, and Mason, 1837), Vol. V, p. 162, from "A Comparison of the Conduct of the Ancient Jews and of the Anti-Federalists in the United States of America."

152. Washington, *Writings* (1932), Vol. XXX, p. 321 n., May 10, 1789.

153. *The Debates in the Several Conventions, on the Adoption of the Federal Constitution*, Jonathan Elliot, editor (Washington: Printed for the Editor, 1836), Vol. II, p. 2, Massachusetts Convention, January 9, 1788.

154. Elliot, *Debates*, Vol. II, p. 207, New York Convention, June 17, 1788.

155. Elliot, *Debates*, Vol. III, p. 1, Virginia Convention, June 2, 1788.

156. Elliot, _Debates_, Vol. IV, p. 1, North Carolina Convention, July 21, 1788; see also Vol. II, p. 2, Masschusetts Convention, January 9, 1788.

157. _The Daily Advertiser_, New York, Thursday, April 23, 1789, p. 2.

158. _Annals of Congress_ (1834), Vol. I, p. 25, April 27, 1789.

159. _Annals of Congress_ (1834), Vol. I, p. 241, April 29, 1789.

160. _Annals of Congress_ (1834) Vol. I, pp. 27-28, April 30, 1789.

161. _Annals of Congress_ (1834) Vol. I, p. 29, April 30, 1789.

162. _Annals of Congress_ (1834) Vol. I, pp. 949-950, September 25, 1789.

163. Washington, _Writings_ (1838), Vol. XII, pp. 119-120, October 3, 1789; see also James D. Richardson, _A Compilation of the Messages and Papers of the Presidents, 1789-1897_ (Published by Authority of Congress, 1899), Vol. I, p. 64, October 3, 1789.

164. Washington, _Writings_ (1838), Vol. XII, p. 167, to the Synod of the Reformed Dutch Church of North America in October 1789.

165. Washington, _Writings_ (1838), Vol. X, pp. 222-223, to John Armstrong on March 11, 1792.

166. George Washington, _Address of George Washington, President of the United States . . . Preparatory to His Declination_ (Baltimore: George and Henry S. Keatinge, 1796), pp. 22-23.

167. James Kent, _Memoirs and Letters of James Kent_, William Kent, editor (Boston: Little, Brown, and Company, 1898), p. 123.

168. _The Documentary History of the Supreme Court of the United States, 1789-1800_, Maeva Marcus, editor (New York: Columbia University Press, 1988), Vol. II, p. 11.

169. _The Documentary History of the Supreme Court_, Vol. II, p. 13, from John Jay to Richard Law on March 10, 1790.

170. _New Hampshire Gazette_ (Portsmouth), May 26, 1791; see also _Documentary History of the Supreme Court_, Vol. II, p. 192.

171. _Columbian Centinel_ (Boston), May 16, 1792, p. 74; see also _Documentary History of the Supreme Court_, Vol. II, p. 276.

172. _The Documentary History of the Supreme Court_, Vol. II p. 412, from the _Newport Mercury_ (Rhode Island) of June 25, 1793.

173. _United States Oracle_ (Portsmouth, NH), May 24, 1800; see also _The Documentary History of the Supreme Court_, Vol. III, p. 436.

174. _The Debates and Proceedings in the Congress of the United States_ (Washington: Gales and Seaton, 1851), Sixth Congress, Second Session, p. 797, December 4, 1800.

175. John Quincy Adams, _Memoirs of John Quincy Adams_, Charles Francis Adams, editor (Philadelphia: J. B. Lippincott and Company, 1874), Vol. I, p. 268, October 30, 1803.

176. John Quincy Adams, _Memoirs_, Vol. I, p. 265, October 23, 1803.

177. Kendall, Vol. I, pp. 3-5.

178. John Quincy Adams, _Memoirs_, Vol. I, p. 251, May 26, 1802.

179. Alexis de Tocqueville, _The Republic of the United States of America and Its Political Institutions, Reviewed and Examined_, Henry Reeves, translator (Garden City, NY: A. S. Barnes & Co., 1851), Vol. I, p. 337.

180. Achille Murat, _A Moral and Political Sketch of the United States_ (London: Effingham Wilson, 1833), p. 142.

181. Murat, pp. 113, 132.

182. Murat, p. 111.

183. Harriet Martineau, _Society in America_ (New York: Saunders and Otley, 1837), Vol. II, pp. 317-318.

184. Martineau, Vol. II, p. 366.

185. _Holy Trinity_ at 465, 470, 471.

Chapter 6
The Religious Nature of the Founding Fathers

1. See Noah Webster's *Sketches of American Policy* (Hartford: Hudson and Goodwin, 1785). James Madison confirms Noah Webster's call as the second, following Pelatiah Webster's call (Pelatiah Webster, *A Dissertation on the Political Union and Constitution of the Thirteen United States* (Hartford: Hudson & Goodwin, 1783)); see also James Madison, *The Papers of James Madison,* Henry D. Gilpin, editor (Washington: Langtree & O. Sullivan, 1840), Vol. II, pp. 706-708, in Madison's preface to his Notes on the Debates in the Convention.

2. See, for example, Noah Webster, *An American Dictionary of the English Language* (Springfield, MA: George and Charles Merriam, 1849), p. xvi, from "Memoir of the Author." Furthermore, Webster's diaries record visits from delegates George Washington, Benjamin Franklin, James Madison, Rufus King, Abraham Baldwin, Edmund Randolph, William Samuel Johnson, Oliver Ellsworth, Roger Sherman, and William Livingston during the Convention.

3. *American Heritage Dictionary, 2nd College Edition,* s.v. "atheism."

4. *Id.,* s.v. "agnostic."

5. *Id.,* s.v. "deism"; see also *American College Dictionary* (1947), s.v. "deism."

6. *Webster's New World Dictionary of the American Language* (1964), see synonym for "deist"; *Webster's Seventh New Collegiate Dictionary* (1963), see synonym for "atheism"; *The Century Dictionary and Cyclopedia* (1895), Vol. I, see synonym for "atheist"; *Funk & Wagnalls Standard Dictionary of the English Language* (1966), see synonyms for "skeptic."

7. Society of Separationists, "Did you know that these great American thinkers all rejected Christianity?" (Austin, TX: American Atheist Center); see also *Los Angeles Times,* August 3, 1995, p. B-9, "America's Unchristian Beginnings," Steven Morris.

8. John Adams, *The Works of John Adams, Second President of the United States,* Charles Francis Adams, editor (Boston: Little, Brown and Company, 1856), Vol. X, p. 254, to Thomas Jefferson on April 19, 1817.

9. *Id.*

10. Thomas Jefferson, *Memoir, Correspondence, and Miscellanies, From the Papers of Thomas Jefferson,* Thomas Jefferson Randolph, editor (Boston: Gray and Bowen, 1830), Vol. IV, p. 301, to John Adams on May 5, 1817.

11. *Naval Documents Related to the United States Wars with the Barbary Powers,* Claude A. Swanson, editor (Washington: Government Printing Office, 1939), Vol. I, p. V.

12. Glen Tucker, *Dawn Like Thunder: The Barbary Wars and the Birth of the U. S. Navy* (Indianapolis: Bobbs-Merrill Company, 1963), p. 127.

13. *A General View of the Rise, Progress, and Brilliant Achievements of the American Navy, Down to the Present Time* (Brooklyn, 1828), pp. 70-71.

14. Tucker, p. 50.

15. President Washington selected Col. David Humphreys in 1793 as sole commissioner of Algerian affairs to negotiate treaties with Algeria, Tripoli and Tunis. He also appointed Joseph Donaldson, Jr., as Consul to Tunis and Tripoli. In February of 1796, Humphreys delegated power to Donaldson and/or Joel Barlow to form treaties. James Simpson, U. S. Consul to Gibraltar, was dispatched to renew the treaty with Morocco in 1795. On October 8, 1796, Barlow commissioned Richard O'Brien to negotiate the treaty of peace with Tripoli. See, for example, Ray W. Irwin, *The Diplomatic Relations of the United States with the Barbary Powers* (Chapel Hill: The University of North Carolina Press, 1931), p. 84.

16. J. Fenimore Cooper, *The History of the Navy of the United States of America* (Philadelphia: Thomas, Cowperthwait & Co., 1847), pp. 123-124; see also *A Compilation of the Messages and Papers of the Presidents: 1789-1897,* James D. Richardson, editor (Washington, D. C.: Published by Authority of Congress, 1899), Vol. I, pp. 201-202, from Washington's Eighth Annual Address of December 7, 1796.

17. See, for example, the treaty with **Morocco:** ratified by the United States on July 18, 1787. *Treaties and Other International Agreements of the United States of America: 1776-1949,* Charles I. Bevans, editor (Washington, D. C.: Department of State, 1968-1976), Vol. IX, pp. 1278-1285; **Algiers:** concluded September 5, 1795; ratified by the U. S. Senate March 2, 1796; see also, "Treaty of Peace and Amity" concluded June 30 and July 6, 1815; proclaimed December 26, 1815, *Treaties and Conventions Concluded Between the United States of America and Other Powers Since July 4, 1776* (Washington, D. C.: Government Printing Office, 1889), pp. 1-15; **Tripoli:** concluded November 4, 1796; ratified June 10, 1797; see also, "Treaty of Peace and Amity" concluded June 4, 1805; ratification advised by the U. S. Senate April 12, 1806. *Treaties, Conventions, International Acts, Protocols and Agreements between the United States of America and Other Powers: 1776-1909,* William M. Malloy, editor (Washington, D. C.: Government Printing Office, 1910), Vol. II, pp. 1785-1793; **Tunis:** concluded August 1797; ratification advised by the Senate, with amendments, March 6, 1798; alterations concluded March 26, 1799; ratification again advised by the Senate December 24, 1799. *Treaties, Conventions, International Acts, Protocols and Agreements between the United States of America and Other Powers: 1776-1909,* William M. Malloy, editor (Washington, D. C.: Government Printing Office, 1910), Vol. II, pp. 1794-1799.

18. Gardner W. Allen, *Our Navy and the Barbary Corsairs* (Boston: Houghton, Mifflin and Company, 1905), pp. 33, 45, 56, 60.

19. Allen, p. 66.

20. Allen, p. 57.

21. Allen, p. 56.

22. (See general bibliographic information from footnote 17 for each of these references) **Morocco:** see Articles 10, 11, 17, and 24; **Algiers:** See Treaty of 1795, Article 17, and Treaty of 1815, Article 17; **Tripoli:** See Treaty of 1796, Article 11, and Treaty of 1805, Article 14; **Tunis:** See forward to Treaty.

23. *Acts Passed at the First Session of the Fifth Congress of the United States of America* (Philadelphia: William Ross, 1797), pp. 43-44.

24. John Jay, *Correspondence and Public Papers of John Jay,* Henry P. Johnston, editor (New York: G. P. Putnam's Sons, 1893), Vol. IV, p. 491, Address to the Annual Meeting of the American Bible Society, May 8, 1823.

25. John Quincy Adams, *An Oration Delivered Before the Inhabitants of the Town of Newburyport at Their Request on the Sixty-First Anniversary of the Declaration of Independence* (Newburyport: Charles Whipple, 1837), p. 17.

26. John Adams, *Works,* Vol. IX, p. 121, in a speech to both houses of Congress, November 23, 1797.

27. Noah Webster, *History of the United States* (New Haven: Durrie & Peck, 1832), p. 339.

28. Daniel Webster, *Mr. Webster's Speech in Defence of the Christian Ministry and In favor of the Religious Instruction of the Young. Delivered in the Supreme Court of the United States, February 10, 1844, in the Case of Stephen Girard's Will* (Washington: Gales and Seaton, 1844), p. 52.

29. John Adams, *Works,* Vol. VIII, p. 407, to Thomas Jefferson on July 3, 1786.

30. John Adams, *Works,* Vol. X, pp. 45-46, to Thomas Jefferson on June 28, 1813.

31. Charles Prentiss, *The Life of the Late Gen. William Eaton: Several Years an Officer in the United States' Army Consul at the Regency of Tunis on the Coast of Barbary, and Commander of the Christian and Other Forces that Marched from Egypt Through the Desert of Barca,*

in 1805, and Conquered the City of Derne, Which Led to the Treaty of Peace Between the United States and the Regency of Tripoli (Brookfield: Merriam & Company, 1813), pp. 92-93, from General Eaton to Timothy Pickering, June 15, 1799.

32. Prentiss, p. 146, from General Eaton to Mr. Smith, June 27, 1800.

33. Prentiss, p. 150, from General Eaton to Timothy Pickering on July 4, 1800.

34. Prentiss, p. 185, from General Eaton to General John Marshall, September 2, 1800.

35. Prentiss, p. 325, from Eaton's journal, April 8, 1805.

36. Prentiss, p. 334, from Eaton's journal, May 23, 1805.

37. Prentiss.

38. Benjamin Franklin, *The Works of Benjamin Franklin,* Jared Sparks, editor (Boston: Tappan, Whittemore and Mason, 1840), Vol. X, pp. 281-282, to Thomas Paine in 1790.

39. John Adams, *Works,* Vol. III, p. 421, diary entry for July 26, 1796.

40. John Adams, *Works,* Vol. IX, p. 73, to John Marshall on August 11, 1800.

41. William V. Wells, *The Life and Public Services of Samuel Adams* (Boston: Little, Brown, and Company, 1865), Vol. III, pp. 372-373, to Thomas Paine on November 30, 1802.

42. Benjamin Rush, *Letters of Benjamin Rush,* L. H. Butterfield, editor (Princeton: Princeton University Press, 1951), Vol. II, p. 770, to John Dickinson on February 16, 1796.

43. Joseph Gurn, *Charles Carroll of Carrollton* (New York: P. J. Kennedy & Sons, 1932), p. 203.

44. John Witherspoon, *The Works of the Reverend John Witherspoon* (Philadelphia: William W. Woodward, 1802), Vol. III, p. 24, n. 2, from "The Dominion of Providence over the Passions of Men," delivered at Princeton on May 17, 1776.

45. John Quincy Adams, *An Answer to Pain's* [sic] *"Rights of Man"* (London: John Stockdale, 1793), p. 13.

46. Elias Boudinot, *The Age of Revelation* (Philadelphia: Asbury Dickins, 1801), pp. xii-xiv, from the prefatory remarks to his daughter, Mrs. Susan V. Bradford.

47. S. G. Arnold, *The Life of Patrick Henry of Virginia* (Auburn and Buffalo: Miller, Orton and Mulligan, 1854), p. 250, to his daughter Betsy on August 20, 1796.

48. George Morgan, *Patrick Henry* (Philadelphia: J. B. Lippincott Company, 1929), p. 366 n; see also, Bishop William Meade, *Old Churches, Ministers, and Families of Virginia* (Philadelphia: J. B. Lippincott Company, 1857), Vol. II, p. 12.

49. John E. O'Conner, *William Paterson: Lawyer and Statesman* (New Brunswick: Rutgers University Press, 1979), p. 244, from a Fourth of July Oration in 1798.

50. Zephaniah Swift, *A System of Laws of the State of Connecticut* (Windham: John Byrne, 1796), Vol. II, pp. 323-324.

51. William Jay, *Life,* Vol. II, p. 266, to the Rev. Uzal Ogden on February 14, 1796.

52. *Dictionary of American Biography,* s.v. "Thomas Paine."

53. Thomas Paine, *The Age of Reason* (Philadelphia: The Booksellers, 1794), p. 8.

54. Noah Webster, *An American Dictionary of the English Language* (1828), s.v. "infidelity."

55. Benjamin Franklin, *Two Tracts: Information to Those Who Would Remove to America and Remarks Concerning the Savages of North America* (London: John Stockdale, 1784), p. 24.

56. Paine, p. 9.

57. Ethan Allen, *Reason the Only Oracle of Man* (Bennington, Vermont: Haswell & Russell, 1784), also called, "The Deist's Bible."

58. Charles Lee, *Anecdotes of the Late Charles Lee, Esq. [and His] Letters* (London: J. S. Jordon, 1797), pp. 189-194; see especially his will.

59. Daniel Dorchester, *Christianity in the United States from the First Settlement Down to the Present Time* (New York: Hunt & Eaton, 1890), pp. 316-317.

60. Copies of these wills are in our files; they may be obtained from various state archives and historical societies.

61. John Adams and John Quincy Adams, *The Selected Writings of John and John Quincy Adams*, Adrienne Koch and William Peden, editors (New York: Alfred A. Knopf, 1946), p. 292, John Quincy Adams to John Adams, January 3, 1817.

62. Gunning Bedford, *Funeral Oration Upon the Death of General George Washington* (Wilmington: James Wilson, 1800), p. 18.

63. Rolla P. Andrae, *A True, Brief History of Daniel Boone* (Defiance, MO: Daniel Boone Home, 1985), p. 59, to Sarah Boone in October 1816.

64. *Letters of the Delegates to Congress: 1774-1789*, Paul H. Smith, editor (Washington, D. C.: Library of Congress, 1992), Vol. XIX, p. 325, from a letter of Elias Boudinot to his daughter, Susan Boudinot, on October 30, 1782; see also, Elias Boudinot, *The Life Public Services, Addresses, and Letters of Elias Boudinot, LL.D., President of Continental Congress* (Boston and New York: Houghton, Mifflin, and Company, 1896), Vol. I, p. 260-262.

65. From an autographed letter in our possession written by Jacob Broom to his son, James, on February 24, 1794, from Wilmington, Delaware.

66. From an autographed letter in our possession written by Charles Carroll to Charles W. Wharton, Esq., on September 27, 1825, from Doughoragen, Maryland.

67. James Iredell, *The Papers of James Iredell*, Don Higginbotham, editor (Raleigh: North Carolina Division of Archives and History, 1976), Vol. I, p. 11 from his 1768 essay on religion.

68. Edwards Beardsley, *Life and Times of William Samuel Johnson* (Boston: Houghton, Mifflin and Company, 1886), p. 184.

69. James Kent, *Memoirs and Letters of James Kent*, William Kent, editor (Boston: Little, Brown, and Company, 1898), p. 277.

70. Hugh A. Garland, *The Life of John Randolph of Roanoke* (New York: D. Appleton & Company, 1853), Vol. II, p. 104, from Francis Scott Key to John Randolph.

71. Robert Treat Paine, *The Papers of Robert Treat Paine*, Stephen T. Riley and Edward W. Hanson, editors (Boston: Massachusetts Historical Society, 1992), Vol. I, p. 48, March/April, 1749.

72. Charles W. Upham, *The Life of Timothy Pickering* (Boston: Little, Brown, and Company, 1873), Vol. IV, p. 390, from his prayer of November 30, 1828.

73. Garland, Vol. II, p. 99, to Francis Scott Key on September 7, 1818.

74. Benjamin Rush, *The Autobiography of Benjamin Rush*, George W. Corner, editor (Princeton: Princeton University Press for the American Philosophical Society, 1948), p. 166.

75. Lewis Henry Boutell, *The Life of Roger Sherman* (Chicago: A. C. McClurg and Company, 1896), pp. 272-273.

76. Swift, *Correspondent*, p. 135.

77. From a proclamation in our possession: *By the Honourable Jonathan Trumbull, Esq; Governor of the English Colony of Connecticut, in New-England, in America. A Proclamation. New Haven, 12th Day of October, 1770.*

78. John Witherspoon, *The Works of John Witherspoon* (Edinburgh: J. Ogle, 1815), Vol. V, p. 276, 278, "The Absolute Necessity of Salvation Through Christ," January 2, 1758.

79. *An Abstract of the American Bible Society* (New York: Daniel Fanshaw, 1830), p. 2.

80. *Report of the Executive Committee of the Bible Society of Massachusetts, prepared for the Anniversary of the Society, June 4, 1818* (Boston: John Eliot, 1818), p. 7.

81. Parker C. Thompson, *The United States Army Chaplaincy: from its European Antecedents to 1791* (Washington: D. C.: Office of the Chief of Chaplins, Department of the Army, 1978), Vol. I, p. 246.

82. *Thompson*, Vol. I, p. 246.

83. *The Second Report of the Managers of the New Jersey Bible Society, Read before the Society at Their Annual Meeting at New Brunswick, August 27, 1811* (Trenton: George Sherman, 1811), p. 11.

84. *Constitution of the American Bible Society* (New York: Printed for the American Bible Society, 1816), p. 7.

85. *Address of the New Jersey Bible Society to the Publick: with an Appendix, Containing the Constitution of the Said Society* (New Brunswick: Abraham Blauvelt, 1810), p. 15.

86. *Report of the American Board of Commissioners for Foreign Missions* (Boston: Crocker & Brewster, 1835), p. 5.

87. Rev. Eliphalet Pearson, *A Sermon Delivered in Boston Before the Massachusetts Society for Promoting Christian Knowledge, November 27, 1811* (Cambridge: Hilliard and Metcalf, 1811), p. 36.

88. Abiel Holmes, *A Discourse Delivered Before the Society for Propagating the Gospel Among the Indians and Others in North America, November 3, 1808* (Boston: Farrand, Mallory, and Co., 1808), p. 66.

89. *The Eighth Report of the Bible Society of Philadelphia* (Philadelpia: William Fry, 1816), p. 44.

90. *Constitution of the American Bible Society,* p. 7; see also W. P. Strickland, *History of the American Bible Society from its Organization to the Present Time* (New York: Harper and Brothers, 1849), p. 34.

91. *The Eighth Report of the Bible Society of Philadelphia,* p. 45.

92. *An Abstract of the American Bible Society* (New York: David Fanshaw, 1818), p. 2.

93. Holmes, p. 65.

94. *An Act to Incorporate the Trustees of the Missionary Society of Connecticut: An Address from said Trustees to the Ministers and People of the State, with a Narrative on the Subject of Missions and a Statement of the Funds of the Society for the Year 1802* (Hartford: Hudson and Goodwin, 1803), name appears in advertisement preceeding the address.

95. John Lathrop, *A Discourse Before the Society for Propagating the Gospel Among the Indians and Others in North America, Delivered on the 19th of January, 1804* (Boston: Manning and Loring, 1804), p. 42.

96. *Constitution of the American Bible Society,* p. 7.

97. *Constitution of the American Bible Society,* p. 7.

98. *An Abstract of the American Bible Society* (New York: Daniel Fanshaw, 1819), p. 2.

99. *Constitution of the American Bible Society,* p. 7.

100. *Constitution of the American Bible Society,* p. 7.

101. Alexander Hamilton, *The Papers of Alexander Hamilton,* Harold C. Syrett, editor (New York: Columbia University Press, 1979), Vol. XXV, pp. 605-610, to James Bayard on April 16-21, 1802.

102. *The Second Report of the Managers of the New-Jersey Bible Society,* p. 14.

103. *An Abstract of the American Bible Society* (New York: Daniel Fanshaw, 1822), p. 2.

104. *Report of the American Board for Foreign Missions,* p. 5.

105. *Constitution of the American Bible Society,* p. 7.

106. William J. Petersen, *A Brief History of the American Sunday-School Union* (Pennsylvania: American Missionary Fellowship, 1969), p. 6.

107. *Constitution of the American Bible Society,* p. 6; see also, Rufus King, *The Life and Correspondence of Rufus King,* Charles R. King, editor (New York: G. P. Putnam's Sons, 1900), Vol. VI, pp. 28-30 (including all notes), from the Rev. Dr. Romeyn of the American Bible Society to R. King on July 17, 1816, and from R. King to the Rev. Dr. Romeyn, July 1816, and from the Rev. Dr. Romeyn of the American Bible Soceity to R. King on July 31, 1816.

108. *Address of the New Jersey Bible Society to the Publick* (New Brunswick: Abraham Blauvelt, 1810), p. 15.

109. *An Abstract of the American Bible Society* (New York: Daniel Fanshaw, 1818), p. 2.

110. Rev. Gailbreth Hall Todd, *The Torch and the Flag* (Philadelphia: American Sunday School Union, 1966), p. 20.

111. *Constitution of the American Bible Society*, p. 7.

112. Holmes, p. 66.

113. Holmes, p. 66.

114. *Constitution of the American Bible Society*, p. 7.

115. *An Abstract of the American Bible Society* (New York: Daniel Fanshaw, 1830), p. 2.

116. Todd, p. 19.

117. Bernard C. Steiner, *One Hundred and Ten Years Of Bible Society Work in Maryland: 1810-1920* (Baltimore: Maryland Bible Society, 1921), pp. 12-13.

118. *An Abstract of the American Bible Society* (New York: Daniel Fanshaw, 1821), p. 2.

119. Todd, p. 20.

120. *Constitution of the American Bible Society*, p. 7.

121. Robert Treat Paine, *Papers*, Vol. I, p. 300, from Paine's commission as chaplain on August 8, 1755.

122. Todd, p. 20.

123. Holmes, p. 64.

124. *A Circular Address from the Bible Society of Massachusetts* (Boston: J. Belcher, 1809), p. 22.

125. *Address of the New Jersey Bible Society to the Publick*, p. 15.

126. *An Abstract of the American Bible Society* (New York: Daniel Fanshaw, 1820), p. 2.

127. Samuel Worchester, D.D., *A Sermon Preached in Boston on the Anniversary of the American Society for Educating Pious Youth for the Gospel Ministry* (Andover: Flagg and Gould, 1816), p. 44.

128. *The Eighth Report of the Bible Society of Philadelphia*, p. 51.

129. *Constitution of the American Bible Society*, p. 7.

130. *Constitution of the American Bible Society*, p. 7.

131. *The Eighth Report of the Bible Society of Philadelphia*, p. 51.

132. *An Address of the Bible Society Established at Philadelphia to the Public* (Philadelphia: By Order of the Society, 1809), p. 24.

133. *Constitution of the American Bible Society*, p. 7.

134. *Biographical Directory of the United States Congress, 1774-1989* (United States Government Printing Office, 1989), p. 1833, s.v. "John Cotton Smith."

135. *The Eighth Report of the Bible Society of Philadelphia*, p. 45.

136. *An Abstract of the American Bible Society* (New York: Daniel Fanshaw, 1832), p. 2.

137. *Report of the American Board of Commissioners for Foreign Missions*, p. 3.

138. *Constitution of the American Bible Society*, p. 7.

139. Holmes, p. 68.

140. Holmes, p. 65.

141. *Constitution of the American Bible Society*, p. 7.

142. *Constitution of the American Bible Society*, p. 7; see also *An Abstract of the American Bible Society* (New York: Daniel Fanshaw, 1817), p. 2.

143. *First Annual Report of the Board of Managers of the American Bible Society* (New York: J. Seymour, 1817), p. 3.

144. *An Act to Incorporate . . . the Missionary Society of Connecticut*, name appears in advertisement preceeding the address.

145. *An Abstract of the American Bible Society* (New York: Daniel Fanshaw, 1825), p. 2.

146. Margaret R. Townsend, *Vice-Presidents of the American Bible Society, 1816-1966* (New York: American Bible Society, 1967), s.v. "Peter Vroom."

147. *Report of the American Board of Commissioners for Foreign Missions*, p. 4.

148. *Constitution of the American Bible Society*, p. 7.

149. Todd, p. 16

150. Todd, p. 18.

151. *Constitution of the American Bible Society*, p. 7.

152. *Constitution of the American Bible Society*, p. 7.

153. *American Heritage*, December 1992, "The Radical Revolution," Gordon Wood, p. 52.

154. *The Los Angeles Times*, August 3, 1995, "America's Unchristian Beginnings," Steven Morris, p. B-9. This article was picked up on wire services and appeared in newspapers across the nation.

155. Thomas Jefferson, *The Writings of Thomas Jefferson*, Albert Ellery Bergh, editor (Washington, D. C.: The Thomas Jefferson Memorial Association, 1904), Vol. XIV, p. 385, to Charles Thompson on January 9, 1816.

156. Jefferson, *Memoir*, Vol. III, p. 506, to Benjamin Rush on April 21, 1803.

157. Benjamin Franklin, *Works of the Late Doctor Benjamin Franklin: Consisting of His Life, Written By Himself, Together With Essays, Humerous, Moral & Literary, Chiefly in the Manner of the Spectator* (Dublin: P. Morgan, P. Byrne, J. Moore, and W. Jones, 1793), p. 76.

158. See, for example, the Rev. Charles Buck, *Theological Dictionary* (Philadelphia: Edwin T. Scott, 1823), pp. 141-142; and John Evans, *A Sketch of the Denominations into Which the Christian World is Divided* (Worcester: Thomas & Sturtevant, 1807), pp. 22-26; and Robert Baird, *Religion in America* (New York: Harper and Brothers, 1845), p. 286.

159. James Madison, *The Papers of James Madison* (Washington, D. C.: Langtree & Sullivan, 1840), Vol. II, pp. 984-986.

160. Noah Webster, *An American Dictionary of the English Language* (1828), s.v. "infidelity."

161. John Adams, *Papers*, Vol. VI, p. 348, to James Warren on August 4, 1778.

162. Rush, *Letters*, Vol. II, p. 799, to Noah Webster on July 20, 1798.

163. Hamilton, *Papers*, Vol. XXI, pp. 402-404, "The Stand No. III," New York, April 7, 1798.

164. William Jay, *Life*, Vol. II, pp. 346-347, to John Bristed on April 23, 1811.

165. Arnold, pp. 249-250.

166. Samuel Adams, *The Writings of Samuel Adams*, Harry Alonzo Cushing, editor (New York: G. P. Putnam's Sons, 1906), Vol. II, p. 381, to William Checkley on December 14, 1772.

167. *Collections of the New York Historical Society for the Year 1821* (New York: E. Bliss and E. White, 1821), p. 34, from "An Inaugural Discourse Delivered Before the New York Historical Society by the Honorable Gouverneur Morris on September 4, 1816."

168. Witherspoon, *Works* (1802), Vol. VI, p. 13, from "An Address to the Senior Class at Princeton College," September 23, 1775.

169. Witherspoon, *Works* (1802), Vol. III, p. 42, "The Dominion of Providence Over the Passions of Men," May 17, 1776.

170. *Appleton's Cyclopedia of American Biography*, James Grant Wilson and John Fiske, editors (New York: D. Appleton and Company, 1888), s. v. "Richard Lee/Richard Henry Lee."

171. Richard Henry Lee, *Memoir of the Life of Richard Henry Lee, and His Correspondence*, Richard Henry Lee, editor (Philadelphia: H. C. Carey and I. Lea, 1825), Vol. I, p. 201.

172. Associated Press, *Dallas Times Herald*, August 6, 1988, B-5, "Public backs 'separation' slogan, but not its results."

Chapter 7
Safeguarding Original Intent

1. *Church of the Holy Trinity* v. *U. S.*, 143 U. S. 457, 459 (1892).
2. John Dickinson, *The Political Writings of John Dickinson* (Wilmington: Bonsal and Niles, 1801), Vol. I, p. 199.
3. *State* v. *Smith Clark*, 5 Dutcher (29 NJ Law) 96, 97-98 (Sup. Ct. NJ 1860).
4. *Clark* at 97.
5. *Clark* at 99.
6. *United States* v. *Kirby*, 74 U. S. 482, 483 (1868).
7. *Kirby* at 484.
8. *Kirby* at 486, 487.
9. *Kirby* at 487.
10. *Holy Trinity* at 472 .

Chapter 8
Rewriting Original Intent

1. *McCollum* v. *Board of Education*, 333 U. S. 203, 207-209 (1948).
2. *McCollum* at 212.
3. *McCollum* at 231, Frankfurter, J. (concurring).
4. *Acts Passed at a Congress of the United States of America, Begun and Held at the City of New-York on Wednesday the Fourth of March in the Year 1789* (Hartford: Hudson and Goodwin, 1791), p. 104.
5. *The Constitutions of the United States of America* (Trenton: Moore and Lake, 1813), p. 364, "An Ordinance of the Territory of the United States Northwest of the River Ohio," Article III; see also *The Public Statutes at Large of the United States of America* (Boston: Charles C. Little and James Brown, 1846), Vol. III, p. 536, December 3, 1818.
6. Thomas Jefferson, *The Writings of Thomas Jefferson*, Albert E. Bergh, editor (Washington D. C.: Thomas Jefferson Memorial Association, 1904), Vol. XVI, p. 19, to Judge Augustus B. Woodward on March 24, 1824.
7. Edwards Beardsley, *Life and Times of William Samuel Johnson* (Boston: Houghton, Mifflin and Company, 1886), pp. 141-142.
8. Samuel Adams, *The Writings of Samuel Adams*, Harry Alonzo Cushing, editor (New York: G. P. Putnam's Sons, 1908), Vol. IV, p. 401, to the Legislature of Massachusetts on January 27, 1797.
9. Samuel Adams, *Writings*, Vol. IV, p. 371, to the Legislature of Massachusetts on January 16, 1795.
10. William V. Wells, *The Life and Public Services of Samuel Adams* (Boston: Little, Brown, and Company, 1865), Vol. III, p. 327, to the Legislature of Massachusetts on January 17, 1794.
11. George Washington, *Address of George Washington, President of the United States . . . Preparatory to His Declination* (Baltimore: George and Henry S. Keatinge, 1796), pp. 22-23.
12. Jared Sparks, *The Life of Gouverneur Morris* (Boston: Gray and Bowen, 1832), Vol. III, p. 483, from his "Notes on the Form of a Constitution for France."
13. Benjamin Rush, *Essays, Literary, Moral and Philosophical* (Philadelphia: Thomas and Samuel F. Bradford, 1798), p. 8, "On the Mode of Education Proper in a Republic."
14. Benjamin Rush, *Letters of Benjamin Rush*, L. H. Butterfield, editor (Princeton, New Jersey: American Philosophical Society, 1951), Vol. I, p. 294, to John Armstrong on March 19,

1783; see also James Henry Morgan, *Dickinson College: The History of One Hundred and Fifty Years 1783–1933* (Carlisle, PA: Dickinson College, 1933), p. 11.

15. Noah Webster, *A Collection of Papers on Political, Literary, and Moral Subjects* (New York: Webster and Clark, 1843), p. 291, from his "Reply to a Letter of David McClure on the Subject of the Proper Course of Study in the Girard College, Philadelphia. New Haven, October 25, 1836."

16. Daniel Webster, *The Works of Daniel Webster* (Boston: Little, Brown and Company, 1853), Vol. II, pp. 107–108, remarks to the ladies of Richmond, October 5, 1840.

17. *Vidal* v. *Girard's Executors,* 43 U. S. 126, 200 (1844).

18. *The Speeches of the Different Governors to the Legislature of the State of New York, Commencing with Those of George Clinton and Continued Down to the Present Time* (Albany: J. B. Van Steenbergh, 1825), p. 108, Governor Daniel Tompkins on January 30, 1810.

19. *McCollum* at 234–235, Jackson, J. (concurring).

20. *McCollum* at 237.

21. *Zorach* v. *Clauson,* 343 U. S. 306 (1952).

22. *Engel* v. *Vitale,* 370 U. S. 421, 422 (1962).

23. *Engel* at 423.

24. *State Board of Education* v. *Board of Education of Netcong,* 262 A. 2d 21, 30 (Sup. Ct. NJ 1970), *cert. denied,* 401 U. S. 1013.

25. *Engel* at 430, 425 (1962).

26. Notice, for example, that the courts invoked *Engel* when striking down adult-led graduation invocations and benedictions in *Lee* v. *Weisman* (120 L. Ed. 2d 467, 1992); when striking down student-led invocations and benedictions in *Harris* v. *Joint School District* (41 F. 3d 447, 9th Cir. 1994); when striking down voluntary silent prayer in *Wallace* v. *Jaffree* (472 U. S. 38, 1985); when striking down student team-prayer before athletic events in *Doe* v. *Duncanville Independent School District* (994 F. 2d 160, 5th Cir. 1993); when striking down equal-access invocations before football games in *Jager* v. *Douglas* (862 F. 2d 824, 11th Cir. 1989; *cert. denied,* 490 U. S. 1090 (1989)); and in virtually every other prayer case of any description.

27. *Engel* at 431.

28. George Washington, *The Writings of George Washington,* Jared Sparks, editor (Boston: Ferdinand Andrews, 1838), Vol. XII, pp. 166–167, to the Synod of the Dutch Reformed Church in North America in October 1789.

29. John Adams, *The Works of John Adams, Second President of the United States,* Charles Francis Adams, editor (Boston: Little, Brown, and Company, 1854), Vol. IX, p. 636, to Benjamin Rush on August 28, 1811.

30. *Independent Chronicle* (Boston), February 22, 1787, Fisher Ames writing as Camillus; see also Fisher Ames, *The Works of Fisher Ames,* Seth Ames, editor (Indianapolis: Liberty Classics, 1983), Vol. I, p. 67.

31. *A Constitution or Frame of Government Agreed Upon By the Delegates of the People of the State of Massachusetts* (Boston: Benjamin Edes & Sons, 1780), p. 7, "Declaration of Rights," Part the First, Article III.

32. *United States Oracle* (Portsmouth, NH), May 24, 1800; see also *The Documentary History of the Supreme Court of the United States, 1789–1800,* Maeva Marcus, editor (New York: Columbia University Press, 1988), Vol. III, p. 436.

33. Jefferson, *Writings* (1904), Vol. XVI, p. 291, to Captain John Thomas on November 18, 1801.

34. Noah Webster, *History of the United States* (New Haven: Durrie & Peck, 1832), p. 339, ¶ 53.

35. William W. Campbell, *The Life and Writings of DeWitt Clinton* (New York: Baker and Scribner, 1849), p. 307, in an address before the American Bible Society on May 8, 1823.

36. Benjamin Rush, *Letters of Benjamin Rush*, L. H. Butterfield, editor (Princeton, New Jersey: American Philosophical Society, 1951), Vol. I, p. 475, to Elias Boudinot on July 9, 1788.

37. John Witherspoon, *The Works of the Rev. John Witherspoon* (Philadelphia: William W. Woodard, 1802), Vol. III, p. 46, "The Dominion of Providence Over the Passions of Men," May 17, 1776.

38. *Engel* at 436.

39. *Engel* at 449-450, Stewart, J. (dissenting).

40. *Abington* v. *Schempp*, 374 U. S. 203, 220-221 (1963).

41. *Abington* at 220-221.

42. Lawrence A. Cremin, *1963 Yearbook*, World Book Encyclopedia, p. 38.

43. Richard L. Worsnop, *Editorial Research Reports*, "Supreme Court: Legal Storm Center," September 28, 1966, pp. 707-708.

44. See generally, *Hearings Before the Subcommittee on Constitutional Amendments of the Committee on the Judiciary, United States Senate, Eighty-Ninth Congress, Second Session on Senate Joint Resolution 148. Relating to Prayer in Public Schools* (Washington, D.C.: U. S. Government Printing Office, 1966), August 1-8, 1966.

45. *Engel* at 431, n. 13.

46. *Hearings*, pp. 687-714, charts demonstrating results of survey regarding religious practices in schools.

47. *Abington* at 213.

48. *Engel* at 445, Stewart, J. (dissenting).

49. *Abington* at 211, n. 4, 207.

50. *Abington* at 207.

51. *Schempp* v. *School District of Abington*, 177 Fed. Supp. 398, 400.

52. *Schempp* at 401.

53. *Abington* at 312-313, Stewart, J. (dissenting).

54. Rush, *Letters*, Vol. I, p. 521, to Jeremy Belknap on July 13, 1789.

55. Benjamin Rush, *Essays*, pp. 94, 100, "A Defence of the Use of the Bible as a School Book."

56. Fisher Ames, *Works of Fisher Ames* (Boston: T. B. Wait & Co., 1809), pp. 134-135.

57. John Adams, *Works*, Vol. II, pp. 6-7, diary entry for February 22, 1756.

58. John Adams, *Works*, Vol. X, p. 85, to Thomas Jefferson on December 25, 1813.

59. Henry Laurens, *The Papers of Henry Laurens*, George C. Rogers, Jr., and David R. Chesnutt, editors (Columbia, S. C.: University of South Carolina Press, 1980), Vol. VIII, pp. 426-427, to James Lawrenson on August 19, 1772.

60. Joseph Story, *A Familiar Exposition of the Constitution of the United States* (New York: Harper and Brothers, 1854), p. 259, §446.

61. John Quincy Adams, *Letters of John Quincy Adams to His Son on the Bible and Its Teachings* (Auburn: James M. Alden, 1850), p. 34.

62. *Collections of the New York Historical Society for the Year 1821* (New York: E. Bliss and E. White, 1821), p. 30, from "An Inaugural Discourse Delivered Before the New York Historical Society by the Honorable Gouverneur Morris on September 4, 1816."

63. William Wirt, *Sketches of the Life and Character of Patrick Henry* (Philadelphia: James Webster, 1818), p. 402; see also George Morgan, *Patrick Henry* (Philadelphia & London: J. B. Lippincott Company, 1929), p. 403.

64. Daniel Webster, *Address Delivered at Bunker Hill, June 17, 1843, on the Completion of the Monument* (Boston: T. R. Marvin, 1843), p. 31; see also W. P. Strickland, *History of the*

American Bible Society from its Organization to the Present Time (New York: Harper and Brothers, 1849), p. 18.

65. John Jay, *John Jay: The Winning of the Peace. Unpublished Papers 1780-1784*, Richard B. Morris, editor (New York: Harper & Row Publishers, 1980), Vol. II, p. 709, to Peter Augustus Jay on April 8, 1784.

66. Noah Webster, *The Holy Bible . . . With Amendments of the Language* (New Haven: Durrie & Peck, 1833), p. v.

67. Bernard C. Steiner, *One Hundred and Ten Years of Bible Society Work in Maryland* (Baltimore: Maryland Bible Society, 1921), p. 14.

68. *Abington* at 217, quoting *Everson* v. *Board of Education*, 330 U. S. 1, 31-32.

69. Washington, *Address . . . Preparatory to His Declination*, pp. 22-23.

70. Moses Coit Tyler, *Patrick Henry* (New York: Houghton Mifflin Co., 1897), p. 409, to Archibald Blair on January 8, 1799.

71. Joseph Story, *Life and Letters of Joseph Story*, William W. Story, editor (Boston: Charles C. Little and James Brown, 1851), Vol. II, pp. 8, 92.

72. James Madison, *The Papers of James Madison*, Henry D. Gilpin, editor (Washington: Langtree & O'Sullivan, 1840), Vol. II, p. 985, June 28, 1787.

73. John Quincy Adams, *An Oration Delivered Before the Inhabitants of the Town of Newburyport at Their Request on the Sixty-First Anniversary of the Declaration of Independence, July 4, 1837* (Newburyport: Charles Whipple, 1837), pp. 5-6.

74. Daniel Webster, *Mr. Webster's Speech in Defence of the Christian Ministry and in Favor of the Religious Instruction of the Young. Delivered in the Supreme Court of the United States, February 10, 1844, in the Case of Stephen Girard's Will* (Washington: Printed by Gales and Seaton, 1844), p. 41.

75. John Witherspoon, *The Works of John Witherspoon* (Edinburgh: J. Ogle, 1815), Vol. V, p. 272, "The Absolute Necessity of Salvation Through Christ," January 2, 1758.

76. James Madison, *A Memorial and Remonstrance Presented to the General Assembly of the State of Virginia at their Session in 1785 in Consequence of a Bill Brought into that Assembly for the Establishment of Religion* (Massachusetts: Isaiah Thomas, 1786), p. 4.

77. John Adams, *Works*, Vol. II, p. 31, from his diary entry for Sunday, August 22, 1756.

78. Rush, *Letters*, Vol. II, pp. 820-821, to Thomas Jefferson on August 22, 1800.

79. Noah Webster, *History*, p. 300, ¶578.

80. *Speeches of the . . . Governors . . . of New York*, p. 47, Governor John Jay on January 6, 1796.

81. *Speeches of the . . . Governors . . . of New York*, p. 136, Governor Daniel Tompkins on November 5, 1816.

82. *Walz* v. *Tax Commission*, 397 U. S. 664, 672 (1970).

83. *Walz* at 672, Brennan, J. (concurring).

84. *Walz* at 716, Douglas, J. (dissenting).

85. Rush, *Letters*, Vol. I, p. 474, to Elias Boudinot on July 9, 1788.

86. Washington, *Writings* (1838), Vol. XII, p. 186, to the Hebrew Congregation of the City of Savannah in May, 1790.

87. John Adams, *Works*, Vol. IX, pp. 609-610, to F. A. Vanderkemp on February 16, 1809.

88. *The Holy Bible* (Trenton: Isaac Collins, 1791), introduction by John Witherspoon.

89. From the will of Elias Boudinot available from the New Jersey State Archives. Or see, for example, excerpts in George Adams Boyd, *Elias Boudinot: Patriot and Statesman* (Princeton: Princeton University Press, 1952), p. 261.

90. Rush, *Essays*, p. 8, "On the Mode of Education Proper in a Republic."

91. Joseph Story, *Commentaries on the Constitution of the United States* (Boston: Hilliard, Gray, and Company, 1833), Vol. III, p. 728, §1871.

92. Washington, *Writings* (1932), Vol. XV, p. 55, from his speech to the Delaware Indian Chiefs on May 12, 1779.

93. Samuel Adams and John Adams, *Four Letters: Being an Interesting Correspondence Between Those Eminently Distinguished Characters, John Adams, Late President of the United States; and Samuel Adams, Late Governor of Massachusetts. On the Important Subject of Government* (Boston: Adams and Rhoades, 1802), pp. 9–10.

94. Bernard C. Steiner, *The Life and Correspondence of James McHenry* (Cleveland: The Burrows Brothers, 1907), p. 475, to James McHenry on November 4, 1800.

95. Jared Sparks, *Lives of William Pinkney, William Ellery, and Cotton Mather* (New York: Harper and Brothers, 1860), from The Library of American Biography, Vol. VI, pp. 138–139.

96. Benjamin Franklin, *Proposals Relating to the Education of Youth in Pennsylvaina* (Philadelphia, 1749), p. 22.

97. John Jay, *The Correspondence and Public Papers of John Jay*, Henry P. Johnston, editor (New York: G. P. Putnam's Sons, 1893), Vol. IV, p. 52, to Lindley Murray on August 22, 1794.

98. Witherspoon, *Works* (1815), Vol. VIII, pp. 33, 38, "On the Truth of the Christian Religion," Lecture IV.

99. K. Alan Snyder, *Defining Noah Webster: Mind and Morals in the Early Republic* (New York: University Press of America, 1990), p. 253, to James Madison on October 16, 1829.

100. John Quincy Adams, *Address Delievered at the Request of the Committee of Arrangements for Celebrating the Anniversary of Independence at the City of Washington on the Fourth of July 1821, Upon the Occasion of Reading the Declaration of Independence* (Cambridge: Hilliard and Metcalf, 1821), p. 28.

101. John Quincy Adams, *An Oration . . . on . . . July 4, 1837*, p. 18.

102. Elias Boudinot, *The Life, Public Services, Addresses, and Letters of Elias Boudinot, LL. D., President of the Continental Congress*, J. J. Boudinot, editor (Boston: Houghton, Mifflin and Co., 1896), Vol. I, p. 19, speech in the First Provincial Congress of New Jersey.

103. Campbell, p. 307, in an address before the American Bible Society on May 8, 1823.

104. B. F. Morris, *The Christian Life and Character of the Civil Institutions of the United States* (Philadelphia: George W. Childs, 1864), p. 323.

105. *Walz* at 681, Brennan, J. (concurring).

106. *Walz* at 702–703, Douglas, J. (dissenting).

107. *Stone* v. *Graham*, 449 U. S. 39 (1980).

108. *Stone* at 41.

109. *Lynch* v. *Donnelly*, 465 U. S. 668, 677 (1984).

110. *County of Allegheny* v. *ACLU*, 106 L. Ed. 2d 472, 533 (1989), Stevens, J. (concurring).

111. *Stone at* 43, 45, Rehnquist, J. (dissenting).

112. *Stone* at 42.

113. *Stone* at 42.

114. John Adams, *A Defence of the Constitution of Government of the United States of America* (Philadelphia: William Young, 1797), Vol. III, p. 217, from "The Right Constitution of a Commonwealth Examined," Letter VI.

115. John Quincy Adams, *Letters . . . to His Son*, p. 61.

116. John Quincy Adams, *Letters . . . to His Son*, pp. 70–71.

117. William Findley, *Observations on "The Two Sons of Oil"* (Pittsburgh: Patterson & Hopkins, 1812), pp. 22–23.

118. Noah Webster, *Collection of Papers*, pp. 291–292, from his "Reply to a Letter of David McClure on the Subject of the Proper Course of Study in the Girard College, Philadelphia. New Haven, October 25, 1836."

119. Campbell, pp. 307, 305.

120. Witherspoon, *Works* (1815), Vol. IV, p. 95, "Seasonable Advice to Young Persons," Sermon XIX, February 21, 1762.

121. Steiner, *One Hundred and Ten Years of Bible Society Work in Maryland* (Baltimore: Maryland Bible Society, 1921), p. 14.

122. Robert Winthrop, *Addresses and Speeches on Various Occasions* (Boston: Little, Brown & Co., 1852), p. 172, from an address delivered May 28, 1849, to the Massachusetts Bible Society.

123. John Quincy Adams, *Letters . . . to His Son*, p. 62.

124. Daniel Webster, *Works*, Vol. I, p. 42, from a discourse delivered December 22, 1820.

125. David Ramsay, *An Oration Delivered in St. Michael's Church Before the Inhabitants of Charleston, South Carolina, on the Fourth of July 1794* (Charleston: W. P. Young, 1794), p. 19.

126. Washington, *Address . . . Preparatory to His Declination*, p. 23.

127. Charles C. Jones, *Biographical Sketches of the Delegates from Georgia to the Continental Congress* (Boston and New York: Houghton, Mifflin and Company, 1891), pp. 6-7.

128. Samuel Adams, *Writings*, Vol. IV, p. 225, to Thomas Wells on November 22, 1780.

129. Noah Webster, *History*, p. 339, ¶53.

130. *Stone* at 45, 46, Rehnquist, J. (dissenting).

131. *Wallace* v. *Jaffree*, 472 U. S. 38, 48, n. 30 (1984).

132. *Wallace* at 43, 44, n. 22.

133. *Wallace* at 41-42.

134. *Wallace* at 86-87, Burger, C. J. (dissenting).

135. *Constitutions* (1813), p. 364, "An Ordinance of the Territory of the United States Northwest of the River Ohio," Article III.

136. *Independent Chronicle* (Boston), November 2, 1780, last page; see also Abram English Brown, *John Hancock, His Book* (Boston: Lee and Shepard, 1898), p. 269.

137. Jones, pp. 6-7.

138. Story, *Familiar Exposition*, p. 260, §442.

139. Witherspoon, *Works* (1815), Vol. VII, pp. 118-119, "Jurisprudence," Lecture XIV.

140. Witherspoon, *Works* (1815), Vol. IV, p. 265, from his "Sermon Delivered at Public Thanksgiving After Peace."

141. Laurens, *Papers*, Vol. XI, p. 200, in a letter to Oliver Hart and Elharan Winchester on March 30, 1776.

142. *The Connecticut Courant* (Hartford), June 7, 1802, p. 3, from "A report of the Committee . . . to the General Assembly of the State of Connecticut" by Oliver Ellsworth.

143. *Speeches of the . . . Governors . . . of New York*, p. 66, Governor John Jay on November 4, 1800.

144. *Wallace* at 85, 89, Burger, C. J. (dissenting).

145. *Wallace* at 106-107, 112, Rehnquist, J. (dissenting).

146. *Wallace* at 113-114 , Rehnquist, J. (dissenting).

147. *Lynch* at 669-670.

148. *County of Allegheny* at 472, 475 (L. Ed. 2d).

149. *County of Allegheny* at 543, Kennedy, J. (concurring in the judgment in part and dissenting in part).

150. *County of Allegheny* at 541.

151. *County of Allegheny* at 547-548, 550, Kennedy, J. (concurring in judgment in part and dissenting in part).

152. *County of Allegheny* at 472, 505.

153. James Otis, *The Rights of the British Colonies Asserted and Proved* (London: J. Williams and J. Almon, 1766), pp. 11, 98.

154. Samuel Adams, *Writings*, Vol. I, p. 269, Samuel Adams in the *Boston Gazette* of December 19, 1768, as "Vindex."

155. William Livingston, *The Papers of William Livingston* (Trenton: New Jersey Historical Commission, 1979), Vol. I, p. 161, in an address from John Hart, October 5, 1776.

156. John Dickinson, *The Political Writings of John Dickinson* (Wilmington: Bonsal and Niles, 1801), Vol. I, p. 111.

157. Witherspoon, *Works* (1815), Vol. IV, p. 270, from his "Sermon Delivered at Public Thanksgiving After Peace."

158. William Jay, *The Life of John Jay: With Selections From His Correspondence and Miscellaneous Papers* (New York: J. & J. Harper, 1833), Vol. I, pp. 457-458, to the Committee of the Corportaion of the City of New York on June 29, 1826.

159. James D. Richardson, *A Compilation of the Messages and Papers of the Presidents, 1789-1897* (Published by Authority of Congress, 1899), Vol. I, p. 561. March 4, 1815.

160. Washington, *Writings* (1932), Vol. XXXV, p. 416, to the Clergy of Different Denominations Residing in and Near the City of Philadelphia on March 3, 1797.

161. John Adams, *Works*, Vol. IX, p. 229, to the Officers of the First Brigade of the Third Division of the Militia of Massachusetts on October 11, 1798.

162. *County of Allegheny* at 549, Kennedy, J. (concurring in judgment in part and dissenting in part).

163. *Wallace* at 106, Rehnquist, J. (dissenting).

164. *Lee* v. *Weisman*, 120 L. Ed. 2d 467, 509 (1992), Scalia, J. (dissenting).

165. *Lee* at 467.

166. *Lee* at 492, Blackman, J. (concurring).

167. Washington, *Writings* (1838), Vol. XII, p. 119, proclamation for a National Thanksgiving on October 3, 1789.

168. John Adams, *Works*, Vol. IX, p. 169, proclamation for a National Thanksgiving on March 23, 1798.

169. Richardson, Vol. I, p. 532. July 23, 1813.

170. Samuel Adams, *By the Governor. A Proclamation for a Day of Public Fasting, Humiliation, and Prayer* (Printed at the State Press: Adams and Larkin, 1795).

171. James Madison, *The Papers of James Madison*, Henry D. Gilpin, editor (Washington: Langtree & O'Sullivan, 1840), Vol. II, pp. 984-986. June 28, 1787.

172. *Speeches of the . . . Governors . . . of New York*, p. 80, Governor George Clinton on January 31, 1804.

173. Jonathan Trumbull, *By His Excellency Jonathan Trumbull, Esq. Governor and Commander in Chief In and Over the State of Connecticut. A Proclamation* (Hudson and Goodwin, 1807).

174. Boudinot, Vol. I, p. 21, to the First Provincial Congress of New Jersey.

175. *Speeches of the . . . Governors . . . of New York*, p. 126, Governor Daniel Tompkins on January 25, 1814.

176. *Lee* at 509, Scalia, J. (dissenting).

177. *Lee* at 505-506, Souter, J. (concurring).

178. *Lee* at 510-511, 516, Scalia, J. (dissenting).

179. *Lee* at 484.

180. *Lee* at 509, 514, Scalia, J. (dissenting).

181. *Lee* at 519, Scalia, J. (dissenting).

182. *Lee* at 518, Scalia, J. (dissenting).

183. *Lee* v. *Weisman*, 728 F. Supp. 68, 75 (D.C. RI 1990).

184. Thomas Jefferson, *Memoir, Correspondence, and Miscellanies, From the Papers of Thomas Jefferson*, Thomas Jefferson Randolph, editor (Boston: Gray and Bowen, 1830), Vol. IV, p. 317, to Judge Spencer Roane on September 6, 1819.

Chapter 9
Ignoring Original Intent

1. *Abington School District* v. *Schempp*, 374 U. S. 203, 220-221 (1963).
2. *Abington School District* v. *Schempp*, 374 U. S. 203 (1963).
3. *Epperson* v. *Arkansas*, 393 U. S. 97 (1968).
4. *Epperson* at 97.
5. *Scopes* v. *State*, 289 S. W. 363 (Sup. Ct. Tenn. 1927).
6. *Board of Education* v. *Allen*, 392 U. S. 236 (1968).
7. *Lemon* v. *Kurtzman*, 403 U. S. 602 (1971).
8. *Lemon* at 602.
9. *Lemon* at 602.
10. *Levitt* v. *Committee for Public Education*, 413 U. S. 472, 474 (1973).
11. *Committee for Public Education* v. *Nyquist*, 413 U. S. 756 (1973).
12. *Stone* v. *Graham*, 449 U. S. 39 (1980).
13. *Marsh* v. *Chambers*, 463 U. S. 783 (1983).
14. *Lynch* v. *Donnelly*, 465 U. S. 668 (1984).
15. *Wallace* v. *Jaffree*, 472 U. S. 38 (1985).
16. *Edwards* v. *Aguillard*, 482 U. S. 578 (1987).
17. *Edwards* at 578.
18. *County of Allegheny* v. *ACLU*, 492 U. S. 472 (1989).
19. *Westside* v. *Mergens*, 496 U. S. 226 (1990).
20. *United States Code, 1988 Edition* (Washington, D. C.: United States Government Printing Office, 1989), p. 883, Equal Access Act: United States Code § 4071-4074.
21. *Lee* v. *Weisman*, 120 L. Ed. 2d 467 (1992).
22. *Lee* at 505-506, Souter, J., (concurring).
23. *Lamb's Chapel* v. *Center Moriches*, 124 L. Ed. 2d 352 (1993).
24. *Zobrest* v. *Catalina Foothills*, 125 L. Ed. 2d 1 (1993).
25. *Rosenberger* v. *Rector and Visitors of University of Virginia*, 115 S. Ct. 2510 (1995).

Chapter 10
The Court's Use of Selective History

1. *World Book Encyclopedia*, 1995, s.v. "Constitution of the United States, Amendment 14," explained it this way: "The principal purpose of this amendment was to make former slaves citizens of both the United States and the state in which they lived."
2. *McCullough* v. *Maryland*, 4 Wheaton 316, 401 (1819).
3. *Church of the Holy Trinity* v. *U. S.*, 143 U. S. 457, 465 (1892).
4. *Cantwell* v. *State of Connecticut*, 310 U. S. 296 (1940).
5. *Murdock* v. *Pennsylvania*, 319 U. S. 105 (1943).
6. *Everson* v. *Board of Education*, 330 U. S. 1 (1947).
7. See the description of this process by Justice William Douglas in his dissenting opinion in *Walz* v. *Tax Commission*, 397 U. S. 664, 701 (1970).
8. *Abington* v. *Schempp*, 374 U. S. 203, 215-216 (1963).
9. *Walz* at 701-703, Douglas, J. (dissenting).
10. Samuel Adams, *The Writings of Samuel Adams*, Harry Alonzo Cushing, editor (New York: G. P. Putnam's Sons, 1908), Vol. IV, p. 332, to Elbridge Gerry on August 22, 1789.

11. Thomas Jefferson, *Memoir, Correspondence, and Miscellanies, From the Papers of Thomas Jefferson*, Thomas Jefferson Randolph, editor (Boston: Gray and Bowen, 1830), Vol. IV, p. 374. In a letter to Judge William Johnson on June 12, 1823.

12. Jefferson, *Memoir*, Vol. IV, pp. 103-104, to the Rev. Samuel Miller on January 23, 1808.

13. *Barron v. Baltimore*, 32 U. S. 243, 249-250 (1833).

14. *McCollum v. Board of Education*, 333 U. S. 203, 218-219, n. 6 (1948).

15. *McCollum* at 218, n. 6.

16. *Everson* at 13.

17. *Engel v. Vitale*, 370 U. S. 421, 428 (1962).

18. *The Constitutions of the Several Independent States of America* (Boston: Norman and Bowen, 1785), pp. 73-74, New Jersey, 1776, Section 19.

19. *Constitutions* (1785), p. 138, North Carolina, 1776, Section 34.

20. *Constitutions* (1785), p. 91, Delaware, 1776, "Declaration of Rights," Section 2.

21. *Constitutions* (1785), p. 67, New York, 1777, Section 38.

22. *Constitutions* (1785), p. 77, Pennsylvania, 1776, "Declaration of Rights," Section 2.

23. *Constitutions* (1785), p. 166, Georgia, 1777, Section 56.

24. *The Constitutions of the Sixteen States* (Boston: Manning and Loring, 1797), p. 250, Vermont, 1786, "Declaration of Rights," Section 3.

25. John V. L. McMahon, *An Historical View of the Government of Maryland* (Baltimore: F. Lucas, Jr. Cushing & Sons, and William & Joseph Neal, 1831), Vol. I, pp. 380-400.

26. *Wallace v. Jaffree*, 472 U. S. 38, 98-99 (1985), Rehnquist, J. dissenting.

27. Thomas Jefferson, *The Writings of Thomas Jefferson*, Albert Ellery Bergh, editor (Washington, D. C.: The Thomas Jefferson Memorial Association, 1904), Vol. X, p. 325, to Dr. Joseph Priestly on June 19, 1802.

28. James Madison, *The Letters and Other Writings of James Madison* (New York: R. Worthington, 1884), Vol. IV, pp. 341-342, to William Cogswell on March 10, 1834.

29. Forrest McDonald, *Novus Ordo Seclorum: The Intellectial Origins of the Constitution* (Lawrence, Kansas, 1985), pp. 208-209, quoting from *The Records of the Federal Convention* of 1787, Max Farrand, editor (New Haven: Yale University Press, 1911).

30. Forrest McDonald, pp. 205-209.

31. James Wilson, *The Works of James Wilson*, Robert Green McCloskey, editor (Massachusetts: The Belknap Press of Harvard University Press, 1967), Vol. I, p. 2, introduction.

32. S. Sidney Olmer, "Charles Pinckney: Father of the Constitution," *South Carolina Law Quarterly 10* (1958), 225-247.

33. Jared Sparks, *The Life of George Washington* (Boston: Ferdinand Andrews, 1839), pp. 403-404; see also Catherine Drinker Bowen, *Miracle at Philadelphia* (Boston: Little, Brown, and Company, 1966), pp. 192-193, quoting from James Monroe to Thomas Jefferson; see also Jay A. Perry, Andrew N. Allison, and W. Cleon Skousen, *The Real George Washington* (D. C.: National Center for Constitutional Studies, 1991), p. 506, again citing James Monroe in a letter to Thomas Jefferson.

34. George Bancroft, *A Plea for the Constitution of the United States Wounded in the House of its Guardians* (New York: Harper, 1886), pp. 2-3.

35. Jefferson, *Writings* (1904), Vol. X, p. 325, to Dr. Joseph Priestly on June 19, 1802.

36. James Madison, *The Papers of James Madison*, Henry D. Gilpin, editor (Washington: Langress and O'Sullivan, 1840), Vol. III, p. 1566, for Wednesday, September 12, 1787; see also George Bancroft, *Bancroft's History of the Formation of the Constitution* (New York: D. Appleton and Company, 1882), Vol. II, pp. 209-210, and Farrand's *Records of The Federal Convention of 1787*, Vol. II, pp. 588, 637.

37. *Debates in the Several State Conventions on the Adoption of the Federal Constitution,* Jonathan Elliot, editor (Washington: Printed for the Editor, 1836), Vol. I, p. 306, September 12, 1787.

38. Elliot's *Debates,* Vol. III, pp. 652-655, June 25, 1788.

39. Elliot's *Debates,* Vol. II, pp. 176-181, February 6, 1788.

40. Joseph B. Walker, *A History of the New Hampshire Convention* (Boston: Cupples & Hurd, 1888), pp. 41-43, June 21, 1788.

41. Elliot's *Debates,* Vol. II, p. 413, July 26, 1788.

42. *Collections of the Rhode Island Historical Society* (Providence: Knowles and Vose, 1843), Vol. V, pp. 320-321, March 24, 1788.

43. Elliot's *Debates,* Vol. IV, pp. 242-251, August 1-2, 1788.

44. Elliot's *Debates,* Vol. III, pp. 616-622, James Madison, June 24, 1788.

45. Kate Mason Rowland, *The Life of George Mason* (New York and London: G. P. Putnam's Sons, 1892), Vol. I, p. 244.

46. Elliot's *Debates,* Vol. III, pp. 655-656, June 25, 1788.

47. Patrick Henry, *Life, Correspondence and Speeches,* William Wirt Henry (New York: Charles Scribner's Sons, 1891), Vol. I, pp. 430-431; see also Kate Mason Rowland, The Life of George Mason (New York: G. P. Putnam's Sons, 1892), Vol. I, p. 244; see also Elliot's *Debates,* Vol. III, p. 659, June 27, 1788.

48. *The Debates and Proceedings in the Congress of the United States* (Washington, D. C.: Gales & Seaton, 1834), First Congress, First Session, pp. 448-450, June 8, 1789; see also *Wallace v. Jaffree,* 472 U. S. 38, 93-99, Rehnquist, J. (dissenting).

49. See *The Debates and Proceedings in the Congress of the United States* (Washington, D. C.: Gales and Seaton, 1834), Vol. I, pp. 440-948, June 8- September 24, 1789.

50. James D. Richardson, *A Compilation of the Messages and Papers of the Presidents, 1789-1897* (Published by Authority of Congress, 1899), Vol. I, pp. 512-513, June 19, 1812; pp. 532-533, July 23, 1813; p. 558, November 16, 1814; pp. 560-561, March 4, 1815.

51. Jefferson, *Memoir,* Vol. IV, pp. 103-104, to the Rev. Samuel Miller on January 28, 1808.

52. Jefferson, *Memoir,* Vol. IV, p. 103-104, to the Rev. Samuel Miller on January 28, 1808.

53. For example, see Jefferson's encouragement of a day for fasting and prayer for June 1, 1774 (Jefferson, *Writings,* Vol. I, pp. 9-10) and the November 11, 1779, proclamation for a day of prayer and thanksgiving he issued while Governor. See *Official Letters of the Governors of the State of Virginia,* H. R. McIlwaine, editor (Richmond: Virginia State Library, 1928), Vol. II, pp. 64-66.

54. James Madison, *The Papers of James Madison,* Robert A Rutland, editor (Chicago: University of Chicago Press, 1973), Vol. VIII, pp. 396.

55. Jefferson, *Writings,* Vol. XIX, pp. 449-450, at a Meeting of the Visitors of the University . . . on Monday the 4th of October, 1824.

56. *Id.*

57. Jefferson, *Memoir,* Vol. IV, pp. 358-359, to Dr. Thomas Cooper on November 2, 1822.

58. Jefferson, *Writings,* Vol. XVI, p. 291, to Captain John Thomas on November 18, 1807.

59. Henry S. Randall, *The Life of Thomas Jefferson* (New York: Derby & Jackson, 1858), Vol. III, pp. 451-452. For an alternative view of the purpose of this book, see *Jefferson's Extracts from the Gospel's,* Dickinson W. Adams, editor (Princeton: Princeton University Press, 1983), p. 28, n. 87.

60. *American State Papers,* Walter Lowrie and Matthew St. Claire Clarke, editors (Washington, D. C.: Gales and Seaton, 1832), Vol. IV, p. 687.

61. *Wallace* at 103, Rehnquist, J. (dissenting).

62. *Debates and Proceedings in the Congress of the United States, Seventh Congress* (Washington, D. C.: Gales and Seaton, 1851), p. 1332, "An Act in Addition to An Act, Entitled, 'An Act in Addition to an Act Regulating the Grants of Land Appropriated for Military Services,

and for the Society of the United Brethren for Propagating the Gospel Among the Heathen' ";
Seventh Congress, Second Session, p. 1602, "An Act to Revive and Continue in Force An Act in
Addition to An Act, Entitled, 'An Act in Addition to an Act Regulating the Grands of Land
Appropriated for Military Services, and for the Society of the United Brethren for Propagating
the Gospel Among the Heathen,' and for Other Purposes"; and *Eighth Congress,* p. 1279, "An
Act Granting Further Time for Locating Military Land Warrants, and for Other Purposes."

63. Madison, *Letters,* Vol. I, pp. 5–6, to William Bradford on November 9, 1772.

64. James Madison, *The Papers of James Madison,* William T. Hutchinson, editor (Illinois:
University of Chicago Press, 1962), Vol. I, p. 66, to William Bradford on September 25, 1773.

65. *The Proceedings of the Convention of Delegates, Held at the Capitol in the City of
Williamsburg, in the Colony of Virginia, on Monday the 6th of May, 1776* (Williamsburg:
Alexander Purdie, 1776), p. 103. Madison on the Committee on May 16, 1776; the "Decla-
ration of Rights" passed June 12, 1776.

66. *Debates and Proceedings* (1834), Vol. I, p. 451, June 8, 1789.

67. *Debates and Proceedings* (1834), Vol. I, pp. 758–759, August 15, 1789.

68. *Debates and Proceedings* (1834), Vol. I, p. 109, April 9, 1789.

69. *The Debates and Proceedings in the Congress of the United States* (Washington: Gales
& Seaton, 1853), Twelfth Congress, Second Session, p. 1325: "An Act for the relief of the
Bible Society of Philadelphia. Be it enacted, &c., That the duties arising and due to the
United States upon certain stereotype plates, imported during the last year into the port of
Philadelphia, on board the ship Brilliant, by the Bible Society of Philadelphia, for the pur-
pose of printing editions of the Holy Bible, be and the same are hereby remitted, on behalf
of the United States, to the said society: and any bond or security given for the securing of
the payment of the said duties shall be cancelled. Approved February 2, 1813."

70. Richardson, Vol. I, p. 513: July 9, 1812; pp. 532–533: July 23, 1813; p. 558: November 16, 1814; pp. 560–561: March 4, 1815.

71. *The William & Mary Quarterly,* Third Series, October 1946, Vol. III, No. 4,
Madison's "Detached Memoranda," edited by Elizabeth Fleet, pp. 534–568.

72. James Madison, *Letters and Other Writings of James Madison* (New York: R. Worthington, 1884), Vol. III, p. 19, to the Rev. Miles King on September 5, 1816.

73. Patrick Henry, *Life, Correspondence, and Speeches,* William Wirt Henry, editor
(New York: Charles Scribner's Sons, 1891), Vol. II, p. 207.

74. James Madison, *A Memorial and Remonstrance Presented to the General Assembly of
the State of Virginia at their Session in 1785 in Consequence of a Bill Brought into that Assembly
for the Establishment of Religion* (Massachusetts: Isaiah Thomas, 1786); see also the text of
Madison's 1813 Presidential proclamation.

75. William C. Rives, *History of the Life and Times of James Madison* (Boston: Little,
Brown, and Company, 1873), Vol. I, p. 602; see also Patrick Henry, *Life, Correspondence and
Speeches,* William Wirt Henry (New York: Charles Scribner's Sons, 1891), Vol. II, p. 210.

76. Madison, *Letters,* Vol. I, p. 111, to James Monroe on November 27, 1784.

77. *A Constitution or Frame of Government Agreed Upon by the Delegates of the People of
the State of Massachusetts-Bay in Convention* (Boston: Benjamin Edes & Sons, 1780), pp. 7–
8, "Declaration of Rights," Article 3.

78. *Constitutions* (1785), p. 4, New Hampshire, 1783, Article 1, Section 6 of the "Bill
of Rights."

79. *Constitutions* (1785), p. 107, Maryland, 1776, "Declaration of Rights," Article XXXIII.

80. Paul C. Vitz, *Censorship: Evidence of Bias in Our Children's Textbooks* (Ann Arbor,
Michigan: Servant Books, 1986), p. 77.

81. Jared Sparks, *The Life of Gouverneur Morris* (Boston: Gray and Bowen, 1832),
Vol. III, p. 483.

82. James Wilson, *The Works of James Wilson*, Bird Wilson, editor (Philadelphia: Bronson and Chauncey, 1804), Vol. I, pp. 104-106, "Of the General Principles of Law and Obligation."

83. *Debates and Proceedings* (1834), Vol. I, p. 796, August 20, 1789.

84. Fisher Ames, *Works of Fisher Ames* (Boston: T. B. Wait & Co., 1809), p. 134-135, "School Books."

85. George Washington, *Address of George Washington, President of the United States . . . Preparatory to His Declination* (Baltimore: George and Henry Keating, 1796), pp. 22-26.

Chapter 11
Establishing the American Philosophy of Government

1. James Madison, *The Papers of James Madison*, Henry D. Gilpin, editor (Washington: Langtree and O'Sullivan, 1840), Vol. II, p. 984, June 28, 1787.

2. Donald S. Lutz, *The Origins of American Constitutionalism* (Baton Rouge, LA: Louisiana State University Press, 1988).

3. Lutz, p. 143.

4. George Bancroft, *Bancroft's History of the United States* (Boston: Little, Brown & Co., 1859), Vol. V, p. 24; see Baron Charles Secondat de Montesquieu, *Spirit of Laws* (Philadelphia: Isaiah Thomas, 1802), Vol. I, p. 18, ad passim.

5. Montesquieu, Vol. II, pp. 125-126.

6. John Quincy Adams, *An Oration Addressed to the Citizens of the Town of Quincy, on the Fourth of July, 1831, The Fifty-Fifth Anniversary of the Independence of the United States of America* (Boston: Richardson, Lord and Holbrook, 1831), p. 27.

7. Montesquieu, Vol. I, p. 181.

8. George Washington, *Address of George Washington, President of the United States . . . Preparatory to His Declination* (Baltimore: George & Henry S. Keatinge, 1796), p. 22.

9. Alexander Hamilton, John Jay, and James Madison, *The Federalist, on the New Constitution Written in 1788* (Philadelphia: Benjamin Warner, 1818) p. 80, Alexander Hamilton, Number XV.

10. John Wingate Thornton, *The Pulpit of the American Revolution* (Boston: Gould and Lincoln, 1860), p. xxvii.

11. *Debates and Proceedings in the Congress of the United States* (Washington: Gales and Seaton, 1849), Third Congress, First Session, p. 65, March 10, 1794.

12. James Madison, *Letters and Other Writings of James Madison* (New York: R. Worthington, 1884), Vol. III, p. 233, to Littell and Henry on October 18, 1821.

13. Sir William Blackstone, *Commentaries on the Laws of England* (Philadelphia: Robert Bell, Union Library, 1771), Vol. I, pp. 39, 41-42.

14. James Iredell's Charge to the Grand Jury in the *Case of Fries* [9 Fed. Cas. 826, no. 5, 126 (C. C. D. Pa. 1799)].

15. *Id.*

16. Thomas Jefferson, *The Writings of Thomas Jefferson* (Washington, D. C.: The Thomas Jefferson Memorial Association, 1904), Vol. XII, p. 392, to Governor John Tyler on May 26, 1810.

17. John Locke, *Two Treatises on Government* (London: J. Whiston, etc., 1772), Book II, p. 252, Chapter VIII, §95.

18. William Findley, *Observations on "The Two Sons of Oil"* (Pittsburgh: Patterson and Hopkins 1812), p. 35.

19. John Locke, *Two Treatises,* Book II, p. 285, Chapter XI, §135.

20. Locke at p. 285, Chapter XI, §135 n., quoting Hooker's *Eccl. Pol.* 1. iii, sect. 9.

21. See Richard Watson, *Theological Institutes: On a View of the Evidences, Doctrines, Morals, and Institutions of Christianity* (New York: Carlton and Porter, 1857), where Watson includes John Locke as a theologian.

22. Noah Webster, *An American Dictionary of the English Language* (New York: S. Converse, 1828), s.v. "infidel."

23. James Wilson, *The Works of the Honourable James Wilson*, Bird Wilson, editor (Philadelphia: Lorenzo Press, 1804), Vol. I, pp. 67-68, "Of the General Principles of Law and Obligation."

24. Locke, *Two Treatises*, passim.

25. Wilson, Vol. I, p. 56, "Of the General Principles of Law and Obligation."

26. Wilson, Vol. I, p. 102, "Of the General Principles of Law and Obligation."

27. Wilson, Vol. I, p. 143, "Of the Law of Nature."

28. Richard Hooker, *The Works of that Learned and Judicious Divine, Mr. Richard Hooker* (Oxford: The University Press, 1845), Vol. I, p. 148.

29. Hooker, Vol. I, p. 230

30. Hooker, Vol. I, p. 427

31. Hooker, Vol. I, p. 207

32. Jefferson, *Writings*, Vol. XVI, pp. 281-282, to the Danbury Baptist Association on January 1, 1802.

33. Benjamin Franklin, *The Works of Benjamin Franklin,* John Bigelow, editor (New York: G. P. Putnam's Son, 1904), Vol. V, pp. 325-326, from David Hume to Benjamin Franklin on February 7, 1772.

34. John Adams, *Diary and Autobiography of John Adams*, L. H. Butterfield, editor (Cambridge, MA: Belknap Press, 1962), Vol. II, p. 391, diary entry of June 23, 1779; see also, John Adams, *The Works of John Adams, Second President of the United States*, Charles Francis Adams, editors (Boston: Charles C. Little and James Brown, 1851), Vol. III, p. 391.

35. Webster, *American Dictionary* (1828), s.v. "libertine."

36. Madison, *Letters*, Vol. IV, p. 58, to N. P. Trist in February 1830.

37. Madison, *Letters*, Vol. IV, p. 464, from his "Essay on Money."

38. John Quincy Adams, *An Oration . . . on the Fourth of July, 1831*, p. 15.

39. Thomas Jefferson, *Memoir, Correspondence, and Miscellanies, From the Papers of Thomas Jefferson*, Thomas Jefferson Randolph, editor (Boston: Gray and Bowen, 1830), Vol. IV, p. 80, to John Norvell on June 11, 1807.

40. Jefferson, *Writings*, Vol. XII, p. 405, to Col. William Duane on August 12, 1810.

41. John Witherspoon, *The Works of John Witherspoon* (Edinburgh: J. Ogle, 1815), Vol. V, p. 242, from "The Absolute Necessity of Salvation Through Christ," January 2, 1758.

42. Benjamin Rush, *Letters of Benjamin Rush*, L. H. Butterfield, editor (New Jersey: Princeton University Press, 1951), Vol. II, p. 748, to James Kidd on May 13, 1794.

43. George Morgan, *Patrick Henry* (Philadelphia: J. B. Lippincott Company, 1929), p. 366; see also, William Meade, *Old Churches, Ministers, and Families of Virginia* (Philadelphia: J. B. Lippincott Company, 1857), Vol. II, p. 12.

44. Watson, Vol. I, p. 227.

45. Alexander Hamilton, *The Papers of Alexander Hamilton*, Harold Syrett, editor (NY: Columbia University Press, 1961), Vol. I, p. 86, from "The Farmer Refuted," February 23, 1775.

46. Witherspoon, *Works* (1815), Vol. VII, p. 152, from "Lecture on Moral Philosophy," Lecture XVI.

47. Hugo Grotius, *Commentary on the Law of Prize and Booty*, translated from the original manuscript of 1604 by Gwladys L. Williams (Oxford: Clarendon Press, 1950), Vol. I, p. 8.

48. Hugo Grotius, *The Truth of Christian Religion* (London: Richard Royston, 1780), p. 20.

49. The Baron Puffendorf, *Of the Law of Nature and Nations, Eight Books,* Basil Kennet, editor (London: R. Sare, 1717), Book 1, p. 68.

50. Puffendorf, Book III, p. 78.

51. Wilson, Vol. I, pp. 120, 137-138, "Of the Law of Nature."

52. Zephaniah Swift, *A System of the Laws of the State of Connecticut* (Windham: John Byrne, 1795), Vol. I, pp. 6-7.

53. Samuel Adams, *The Writings of Samuel Adams,* Harry Alonzo Cushing, editor (New York: G. P. Putnam's Sons, 1908), Vol. IV, p. 356, to the Legislature of Massachusetts on January 17, 1794.

54. John Quincy Adams, *The Jubilee of the Constitution* (New York: Published by Samuel Colman, 1839), pp. 13-14.

55. Hamilton, *Papers,* Vol. I, p. 87, from "The Farmer Refuted," February 23, 1775, quoting from Blackstone.

56. Noah Webster, *An American Dictionary of the English Language* (New York: S. Converse, 1828), s.v. "law," definition #3 and #6.

57. John Jay, *The Life of John Jay,* William Jay, editor (New York: J. & J. Harper, 1833), Vol. II, p. 385, to John Murray on April 15, 1818.

58. Findley, p. 33.

59. Rufus King, *The Life and Correspondence of Rufus King,* Charles R. King, editor (New York: G. P. Putnam's Sons, 1900), Vol. VI, p. 276, to C. Gore on February 17, 1820.

60. Wilson, Vol. I, p. 64, "Of the General Principles of Law and Obligation."

61. Lutz, p. 141.

62. Lutz, p. 141.

63. Kenneth Woodward and David Gates, "How the Bible Made America," *Newsweek,* December 27, 1982, p. 44.

Chapter 12
A Changing Standard—Toward a New Constitution

1. *The Encyclopedia of Religion* (NY: MacMillan Publishing Co. 1987), Vol. XII, p. 274, see "Relativism," by Richard H. Popkin.

2. John Eidsmoe, *Christianity and the Constitution* (MI: Baker Book House, 1987), p. 394.

3. John Dewey, *The Public and Its Problems* (NY: Henry Holt and Company, 1927), p. 34.

4. *Columbia Law Review,* Vol. 8, No. 8, December 1908, p. 609, "Mechanical Jurisprudence" by Roscoe Pound.

5. Oliver Wendell Holmes, Jr., *Collected Legal Papers* (NY: Harcourt, Brace and Company, 1920), p. 225, "The Law in Science—Science in Law."

6. Oliver Wendell Holmes, Jr., *The Common Law* (originally published 1881, reprinted Cambridge, MA: Harvard University Press, 1963), p. 5.

7. *New State Ice Company* v. *Liebmann,* 285 U. S. 262, 311 (1932), Louis Brandeis, J. (dissenting).

8. Benjamin Cardozo, *The Growth of the Law* (New Haven: Yale University Press, 1924), p. 49.

9. Benjamin Cardozo, *The Nature of the Judicial Process* (New Haven: Yale University Press, 1921), p. 10.

10. Charles Evans Hughes, *The Autobiographical Notes of Charles Evans Hughes,* David J. Danelski and Joseph S. Tulchin, editors (Cambridge: Harvard University Press, 1973), p. 144, speech at Elmira on May 3, 1907.

11. *Trop* v. *Dulles,* 356 U. S. 86, 101 (1958).

12. *Abington* v. *Schempp*, 374 U. S. 203, 220-221 (1963).

13. Samuel Adams, *The Writings of Samuel Adams*, Harry Alonzo Cushing, editor (New York: G. P. Putnam's Sons, 1904), Vol. IV, p. 388, to the Legislature of Massachusetts on January 19, 1796.

14. George Washington, *Address of George Washington, President of the United States . . . Preparatory to His Declination* (Baltimore: George and Henry S. Keatinge, 1796), p. 22.

15. Thomas Jefferson, *The Writings of Thomas Jefferson*, Albert Ellery Bergh, editor (Washington D. C.: The Thomas Jefferson Memorial Association, 1904), Vol. XV, p. 277, to William Charles Jarvis on September 28, 1820.

16. See, for example, the 25th Annual Gallup Poll, October 1993; see also the September 8, 1993 poll of Fabrizio, McLaughlin, & Associates, Inc.; see also the various polls from Yankelovich, Clancy, & Shulman; see also the annual polling done by the Princeton Religion Research Center in New Jersey. Gallup Poll, November 1994; see also, CNN/USA Today/Gallup Poll: Top-Line, November 28-29, 1994.

17. *Congressional Record*, June 29, 1987, H. 3511, citing *General Social Survey Annual* of the National Opinion Research Center.

18. U. S. House of Representatives, *What America Believes: The Rest of the Story* (Republican Staff of the Select Committee on Children, Youth, and Families, U. S. House of Representatives, 1990), p. 12, citing the *Boston Globe*, October 31, 1989.

Chapter 13
A Constitution In a State of Flux

1. *Marsh* v. *Chambers*, 463 U. S. 783 (1983).

2. *State Board of Education* v. *Board of Education of Netcong*, 262 A. 2d 21 (Sup. Ct. NJ 1970), *cert. denied*, 401 U. S. 1013.

3. *Anderson* v. *Salt Lake City Corporation*, 475 F. 2d 29, 33, 34 (10th Cir. 1973), *cert. denied*, 414 U. S. 879.

4. *Stone* v. *Graham*, 449 U. S. 39 (1980).

5. *Harvey* v. *Cobb County*, 811 F. Supp. 669 (N.D. Ga. 1993); *affirmed*, 15 F. 3d 1097 (11th Cir. 1994); *cert. denied*, 114 S. Ct. 2138 (1994).

6. *Bogen* v. *Doty*, 598 F. 2d 1110 (1979).

7. *Marsh* v. *Chambers*, 463 U. S. 783 (1983).

8. *Lee* v. *Weisman*, 120 L. Ed. 2d 467 (1992).

9. *Harris* v. *Joint School District*, 41 F. 3d 447 (9th Cir. 1994).

10. *Lynch* v. *Donnelly*, 465 U. S. 668, 669-670 (1985).

11. *County of Allegheny* v. *ACLU*, 106 L. Ed. 2d 472, 475 (1989).

12. George Bancroft, *Bancroft's History of the United States* (Boston: Little, Brown & Co., 1859), Vol. V, p. 24; see also Baron Charles Secondat de Montesquieu, *Spirit of Laws* (Philadelphia: Isaiah Thomas, 1802), Vol. I, p. 18, ad passim; and Benjamin Rush, *Letters of Benjamin Rush*, L. H. Butterfield, editor (Princeton: The American Philosophical Society, 1951), Vol. I, p. 454, to David Ramsay, March or April 1788.

13. *Bishop* v. *Colaw*, 450 F. 2d 1069, 1072, 1075 (8th Cir. 1971).

14. *Wallace* v. *Ford*, 346 F. Supp. 156, 162 (D.C. Ark. 1972).

15. *Finot* v. *Pasadena City Board of Education*, 58 Cal. Rptr. 520, 522 (Ct. App. 2nd Dist. Cal. 1967).

16. *Jones* v. *Clear Creek Independent School District*, 977 F. 2d 964, 965 (5th Cir. 1992).

17. *Harris* at 454.

18. *Pierce* v. *Society of Sisters*, 268 U. S. 510, 535 (1925).

19. *Reed* v. *van Hoven,* 237 F. Supp. 48, 51 (W.D. Mi. 1965).

20. *State Board of Education* v. *Board of Education of Netcong,* 262 A. 2d 21, 26 (Sup. Ct. NJ 1970), *cert. denied,* 401 U. S. 1013.

21. *Harris* at 447.

22. *Cohen* v. *California,* 403 U. S. 15, 18, 20, 25 (1971).

23. *People* v. *Ruggles,* 8 Johns 545, 546 (Sup. Ct. NY 1811).

24. *Erznoznik* v. *City of Jacksonville,* 422 U. S. 205. (1975).

25. *Commonwealth* v. *Jesse Sharpless and Others,* 2 Serg. & R. 91, 103, 104 (Sup. Ct. Penn. 1815).

26. *Grove* v. *Mead School District,* 753 F. 2d 1528, 1540 (9th Cir. 1985), *cert. denied,* 474 U. S. 826.

27. *People* v. *Ruggles,* 8 Johns 545, 546 (Sup. Ct. NY 1811).

28. *Walz* v. *Tax Commission,* 397 U. S. 664, 695 (1970), Harlan J. (concurring).

29. *Davis* v. *Beason,* 133 U. S. 333, 343 (1890).

30. *Commwealth* v. *Nesbit,* 84 Pa. 398, 406 (Pa. Sup. Ct. 1859).

31. *County of Allegheny* at 492.

32. *Theriault* v. *Silber,* 547 F. 2d 1279 (5th Cir. 1977).

33. *Malnak* v. *Yogi,* 440 F. Supp. 1284, 1287 (D.C. NJ 1977).

34. *Grove* at 1534.

35. *Torcaso* v. *Watkins,* 367 U. S. 488, 495, n. 11.

36. *Commonwealth* v. *Abner Kneeland,* 37 Mass. (20 Pick) 206, 233, 234 (Sup. Ct. Mass. 1838).

37. Noah Webster, *An American Dictionary of the English Language* (1828), s.v. "religion."

38. *Walz* at 695, Harlan, J. (concurring).

39. *Epperson* v. *Arkansas,* 393 U. S. 97 (1968).

40. *Wallace* v. *Jaffree,* 472 U. S. 38, 107 (1985), Rehnquist, J. (dissenting).

41. *Wallace* at 110-111, Rehnquist, J. (dissenting).

Chapter 14
Identifying the Spirit of the Constitution

1. *Benchmark,* Vol. 2, No. 1, January-February 1986, p. 6, "Toward a Jurisprudence of Original Intention," by Attorney General Edwin Meese, III.

2. John Witherspoon, *The Works of John Witherspoon* (Edinburgh: J. Ogle, 1815), Vol. V, p. 314, "The Trial of Religious Truth by Its Moral Influence," October 9, 1759.

3. Samuel Adams, *The Writings of Samuel Adams,* Harry Alonzo Cushing, editor (New York: G. P. Putnam's Sons, 1908), Vol. IV, p. 357, to the Legislature of Massachusetts on January 17, 1794.

4. James D. Richardson, *A Compilation of the Messages and Papers of the Presidents* 1789-1897 (Authority of Congress, 1899), Vol. I, p. 80, August 14, 1790.

5. Richardson, Vol. I, p. 249, July 22, 1797.

6. Richardson, Vol. I, p. 357, July 16, 1803.

7. Richardson, Vol. I, p. 473, August 9, 1809.

8. Richardson, Vol. II, p. 36, April 28, 1818.

9. Richardson, Vol. II, p. 376, March 17, 1827.

10. Richardson, Vol. II, p. 440, May 11, 1829.

11. *The Statutes at Large, Treaties, and Proclamations of the United States of America,* George P. Sanger, editor (Boston: Little, Brown, and Company, 1866), Vol. XIII, p. 33, Thirty-Eighth Congress, Session 1, Chapter 37, Section 4, Colorado's enabling act of March 21, 1864.

12. *Id.* at Vol. XIII, p. 31, Chapter 36, Section 4, Nevada's enabling act of March 21, 1864.

13. *Id.* at Vol. XIII, p. 48, Chapter 59, Section 4, Nebraska's enabling act of April 19, 1864.

14. *The Statutes at Large of the United States of America* (Washington: Government Printing Office, 1907), Vol. XXXIV, Part 1, p. 269, Fifty-Ninth Congress, Session 1, Chapter 3335, Section 3, Oklahoma's enabling act of June 16, 1906.

15. John Quincy Adams, *The Jubilee of the Constitution* (New York: Samuel Colman, 1839), p. 54.

16. Abraham Lincoln, *The Works of Abraham Lincoln: Speeches and Debates,* John H. Clifford, editor (New York: The University Society Inc., 1908), Vol. III, pp. 126-127, August 17, 1858.

17. *Gulf, Colorado and Santa Fe Railway Company* v. *Ellis,* 165 U. S. 150, 160 (1897).

Chapter 15
Maintaining Constitutional Integrity:
A Government of the People

1. Albert J. Beveridge, *The Life of John Marshall* (Boston: Houghton Mifflin, 1919), Vol. III, p. 121, n; see also the information from *The Proceedings of the American Philosophical Society* (Philadelphia: The American Philosophical Society, 1936), Vol. LXXVI, pp. 543-596, from "The First Homes of the Supreme Court of the United States," by Robert P. Reeder.

2. James Madison, *The Writings of James Madison,* Gaillard Hunt, editor (New York and London: G.P. Putnam's Sons, 1910), Vol. IX, p. 219, to Thomas Jefferson on February 8, 1825.

3. Alexander Hamilton, John Jay, James Madison, *The Federalist, on The New Constitution* (Philadelphia: Benjamin Warner, 1818), p. 281, Federalist #51 by Alexander Hamilton.

4. *The Federalist,* pp. 419-420, Federalist #78 by Alexander Hamilton; see also *The Federalist,* p. 398, Federalist #73 by Alexander Hamilton.

5. John Locke, *Two Treatises of Government,* (London: J. Whiston, 1772), p. 282, § 134, "Of the Extent of the Legislative Power."

6. Baron Charles Secondat de Montesquieu, *The Spirit of Laws* (Worcester: Isaiah Thomas, 1802), Vol. I, pp. 181, 185.

7. *The Constitutions of the Sixteen States* (Boston: Manning & Loring, 1797), p. 166, Pennsylvania, 1790, Article IX, Section II.

8. *Constitutions* (1797), p. 237, South Carolina, 1790, Article IX, Section I.

9. *The Constitutions of the Several Independent States of America* (Boston: Norman and Bowen, 1785), p. 55, New York, 1777, Article I.

10. *Constitutions* (1785), p. 130, North Carolina, 1776, "Declaration of Rights," Article I.

11. *The Constitutions of the United States of America* (Trenton: Moore and Lake, 1813), p. 165, Delaware, 1792, Preamble.

12. *Constitutions* (1797), p. 250, Vermont, 1786, "Declaration of Rights," Article VI.

13. *The Constitutions of the Several States Composing the Union* (Philadelphia: Hogan and Thompson, 1838), p. 179; Bill of Rights to the Virginia Constitution of 1776, Section 2.

14. *Constitutions* (1785), p. 3, New Hampshire, 1784, Part I, Bill of Rights, Article I.

15. *A Constitution or Frame of Government Agreed Upon by the Delegates of the People of the State of Massachusetts-Bay* (Boston: Benjamin Edes & Sons, 1780), p. 9, Massachusetts, 1780, Part I, Article V.

16. *Constitutions* (1785), p. 103, Maryland, 1776, "Declaration of Rights," Article I.

17. *The Federalist,* p. 275, Federalist #49 by Alexander Hamilton.

18. *The Federalist,* p. 424, Federalist #78 by Alexander Hamilton.

19. James Madison, *The Papers of James Madison,* Henry D. Gilpin, editor (Washington: Langtree & O'Sullivan, 1840), Vol. II, p. 1184, James Madison during the debates of Monday, July 23, 1787.

20. *Debates in the Several State Conventions on the Adoption of the Federal Constitution*, Jonathan Elliot, editor (Washington: Printed for the Editor, 1836), Vol. II, p. 446, James Wilson at the Pennsylvania Ratification Debates on Saturday, December 1, 1787.

21. Elliot's *Debates*, Vol. III, p. 553, John Marshall at the Virginia Ratification Debates on Friday, June 20, 1788.

22. *The Documentary History of the Supreme Court of the United States, 1789–1800*, Maeva Marcus, editor (New York: Columbia University Press, 1990), Vol. III, p. 412, from Justice Samuel Chase's "Charge to the Grand Jury of the Circuit Court for the District of Pennsylvania on April 12, 1800."

23. Madison, *Papers*, Vol. II, p. 1168, George Mason quoting Luther Martin during the debates on Saturday, July 21, 1787.

24. *The Federalist*, p. 421, Federalist #78 by Alexander Hamilton.

25. James Kent, *Commentaries on American Law* (New York: O. Halsted, 1826), Vol. I, p. 421.

26. Joseph Story, *Commentaries on the Constitution of the United States* (Boston: Hillard, Gray, and Company, 1833), Vol. III, p. 428, § 1570.

27. Madison, *Papers*, Vol. III, p. 1333, John Mercer during the debates of Wednesday, August 15, 1787.

28. Madison, *Papers*, Vol. III, p. 1334, John Dickinson during the debates of Wednesday, August 15, 1787; see also Beveridge, Vol. III, p. 116.

29. Madison, *Papers*, Vol. II, p. 783, Elbridge Gerry during the debates on Monday, June 4, 1787.

30. Raoul Berger, *Government by Judiciary: The Transformation of the Fourteenth Amendment* (Massachusetts: Harvard University Press, 1977), p. 360.

31. Story, Vol. I, p. 363, § 390.

32. *The Federalist*, p. 436, Federalist #81 by Alexander Hamilton.

33. Kent, Vol. I, p. 421.

34. *The Federalist*, p. 435, Federalist #81 by Alexander Hamilton.

35. James Madison, *Letters and Other Writings of James Madison* (New York: Published by Order of Congress, 1884), Vol I, p. 194, from his remarks on Mr. Jefferson's "Draught of a Constitution for Virginia," sent from New York to Mr. John Brown, Kentucky, October 1788.

36. *The Records of the Federal Convention of 1787*, Max Farrand, editor (New Haven: Yale University Press, 1911), Vol. I, p. 108, from Rufus King's records of the Convention from Monday, June 4, 1787.

37. *The Federalist*, p. 423, Federalist #78 by Alexander Hamilton.

38. Samuel Adams, *The Writings of Samuel Adams*, Harry Alonzo Cushing, editor (New York: G. P. Putnam's Sons, 1904), Vol. I, p. 3, from his "Instructions of the Town of Boston to its Representatives in the General Court, May 1764"; Vol. I, p. 144, from his "The House of Representatives of Massachusetts to Dennys Berdt, January 12, 1768"; Vol. I, p. 193, from his "The House of Representative of Massachusetts to Henry Seymour Conway on February 13, 1768"; Vol. II, pp. 343-344, from a letter to Arthur Lee on November 3, 1772; Vol. II, pp. 369-370, from his "A Letter of Correspondence to the Other Towns, November 20, 1772"; Vol. III, p. 4, from his "A Report to the Town of Boston, March 23, 1773"; Vol. III, p. 49, from a letter to Arthur Lee on June 28, 1773; Vol. III, pp. 50-51, from his "The Committee of Correspondence of Boston to the Committee of Correspondence of Worcester on September 11, 1773"; Vol. III, p. 80, from his "Resolution of the House of Representatives of Massachusetts, March 1, 1774"; Vol. III, p. 85, from his "Committee of Correspondence of Massachusetts to Benjamin Franklin, March 31, 1774"; and Vol. III, p. 97, from a letter to Arthur Lee on April 4, 1774.

39. Samuel Adams, _Writings,_ Vol. I, p. 144, from his "The House of Representatives of Massachusetts to Dennys Berdt, January 12, 1768" and Vol. I, p. 172, from his "The House of Representatives of Massachusetts to the Marquis of Rockingham, January 22, 1768."

40. _Boston Gazette,_ January 20, 1772, Samuel Adams writing as "Candidus."

41. Madison, _Papers,_ Vol. II, p. 1166, Luther Martin during the debates of Saturday, July 21, 1787.

42. _Commonwealth_ v. _Abner Kneeland,_ 37 Mass. (20 Pick) 206, 227, 232 (Sup. Ct. Mass. 1838).

43. William Rawle, _A View of the Constitution of the United States of America_ (Philadelphia: Philip H. Nicklin, 1829), p. 201.

44. _The Federalist,_ pp. 419-420, Federalist #78 by Alexander Hamilton.

45. Thomas Jefferson, _Writings of Thomas Jefferson,_ Albert Ellery Bergh, editor (Washington D. C.: Thomas Jefferson Memorial Association, 1904), Vol. XV, pp. 331-332, to Charles Hammond on August 18, 1821.

46. Thomas Jefferson, _Memoir, Correspondence, and Miscellanies, From the Papers of Thomas Jefferson,_ Thomas Jefferson Randolph, editor (Boston: Gray and Bowen, 1830), Vol. IV, p. 374, to Judge William Johnson on June 12, 1823.

47. Jefferson, _Writings,_ Vol. XV, p. 332, to Charles Hammond on August 18, 1821.

48. _Griswold_ v. _Connecticut,_ 381 U. S. 479, 483-484 (1965).

49. Berger, p. 2.

50. Elliot's _Debates,_ Vol. II, p. 446, James Wilson at the Pennsylvania Ratification Debates on Saturday, December 1, 1787.

51. Jefferson, _Writings,_ Vol. XI, p. 42, to Mrs. John Adams on July 22, 1804.

52. Jefferson, _Memoir,_ Vol. IV, p. 27, to Abigail Adams on September 11, 1804.

53. Madison, _Papers,_ Vol. II, p. 1166, Luther Martin during the debates of Saturday, July 21, 1787.

54. _The Debates and Proceedings in the Congress of the United States_ (Washington, D. C.: Gales and Seaton, 1834), Vol. I, p. 520, James Madison on June 17, 1789.

55. _Debates and Proceedings,_ Vol. I, p. 568, James Madison on June 18, 1789.

56. _The Debates and Proceedings in the Congress of the United States_ (Washington: Gales and Seaton, 1851), Seventh Congress, First Session, p. 661, February 20, 1802.

57. Jefferson, _Writings,_ Vol. XV, p. 215, to Spencer Roane on September 6, 1819.

58. Jefferson, _Writings,_ Vol. XV, p. 215, to Spencer Roane on September 6, 1819.

59. Jefferson, _Memoir,_ Vol. IV, p. 27, to Abigail Adams on September 11, 1804.

60. Jefferson, _Writings,_ Vol. XV, p. 277, to William Charles Jarvis on September 28, 1820.

61. Jefferson, _Memoir,_ Vol. IV, p. 27, to Abigail Adams on September 11, 1804.

62. James D. Richardson, _A Compilation of the Messages and Papers of the Presidents, 1789-1897_ (Published by Authority of Congress, 1899), Vol. VI, p. 9, "Inaugural Address" on March 4, 1861.

63. _Dred Scott_ v. _Sandford,_ 60 U. S. 393 (1857)

64. _The Debates and Proceedings of the Second Session of the Thirty-Seventh Congress,_ John C. Rives, editor (Washington D. C.: Congressional Globe Office, 1862), p. 2618, June 9, 1862.

65. Rawle, pp. 200-202.

66. Story, Vol. I, p. 346 § 374.

67. Henry St. George Tucker, _Lectures on Government_ (Charlottesville: Published by James Alexander, 1844), pp. 70-71.

68. Madison, _Papers,_ Vol. II, pp. 1161-62, James Wilson during the debates of Saturday, July 21, 1787.

69. Madison, *Papers,* Vol. II, pp. 1162-66, Elbridge Gerry, Caleb Strong, and Luther Martin during the debates of Saturday, July 21, 1787.

70. Madison, *Papers,* Vol. II, p. 791, debates of Monday, June 4, 1787; Vol. II, p. 812, debates of Wednesday, June 6, 1787; Vol. II, p. 1171, debates of Saturday, July 21, 1787; and Vol. III, p. 1331, debates of Wednesday, August 15, 1787.

71. *Marbury* v. *Madison,* 1 Cranch 137 (1803).

72. *Dictionary of American Biography,* s.v. "John Marshall."

73. John Marshall, *The Papers of John Marshall,* Charles Hobson, editor (Chapel Hill: University of North Carolina Press, 1990), Vol. VI, p. 90, from a letter to James Marshall on March 18, 1801.

74. Beveridge, Vol. III, p. 129, n. 1-4, p. 130, n. 1-2

75. Beveridge, Vol. III, pp. 128-129.

76. Beveridge, Vol. III, pp. 128-129.

77. Jefferson, *Writings,* Vol. XV, p. 447, to Judge William Johnson on June 12, 1823.

78. See *Cherokee Nation* v. *Georgia,* 8 L. Ed. 25 (1831), and *Worcester* v. *Georgia,* 31 U. S. 515 (1832).

79. Richardson, Vol. II, p. 582, "Veto Message" on July 10, 1832.

80. Richardson, Vol. II, p. 582, "Veto Message" on July 10, 1832.

81. *McCulloch* v. *Maryland,* 17 U. S. 316 (1819).

82. *Osborn* v. *United States Bank,* 22 U. S. 738 (1824).

83. J. G. Holland, *Life of Abraham Lincoln* (Springfield, MA: Gurdon Bill, 1866), p. 175.

84. George Washington, *Address of George Washington, President of the United States, and Late Commander in Chief of the American Army, to the People of the United States, Preparatory to His Declination* (Baltimore: George and Henry S. Keatinge, 1796), p. 22.

85. *The Federalist,* p. 80, Federalist #15 by Alexander Hamilton.

86. Jefferson, *Memoir,* Vol. IV p. 375, to Judge William Johnson on June 12, 1823.

87. George Washington, *Address . . . Preparatory to his Declination,* pp. 21-22.

88. James Madison, *A Memorial and Remonstrance Presented to the General Assembly of the State of Virginia at their Session in 1785 in Consequence of a Bill Brought into that Assembly for the Establishment of Religion* (Massachusetts: Isaiah Thomas, 1786), pp. 4-5.

89. Samuel Adams, *Writings,* Vol. IV, pp. 388-389, to the Legislature of Massachusetts on January 19, 1796.

90. *The Federalist,* p. 397, Federalist #73 by Alexander Hamilton.

91. Elliot's *Debates,* Vol. II, p. 196, Oliver Ellsworth at the Connecticut Ratification Debates of January 7, 1788.

92. *The Federalist,* p. 438, Federalist #81 by Alexander Hamilton.

93. *The Federalist,* p. 435, Federalist #81 by Alexander Hamilton.

94. *The Federalist,* p. 438, Federalist #81 by Alexander Hamilton.

95. James Wilson, *The Works of the Honorable James Wilson,* Bird Wilson, editor (Philadelphia: Bronson and Chauncey, 1804), Vol. II, p. 166, "Of the Constitution of the United States and of Pennsylvania—of the Legislative Department."

96. Story, Vol. II, pp. 233-234, § 762.

97. Madison, *Papers,* Vol. III, p. 1528, George Mason during the debates on Saturday, September 8, 1787.

98. *The Federalist,* p. 352, Federalist #65 by Alexander Hamilton.

99. Madison, *Papers,* Vol. III, p. 1528, Elbridge Gerry during the debates on Saturday, September 8, 1787.

100. Rawle, p. 211.

101. Rawle, p. 210.

102. Story, Vol. II, p. 268, § 798.

103. *The Federalist*, p. 353, Federalist #65 by Alexander Hamilton.

104. Elliot's *Debates*, Vol. IV, p. 32, James Iredell at North Carolina's Ratification Convention on Thursday, July 24, 1788

105. Story, Vol. II, p. 172, § 687.

106. George Washington, *The Writings of George Washington*, Jared Sparks, editor (Boston: Russell, Odiorne and Metcalf, 1835), Vol. IX, p. 279, to Bushrod Washington on November 10, 1787.

107. Jefferson, *Writings*, Vol. XV, p. 278, to William Charles Jarvis on September 28, 1820.

108. Richardson, Vol. I, p. 164, from the "Sixth Annual Address" of November 19, 1794.

109. Thomas Jefferson, *The Papers of Thomas Jefferson*, Julian P. Boyd, editor (NJ: Princeton University Press, 1961), Vol. XVI, p. 179, "Response to the Citizens of Albermarle," February 12, 1790.

110. Richardson, Vol. I, p. 322, from Jefferson's First Inaugural on March 11, 1801.

111. Samuel Adams, *Writings*, Vol. IV, p. 246, to Mrs. Adams on February 1, 1781.

112. *Compassion in Dying* v. *Washington*, No. 94-35534 (9th Cir. 1996), and *Quill* v. *Vacco*, No. 95-7028 (2nd Cir. 1996).

113. *Romer* v. *Evans*, 64 L.W. 4353 (1996).

114. *U. S. Term Limits* v. *Thornton*, 131 L. Ed. 2d 881 (1995), and *Thorsted* v. *Munro*, 75 F. 3d 454 (9th Cir. 1996).

115. *Coalition for Economic Equity* v. *Pete Wilson*, No. C-964024 TEH (U.S.D.C., N.D. Cal. 1996); *LULAC* v. *Wilson*, *908* F. Supp. 755 (C.D. Cal. 1995); and *Gregorio T.* v. *Wilson*, 59 F. 3d 1002 (9th Cir. 1996).

116. *Yniguez* v. *Arizona*, 69 F. 3d 920 (9th Cir.. 1995).

117. *Missouri* v. *Kalima Jenkins*, 58 L.W. 4480 (1990).

Chapter 16
Revisionism: A Willing Accomplice

1. Robert Ingersoll, *Ingersollia, Gems of Thought*, edited by Elmo (Chicago: Belford, Clarke & Co., 1882), pp.49-54.

2. Charles A. Beard and Mary R. Beard, *The Rise of American Civilization* (New York: The MacMillan Company, 1930), p. 439.

3. The Beards, *Rise*, p. 439.

4. *Church of the Holy Trinity* v. *U. S.*, 143 U. S. 457, 467-468 (1892).

5. W. E. Woodward, *George Washington: The Image and the Man* (New York: Boni and Liverlight, 1926), p. 142.

6. George Washington, *The Writings of Washington*, John C. Fitzpatrick, editor (Washington, D. C.: U. S. Government Printing Office, 1932), Vol. XV, p. 55, from his speech to the Delaware Indian Chiefs on May 12, 1779.

7. *Fac-Similie of Manuscript Prayer-Book Written by George Washington* (Philadelphia: 1891). According to the information from this book, the handwritten prayer book was bequeathed, with Washington's "other papers, to Judge Bushrod Washington from whom it descended to Col. John Augustine Washington, the last private owner of Mt. Vernon, who left it to his son Lawrence Washington, under whose direction the fac-similie has been most carefully prepared."

8. The Beards, *Rise*, p. 439.

9. John Frederick Schroeder, *Maxims of George Washington* (Mount Vernon, Virginia: The Mount Vernon Ladies' Association, 1989), p. 164.

10. Woodward, *George Washington*, p. 142.

11. *The Los Angeles Times,* August 3, 1995, "America's Unchristian Beginnings" Steven Morris, p. B-9. This article was picked up on wire services and appeared in newspapers across the nation.

12. For examples of ministers who used both clear evangelical terms as well as what today are errantly considered "deistic" descriptions for God, see Samuel Stanhope Smith, *The Divine Goodness to the United States of America—A Discourse on the Subjects of National Gratitude* (Philadelphia: William Young, 1795); Jonathan French, *A Sermon Delivered on the Anniversary of Thanksgiving, November 29, 1798* (Andover: Ames and Parker, 1799); Rev. Joseph Willard, *A Thanksgiving Sermon Delivered at Boston December 11, 1783* (Boston: T. and J. Fleet, 1784); William Hazlitt, *A Thanksgiving Sermon Preached at Hallowell, December 15, 1785* (Boston: Samuel Hall, 1786); John Evans, *The Happiness of American Christians, A Thanksgiving Sermon preached on Thursday the 24th of November 1803* (Hartford: Hudson and Goodwin, 1804); Isaac Backus, *An Appeal to the Public for Religious Liberty* (Boston: John Boyle, 1783); et. al.

13. George Washington, *The Writings of George Washington,* Jared Sparks, editor (Boston: Ferdinand Andrews, 1838), Vol. XII, pp. 406-407, from Washington's adopted daughter to Jared Sparks on February 26, 1833.

14. Gunning Bedford, *Funeral Oration upon the Death of General George Washington* (Wilmington: Franklin Press, 1800), p. 15.

15. John Frederick Schroeder, *Maxims of Washington; Political, Social, Moral, and Religious* (New York: D. Appleton and Company, 1855), p. 340.

16. Abiel Holmes, *The Counsel of Washington, Recommended in a Discourse Delivered at Cambridge, February 22, 1800* (Boston: Samuel Hall, 1800), p. 20.

17. *Eulogies and Orations on the Life and Death of General George Washington* (Boston: Manning and Loring, 1800), p. 37, from an eulogy by Jonathan Mitchell Sewall on December 31, 1799.

18. *Eulogies,* p. 190, from an oration delivered by Jeremiah Smith on February 22, 1800.

19. *The Charlotte Observer,* Friday, January 15, 1993, "Founding Fathers weren't devout," Michael A. Macdonald, p. 7A.

20. John Witherspoon, *The Works of John Witherspoon* (Edinburgh: J. Ogle, 1815), Vol. VI, p. 237, from "A Serious Apology for the Ecclesiastical Characteristics."

21. The Beards, *Rise,* Vol. I, p. 439.

22. Kenneth C. Davis, *Don't Know Much About History* (New York: Avon Books, 1990), p. 61.

23. Davis, p. 21.

24. Patrick Henry, *Patrick Henry: Life, Correspondence and Speeches,* William Wirt Henry, editor (New York: Charles Scribner's Sons, 1891), Vol. I, p. 266; see also *Orations of American Orators* (New York: The Colonial Press, 1900), Vol. I, p. 59.

25. *Documentary Source Book of American History 1606-1898,* William McDonald, editor (New York: The MacMillan Company, 1909), p. 19.

26. *Documents of American History,* Henry Steele Commager, editor (New York: Appleton-Century-Crofts, Inc., 1948), p. 117.

27. *Select Documents Illustrative of the History of the United States, 1776-1861,* William MacDonald, editor (New York: The MacMillan Company, 1898), p. 16.

28. *Documentary Source Book,* p. 80.

29. *A Collection of Charters and Other Public Acts Relating to the Province of Pennsylvania* (Philadelphia: B. Franklin, 1740), p. 1.

30. Alexis de Tocqueville, *Democracy in America: Specially Edited and Abridged for the Modern Reader,* Richard D. Heffner, editor (New York: Penguin Books, 1984).

31. Alexis de Tocqueville, *Democracy in America [The Republic of the United States of America and its Political Institutions, Reviewed and Examined]* (New York: A. S. Barnes, Co., 1851), Vol. I, p. 332.

32. de Tocqueville (1851) at Part I, 337.

33. de Tocqueville (1851) at Part I, 335.

34. Paul C. Vitz, *Censorship: Evidence of Bias in Our Children's Textbooks* (Michigan: Servant Books, 1986), p. 3.

35. Vitz, pp. 18-19.

36. Vitz, pp. 49-50.

37. Vitz, pp. 53-54.

38. Vitz, passim.

39. Charles Coffin, *The Story of Liberty* (New York: Harper & Brothers, 1878), p. 9.

40. *Richmond Times-Dispatch*, Tuesday, August 17, 1993, "Shadowboxing" p. A-8.

41. *Id.*

42. *Roanoke Times World-News,* September 1, 1993, "Sleaze in Salem," p. A-6.

43. W. E. Woodward, *A New American History* (New York: The Literary Guild, 1937), pp. 86-87.

44. Woodward, *George Washington*, p. 143.

45. Fairfax Downey, *Our Lusty Forefathers* (New York: Charles Scribner's Sons, 1947), p. 40, n.

46. Frank Moore, *Materials for History Printed From Original Manuscripts, the Correspondence of Henry Laurens of South Carolina* (New York: Zenger Club, 1861), p. 20, to John Laurens on August 14, 1776.

47. John Jay, *The Correspondence and Public Papers of John Jay,* Henry P. Johnston, editor (New York: G. P. Putnam's Sons, 1891), Vol. III, p. 342, to the English Anti-Slavery Society in June 1788.

48. Thomas Jefferson, *The Writings of Thomas Jefferson*, Albert Ellery Bergh, editor (Washington, D. C.: Thomas Jefferson Memorial Assoc., 1903), Vol. I, p. 34.

49. Benjamin Franklin, *The Works of Benjamin Franklin,* Jared Sparks, editor (Boston: Tappan, Whittemore, and Mason, 1839), Vol. VIII, p. 42, to the Rev. Dean Woodward on April 10, 1773.

50. John Quincy Adams, *An Oration Delivered Before The Inhabitants Of The Town Of Newburyport at Their Request on the Sixty-First Anniversary of the Declaration of Independence, July 4, 1837* (Newburyport: Charles Whipple, 1837), p. 50.

51. Jefferson, *Writings,* Vol. I, p. 4.

52. Jefferson, *Writings,* Vol. I, p. 28, from his autobiography; see also James Madison, *The Papers of James Madison* (Washington: Langtree and O'Sullivan, 1840), Vol. III, p. 1395, August 22, 1787; see also James Madison, *The Writings of James Madison,* Gaillard Hunt, editor, (New York: G. P. Putnam's Sons, 1910), Vol. IX, p. 2, to Robert Walsh on November 27, 1819.

53. *The Debates and Proceedings in the Congress of the United States* (Washington, D. C.: Gales and Seaton, 1834), First Congress, Second Session, p. 1518, March 22, 1790; see also George Adams Boyd, *Elias Boudinot, Patriot and Statesman* (Princeton, New Jersey: Princeton University Press, 1952), p. 182.

54. John Adams, *The Works of John Adams, Second President of the United States,* Charles Francis Adams, editor (Boston: Little, Brown, and Company, 1854), Vol. IX, pp. 92-93, to George Churchman and Jacob Lindley on January 24, 1801.

55. Kate Mason Rowland, *Life and Correspondence of Charles Carroll of Carrollton* (New York & London: G. P. Putnam's Sons, 1898), Vol. II, p. 321, to Robert Goodloe Harper, April 23, 1820.

56. Charles J. Stille, *The Life and Times of John Dickinson* (Philadelphia: J. P. Lippincott Company, 1891), p. 324, to George Logan on January 30, 1804.

57. John Jay, *The Life and Times of John Jay,* William Jay, editor (New York: J. & S. Harper, 1833), Vol. II, p. 174, to the Rev. Dr. Richard Price on September 27, 1785.

58. Thomas Jefferson, *Notes on the State of Virginia* (Philadelphia: Matthew Carey, 1794), Query XVIII, pp. 236-237.

59. Richard Henry Lee, *Memoir of the Life of Richard Henry Lee, and His Correspondence With the Most Distinguished Men in America and Europe, Illustrative of Their Characters, and of the American Revolution,* Richard Henry Lee, editor (Philadelphia: H. C. Carey and I. Lea, 1825), Vol. I, p. 19, the first speech of Richard Henry Lee in the House of Burgesses of Virginia.

60. William Livingston, *The Papers of William Livingston,* Carl E. Prince, editor (New Brunswick: Rutgers University Press, 1988), Vol. V, p. 358, to James Pemberton on October 20, 1788.

61. Luther Martin, *The Genuine Information Delivered to the Legislature of the State of Maryland Relative to the Proceedings of the General Convention Lately Held at Philadelphia* (Philadelphia: Eleazor Oswald, 1788), p. 57; see also *Debates in the Several State Conventions on the Adoption of the Federal Constitution,* Jonathan Elliot, editor (Washington: Printed for the Editor, 1836), Vol. I, p. 377.

62. Elliot's *Debates,* Vol. III, pp. 452-454, George Mason, June 15, 1788.

63. William Armor, *Lives of the Governors of Pennsylvania* (Norwich, Conn.: T. H. Davis & Co., 1874), p. 223.

64. Benjamin Rush, *Minutes of the Proceedings of a Convention of Delegates from the Abolition Societies Established in Different Parts of the United States Assembled at Philadelphia* (Philadelphia: Zachariah Poulson, 1794), p. 24.

65. Noah Webster, *Effect of Slavery on Morals and Industry* (Hartford: Hudson and Goodwin, 1793), p. 48.

66. James Wilson, *The Works of the Honorable James Wilson,* Bird Wilson, editor (Philadelphia: Lorenzo Press, 1804), Vol. II, p. 488, lecture on "The Natural Rights of Individuals."

67. Witherspoon, *Works* (1815), Vol. VII, p. 81, from "Lectures on Moral Philosophy," Lecture X on Politics.

68. Livingston, *Papers,* Vol. V, p. 255, to the New York Manumission Society on June 26, 1786.

69. *A Constitution or Frame of Government Agreed Upon by the Delegates of the People of the State of Massachusetts-Bay* (Boston: Benjamin Edes and Sons, 1780), p. 7, Article I, "Declaration of Rights" and *An Abridgement of the Laws of Pennsylvania,* Collinson Read, editor, (Philadelphia: Printed for the Author, 1801), pp. 264-266, Act of March 1, 1780.

70. *The Public Statue Laws of the State of Connecticut* (Hartford: Hudson and Goodwin, 1808), Book I, pp. 623-625, Act passed in October 1777 and *Rhode Island Session Laws* (Providence: Wheeler, 1784), pp. 7-8, Act of February 27, 1784.

71. *Constitutions* (1797), p. 249, Vermont, 1786, Article I, "Declaration of Rights."

72. *The Constitutions of the Sixteen States* (Boston: Manning and Loring, 1797), p. 50, New Hampshire, 1792, Article I, "Bill of Rights."

73. *Laws of the State of New York, Passed at the Twenty-Second Session, Second Meeting of the Legislature* (Albany: Loring Andrew, 1798), pp. 721-723, Act passed on March 29, 1799.

74. *Laws of the State of New Jersey, Complied and Published Under the Authority of the Legislature,* Joseph Bloomfield, editor (Trenton: James J. Wilson, 1811), pp. 103-105, Act passed February 15, 1804.

75. Rufus King, *The Life and Correspondence of Rufus King,* Charles King, editor (New York: G. P. Putnam's Sons, 1894), Vol. I, pp. 288-289.

76. *Acts Passed at a Congress of the United States of America* (Hartford: Hudson and Goodwin, 1791), p. 104, August 7, 1789.

77. *The Constitutions of the United States* (Trenton: Moore and Lake, 1813), p. 366, "An Ordinance for the Government of the Territory of the United States Northwest of the River Ohio," Article VI.

78. Washington, *Writings* (1932), Vol. XXVIII, pp. 407-408, to Robert Morris on April 12, 1786.

79. Richard Allen, *The Life Experience and Gospel Labors of the Rt. Rev. Richard Allen* (Nashville: Abingdon Press, 1983), p. 73, from his "Address to the People of Color in the United States."

80. *Principles: A Quarterly Review for Teachers of History and Social Science* (Claremont, CA: The Claremont Institute Spring/Summer 1992), Thomas G. West, "Was the American Founding Unjust? The Case of Slavery," p. 5.

81. Walter E. Williams, Creators Syndicate, Inc., May 26, 1993, "Some Fathers Fought Slavery."

82. Williams, May 26, 1993, "Some Fathers Fought Slavery."

83. Frank Swancara, *Obstruction of Justice by Religion* (Colorado: W. H. Courtwright Publishing Company, 1936), p. 3.

84. R. J. Rummel, *Death By Government* (New Brunswick: Transaction Publishers, 1994), p. 4.

85. Rummel, p. 8.

86. Daniel Dorchester, *Christianity in the United States* (New York: Hunt and Eaton, 1890), p. 124.

87. Witherspoon, *Works* (1815), Vol. V, pp. 325-326, "The Trial of Religious Truth by Its Moral Influence," October 9, 1759.

88. Benjamin Franklin, *The Works of Benjamin Franklin*, Jared Sparks, editor (Boston: Tappan, Whittemore, and Mason, 1840), Vol. X, p. 281-282, to Thomas Paine.

89. James Thomas Flexner, *George Washington: The Forge of Experience* (1732-1775), (Boston: Little, Brown and Company 1965), p. 39.

90. Washington, *Writings* (1836), Vol. XI, p. 232, to Mrs. S. Fairfax on May 16, 1798.

91. Washington, *Writings* (1938), Vol. XXVIII, p. 83, to George William Fairfax on February 27, 1785.

92. Washington, *Writings* (1836), Vol. XI, p. 232, to Sarah Cary Fairfax on May 16, 1798.

93. Flexner, p. 157.

94. See, for example, John Adams, *Works of John Adams, Second President of the United States* (Boston: Charles C. Little and James Brown, 1851), Vol. III, pp. 170-171, diary entry for June 2, 1778; see also Noah Webster, *The Revolution in France Considered in Respect to its Progress and Effects* (New York: George Bunce, 1794), p. 18; see also *Correspondence of the American Revolution; Being Letters of Eminent Men to George Washington,* Jared Sparks, editor (Boston: Little, Brown, and Company, 1853), Vol. IV, pp. 256-257, from Gouverneur Morris to George Washington, April 29, 1789.

95. de Tocqueville (1851), Vol. I, p. 332.

96. Washington, *Writings* (1835), Vol. IX, p. 190, to the Marquis de la Rourie on August 10, 1786.

97. George Washington Parke Custis, *Recollections and Private Memoirs of Washington, by His Adopted Son, George Washington Parke Custis, with a Memoir of the Author, by his Daughter; and Illustrative and Explanatory Notes, by Benson J. Lossing* (New York: Derby & Jackson, 1860), pp. 472-473.

98. John Marshall, *The Life of George Washington, Commander-in-Chief of the American Forces, During the War Which Established the Independence of His Country, and First President of the United States* (Philadelphia: C. P. Wayne, 1807), Vol. V, pp. 761-762.

99. *The Medical Repository,* Samuel L. Mitchill, M. D., and Edward Miller, M. D., editors (New York: T. & J. Swords, 1800), Vol. III, pp. 311-312, from *The Times,* a newspaper printed in Alexandria (Virginia), dated in December 16, 1799, by James Craik and Elisha C. Dick, attending physicians.

100. *Eulogies,* p. 91, from an oration by David Ramsay, M. D., on January 15, 1800.

101. *Eulogies,* p. 190, from an oration delivered by Jeremiah Smith on February 22, 1800.

102. *Eulogies,* pp. 36-37, from an eulogy by Jonathan Mitchell Sewell on December 31, 1799.

103. *Eulogies,* p. 17, from an oration by Major-General Henry Lee on December 26, 1799.

104. John Quincy Adams, *Writings of John Quincy Adams,* Worthington Chauncey Ford, editor (NY: The MacMillan Company, 1913), Vol. II, p. 451, n., to Joseph Pitcairn on February 4, 1800.

105. Charles Caldwell, *Character of General Washington* (Philadelphia: Printed at the office of "The True American," 1801), p. 7.

106. Alfred W. McCann, *Greatest of Men—Washington* (New York: The Devin-Adair Company, 1927), pp. 3, 5, 207.

107. Barbara Chase-Riboud, *Sally Hemings* (New York: The Viking Press, 1979), Book Jacket.

108. Virginius Dabney, *The Jefferson Scandals: A Rebuttal* (New York: Dodd, Mead and Company, 1981), p. 6.

109. *Dictionary of American Biography,* s.v. "James Thomson Callender."

110. *Dictionary of American Biography,* s.v. "James Thomson Callender."

111. *Dictionary of American Biography,* s.v. "James Thomson Callender."

112. Dabney, pp. 15, 34.

113. Dabney, p. 6.

114. *Newsweek,* February 1, 1993, p. 59, "What's Fair in Love and War," Randy Shilts.

115. John McAuley Palmer, *General Von Steuben* (New Haven: Yale University Press, 1937), p. 94.

116. Washington, *Writings* (1934), Vol. XI, pp. 83-84, from General Orders at Valley Forge on March 14, 1778.

117. Sir William Blackstone, *Commentaries on the Laws of England* (Oxford: Clarendon Press, 1769), Vol. IV, pp. 215-216.

118. James Wilson, *The Works of James Wilson* (Cambridge: Belknap Press of Harvard University Press, 1967), Vol. II, p. 656.

119. Zephaniah Swift, *A System of Laws of the State of Connecticut* (Windham: John Byrne, 1796), Vol. II, p. 311.

120. *Laws of the State of New York... Since the Revolution* (New York: Thomas Greenleaf, 1798), Vol., I, p. 336, Chap. XXI, February 14, 1787, in which the penalty was hanging; *The Public Statute Law of the State of Connecticut* (Hartford: Hudson and Goodwin, 1808), Book I, p. 295, Title LXVI, Chap. I, § 2, in which the penalty was death; *Alphabetical Digest of the Public Statute Laws of South Carolina* (Charleston: John Hoff, 1814), Vol. I, p. 99, Title 28, in which the penalty was death as well as the forfeiture of possessions; *Statutes of the State of Vermont* (Bennington, 1791), p. 74, March 8, 1787, in which the penalty was death.

121. *A Digest of the Laws of the State of Georgia* (Milledgeville: Grantland and Orme, 1822), p. 350, Section XXXV, in which the penalty was life in prison at hard labor; *Laws of the State of Maine* (Hallowell: Goodale, Glazier and Company, 1822), p. 58, Chapter V, Febrary 19, 1821, in which the penalty was solitary confinement for up to one year and imprisonment at hard labor for up to ten years; *Laws of the Commonwealth of Pennsylvania* (Philadelphia: John Bioren, 1810), Vol. I, p. 113, Chapter CCXXXVI, Section VII, in which the penalty was imprisonment at hard labor.

122. Thomas Jefferson, *Notes on the State of Virginia* (Philadelphia: Matthew Carey, 1794), p. 211, Query XIV.

123. Jefferson, *Writings,* Vol. I, pp. 226–227, from Jefferson's "For Proportioning Crimes and Punishments."

124. Peter Stone, *1776: A Musical Play* (New York: The Viking Press, 1970), p. 153.

125. Stone, p. 78.

126. Stone, p. 74.

127. Stone, p. 28.

128. Stone, p. 81.

129. Charles A. Goodrich, *Lives of the Signers of the Declaration of Independence* (New York: William Reed & Co., 1829), p. 153.

130. John Sanderson, *Biography of the Signers of the Declaration of Independence* (Philadelphia: R.W. Pomeroy, 1824), Vol. VI, pp. 253, 260.

131. Benson J. Lossing, *Eminent Americans* (New York: American Book Exchange, 1881), p. 320.

132. Chase-Riboud, Book Jacket.

133. Chase-Riboud, pp. 123–124.

134. Mary Higgins Clark, *Aspire To The Heavens: A Portrait of George Washington* (Cutchogue, NY: Buccaneer Books, 1968), p. 44.

135. Richard M. Rollins, *The Long Journey of Noah Webster* (PA: University of Pennsylvaina Press, 1980), pp. 107–108.

136. Noah Webster, *Letters of Noah Webster,* Harry R. Warfel, editor (New York: Library Publishers, 1953), pp. 309–315, to Thomas Dawes on December 20, 1808.

137. Fawn M. Brodie, *Thomas Jefferson: An Intimate History* (New York: W.W. Norton and Company, 1974), p. 229.

138. Brodie, p. 229.

139. Mark Noll, Nathan Hatch, George Marsden, *The Search for Christian America* (Colorado Springs: Helmers & Howard, 1989), p. 90.

140. See, for example, John Witherspoon's numerous works, including *The Dominions of Providence Over the Passions of Men* (Philadelphia: R. Aitken, 1776); *Ecclesiastical Characteristics* (Philadelphia: William and Thomas Bradford, 1767); *Christian Magnanimaty* (Princeton: James Tod, 1787); *A Sermon on the Religious Education of Children* (New York: M'Lean, etc., 1789); *Sermons on Practical Subjects* (Glasgow: A. Duncan and Company, 1768); *Letters on the Education of Children and Marriage* (Andover: Flagg and Gould, 1817); *The Works of the Rev. John Witherspoon* (Philadelphia: William W. Woodward, 1802) in four volumes; *The Works of John Witherspoon* (Edinburgh: J. Ogle, 1815) in ten volumes; etc.

141. Noah Webster, *The Holy Bible . . . With Amendments of the Language* (New Haven: Durrie & Peck, 1833), p. iii.

142. *Random House Dictionary of the English Language* (1987), s.v. "religion."

143. *United States* v. *Seeger,* 380 U. S. 163 (1965).

144. Noah Webster, *An American Dictionary of the English Language* (1828), s.v. "religion."

145. The Beards, *Rise,* pp. 448–449.

146. *The Concise Columbia Encyclopedia* (1983), p. 872.

147. Rev. Charles Buck, *A Theological Dictionary Containing Definitions of All Religious Terms* (Philadelphia: Edwin T. Scott, 1823), p. 582.

148. "An Answer to the Question, Why do you attend a Unitarian Church?" (Published at the Christian Register Office-John B. Russell, printer), circa 1840.

149. Daniel Rupp, *An Original History of the Religious Denominations at Present Existing in the United States* (Philadelphia: J. Y. Humphrys, 1844), p. 711.

150. *Dictionary of American History*, James Truslow Adams, editor (New York: Charles Scribner's Sons, 1940), p. 345.

151. Rupp, pp. 704-705.

152. Noll, Hatch, Marsden.

Chapter 17
Religion and Morality: The Indispensable Supports

1. George Washington, *Address of George Washington, President of the United States . . . Preparatory to his Declination* (Baltimore: George and Henry S. Keatinge, 1796), pp. 22-23.

2. John Adams, *The Works of John Adams, Second President of the United States,* Charles Frances Adams, editor (Boston: Little, Brown and Company, 1854), Vol. IX, p. 229, to the Officers of the First Brigade of the Third Division of the Militia of Massachusetts on October 11, 1798.

3. John Adams, *Works,* Vol. IX p. 401, to Zabdiel Adams on June 21, 1776.

4. John Adams, *Works,* Vol. IX p. 636, to Benjamin Rush on August 28, 1811.

5. John Quincy Adams, *Letters of John Quincy Adams to His Son on the Bible and its Teachings* (Auburn: James M. Alden, 1850), pp. 22-23.

6. Samuel Adams, *The Writings of Samuel Adams,* Harry Alonzo Cushing, editor (New York: G. P. Putnam's Sons, 1905), Vol. IV, p. 74, to John Trumbull on October 16, 1778.

7. William V. Wells, *The Life and Public Service of Samuel Adams* (Boston: Little, Brown, & Co., 1865), Vol. I, p. 22, quoting from a political essay by Samuel Adams published in *The Public Advertiser,* 1748.

8. Samuel Adams, *Writings,* Vol. IV, p. 124, to James Warren on February 12, 1779.

9. *Independent Chronicle* (Boston), February 22, 1787, Fisher Ames writing as Camillus; see also Fisher Ames, *The Works of Fisher Ames,* Seth Ames, editor (Indianapolis: Liberty Classics, 1983), Vol. I, p. 67.

10. Charles C. Jones, *Biographical Sketches of the Delegates from Georgia to the Continental Congress* (Boston and New York: Houghton, Mifflin and Company, 1891), pp. 6-7.

11. Bernard C. Steiner, *The Life and Correspondence of James McHenry* (Cleveland: The Burrows Brothers Company, 1907), p. 475, Charles Carroll to James McHenry on November 4, 1800.

12. *Connecticut Courant,* June 7, 1802, p. 3.

13. Benjamin Franklin, *The Works of Benjamin Franklin,* Jared Sparks, editor (Boston: Tappan, Whittemore and Mason, 1840), Vol. X, p. 297, to Messrs. The Abbes Chalut and Arnaud on April 17, 1787.

14. Nathanael Greene, *The Papers of General Nathanael Greene,* Richard K. Showman, editor (Chapel Hill: University of North Carolina Press, 1976), Vol. I, p. 182, to Catherine Ward Greene on January 13, 1776.

15. *The Independent Chronicle* (Boston: Nathaniel Willis) on November 2, 1780, Vol. XIII, p. 4, from John Hancock's Inaugural Address as Governor of Massachusetts; see also Abram English Brown, *John Hancock, His Book* (Boston: Lee and Shepard Publishers, 1898), p. 269.

16. Patrick Henry, *Patrick Henry: Life, Correspondence and Speeches,* William Wirt Henry, editor (New York: Charles Scribner's Sons, 1891), Vol. I, p. 82, from a handwritten endorsement on the back of the paper containing the resolutions of the Virginia Assembly in 1765 concerning the Stamp Act.

17. Henry, *Correspondence,* Vol. II, p. 592, to Archibald Blair on January 8, 1799.

18. Henry, *Correspondence,* Vol. II, p. 185, from George Mason to Patrick Henry, May 6, 1783.

19. Thomas Jefferson, *The Writings of Thomas Jefferson*, Albert Ellery Bergh, editor (Washington, D. C.: The Thomas Jefferson Memorial Association, 1904), Vol. XII, p. 315, to James Fishback, September 27, 1809.

20. Richard Henry Lee, *The Letters of Richard Henry Lee*, James Curtis Ballagh, editor (New York: The MacMillan Company, 1914), Vol. II, p. 411, to Colonel Martin Pickett on March 5, 1786.

21. Bernard C. Steiner, *One Hundred and Ten Years of Bible Society Work in Maryland, 1810-1920* (Baltimore: The Maryland Bible Society, 1921), p. 14.

22. Gouverneur Morris, *A Diary of the French Revolution* (Boston: Houghton Mifflin Co., 1939), Vol. II, p. 172, April 29, 1791.

23. Morris, *Diary*, Vol. II, p. 452, to Lord George Gordon, June 28, 1792.

24. Jared Sparks, *The Life of Gouverneur Morris* (Boston: Gray and Bowen, 1832), Vol. III, p. 483, from his "Notes on the Form of a Constitution for France."

25. *United States Oracle* (Portsmouth, NH), May 24, 1800; see also *The Documentary History of the Supreme Court of the United States, 1789-1800*, Maeva Marcus, editor (New York: Columbia University Press, 1988), Vol. III, p. 436.

26. David Ramsay, *An Oration, Delivered in St. Michael's Church Before the Inhabitants of Charleston, South-Carolina, on the Fourth of July, 1794, in Commemoration of American Independence* (Charleston: W. P. Young, 1794), p. 19.

27. Benjamin Rush, *Essays, Literary, Moral and Philosophical* (Philadelphia: Thomas and Samuel Bradford, 1798), p. 8, "On the Mode of Education Proper in a Republic."

28. Benjamin Rush, *Letters of Benjamin Rush*, L. H. Butterfield, editor (Princeton: The American Philosophical Society, 1951), Vol. I, p. 505, "To American Farmers About to Settle in New Parts of the United States," March 1789.

29. *A Selection of Orations and Eulogies . . . In Commemoration of the Life . . . of Gen. George Washington*, Charles Humphrey Atherton, editor (Amherst: Samuel Preston, 1800), p. 81, from an oration by Jeremiah Smith, February 22, 1800.

30. Joseph Story, *Commentaries on the Constitution of the United States* (Boston: Hillard, Gray, and Company, 1833), Vol. III, pp. 722-723, § 1865.

31. Story, *Commentaries*, Vol. III, p. 727, § 1869.

32. John Sanderson, *Biography of the Signers to the Declaration of Independence* (Philadelphia: R. W. Pomeroy, 1824), Vol. IX, p. 333, Thomas Stone to his son, October 1787.

33. Washington, *Address . . . Preparatory to his Declination*, pp. 22-23.

34. George Washington, *The Writings of George Washington*, John C. Fitzpatrick, editor (Washington: U. S. Government Printing Office, 1936), Vol. XIII, p. 118, from General Orders, October 21, 1778.

35. Washington, *Writings* (1939), Vol. XXIX, p. 410, to Marquis de Lafayette on February 7, 1788.

36. George Washington, *The Writings of George Washington*, Jared Sparks, editor (Boston: Ferdinand Andrews, 1838), Vol. XII, p. 167, to the Synod of the Reformed Dutch Church in North America, October, 1789.

37. Washington, *Writings* (1940), Vol. XXXV, p. 416, to the Clergy of Different Denominations Residing in and Near the City of Philadelphia, on March 3, 1797.

38. Daniel Webster, *The Works of Daniel Webster* (Boston: Little, Brown, & Co., 1853), Vol. II, p. 615, from an address delivered at the Laying of the Cornerstone of the Addition to the Capitol on July 4, 1851.

39. Daniel Webster, *Works*, Vol. I, p. 44, from a Discourse Delivered at Plymouth on December 22, 1820.

40. Noah Webster, *History of the United States* (New Haven: Durrie & Peck, 1832), p. 6.

41. Noah Webster, *History*, p. 339, ¶ 53.

42. James Wilson, *The Works of the Honourable James Wilson*, Bird Wilson, editor (Philadelphia: Bronson and Chauncey, 1804), Vol. I, pp. 104-106, "Of the General Principles of Law and Obligation."

43. John Witherspoon, *The Works of John Witherspoon* (Edinburgh: J. Ogle, 1815), Vol. IX, p. 231, from "The Druid," Number I.

44. John Witherspoon, *The Works of the Rev. John Witherspoon* (Philadelphia: William W. Woodard, 1802), Vol. III, pp. 41-42, 46, "The Dominion of Providence Over the Passions of Men," May 17, 1776.

45. *Journals of the American Congress: From 1774 to 1788* (Washington: Way and Gideon, 1823), Vol. III, p. 85, October 12, 1788.

46. *Runkel* v. *Winemiller*, 4 H & McH. 276, 288 (Sup. Ct. MD 1799)

47. *People* v. *Ruggles*, 8 Johns 545, 546 (Sup. Ct. NY 1811).

48. *Updegraph* v. *Commonwealth*, 11 Serg. & R. 393, 406 (Sup. Ct. Penn. 1824).

49. *Vidal* v. *Girard's Executors*, 43 U. S. 126, 200 (1844).

50. *City Council of Charleston* v. *S. A. Benjamin*, 2 Strob. 508, 520 (Sup. Ct. SC 1846).

51. *Reports of Committees of the House of Representatives Made During the First Session of the Thirty-Third Congress* (Washington: A. O. P. Nicholson, 1854), H. Rep. 124, p. 8, March 27, 1854.

52. *Church of the Holy Trinity* v. *U. S.*, 143 U. S. 457, 469 (1892).

53. *Ruggles* at 546.

54. *Commonwealth* v. *Jesse Sharpless and Others*, 2 Serg. & R. 91, 103 (Sup. Ct. Penn. 1815), Yeates, J., (concurring).

55. *Updegraph* at 398-399, 405 (Sup. Ct. Penn. 1824).

56. *City of Charleston* at 523.

57. *Reports of Commitee of the House of Representatives*, p. 8.

58. B. F. Morris, *Christian Life and Character of the Civil Institutions of the United States* (Philadelphia: George W. Childs, 1864), p. 328.

59. Thomas Jefferson, *Memoir, Correspondence, and Miscellanies, From the Papers of Thomas Jefferson*, Thomas Jefferson Randolph, editor (Boston: Gray and Bowen, 1830), Vol. III, p. 509, to Benjamin Rush on April 21, 1803, Jefferson's "Syllabus of an Estimate of the Merit of the Doctrines of Jesus, Compared with Those of Others." See also William Linn, *The Life of Thomas Jefferson* (Ithaca, New York: Mack & Andrus, 1834), p. 265.

60. John Quincy Adams, *Letters . . . to His Son*, p. 62.

61. Zephaniah Swift, *The Correspondent* (Windham: Printed by John Byrne, 1793), p. 119.

62. Jones, pp. 6-7.

63. Witherspoon, *Works* (1815), Vol. VII, pp. 118-119, from his Lectures on Moral Philosophy, Lecture 14, on Jurisprudence.

64. James Otis, *The Rights of the British Colonies Asserted and Proved* (Boston and London: J. Williams and J. Almon, 1766), p. 4.

65. Robert Winthrop, *Addresses and Speeches on Various Occasions* (Boston: Little, Brown and Co., 1852), p. 172, from an Address Delivered at the Annual Meeting of the Massachusetts Bible Society in Boston, May 28, 1849.

66. Daniel Webster, *Works*, Vol. I, pp. 41-42, from a speech at Plymouth on December 22, 1820.

67. Rush, *Essays*, p. 112, "Defense of the Use of the Bible as a School Book."

68. Alexis de Tocqueville, *Democracy in America, The Republic of the United States of America and Its Political Institutions, Reviewed and Examined*, Henry Reeves, translator (New York: A. S. Barnes & Co., 1851), Vol. II, p. 130.

Chapter 18
Returning to Original Intent

1. *The Constitutions of the Several Independent States of America* (Boston: Norman and Bowen, 1785), p. 81, Pennsylvania, 1776, Chapter II, Section 10.

2. *The Constitutions of the Sixteen States* (Boston: Manning and Loring, 1797), p. 257, Vermont, 1792, Chapter II, Section XII.

3. *Constitutions* (1785), p. 146, South Carolina, 1776, Section 13.

4. *Constitutions* (1797), p. 274, Tennessee, 1796, Article VIII, Section II.

5. *Reports of the Proceedings and Debates of the Convention of 1821, Assembled for the Purpose of Amending the Constitution of the State of New York* (Albany: E. and E. Hosford, 1821), p. 575, Rufus King, October 30, 1821.

6. Matthias Burnet, *An Election Sermon, Preached at Hartford, on the Day of the Anniversary Election, May 12, 1803* (Hartford: Hudson and Goodwin, 1803), pp. 7-9.

7. John Adams, *The Works of John Adams, Second President of the United States,* Charles Francis Adams, editor (Boston: Charles C. Little and James Brown, 1850), Vol. II, p. 294, diary entry for February 9, 1772.

8. Samuel Adams, *The Writings of Samuel Adams,* Harry Alonzo Cushing, editor (New York: G. P. Putnam's Sons, 1907), Vol. III, p. 286, to John Scollay on April 30, 1776.

9. James Madison, *The Papers of James Madison,* Henry Gilpin, editor (Washington: Langtree and O'Sullivan, 1840), Vol. III, p. 1391, August 22, 1787.

10. *The Debates in the Several State Conventions,* Jonathan Elliot, editor (Washington: Jonathan Elliot, 1836), Vol. I, p. 374, Luther Martin, January 27, 1788.

11. Chandler Robbins, *A Sermon Preached Before His Excellency John Hancock, Esq Governour; His Honor Samuel Adams, Esq. Lieutenant Governour; the Honourable the Council, and the Honourable the Senate and House of Representatives of the Commonwealth of Massachusetts, May 25, 1791, Being the Day of General Election* (Boston: Thomas Adams, 1791), p. 32.

12. *The Daily Advertiser* (New York), May 1, 1789, p. 2; see also *American State Papers: Documents Legislative and Executive, of the Congress of the United States* (Washington: Gales and Seaton, 1833), Vol. I, pp. 9-10, April 30, 1789.

13. Madison, *Papers* (1840), Vol. II, p. 985, June 28, 1787.

14. Thomas Jefferson, *Notes on State of Virginia* (Philadelphia: Mathew Carey, 1794), p. 237, Query XVIII.

15. An example of this is demonstrated in the anecdote where, having concluded their work on the Constitution, Benjamin Franklin walked outside and seated himself on a public bench. A woman approached him and inquired, "Well, Dr. Franklin, what have you done for us?" Franklin quickly responded, "My dear lady, we have given to you a republic—if you can keep it." Taken from "America's Bill of Rights at 200 Years," by former Chief Justice Warren E. Burger, printed in *Presidential Studies Quarterly,* Vol. XXI, No. 3, Summer 1991, p. 457. This anecdote appears in numerous other works as well.

16. Alexander Hamilton, John Jay, James Madison, *The Federalist on the New Constitution* (Philadelphia: Benjamin Warner, 1818), p. 53, #10, James Madison.

17. John Adams, *Works,* Vol. VI, p. 484, to John Taylor on April 15, 1814.

18. Fisher Ames, *Works of Fisher Ames* (Boston: T. B. Wait & Co., 1809), p. 24, Speech on Biennial Elections, delivered January, 1788.

19. Ames, *Works,* p. 384, "The Dangers of American Liberty," February 1805.

20. Gouverneur Morris, *An Oration Delivered on Wednesday, June 29, 1814, at the Request of a Number of Citizens of New-York, in Celebration of the Recent Deliverance of Europe from the Yoke of Military Despotism* (New York: Van Winkle and Wiley, 1814), pp. 10, 22.

21. John Quincy Adams, *The Jubilee of the Constitution. A Discouse Delivered at the Request of the New York Historical Society, in the City of New York, on Tuesday, the 30th of April 1839; Being the Fiftieth Anniversary of the Inauguration of George Washington as President of the United States, on Thursday, the 30th of April, 1789* (New York: Samuel Colman, 1839), p. 53.

22. Benjamin Rush, *The Letters of Benjamin Rush*, L. H. Butterfield, editor (Princeton: Princeton University Press for the American Philosophical Society, 1951), Vol. I, p. 523, to John Adams on July 21, 1789.

23. Noah Webster, *The American Spelling Book: Containing an Easy Standard of Pronunciation: Being the First Part of a Grammatical Institute of the English Langauage, To Which is Added, an Appendix, Containing a Moral Catechism and a Federal Catechism* (Boston: Isaiah Thomas and Ebenezer T. Andrews, 1801), pp. 103–104.

24. Witherspoon, Works (1815), Vol. VII, p. 101, Lecture 12 on Civil Society.

25. Zephaniah Swift, *A System of the Laws of the State of Connecticut* (Windham: John Byrne, 1795), Vol. I, p. 19.

26. See, for example, Benjamin Rush, *Letters*, Vol. I, p. 498, to John Adams on January 22, 1789.

27. Noah Webster, *History of the United States* (New Haven: Durrie & Peck, 1832), p. 6.

28. George Bancroft, *History of the United States from the Discovery of the American Continent* (Boston: Little, Brown & Co., 1859), Vol. V, p. 24; see also Baron Charles Secondat de Montesquieu, *Spirit of the Laws* (Philadelphia: Isaiah Thomas, 1802), Vol. I, pp. 17–23, and ad passim.

29. Rush, *Letters*, Vol. I, p. 454, to David Ramsay, March or April 1788.

30. Sir William Blackstone, *Commentaries on the Laws of England* (Philadelphia: Robert Bell, 1771), Vol. I, pp. 42–43.

31. James Wilson, *The Works of the Honourable James Wilson*, Bird Wilson, editor (Philadelphia: Lorenzo Press, 1804), Vol. I, pp. 103–105, "Of the General Principles of Law and Obligation."

32. Alexander Hamilton, *The Papers of Alexander Hamilton*, Harold C. Syrett, editor (New York: Columbia University Press, 1961), Vol. I, p. 87, February 23, 1775, quoting William Blackstone, *Commentaries on the Laws of England* (Philadelphia: Robert Bell, 1771), Vol. I, p. 41.

33. Rufus King, *The Life and Correspondence of Rufus King*, Charles R. King, editor (New York: G. P. Putnam's Sons, 1900), Vol. VI, p. 276, to C. Gore on February 17, 1820.

34. John Adams, *The Papers of John Adams*, Robert J. Taylor, editor (Cambridge: Belknap Press, 1977), Vol. I, p. 83, from "An Essay on Man's Lust for Power, with the Author's Comment in 1807," written on August 29, 1763, but first published by John Adams in 1807.

35. William J. Bennett, *American Education Making It Work* (Washington, D. C.: U. S. Government Printing Office, 1988), p. 10.

36. *The Common School Almanac* (New York: The American Common School Society, 1839), p. 1, Maxim 11.

37. Thomas Jefferson, *Writings of Thomas Jefferson*, Albert Bergh, editor (Washington, D. C.: Thomas Jefferson Memorial Assoc., 1904), Vol. XIV, p. 384, in a letter to Colonel Charles Yancey on January 6, 1816.

38. John Adams, *Papers*, Vol. I, p. 81, from "'U' to the Boston Gazette" written on August 29, 1763.

39. John Jay, *The Correspondence and Public Papers of John Jay*, Henry P. Johnston, editor (New York: G. P. Putnam's Sons, 1890), Vol. I, pp. 163–164, from his Charge to the Grand Jury of Ulster County, September 9, 1777.

40. *Debates in the Several State Conventions on the Adoption of the Federal Constitution*, Jonathan Elliot, editor (Washington: Printed for the Editor, 1836), Vol. II, p. 200, Governor Samuel Huntington, January 9, 1788.

41. Edward C. Reynolds, _The Maine Scholars' Manual_ (Portland, Maine: Dresser, McLellan and Co., 1880), preface.

42. Pat Robertson, _America's Dates with Destiny_ (Nashville: Thomas Nelson Publishers, 1986) p. 95.

43. H. R. Warfel, _Noah Webster, Schoolmaster to America_ (NY: MacMillan Co, 1936), pp. 181-82.

44. Rush, _Letters_, Vol. II, p. 1103, to John Adams on September 4, 1811.

45. Thomas Clarkson, _Memoirs of the Private and Public Life of William Penn_ (London: Richard Taylor and Co., 1813) Vol. I, p. 303.

46. _United States Oracle_ (Portsmouth, NH), May 24, 1800; see also _The Documentary History of the Supreme Court of the United States, 1789-1800_, Maeva Marcus, editor (New York: Columbia University Press, 1988), Vol. III, p. 436.

47. Noah Webster, _History_, pp. 336-337, ¶ 49.

48. Noah Webster, _Letters to a Young Gentleman Commencing His Education_ (New Haven: S. Converse, 1823), pp. 18-19, Letter 1.

49. Robbins, p. 18.

50. Burnet, pp. 16, 27.

51. Samuel Adams, _Writings_, Vol. III, pp. 236-237, to James Warren on November 4, 1775.

52. _Collections of the New York Historical Society for the Year 1821_ (New York: E. Bliss and E. White, 1821), pp. 32, 34, from "An Inaugural Discourse Delivered Before the New York Historical Society by the Honorable Gouverneur Morris, (President,) 4th September, 1816."

53. Witherspoon, _Works_ (1815), Vol. IV, pp. 266-267, from "A Sermon Delivered at a Public Thanksgiving after Peace."

54. William Jay, _The Life of John Jay_ (New York: J. & J. Harper, 1833), Vol. II, p. 376, to John Murray, Jr. on October 12, 1816.

55. Burnet, p. 27.

56. Witherspoon, _Works_ (1815), Vol. IV, p. 267, from "A Sermon Delivered at a Public Thanksgiving after Peace."

57. Jay, _Correspondence_, Vol. I, p. 161, from his "Charge to the Grand Jury of Ulster County" on September 9, 1777.

58. Samuel Adams, _Writings_, Vol. IV, p. 253, in the _Boston Gazette_ on April 2, 1781.

59. Samuel Adams, _Writings_, Vol. IV, p. 256, in the _Boston Gazette_ on April 16, 1781.

60. Daniel Webster, _The Works of Daniel Webster_ (Boston: Little, Brown, and Company, 1853), Vol. II, p. 108, from remarks made at a public reception by the ladies of Richmond, Virginia, on October 5, 1840.

61. Noah Webster, _Letters to a Young Gentleman_, p. 19, Letter 1.

62. George Washington, _The Writings of George Washington_, Jared Sparks, editor (Boston: Russell, Odiorne, and Metcalf; and Hilliard, Gray, and Co., 1835), Vol. IX, pp. 391-392, to Benjamin Lincoln on June 29, 1788.

63. John Witherspoon, _The Works of the Rev. John Witherspoon_ (Philadelphia: William W. Woodward, 1802), Vol. III, p. 37, sermon at Princeton on May 17, 1776, "Dominion of Providence Over the Passions of Men."

64. Witherspoon, _Works_ (1815), Vol. IX, p. 129, from his "Speech in Congress upon the Confederation."

65. Samuel Adams, _Writings_, Vol. IV, p. 225, to Thomas Wells on November 22, 1780.

66. Samuel Adams, _Writings_, Vol. IV, p. 252, in the _Boston Gazette_ on April 2, 1781.

67. Daniel Webster, _The Writings and Speeches of Daniel Webster_ (Boston: Little, Brown, & Company, 1903), Vol. XIII, pp. 492-493, from a speech on February 23, 1852.

68. John Dickinson, *The Political Writings of John Dickinson* (Wilmington: Bonsal and Niles, 1801), Vol. I, p. 277, quoting from Montesquieu, Vol. I, p. 272.

69. Samuel Adams, *Writings*, Vol. II, p. 287, in the *Boston Gazette* on December 9, 1771.

70. Daniel Webster, *Works*, Vol. I, p. 403.

71. John M. Taylor, *Garfield of Ohio: The Available Man* (New York: W. W. Norton and Company, Inc., 1970), p. 180, quoted from "A Century of Congress," by James A. Garfield, *Atlantic*, July 1877.

72. Charles G. Finney, *Lectures on Revivals of Religion* (New York: Fleming H. Revell Company, 1868, first published in 1835), Lecture XV, pp. 281-282.

73. George Washington, *Address of George Washington, President of the United States . . . Preparatory to His Declination* (Baltimore: George and Henry S. Keatinge, 1796), pp. 19-21.

74. David Ramsay, *An Eulogium Upon Benjamin Rush, M.D.* (Philadelphia: Bradford and Inskeep, 1813), p. 103.

75. Burnet, pp. 26-27.

76. John R. Musick, *Great Americans of History—John Hancock* (Chicago: Union School Furnishing Company 1898), pp. 116-117.

Appendix E:
List of Cases Cited

Abington v. *Schempp,* 374 U. S. 203 (1963).

Alexander v. *Nacogdoches School District,* Civil Action 9:91CV144 (U.S.D.C., E.D. Tx. 1991).

American Federation of Labor v. *American Sash & Door Co.,* 335 U. S. 538 (1949).

Anderson v. *Salt Lake City Corporation,* 475 F. 2d 29 (10th Cir. 1973), *cert. denied,* 414 U. S. 879.

Baer v. *Kolmorgen,* 181 N. Y. S. 2d. 230 (Sup. Ct. NY 1958).

Barron v. *Baltimore,* 32 U. S. 243 (1833).

Bebout v. *Leimbaugh,* 93-C-1079 J (C.D. Utah 1993).

Bishop v. *Aronov,* 926 F. 2d 1066 (11th Cir. 1991).

Bishop v. *Colaw,* 450 F. 2d 1069 (8th Cir. 1971).

Board of Education v. *Allen,* 392 U. S. 236 (1968).

Bogen v. *Doty,* 598 F. 2d 1110 (8th Cir. 1979).

Cantwell v. *State of Connecticut,* 310 U. S. 296 (1940).

Case of Fries 9 Fed. Cas. 826, no. 5, 126 (C.C.D. Pa. 1799).

Cherokee Nation v. *Georgia,* 8 L. Ed. 25 (1831).

Church of the Holy Trinity v. *U. S.,* 143 U. S. 457 (1892).

City Council of Charleston v. *S. A. Benjamin,* 2 Strob. 508 (Sup. Ct. SC 1846).

Coalition for Economic Equity v. *Pete Wilson,* No. C-964024 TEH (U.S.D.C., N.D. Cal. 1996).

Cohen v. *California,* 403 U. S. 15 (1971).

Collins v. *Chandler Unified School District,* 644 F. 2d 759 (9th Cir. 1981), *cert. denied,* 454 U. S. 863.

Commissioner of Education v. *School Committee of Leyden,* 267 N. E. 2d 226 (Sup. Ct. Mass. 1971), *cert. denied,* 404 U. S. 849 (1971).

Committee for Public Education v. *Nyquist,* 413 U. S. 756 (1973).

Commonwealth v. *Chambers,* 599 A. 2d 630 (Sup. Ct. Pa. 1991), *cert. denied,* case no. 91-1597, May 26, 1992, petition for rehearing denied August 18, 1992.

Commonwealth v. *Has* (1877).

Commonwealth v. *[Abner] Kneeland,* 37 Mass. (20 Pick) 206 (Sup. Ct. Mass. 1838).

Commonwealth v. *Nesbit,* 84 Pa. 398 (Pa. Sup. Ct. 1859).

Commonwealth v. *[Jesse] Sharpless and Others,* 2 Serg. & R. 91 (Sup. Ct. Penn. 1815).

Commonwealth v. *Wolf,* 3 Serg. & R. 48 (Sup. Ct. Penn. 1817).

Compassion in Dying v. *Washington,* No. 94-35534 (9th Cir. 1996).

County of Allegheny v. *American Civil Liberties Union,* 106 L. Ed. 2d 472 (1989).

Dartmouth College v. *Woodward,* 17 U. S. 518 (1819).

Davis v. *Beason,* 133 U. S. 333 (1890).

Doe v. *Aldine Independent School District,* 563 F. Supp. 883 (U.S.D.C., S.D. Tx. 1982).

Doe v. *Duncanville Independent School District,* 994 F. 2d 160 (5th Cir. 1993).

[Jane] Doe v. *Santa Fe Independent School District,* Civil Action No. G-95-176 (U.S.D.C., S.D. Tx. 1995).

Duran v. *Nitsche,* 780 F. Supp. 1048 (E.D. Pa. 1991).

Edwards v. *Aguillard,* 482 U. S. 578 (1987).

Engel v. *Vitale,* 370 U. S. 421 (1962).

Epperson v. *Arkansas,* 393 U. S. 97 (1968).

Erznoznik v. *City of Jacksonville,* 422 U. S. 205 (1975).

Everson v. *Board of Education,* 330 U. S. 1 (1947).

Finot v. *Pasadena City Board of Education,* 58 Cal. Rptr. 520 (Ct. App. 2nd Dist. Cal. 1967).

Florey v. *Sioux Falls School District,* 464 F. Supp. 911 (U.S.D.C., SD 1979), *cert. denied,* 449 U. S. 987 (1980).

Florida v. *George T. Broxson,* Case no. 90-0293-CF (1st Jud. Cir. Ct., Walton County, Fl., 1992).

Friedman v. *Board of County Commissioners,* 781 F. 2d 777 (10th Cir. 1985), *cert. denied,* 476 U. S. 1169 (1986).

Gearon v. *Loudoun County School Board,* 844 F. Supp. 1097 (U.S.D.C., E.D. Va. 1993).

Gierke v. *Blotzer,* CV-88-0-883 (U.S.D.C. Neb. 1989).

Graham v. *Central Community School District of Decatur County,* 608 F. Supp. 531 (U.S.D.C. Iowa 1985).

Gregorio T. v. *Wilson,* 59 F. 3d 1002 (9th Cir. 1996).

Griswold v. *Connecticut,* 381 U. S. 479 (1965).

Grove v. *Mead School District,* 753 F. 2d 1528 (9th Cir. 1985), *cert. denied,* 474 U. S. 826.

Gulf, Colorado and Santa Fe Railway Company v. *Ellis,* 165 U. S. 150 (1897).

Harris v. *City of Zion,* 927 F. 2d 1401 (7th Cir. 1991), *cert. denied,* 112 S. Ct. 3054 (1992).

Harris v. *Joint School District,* 41 F. 3d 447 (9th Cir. 1994).

Harvey v. *Cobb County,* 811 F. Supp. 669 (N.D. Ga. 1993), *affirmed,* 15 F. 3d 1097 (11th Cir. 1994), *cert. denied,* 114 S. Ct. 2138 (1994).

[Gloria] Iverson v. *Forbes,* 93-3-232 (Or. Cir. Ct. 1993).

Jager v. *Douglas,* 862 F. 2d 824 (11th Cir. 1989), *cert. denied,* 490 U. S. 1090 (1989).

Johnston v. *The Commonwealth,* 22 Pa 102 (Sup. Ct. Penn. 1853).

Jones v. *Clear Creek Independent School District,* 977 F. 3d 963 (5th Cir. 1992).

Kay v. *Douglas School District,* 719 P. 2d 875 (Or. App. 1986).

Kuhn v. *City of Rolling Meadows*, 927 F. 2d 1401 (7th Cir. 1991), *cert. denied*, 112 S. Ct. 3025 (1992).

Lamb's Chapel v. *Center Moriches*, 124 L. Ed. 2d 352 (1993).

Lanner v. *Wimmer*, 662 F. 2d 1349 (10th Cir. 1981).

[Robert E.] Lee v. *Daniel Weisman*, 112 S. Ct. 2649, 120 L. Ed. 2d 467 (1992).

Lemon v. *Kurtzman*, 403 U. S. 602 (1971).

Levitt v. *Committee for Public Education*, 413 U. S. 472 (1973).

Lindenmuller v. *The People*, 33 Barb 548 (Sup. Ct. NY 1861).

Lowe v. *City of Eugene*, 451 P. 2d 117 (Sup. Ct. Or. 1969), *cert. denied*, 434 U. S. 876.

LULAC v. *Wilson*, 908 F. Supp. 755 (C.D. Cal. 1995).

Lynch v. *Donnelly*, 465 U. S. 668 (1984).

M'Creery's Lessee v. *Allender*, 4 H. & McH. 258 (Sup. Ct. Md. 1799).

Malnak v. *Yogi*, 440 F. Supp. 1284 (D.C. NJ 1977).

Marsh v. *Chambers*, 463 U. S. 783 (1983).

McCulloch v. *Maryland*, 17 U. S. 316 (1819).

McCollum v. *Board of Education*, 333 U. S. 203 (1948).

Melvin v. *Easley*, 52 N.C. 276 (Sup. Ct. NC 1860).

Missouri v. *Kalima Jenkins*, 58 L.W. 4480 (1990).

Murdock v. *Pennsylvania*, 319 U. S. 105 (1943).

Murphy v. *Ramsey*, 114 U. S. 15 (1885).

New State Ice Company v. *Liebmann*, 285 U. S. 262 (1932).

Osborn v. *United States Bank*, 22 U. S. 738 (1824).

People v. *Ruggles*, 8 Johns 545 (Sup. Ct. NY. 1811).

Pierce v. *Society of Sisters*, 268 U. S. 510 (1925).

Quill v. *Vacco*, No. 95-7028 (2nd Cir. 1996).

Reed v. *van Hoven*, 237 F. Supp. 48 (W.D. Mich. 1965).

[Terry] Reidenbach v. *Pethtel*, 3:93CV632 (E.D. Va. 1993).

Reynolds v. *United States*, 98 U. S. 145 (1878).

Ring v. *Grand Forks Public School District*, 483 F. Supp. 272 (D.C. ND 1980).

Roberts v. *Madigan*, 702 F. Supp. 1505 (D.C. Colo. 1989), 921 F. 2d 1047 (10th Cir. 1990), *cert. denied*, 112 S. Ct. 3025, 120 L. Ed. 2d 896.

Robinson v. *City of Edmond*, 68 F. 3d 1226 (10th Cir. 1995).

Romer v. *Evans*, 64 L.W. 4353 (1996).

Rosenberger v. *Rector and Visitors of University of Virginia*, 115 S. Ct. 2510 (1995).

Runkel v. *Winemiller*, 4 H. & McH. 276 (Sup. Ct. Md. 1799).

Appendix F:
Bibliography
Books

[An] Abridgement of the Laws of Pennsylvania, Collinson Read, editor. Philadelphia: 1801.

[An] Abstract of the American Bible Society. New York: Daniel Fanshaw, 1816.

[An] Abstract of the American Bible Society. New York: Daniel Fanshaw, 1817.

[An] Abstract of the American Bible Society. New York: Daniel Fanshaw, 1818.

[An] Abstract of the American Bible Society. New York: Daniel Fanshaw, 1819.

[An] Abstract of the American Bible Society. New York: Daniel Fanshaw, 1820.

[An] Abstract of the American Bible Society. New York: Daniel Fanshaw, 1821.

[An] Abstract of the American Bible Society. New York: Daniel Fanshaw, 1822.

[An] Abstract of the American Bible Society. New York: Daniel Fanshaw, 1825.

[An] Abstract of the American Bible Society. New York: Daniel Fanshaw, 1830.

[An] Abstract of the American Bible Society. New York: Daniel Fanshaw, 1832.

[An] Act to Incorporate the Trustees of the Missionary Society of Connecticut: An Address from said Trustees to the Ministers and People of the State, with a Narrative on the Subject of Missions and a Statement of the Funds of the Society for the Year 1802. Hartford: Hudson and Goodwin, 1803.

Acts Passed at a Congress of the United States of America Begun and Held at the City of New-York, on Wednesday the Fourth of March, in the Year 1789. Hartford: Hudson and Goodwin, 1791.

Acts Passed at the First Session of the Fifth Congress of the United States of America. Philadelphia: William Ross, 1797.

Adams, John; Bowdoin, John. *An Address of the Convention for Framing a New Constitution of Government for the State of Massachusetts-Bay to their Constituents*. Boston: White and Adams, 1780.

Adams, John. *A Defence of the Constitution of Government of the United States of America*. Philadelphia: William Young, 1797. Three volumes.

Adams, John. *Diary and Autobiography of John Adams*, L. H. Butterfield, editor. Cambridge: Belknap Press, 1962. Four volumes.

Adams, John; Adams, Samuel. *Four Letters: being an Interesting Correspondence Between Those Eminently Distinguished Characters, John Adams, Late President of the United States; and Samuel Adams, Late Governor of Massachusetts. On the Important Subject of Government*. Boston: Adams and Rhoades, 1802.

Adams, John. *Letters of John Adams, Addressed to His Wife*, Charles Francis Adams, editor. Boston: Charles C. Little and James Brown, 1841. Two volumes.

Adams, John. *The Papers of John Adams*, Robert J. Taylor, editor. Cambridge: Belknap Press, 1977-1989. Eight volumes.

Adams, John. *The Works of John Adams, Second President of the United States*, Charles Francis Adams, editor. Boston: Charles C. Little and James Brown, 1850-1856. Ten volumes.

Adams, John; Adams, John Quincy. *The Selected Writings of John and John Quincy Adams*, Adrienne Koch and William Peden, editors. New York: Alfred A. Knopf, 1946.

Adams, John Quincy. *An Answer to Pain's* [sic] *"Rights of Man."* London: John Stockdale, 1793.

Adams, John Quincy. *Address Delievered at the Request of the Committee of Arrangements for Celebrating the Anniversary of Independence at the City of Washington on the Fourth of July 1821, upon the Occasion of Reading the Declaration of Independence.* Cambridge: Hilliard and Metcalf, 1821.

Adams, John Quincy. *An Oration Addressed to the Citizens of the Town of Quincy, on the Fourth of July, 1831, the Fifty-Fifth Anniversary of the Independence of the United States of America.* Boston: Richardson, Lord, and Holbrook, 1831.

Adams, John Quincy. *An Oration Delivered Before the Inhabitants of the Town of Newburyport at their Request on the Sixty-First Anniversary of the Declaration of Independence, July 4, 1837.* Newburyport: Charles Whipple, 1837.

Adams, John Quincy. *The Jubilee of the Constitution. A Discouse Delivered at the Request of the New York Historical Society, in the City of New York, on Tuesday, the 30th of April 1839; being the Fiftieth Anniversary of the Inauguration of George Washington as President of the United States, on Thursday, the 30th of April, 1789.* New York: Samuel Colman, 1839.

Adams, John Quincy. *Letters of John Quincy Adams to His Son on the Bible and Its Teachings.* Auburn: James M. Alden, 1850.

Adams, John Quincy. *Memoirs of John Quincy Adams,* Charles Francis Adams, editor. Philadelphia: J. B. Lippincott and Company, 1874-1877. Twelve volumes.

Adams, John Quincy. *Writings of John Quincy Adams,* Worthington Chauncey Ford, editor. New York: The MacMillan Company, 1913-1916. Six volumes.

Adams, Samuel. *The Life and Public Services of Samuel Adams,* William V. Wells, editor. Boston: Little, Brown, and Company, 1865. Three volumes.

Adams, Samuel. *The Writings of Samuel Adams,* Harry Alonzo Cushing, editor. New York: G. P. Putnam's Sons, 1904-1908. Four volumes.

[An] Address of the Bible Society Established at Philadelphia to the Public. Philadelphia: By Order of the Society, 1809.

Address of the New Jersey Bible Society to the Publick: with an Appendix, Containing the Constitution of the Said Society. New Brunswick: Abraham Blauvelt, 1810.

Allen, Ethan. *Reason, the Only Oracle of Man.* Bennington, Vermont: Haswell & Russell, 1784.

Allen, Gardner W. *Our Navy and the Barbary Corsairs.* Boston: Houghton, Mifflin and Company, 1905.

Allen, Richard. *The Life Experience and Gospel Labors of the Rt. Rev. Richard Allen.* Nashville: Abingdon Press, 1983.

Allison, Andrew N.; Perry, Jay A.; Skousen, W. Cleon. *The Real George Washington.* Washington, D. C.: National Center for Constitutional Studies, 1991.

Alphabetical Digest of the Public Statute Laws of South Carolina. Charleston: John Hoff, 1814. Three volumes.

American College Dictionary. New York: Random House, 1947.

American Heritage Dictionary, 2nd College Edition. New York: Bantam Doubleday Dell, 1983.

American State Papers: Documents Legislative and Executive, of the Congress of the United States, Walter Lowrie and Matthew St. Claire Clarke, editors. Washington, D.C.: Gales and Seaton, 1832-1861. Thirty-eight volumes.

Ames, Fisher. *The Works of Fisher Ames.* Boston: T. B. Wait & Co., 1809.

Ames, Fisher. *The Works of Fisher Ames,* Seth Ames, editor. Indianapolis: Liberty Classics, 1983. Two volumes.

Andrae, Rolla P. *A True, Brief History of Daniel Boone.* Defiance, Missouri: Daniel Boone Home, 1985.

Andrews, Israel Ward. *Manual of the Constitution of the United States.* New York: Wilson, Hinkle & Co., 1874.

Appleton's Cyclopedia of American Biography, James Grant Wilson and John Fiske, editors. New York: D. Appleton and Company, 1888-1889. Six volumes.

Armor, William. *Lives of the Governors of Pennsylvania.* Norwich, Connecticut: T. H. Davis & Co., 1874.

Arnold, A. G. *The Life of Patrick Henry of Virginia.* Auburn and Buffalo: Miller, Orton and Mulligan, 1854.

Backus, Isaac. *An Appeal to the Public for Religious Liberty.* Boston: John Boyle, 1783.

Baird, Robert. *Religion in America.* New York: Harper and Brothers, 1845.

Bancroft, George. *Bancroft's History of the Formation of the Constitution.* New York: D. Appleton and Company, 1882. Two volumes.

Bancroft, George. *History of the United States.* Boston: Little, Brown & Co., 1858-1875. Ten volumes.

Bancroft, George. *A Plea for the Constitution of the United States Wounded in the House of its Guardians.* New York: Harper, 1886.

Banvard, Joseph. *Tragic Scenes in the History of Maryland and the Old French War.* Boston: Gould and Lincoln, 1856.

Beard, Charles A. and Mary R. *The Rise of American Civilization.* New York: The MacMillan Company, 1930.

Beardsley, Edwards. The *Life and Times of William Samuel Johnson.* Boston: Houghton, Mifflin and Company, 1886.

Bedford, Gunning. *Funeral Oration upon the Death of General George Washington.* Wilmington: James Wilson, 1800.

Bennett, William J. *American Education: Making It Work.* Washington, D. C.: U. S. Government Printing Office, 1988.

Berger, Raoul. *Government by Judiciary: The Transformation of the Fourteenth Amendment.* Massachusetts: Harvard University Press, 1977.

Beveridge, Albert J. *The Life of John Marshall.* Boston: Houghton Mifflin, 1916-1919. Four volumes.

Biographical Directory of the United States Congress, 1774-1989. United States Government Printing Office, 1989.

Blackstone, William. *Commentaries on the Laws of England.* Oxford: Clarendon Press, 1769-1771. Four volumes.

Boudinot, Elias. *The Age of Revelation.* Philadelphia: Asbury Dickins, 1801.

Boudinot, Elias. *The Life, Public Services, Addresses, and Letters of Elias Boudinot, LL. D., President of the Continental Congress,* J. J. Boudinot, editor. Boston: Houghton, Mifflin & Co., 1896. Two volumes.

Boutell, Lewis Henry. *The Life of Roger Sherman*. Chicago: A. C. McClurg and Company, 1896.

Bouvier, John. *A Law Dictionary*. Philadelphia: George W. Childs, 1870. Two volumes.

Bowen, Catherine Drinker. *Miracle at Philadelphia*. Boston: Little, Brown, and Company, 1966.

Boyd, George Adams. *Elias Boudinot, Patriot and Statesman*. Princeton: Princeton University Press, 1952.

Bradford, William. *History of Plymouth Plantation*. Boston: Little, Brown, and Company, 1856.

Bridenbaugh, Carl. *Mitre and Sceptre*. New York: Oxford University Press, 1962.

Brodie, Fawn M. *Thomas Jefferson: An Intimate History*. New York: W. W. Norton and Company, 1974.

Brown, Abram English. *John Hancock, His Book*. Boston: Lee and Shepard, 1898.

Buck, Rev. Charles. *A Theological Dictionary Containing Definitions of All Religious Terms*. Philadelphia: Edwin T. Scott, 1823.

Burnet, Matthias. *An Election Sermon, Preached at Hartford, on the Day of the Anniversary Election, May 12, 1803*. Hartford: Hudson and Goodwin, 1803.

Caldwell, Charles. *Character of General Washington*. Philadelphia: Printed at the office of "The True American," 1801.

Campbell, William W. *The Life and Writings of De Witt Clinton*. New York: Baker and Scribner, 1849.

Cardozo, Benjamin. *The Growth of the Law*. New Haven: Yale University Press, 1924.

Cardozo, Benjamin. *The Nature of the Judicial Process*. New Haven: Yale University Press, 1921.

[The] Century Dictionary and Cyclopedia. New York: The Century Co., 1895.

[The] Catalogue of the Library of Yale College in New Haven. New London: T. Green, 1743.

[The] Catalogue of the Library of Yale College in New Haven. New Haven: James Parker, 1755.

[The] Charter of Dartmouth College. Dresden: Isaiah Thomas, 1779.

Chase-Riboud, Barbara. *Sally Hemings*. New York: The Viking Press, 1979.

Choate, Rufus. *A Discourse Delivered before The Faculty, Students, and Alumni of Dartmouth College*. Boston: James Monroe and Company, 1853.

[A] Circular Address from the Bible Society of Massachusetts. Boston: J. Belcher, 1809.

Clark, Mary Higgins. *Aspire To The Heavens: A Portrait of George Washington*. Cutchogue, New York: Buccaneer Books, 1968.

Clarkson, Thomas. *Memoirs of the Private and Public Life of William Penn*. London: Longman, 1813. Two volumes.

[The] Code of 1650, being a Compilation of the Earliest Laws and Orders of the General Court of Connecticut. Hartford: Silus Andrus, 1822.

Coffin, Charles. *The Story of Liberty*. New York: Harper & Brothers, 1878.

[A] Collection of Charters and Other Public Acts Relating to the Province of Pennsylvania. Philadelphia: B. Franklin, 1740.

Collections of the New York Historical Society for the Year 1821. New York: E. Bliss and E. White, 1821.

Collections of the Rhode Island Historical Society. Providence: Knowles and Vose, 1827-1867. Six volumes.

Columbia Rules. New York: Samuel Loudon, 1785.

Columbus, Christopher. *Christopher Columbus's Book of Prophecies*, Kay Brigham, translator. Barcelona, Spain: CLIE, 1990; Ft. Lauderdale: TSELF, 1991.

[The] Common School Almanac. New York: The American Common School Society, 1839.

[The] Concise Columbia Encyclopedia, Judith S. Levey and Agnes Greenhall, editors. Avon Publishers, 1983.

[The] Constitutions of All the United States. Lexington, Kentucky: Thomas T. Skillman, 1817.

Constitution of the American Bible Society. New York: Printed for the American Bible Society, 1816.

[The] Constitutions of the Several Independent States of America. Boston: Norman and Bowen, 1785.

[The] Constitutions of the Several States Composing the Union. Philadelphia: Hogan and Thompson, 1838.

[The] Constitutions of the Sixteen States. Boston: Manning and Loring, 1797.

[The] Constitution of the State of Nebraska. Lincoln: Allen J. Beermann, Secretary of State, 1992.

[The] Constitution of the State of North Carolina. Raleigh: Rufus L. Edmisten, Secretary of State, 1989.

[The] Constitutions of the United States with the Latest Amendments. Trenton: Moore and Lake, 1813.

[A] Constitution or Frame of Government agreed upon by the Delegates of the People of the State of Massachusetts-Bay. Boston: Benjamin Edes & Sons, 1780.

Cooper, J. Fenimore. *The History of the Navy of the United States of America.* Philadelphia: Thomas, Cowperthwait & Co., 1847.

Correspondence of the American Revolution; being Letters of Eminent Men to George Washington, Jared Sparks, editor. Boston: Little, Brown, and Company, 1853. Four volumes.

Cremin, Lawrence A. *1963 Yearbook*, World Book Encyclopedia.

Cubberley, E. P. *Public Education in the United States.* Boston: Houghton, Mifflin Co., 1919.

Custis, George Washington Parke. *Recollections and Private Memoirs of Washington, by His Adopted Son, George Washington Parke Custis, with a Memoir of the Author, by His Daughter; and Illustrative and Explanatory Notes, by Benson J. Lossing.* New York: Derby & Jackson, 1860.

Dabney, Virginius. *The Jefferson Scandals: A Rebuttal.* New York: Dodd, Mead and Company, 1981.

Davis, Kenneth C. *Don't Know Much about History.* New York: Avon Books, 1990.

de Tocqueville, Alexis. *Democracy in America: Specially Edited and Abridged for the Modern Reader*, Richard D. Heffner, editor. New York: Penguin Books, 1984.

de Tocqueville, Alexis. *[Democracy in America] The Republic of the United States of America and Its Political Institutions, Reviewed and Examined*, Henry Reeves, translator. Garden City, New York: A. S. Barnes & Co., 1851. Two volumes.

Deane, Silas. *The Deane Papers: Collections of the New York Historical Society for the Year 1886.* New York: Printed for the Society, 1887-1891. Five volumes.

[The] Debates and Proceedings in the Congress of the United States (1789-1824). Washington, D. C.: Gales and Seaton, 1834-1856. Forty volumes.

[The] Debates and Proceedings of the Second Session of the Thirty-Seventh Congress, 1861-62, John C. Rives, editor. Washington D. C.: Congressional Globe Office, 1862. Four volumes.

[The] Debates in the Several State Conventions on the Adoption of the Federal Constitution, Jonathan Elliot, editor. Washington, D. C.: Jonathan Elliot, 1836. Four volumes.

Dewey, John. *The Public and Its Problems.* New York: Henry Holt and Company, 1927.

Dickinson, John. *The Political Writings of John Dickinson.* Wilmington: Bonsal and Niles, 1801. Two volumes.

Dictionary of American Biography, Allen Johnson and Dumas Malone, editors. New York: Charles Scribner's Sons, 1928-1936. Twenty volumes.

Dictionary of American History, James Truslow Adams, editor. New York: Charles Scribner's Sons, 1940. Six volumes.

[A] Digest of the Laws of the State of Georgia. Milledgeville: Grantland and Orme, 1822.

[The] Documentary History of the Supreme Court of the United States, 1789-1800, Maeva Marcus, editor. New York: Columbia University Press, 1985-88. Three volumes.

Documentary History of Yale University, Franklin B. Dexter, editor. New Haven: Yale University Press, 1916.

Documentary Source Book of American History 1606-1898, William McDonald, editor. New York: The MacMillan Company, 1909.

Documents of American History, Henry Steele Commager, editor. New York: Appleton-Century-Crofts, Inc., 1948.

Dorchester, Daniel. *Christianity in the United States.* New York: Hunt and Eaton, 1890.

Downey, Fairfax. *Our Lusty Forefathers.* New York: Charles Scribner's Sons, 1947.

Eidsmoe, John. *Christianity and the Constitution.* Michigan: Baker Book House, 1987.

[The] Eighth Report of the Bible Society of Philadelphia. Philadelpia: William Fry, 1816.

[The] Encyclopedia of Religion. New York: MacMillan Publishing Co. 1987. Sixteen volumes.

Eulogies and Orations on the Life and Death of General George Washington. Boston: Manning and Loring, 1800.

Evans, John. *The Happiness of American Christians, a Thanksgiving Sermon Preached on Thursday the 24th of November 1803.* Hartford: Hudson and Goodwin, 1804.

Evans, John. *A Sketch of the Denominations into Which the Christian World is Divided.* Worcester: Thomas & Sturtevant, 1807.

Fac-Similie of Manuscript Prayer-Book Written by George Washington. Philadelphia: 1891.

Findley, William. *Observations on "The Two Sons of Oil."* Pittsburgh: Patterson & Hopkins, 1812.

Finney, Charles G. *Lectures on Revivals of Religion.* New York: Fleming H. Revell Company, 1868. First published in 1835.

First Annual Report of the Board of Managers of the American Bible Society. New York: J. Seymour, 1817.

Fiske, John. *The Beginnings of New England.* Boston: Houghton, Mifflin & Co., 1898.

Flexner, James Thomas. *George Washington: The Forge of Experience.* Boston: Little, Brown and Company, 1965.

Franklin, Benjamin. *Proposals Relating to the Education of Youth in Pennsylvania.* Philadelphia, 1749.

Franklin, Benjamin. *Two Tracts: Information to Those Who Would Remove to America and Remarks Concerning the Savages of North America.* London: John Stockdale, 1784.

Franklin, Benjamin. *The Works of Benjamin Franklin,* Jared Sparks, editor. Boston: Tappan, Whittemore, and Mason, 1836-1840. Ten volumes.

Franklin, Benjamin. *The Works of Benjamin Franklin,* John Bigelow, editor. New York: G. P. Putnam's Sons, 1904. Twelve volumes.

Franklin, Benjamin. *Works of the Late Doctor Benjamin Franklin: Consisting of His Life, Written by Himself, Together with Essays, Humorous, Moral & Literary, Chiefly in the Manner of the Spectator.* Dublin: P. Morgan, P. Byrne, J. Moore, and W. Jones, 1793.

French, Jonathan. *A Sermon Delivered on the Anniversary of Thanksgiving, November 29, 1798.* Andover: Ames and Parker, 1799.

Frothingham, Richard. *Rise of the Republic of the United States.* Boston: Little, Brown & Co., 1872.

Funk & Wagnalls Standard Dictionary of the English Language. Funk & Wagnalls Company, 1966.

Garland, Hugh A. *The Life of John Randolph of Roanoke.* New York: D. Appleton & Company, 1850. Two volumes.

[A] General View of the Rise, Progress, and Brilliant Achievements of the American Navy, Down to the Present Time. Brooklyn, 1828.

Goodrich, Charles A. *Lives of the Signers of the Declaration of Independence.* New York: William Reed & Co., 1829.

[The] Grants, Concessions, and Original Constitutions of the Province of New-Jersey, Aaron Leaming and Jacob Spicer, editors. Philadelphia: W. Bradford, 1758.

Greene, Nathanael. *The Papers of General Nathanael Greene,* Richard K. Showman, editor. Chapel Hill: University of North Carolina Press, 1976-1991+. Eight volumes.

Grotius, Hugo. *Commentary on the Law of Prize and Booty,* translated from the original manuscript of 1604 by Gwladys L. Williams. Oxford: Clarendon Press, 1950. Two volumes.

Grotius, Hugo. *The Truth of Christian Religion.* London: Richard Royston, 1780.

Gurn, Joseph. *Charles Carroll of Carrollton.* New York: P. J. Kennedy & Sons, 1932.

Hamilton, Alexander; Jay, John; Madison, James. *The Federalist on the New Constitution.* Philadelphia: Benjamin Warner, 1818.

Hamilton, Alexander. *The Papers of Alexander Hamilton,* Harold C. Syrett, editor. New York: Columbia University Press, 1961-1987. Twenty-seven volumes.

Hatch, Nathan; Marsden, George; Noll, Mark. *The Search for Christian America.* Colorado: Helmers & Howard, 1989.

Hazlitt, William. *A Thanksgiving Sermon Preached at Hallowell, December 15, 1785.* Boston: Samuel Hall, 1786.

Headly, J. T. *The Chaplains and Clergy of the Revolution.* Massachusetts: G. & F. Bill, 1861.

Hearings Before the Subcommittee on Constitutional Amendments of the Committee on the Judiciary, United States Senate, Eighty-Ninth Congress, Second Session on Senate Joint Resolution 148. Relating to Prayer in Public Schools. Washington, D. C.: U. S. Government Printing Office, 1966.

Henry, Patrick. *Patrick Henry: Life, Correspondence and Speeches,* William Wirt Henry, editor. New York: Charles Scribner's Sons, 1891. Three volumes.

Historical Collections: Consisting of State Papers and Other Authentic Documents: Intended as Materials for an History of the United States of America, Ebenezer Hazard, editor. Philadelphia: T. Dobson, 1792. Two volumes.

Holland, J. G. *Life of Abraham Lincoln.* Springfield, Massachusetts: Gurdon Bill, 1866.

Holmes, Abiel. *The Counsel of Washington, Recommended in a Discourse Delivered at Cambridge, February 22, 1800.* Boston: Samuel Hall, 1800.

Holmes, Abiel. *A Discourse Delivered before the Society for Propagating the Gospel among the Indians and Others in North America, November 3, 1808.* Boston: Farrand, Mallory, and Co., 1808.

Holmes, Oliver Wendell, Jr. *The Common Law.* Originally published 1881, reprinted Cambridge: Harvard University Press, 1963.

Holmes, Oliver Wendell, Jr. *"The Law in Science—Science in Law," Collected Legal Papers.* New York: Harcourt, Brace and Company, 1920.

[The] Holy Bible as Printed by Robert Aitken and Approved & Recommended by the Congress of the United States of America in 1782. Philadelphia: R. Aitken, 1782.

Hooker, Richard. *The Works of Richard Hooker.* Oxford: University Press, 1845. Two volumes.

Hopkins, Stephen. *The Rights of Colonies Examined.* Providence: William Goddard, 1765.

Hopkinson, Francis. *The Miscellaneous Essays and Occasional Writings of Francis Hopkinson, Esq.* Philadelphia: T. Dobson, 1792. Three volumes.

Hughes, Charles Evans. *The Autobiographical Notes of Charles Evans Hughes,* David J. Danelski and Joseph S. Tulchin, editors. Cambridge: Harvard University Press, 1973.

Ingersoll, Robert. *Ingersollia, Gems of Thought,* edited by Elmo. Chicago: Belford, Clarke & Co., 1882.

Iredell, James. *The Papers of James Iredell,* Don Higginbotham, editor. Raleigh: North Carolina Division of Archives and History, 1976+. Two volumes to date.

Irwin, Ray W. *The Diplomatic Relations of the United States with the Barbary Powers.* Chapel Hill: The University of North Carolina Press, 1931.

Ives, J. Moss. *The Ark and the Dove.* New York: Cooper Square Publishers, Inc., 1936, 1969.

Jay, John. *The Correspondence and Public Papers of John Jay,* Henry P. Johnston, editor. New York and London, 1890-1893. Four volumes.

Jay, John. *John Jay: The Winning of the Peace. Unpublished Papers 1745-1784,* Richard B. Morris, editor. New York: Harper & Row Publishers, 1975, 1980. Two volumes.

Jay, William. *The Life of John Jay: With Selections From His Correspondence and Miscellaneous Papers.* New York: J. & J. Harper, 1833. Two volumes.

Jefferson's Extracts from the Gospel's, Dickinson W. Adams, editor. Princeton: Princeton University Press, 1983.

Jefferson, Thomas. *Memoir, Correspondence, and Miscellanies, From the Papers of Thomas Jefferson,* Thomas Jefferson Randolph, editor. Boston: Gray and Bowen, 1830. Four volumes.

Jefferson, Thomas. *Notes on the State of Virginia.* Philadelphia: Mathew Carey, 1794.

Jefferson, Thomas. *The Papers of Thomas Jefferson,* Julian P. Boyd, editor. New Jersey: Princeton University Press, 1950-1995. Twenty-six volumes.

Jefferson, Thomas. *Writings of Thomas Jefferson,* Albert Bergh, editor. Washington, D. C.: Thomas Jefferson Memorial Assoc., 1903-1904. Twenty volumes.

[The] Jeffersonian Cyclopedia, John P. Foley, editor. New York: Funk & Wagnalls, 1900.

Jones, Charles C. *Biographical Sketches of the Delegates from Georgia to the Continental Congress.* Boston and New York: Houghton, Mifflin and Company, 1891.

[A] Journal of the Honorable House of Representatives. Watertown, Massachusetts: 1776.

[The] Journals of Each Provincial Congress of Massachusetts in 1774 and 1775, William Lincoln, editor. Boston: Dutton and Wentworth, 1838.

Journals of the American Congress, from 1774 to 1788. Washington, D. C.: Way and Gideon, 1823. Four volumes.

Journals of the Continental Congress. Washington: Government Printing Office, 1904-1937. Thirty-four volumes.

Kendall, Edward. *Kendall's Travels.* New York: I. Riley, 1809. Three volumes.

Kent, James. *Commentaries on American Law.* New York: O. Halsted, 1826-1830. Four volumes.

Kent, James. *Memoirs and Letters of James Kent,* William Kent, editor. Boston: Little, Brown, and Company, 1898.

King, Rufus. *The Life and Correspondence of Rufus King,* Charles R. King, editor. New York: G. P. Putnam's Sons, 1894-1900. Six volumes.

Lathrop, John. *A Discourse Before the Society for Propagating the Gospel among the Indians and Others in North America, Delivered on the 19th of January, 1804.* Boston: Manning and Loring, 1804.

Laurens, Henry. *The Papers of Henry Laurens,* George C. Rogers, Jr., and David R. Chesnutt, editors. Columbia: University of South Carolina Press, 1968-1992+. Thirteen volumes to date.

Laws of Arkansas Territory, Compiled and Arranged by J. Steele and J. M'Campbell Esq's. (Attorneys and Counsellors at Law;) Under the Direction and Superintendance of John Pope, Esq., Governor of the Territory of Arkansas. Little Rock, Ark. Ter.: J. Steele, Esq., 1835.

[The] Laws of the College of New-Jersey. Trenton: Isaac Collins, 1794.

Laws of the Commonwealth of Pennsylvania. Philadelphia: John Bioren, 1810.

[The] Laws of Harvard College. Boston: Samuel Hall, 1790.

Laws of the State of Maine. Hallowell: Goodale, Glazier and Company, 1822.

Laws of the State of New York, Passed at the Twenty-Second Session, Second Meeting of the Legislature. Albany: Loring Andrew, 1798.

Laws of the State of New York, Comprising the Constitution, and the Acts of the Legislature, since the Revolution. New York: Thomas Greenleaf, 1798. Three volumes.

Laws of the State of New Jersey, Complied and Published under the Authority of the Legislature, Joseph Bloomfield, editor. Trenton: James J. Wilson, 1811.

[The] Laws of Yale College in New Haven in Connecticut. New Haven: Josiah Meigs, 1787.

Lee, Charles. *Anecdotes of the Late Charles Lee, Esq. and His Letters.* London: J. S. Jordon, 1797.

Lee, Richard Henry. *The Letters of Richard Henry Lee,* James Curtis Ballagh, editor. New York: The MacMillan Company, 1911-1914. Two volumes.

Lee, Richard Henry. *Memoir of the Life of Richard Henry Lee, and His Correspondence With the Most Distinguished Men in America and Europe, Illustrative of Their Characters, and of the American Revolution,* Richard Henry Lee, editor. Philadelphia: H. C. Carey and I. Lea, 1825. Two volumes.

Letters of Delegates to Congress, 1774-1789, Paul H. Smith, editor. Washington D. C.: Library of Congress, 1976-1994+. Twenty-one volumes to date.

Lincoln, Abraham. *Letters and Addresses of Abraham Lincoln,* Mary Maclean, editor. NY: Unit Book Publishing Co., 1907.

Lincoln, Abraham. *The Works of Abraham Lincoln: Speeches and Debates,* John H. Clifford, editor. New York: The University Society Inc., 1908. Eight volumes.

Linn, William. *The Life of Thomas Jefferson.* Ithaca, New York: Mack & Andrus, 1834.

Livingston, William. *The Papers of William Livingston,* Carl E. Prince, editor. New Brunswick: Rutgers University Press, 1979-1988+. Five volumes to date.

Locke, John. *A Collection of Several Pieces of Mr. John Locke Never Before Printed or not Extant in His Works.* London: J. Bettenham for R. Francklin, 1720.

Locke, John. *Two Treatises of Government.* London: J. Whiston, 1772.

Lossing, Benson J. *Eminent Americans.* New York: John B. Alden, 1886.

Lutz, Donald S. *The Origins of American Constitutionalism*. Baton Rouge: Louisiana State University Press, 1988.

Madison, James. *A Memorial and Remonstrance Presented to the General Assembly of the State of Virginia at their Session in 1785 in Consequence of a Bill Brought into that Assembly for the Establishment of Religion*. Massachusetts: Isaiah Thomas, 1786.

Madison, James. *The Letters and Other Writings of James Madison*. New York: R. Worthington, 1884. Four volumes.

Madison, James. *The Papers of James Madison*, Henry D. Gilpin, editor. Washington: Langtree & O'Sullivan, 1840. Three volumes.

Madison, James. *The Papers of James Madison*, William T. Hutchinson, editor. Illinois: University of Chicago Press, 1962-1977. Ten volumes.

Madison, James. *The Writings of James Madison*, Gaillard Hunt, editor. New York and London: G. P. Putnam's Sons, 1900-1910. Nine volumes.

Manning, Leonard F. *The Law of Church-State Relations in a Nutshell*. St. Paul: West Publishing Co., 1981.

Marshall, John. *The Life of George Washington, Commander-in-Chief of the American Forces, During the War Which Established the Independence of His Country, and First President of the United States*. Philadelphia: C. P. Wayne, 1807. Five volumes.

Marshall, John. *The Papers of John Marshall*. Chapel Hill: University of North Carolina Press, 1990. Seven+ volumes.

Martin, Luther. *The Genuine Information Delivered to the Legislature of the State of Maryland Relative to the Proceedings of the General Convention Lately Held at Philadelphia*. Philadelphia: Eleazor Oswald, 1788.

Martineau, Harriet. *Society in America*. New York: Saunders and Otley, 1837. Two volumes.

McCann, Alfred W. *Greatest of Men—Washington*. New York: The Devin-Adair Co., 1927.

McDonald, Forrest. *Novus Ordo Seclorum: The Intellectual Origins of the Constitution*. Lawrence, Kansas: 1985.

McMahon, John V. L. *An Historical View of the Government of Maryland*. Baltimore: F. Lucas, Jr., Cushing & Sons, and William & Joseph Neal, 1831.

Meade, Bishop William. *Old Churches, Ministers, and Families of Virginia*. Philadelphia: J. B. Lippincott Company, 1857. Two volumes.

[The] Medical Repository, Samuel L. Mitchill, M. D. and Edward Miller, editors. New York: T. & J. Swords, 1800.

Mitchell, James Coffield. *The Tennessee Justice's Manual and Civil Officer's Guide*. Nashville: Mitchell and C. C. Norvell, 1834.

Montesquieu, Baron Charles Secondat de. *Spirit of Laws*. Philadelphia: Isaiah Thomas, 1802. Two volumes.

Moore, Frank. *Materials for History Printed from Original Manuscripts, the Correspondence of Henry Laurens of South Carolina*. New York: Zenger Club, 1861.

Moore, Hugh. *Memoir of Col. Ethan Allen*. Plattsburgh, New York: O. R. Cook, 1834.

Morgan, George. *Patrick Henry*. Philadelphia: J. B. Lippincott Company, 1929.

Morgan, James Henry. *Dickinson College: The History of One Hundred and Fifty Years, 1783-1933*. Carlisle, Pennsylvania: Dickinson College, 1933.

Morris, B. F. *The Christian Life and Character of the Civil Institutions of the United States.* Philadelphia: George W. Childs, 1864.

Morris, Gouverneur. *A Diary of the French Revolution.* Boston: Houghton Mifflin Co., 1939. Two volumes.

Morris, Gouverneur. *An Oration Delivered on Wednesday, June 29, 1814, at the Request of a Number of Citizens of New-York, in Celebration of the Recent Deliverance of Europe from the Yoke of Military Despotism.* New York: Van Winkle and Wiley, 1814.

Muhlenberg, Henry A. *The Life of Major-General Peter Muhlenberg of the Revolutionary Army.* Philadelphia: Carey and Hart, 1849.

Murat, Achille. *A Moral and Political Sketch of the United States.* London: Effingham Wilson, 1833.

Musick, John R. *Great Americans of History—John Hancock.* Chicago: Union School Furnishing Company, 1898.

Naval Documents Related to the United States' Wars with the Barbary Powers, Claude A. Swanson, editor. Washington: Government Printing Office, 1939-1944. Six volumes.

[The] New Annual Register, or a View of the History, Politics, and Literature, from the Year 1775. London: J. Dodsley, 1776.

[The] New Annual Register, or General Repository of History, Politics, and Literature, for the Year 1781. London: G. Robinson, 1782.

[The] New Annual Register or General Repository of History, Politics, and Literature, for the Year 1783. London: G. Robinson, 1784.

Niles, Hezekiah. *Principles and Acts of the Revolution in America.* Baltimore: William Ogden Niles, 1822.

North Carolina History, Hugh Talmage Lefler, editor. Chapel Hill: University of North Carolina Press, 1934, 1956.

O'Conner, John E. *William Paterson: Lawyer and Statesman.* New Brunswick: Rutgers University Press, 1979.

Official Letters of the Governors of the State of Virginia, H. R. McIlwaine, editor. Richmond: Virginia State Library, 1926-1929. Three volumes.

Ohio Revised Code Annotated. Cincinnati: Anderson Publishing Co., 1994.

Oliver, Peter. *Peter Oliver's Origin & Progress of the American Rebellion,* Douglass Adair and John Schutz, editors. California: The Huntington Library, 1961.

Orations of American Orators. New York: The Colonial Press, 1900. Two volumes.

Otis, James. *The Rights of the British Colonies Asserted and Proved.* Boston: J. Williams 1766.

[The] Pageant of America, Ralph Henry Gabriel, editor. Yale University Press, 1925-29. Fifteen volumes.

Paine, Thomas. *The Age of Reason.* Philadelphia: The Booksellers, 1794.

Paine, Robert Treat. *The Papers of Robert Treat Paine,* Stephen T. Riley and Edward W. Hanson, editors. Boston: Massachusetts Historical Society 1992. Two volumes.

Palmer, John McAuley, *General Von Steuben.* New Haven: Yale University Press, 1937.

[The] Patriot Preachers of the American Revolution, With Biographical Sketches, 1766-1783. New York: Printed for the Subscribers, 1860.

Pearson, Rev. Eliphalet. *A Sermon Delivered in Boston Before the Massachusetts Society for Promoting Christian Knowledge, November 27, 1811.* Cambridge: Hilliard and Metcalf, 1811.

Petersen, William J. *A Brief History of the American Sunday-School Union.* Pennsylvania: American Missionary Fellowship, 1969.

Pierce, Benjamin. *A History of Harvard University.* Cambridge, Massachusetts: Brown, Shattuck, and Company, 1833.

Powers, Peter. *Jesus Christ the True King and Head of Government. A Sermon Preached Before the General Assembly of the State of Vermont, on the Day of their First Election, March 12, 1778 at Windsor.* Newburyport: John Mycall, 1778.

Prentiss, Charles. *The Life of the Late Gen. William Eaton: Several Years an Officer in the United States' Army, Consul at the Regency of Tunis on the Coast of Barbary, and Commander of the Christian and Other Forces that Marched from Egypt through the Desert of Barca, in 1805, and Conquered the City of Derne, which Led to the Treaty of Peace Between the United States and the Regency of Tripoli.* Brookfield: Merriam & Company, 1813.

[The] Proceedings of the American Philosophical Society. Philadelphia: The American Philosophical Society, 1840-1995. One hundred thirty nine volumes.

[The] Proceedings of the Convention of Delegates, Held at the Capitol in the City of Williamsburg, in the Colony of Virginia, on Monday the 6th of May, 1776. Williamsburg: Printed by Alexander Purdie, Printer to the Commonwealth, 1776.

[The] Public Statute Laws of the State of Connecticut. Hartford: Hudson and Goodwin, 1808-1820. Two volumes.

[The] Public Statutes at Large of the United States of America, Richard Peters, editor. Boston: Little, Brown and Company, 1854.

Puffendorf, Baron Samuel de. *Of the Law of Nature and Nations, Eight Books,* Basil Kennet, editor. London: R. Sare, 1717.

Ramsay, David. *An Eulogium upon Benjamin Rush, M. D.* Philadelphia: Bradford & Inskeep, 1813.

Ramsay, David. *An Oration Delivered in St. Michael's Church before the Inhabitants of Charleston, South Carolina, on the Fourth of July 1794.* Charleston: W. P. Young, 1794.

Ramsay, David. *The History of the American Revolution.* Dublin: William Jones, 1795. Two volumes.

Randall, Henry S. *The Life of Thomas Jefferson.* New York: Derby & Jackson, 1858. Three volumes.

Random House Dictionary of the English Language, unabridged 2nd edition. New York: Random House, 1987.

Rawle, William. *A View of the Constitution of the United States of America.* Philadelphia: Philip H. Nicklin, 1829.

[The] Records of the Federal Convention of 1787, Max Farrand, editor. New Haven: Yale University Press, 1911. Three volumes.

Register of Debates in Congress. Washington D. C.: Gales and Seaton, 1825-1837. Twenty-nine volumes.

Report of the American Board of Commissioners for Foreign Missions. Boston: Crocker & Brewster, 1835.

Report of the Executive Committee of the Bible Society of Massachusetts, Prepared for the Anniversary of the Society, June 4, 1818. Boston: John Eliot, 1818.

Reports of the Proceedings and Debates of the Convention of 1821, Assembled for the Purpose of Amending The Constitution of the State of New York. Albany: E. and E. Hosford, 1821.

Republican Staff of the Select Committee on Children, Youth, and Families. *What America Believes: The Rest of the Story.* U. S. House of Representatives, 1990.

Reynolds, Edward C. *The Maine Scholars' Manual.* Portland, Maine: Dresser, McLellan and Co., 1880.

Rhode Island Session Laws. Providence: Wheeler, 1784.

Richardson, James D. *A Compilation of the Messages and Papers of the Presidents, 1789-1897.* Published by Authority of Congress, 1899. Ten volumes.

Rives, William C. *History of the Life and Times of James Madison.* Boston: Little, Brown, and Company, 1873. Three volumes.

Robbins, Chandler. *A Sermon Preached before His Excellency John Hancock, Esq., Governour; His Honor Samuel Adams, Esq., Lieutenant Governour; the Honourable the Council, and the Honourable the Senate and House of Representatives of the Commonwealth of Massachusetts, May 25, 1791, being the Day of General Election.* Boston: Thomas Adams, 1791.

Robertson, Pat. *America's Dates with Destiny.* Nashville: Thomas Nelson Publishers, 1986.

Rollins, Richard M. *The Long Journey of Noah Webster.* University of Pennsylvaina Press, 1980.

Rowland, Kate Mason. *The Life of Charles Carroll of Carrollton, 1737-1832, with His Correspondence and Public Papers.* New York: G. P. Putnam's Sons, 1898. Two volumes.

Rowland, Kate Mason. *The Life of George Mason.* New York: G. P. Putnam's Sons, 1892. Two volumes.

Rummell, R. J. *Death by Government.* New Brunswick: Transaction Publishers, 1994.

Rupp, Daniel. *An Original History of the Religious Denominations at Present Existing in the United States.* Philadelphia: J. Y. Humphrys, 1844.

Rush, Benjamin. *The Autobiography of Benjamin Rush,* George W. Corner, editor. Princeton: Princeton University Press for the American Philosophical Society, 1948.

Rush, Benjamin. *Essays, Literary, Moral and Philosophical.* Philadelphia: Thomas & Samuel F. Bradford, 1798.

Rush, Benjamin. *Letters of Benjamin Rush,* L. H. Butterfield, editor. Princeton University Press, 1951. Two volumes.

Rush, Benjamin. *Minutes of the Proceedings of a Convention of Delegates from the Abolition Societies Established in Different Parts of the United States Assembled at Philadelphia.* Philadelphia: Zachariah Poulson, 1794.

Rutgers' Fact Book of 1965. New Jersey: Rutgers University, 1965.

Sanderson, John. *Biography of the Signers to the Declaration of Independence.* Philadelphia: R. W. Pomeroy, 1823-1824. Nine volumes.

Schroeder, John Frederick. *Maxims of George Washington.* Mount Vernon, Virginia: The Mount Vernon Ladies' Association, 1989.

Schroeder, John Frederick. *Maxims of Washington; Political, Social, Moral, and Religious.* New York: D. Appleton and Company, 1855.

[The] Second Report of the Managers of the New Jersey Bible Society, Read before the Society at Their Annual Meeting at New Brunswick, August 27, 1811. Trenton: George Sherman, 1811.

Select Charters and Other Documents, William MacDonald, editor. New York: The Mac Millan Company, 1899.

Select Documents Illustrative of the History of the United States, 1776-1861, William MacDonald, editor. New York: The MacMillan Company, 1898.

[A] Selection of Orations and Eulogies Pronounced in Different Parts of the United States In Commemoration of the Life, Virtue, and Preeminent Services of Gen. George Washington. Amherst: Samuel Preston, 1800.

Smith, Samuel Stanhope. *The Divine Goodness to the United States of America—A Discourse on the Subjects of National Gratitude.* Philadelphia: William Young, 1795.

Smylie, James Hutchinson. *American Clergyman and the Constitution of the United States of America.* Princeton, 1954.

Snyder, K. Alan. *Defining Noah Webster: Mind and Morals in the Early Republic.* New York: University Press of America, 1990.

Sparks, Jared. *The Life of Gouverneur Morris.* Boston: Gray and Bowen, 1832. Three volumes.

Sparks, Jared. *Lives of William Pinkney, William Ellery, and Cotton Mather.* New York: Harper and Brothers, 1860.

[The] Speeches of the Different Governors to the Legislature of the State of New York, Commencing with Those of George Clinton and Continued Down to the Present Time. Albany: J. B. Van Steenbergh, 1825.

[The] Statutes at Large of the United States of America. Washington: Government Printing Office, 1907.

[The] Statutes at Large and Treaties of the United States of America. Boston: Charles C. Little and James Brown, 1846.

[The] Statutes at Large, Treaties, and Proclamations of the United States of America, George P. Sanger, editor. Boston: Little, Brown, and Company, 1866.

Statutes of the State of Vermont. Bennington, 1791.

Steiner, Bernard C. *One Hundred and Ten Years of Bible Society Work in Maryland.* Baltimore: Maryland Bible Society, 1921.

Steiner, Bernard C. *The Life and Correspondence of James McHenry.* Cleveland: The Burrows Brothers, 1907.

Stille, Charles J. *The Life and Times of John Dickinson.* Philadelphia: J. P. Lippincott Company, 1891.

Stone, Peter. *1776: A Musical Play.* New York: The Viking Press, 1970.

Story, Joseph. *A Familiar Exposition of the Constitution of the United States.* New York: Harper & Brothers, 1854.

Story, Joseph. *Commentaries on the Constitution of the United States.* Boston: Hilliard, Gray, and Company, 1833. Three volumes.

Story, Joseph. *Life and Letters of Joseph Story,* William W. Story, editor. Boston: Charles C. Little and James Brown, 1851.

Strickland, W. P. *History of the American Bible Society from its Organization to the Present Time.* New York: Harper and Brothers, 1849.

Sullivan, William. *The Political Class Book.* Boston: Richardson, Lord, and Holbrook, 1831.

Swancara, Frank. *Obstruction of Justice by Religion.* Colorado: W. H. Courtwright Publishing Company, 1936.

Swift, Zephaniah. *The Correspondent.* Windham: John Byrne, 1793.

Swift, Zephaniah. *A System of Laws of the State of Connecticut.* Windham: John Byrne, 1795-1796. Two volumes.

Taylor, John M. *Garfield of Ohio: The Available Man.* New York: W. W. Norton and Company, Inc., 1970.

[The] Territorial Papers of the United States, Clarence Edwin Carter, editor. Washington,   D. C.: U. S. Government Printing Office, 1934-1948. Thirteen volumes.

Thacher, James. *A Military Journal During the American Revolutionary War.* Boston: Richardson and Lord, 1823.

Thompson, Parker C. *The United States Army Chaplaincy: from its European Antecedents to 1791.* Washington: D. C.: Office of the Chief of Chaplains, Department of the Army, 1978.

Thornton, John Wingate. *Pulpit of the American Revolution.* Boston: Gould and Lincoln, 1860.

Todd, Rev. Gailbreth Hall. *The Torch and the Flag.* Philadelphia: American Sunday School Union, 1966.

Townsend, Margaret R. *Vice-Presidents of the American Bible Society, 1816-1966.* New York: American Bible Society, 1967.

Treaties and Conventions Concluded Between the United States of America and Other Powers Since July 4, 1776. Washington, D. C.: Government Printing Office, 1889.

Treaties, Conventions, International Acts, Protocols and Agreements Between the United States of America and Other Powers: 1776-1909, William M. Malloy, editor. Washington, D. C.: Government Printing Office, 1910. Eleven volumes.

Treaties and Other International Agreements of the United States of America: 1776-1949, Charles I. Bevans, editor. Washington, D. C.: Department of State, 1968-1976. Thirteen volumes.

True, M. B. C. *A Manual of the History and Civil Government of the State of Nebraska.* Omaha: Gibson, Miller, & Richardson, 1885.

Trumbull, Benjamin. *A Complete History of Connecticut, Civil and Ecclesiastical, from the Emigration of its First Planters from England.* Hartford: Hudson & Goodwin, 1797.

Tucker, Henry St. George. *Lectures on Government.* Charlottesville: James Alexander, 1841.

Tucker, Glen. *Dawn Like Thunder: The Barbary Wars and the Birth of the U. S. Navy.* Indianapolis: Bobbs-Merrill Company, 1963.

Tucker, John Randolph. *The Constitution of the United States.* Chicago: Callaghan & Co., 1899.

Tyler, Moses Coit. *Patrick Henry.* New York: Houghton Mifflin Co., 1897.

[The] United States Code, 1988 Edition. Washington, D. C.: United States Government Printing Office, 1989.

[The] United States Code Annotated. St. Paul: West Publishing Co., 1987.

Upham, Charles W. *The Life of Timothy Pickering.* Boston: Little, Brown, and Company, 1867-1873. Four volumes.

Vitz, Paul C. *Censorship: Evidence of Bias in Our Children's Textbooks.* Michigan: Servant Books, 1986.

Walker, Joseph B. *A History of the New Hampshire Convention.* Boston: Cupples & Hurd, 1888.

Wallace, Paul. *The Muhlenbergs of Pennsylvania.* Philadelphia: Univ. of Pennsylvania Press, 1950.

Warfel, H. R. *Noah Webster, Schoolmaster to America.* New York: MacMillan Co, 1936.

Warner, John. *Warner's Almanack for 1737.* Williamsburg, Virginia: William Parks, 1736.

Warren, Mercy Otis. *History of the Rise, Progress and Termination of the American Revolution, Interspersed with Biographical, Political and Moral Observations.* Boston: E. Larkin, 1805. Three volumes.

Washington, George. *Address of George Washington, President of the United States and Late Commander-in-Chief of the American Army, to the People of the United States, Preparatory to His Declination.* Baltimore: George and Henry S. Keatinge, 1796.

Washington, George. *The Diaries of George Washington,* John C. Fitzpatrick, editor. New York: Houghton Mifflin Co., 1925. Four volumes.

Washington, George. *The Last Official Address of His Excellency General Washington, to the Legislatures of the United States.* Hartford: Hudson and Goodwin, 1783.

Washington, George. *The Writings of George Washington,* Jared Sparks, editor. Boston: Ferdinand Andrews, 1834-1838. Twelve volumes.

Washington, George. *The Writings of Washington,* John C. Fitzpatrick, editor. Washington, D. C.: U. S. Government Printing Office, 1931-1944. Thirty-nine volumes.

Watson, Richard. *Theological Institutes: On a View of the Evidences, Doctrines, Morals, and Institutions of Christianity.* New York: Carlton and Porter, 1857. Two volumes.

Webster, Daniel. *Address Delivered at Bunker Hill, June 17, 1843, on the Completion of the Monument.* Boston: T. R. Marvin, 1843.

Webster, Daniel. *Mr. Webster's Speech in Defence of the Christian Ministry and in Favor of the Religious Instruction of the Young. Delivered in the Supreme Court of the United States, February 10, 1844, in the Case of Stephen Girard's Will.* Washington: Gales and Seaton 1844.

Webster, Daniel. *The Works of Daniel Webster.* Boston: Little, Brown and Company, 1853. Six volumes.

Webster, Daniel. *The Writings and Speeches of Daniel Webster.* Boston: Little, Brown, & Company, 1903. Eighteen volumes.

Webster, Noah. *An American Dictionary of the English Language.* New York: S. Converse, 1828. Two volumes.

Webster, Noah. *An American Dictionary of the English Language.* Springfield, Massachusetts: George and Charles Merriam, 1849.

Webster, Noah. *The American Spelling Book: Containing an Easy Standard of Pronunciation: being the First Part of a Grammatical Institute of the English Langauage, to Which is Added, an Appendix, Containing a Moral Catechism and a Federal Catechism.* Boston: Isaiah Thomas and Ebenezer T. Andrews, 1801.

Webster, Noah. *A Collection of Papers on Political, Literary and Moral Subjects.* New York: Webster & Clark, 1843.

Webster, Noah. *Effect of Slavery on Morals and Industry.* Hartford: Hudson and Goodwin, 1793.

Webster, Noah. *History of the United States.* New Haven: Durrie & Peck, 1832.

Webster, Noah. *The Holy Bible Containing the Old and New Testaments, in the Common Version. With Amendments of the Language.* New Haven: Durrie & Peck, 1833.

Webster, Noah. *Letters of Noah Webster,* Harry R. Warfel, editor. New York: Library Publishers, 1953.

Webster, Noah. *Letters to a Young Gentleman Commencing His Education.* New Haven: Howe & Spalding, 1823.

Webster, Noah. *The Revolution in France Considered in Respect to its Progress and Effects.* New York: George Bunce, 1794.

Webster, Noah. *Sketches of American Policy.* Hartford: Hudson and Goodwin, 1785.

Webster, Pelatiah. *A Dissertation on the Political Union and Constitution of the Thirteen United States.* Hartford: Hudson & Goodwin, 1783.

Webster's New World Dictionary of the American Language. Cleveland and New York: The World Publishing Company, 1964.

Webster's Seventh New Collegiate Dictionary. Springfield, Massachusetts: G. & C. Merriam Company, 1963.

Willard, Rev. Joseph. *A Thanksgiving Sermon Delivered at Boston, December 11, 1783.* Boston: T. and J. Fleet, 1784.

William & Mary Rules. Richmond: Augustine Davis, 1792.

Wilson, James. *The Works of the Honourable James Wilson,* Bird Wilson, editor. Philadelphia: Bronson and Chauncey, 1804. Three volumes.

Wilson, James. *The Works of James Wilson,* Robert Green McCloskey, editor. Massachusetts: The Belknap Press of Harvard University Press, 1967. Two volumes.

Winthrop, John. *The Winthrop Papers,* Stewart Mitchell, editor. Massachusetts Historical Society, 1929-1947. Five volumes.

Winthrop, Robert. *Addresses and Speeches on Various Occasions.* Boston: Little, Brown & Co., 1852.

Wirt, William. *Sketches of the Life and Character of Patrick Henry.* Philadelphia: James Webster, 1818.

Witherspoon, John. *Christian Magnanimity.* Princeton: James Tod, 1787.

Witherspoon, John. *The Dominion of Providence Over the Passions of Men.* Philadelphia: R. Aitken, 1776.

Witherspoon, John. *Ecclesiastical Characteristics.* Philadelphia: William and Thomas Bradford, 1797

Witherspoon, John (authored the introduction). *The Holy Bible.* Trenton: Isaac Collins, 1791.

Witherspoon, John. *Letters on the Education of Children and Marriage.* Andover: Flagg and Gould, 1817.

Witherspoon, John. *Sermons on Practical Subjects.* Glasgow: A. Duncan and Company, 1768.

Witherspoon, John. *A Sermon on the Religious Education of Children.* New York: M'Lean, 1789.

Witherspoon, John. *The Works of the Reverend John Witherspoon.* Philadelphia: William W. Woodward, 1802. Four volumes.

Witherspoon, John. *The Works of John Witherspoon.* Edinburgh: J. Ogle, 1815. Ten volumes.

Woodward, W. E. *A New American History.* New York: The Literary Guild, 1937.

Woodward, W. E. *George Washington: The Image and the Man.* New York: Boni & Liverlight, 1926.

Worchester, Samuel. *A Sermon Preached in Boston on the Anniversary of the American Society for Educating Pious Youth for the Gospel Ministry.* Andover: Flagg and Gould, 1816.

World Book Encyclopedia. Chicago, 1995. Twenty-two volumes.

Documents

ACLU. A letter dated April 18, 1988 by the ACLU California Legislative Office to California State Senator Newton Russell.

Adams, Samuel. *A Proclamation by the Governor for a Day of Public Fasting, Humiliation, and Prayer.* Printed at the State Press: Adams and Larkin, 1795.

[An] Answer to the Question, "Why do you attend a Unitarian Church?". Published at the Christian Register Office-John B. Russell, printer, circa 1840.

Broom, Jacob. An autographed letter in our possession written by Jacob Broom to his son, James, on February 24, 1794, from Wilmington, Delaware.

Carroll, Charles. An autographed letter in our possession written by Charles Carroll to Charles W. Wharton, Esq., on September 27, 1825, from Doughoragen, Maryland.

CNN/USA Today/Gallup Poll: Top-Line, November 28-29, 1994.

Congressional Record, June 29, 1987, H. 3511, citing *General Social Survey Annual* of the National Opinion Research Center.

Dickinson, John. *Thanksgiving Proclamation of October 30, 1783 by the President and the Supreme Executive Council of the Commonwealth of Pennsylvania, A Proclamation.* Philadelphia: Francis Bailey, 1783.

Fabrizio, McLaughlin, & Associates, Inc. Poll, September 8, 1993.

Gallup. The 25th Annual Gallup Poll, October 1993.

Hancock, John. *A Proclamation for a Day of Thanksgiving.* Boston, 1783.

Jefferson, Thomas. Thomas Jefferson Papers Manuscript Division, Library of Congress, Washington, D. C.

Livingston, William. *Thanksgiving Proclamation of November 11, 1783.* Trenton, New Jersey: Issac Collins, 1783.

Princeton Religion Research Center in New Jersey. The annual polling.

Society of Separationists, "Did you know that these great American thinkers all rejected Christianity?" Austin, TX: American Atheist Center.

Trumbull, Jonathan. *A Proclamation by His Excellency Jonathan Trumbull, Esq. Governor and Commander in Chief In and Over the State of Connecticut.* Hudson and Goodwin, 1807.

Trumbull, Jonathan. A proclamation in our possession: *by the Honourable Jonathan Trumbull, Esq; Governor of the English Colony of Connecticut, in New-England, in America. New Haven, 12th Day of October, 1770.*

Yankelovich, Clancy, & Shulman. Various polls.

Reports/Legal Reviews

Benchmark, Vol. 2, No. 1, "Toward a Jurisprudence of Original Intention," Attorney General Edwin Meese, III, January-February 1986.

Columbia Law Review, Vol. 8, No. 8, "Mechanical Jurisprudence," Roscoe Pound, December 1908.

Editorial Research Reports, "Supreme Court: Legal Storm Center," Richard L. Worsnop, September 28, 1966.

House Report 154, March 27, 1854, House Judiciary Committee.

House of Representatives, Mis. Doc. No. 44, 35th Congress, 2nd Session, February 2, 1859.

Presidential Studies Quarterly, Vol. XXI, No. 3, "America's Bill of Rights at 200 Years," Chief-Justice Warren E. Burger, Summer 1991.

South Carolina Law Quarterly 10 (1958), "Charles Pinckney: Father of the Constitution," S. Sidney Olmer.

[The] Reports of Committees of the House of Representatives Made During the First Session of the Thirty-Third Congress. Washington: A. O. P. Nicholson, 1854.

[The] Reports of Committees of the Senate of the United States for the Second Session of the Thirty-Second Congress, 1852-53. Washington: Robert Armstrong, 1853.

Periodicals

American Heritage, December 1992, "The Radical Revolution," Gordon Wood.

Atlantic, July 1877, "A Century of Congress," James A. Garfield.

Boston Gazette, January 20, 1772.

Boston Gazette, September 26, 1774.

Boston Globe, October 31, 1989.

California Voter's Guide, Vol. 5, No. 10, "Governor Signs Abstinence Bill," Sacramento: California Coalition for Traditional Values, Fall 1988.

Charlotte Observer, January 15, 1993, "Founding Fathers weren't devout," Michael A. Macdonald.

Columbian Centinel. Boston, May 16, 1792.

Connecticut Courant, June 7, 1802.

Daily Advertiser (New York), May 1, 1789.

Dallas Morning News, "Court rejects case of girl who wrote Jesus paper," November 28, 1995.

Dallas Times Herald, August 6, 1988.

[The] Harvard Graduates' Magazine. "Harvard Seals and Arms," Samuel Eliot Morison, Manesh, WI: George Barna Publishing Co., September 1933.

Independent Chronicle (Boston), November 2, 1780.

Independent Chronicle (Boston), February 22, 1787.

Los Angeles Times, "America's Unchristian Beginnings," Steven Morris, August 3, 1995.

New American, June 20, 1988, "America Without God."

New Hampshire Gazette. Portsmouth, May 26, 1791.

New York Daily Advertiser, April 23, 1789.

Newport Mercury, Rhode Island, June 25, 1793.

Newsweek, December 27, 1982, "How the Bible Made America," Kenneth L. Woodward and David Gates.

Newsweek, February 1, 1993, "What's Fair in Love and War," Randy Shilts.

Olean Times Herald, "Commandments Must Be Covered for Trial," Monday, April 6, 1992.

Principles: A Quarterly Review for Teachers of History and Social Science, Spring/Summer 1992, "Was the American Founding Unjust? The Case of Slavery," Thomas G. West.

Richmond Times-Dispatch, Tuesday, August 17, 1993, "Shadowboxing."

Roanoke Times World-News, September 1, 1993, "Sleaze in Salem."

United States Oracle (Portsmouth, New Hampshire), May 24, 1800.

Washington Times, December 12, 1988, "Parent silences teaching of carols" and "School officials deny banning Bible."

The William & Mary Quarterly, Third Series, Vol. III, No. 4, Madison's "Detached Memoranda," edited by Elizabeth Fleet, October 1946.

Williams, Walter E., Creators Syndicate, Inc., May 26, 1993, "Some Fathers Fought Slavery."

Original Intent Index

~ A ~

~ Y ~

~ Z ~

NOTES

NOTES

NOTES

NOTES

WallBuilders Resources

P.O. Box 397 • Aledo, TX 76008 • To place a MasterCard or Visa order, call

1-800-873-2845

Prices subject to change without notice. Quantity & case-lot discounts available.

Videos

The Spiritual Heritage of the U.S. Capitol (2 hours) (V06) $39.00*
A personal tour of the U.S. Capitol with WallBuilders founder David Barton complete with dramatic reenactments. *Donation (Do not add sales tax and shipping.)

The Spiritual Heritage of the U.S. Capitol (1 hour) (V06A) $24.00*
Shorter version of above video. *Donation (Do not add sales tax and shipping.)

America's Godly Heritage (60 min.) (V01) $19.95
Explains the Founding Fathers' beliefs concerning the role of Christian principles in the public affairs of the nation.

Keys to Good Government (59 min.) (V05) $19.95
Presents beliefs of the Founders concerning the proper role of Biblical thinking in education, government, and public affairs.

Education and the Founding Fathers (60 min.) (V02) $19.95
A look at the educational system which produced America's great heroes.

Spirit of the American Revolution (53 min.) (V04) $19.95
A look at the motivation that caused the Founders to pledge their "lives, fortunes, and sacred honor" to establish our nation.

Foundations of American Government (25 min.) (V03) $9.95
Surveys the historical statements and records surrounding the drafting of the First Amendment, showing the Founders' intent.

Books

Benjamin Rush: Hardback (B20A) $15.95
Signer of the Declaration of Independence Paperback (B20) $9.95
Features the life and writings of this dedicated Christian statesman, including numerous historical illustrations.

Original Intent Hardback (B24) $19.95 • Paperback (B16) $12.95
Reveals how the Court has reinterpreted the Constitution, diluting the principles upon which it was based. Allows the Founders to speak for themselves.

A Spiritual Heritage Tour of the U.S. Capitol (B22) $6.95
A self-guided tour of the U.S. Capitol Building which focuses on the Godly heritage found in artwork, statues, etc., throughout the building.

Ethics: An Early American Handbook (B23) $7.95
An historical reprint of an 1890 textbook that taught character to America's young people. Great for all ages!

Documents of Freedom (B21) $3.95
Pocket-size copy of the Declaration of Independence, the U.S. Constitution, and George Washington's Farewell Address.

America: To Pray or Not to Pray   **(B01A) $7.95**
A statistical look at what has happened when religious principles were separated from public affairs by the Supreme Court in 1962.

Lives of the Signers of the Declaration of Independence   **(B14A) $10.95**
This reprint of an 1848 original features biographic sketches on the lives of each of the 56 men who signed the Declaration of Independence.

Wives of the Signers   **(B18A) $10.95**
This reprint describes those women who, alongside their husbands, experienced the struggle for independence and the building of a new nation.

Impeachment! Restraining an Overactive Judiciary   **(B17) $6.95**
This book reveals how the Founders restrained overactive courts via impeachment. Learn how we can do the same with our judges today.

Lessons From Nature for Youth   **(B13) $6.95**
This 1836 reprint will teach young people admirable traits once taught in our schools. Learn loyalty from a buffalo, gratitude from a lion, etc. Great for all ages!

The Bulletproof George Washington   **(B05) $6.95**
An account of God's miraculous protection of Washington in the French and Indian War and of Washington's open gratitude for God's Divine intervention.

The New England Primer   **(B06) $6.95**
A reprint of the 1777 textbook used by the Founding Fathers. It was the first textbook printed in America (1690) and was used for 200 years to teach reading and Bible lessons in school.

Noah Webster's "Advice to the Young"   **(B10A) $6.95**
Founder Noah Webster stated that this work "will be useful in enlightening the minds of youth in religious and moral principles."

Bible Study Course – New Testament   **(B09) $4.95**
A reprint of the 1946 N.T. survey text used by the Dallas Public High Schools.

Bible Study Course – Old Testament   **(B12) $4.95**
A reprint of the 1954 O.T. survey text used by the Dallas Public High Schools.

Video Transcripts

America's Godly Heritage (See video)	**(TSC01) $3.95**
Keys to Good Government (See video)	**(TSC04) $3.95**
Education and the Founding Fathers (See video)	**(TSC02) $3.95**
Spirit of the American Revolution (See video)	**(TSC05) $3.95**
Foundations of American Government (See video)	**(TSC03) $2.95**

American Heritage Poster Series

A series of posters designed to give an enjoyable overview of great men, women, and events in America's history. These beautiful 16 x 20 informational posters are excellent for use in schools or homeschool classrooms.

George Washington Carver	**(P02)**	**$4.95**
Thomas Jefferson	**(P03)**	**$4.95**

Abraham Lincoln .... (P04) $4.95
Pocahontas .... (P05) $4.95
George Washington .... (P06) $4.95
First Prayer in Congress .... (P07) $4.95
First Thanksgiving .... (P08) $4.95
The Signing of the Declaration of Independence .... (P10) $4.95
Poster Set (Any 5 – Write selections on order form) .... (P01) $19.95
Complete Poster Set (All 8 posters) .... (PS8) $27.95

Authentic Historical Documents

Beautiful parchment replicas of significant documents which add an historical atmosphere to any classroom, home, or study

Declaration of Independence .... (D01) $3.95
Bill of Rights .... (D02) $3.95
Northwest Ordinance of 1787 .... (D03) $3.95
Mayflower Compact of 1620 .... (D04) $3.95
Patrick Henry's "Liberty or Death" Speech .... (D05) $3.95
U.S. Constitution (4 pages) .... (D06) $9.95

Audio Cassettes

Religion & Morality, Indispensable Supports　　　　　　　(A14) $4.95
Documents the Founding Fathers' belief that religion and morality are indispensable supports for American society.

Thinking Biblically, Speaking Secularly　　　　　　　　　(A13) $4.95
Provides guidelines for Biblically thinking individuals to effectively communicate truths in today's often anti-Biblical environment.

The Founding Fathers　　　　　　　　　　　　　　　　(A11) $4.95
Highlights accomplishments and notable quotes of Founding Fathers which show their strong belief in Christian principles.

The Laws of the Heavens　　　　　　　　　　　　　　　(A03) $4.95
An explanation of the eight words in the Declaration of Independence on which the nation was birthed.

America: Lessons from Nehemiah　　　　　　　　　　　　(A05) $4.95
A look at the Scriptural parallels between the rebuilding of Jerusalem in the book of Nehemiah and that of America today.

Principles for Reformation　　　　　　　　　　　　　　(A10) $4.95
Explores the Biblical guidelines for restoring Christian principles to society and public affairs.

Is America a Christian Nation?　　　　　　　　　　　　(A16) $4.95
An examination of the writings of the Framers of the Constitution and of the Supreme Court's own records.

The Importance of Duty　　　　　　　　　　　　　　　(A17) $4.95
Highlights how stewardship of rights and performance of responsibilities is the duty of each Christian.

The Practical Benefits of Christianity   (A18) $4.95
Demonstrates the positive and powerful societal influences which the Founding Fathers believed Christianity provided.

The Changing First Amendment   (A19) $4.95
Shows how the courts have reinterpreted the First Amendment resulting in rulings opposed to the Founders' intent.

America's Godly Heritage – Part One (See video)   (A01) $4.95

America's Godly Heritage – Part Two   (A15) $4.95
An expanded look at the Founding Fathers' beliefs concerning the role of Christian principles in the public affairs of the nation.

The Bible and the Judiciary   (A22) $4.95
Discover the role the Bible has historically played in America's courts and how it's been removed today.

Faith, Character, and the Constitution   (A21) $4.95
Does character matter? Does religious faith have a part in today's society? Learn what the Founders believed on both issues.

America's Birthday: The Fourth of July   (A20) $4.95
A fascinating look at our nation's birth and the great men and events involved in bringing us to the occasion.

Impeachment: Restraining an Overactive Judiciary (See book)   (A23) $4.95
Keys to Good Government (See video)   (A09) $4.95
Education and the Founding Fathers (See video)   (A08) $4.95
The Spirit of the American Revolution (See video)   (A02) $4.95
Foundations of American Government (See video)   (A12) $4.95
America: To Pray or Not To Pray? (See book)   (A07) $4.95

Pamphlets

The Truth About Jefferson & the First Amendment   (PAM01) $.50
Explains a common misconception concerning Jefferson's role with the First Amendment and points out those who did influence it.

The Bible in Schools (25 count)   (PAM04) $3.95
A reprint of an essay by Founding Father Benjamin Rush on why the Bible should be taught in schools.

America: God Shed His Grace on Thee (25 count)   (PAM02) $2.95
Gives quotes from the Founders highlighting their belief in government based upon Biblical principles.